P9-DNY-110

Amalfi Coast with Naples, Capri & Pompeii

3rd Edition

by Bruce Murphy & Alessandra de Rosa

WILEY

Wiley Publishing, Inc.

Published by:

WILEY PUBLISHING, INC.

111 River St.
Hoboken, NJ 07030-5774

ISBN 978-0-470-49734-0

Editor: Alexia Travaglini
Production Editor: Jonathan Scott
Cartographer: Guy Ruggiero
Photo Editor: Richard Fox

Production by Wiley Indianapolis Composition Services

Front cover photo: Hillside in Positano © Ray Juno/Corbis
Back cover photo: Galleria Umberto, Naples © Thomas Schmitt / Getty Images

For information on our other products and services or to obtain technical support, please contact our Customer Care Department within the U.S. at 877/762-2974, outside the U.S. at 317/572-3993 or fax 317/572-4002.

Wiley also publishes its books in a variety of electronic formats. Some content that appears in print may not be available in electronic formats.

Manufactured in the United States of America

5   4   3   2   1

CONTENTS

LIST OF MAPS

ABOUT THE AUTHORS

Bruce Murphy has lived and worked in New York City, Boston, Chicago, Dublin, Rome, and Sicily. His work has appeared in magazines ranging from *Cruising World* to *Critical Inquiry*. In addition to guidebooks, he has published fiction, poetry, and criticism, most recently the *Encyclopedia of Murder and Mystery* (St. Martin's Press).

Alessandra de Rosa was born in Rome and has lived and worked in Rome, Paris, and New York City. She did her first cross-Europe trip at age 2, from Rome to London by car. She has continued in that line ever since, exploring three out of seven continents so far. Her beloved Italy remains her preferred destination.

HOW TO CONTACT US

In researching this book, we discovered many wonderful places—hotels, restaurants, shops, and more. We're sure you'll find others. Please tell us about them, so we can share the information with your fellow travelers in upcoming editions. If you were disappointed with a recommendation, we'd love to know that, too. Please write to:

Frommer's Amalfi Coast with Naples, Capri & Pompeii, 3rd Edition
Wiley Publishing, Inc. • 111 River St. • Hoboken, NJ 07030-5774

AN ADDITIONAL NOTE

Please be advised that travel information is subject to change at any time—and this is especially true of prices. We therefore suggest that you write or call ahead for confirmation when making your travel plans. The authors, editors, and publisher cannot be held responsible for the experiences of readers while traveling. Your safety is important to us, however, so we encourage you to stay alert and be aware of your surroundings. Keep a close eye on cameras, purses, and wallets, all favorite targets of thieves and pickpockets.

FROMMER'S STAR RATINGS, ICONS & ABBREVIATIONS

Every hotel, restaurant, and attraction listing in this guide has been ranked for quality, value, service, amenities, and special features using a **star-rating system.** In country, state, and regional guides, we also rate towns and regions to help you narrow down your choices and budget your time accordingly. Hotels and restaurants are rated on a scale of zero (recommended) to three stars (exceptional). Attractions, shopping, nightlife, towns, and regions are rated according to the following scale: zero stars (recommended), one star (highly recommended), two stars (very highly recommended), and three stars (must-see).

In addition to the star-rating system, we also use **seven feature icons** that point you to the great deals, in-the-know advice and unique experiences that separate travelers from tourists. Throughout the book, look for:

(Finds)	Special finds—those places only insiders know about
(Fun Facts)	Fun facts—details that make travelers more informed and their trips more fun
(Kids)	Best bets for kids, and advice for the whole family
(Moments)	Special moments—those experiences that memories are made of
(Overrated)	Places or experiences not worth your time or money
(Tips)	Insider tips—great ways to save time and money
(Value)	Great values—where to get the best deals

The following **abbreviations** are used for credit cards:

AE	American Express	**DISC**	Discover	**V**	Visa
DC	Diners Club	**MC**	MasterCard		

TRAVEL RESOURCES AT FROMMERS.COM

Frommer's travel resources don't end with this guide. Frommer's website, **www.frommers.com**, has travel information on more than 4,000 destinations. We update features regularly, giving you access to the most current trip-planning information and the best airfare, lodging, and car-rental bargains. You can also listen to podcasts, connect with other Frommers.com members through our active-reader forums, share your travel photos, read blogs from guidebook editors and fellow travelers, and much more.

The Best of Campania & the Amalfi Coast

Campania—the region that encompasses Naples and the Amalfi Coast—is, for many tourists, terra incognita. A land of myth and legends, coveted since antiquity for the fertility of its countryside and the beauty of its coasts. In this chapter, we'll help you discover the best of Campania by pointing you toward its major treasures.

1 THE BEST TRAVEL EXPERIENCES

- **Walking through Naples's Historic District:** Maybe it is a bit defiant, given all the negative press about garbage and mafia here, but we find it exhilarating to be able to enjoy Naples's stunning art after it was literally hidden in grime for decades. Its collection of exquisite frescoes, paintings, and sculptures are now available to visitors at its numerous monasteries, palaces, churches, and museums. Kings and noble families have lavished art on the city as nowhere else in Italy except Rome, making Naples a competitor with Florence and Venice. A key stop for art lovers during the Grand Tour, Naples was later forgotten due to the complete abandonment of its monuments. But thanks to sustained efforts over the past 15 years, Naples is again experiencing a tourism boom. See "Exploring Naples," in chapter 5.

- **Exploring Capri:** This renowned island remains a magical destination, in spite of the crowds of tourists that flock to its shores. Of course, for the best experience, come early in the season and plan to stay overnight.

- **Arriving in Naples by Boat:** You don't have to book a transatlantic cruise to have this marvelous experience. While arriving in Naples by car can be nerve-racking, confusing, and hot, with most

landmarks annoyingly out of view, gliding into the Bay, with a sea breeze behind you and the city spread out ahead of you, can be magnificent. The majestic and somewhat ominous presence of Mount Vesuvius looming over the Bay makes it that much more dramatic. You can arrive by regular ferry from one of the islands or even from one of the other harbors in Campania, such as Salerno or Sorrento. We highly recommend arriving during the very early morning or in the evening, when the sun is sinking below the horizon, bathing the city in gold and orange; this is when the view is most magical. Upon soaking in the sight, you'll instantly understand the motivation behind the old saying, "See Naples and die." See "Getting There," in chapter 5.

- **Hiking the Ancient Paths of the Amalfi Coast:** Taking a stroll on one of the Amalfi Coast's footpaths—once the only means of communication between the region's towns—is the best way to soak in the intensity of this amazing seascape. No matter your level of fitness, you'll find a stretch of path that's right for you. The region's main road—the famed Amalfi Drive—was built in 1840 and made the area more accessible, perhaps too much so. The old trails, on the other hand, are unique, and lead you through the Amalfi Coast missed by so many tourists. Trails come in all levels of difficulty, from flat stretches (such as the footpath from Amalfi to Atrani) to downhill ones (such as the footpath from Ravello to Minori) to more demanding ones (such as the Sentiero degli Dei and the Via degli Incanti from Positano). See chapter 8.

- **Exploring Greek Ruins in Paestum:** The first colony the Greeks established in Italy was Cuma, near Pozzuoli. From there, they expanded south to the rest of the Campanian coast. The heritage they left in Campania is immense— rivaled in Italy only by Sicily—and in a state of conservation seen only in Greece itself. This is Magna Grecia, where ancient Greece first spread its influence into Italy, setting the stage for what we call Western culture. In these temples and towns, you literally get the chance to walk in the footsteps of Plato and Aristotle's contemporaries. See chapters 6 and 10.

- **Eating the Best Pizza:** Pizza was invented here, in the narrow lanes of Naples's historic district, and for Neapolitans, their pizza is the only "real" one, thick crusted and fragrant. Whether you prefer a simple pizza joint or an elaborate restaurant, you'll share the pride Neapolitans feel for their invention, now taken over by the whole planet. The decor may be simple and traditional (sometimes nonexistent), and, in the most authentic restaurants, you'll have a modest choice of toppings—only two at Da Michele, reputed to make the best pizza in Naples. Yet whichever place you choose, the outcome will be tasty, satisfying, and distinctive, because in Naples, no two pizzas are alike. See "Where to Dine," in chapter 5.

- **Shopping in Positano:** The best exclusive shopping in the region can be found at this trendy resort, which stocks treasure troves of unique, hand-made clothes and shoes. You can still find tailors and cobblers who will make you garments or sandals on the spot, while you wait—or, even better, while you go for a swim. See chapter 8 for addresses.

- **Wandering Through Ancient Roman Lanes in Pompeii:** Walking among ancient ruins is romantic and sad, and even a little creepy at times. Campania affords you many opportunities to live this unique experience. Of all the sites in the region, Pompeii and Hercula-neum are justly famous: Walking their streets gives you a particularly eerie feeling. At the center of the lanes' mesmeric attraction is the knowledge that their violent destruction and miraculous preservation both happened on one terrible day nearly 2,000 years ago. And somehow it feels as if it is *always* that day here. Imagination easily bridges the gap to the time when these rooms resounded with talk and laughter (or, for more morbid minds, screams and cries of terror). Yet the best sites in the region might be some of the lesser known, such as the magnificent Villa di Poppea, in Oplontis, with its wonderful frescoes; the Villa Arianna and the Villa di San Marco, in Castellammare di Stabia; and the Villa Romana of Minori. See chapters 6, 7, and 8.

- **Listening to a Concert in a Medieval Cloister:** The unique blend of cultures operating in Campania gave birth to some of the most splendid medieval cloisters ever built. Intertwined arches of Sicilian-Norman architecture are used here to support the loggias of delightful inner gardens, where the sun, more often than not, is shining on fruit-laden citrus trees and ancient stone and tile work. During the summer, music festivals are held in most coastal towns to take advantage of these

magical spaces. The best of these medieval marvels are the Chiostro del Paradiso in Amalfi, the Villa Rufolo cloister in Ravello, and the cloister of San Francesco in Sorrento. See chapters 7 and 8.

2 THE BEST RUINS

- **The Temples of Paestum:** This site's complete set of walls and three temples are simply the best Greek ruins in existence outside Greece. One of the three temples—the grandiose **Temple of Neptune,** whose restoration was finished in 2004—is actually the best-preserved Greek temple in the world, along with the Theseion in Athens. We highly recommend timing your visit in spring or fall, when the roses are in bloom and the ruins are at their most romantic. The site is also stunning at dawn and sunset in any season, when the temples' surfaces glow golden in the sun. See chapter 10.

- **The Acropolis of Cuma:** The first Greek colony in Italy and a beacon of Greek culture, Cuma was built on one of the most picturesque promontories in Campania. In the once enchanting area of the Phlegrean Fields, where so many myths reside (the Cave of the Sybil, Lake Averno and the entrance to the underworld, and so on), Cuma offers a stunning panorama and atmospheric ruins. See "Phlegrean Fields," in chapter 6.

- **The Anfiteatro Campano of Santa Maria Capua Vetere:** The largest Roman amphitheater after the Colosseum, this splendid ruin offers a glimpse at ancient artistry in spite of the active pillage that occurred here from the 9th century onward. On-site is the Museo dei Gladiatori, a permanent exhibit reconstructing the life of a gladiator; it is housed in a building located on the probable site of Capua's Gladiator School—whose most famous graduate was Spartacus, the slave made famous by the 1960 Stanley Kubrick film. It is located in Santa Maria Capua Vetere, which occupies the grounds of Roman Capua, the city that Cicero considered second only to Rome in the entire ancient world. The area is rich in other noteworthy ruins, such as the splendid Mitreo (Temple to the Persian god Mithras), and museum collections. See chapter 11.

- **Pompeii and Herculaneum:** Will enough ever be said to describe these incredible sites? Even if you have already visited them in the past, new findings are reason enough for a return visit. The magnificent Villa dei Papiri in Herculaneum was opened to the public for the first time in 2004; the Terme Suburbane in Pompeii was opened in 2002. The riches of the archaeological area are best complemented by a visit to the Museo Archeologico Nazionale in Naples, to view its massive array of frescoes and mosaics from earlier excavations at both sites. See chapter 6.

- **Oplontis:** Also called the Villa of Poppea, these are the ruins of a splendid Roman villa—believed to be that of Nero's wife—with magnificent frescoes and decorations. Lesser known than other sites and often skipped by hurried tourists who stop only in Pompeii or Herculaneum, this villa is unique, not only for its state of conservation, but also because modern archaeology requires materials to be left *in situ*. The frescoes and statuary grant you a fuller experience of the Romans' daily lives. See chapter 6.

- **Trajan's Arch in Benevento:** This little-known and out-of-the-way find is the world's best-preserved example of an ancient Roman triumphal arch.

Recently restored—it took 14 years of work before the arch was opened again to the public in 2001—it is a masterpiece of carving that depicts the deeds of the admired (and fairly benevolent) Roman emperor Trajan. Careful cleaning has eliminated darker areas in the marble, making the reliefs much easier to read. Inside a little Longobard church nearby is a permanent exhibit on the arch, its restoration, and Roman life under Trajan. See chapter 11.

- **Pozzuoli:** The ruins of the ancient Roman town of Puteoli have been difficult to excavate because the busy modern town occupies exactly the same area as the original (much as Rome does). In the splendid frame of Pozzuoli's bay, you'll find an underground Pompeii—buried not by a volcanic explosion, but by sinking under unstable volcanic ground. The main attractions are the Rione Terra, with Roman streets and shops; the 1st-century Greco-Roman market (Serapeo); and the Roman amphitheater (Anfiteatro Flavio), where musical performances are held during summer. See chapter 6.
- **The Underwater Archeological Park of Baia:** Due to subsiding ground, a large part of the ancient Roman town of Baia was submerged by the sea. Excavated and transformed into an archaeological park, it can now be visited with scuba equipment or—if you don't like to get wet—in a glass-bottomed boat. The itinerary leads you through the streets of the ancient town and inside its beautiful villas, now water-filled. This magical experience truly deserves the word *unique*. See "Pozzuoli" and "Phlegrean Fields," in chapter 6.
- **Velia:** Overshadowed by Paestum and just a bit too far from Naples for a day trip, Velia was the site of an important Greek settlement started around 540 B.C. It gave birth to one of antiquity's most important philosophical schools of thought—the Eleatic doctrines of Parmenides and Zeno. Velia is one of the only Greek archaeological sites showing remains not only of an acropolis with its ruined temples, but also of a lower town with some houses. Portions of the walls here date from the 5th and 4th centuries B.C. A stretch of the original Greek pavement climbs toward the town gate, the famous Porta Rosa. A highlight of the Roman period is the thermal baths. See chapter 10.

3 THE BEST CHURCHES & CATHEDRALS

- **Casertavecchia Cathedral:** This medieval church is one of the most beautiful extant examples of Arabo-Norman architecture, built with two colors of tufa stone and white marble, and dotted with strange human and animal figures. See chapter 11.
- **Naples's Duomo:** The most splendid of Naples's churches, and home of superb artwork, you'll find that the Duomo is three churches in one. The Cappella di San Gennaro is really a church in its own right, with a fantastic treasure on display in the attached museum. Santa Restituta, the original 6th-century church, contains a magnificent 4th-century baptistery. See chapter 5.
- **Complesso Monumentale di Santa Chiara:** Another star on the Neapolitan scene, this splendid church-cum-monastery holds splendid examples of 14th-century sculpture that escaped the tragic bombing of World War II. (Other parts of the massive structure were not so lucky but have since been restored.) The spacious majolica cloister holds a

plethora of mythological, pastoral, and whimsical scenes enchanting to behold in the open air. See chapter 5.

- **San Lorenzo Maggiore:** Originally built in the 6th century, this lesser-known church in Naples is famous for its literary guests: from Boccaccio, who met his darling Fiammetta here, to Francesco Petrarca and others. It holds splendid Renaissance masterpieces and a multilayered archaeological site, where you can descend like a time traveler through layers of buildings all the way down to a paleochristian basilica and the 1st-century Roman Macellum (market). See chapter 5.

- **Chiesa della Santissima Annunziata:** This church is located in Minuto, one of the medieval hamlets of the township of Scala, which stretches along the cliffs of the Amalfi Coast. The church offers not only some of the region's best examples of Romanesque architecture and beautiful 12th-century frescoes, but also a superb panorama. See chapter 8.

- **Duomo di Santa Maria Capua Vetere:** Dating originally from the 5th century,

this beautiful paleochristian church has been redecorated in later centuries, but it contains artworks reaching back to Roman times (its columns and capitals), as well as examples of Renaissance frescoes and carvings. See chapter 11.

- **Sant'Angelo in Formis:** This is one of the most important Romanesque churches in the entire country. Its entire interior is graced with beautiful frescoes. The church's lovely setting is Mount Tifata, near Capua. See chapter 11.

- **Santa Sofia:** Dating back to the early Longobard kingdom in Benevento, this small medieval church is famous for its unique star-shaped floor plan and the integration of Longobard and Catholic symbols. See chapter 11.

- **Certosa di Padula (Carthusian Monastery of San Lorenzo):** Begun in the 14th century, this magnificent monastery—one of the largest in the world—is a baroque masterpiece, chock-full of art and architectural details. Off the beaten path, but only a short distance from Salerno, it is a destination not to be missed. See chapter 10.

4 THE BEST CASTLES & PALACES

- **Castel dell'Ovo:** The symbol of Naples and the most picturesque icon of the Naples waterfront, this castle is the city's oldest fortification—its foundation dates back to the 9th century B.C. Greek settlement. It is supposedly built over a magic egg hidden by the poet-magician Virgil for the defense of the city (which will crumble into ruin if the egg is destroyed). See chapter 5.

- **Reggia di Caserta:** The Versailles of Italy, this splendid royal palace was built by the famous architect Vanvitelli for the Bourbon kings in the 18th century. It holds fantastic works of art and the decorations—walls and floors included—are magnificent. The Reggia

is also justly famed for its massive Italian garden, one of the most beautiful in the world. See chapter 11.

- **Castel Nuovo (Maschio Angioino):** This 13th-century castle was the residence of Neapolitan kings until the 17th century. Although a fire in the 16th century destroyed its frescoes by Giotto, there is still enough in this majestic fortress to impress visitors. See chapter 5.

- **Palazzo Reale:** The beautiful Royal Palace of Naples dominates wide Piazza del Plebiscito with its neoclassical facade and statues of kings. Inside, you'll find a rich collection of art and decorations as well as a wonderful library. See chapter 5.

- **Castel Lauritano:** This ruined castle in Agerola, a town on the Amalfi Coast, is incredibly picturesque and offers extensive views over both the coast and the interior. See chapter 8.
- **Villa Rufolo:** This splendid villa in Ravello has been made famous by its terrace and gardens, which inspired Wagner to write some of his *Parsifal*, so moved was he by its vistas. Today, you can listen to concerts of Wagner's work in the same setting. See chapter 8.
- **Villa Cimbrone:** The second most famous villa in Ravello, also with a splendid panoramic terrace, the Villa Cimbrone has another attraction: It houses a small hotel and a restaurant, which was opened to the public in 2005. See chapter 8.

5 THE BEST MUSEUMS

- **Museo Nazionale di Capodimonte:** Created by the Bourbon kings, this picture gallery is one of the best in the world, holding paintings from the 13th century onward. The catalog looks like a book on art history, complete with all the famous names of Italian art and many members of the Flemish school. The regular special exhibits draw visitors from all over Italy, Europe, and the world. (The success of these special exhibits is such that you'll need advance reservations to get in, unless you don't mind standing in line for several hours.) See chapter 5.
- **Museo Archeologico Nazionale:** Even if you are only mildly interested in archaeology, you should not miss this unique museum, which holds the largest collection of ancient Roman artifacts in the world. Created in the 17th century—with original Roman mosaics reused in the floors and statues incorporated in the facade decoration—this is where the best finds from Pompeii and other local sites are on display. The huge quantity of frescoes, statuary, and precious objects has greatly benefited from a reorganization, which was finished in 2005. See chapter 5.
- **Museo Nazionale della Ceramica Duca di Martina:** Housed in the elegant Villa Floridiana up in Naples's Vomero neighborhood, this rich ceramic collection includes the most important assemblage of Capodimonte porcelain in the world. See chapter 5.
- **Museo Campano:** This museum in Capua has a tall order, as the repository of the history and culture of the whole Campania region. It does a great job, though, with its several collections, covering the whole ancient history of the area, from the Oscans (about 6th century B.C.) to the Renaissance. It has a magnificent collection of parchment and illuminated manuscripts. See chapter 11.
- **Museo del Duomo:** This museum in Salerno is not large, but it holds a number of invaluable masterpieces ranging from Roman times to the Renaissance and baroque periods. It includes a unique collection of ivory carvings, a great picture gallery, and a rich collection of illuminated manuscripts. See chapter 10.
- **Museo del Sannio:** Housed in the atmospheric cloister of Santa Sofia in Benevento, this is a small but well-rounded collection of artifacts from local sites. It includes the largest collection of Egyptian art found at one Italian archaeological site, a local temple. See chapter 11.
- **Museo Irpino:** This modern museum displays a collection of artifacts found in the rich archaeological sites in the

outlying region of Avellino. The objects date back into the distant past long before the Romans (or even the Greeks) came to the region—as far back as 4000 B.C. See chapter 11.

- **Museo Archeologico dei Campi Flegrei:** Housed in the picturesque Aragonese Castle of Baia, this is another great treasure trove of Roman and Greek art in the vicinity of Naples. See chapter 5.

6 THE BEST SWIMMING & SUNBATHING SPOTS

- **Vico Equense:** This lesser-known resort town on the Sorrentine peninsula is blessed with several beaches—most of them small and hidden away inside picturesque coves—such as **Marina di Equa,** dominated by a powerful 17th-century tower. See chapter 7.
- **Punta del Capo:** This lovely beach near Sorrento under the cliffs has attracted visitors from time immemorial. Nearby, you'll find the ruins of a Roman villa and a small pool of water enclosed by rocks, known as the Bath of Queen Giovanna. See chapter 7.
- **Bay of Ieranto:** Part of the Marine Preserve of Punta Campanella, this unique fjord was almost lost to developers, who would have spoiled its beauty forever. When the light is just right at day's end, the clarity of the waters here creates the illusion of boats floating in midair. See chapter 7.
- **Grotta dello Smeraldo:** Although this grotto in the village of Conca dei Marini on the Amalfi Coast is usually visited by boat, it is also the destination of a scuba procession on Christmas night. The pretty beach can be visited anytime, however. See chapter 8.

- **Positano:** The most famous resort on the Amalfi Coast, Positano has several picturesque beaches—although they're hardly deserted. Besides the central **Spiaggia Grande** by the marina, you'll find **Fornillo** to the west of town, and **La Porta, Ciumicello, Arienzo,** and **Laurito** to the east. See chapter 8.
- **Spiaggia di Citara:** This is the most scenic beach on the island of Ischia, near the little town of Forio. Besides the lovely scenery, there are several natural thermal springs. See chapter 9.
- **Marina di Paestum:** Greek temples are not the only reason to come to Paestum. The sandy beach here is one of the best in Italy, extending for miles along the clear blue sea. See chapter 10.
- **Baia della Calanca:** In beautiful Marina di Camerota, this is one of the nicest beaches in the Cilento, and it is famed for its clear waters. See chapter 10.
- **Bagni di Tiberio:** This is the best of the rare and tiny beaches of Capri. As the name suggests, it lies near the ruins of one of Emperor Tiberius's notorious pleasure palaces. It is accessible by a rocky steep path or by boat. See chapter 9.

7 THE BEST SPAS

- **Parco Termale Giardini Poseidon:** This is our favorite thermal spa. On beautiful Ischia, the Poseidon boasts scenic outdoor thermal pools from

which you can enjoy great views and a variety of aesthetic and health treatments. See chapter 9.

- **Ischia Thermal Center:** In the small town of Ischia, this is one of the most modern spas on the island, where you can enjoy a variety of state-of-the-art modern services. See chapter 9.
- **Terme della Regina Isabella:** Among the most famous and elegant spas on Ischia, this historical establishment in exclusive Lacco Ameno offers state-of-the-art facilities. See chapter 9.
- **Castellammare di Stabia:** This pleasant seaside resort is blessed with 28 natural thermal springs which you can enjoy at one of the two public spas: the historical one built by the Bourbon kings or the modern establishment on the slopes of Mount Faito. Both offer a wide range of services, from beauty and relaxation treatments to medical ones. See chapter 7.
- **Scrajo Terme:** At the beginning of the Sorrentine peninsula, just outside the pleasant resort town of Vico Equense, you'll find this historic thermal establishment dating back to the 19th century. Guest rooms are available so visitors can "take the waters" in style. See chapter 7.
- **Telese Terme:** Little known to foreign visitors, this charming thermal spa and resort is a short distance west of Benevento and affords luxury and quiet. See chapter 11.

---

8 THE BEST VISTAS

- **Lungomare di Salerno:** Italy's best-kept secret may be the seaside promenade of laid-back Salerno. A splendid and completely pedestrian walkway lined with palm trees, it offers views encompassing the whole bay from Capri to Punta Licosa in the Cilento. See chapter 10.
- **Deserto:** From the terraces of this Carmelite hermitage near Sant'Agata dei Golfi, you can enjoy the famous, unique circular panorama encompassing both the Gulf of Naples, with Sorrento and the islands, and the Gulf of Salerno, with the Amalfi Coast. On a good day, you can see almost the entire region, from the Cilento—way off to the south of Paestum—to Capo Miseno, to the islands of Ischia and Procida, and to Capri. See chapter 7.
- **Belvedere dello Schiaccone:** This is the best lookout along the whole Amalfi Drive, located immediately west of Positano and accessible from the road; the views are indeed superb. See chapter 8.
- **Lake Fusaro:** In the once picturesque Phlegrean Fields, not far from Pozzuoli, this beautiful lake was chosen by the Bourbon kings as the site for the Casina Reale, a structural jewel designed by the architect Vanvitelli. Today, as back then, the Casina Reale commands royal views perfect for picture taking. See chapter 6.
- **Monte Cervati:** The highest peak of the Cilento massif, Cervati is famous for its beauty in summer—when it turns purple with lavender fields—and for the magnificent views from its top. See chapter 10.
- **Agropoli:** From the walls of the medieval citadel, you can look down on vast stretches of coastline—a view that helped the Saracens hold onto Agropoli as the base for their incursions, until they were finally dislodged in the 11th century. See chapter 10.

- **Don Alfonso 1890** (✆ **081-8780026**): This is one of the top Italian gourmet addresses and the best restaurant south of Naples, created and maintained by hosts Lidia and Alfonso Iaccarino. The restaurant, a member of the Relais & Châteaux association, has a luxurious decor and offers superb food made of ingredients mainly from the chefs' own organic farm. See chapter 7.

- **Oasi Olimpia Relais** (✆ **081-8080560**): Competing for the title of best restaurant on the Sorrento peninsula with Don Alfonso 1890, this is our favorite spot to eat in the area. It might not have the over-the-top elegance of Don Alfonso (though it's not a place to drop by in your bathing attire, either); it has a more down-to-earth atmosphere and an enthusiasm for homegrown food that we find irresistible. The alfresco dining under the arbor is a plus. See chapter 7.

- **Faro di Capo d'Orso** (✆ **089-877022**): Owned by a young, emerging chef— Rocco Iannone—the Faro (Lighthouse) is one of the culinary highlights of the Amalfi Coast, supplemented by a unique location that offers stunning views of this stretch of coast. See chapter 8.

- **Il San Pietro di Positano** (✆ **800/- 735-2478**): The restaurant of the famous hotel in Positano with the same name, Il San Pietro offers the fine cuisine of Chef Alois Vanlangenacker—all based on ingredients from the hotel's own farm—and a delightfully romantic setting that is worth a visit all by itself. See chapter 8.

- **George's** (✆ **081-7612474**): On the roof terrace of the Grand Hotel Parker's, this is a truly elegant restaurant happily devoid of stuffiness or ostentation. There's no snobbery here, only the best that money can buy. Chef Baciòt brings together the ingredients of tasty and healthy dishes that marry tradition with nutrition. The service and surroundings are impeccable, and the wine list is among the best in Italy. See chapter 5.

- **La Cantinella** (✆ **081-7648684**) This well-known restaurant proudly serves a classic version of traditional Neapolitan cuisine, with a large share of the menu dedicated to seafood. Make reservations well ahead, as it is very popular with local crowds. See chapter 5.

- **Relais Blu Belvedere** (✆ **081-8789552**): This restaurant-cum-small-hotel is a hot address on the Sorrento peninsula. The delightful manager-host will introduce you to the flavors of his beloved native peninsula, be it for predinner drinks, which are served with creative nibbles based on local ingredients, or for a perfectly romantic dinner. High above the rocky coast overlooking Capri, the open-air terrace is spectacular. See chapter 7.

- **Olivo of the Capri Palace** (✆ **081- 9780111**): This restaurant, at the stylish Capri Palace hotel, is a haven of elegance and good taste, from the furnishings and table settings to the impeccable service and superb creative cuisine. See chapter 9.

- **Rossellinis** (✆ **089-818181**): A truly elegant and satisfactory experience awaits you at this restaurant in the exclusive Palazzo Sasso in Ravello, where the finest local ingredients are transformed into delectable meals by the talented chef. See chapter 8.

10 THE BEST LUXURY STAYS

- **Grand Hotel Parker's** (✆ 081-7612474): This is Naples's most romantic luxury hotel, competing with the Grand Hotel Vesuvio for the title of best hotel in town. Housed in a magnificent Liberty-style building, it offers superb service, classy accommodations, and one of the best restaurants in the country. See chapter 5.
- **Grand Hotel Vesuvio** (✆ 081-7640044): This is generally considered the best hotel in Naples, offering palatial accommodations and exquisite service. You will be pampered the moment you step through the doors. The turndown service includes fine small-batch signature chocolates, the linens are royalty class, and the sumptuous breakfast is served in the most panoramic room you can imagine, with views over the picturesque Castel dell'Ovo. The gourmet roof-restaurant is another plus. Every detail here is truly first-class. See chapter 5.
- **Hotel San Pietro Positano** (✆ 800/735-2478): A member of the Relais & Châteaux group, this elegant hotel tops our list of favorite places to stay in the whole of Italy. You'll understand why as soon as you step inside. The kind and attentive service, the tastefully colorful furnishing details, the romantic views from the terraces—we love everything about this place. See chapter 8.
- **Grand Hotel Excelsior Vittoria** (✆ 081-8071044): This gorgeous hotel is the best in Sorrento, housed in what once was a palatial residence overlooking the sea. The antiques in the guest rooms, the picturesque terraces, and the service make this an ideal hotel, right in the center of town (with its own elevator down to a private beach). See chapter 7.
- **Hotel Santa Caterina** (✆ 089-871012): Amalfi's most luxurious hotel, on a cliff just out of town, this is where you'll want to come to be pampered away from the crowds—and to enjoy the hotel's beautiful private beach, swimming pool, and lush gardens. See chapter 8.
- **Hotel Le Sirenuse** (✆ 089-875066): Competing for the title of best hotel in Positano with the Hotel San Pietro, this gorgeous hotel is housed in a beautiful 18th-century villa overlooking the sea. It offers palatial accommodations and fine service. See chapter 8.
- **Grand Hotel Quisisana** (✆ 081-8370788): The glitziest resort on Capri, this luxury hotel provides its guests with splendid accommodations and exquisite service. The hotel's bar and restaurant are popular spots for visiting socialites, so it's worth stopping by just to enjoy the atmosphere. See chapter 9.
- **Mezzatorre Resort & Spa** (✆ 081-986111): Taking its name from the 15th-century watchtower that houses part of the hotel, the Mezzatorre is the most splendid resort in Ischia. On its own secluded promontory off the exclusive town of Lacco Ameno and not far from Forio, it pampers its guests in perfect elegance and style. The views from the park and the swimming pool are breathtaking. See chapter 9.
- **Palazzo Sasso** (✆ 089-818181): The most exclusive hotel in the finest resort on the Amalfi Coast, this authentic 12th-century palace was the home of one of the noblest families in town—and you will be treated accordingly. See chapter 8.

2

Campania & the Amalfi Coast in Depth

A land of ancient civilizations, Campania has been inhabited since at least 4000 B.C., as shown by the many excavated necropolises here. A wonderful and fertile land, it attracted many people, who frequently fought for possession of it over the past 3,000 years. Its three main sections each had slightly different historical fates: the plains in the region's northern part and the hinterland of Naples—the *Campania Felix* of the Romans; the mountainous Sannio dominated by Benevento; and, to the south, the Amalfi Coast and the Cilento.

1 A LOOK AT THE PAST

This brief survey of Campania's long and complex history is oriented toward the Amalfi Coast, but the rest of Campania is covered as well. Once we hit the Renaissance, the focus shifts primarily to Naples and its surroundings, which became the center of power in the region.

THE GREEKS
After a short stop on the island of Ischia, Calcidians founded the city of Cuma in 750 B.C., the first Greek city of Magna Grecia—the Greek cities outside the mainland. Cuma became a beacon of Greek civilization in Italy. Greek expansion into the region, though, was contested by the Etruscans (see "The Etruscans," below). In spite of this, the Greeks established other important colonies in the current area of Naples: first Partenope around 680 B.C., then Dicearchia (Pozzuoli) in 531 B.C., and then Neapolis in 470 B.C. In the meantime, Greeks from Sibari founded Posidonia (Paestum) in 600 B.C. and Elea (Velia) in 540 B.C.

Greeks won two major battles in Cuma against the Etruscans, one in 524 B.C. and

the other in 474 B.C. Weakened by their fights with the Etruscans, they could not resist the Sannite invasion in the 5th century B.C.

THE ETRUSCANS
While the Greeks colonized Campania's coast, the Etruscans colonized the inner plains, the rich agricultural areas around Capua, which they founded in the 9th century B.C., and south all the way down to the hinterland of Paestum. They, too, were weakened by their fights for supremacy in the region against the Greeks, so that when the Sannites began their expansion, Etruscan power in the area came to an end.

THE SANNITES
This mountain people, originally from nearby Abbruzzo, had been expanding south in the Appennines, with an economy based on sheep husbandry. Also a warrior culture, they established a flourishing civilization in Benevento and then moved toward the coast in the 5th century B.C., causing conflict with both Greeks and Etruscans.

Sannite attacks were successful; they took over Capua in 424 B.C. and then took Cuma 3 years later in 421 B.C. Their influence quickly expanded to other cities, such as Neapolis, Pompeii, and Herculaneum, and gave birth to a new civilization, the Oscans (see "The Oscans," below).

The inland Sannites of Beneventum, in the meantime, came into opposition with the Romans who, by the 4th century B.C., had started their expansion southward. This led to the three famous Sannite wars. It took Rome from 343 B.C. to 290 B.C. to overcome the Sannites. The strongly independent Sannites, however, kept creating problems for the Romans. Finally, Beneventum was destroyed and later rebuilt as a Roman colony.

THE LUCANIANS

Another Italic mountain population, the Lucanians came from the nearby region of Basilicata. Slightly less belligerent than their Sannite cousins, they also started a migration toward the coast. They took over Posidonia (Paestum) in 400 B.C., but failed to overcome Elea (Velia). Like the Sannites farther north, they merged with the existing Greek population into the cultural melting pot that became the Oscans.

THE OSCANS

After their victories over the Greeks and Etruscans, the Sannites in the plains merged culturally with Etruscans and Greeks, giving birth to the Oscan civilization. This original population had strong Sannite roots, blending important cultural elements of the other two civilizations in a way that created a unique individual character with its own language. They made their capital in Capua.

Over time, the Oscans became so distinct from the original Sannites, however, that they actually shifted their support to Rome during its conquest of Campania.

THE ROMANS

The Romans took advantage of the opposition between the Oscans and the Sannites to extend their influence in the region. In exchange for allegiance to the Republic, Rome bestowed Roman citizenship, with the right to vote and decide on public affairs (but with the obligation of military service). Citizen colonies were set up as settlements of Roman farmers after the original people had given allegiance (voluntarily, or by sheer force). This worked better with the Oscans than with the Sannites, who continued to oppose Rome even after they lost the war. The Romans founded Paestum in 273 B.C., Beneventum in 268 B.C., then Salernum and Puteoli (modern Pozzuoli) in 194 B.C. These cities were fortified and linked to Rome by the famous Roman roads, such as the Appian Way, which led to Capua, then Beneventum, and then all the way to Brindisi, on the Ionian Sea on Italy's eastern coast.

In this way, a stern Roman culture was added to the preexisting local mixture. The social war from 91 B.C. to 88 B.C.— and, even more so, the civil war instigated by the dictator Sulla from 82 B.C to 81 B.C.—caused great destruction in Campania, especially to the rebellious Sannio region, which was almost completely wiped out. Peace came again with the advent of Rome's first emperor, Gaius Octavius Augustus.

Under the empire, Campania was completely Romanized, but its agricultural strength was slowly supplanted by the production of Africa and Spain, leading to a strong local recession.

When the empire ended in A.D. 395, the richest plains of Capua and Paestum had been abandoned and were in the throes of a malaria epidemic; the population was forced to found new villages up in the mountains, a situation that would not improve dramatically until the 20th century.

THE BYZANTINE & THE LONGOBARDS

With the end of the Roman Empire, barbarian invasions began. The Goths from the north invaded the region in 410, while the Vandals from Africa sacked and destroyed Capua in 456; the Byzantines counterattacked against the Goths and finally drove them out in 555; but (only a few years later, in 570), the Longobards arrived from the Appennines and took over the interior. The Byzantines struggled to maintain power but eventually lost, keeping only the harbors of Naples, Sorrento, and Amalfi; even Salerno was occupied by the Longobards in 630.

The Longobards' aristocracy oppressed Latin populations, but the yoke was lifted a bit when the Longobards converted to Catholicism thanks to the bishop of Benevento, Barbato; the conversion allowed the monasteries to begin operating again, and their role in preserving classical culture was immense. Later (in the 13th century), the Abbey of Monte Cassino, in northern Campania, would be, for a time, the home of the greatest philosopher-theologian in Europe, St. Thomas Aquinas.

In the second half of the 8th century, the Longobard prince Arechi II moved his court from Benevento to Salerno, causing an increasing tension between the two towns, which resulted in civil war and the splitting of the Longobard realm into two independent principalities in 849. This marked the beginning of the end for the Longobards; in the 10th century, Capua also became an independent principality, after having been destroyed by the Saracens in 841 and refounded on more secure grounds.

In the meantime, Amalfi became independent from the Byzantine Duchy of Naples and started gaining strength and power as a maritime commercial republic, maintaining strong contact with both the Byzantine and the Muslims in the East.

THE SARACENS

The Arab period in Sicily began in 827. Taking advantage of the Longobards' civil war, the Saracens—Arabs who had started out in the region as mercenaries—took over a few small harbor towns (particularly Agropoli in 882), and started attacking and sacking the other towns along the coast.

Under these repeated assaults, the once-prosperous coastal towns of Campania became deserted, as the people sought refuge in the hills and the countryside. Some of the towns were then reborn, often in more defensive locations and surrounded by heavy fortifications.

THE NORMANS, SWABIANS & ANGEVINS

Things changed with the arrival of the Normans, who reintroduced the concept of central government and unity in southern Italy. Their first base was Aversa, near Naples, established in 1029, and from there they rapidly expanded their conquest to Capua in 1062, Amalfi in 1073, and Salerno in 1076, where they established their capital until Naples was also annexed to the kingdom in 1139. The Normans then proceeded south and won over Sicily, displacing the Arabs who had ruled the island for 2 centuries.

Salerno became a splendid town and a beacon of culture and learning, thanks to the development of its medical school, the first and most important medical center of the whole Western world. Benevento, on the other hand, had passed appraisal by the power of the Popes in 1051 and stayed so until the unification of Italy in 1860.

The Normans introduced feudalism, a repressive social system that discouraged individual economic initiative, and which undermined the very base of the kingdom. When the dynasty became weaker, it passed to the Swebians and then to the Angevins. The feudal chiefs in Sicily revolted and attacked the central monarchy in the famous "Sicilian Vespers" of 1282. Led by Aragonese elements, the Angevins resisted and succeeded in retaining their power in Campania, but the Cilento—right at the border of the reduced kingdom—and the coastal towns suffered immense casualties and depopulation.

In the mid–13th century, the Angevins had established the capital in Naples, which flourished, but the kingdom's interior was abandoned to heavy feudal rule, which smothered commerce and economic activity and led to extreme poverty, which in turn fostered the growth of groups of bandits in the hills who made all road communication unsafe. The legacy of these centuries of stagnation and misrule persists to this day. The situation worsened still when the rule of the kingdom shifted to Spain.

SPANISH RULE

Spanish rule was seemingly so backward that even many histories of Naples contain a large blank spot for this 2-centuries-long period. The main events of Spanish rule were revolts against it—in 1547, 1599, 1647, and 1674, to name the major ones. The former kingdom of Naples was ruled by a Spanish viceroy, and the resulting extraction of taxes and the imposition of authoritarian rule were onerous. Philip IV called Naples "a gold mine, which furnished armies for our wars and treasure for their protection." The Spanish did build some great palaces and churches, though it is perhaps symbolic that Naples's Palazzo Reale was built for King Philip III, who never lived here. The great plague also occurred during this period, and wiped out half the population.

THE BOURBONS

During the tangled period of the War of Spanish succession in the early 18th century, Naples was ruled by Austrians for 27 years. Naples regained its independence in 1734, with Carlo di Borbone. The independence of the kingdom of Naples was at last recognized by Spain and the Papacy. Carlo revitalized the kingdom, improving the roads, draining the marshes in the area of Caserta, and creating new industries—such as the silk manufacturers in San Leucio, the ceramic artistry in Capodimonte, and the cameo and coral industries in Torre del Greco. The improvements continued during the 10 years of Napoleonic power, when the feudal system was completely dismantled and land was redistributed, creating new administrative and judicial structures. This gave new life to the provinces but, once the Bourbons returned, they were unable to strike a balance with the developing bourgeoisie. The region was thus poised for rebellion when Garibaldi arrived and brought about the unification of Italy in 1861.

A UNITED ITALY

Thanks to the brilliant efforts of Camillo Cavour (1810–61) and Giuseppe Garibaldi (1807–82), the kingdom of Italy was proclaimed in 1861. Victor Emmanuel (Vittorio Emanuele) II of the House of Savoy, king of Sardinia, became the head of the new monarchy.

Unfortunately, while the new kingdom was politically good for Campania, it was disastrous for Campania's economy: The northern government imposed heavy taxes, and the centralized administration paid little attention to local differences and needs. This killed the burgeoning industry that had been developing thanks to the Bourbons' paternalism and protection. Despite these setbacks, though, toward the end of the 19th century the coastal area started to develop the agricultural specialties that still exist today.

FASCISM & WORLD WAR II

Fascism achieved little success outside the urban area of Naples and was mostly embraced by prefects and notables in the rest of Campania. The region paid a heavy toll during World War II, when it was heavily bombarded in preparation for the Allied landing on September 8, 1943, when 55,000 Allied troops stormed ashore. Known as the Salerno Invasion, it actually involved landings in a long arc from Sorrento and Amalfi to as far south as the area of Paestum. The Nazis occupied the region and set up a desperate resistance, retreating slowly for long months just north of Caserta along the Garigliano River. This involved one of the war's most notorious battles, the several-months-long siege of Monte Cassino, which left the ancient monastery a heap of rubble. The Nazis destroyed as much as they could during their retreat, sacking and vandalizing everything—even the most important section of the Naples State Archives was burned.

In September 1943, Naples revolted and managed to chase out the occupiers, only days before the Allied forces arrived in the city. Other towns' insurrections resulted in horrible massacres; men and women organized guerrilla groups against the Nazis, hiding out in the mountains and hills and striking mostly at night, while the Allies bombarded their towns and cities. After many hard months of fighting, Campania was finally freed in June 1944.

THE POSTWAR YEARS

In 1946, Campania became part of the newly established Italian Republic—although Naples had given its preference to the monarchy in the referendum—and reconstruction began. Even though the war had left Italy ravaged, the country succeeded in rebuilding its economy. By the

1960s, as a member of the European Community (founded in Rome in 1957), Italy had become one of the world's leading industrialized nations, prominent in the manufacture of automobiles and office equipment. Campania was slow to recover; the terrible destruction that it suffered, the plague of corruption, plus the rising development of the Camorra, Campania's Mafia-like organization, hindered the region's development more than others.

The great earthquake (10 on the Mercalli, Cancani, Sieberg scale) that hit the region on November 23 gave it another push back, causing great destruction and economic hardship—over 3,000 people died, especially in the provinces of Avellino and Salerno, at the heart of the quake.

In the 1990s, a new Naples mayor and new regional government began investing more time and money in the restoration of Campania's artistic treasures, the reorganization of old museums, and the creation of new museums throughout the region. Just as important, the new government declared war on corruption and criminality. The millennium celebrations and the Papal Jubilee of 2000 brought about further renovations. Results have been spectacular; the center of Naples has been transformed from a depressed state into a sort of open-air museum, with tons of artistic and historical attractions.

At the same time, the escalating war against the Camorra in Naples has attracted much press attention over the past year or so, casting doubt on the city's safety. In our opinion, however, the accounts are sensationalized. Life in the historical part of the city has remained virtually untouched by Camorra violence, and improvements continue to be made, to the extent that Naples's artistic treasures, as well as the attractions of the whole Campania region, become more and more accessible to visitors every day.

2 ART & ARCHITECTURE IN CAMPANIA

ITALIAN ARCHITECTURE AT A GLANCE

While each architectural era has its own distinctive features, there are some elements, general floor plans, and terms common to many. Also, some features might appear near the end of one era and continue through several later ones.

From the Romanesque period on, most churches consist either of a single wide **aisle** or a wide central **nave,** flanked by two narrow aisles. The aisles are separated from the nave by a row of **columns** or by square stacks of masonry called **piers,** usually connected by **arches.**

This main nave/aisle assemblage is usually crossed by a perpendicular corridor called a **transept** near the far east end of the church so that the floor plan looks like a **Latin Cross** (shaped like a crucifix). The shorter, east arm of the nave is the holiest area, called the **chancel;** it often houses the stalls of the **choir** and the **altar.** If the far end of the chancel is rounded off, it's called an **apse.** An **ambulatory** is a curving corridor outside the altar and choir area, separating it from the ring of smaller chapels radiating off the chancel and the apse.

Some churches, especially after the Renaissance when mathematical proportion became important, were built on a **Greek Cross plan,** with each axis the same length, like a giant "+" (plus sign). By the baroque period, funky shapes became popular, with churches built in the round or as ellipses.

It's worth pointing out that very few buildings (especially churches) were built in only one particular style. Massive, expensive structures often took centuries to complete, during which time tastes changed and plans were altered.

Classical: Greeks & Romans (6th Century B.C. to A.D. 4th Century)

The **Greeks** settled Sicily and southern Italy, and left behind some of the best-preserved ancient temples in the world.

The **Romans** made use of certain Greek innovations, particularly architectural ideas. The first to be adopted was post-and-lintel construction (essentially, a weight-bearing frame, like a door). The Romans then added the load-bearing arch. Roman builders were inventive engineers, developing hoisting mechanisms and a specially trained workforce.

Identifiable Classical architectural features include these:

- **Classical orders.** These were usually simplified into types of column capitals, with the least ornate used on a building's ground level and the most ornate used on the top: Doric (a plain capital), Ionic (a capital with a scroll), and Corinthian (a capital with flowering acanthus leaves).
- **Brick and concrete.** Although marble is traditionally associated with Roman architecture, Roman engineers could also do wonders with bricks or even prosaic concrete—concrete seating made possible such enormous theaters as Rome's 2.4-hectare (6-acre), 45,000-seat Colosseum.

Most **Greek Temples** in the *Magna Graecia* of southern Italy were built in the 5th century B.C., Doric style, including those at **Paestum** south of Naples, and in Sicily at **Segesta** and **Agrigento,** including the remarkably preserved Temple of Concord. **Greek theaters** survive in Sicily at Taormina, Segesta, and Syracuse (which was the largest in the ancient world).

One of the best places to see **Roman architecture**, of course, is Rome itself, where examples of most major public buildings still exist. These include the sports stadium of the **Colosseum** (A.D. 1st c.), which perfectly displays the use of the Classical orders; Hadrian's marvel of engineering, the **Pantheon** (A.D. 1st c.); the brick public **Baths of Caracalla** (A.D. 3rd c.); and the **Basilica of Constantine and Maxentius** in the Roman Forum (A.D. 4th c.). By the way, Roman basilicas, which served as law courts, took the form of rectangles supported by arches atop columns along both sides of the interior, with an apse at one or both ends; the form was later adopted by early Christians for their first grand churches.

Three **Roman cities** have been preserved, with their street plans and, in some cases, even buildings remaining intact. These are famous, doomed **Pompeii** and its neighbor **Herculaneum** (both buried by Vesuvius's A.D. 79 eruption), as well as Rome's ancient seaport **Ostia Antica.**

Romanesque (A.D. 800 to 1300)

The Romanesque took its inspiration and rounded arches from ancient Rome (hence the name). Romanesque architects concentrated on building large churches with wide aisles to accommodate the masses, who came to hear the priests say Mass but mainly to worship at the altars of various saints. To support the weight of all that masonry, walls had to be thick and solid (meaning they could be pierced only by few and rather small windows), resting on huge piers, giving churches a dark, somber, mysterious, and often oppressive feeling.

Identifiable Romanesque features include:

- **Rounded arches.** These load-bearing architectural devices allowed architects to open up wide naves and spaces, channeling all the weight of the stone walls and ceiling across the curve of the arch and down into the ground via the columns or pilasters.
- **Thick walls.**
- **Infrequent and small windows.**
- **Huge piers.**
- **Blind arcades.** A range of arches was carried on piers or columns and attached to a wall. Set into each arch's curve was often a lozenge, a diamond-shaped decoration, sometimes inlaid with colored marbles.
- **Stripes.** Created by alternating layers of white and light-gray stones, this banding was typical of the Pisan-Romanesque style prominent in Pisa and Lucca. The gray got darker as time went on; by the late Romanesque/early Gothic period, the pattern often became a zebra of black and white stripes.
- **Stacked facade arcades.** Another typical Pisan-Romanesque feature was a tall facade created by stacking small, open-air loggias with columns of different styles on top of one another to a height of three to five levels.

Modena's Duomo (12th c.) marks one of the earliest appearances of rounded arches, and its facade is covered with great Romanesque reliefs. **Abbazia di Sant'Antimo** (1118), outside **Montalcino,** is a beautiful example of French Romanesque style. **Milan's Basilica di San Ambrogio** (11th–12th c.) is festooned with the tiered loggias and arcades that became hallmarks of the Lombard Romanesque.

Pisa's Cathedral group (1153–1360s) is typical of the Pisan-Romanesque style, with stacked arcades of mismatched columns in the cathedral's facade (and wrapping around the famous Leaning Tower of Pisa) and blind arcading set with lozenges. **Lucca's Cattedrale di San Martino and**

San Michele in Foro (11th–14th c.) are two more prime examples of the style.

Gothic (Late 12th to early 15th centuries)

By the late 12th century, engineering developments freed architecture from the heavy, thick walls of the Romanesque and allowed ceilings to soar, walls to thin, and windows to proliferate.

In place of the dark, somber, relatively unadorned Romanesque interiors that forced the eyes of the faithful toward the altar, where the priest stood droning on in unintelligible Latin, the Gothic interior enticed the churchgoers' gaze upward to high ceilings filled with light. The priests still conducted Mass in Latin, but now peasants could "read" the Gothic comic books of stained-glass windows.

The style began in France and was popular in Italy only in the northern region. From Florence south, most Gothic churches were built by the preaching orders of friars (Franciscans and Dominicans) as cavernous, barnlike structures.

Identifiable features of the French Gothic include:

- **Pointed arches.** The most significant development of the Gothic era was the discovery that pointed arches could carry far more weight than rounded ones.
- **Cross vaults.** Instead of being flat, the square patch of ceiling between four columns arches up to a point in the center, creating four sail shapes, sort of like the underside of a pyramid. The "X" separating these four sails is often reinforced with ridges called ribbing. As the Gothic progressed, four-sided cross vaults became six-sided, eight-sided, or multisided as architects played with the angles.
- **Tracery.** These lacy spider webs of carved stone grace the pointy ends of

windows and sometimes the spans of ceiling vaults.

- **Flying buttresses.** These free-standing exterior pillars connected by graceful, thin arms of stone help channel the weight of the building and its roof out and down into the ground. To help counter the cross forces involved in this engineering sleight of hand, the piers of buttresses were often topped by heavy pinnacles, which took the form of minispires or statues.
- **Stained glass.** Because pointy arches can carry more weight than rounded ones, windows could be larger and more numerous. They were often filled with Bible stories and symbolism written in the colorful patterns of stained glass.

The only truly French-style Gothic church in Italy is **Milan's massive Duomo & Baptistry** (begun ca. 1386), a lacy festival of pinnacles, buttresses, and pointy arches. **Siena's Duomo** (1136–1382), though started in the late Romanesque, has enough Giovanni Pisano sculptures and pointy arches to be considered Gothic. **Florence** has two of those barnlike Gothic churches: **Basilica di Santa Maria Novella** (1279–1357) and **Basilica di Santa Croce** (1294). The decorations inside **Santa Maria Sopra Minerva** (1280–1370), **Rome's** only Gothic church, are all of a later date, but the architecture itself is all pointy arches and soaring ceilings (though, hemmed in by other buildings, its interior is much darker than most Gothic places).

Renaissance (15th to 17th centuries)

As in painting, Renaissance architectural rules stressed proportion, order, classical inspiration, and mathematical precision to create unified, balanced structures. It was probably an architect, **Filippo Brunelleschi,** in the early 1400s, who first truly grasped the concept of "perspective" and provided artists with ground rules for creating the illusion of three dimensions on a flat surface.

Some identifiable Renaissance features include:

- A sense of proportion
- A reliance on symmetry
- The use of classical orders

One of the first great Renaissance architects was Florence's Filippo Brunelleschi (1377–1476). He often worked in the simple scheme of soft white plaster walls with architectural details and lines in pale gray *pietra serena* stone. Among his masterpieces in **Florence** are the Basilica di Santa Croce's **Pazzi Chapel** (1442–46), decorated with Donatello roundels; the interior of the **Basilica di San Lorenzo** (1425–46); and, most famous, the ingenious **dome** capping **Il Duomo** (1420–46). This last truly exemplifies the Renaissance's debt to the ancients. Brunelleschi traveled to Rome and studied the Pantheon up close to unlock the engineering secrets of its vast dome to build his own.

Urbino architect **Bramante** (1444–1514) was perhaps the most mathematical and classically precise of the early High Renaissance architects, evident in his (much-altered) plans for **Rome's St. Peter's Basilica** (his spiral staircase in the Vatican Museums has survived untouched). Also see his jewel of perfect Renaissance architecture, the textbook **Tempietto** (1502) at San Pietro in Montorio on the slopes of Rome's Gianicolo Hill, where church officials once thought that St. Peter had been crucified (as a plus, the little crypt inside is a riotous rococo grotto).

Renaissance man **Michelangelo** (1475–1564) took up architecture late in life, designing **Florence's Medici Laurentian Library** (1524) and **New Sacristy**

(1524–34), which houses the Medici Tombs at Basilica di San Lorenzo. In **Rome,** you can see his facade of the **Palazzo Farnese** (1566) and one of his crowning glories, the soaring **dome of St. Peter's Basilica,** among other structures.

The fourth great High Renaissance architect was **Andrea Palladio** (1508–80), who worked in a much more strictly classical mode of columns, porticoes, pediments, and other ancient temple–inspired features. His masterpieces include **Villa Foscari** and the great **Villa Rotonda,** both in the **Veneto** countryside around Vicenza. His final work is **Vicenza's Olympic Theater** (1580), an attempt to reconstruct a Roman theater stage as described in ancient writings. Other designs include the Venetian church **San Giorgio Maggiore** (1565–1610). He had great influence on architecture abroad as well; his "Palladian" style informed everything from British architecture to Thomas Jefferson's Monticello.

Baroque & Rococo (17th to 18th Centuries)

More than any other movement, the **baroque** aimed toward a seamless meshing of architecture and art. The stuccoes, sculptures, and paintings were all carefully designed to complement each other—and the space itself—to create a unified whole. This whole was both aesthetic and narrative, with the various art forms all working together to tell a single biblical story (or often to subtly relate the deeds of the commissioning patron to great historic or biblical events). Excessively complex and dripping with decorative tidbits, **rococo** is kind of a twisted version of the baroque.

Some identifiable baroque features include:

- **Classical architecture rewritten with curves.** The baroque is similar to Renaissance, but many of the right angles and ruler-straight lines are exchanged for curves of complex geometry and an interplay of concave and convex surfaces. The overall effect is to lighten the appearance of structures and add movement of line and vibrancy to the static look of the classical Renaissance.

- **Complex decoration.** Unlike the sometimes severe and austere designs of the Renaissance, the baroque was playful. Architects festooned exteriors and encrusted interiors with an excess of decorations intended to liven things up—lots of ornate stucco work, pouty cherubs, airy frescoes, heavy gilding, twisting columns, multicolored marbles, and general frippery.
- **Multiplying forms.** Why use one column when you can stack a half-dozen partial columns on top of each other, slightly offset, until the effect is like looking at a single column though a fractured kaleidoscope? The baroque loved to pile up its forms and elements to create a rich, busy effect, breaking a pediment curve into segments so that each would protrude farther out than the last, or building up an architectural feature by stacking short sections of concave walls, each one curving to a different arc.

The baroque flourished across Italy. Though relatively sedate, Carlo Maderno's facade and Bernini's sweeping elliptical colonnade for **Rome's St. Peter's Square** make one of Italy's most famous baroque assemblages. One of the quirkiest and most felicitous baroque styles flourished in the churches of the Apulian city **Lecce.** When an earthquake decimated the Sicilian town of **Noto** near Syracuse, it was rebuilt from scratch on a complete baroque city plan; the streets and squares made viewing platforms for the theatrical backdrops of its churches and palaces.

For the rococo—more a decorative than architectural movement—look no further than **Rome's Spanish Steps** (1726), by architect de Sanctis, or the **Trevi Fountain** (1762), by Salvi.

Neoclassical to Modern (18th to 21st Centuries)

As a backlash against the excesses of the baroque and rococo, architects began turning to the austere simplicity and grandeur of the classical age and inaugurated the **neoclassical** style by the middle of the 18th century. Their work was inspired by the rediscovery of Pompeii and other ancient sites.

In the late 19th and 20th centuries, Italy's architectural styles went in several directions. The **Industrial Age** of the 19th century brought with it the first genteel shopping malls of glass and steel. The country's take on the early-20th-century Art Nouveau movement was called **Liberty Style.** Mussolini made a spirited attempt to bring back ancient Rome in what can only be called **Fascist architecture.** Since then, Italy has built mostly concrete and glass **skyscrapers,** like the rest of the world, although a few architects in the medium have stood out.

Some identifiable features of each of these movements include:

- **Neoclassical.** The classical ideals of mathematical proportion and symmetry, first rediscovered during the Renaissance, are the hallmark of every classically styled era. Neoclassicists reinterpreted ancient temples as buildings and as decorative, massive colonnaded porticos.
- **Liberty Style.** Like Art Nouveau practitioners in other countries, Italian decorators rebelled against the era of mass production by stressing the uniqueness of craft. They created asymmetrical,

curvaceous designs based on organic inspiration (plants and flowers), and they used such materials as wrought iron, stained glass, tile, and hand-painted wallpaper.

- **Fascist.** Deco meets Caesar. This period produced monumentally imposing and chillingly stark, white marble structures surrounded by statuary in the classical style.

Of the **neoclassical, Caserta's Royal Palace** (1752–74), outside Naples, was a conscious attempt to create a Versailles for the Bourbon monarchs, while the unbelievably huge (and almost universally derided) **Vittorio Emanuele Monument** (1884–1927) in Rome, which has been compared to a wedding cake or a Victorian typewriter, was Italy's main monument to reaching its *Risorgimento* goal of a unified Italy.

The **Industrial Age** created glass-domed shopping arcades in giant "X" shapes in both **Milan** and **Naples. Liberty** style never produced any surpassingly important buildings, although you can glimpse it occasionally in period store-fronts.

Fascist architecture still infests corners of Italy (although most of the right-wing reliefs and the repeated engravings of DVCE—Mussolini's nickname for himself—have long since been chipped out). You can see it at its best in Rome's planned satellite community called **EUR,** which includes a multistory "square Colosseum" so funky that it has been featured in many a film and music video, and in **Rome's Stadio Olimpico** complex.

The **mid–20th century** was dominated by **Pier Luigi Nervi** (1891–1979) and his reinforced concrete buildings, **Florence's Giovanni Berta Stadium** (1932), **Rome's Palazzeto dello Sport stadium** (1960), and **Turin's Exposition Hall** (1949).

ART & ARCHITECTURE IN DEPTH

Campania's fertile and rich lands have attracted various peoples since prehistoric times, so it's not surprising that the territory bears the marks of many civilizations. Campania boasts Italy's richest trove of monuments from antiquity, with superb Greek ruins and unique Roman remains. You'll also find medieval castles and towns, Longobard, Norman, and Norman-Sicilian (or Arabo-Norman) architecture, and some of the richest collections of Renaissance and baroque monuments in Italy. However, art here didn't die with modern times—Naples continues to be a lively center of artistic life, especially in music and the figurative arts.

Prehistory

The islands and mountains of Campania are home to a huge trove of prehistoric art, from the grottoes of Palinuro and Marina di Camerota, to the necropolis of Mirabella Eclano, to the beautiful painted terra cottas of the Grotta delle Felci in Capri, to the rich Grotta di Pertosa near Salerno. Prehistoric Italy is probably the least appreciated aspect of Italian history, but it's fascinating.

The Legacy of the Etruscans & the Greeks on Local Italic Art

The Greeks and the Etruscans started to introduce their artistic styles to Campania in the 9th century B.C. From the ruins of **Cuma**—the first Greek colony in Italy—to the wonderful temples of **Paestum,** to the acropolis of **Velia,** Campania is rich with examples of Greek architecture, and the region's jewelry and metal work bear the mark of Etruscan influence. Etruscan and Greek styles were deeply embedded in the art of the local Italic populations when the Sannites took over the region in the 5th century B.C. The best examples of Italic art are the marvelous statues from the Sanctuary of the Goddess Matuta in **Santa Maria Capua Vetere;** and in particular the superb wall paintings from the tombs of **Cuma, Capua,** and **Paestum,** in the archaeological museums of Naples, Capua, and Paestum.

The Romans

With its harbors, fertile plains, and thermal waters, Campania was a key region for the Romans when it came to local artistic development. To the great private homes built along the coasts and on the islands—especially in **Herculaneum, Pompeii, Oplontis,** and **Boscoreale**—Rome added many grand public buildings, such as the amphitheater in **Capua Vetere;** the triumphal arch in **Benevento;** the villas of **Minori, Pozzuoli, Baia;** and the rich collections now in the museums of Naples, Capua, and Salerno.

The Byzantines, the Normans & the Longobards

Most of the early examples of art and architecture of the Middle Ages suffered from extensive damage, particularly by the Longobards. Only with the citizens' conversion to Catholicism and then with the arrival of the Normans did Byzantine art have a rebirth. The cathedrals of **Capua, Salerno,** and **Amalfi** are the richest examples of medieval art in the area, together with the **Basilica of Sant'Angelo in Formis,** the cathedral of **Sant'Agata dei Goti,** and the cathedral of **Casertavecchia,** as well as the Sanctuary of **Montevergine** and the cloister of Sant'Antonio in **Ravello.**

Campania also boasts several examples of magnificent medieval bronze doors, such as the ones in the cathedrals of Amalfi, Atrani, and Salerno. Classic Romanesque and Arab and Sicilian architecture intersect in these cathedrals. So do

many of Campania's local cloisters, such as Amalfi's cathedral and the ex-convent of the Capuchins, Ravello's Palazzo Rufolo, and Sorrento's cloister of Saint Francis.

Renaissance & Baroque

When the Angevins moved the capital of their kingdom to Naples, the enormous artistic development that was the Renaissance exploded in Campania. Famous artists came here from Tuscany—Lello da Orvieto, Giotto, Tino da Camaino, and Donatello—while local artists emerged on the scene, including Roberto d'Oderisio, Niccolò di Bartolomeo da Foggia, and Colantonio, the teacher of Antonello da Messina. The results are visible in the many churches of Naples and in the Castel Nuovo.

In Salerno, the local painter Antonio Sabatini da Salerno gained renown in the early 16th century. Some of the most powerful examples of Campanian High Renaissance style are in Naples, where many Italian artists were active, including Rossellino, Benedetto and Giuliano da Maiano, Fra Giovanni Giocondo, Fra Giovanni da Verona, Pietro Bernini, Giorgio Vasari, Polidoro da Caravaggio, and Antonio Solaro. The chapels of Monteoliveto and the Duomo in Naples are some of the best from this period.

In the 17th century, Caravaggio visited Naples and gave birth to the Neapolitan school of painting, which flourished in the 17th and 18th centuries under such names as Battistello Caracciolo, Andrea Vaccaro, Francesco Guarini, and Luca Giordano. Other Italian artists active in Naples during that period were Artemisia Gentileschi and Domenichino.

As with the rest of Italy, baroque art eventually gained dominance in Naples. The painter Francesco Solimena, together with sculptors Domenico Antonio Vaccaro (son of Lorenzo) and Giuseppe Sanmartino, were among its most famous practitioners. Among the many area architects, Luigi Vanvitelli, with his work on the Reggia di Caserta, emerged as the preeminent figure. Music by such important artists as G. B. Pergolesi and Domenico Cimarosa was also produced during this period.

Contemporary Art

The 19th and 20th centuries saw the continuation of Campania's artistic potential, with the School of Posillipo (Anton Pitloo, Salvatore Fergola) and later the Scuola di Resina in the 19th century, the Gruppo Sud, and the Gruppo 1858 in the 20th century. Modern painters such as Domenico Morelli and Francesco Paolo Michetti, along with sculptors such as Francesco Jerace, gained fame in the early 20th century, while one of the more contemporary artists to emerge is the painter Gianni Pisani. While the most famous composers of Italian opera generally hailed from other cities, the region did produce probably the most famous operatic performer of all time: Enrico Caruso, who was born in Naples in 1873.

3 A TASTE OF CAMPANIA

Food has always been one of life's great pleasures for the Italians. This has been true even from the earliest days: To judge from the lifelike banquet scenes found in Etruscan tombs, the Etruscans loved food and took delight in enjoying it. The Romans became famous for their never-ending banquets and for their love of exotic and even decadent treats, such as flamingo tongues.

Much of Naples's cuisine (spaghetti with clam sauce, or with *ragù* [meat sauce], meatballs, pizzas, fried calamari, and so forth) is already familiar to North Americans because so many Neapolitans moved to the New World and opened restaurants. However, Campanian cuisine has a list of specialties that are much lesser known. **Avellino,** for example, has a number of unique dishes that come from the mountain tradition, such as those flavored with **truffles,** and the delicious cakes made with **chestnuts. Benevento** has a completely different cuisine, reflecting its distinct history—it was part of the church's kingdom from the Renaissance onward—and its strong Sannite heritage. Beneventan cuisine favors meat over fish and includes a large number of specialties made with pork and wild boar. **Salerno** is the homeland of *mozzarella di bufala* and the famous Amalfi lemons.

DINING IN CAMPANIA

Dining hours tend to be later in Campania than in the United States: Lunch is between 1 and 3pm, and dinner between 8 and 10pm. Restaurants will rarely open before 12:30pm or 7:30pm, and often they'll only be setting up at that time.

The Passeggiata

This time-honored tradition takes place nightly in every town in Italy. Shortly after 6pm, men and women, young and old alike, stroll before dinner in the town center, usually through the main piazza and surrounding streets. Often members of the same sex link arms or kiss each other in greeting. There's no easier way to feel a part of everyday life in Italy than to make the passeggiata part of your evening routine.

Impressions

In Italy, the pleasure of eating is central to the pleasure of living. When you sit down to dinner with Italians, when you share their food, you are sharing their lives.

—Fred Plotkin, *Italy for the Gourmet Traveler* (1996)

The typical meal starts with a first course of pasta, or rice *(primo)*, or with an appetizer (antipasto)—sometimes both—which is then followed by a second course of meat or fish *(secondo)*, and/or a vegetable side dish or a salad *(contorno)*. Italians will finish a meal with cheese *(formaggio)*, or a piece of fruit *(frutta)*, and, of course, *caffè* (coffee). They'll have dessert *(dolce)* only occasionally, often opting instead for a gelato at a nearby ice-cream parlor.

Note: Ordering a cappuccino after lunch or dinner is a social blunder: Cappuccino is a breakfast or midmorning drink. Also, know that a latte here is a glass of plain milk, not the milk and coffee concoction you are used to.

Fast-food American style is replaced here by specialized restaurants that serve at the counter: *Spaghetterie* serve a large variety of pasta dishes; they are usually youth-oriented hangouts; *pizza a metro* and *pizza a taglio* are casual pizza parlors where pizza is sold by weight, with limited or nonexistent seating. A *tavola calda* (literally "hot table") serves ready-made hot foods you can take away or eat at one of the few small tables. A *rosticceria* is the same type of place; you'll see chickens roasting on a spit in the window. *Friggitoria* usually sell pizza and deep-fried calzone.

For a quick bite, you can also go to a **bar.** Although bars in Italy do serve alcohol, they function mainly as cafes. *Al banco* is the price you pay standing at the bar counter, while *al tavolo* means you are charged two to four times as much for sitting at a table where you'll be waited on.

In bars, you can find local pastries, panino sandwiches on various kinds of rolls, and *tramezzini* (white-bread sandwich triangles with the crusts cut off). The sandwiches run 1€ to 3€ and are traditionally put in a press to flatten and toast them.

A **pizzeria** is a restaurant specializing in individual pizzas, usually cooked in wood-burning ovens. They will also sometimes serve pasta dishes, and, typically, the menu includes an array of appetizers as well. A full-fledged restaurant is called an **osteria,** a **trattoria,** or a **ristorante.** Once upon a time, these terms meant something—osterias were basic places where you could get a plate of spaghetti and a glass of wine; trattorie were casual places serving full meals of filling peasant fare; and ristoranti were fancier places, with waiters in bow ties, printed menus, wine lists, and hefty prices. Nowadays, fancy restaurants often call themselves a trattoria to cash in on the associated charm factor; trendy spots use osteria to show they're hip; and simple, inexpensive places sometimes tack on ristorante to ennoble themselves. Many restaurants double as pizzerias, with a regular menu and a separate selection for pizza, sometimes offering a separate casual dining area as well.

The **enoteca** is a marriage of a wine bar and an osteria; you can sit and order from a host of good local and regional wines by the glass while snacking on appetizers or eating from a full menu featuring local specialties. Relaxed and full of ambience, these are great spots for light inexpensive lunches—or simply recharging your batteries.

Listen Up: Restaurant Lingo

Sezione fumatori o non fumatori?	Smoking or nonsmoking?	seh-TSYOH-neh foo-mah-TOHree oh nohn foo-mah-TOH-ree
È necessaria la giacca.	You'll need a jacket.	EH neh-chehs-SAH-ryah lah JAHK-kah
Mi dispiace, non sono permessi i pantaloni corti.	I'm sorry, no shorts are allowed.	mee dee-SPYAH-cheh nohn SOH-noh pehr-MEHS-see ee pahn-tah-loh-nee KOHR-tee
Posso portarle qualcosa da bere?	May I bring you something to drink?	POHS-soh pohr-TAHR-leh kwahl-KOH-zah dah BEH-reh
Gradisce la carta dei vini?	Would you like to see a wine list?	grah-DEESH-eh lah KAHR-tah day VEE-nee
Vuol sentire le nostre specialità?	Would you like to hear our specials?	vwol sehn-TEE-reh leh NOHStreh speh-chah-lee-TAH
È pronto/a per ordinare?	Are you ready to order?	EH PROHN-toh/ah pehr ohr-dee-NAH-reh
Mi dispiace signore / signora, ma la sua carta di credito è stata rifiutata.	I'm sorry sir/madame, your credit card was declined.	mee dee-SPYAH-cheh seen-NYOHreh / seen-NYOH-rah mah lah SOO-ah KAHR tah dee KREH-dee-toh EH STAH-tah ree-few-TAH-tah

The **pane e coperto** (bread and cover charge) is a 1€ to 3€ cover charge that you must pay at most restaurants for the mere privilege of sitting at a table. To request the bill, say, "Il conto, per favore" (eel *con*-toh, pore fah-*vohr*-ay). A tip of 15% is usually included in the bill these days but, if you're unsure, ask, "È incluso il servizio?" (ay een-*cloo*-soh eel sair-*vee*-tsoh?).

At many restaurants, especially larger ones and in cities, you'll find a **menu turistico** (tourist's menu), sometimes called **menu del giorno** (menu of the day) or **menu à prezzo fisso** (fixed-price menu). This set-price menu usually covers all meal incidentals—cover charge and 15% service charge—along with a first course *(primo)* and second course *(secondo),* and sometimes even a drink, but it almost always offers an abbreviated selection of pretty commonplace dishes. The above menu should not be confused with the **menu degustazione** (tasting menu) offered by more elegant gourmet restaurants: That's usually the way to go for the best selection of food at the best price. Except in those special restaurants, ordering a la carte will offer you the best chance of a memorable meal. Even better, forego the menu entirely and put yourself in the capable hands of your waiter.

PASTA, MOZZARELLA & PIZZA

The stars of Campanian cuisine are so well-known, they have become epicurean symbols of the nation: Italian cuisine as a whole is associated with pasta, pizza, and mozzarella. Yet these three creations were a direct consequence of the fertility and characteristics of Campania, defined by the Romans as "Campania Felix," or the happiest and most perfect of countrysides. To this day, Campania is considered one of the most important and even ideal agricultural provinces around.

Famous for the quality of their **pasta** since the 16th century, the many mills of the Monti Lattari, at the beginning of the Sorrento peninsula, are counted among the best producers of pasta in the world (the ones in Gragnano are particularly renowned). The pasta here is still *trafilata a bronzo* (extruded through bronze forms), a procedure that leaves the pasta slightly porous, allowing for a better penetration of the sauce for tastier results (as opposed to steel forms, which makes the pasta perfectly smooth).

This region created the kinds of pasta that we eat today—penne, fusilli, rigatoni, and so on, each type strictly defined: Spaghetti is thicker than vermicelli, and both are thicker than capellini.

The warm plains of Campania are also home to the rare native buffalo, which is still raised in the provinces of Caserta and Salerno. Campanians have made **mozzarella** with delicious buffalo milk for centuries and look with disdain on what we all know as mozzarella—the similar cheese made with cow's milk—for which they use a different name, *fiordilatte* (literally, "flower of milk"). Indeed, once you've tasted the real **mozzarella di bufala,** with its unique delicate flavor and lighter texture, you'll surely be converted too, and will look down on regular mozzarella as an inferior kind of cheese. It's delicious as is, or try it in the *caprese,* a simple salad of sliced mozzarella, fresh tomatoes, and basil seasoned with extra-virgin olive oil.

Putting together the wheat, the mozzarella, and the third-famous produce of this region, the tomato, Neapolitans one day invented **pizza.** The unique local tomatoes—especially those produced on the slopes of Mount Vesuvius—have basically no seeds: Imagine a tomato with no central cavity (no spongy, white stuff, either), but filled just with fruit meat, both flavorful and juicy. These are the *pomodoretti,* or small tomatoes of Mount Vesuvius. Obviously the result couldn't be anything but a bestseller, and pizza quickly spread from Naples throughout the world.

Be forewarned that many tourists, however, are disappointed by Neapolitan pizza. Here the dough and the tomatoes are the key ingredients—together with the olive oil, of course—and cheese is an option. If you ask for a Neapolitan pizza in Naples, you'll be offered a "marinara": a thick crust that is crunchy on the outside and covered with fresh tomatoes, olive oil, and oregano, with no cheese at all. Funny enough, what Romans and the rest of Italy call Neapolitan pizza (pizza Napoletana, with tomatoes, cheese, and anchovies) is referred to here in Naples as "Roman pizza" (à la Romana).

The second-most traditional pizza in Naples is the *margherita.* Named after Margherita di Savoia, queen of Italy, who asked to taste pizza during her residence in the Royal Palace of Naples before the capital was moved to Rome, the pizza bears the colors of the Italian flag: basil for the green, mozzarella for the white, and red for the tomatoes. The new pizza met with immediate favor, eventually surpassing the popularity of its older counterpart. Pizza evolved with the addition of a large variety of other toppings, but purist pizzerias in Naples (such as Da Michele in Naples; see chapter 5) serve only these two types. In Naples, you can also taste another wonderful type of pizza: **pizza fritta.** This wonderful creation is served only in truly old-fashioned places where a double round of pizza dough is filled with ricotta, mozzarella, and ham, and deep-fried in a copper cauldron of scalding olive oil. It arrives as puffy as a ball, but as you poke into it, the pizza flattens out, allowing you to delve into the delicious (though not exactly cholesterol-free) dish.

ANTIPASTI E CONTORNI

Italian delight in food has remained strong in Campania throughout the centuries, seemingly in spite of the region's poverty. In fact, the region's poverty prompted the development of an important local characteristic when it comes to food: expediency. Ease and quickness, and making something out of almost nothing, were the driving forces behind Campanians coming up with some of the most delicious, yet simplest, concoctions in the history of cuisine. Check out the *antipasti* buffet of any good restaurant, and you'll be certain to find variety, from scrumptious vegetable dishes to seafood preparations such as sauté of shellfish, delicious mussels and clams sautéed in a pan with garlic and olive oil. Alternatively, go for *polipetti in cassuola* or *affogati* (squid cooked with a savory tomato-and-olive sauce inside a terra-cotta small casserole). Among the vegetables, do not miss the typical *zucchine a scapece,* a round of zucchini fried in olive oil and seasoned with tangy vinegar and fresh mint dressing (the same preparation is sometimes used for eggplant); or *involtini di melanzane* (a roll of deep-fried

eggplant slices, filled with pine nuts and raisins, and warmed up in a tomato sauce) and, when in season, the *friarelli,* a local vegetable that is a cousin to broccoli but much thinner; it's often sautéed with garlic and red pepper, and is at its best paired with local sausages.

SOUPS & PRIMI

One of the most surprising and delicious associations you'll come across here is the delicious *zuppa di fagioli e cozze* (beans and mussels soup), which is common south of Naples and on Capri; another good and unique soup is the *minestra maritata,* a thick concoction of pork meat and a variety of fresh vegetables. The simple comfort food *pasta e patate* (pasta and potatoes smothered with cheese) will surprise you by how tasty it is. At the other end of the spectrum, the elaborated *sartù* (a typical Neapolitan baked dish made with seasoned rice, baby meatballs, sausages, chicken liver, mozzarella, and mushrooms) matches the difficulty of its preparation with the satisfaction of eating it.

Our preferred dish is the local pasta, including *scialatielli* (a fresh, homemade, eggless kind of noodles), served with sautéed seafood *(ai frutti di mare).* Another delicious, but more difficult-to-find pasta, is homemade fusilli. They can be served with all the traditional sauces: *con le vongole* (with clams), *zucchine e gamberi* (shrimp and zucchini), or *al ragù* (a meat sauce, where many kinds of meat can be cooked with tomatoes, including *braciole,* a meat *involtini* with pine nuts and raisins).

SECONDI

The cuisine of Naples—shared by most of Campania's coast—focuses on seafood, and some of the best main courses are made with fish. The *frittura (fritto misto* elsewhere in Italy) of shrimp and calamari is always a great pleasure, and here you will also find other kinds, such as the *fragaglie* (very small fish). The local version of

Ice Cream in Campania: A User's Guide to Gelato

Gelato is the Italian version of ice cream. It is milk or egg white–based, with cream used only for certain flavors, which makes it much easier to digest and in general less caloric, particularly the fruit flavors, which are made with fresh fruit (technically, these are usually water-based, making them *sorbetto,* or sorbet). Also, the fresh-made gelato contains less sugar than most ice cream, and is cholesterol free.

The number of flavors you get depends on the size (2 scoops for the small and up to 4 for the large); you can choose to have it served in a cone *(cono)* or cup *(coppetta).* Locals usually ask for a dollop of whipped cream *(panna)* on top: Specify if you don't want it: *senza panna* (sen-zah pan-nah).

Here are some important tips to help you spot the best gelato parlors:

- The bar or parlor bears a sign saying PRODUZIONE PROPRIA or PRODUZIONE ARTIGIANALE, which means it is made fresh, in small batches, and from fresh, mostly local, ingredients (no large-scale industrial production).
- The colors are not overly bright—no neon green for pistachio, for instance, or bright yellow for lemon. Natural colors are off-white for banana, pale green for pistachio, white for lemon, and so on.
- The flavors on offer include seasonal fruits, such as peach, apricot, and watermelon in summer, and orange and mandarin in winter.
- They tend to be gelato specialists: Gelato is all they sell, or at least, the section devoted to it is substantial, with a large cold counter well in view.

Another cold treat is *granita,* a close cousin to slushies. The classic is made from frozen lemon juice or coffee, but other flavors are sometimes available, such as almond milk or watermelon. Coffee-flavored *granite* are usually served with *panna.* You'll also see street carts selling shaved ice with flavored syrup, which they call *granita* as well. Though still a refreshing treat, it's not quite the same thing.

zuppa di pesce is not often offered, but it is a delicious fish stew. Much more common and equally delicious are the *polpi affogati* or *in cassuola,* squid or octopus slowly stewed with tomatoes and parsley. Large fish is served grilled, with a tasty dressing of herbs and olive oil; *all'acqua pazza,* poached in a light broth made of a few tomatoes and herbs; or *alle patate* (baked over a bed of thinly sliced potatoes, and absolutely delicious). You might also find it *al sale* (cooked inside a crust of salt) to retain its moisture and flavors. Finally, if you have a taste for lobster, you should not miss out on the rare and expensive local clawless variety—*astice.*

For the turf, you might try *coniglio alla cacciatora* (rabbit with wine and black olives), a very tasty creation typical of Ischia; *brasato,* beef slowly stewed with wine and vegetables; *braciola di maiale,* a pork cutlet rolled and filled with prosciutto, pine nuts, and raisins cooked in a tomato sauce; or the simpler meat *alla pizzaiola,* a beef cutlet sautéed in olive oil and cooked with fresh tomatoes and oregano.

SWEETS

If Sicilians are famous for having a sweet tooth, Neapolitans come in a close second, with many delicious specialties on offer. Naples is famous for its *pastiera,* a cake traditionally prepared for Easter but so good that it is now offered year-round in most restaurants. Whole-grain wheat is soaked, boiled, and then used to prepare a delicious creamy filling with ricotta and orange peel in a thick pastry shell.

Another famous dessert is *babà,* a soft, puffy cake soaked in sweet syrup with rum and served with pastry cream. The famous *sfogliatelle* (flaky pastry pockets filled with a sweet ricotta cream) are so good with typical Neapolitan coffee that you shouldn't leave without tasting them; a special kind from Conca dei Marini on the Amalfi Coast is the *sfogliatella Santa Rosa,* filled with pastry cream and *amarene* (candied sour cherries in syrup) instead of ricotta, which was invented in the 14th-century Convento di Santa Rosa.

Each town in Campania, including the smaller villages, has some kind of sweet specialty, such as the *biscotti di Castellammare,* shaped like thick fingers in several flavors, and the several lemon-based pastries from the Sorrento and Amalfi regions: *ravioli al limone* (filled with a lemon-flavored ricotta mixture) from Positano; the *Sospiri* (Sighs)—also called *Zizz'e Nonache* (Nuns' Breasts) depending on which aspect you focus, the taste or the look. The dome-shaped small, pale pastries filled with lemon cream come from Maiori and Minori; and *dolcezze al limone,* the typical lemon pastries of Sorrento, are small puff pastries filled with lemon-flavored cream.

AND SOME VINO TO WASH IT ALL DOWN

Italy is the largest wine-producing country in the world (more than 1.6 million hectares/4 million acres of soil are cultivated as vineyards). Grapes were cultivated as far back as 800 B.C., probably introduced by the Greeks, and wine has been produced ever since. However, it wasn't until 1965 that laws were enacted to guarantee consistency in winemaking and to defend

specific labels. Winemakers have to apply to have the right to add "D.O.C." *(Denominazione di Origine Controllata)* on their labels, and only consistently good wines from specific areas receive this right. The "D.O.C.G." on a label (the "G" means *garantita*) applies to even better wines from even more strictly defined producing areas. Vintners who are presently limited to marketing their products as unpretentious table wines—*vino da tavola*—often expend great efforts lobbying for an elevated status as a D.O.C.

Of Campania's five provinces, Benevento is the one with the largest number of D.O.C. wines, including the ***Aglianico del Taburno, Solopaca, Guardiolo, Sannio, Sant'Agata dei Goti,*** and ***Taburno,*** but Avellino is the only one with three D.O.C.G. wines: the wonderful ***Taurasi,*** considered to be one of the best Italian red wines, up there with Brunello and Barolo; the ***Greco di Tufo,*** straw-yellow and dry, with a delicate peach-almond flavor; and the ***Fiano di Avellino,*** a dry and refreshing white wine, which received its D.O.C.G. label only in 1993.

From the volcanic soil of Mount Vesuvius comes the amber-colored ***Lacrima Christi*** (Tears of Christ), and from the area of Pozzuoli, the D.O.C. ***Campi Flegrei.*** With meat dishes, try the dark mulberry-colored ***Gragnano,*** in the Sorrento peninsula, which has a faint bouquet of faded violets, and ***Penisola Sorrentina.*** From the islands come the ***Ischia*** red and white, and the ***Capri.***

The Amalfi Coast also has its share of D.O.C. wines. The ***Costa d'Amalfi*** includes the ***Furore***—white, red, and dry rosé—the red ***Tramonti,*** and the ***Ravello***—white and dry with an idea of gentian, the rosé dry with a delicate violet and raspberry bouquet and with a slightly fuller body, and a red with the most body.

Produced in the Salerno area, the ***Castel San Lorenzo*** red and rosé are D.O.C.,

Campanian Nightlife

By American and British standards, nightlife in Campania's provincial towns tends to be dull. There isn't a bar culture in southern Italy, and often what's called a pub here is a rather pale imitation. Cultural and social life, though, are always lively, from strolling along the main street or going out for dinner, to having an *aperitivo*, eating handmade gelato, or going to the theater or a movie.

While there are some great nightclubs in Naples, the situation is quite different in the rest of the region. You'll find some good clubs along the Amalfi Coast in summer, but things are quieter in the evening in the country. Your best option will often be a concert. Musical events (both classical and Italian pop) are sometimes staged in even the most remote little towns and villages.

but there is also a *barbera* (fizzy red), a white, and a *moscato* (sweet). Farther south is the **Cilento,** another excellent D.O.C. wine.

From Caserta come the **Falerno,** the D.O.C. **Galluccio,** and the D.O.C. **Asprino d'Aversa,** which is light and slightly fizzy.

OTHER DRINKS

Italians drink other libations as well. The most famous Italian drink is **Campari,** bright red in color and flavored with herbs; it has a quinine bitterness to it. It's customary to serve it with ice cubes and soda.

Campania also excels at the preparation of *Rosolio,* sweet liquor usually herb or fruit flavored, prepared according to recipes passed down by families for generations. The most famous is **limoncello,** a bright yellow drink made by infusing pure alcohol with the famous lemons from the Amalfi Coast, but others deserve similar fame, like the rare *nanassino,* made with prickly pears; and the *finocchietto,* made with wild fennel. Limoncello has become Italy's second-most popular drink (p. 30). It has long been a staple in the lemon-producing region of Capri and Sorrento, and recipes for the

sweetly potent concoction have been passed down by families there for generations. About a decade ago, restaurants in Sorrento, Naples, and Rome started making their own versions. Visitors to those restaurants as well as the Sorrento peninsula began singing limoncello's praises and requesting bottles to go. Now it's one of the most up-and-coming liqueurs in the world, thanks to heavy advertising promotions.

Beer, once treated as a libation of little interest, is still far inferior to wines produced domestically, but foreign beers, especially those of Ireland and England, are gaining great popularity with Italian youth, especially in Rome. This popularity is mainly because of atmospheric pubs, which now number more than 300 in Rome alone, where young people linger over a pint and a conversation. Most pubs are in the Roman center, and many are licensed by Guinness and its Guinness Italia operations. In a city with 5,000 watering holes, 300 pubs might seem like a drop, but because the clientele is young, the wine industry is trying to devise a plan to keep that drop from becoming a steady stream of Italians who prefer grain to grapes.

2

High-proof **grappa** is made from the "leftovers," after the grapes have been pressed. Many Italians drink this before or after dinner (some put it into their coffee). It's an acquired taste—to an untrained foreign palate, it often seems rough and harsh.

4 RECOMMENDED BOOKS

General

Besides his more famous *Italian Neighbors,* Tim Parks wrote a delightful account of his encounters with Italian culture (his wife is Italian), full of humor and insight, in *Italian Education.*

True Stories

If you want to bone up on the ancient Romans, Edward Gibbon's *History of the Decline and Fall of the Roman Empire* (begun in 1776) is still unrivaled today, but it will take you a minimum of 3 months to get through the several volumes.

Among the many travel books about this region, one of the first is also one of the best and most charming: Johann Wolfgang von Goethe's *Italian Journey.* Goethe much preferred Naples to Rome and writes vividly about a wide range of social and natural phenomena, from his mingling with the aristocracy to a trip up Mount Vesuvius during an eruption. The 19th century saw an explosion of travel writing by eminent authors on the "Grand Tour"; William Dean Howells recorded his impressions in *Roman Holidays and Others.* The impoverished English "slum novelist" George Gissing was finally able to travel to Italy toward the end of his life and wrote with great enthusiasm about his experiences in *By the Ionian Sea.* Henry James's *Italian Hours* is a collection of essays, one of which describes the novelist's visit to the Bay of Naples and its islands. Barbara Grizzuti Harrison describes her time in Italy, including a stay in Naples, in *Italian Days.* Most recently, Frommer's author Marc Llewellyn penned

Finding Nino, a memoir of his time spent living with his family as a fisherman on Lipari, in the Aeolian Islands, or the "Islands of the Wind."

Art History

For a modern history of art, the touchstone is the massive *History of Italian Renaissance Art,* by Frederick Hartt. Naples was not central to the art of that great period—Rome, Florence, and Venice were the major focal points—but you will find an interesting treatment of Naples's Renaissance legacy in Laurie Scheider Adams's *Italian Renaissance Art.* To home in on Naples's baroque heritage, try John Varriano's *Italian Baroque and Rococo Architecture.* Giorgio Vasari's *Lives of the Artists Vols. I and II* is a collection of biographies of the great artists from Cimabue up to Vasari's own 16th-century contemporaries.

FICTION

The English writer Norman Douglas came to the Bay of Naples early in the 20th century and was gripped by a lifelong fascination with the region. His most famous novel, *South Wind,* is set on a fictional version of Capri, and reproduces the glamorous and eccentric expatriate community. Susan Sontag's historical novel, *The Volcano Love,* is set in the Napoleonic era, and is based on the true story of the love triangle between Sir William Hamilton (British ambassador to the Kingdom of the Two Sicilies), his wife, and her lover, Lord Horatio Nelson. *The Uncle from Rome,* by American author Joseph Caldwell, is the story of an opera singer from Indiana who comes to Naples to play a role. He befriends a family of Neapolitans, and becomes involved in family dynamics at least as theatrical as his stage performance. For a look at Naples's dark side, there is the tragicomic *Così fan Tutti,* a mystery by English novelist Michael Dibdin in his detective Aurelio Zen series.

Several Italian authors have written movingly of the harsh and beautiful rural life of southern Italy. Most famous perhaps is Carlo Levi's *Christ Stopped at Eboli,* about the author's sojourn in a small village where he was exiled during the Fascist period.

3

Planning Your Trip to Campania & the Amalfi Coast

Italy is an easy country to tour, and Campania is a tourist- and family-friendly destination, whatever your traveling style and needs. The bulk of your planning will be focused on prioritizing which destinations you'll visit and which you'll leave for your next Campanian vacation. Remember: The laidback *dolce vita* reigns here and you don't want to put too much on your plate—unless it's the local food.

This relaxed culture has the unfortunate (for tourists) side effect that in certain seaside destinations—in particular Capri and the Amalfi and Cilento coasts—many low-end hotels and restaurants close for the entire winter (usually Nov–Mar), with the occasional exception for the Christmas and New Year's holidays. This is a mixed blessing, because you'll enjoy this splendid coast without the summer crowds, but your choices of accommodations and entertainment will be reduced.

For additional help in planning your trip and for more on-the-ground resources in Campania and the Amalfi Coast, turn to chapter 12.

1 WHEN TO GO

April to June and **September to October** are generally the best times to visit Campania; temperatures are usually mild, and the crowds aren't quite so intense. Starting in mid-June, the summer rush begins, especially at the seaside resorts; and from **July to August,** the coast teems with visitors. **Mid-August** is the worst on the coast in terms of crowds: The entire country goes on vacation around the holiday of **Ferragosto,** on August 15; while the cities tend to be deserted—in Naples, Benevento, Avellino, Caserta, and Salerno many restaurants and shops will be closed—the seaside towns and island resorts buzz with activity. By contrast, the region's interior never gets really crowded. From **November to Easter,** most attractions go to shorter winter hours or are closed for renovation, while a number of

hotels and restaurants close or take extended vacations. Especially between **November and February,** spa and beach destinations become padlocked ghost towns. Also, it can get much colder than you'd expect (it might even snow).

High season on most airline routes to Naples usually stretches from June to the beginning of September. This is the most expensive and most crowded time to travel. **Shoulder season** is from April to May, early September to October, and December 15 to January 14. **Low season** is from November 1 to December 14 and from January 15 to March 31.

WEATHER

Campania enjoys four well-defined seasons. Winters are mild, spring and fall are pleasant, and summers are hot. July and

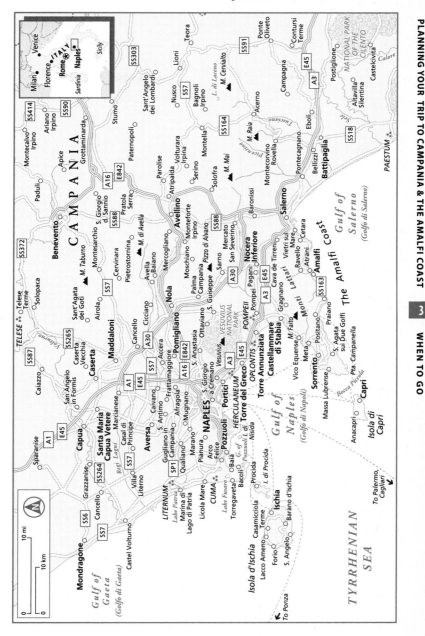

Naples	Jan	Feb	Mar	Apr	May	June	July	Aug	Sept	Oct	Nov	Dec
Temp. (°F)	48	48	52	56	64	71	76	76	71	63	54	50
Temp. (°C)	8	8	11	13	17	21	24	24	21	17	12	10
Rainfall (in.)	3.8	3.2	3	3	2	1.5	0.9	1.2	3.1	5.2	5	4.7
Salerno	Jan	Feb	Mar	Apr	May	June	July	Aug	Sept	Oct	Nov	Dec
Temp. (°F)	50	53	55	60	66	75	78	81	75	66	59	55
Temp. (°C)	10	11	13	16	19	24	26	27	24	19	15	13
Rainfall (in.)	6.2	5.4	4.5	3.7	2.9	1.5	.7	1.1	4.1	6.5	7.5	7.1
Sorrento	Jan	Feb	Mar	Apr	May	June	July	Aug	Sept	Oct	Nov	Dec
Temp. (°F)	50	50	51	57	62	69	75	75	71	64	57	51
Temp. (°C)	10	10	11	14	17	21	24	24	22	18	14	11
Rainfall (in.)	2.9	2.1	2.1	1.6	1.2	0.6	0.7	1.2	2	2.7	3.9	3.4
Benevento	Jan	Feb	Mar	Apr	May	June	July	Aug	Sept	Oct	Nov	Dec
Temp. (°F)	45	46	52	57	64	71	77	77	71	63	54	50
Temp. (°C)	7	8	11	14	18	22	25	25	22	17	12	10
Rainfall (in.)	2.8	2.8	2.1	2	2.1	1.4	.6	1.2	2.1	3	3.7	3.5

August are very hot, especially in low-lying areas. The high temperatures (measured in Italy in degrees Celsius) begin in Naples in May, often lasting until sometime in October. For the most part, the humidity is lower in Campania than, say, in Washington, D.C., so high temperatures don't seem as oppressive. In Naples, temperatures can stay in the 90°F (30°C) range for days, but nights are often comfortably cooler.

Winters are mild by the sea, with temperatures averaging 50°F (10°C), but it gets much colder in the interior and the mountains, which often are subject to rain and snow. Precipitations tend to be rare in summer but increase abruptly in the fall, which tends to be the wetter season. They are somewhat lower in winter and dwindle in spring.

CAMPANIA CALENDAR OF EVENTS

For an exhaustive list of events beyond those listed here, check http://events.frommers.com, where you'll find a searchable, up-to-the-minute roster of what's happening in cities all over the world.

For major events in which tickets should be procured well before your arrival, we prefer using Italy-based services; they are often cheaper and have more comprehensive event offerings (see "Before You Leave Home: Tickets & Seats in Advance," below). You can also check with **Global Edwards & Edwards,** in the United States, at © **800-223-6108.**

JANUARY

Il Presepe nel Presepe (**Manger in a Manger**), Morcone. This suggestive little town near Benevento is a natural background for the reenactment of Jesus' birth. Each January, the villagers

here transform their town into a version of Bethlehem, and open their homes to visitors. January 3.

Epiphany celebrations, regionwide. All Roman Catholic holidays are deeply felt in Campania, and festive celebrations for the Epiphany include numerous fairs and processions celebrating the arrival of the Three Kings at Christ's manger. January 6.

Festival Internazionale della Canzone Napoletana ed Italiana (International Festival of Italian and Neapolitan Song), Capua. Gathering performers and lovers of Italian and Neapolitan music for more than 3 decades (the festival reached its 30th anniversary in 2007), this 3-day event is a celebration of Italian folk music, both new and traditional. End of January.

FEBRUARY

Carnival, regionwide. During the period before Lent, float parades and histrionic traditional shows take place in most towns, big and small, throughout the region. Some of the best are in Capua, which puts on a grand parade and cabaret and theater performances (call the tourist office at (✆ 0823-321137), and in Montemarano, where celebrations start on January 17 (call the tourist office at (✆ 082-524013, for a schedule of events). Paestum schedules great parade and dance shows (call the tourist office at (✆ 0828-811016). Dates vary, but it's generally held the week before Ash Wednesday.

Carnevale Irpino, Avellino. This festival includes traditional representations, such as the famous *Zeza*, a musical farce; parades; and the Concorso della Zeza, a large competition for group mummers (masked performers). Contact the EPT ((✆ 0825-74732 or 0825-74695) for a schedule of the events. The 2 weeks before Ash Wednesday.

MARCH

Nauticsud, Mostra d'Oltremare, Napoli. Spanning both land and water, this boat show boasts displays of the latest motor and sailing boats and equipment. Check the website for information at www.nauticsud.info. Mid-March.

Comicon—International Comics Festival, Napoli. This international event at Castel Sant'Elmo, in its 11th year in 2009, is a must see for fans of comic books and animation. Each year the fair is organized around a main theme—Japanese comics and mystery were the last two—and includes previews and presentations of new productions spanning the spectrum. Contact the organization for a schedule of events ((✆ 081-4238127; www.comicon.it). March and April.

Primavera Sorrentina, Sorrento. The town celebrates the spring and then the summer with an array of events, including various flower fairs, food fairs, and a few musical venues. March through July.

APRIL

Pasqua (Easter), regionwide. Celebrations for the resurrection of Christ include several events: Processions for the benediction of the symbolic palm—usually olive tree branches—take place on the Sunday before Easter Sunday; Stations of the Cross processions (reenacting Jesus' ascent to Golgotha) are staged in almost every church on Holy Friday; finally, Easter Sunday is marked by special religious celebrations. Various dates between end of March and April.

Pasqua a Sorrento (Easter in Sorrento), Sorrento. These Easter celebrations last a whole week; religious processions and concerts are scheduled in the town's cathedral and in the delightful cloister of San Francesco. Other processions take place on the night of Holy Thursday through Holy Friday in the towns surrounding Sorrento: Meta, Piano di Sorrento, and Sant'Agnello. Week before Easter.

Processione dei Misteri (Procession of the Mysteries), Procida. This is one of the most famous traditional religious events in Campania, a procession of plastic scenes from the Passion of Christ sculpted by local craftspeople. Evolving from its original procession in 1627, it is now a glorious show of entire scenes depicting the betrayal of Judas, the Last Supper, and so on, as well as large statues of Christ and the Madonna. Holy Thursday night into Holy Friday morning.

Linea d'ombra Salerno—Festival Culture Giovani, Salerno. This major international event, in its 14th year in 2009, is dedicated to new talent in Europe and focuses on the passage from adolescence to adulthood—the "shadow line," written about by Joseph Conrad—through film, music, visual and performing arts, and literature. Contact the festival office (📞 **089-2753673;** fax 089-2571125; www.festivalculture giovani.it). Varying week in April.

MAY

Feast of San Costanzo, Marina Grande, Capri. This day honors St. Costanzo, whose remains, preserved in the local basilica, protected the island from the Saracens' attacks during the Middle Ages. Bishop Costanzo died on the island during his apostolic mission in Capri on his way to Constantinople around A.D. 677. Call the local tourist office for a program, at 📞 **081-8370424.** Third week of May.

Maggio dei Monumenti **(Monuments in May),** Napoli. The *centro storico* (city center) of Naples comes alive with cultural events and extraordinary openings of private collections and monuments for a whole week. This successful special event marked its 14th anniversary in 2008. Contact the tourist office for a schedule. Last week of May.

JUNE

Historic Regatta of the Maritime Republics, Amalfi. Each of Italy's four historical towns—Genova, Pisa, Venice, and Amalfi—alternate turns hosting

this annual regatta. Amalfi's turn was in 2009 and will occur again in 2013. Contact the tourist office (📞 **089-871107**). First Sunday in June.

Il Trionfo del Tempo e del Disinganno **(The Triumph of Time and Enlightenment),** provinces of Caserta and Benevento. Reaching its 17th year in 2010, this festival of medieval, Renaissance, and baroque music is beloved by connoisseurs, who delight not only in the high quality of the performances, but also in the venues: All concerts are held in little-known historical buildings, some of which are not usually open to the general public, and can be visited with a guide just before the concert. Check http://trionfo.altervista.org for a schedule of events. Second half of June through the end of August.

Concerti al Tramonto, Anacapri. Each summer, the Foundation Axel Munthe organizes a series of sunset concerts (classical and jazz) in the Villa San Michele, in a spectacular setting overlooking the island and the sea. Contact the tourist office for details (📞 **081-8371401;** www.sanmichele.org). June through August.

Leuciana Festival, Caserta. With a rich program of musical, theatrical, and dance performances held in Caserta's Reggia and in the scenic Belvedere di San Leucio, this festival celebrated its 10-year anniversary in 2008. For more information, call 📞 **0823-444234** or visit www.leuciana.org. June through August.

Music in the Cloister, Amalfi. Organized by the town of Amalfi, this series of concerts, held in the splendid Chiostro del Paradiso at Amalfi's cathedral, is one of our favorite events. Contact the tourist office (📞 **089-871107**) for a program. Usually on Friday at 9pm. Beginning of August to mid-September.

Sagra del Limone (Lemon Fair), Massa Lubrense. Celebrating the fruit that characterizes so much of the local culture and cuisine, this 4-day festival (celebrating 34 years in 2008) includes walks in the countryside, farm visits, and culinary events. First weekend in July.

Benevento Citta' Spettacolo, Benevento. The ancient Roman theater of Benevento is the venue for a full-fledged summer season of opera and drama. Contact the tourist office (✆ **0824-319911**). July through August.

Neapolis Festival, Naples. Rock might be old-fashioned these days, but this 2-day festival is still hot. It stages the best groups in Italy and the world. Call or check the website for the program (✆ **081-7258025;** www.neapolis.it). July.

Ischia Film Festival, Ischia. Already preparing for the eighth edition in 2010, this growing event staged 100 films from 23 different countries in 2009. Visit www.ischiafilmfestival.it for more information. One week in July.

Ravello Festival, Ravello. This internationally renowned festival includes classical music, jazz, dance, and visual arts, with shows by artists of world fame. You must make reservations well in advance. Contact the festival office (✆ **089-858422** or 334-6264222; www.ravellofestival.com) for reservations. July through September.

Estate a Minori, Minori. Artists from around the world come to perform with the Amalfi Coast as their backdrop, and the Teatro del Mare inaugurated this year provides an additional stage right on the beach. Contact the local tourist office for the program (✆/fax **089-877087;** www.proloco.minori.sa.it). July through August.

Festival Ville Vesuviane, Ercolano. Reaching its 23rd edition in 2010, this music festival takes the stage in the splendid villas of the Miglio d'Oro—the stretch of some 122 elegant villas built at the foot of Mount Vesuvius during the 18th century by the Bourbon court. Contact the Ente Ville Vesuviane (✆ **081-7322134;** www.villevesuviane.net) for a schedule of events. July.

Festa del Mare, town of Ischia. These spectacular celebrations mark the occasion of the Festival of Sant'Anna. A procession of boats and floats crosses the harbor under the town's illuminated castle. July 26.

Sagra della Sfogliatella di Santa Rosa, Conca dei Marini. This event celebrates the local version of *sfogliatella,* the most famous of Neapolitan pastries, filled with pastry cream and a sour cherry confection. August.

Festival of the Assunta, Positano. In the 9th and 10th centuries A.D., when the Saracens established themselves in nearby Agropoli (see chapter 8), the whole coast was endangered by their repeated incursions and bloody robberies. This festival reenacts the Saracens' attack on Positano and the miraculous intervention of the Madonna who, as legend has it, saved the town. August 14 and August 15.

Surrentum Grandi Eventi, Sorrento. The rich program of this recurring festival—at its 14th edition in 2010—is centered on dance, theater, and music. The additional draw is the setting: All performances are staged in beautiful Villa Fiorentino. Contact the villa (✆ **081-8782284**) or check their website (www.festivaldellospettacolo.it) for a schedule of events. August.

Musica negli Scavi Archeologici, Ercolano. Top-quality concerts are

(Tips)   Before You Leave Home: Tickets & Seats in Advance

You absolutely need advance reservations for the Capodimonte Museum in Naples (the one museum in Campania where lines are always several hours long because of the many special exhibits) and for special guided tours of Pompeii, but you might want to make reservations for a number of other attractions and events as well. The best place to make reservations is **Pierreci** (✆ 063-9967050; www.pierreci.it), the official advance reservation service for a number of museums and events in Campania and in Italy. To get tickets for all kinds of events, the best Italy-based operators are **TicketOne** (✆ 023-92261 for an English-speaking operator; www.ticketone.it); and **Viva Ticket** (www.vivaticket.it). They have English-language websites where you can make reservations and purchase tickets. U.S.-based companies offering advance tickets for a variety of museums and events in Italy are convenient, but they are usually more expensive and cover only a small selection of monuments and events. The best of these is **Cultural italy.com** (✆ 800/380-0014; fax 928/639-0388; www.culturalitaly.com), a Los Angeles–based company that offers seats and reservations for operatic performances in Naples, special guided tours in Pompeii, and even tickets to the famed Festival of Ravello. Most reservations carry a $10 fee, plus the cost of the event.

staged in the magic scenery of the ruins of Herculaneum and in the 18th-century Villa Campolieto. We hope this event, which reached its fourth edition in 2009, will continue for many years. Contact the tourist office of Ercolano (✆ **081-7881274** or 081-7881243) for a schedule of events. August through September.

Scala Meets New York, Scala. This festival stages internationally renowned artists as well as political and cultural personalities to mark the solidarity of the oldest town on the Amalfi Coast with the most modern city in the world. The festival—in its 8th year in 2010—has a rich calendar of events. For more info see the websites of the two organizing associations (www.italiausa.org and www.scalanelmondo.org). August 11 to September 11.

Incontri Musicali Sorrentini **(Sorrentine Musical Encounters),** Sorrento. Sorrento offers unending cultural events throughout the year, but this

festival—in its 38th edition in 2010—is when the peaceful cloister at St. Francis Church comes alive for 3 weeks of classical concerts. Ask the tourist office (✆ **081-8074033;** www.sorrentotourism.com) for a schedule of events. August through September.

SEPTEMBER

Settembre al Borgo (September in the Village), Casertavecchia. In the romantic setting of a medieval town, this festival will celebrate its 40th year in 2010. For 10 days, the ancient bourg comes alive with music and other performances focusing on a different theme each year. Contact the Caserta tourist office (✆ **0823-550011**), or visit www.casertamusica.com for a schedule of events. End of August to the beginning of September.

Festa di Piedigrotta, Naples. This centuries-old religious and musical festival was successfully revived in 2007 after years of neglect. It was at the 1898 edition of this festival that the world-famous song

"O Sole Mio" was presented for the first time, and the festival went strong for decades until it lost its following in the 1980s. It is now back full strength, featuring religious and musical events as well as a children's program and a parade of floats. For more information, visit www.festadipiedigrotta.it. First 2 weeks in September.

Santa Maria della Libera, Capri. Starting from the St. Costanzo in Marina Grande church and crossing the town of Capri, grand processions are staged at this festival, which includes music, fireworks, and market stalls. Contact the tourist office ((C) **081-8375308**) for more information. The Sunday closest to September 12.

Ischia Jazz Weekend, Ischia. This event is organized by the famous Umbria Jazz group, with important international performers. Call (C) **081-4972777** for information. Usually second weekend of September.

OCTOBER

Le lune di Pompei, Pompeii Archeological Area. This is *the* most romantic guided tour of Pompeii's ruins. The tour rotates on seven themes and is scheduled every night for 2 weeks in August and then every weekend night throughout October and November. You can book directly online at www.lelunedipompei.com, or contact the booking office for information ((C) **081-19303885**). August through November.

NOVEMBER

Feast of St. Andrew, Amalfi. St. Andrew, the patron of Amalfi and the protector of fishermen, is honored annually by local fishermen, who run with a heavy statue of him on their shoulders from the beach up the cathedral's hundreds of steps, and then present the saint with offerings of fish—both fresh and carved. The town also celebrates with games, folk shows,

and magnificent fireworks. The feast is repeated in a mellower form on June 27, the anniversary of the day the saint miraculously saved the town from an attack by Saracen pirates. November 30.

DECEMBER

Sagra della Salsiccia e Ceppone (Sausage and Bonfire Fair), Sorrento. In this celebration of Saint Lucia, locals and visitors cook—and eat—about 91 kilograms (200 lbs.) of delicious local sausages barbecued over a huge fire (prepared in the heart of the Santa Lucia neighborhood). The food is accompanied by bottles of excellent local wine. December 13.

Avellino Christmas Concerts, Avellino. For 5 days, the town is alive with music, as local choirs give concerts inside the town's beautiful cathedral. Contact the tourist office ((C) **0825-74695**) for a program. Usually December 13 through December 18.

Feast of the *Torrone*, San Marco dei Cavoti. The typical Christmas candy, the *torrone*, becomes an occasion for celebrations in the little town that has been famous for making its special version—the *croccantino*—since the Middle Ages. You can taste all the variations of the treat along Via del Torrone (Via Roma), and then watch the building of a giant *croccantino* by local masters in the town's main square. Call the tourist office at (C) **0824-984009** for more information. December 8 and the following weekends until Christmas.

Divers' Procession to Grotta dello Smeraldo, Conca dei Marini. Each December and January, a special pilgrimage embarks to this town's greatest attraction, Grotta dello Smeraldo. Local and guest scuba divers swim from the beach to an underwater manger inside the grotto (see chapter 8). Call the visitor center in Amalfi at (C) **089-871107** for more information. December 24 and January 6.

Live Manger, Belvedere di San Leucio, Caserta. Come to see this hamlet turn the clock back to the 18th century with historical reenactments, music, and performances during the Christmas period. Contact © **333-8283690,** or e-mail info@presepevaccheria.it for information. December 25 to January 6.

Live Manger, Pietrelcina. This picturesque little town near Benevento hosts a reenactment of Christmas involving the whole town, with events spread over several days. December 27 through December 29.

Sagra della Zeppola **(Feast of the Zeppola),** Positano. Celebrants at this feast ring in the new year by feasting on *zeppolas,* delicious fried sweet pastries, and by enjoying the Kermesse of dances, music, and fireworks on the beach of Marina Grande. December 31 through January 1.

2 ENTRY REQUIREMENTS

Italy is part of the Schengen area. For more information, please visit the European Union's website, www.europa.eu and click on "About the E.U." Entry requirements are specified under "Your Life in the E.U.", "Traveling in Europe."

PASSPORTS

You'll need a **valid passport** to enter Italy and Campania (the passport should be valid for at least 3 months beyond the period of stay). The length of your stay is determined by your **visa** (see "Visas," below) and the fulfillment of the other entry requirements (see "Other Entry Requirements," below). American, Canadian, Australian, New Zealand citizens, and those from a few other countries (check the list at www.esteri.it/visti) can stay up to 90 days without a visa; citizens from a country belonging to the Schengen area can enter with a simple identification card; other E.U. citizens, including Irish and British citizens, will need a passport.

For information on how to get a passport for U.S., Australian, New Zealand, Ireland, and U.K. citizens, please see "Passports" in chapter 12—the websites listed provide downloadable passport applications as well as the current fees for processing passport applications.

VISAS

European Union citizens, including U.K. and Ireland—do not need a visa.

Citizens from the United States, Canada, Australia, New Zealand, and from a few other countries, don't need a visa to enter Italy or Campania if they don't expect to stay more than 90 days and don't expect to work or study there. *Note:* The 90 days refer to your **total** stay in the Schengen area, so if you are coming to Campania as part of a longer trip in Europe, make sure you do not exceed the time limit, or you'll need to obtain a visa before entering.

Citizens from all other countries need a visa for stays of any length.

Note: At the border you may be asked to produce the documents you presented to obtain your visa. Remember to carry them with you and have them handy at the border check.

Visit the website of the Italian Foreign Affairs Ministry at www.esteri.it/visti to find out if you need a visa.

For more information on obtaining a Visa, please see chapter 12.

CUSTOMS
What You Can Bring Into Italy & Campania

Rules governing what tourists can bring in duty-free are detailed at www.agenziado gane.it (click on "Publications" and then "Traveler's customs card"). Foreign visitors from outside the European Union can bring up to 175€ worth of goods for personal use (visitors under 15 years of age can bring up to 90€). Visitors over 17 years of age can also bring up to 200 cigarettes or 100 cigarillos (up to 3g each) or 50 cigars or loose tobacco not exceeding 250 grams; and up to 2 liters of alcoholic beverages under 22% by volume or under 1 liter. Visitors over 15 years of age can also bring up to 500 grams of coffee; and all visitors can bring up to 100grams of tea, 50 grams of perfume, and 25 centiliters of eau de toilette. Meat, meat products, milk, and milk products are not allowed.

If you are carrying currency in excess of a value of 10,000€, you will need to fill out a Customs declaration.

What You Can Take Home from Campania

While there is no special limit on how much you can take out of Italy, certain items are restricted, in particular art objects: You'll need special permits for the export of objects more than 50 years old. *Note:* Italy adheres to CITES (Convention on International Trade in Endangered Species of Wild Fauna and Flora), which means the purchase and export of protected species is prohibited. So is the purchase and export of copies of fashion items (think Vuitton or Chanel and the like) and other copyrighted material. The fines are steep; do not break the law!

For information on what you're allowed to take home, contact one of the following agencies:

U.S. Citizens: U.S. Customs & Border Protection, 1300 Pennsylvania Ave., NW,

Washington, DC 20229 (℃ 877/287-8667; www.cbp.gov).

Canadian Citizens: Canada Border Services Agency, Ottawa, ON, K1A 0L8, Canada (℃ 800/461-9999 in Canada, or 204/983-3500; www.cbsa-asfc.gc.ca).

U.K. Citizens: HM Customs & Excise Crownhill Court, Tailyour Road, Plymouth, PL6 5BZ (℃ 0845-010-9000, or 020-8929-0152 from outside the U.K.; www.hmce.gov.uk).

Australian Citizens: Australian Customs Service, Customs House, 5 Constitution Ave., Canberra City, ACT 2601 (℃ 1300-363-263; www.customs.gov.au).

New Zealand Citizens: New Zealand Customs, The Customhouse, 17–21 Whitmore St., Box 2218, Wellington 6140 (℃ 04/473-6099 or 0800-428-786; www.customs.govt.nz).

MEDICAL REQUIREMENTS

Unless you're arriving from an area known to be suffering from an epidemic (particularly cholera or yellow fever), inoculations or vaccinations are not required for entry into Italy and Campania. All travelers to Italy though are required to have valid medical insurance coverage in case they need medical care during their trip. See tips on purchasing travel medical insurance on p. 320.

OTHER ENTRY REQUIREMENTS
Means of Subsistence

To enter Italy and Campania you need to prove that you have adequate means of subsistence. That includes a place to stay, enough money to live during your stay and to return to your country, and medical insurance (see "Medical Requirements," above). At the border, you may be asked to show your return ticket as well as a hotel voucher or equivalent, and cash, traveler's checks, and credit or debit cards (or a bank account in Italy), with resources proportionate to the length of your stay.

Permit or Declaration of Stay

Foreigners entering Italy from a country outside the Schengen area and planning to stay more than 8 days also need to file a *permesso di soggiorno* (permit of stay). If you have already filed a permit of stay in another country in the Schengen area for this trip, you'll need to file a *dichiarazione di soggiorno* (declaration of stay) within 3 days of your entry in Italy. If you are flying from a country outside the Schengen area, the stamp you obtain on your passport at the airport is the equivalent of a permit of stay, but if you are entering Italy from a country within the Schengen area, you will need to file with the local police (you can also present the form at the local post office). *Note:* If you are staying in a hotel, the declaration of stay is automatically done for you by the hotel. But if you are staying in a private house, you'll need to handle the procedure yourself. Note also that failure to file is punished with expulsion from Italy. For the permit and declaration, you'll need a photocopy of your passport, two photographs, proof of medical insurance, proof of adequate means of financial support, and a photocopy of your return ticket. It is a simple routine check, and you should be able to breeze through this formality; just remember to bring all your documentation, including the documents you presented to obtain your **visa,** if you needed one.

3 GETTING THERE & GETTING AROUND

GETTING TO CAMPANIA
By Plane

Campania is served by Naples's **Capodichino Airport** (✆ 081-7896259; www.gesac.it); its international airport code is **NAP.** This is the most convenient, as all attractions in the region are a short distance away.

Only a few international airlines fly directly to Naples and you may also decide to enjoy the wider choice offered by Rome's Fiumicino-Leonardo da Vinci airport (international airport code **FCO**). You'll then have to transfer to the train (see "By Train," below).

In addition to several low-cost companies, a few major airlines offer international flights to Naples from their European hubs: Alitalia, Air France, Air Lingus, Austrian Airlines, British Airways, and Lufthansa. The only intercontinental nonstop flights to Naples are those offered by **Meridiana** from New York (Meridiana recently purchased Eurofly from Alitalia). From elsewhere in North America and from Australia and New Zealand, you will have to take a connecting flight (Rome is only 50 min. away, Milan about 90 min., and most European hubs about 2 hr.).

To find out which airlines travel to Italy and Campania, please see "Airline, Hotel & Car-Rental Websites," p. 324.

FROM THE AIRPORT About 7km (4 miles) from Naples's city center, the airport is only 20 minutes away from the downtown area and the harbor. The easiest way to get to your destination is by taking a **taxi** directly to your hotel: The flat rate for Naples is 19€ plus gratuities, 100€ for Sorrento, 120€ for Positano, 130€ for Amalfi and 135€ for Ravello. Most hotels and resorts along the coast offer airport pickup: For a limousine booked through your hotel, you'll pay about 30€ for Naples and about 90€ for Sorrento and 115€ for Amalfi. You might get better rates, though, contacting a car service directly (see "By Car," in "Getting Around" later in this chapter).

If you don't have too much luggage, the **Alibus shuttle bus** (© 800-639525; www. anm.it) to Naples is a cheaper alternative at 3€. With departures every 20 minutes, it stops on Corso Garibaldi near Napoli Centrale train station, and in Piazza Municipio at the heart of the historic district. Shuttle bus service to other nearby towns (Sorrento and Castellammare di Stabia, for instance) is also available.

By Train

Italy enjoys an excellent railway system and trains often are the most convenient way to get from one destination to another. Naples is on Italy's main southern corridor, making it easily accessible from other Italian and European towns. Electric high-velocity trains have made travel within Europe and Italy faster and more comfortable than ever. The national railroad company **FS-Trenitalia** (© **892021** from anywhere in Italy, 39-06-68475475 from abroad; www.trenitalia.it) offers local trains as well as the faster, more expensive AltaVelocità, EuroStar, and InterCity trains (designated AV, ES, and IC on train schedules, respectively), which make limited stops. AV trains—Italy's fastest—travel at speeds of up to 300kmph (186 mph). The new AV train takes only 87 minutes between Rome and Naples, and 5 hours and 35 minutes from Milan, making it by far the best way to move between these cities; regular trains take about 2½ and 9 hours respectively for the same connections.

Train fares are not cheap, but there are specials if you book online and in advance directly on the **Trenitalia** website (www. trenitalia.it). Children ages 5 to 11 receive a discount of 50%, and children ages 4 and younger travel free with their parents. Seniors and youths ages 25 and under can purchase discount cards. Advance seat reservations, which are obligatory on all AV, ES, and IC trains, are highly recommended for other trains during peak season and on weekends and holidays.

If you plan to travel extensively in Europe by train, it may be cheaper to purchase a **Eurail Pass,** a prepaid train pass for sale at all major rail stations and online (www.eurail.com). You can choose among several possible combinations, including an Italy-only pass granting 3 to 10 unlimited travel days within a 2-month period. Adult rates vary from between 148€ to 335€ depending on time and class. You will need to pay an extra fee for compulsory seat reservations on the faster trains and sleepers, but you'll be entitled to reductions on certain bus and ferry lines of up to 20%. If you prefer to discuss your options with a travel agent, contact **Rail Europe** (© **877/272-RAIL** [7245]; www. raileurope.com) or your own travel agent, but they'll charge a commission. Savings are available for youths ages 25 and younger and for groups.

By Boat

Italy is well served by international ferries and a regular stop on most cruise-ship lines. Two of its major ports are Naples and Salerno, both in Campania. Naples is the main port of central Italy, receiving daily ships and ferries from international destinations. Salerno is only slightly smaller.

Arriving in Naples by ship is a magnificent experience and the best approach to Campania. You'll land at **Stazione Marittima,** only steps from the Maschio Angioino, in the heart of the historical district, the *città antica.* Salerno's harbor is also only a short distance from the historic district.

A number of cruise-ship companies sail to Naples, especially in the good season, from spring well into fall. One of our favorites is **MSC Cruises** (www.msc cruises.com), both for the quality of ships and cruises and for the company's commitment to sustainable tourism and minimal ecological impact. Another favorite, both for the quality of its ships and service and its commitment to the protection of the environment, is **Costa Cruises** (www. costacruise.com). Other reliable companies offering cruises to Campania are **Regent Seven Seas Cruises** (www.rssc. com); **Norwegian Cruise Line** (www.ncl. eu); and **Oceania Cruises** (www.oceania cruises.com).

The major ferry companies offering regular service to Naples are **Tirrenia** (© 199-123199 or 081-2514711; www. tirrenia.it), with boats to Sardinia (Cagliari) and Sicily (Palermo); **Siremar** (© 081-5800340; www.siremar.it), with ships to the Aeolian Islands and Sicily (Milazzo); **TTTLines** (© 800-915365), with ships to Sicily (Catania and Palermo); **Medmar** (© 081-5513352), with boats to Tunisia (Tunis); **SNAV** (© 081-4285555 or 081-4285111; www.snav.it), with boats to Sicily, Sardinia, and the Aeolian and Pontine islands. Major companies operating from Salerno are **Grimaldi Lines** (© 081-496444; www.grimaldi-ferries.com), with regular service to Spain (Valencia), Malta (La Valletta), Tunisia (Tunis), and Sicily (Palermo); and **Caronte & Tourist** (© 800-627414 toll-free within Italy, or 089-2582528; www.caronte tourist.it), with boats to Sicily (Catania and Messina).

Of course, you could also cruise to another of the Italian harbors and then get to Campania by other means. Major navigation companies serving other Italian ports are **Blue Star Ferries** (www.bluestar ferries.gr) and **Superfast Ferries** (www. superfast.com), from Greece; **Marmara Lines** (www.marmaralines.com), from Turkey; **Grandi Navi Veloci** (www.gnv.it), from Spain; and **Virtu Ferries** (www.virtu ferries.com), from Malta.

By Car

To drive a car in Italy, you will need an **International Driving Permit (IDP)** which is an official translation of your license. Apply in the United States at any **American Automobile Association**

(AAA) branch; contact **AAA's national headquarters** (© 800/222-4357 or 407/444-4300; www.aaa.com). Canadians can get the address of the nearest **Canadian Automobile Association** by calling © 613/247-0117, or by visiting www. caa.ca. Remember that an international permit is valid only if physically accompanied by your home country–issued driver's license and only if signed on the back.

Most car-rental companies require a minimum age of 23 or 25, but a few will accept a minimum age of 21 for their cheaper models. Most rental companies will not rent a car to drivers 76 and older. Insurance on all vehicles is compulsory and can be purchased at any reputable rental firm. You will also need a valid credit card (not a prepaid or debit card) for a standard model and two credit cards for a deluxe model; cash payments will not be accepted.

Car rental in Italy is more expensive then in the United States. Your best bet is to check for specials on companies' websites. Prices vary with car size and special offers, but a compact car will generally rent for between 60€ and 100€ per day.

All of the major international rental companies operate in Italy: **Avis** (© 800/ 331-1212; www.avis.com), **Budget** (© 800/472-3325; www.budget.com), **Hertz** (© 800/654-3131; www.hertz. com), and **National** in the U.S. (© 800/ CAR-RENT [227-7368]; www.national car.com). National is associated with Italy's primary rental company, **Maggiore** (© 1478-67067 toll-free in Italy; www. maggiore.it). A newer, reputable, and sometimes cheaper company is **Sixt** (© 888/749-8227 in the United States; 199-100666 in Italy; www.sixt.it, or www. sixtusa.com for U.S. citizens). If you need a long-term rental, **Auto Europe** (© 800/223-5555; www.autoeurope. com), **Europe by Car** (© 800/223-1516, or 212/581-3040 in New York; www. europebycar.com), and **Kemwel Holiday**

Public Transportation Strikes

You might have heard it before—even the U.S. travel advisory for Italy warns of it—strikes are a common occurrence in Italy and can hamper public transportation. While strikes do happen, they remain a rare occurrence, and planned walk-outs are often canceled at the last minute because the parties reach an agreement. Should it actually happen, minimum service is guaranteed and alternate transportation is always made available. The bottom line is that strikes are no reason to forgo public transportation in favor of driving.

Auto (© **800/678-0678;** www.kemwel.com), might offer better rates. It is worth asking when you book if your American Automobile Association (AAA) or AARP membership will give you a discount. Renting online usually will get you the best prices, but it is worth checking with the local rental office for a better deal. Package discounts are sometimes available when you book your car together with your flight.

Cars in Italy have manual shift, but you can request a car with automatic shift; they usually rent at a premium.

If you are driving to Italy from abroad, you will have to pass the Alps. There are only two tunnels (Mont Blanc from France and Grand St. Bernard from Switzerland, both leading to the A5 highway to Turin and Milan) and a few passes (the main one is the Brenner from Austria, leading to the A22 highway to Bologna). Traffic at the border can be delayed by bad weather or at times of mass exodus (such as the beginning and end of school vacations).

Limited-access express highways in Italy are called autostrada and numbered from A1 on. They sometimes are also marked with the European number, starting with the letter E. Autostrade are toll roads; they are quality roads with modern gas stations at sensible intervals, and high-quality restoration. Tariffs depend on your vehicle (up to 1.3m/4.3 ft. in height—your average car and any motorcycle being the cheapest, followed by taller cars, such as

SUVs and vans, and then various categories of trucks and caravans) and on the type of road, as mountain roads are more expensive to maintain, hence the toll is higher. Regular cars pay .056€ per kilometer on the flat, and .066€ per kilometer on mountains, to which you need to add a small surcharge and rounding. To give you an example, Rome–Salerno will cost you a minimum of 13.20€. The official website, www.autostrade.it, offers a tool to calculate your costs and organize your trip, but, for the moment, it is in Italian only.

The Autostrada del Sole A1 from Milan to Naples is the highway to Campania. From Naples, the A3 leads to Salerno. Italy develops lengthwise and it is a long drive to reach the south from the north. Driving from Milan to Naples will take you about 9 hours on average, and about 10 to Sorrento. But be forewarned, driving in Campania is notorious in Italy, see "By Car," in the "Getting Around" section below for a few useful tips.

GETTING AROUND
By Train

With easy connections between the region's major towns—Naples, Sorrento, Salerno, Caserta, Benevento——and the Vesuvian attractions of Herculaneum and Pompeii, the train is an excellent way to move between these destinations. Local trains are cheap and frequent and you don't need advance reservation: You can buy your ticket at the automatic machines

The Unico Travel Pass

Traffic might be bad in the region, but paying for public transportation just became a lot easier. With one ticket for the specific area you are visiting, you can board all forms of transportation, from trains and the Metro, to buses and ferries. The "**Unico**" is offered in several denominations (usually 45 min., 90 min., 24 hr., and 3 days) and is for sale at stations as well as tobacconists and newsstands near transportation hubs.

Naples's Unico is the most complicated because you can choose between several *zone* (zones), with a U1 covering the historic district, Pozzuoli, and the island of Procida; U2 extending to Ercolano, Baia, and Ischia; U3 to Pompei; U4 Capua and Vicco Equense; and U5 encompassing Naples to Sorrento, the Amalfi Coast, and Salerno. U1 costs 1.10€ for the 90-minute version and 3.10€ for the 24-hr. pass (2.60€ on Sun); U5 costs 3.30€ for the 90-minute version and 6.60€ for the 24-hour pass (5.30€ on Sun).

The **Unico Campania 3T** covers the whole region, including the Alibus shuttle from Naples's Capodichino Airport to the city center, plus public trains, buses, and funiculars on the mainland, Ischia, and Procida. To give you an idea, it includes the Circumvesuviana train to Pompei or Sorrento, the funicular and bus in Naples, as well as the Sita buses on the Amalfi Coast, the FS train to Benevento and the local bus there. The pass is valid for 3 days, from the first stamp to midnight of the third day, and costs 20€.

The **Unico Costiera** covers all the towns along the Sorrento and Amalfi coasts, from Meta di Sorrento to Salerno. The best deals are the 24-hour pass and the 3-day pass (respectively 6€ and 15€), which also include one ride on the City Sightseeing tour buses between Amalfi and Ravello or Amalfi and Maiori. The Unico is also available in 45-minute and 90-minute increments, respectively 2€ and 3€. Any of the passes will allow you unlimited rides on SITA buses and the Circumvesuviana trains connecting Meta with Sorrento and stations in between.

For more information, visit www.unicocampania.it.

inside the station and hop on the train. The advantage is also that the rail station is usually in the center of town, walking distance from the major attractions and well connected by public transportation and taxis.

The national railway system **FS-Trenitalia** (② 892021 from anywhere in Italy; www.trenitalia.it) serves the area together with the local lines **Alifana** (② 800-127157 or 081-5993254; www.alifana.it), covering Benevento and surrounding areas; **Circumvesuviana** (② 800-053939; www.vesuviana.it), connecting Naples with the Vesuvian area including Ercolano, Pompei, Castellammare di Stabia, and Sorrento; and **Metronapoli** (② 800-568866; www.metro.na.it), connecting Naples with Pozzuoli and the Phlegrean Fields.

National and regional lines serve most major tourist destination, sometimes in parallel, with the result that even relatively small towns have two stations, one for the national railroad, F.S.—Ferrovie dello

Stato (of which Trenitalia is a division), and one for the local line: Circumvesuviana railroad, for Pompei (with the Pompeii archaeological site), Ercolano (with Herculaneum), and Sorrento; Cumana railroad, for Cuma and Pozzuoli; and Naples's Metro line, which extends out of town to the city suburbs, offering an additional way to reach Pozzuoli, for example. You will find all the options in the section "Getting There" in each destination chapter in this book.

By Bus

Local bus companies operate throughout Campania, and are a handy resource particularly in hilly and mountainous areas where rail service isn't available. We recommend using the bus, for example, in the Amalfi Coast, where the frequent service offers a good alternative to driving. **SITA** (see below) schedules numerous runs between Salerno, Naples, and Sorrento, with extra lines between Amalfi, Positano, and Sorrento, as well as secondary lines from Amalfi and Sorrento to minor destinations along the Costiera. These provide not only convenient but also cheap transport, as you can buy a single pass valid on public transportation for the whole Costiera (see "The Unico Travel Pass," above).

The leading bus operators in the region are **SITA** (© 081-5522176; www.sitabus.it), serving the Sorrento peninsula and the Amalfi Coast; **SEPSA** (© 800-001616; www.sepsa.it), serving Pozzuoli, Baia, Cuma, and Miseno, as well as Procida and Ischia; **CTP** (© 800-482644; www.ctpn.it), serving Naples and linking it with neighboring towns; **AIR** (© 0825-204250; www.air-spa.it), connecting the Avellino area with Naples; and **CSTP** (© 800-016659 or 089-487001; www.cstp.it), with trains in Salerno, Paestum, and the Cilento.

For more information, see "Getting There" in the destination chapters throughout this book.

By Ferry

Ferries are a great way to get around this region's coastal destinations and, obviously, crucial to reaching its islands. They are a fantastic option particularly during the summer, when the narrow coastal roads become overly congested. Several companies connect the region's top destinations. Hydrofoil service is the fastest, but is suspended in winter and operates only between selected harbors—chiefly Naples, Capri, Ischia, Sorrento, Positano, Amalfi, and Salerno. Other options include large ferries with transport of vehicles, and smaller motorboats, which can reach smaller harbors. All companies charge similar rates for similar service. The only relevant difference is the time schedule.

Naples's two harbors—Stazione Marittima, downtown, and Terminal Aliscafi, in Mergellina—along with **Salerno's** are the region's main hubs, followed by **Amalfi, Sorrento,** and **Pozzuoli.** All offer multiple daily connections to the islands (**Capri, Ischia,** and **Procida**) and the smaller towns of the Amalfi Coast, including **Positano.**

Companies offering local service are **Alilauro** (© 081-4972238; www.alilauro.it), with hydrofoils to Ischia and Positano; **Caremar** (© 081-5513882; www.caremar.it), with ferries and hydrofoils to Ischia, Capri, and Procida; **LMP** (© 081-5513236; www.consorziolmp.it), with hydrofoils to Sorrento; **Medmar** (© 081-3334411; www.medmargroup.it), with ferries to Ischia; **Metrò del Mare** (© 199-446644; www.metrodelmare.com), with commuter-style service between Bacoli and Salerno, with intermediary stops in Pozzuoli, Naples, Vico Equense, Sorrento, Positano, and Amalfi, and summer service to the islands; **NLG** (© 081-5527209; www.navlib.it), with hydrofoils to Capri; **SNAV** (© 081-4285555 or 081-4285111; www.snav.it), with hydrofoils to Ischia, Capri, and Procida; and **Volaviamare** (© 081-4972211; www.volaviamare.it), with fast boats between Naples, Sorrento, Amalfi, Positano, Salerno, Ischia, and Capri.

Companies offering minicruises and excursions are also great resources for moving around the region: We recommend **Blue Cruises** (© 081-4972222; www.blucruises.it) and **Capitan Morgan** (© 081-985080; www.capitanmorgan.it).

Taxi del Mare (© 081-8773600; www.taxidelmare.it) is a water taxi that takes passengers to any destination in Naples and Salerno bays. Prices vary depending on the distance: The most expensive ride, at presstime, was Naples to Amalfi for 905€, while the cheapest was Capri to Nerano for 356€.

By Limousine/Car Service & Taxi

A good alternative to renting a car is using a **taxi** or a **car service**—Make sure they use cars and minivans with air-conditioning (very important in summer), as well as trained, English-speaking drivers. Official taxis are at the airport and the train station. They are white and have a taxi sign on the roof, a city logo, and a card clearly detailing the official rates inside. The Municipality of Naples has established flat rates for major tourist destinations in the region. These rates are cheaper than if the meter was used, and you have to ask for it before departure. A round-trip to Herculaneum, with a 2-hour wait (during which you visit the ruins), is 70€; Pompeii and a 2-hour wait is 90€; a round-trip tour of the Amalfi Coast (Positano, Ravello, Amalfi, and Sorrento), for an entire day, is 220€; a round-trip to Mount Vesuvius, with a 2-hour wait, is 90€; round-trip to Baia (Scavi Archeologici) and Solfatara, with a 3-hour wait, is 85€; a tour of Naples is 70€.

The best companies are **Radio Taxi Napoli** (© 081-444444, 081-5555555, or 081-5564444; www.consorziotaxinapoli.it), **Cooperativa Partenopea** (© 081-5606666, 081-5515151, or 081-5560202;

www.radiotaxilapartenope.it), **Radio Taxi La 570** (© 081-5707070; www.la570.it), and **Consortaxi** (© 081-202020). Taxis operate from the airport or various taxi stands at major destinations in and around the city. You can just go to one of these stands and grab a taxi, but book in advance for longer excursions.

Car services tend to be based on the Sorrento peninsula and Amalfi Coast. They are often cheaper than taxis, and drivers also act as guides. Car services we recommend are **Sorrento Limo** (www.sorrentolimo.com), **APTours** (www.aptours.it), **Cuomo Limousine** (www.carsorrento.it), and **Paolo Bellantonio** (www.bellantoniolimoservice.com), all based in Sorrento; **Benvenuto Limos & Tours** (www.benvenutolimos.com), based in Praiano; and **Avellino Car Service** (www.amedeoavellino.com), based in Vico Equense. We also like two private drivers: **Francesco Marrapese** (www.francescomarrapese.com) and **Angelo** (www.angelodriver.com).

Recommended providers in Naples are **ANA Limousine Service,** Piazza Garibaldi 73 (© 081-282000), and **Italy Limousine** (© 081-8016184, 335-6732245, or 338-9681866; www.italylimousine.it). Check individual chapters for more options.

By Car

Distances within Campania on the autostrada (limited-access, toll-express highways) are short: Naples to Salerno is about 30 minutes, and Salerno to Avellino only 20 minutes. Local routes tend to be much more congested, especially in the summer. Driving from Sorrento to Amalfi in the off-season will take you less than an hour, but, with summer traffic, a 2-hour ride is more like it. Renting a motorcycle is a good way to get around as well.

Before renting a car or a motorcycle, though, know that Neapolitans have truly earned their reputation for aggressive and daring driving. You need to be a skilled and alert driver, if you want to navigate Italian roads, with super-high speeds on the autostrade and super-narrow streets in the cities and towns. You will literally be taking your life into your hands, as Italy's roads have one of the highest fatality rates in Europe. The situation gets worse in Naples and surrounding areas, where roads have guardrails only when the road is on a cliff and breaking speed limits and other rules of the road is a local sport. Motor scooters are extremely prevalent and their drivers often do not obey traffic laws, so be mindful of them as they zoom and swerve between cars.

Also, driving is not cheap: In addition to high tolls on the autostrada, gasoline prices and parking fees are steep.

If you are planning to visit only major destinations in the region, you'll be better off using public transportation or hiring a car with a driver. However, driving will allow you to see much more of the countryside at your own pace, and it makes sense if you have the time to go exploring off the beaten path.

The two primary Italian car-rental companies are **Maggiore** (www.maggiore.it) and **Travelcar** (www.travelcar.it), but all major international car-rental companies operate here (see "Getting There," p. 44 and "Airline, Hotel & Car-Rental Websites," p. 324). In addition, you'll also find a number of local companies that rent cars (with or without driver) as well as scooters or motorcycles. We list them for each destination in the "Getting Around" section in each chapter.

RULES OF THE ROAD   In Italy, driving is on the right-hand side of the road. Unless otherwise marked, **speed limits** are 50kmph (31 mph) in urban areas, 90kmphto 110kmph (56–68 mph) in suburban areas, and 110kmph to 130kmph (68–81 mph) on limited-access highways. Speed limits for trailers, or towed vehicles, are lower: 70 kmph (43 mph) outside urban areas and 80 kmph

(50 mph) on autostrada (100 kmph/62 mph for auto-caravans, or mobile homes). Automatic speed controls are installed on most roads, and you may be ticketed for driving faster than the posted limit.

It is mandatory to have your **headlights** on at all times outside urban areas and to use **seat belts** (front and rear) and age-appropriate **car seats** for children. High-beam headlights are sometimes used to signal to fellow drivers: If you are in the left passing lane and a driver flashes you from behind, you need to move out of the way. If an oncoming car signals you, it means that some danger is ahead, so slow down. If cars ahead of you put on their hazard lights, slow down: The traffic is completely stopped ahead. Horns cannot be used in urban areas except in an emergency.

Only motorcycles and scooters with engines above 150 cubic centimeters can use the autostrade. **Helmet use** is mandatory on all roads.

Drinking and driving is severely punished and there are fines for talking on your mobile phone while driving and for illegal parking.

FINDING YOUR WAY   Road signs are posted with one sign about 1.6km (1 mile) before an exit, and then another right at the exit. Destination signs are blue for local roads and green for the toll highway. Destinations of cultural interest (such as monuments and archaeological areas) are posted on brown signs. Often, only the major town on a local road is marked, while smaller towns and villages on the way will not be posted. See p. 321 for information on buying some reliable maps.

GASOLINE   Gas stations are distributed along local roads at sensible intervals, however, large stretches of countryside are without stations. Pumps are generally open Monday to Saturday from 7 or 8am to 1pm and 3 or 4pm to 7 or 8pm (some have a self-service pump accessible after hours). On toll highways gas stations are positioned every 32km or 48km (20 or 30 miles) and are open 24 hours daily. Most cars take *benzina senza piombo* (unleaded fuel) or diesel (*diesel* or *gasolio*). Among diesel cars, only the newest models take the ecofuel labeled *blu diesel* (blue diesel) Be prepared for sticker shock every time you fill up—even in a medium-size car— as fuel is priced throughout the country at around 6€ per gallon (diesel is cheaper, selling around 5€ per gallon). Make sure the pump registers zero before an attendant starts filling your tank: A common scam involves filling your tank before resetting the meter (so that you also pay the charges run up by the previous motorist), and it is still performed by some dishonest attendants.

BREAKDOWNS & ASSISTANCE Roadside aid in Italy is excellent. For 24-hour emergency assistance, contact the national department of motor vehicles, Automobile Club d'Italia (& 803-116 toll-free within Italy; www.aci.it).

PARKING Parking is always limited, particularly during the high season and near major attractions. Parking lots and areas are indicated with a square sign bearing a large white P on a blue background.

Parking spots are marked on the pavement with painted lines of various colors depending on the type of parking: Yellow is for reserved parking (deliveries, drivers with disabilities, taxis, and so on); white is free parking (very limited—you won't find many of those on the Costiera); blue is paid parking. Rates vary as they are established by each municipality: Check the sign at the beginning and end of the stretch of parking spots and the sign on the automatic parking machines (usually located at a more or less reasonable distance from your parking spot; look for a gray/white box on a post or on a wall). Machines usually accept only coins, so come prepared (prices usually range 1€–3€ per hr.). The timer shows the current time, and as you insert money, it will show you what time you are paid through. When you're done, press the green button, collect the receipt, and place it on your dashboard in a visible spot. Do not even think about skipping this, particularly in tourist areas, authorities are very vigilant.

The alternative is a private parking lot. These are usually located near the historic district (or attractions) in most towns. They are often underground, and attendants will park your car for you. Expect to pay 20€ to 50€ per day, depending on the location.

4 MONEY & COSTS

The Value of the Euro versus Other Popular Currencies

Euro	US$	Can$	UK£	Aus$	NZ$
1€	$1.40	C$1.56	£0.70	A$1.72	NZ$2.11

The currency conversions quoted above were correct at presstime. However, rates fluctuate, so before departing consult a currency exchange website such as **www.oanda.com/convert/classic** to check up-to-the-minute rates.

You'll be glad to hear that Campania is still an affordable destination in Italy: The cost of living and traveling is lower then say Tuscany or Milan, and quite a bit lower then some northern Europe destinations, such as London, Copenhagen, and Amsterdam.

ATMs (automated teller machines) are common and present in all but the most remote localities in the region. The **Cirrus**

What Things Cost in Naples

Item	Euro €
A metro or city bus ride	1.00
Can of soda	2.00
Pay-phone call	0.20
Movie ticket	8.00
Caffè lungo (American-style espresso)	1.00
Ticket to the Museo Nazionale Capodimonte (including reservation)	9.00
Gasoline/petrol (per gal.)	6.00
Taxi from the airport	20.00
Moderate 3-course dinner for one without alcohol	30.00
Moderate hotel room (double)	225.00
Liter of house wine in a restaurant	10.00
First-class letter to the United States (or any overseas country)	0.85

(© 800/424-7787; www.mastercard.com) and **PLUS** (© 800/843-7587; www.visa.com) networks are the most common. Go to your bank card's website to find ATM locations at your destination. Be sure you know your daily withdrawal limit before you depart. *Note:* Many banks impose a fee every time you use a card at another bank's ATM, and that fee can be higher for international transactions (up to $5 or more). In addition, the bank from which you withdraw cash may charge its own fee. For international withdrawal fees, ask your bank. Deutsche Bank and BNL (Banca Nazionale del Lavoro) are those that do not charge transaction fees at other Alliance member ATMs (these include Bank of America, Scotiabank, and Barclays).

Most ATMs accept **four-** and **five-digit codes** (six digits may not work), so if you have a six-digit code you'll want to go into your bank and get a new PIN for your trip.

Credit and debit cards in Italy have chips instead of a swiping magnetic band, but "swipe" cards are widely accepted and you should not have a problem with this. Do keep cash on hand though, as many shops have a higher minimum than in the U.S. for credit card use (most often they will not accept credit or debit cards for amounts below 15€).

5 HEALTH

STAYING HEALTHY

There are no particular health concerns in Campania. It is always, however, a good idea to protect yourself from mosquito bites even in the most developed countries, as an increasing number of diseases previously contained within the tropical areas of the world have started spreading. The World Health Organization recommends hepatitis A and B vaccines for travelers to any country in the world, including Europe and Italy, and to keep up-to-date with boosters for your childhood vaccinations.

During the past couple of years, Naples and its suburbs—and occasionally other areas of the region—have been struggling with a garbage collection crisis due to the enmeshment of the local Camorra (a Mafia-like secret society) with the local contractors. As a result, refuse cyclically accumulates in many areas. As a form of protest, residents resorted to burning the piles of garbage, creating toxic fumes, which are particularly dangerous in summer. The authorities have largely tackled the problem, but, should it reoccur during your visit, avoid the fumes as they can aggravate respiratory problems.

General Availability of Health Care

Over-the-counter medicines are widely available in Campania, and **prescriptions** are easily filled in any pharmacy. **Pharmacies** are abundant: Even small towns will have one. Names of products will be different, so make sure you know the active ingredient of your brand and that your doctor writes the prescription clearly, mentioning both the generic name and its dosage. Most likely you will find a pharmacist who will be able to assist you in finding an English-speaking doctor.

Contact the **International Association for Medical Assistance to Travelers (IAMAT;** ✆ **716-754-4883,** 416-652-0137 in Canada; www.iamat.org) for tips on travel and health concerns in the countries you're visiting, and for lists of local, English-speaking doctors. The United States' **Centers for Disease Control and Prevention** (✆ **800/311-3435;** www.cdc.gov) provides up-to-date information on health hazards by region or country and offers tips on food safety. **Travel Health Online** (www.tripprep.com), sponsored by a consortium of travel medicine practitioners, may also offer helpful advice on traveling abroad. You can find listings of reliable medical clinics overseas at the **International Society of Travel Medicine** (www.istm.org).

COMMON AILMENTS

DIETARY RED FLAGS You should always exercise caution when eating seafood, especially in summer when improperly refrigerated seafood spoils faster. Also, be cautious of street food, only buying from vendors whose facilities look neat and clean. Water in Campania's cities and towns is potable. The quality varies in some areas of Naples, but hotels, restaurants, and bars all have their own water-purification systems. If you're still concerned, order bottled water.

Non–meat eaters can go into any restaurant in Campania, even those specializing in meat and fish, and find a variety of vegetarian dishes on the menu—from *antipasti* to pasta dishes. Most restaurants will try their best to accommodate your dietary restrictions.

Wheat intolerance and celiac disease are getting increased attention, and many of the restaurants in the more-expensive bracket carry gluten-free pasta, bread, and crackers. Supermarkets have also started to carry such products, which were previously only available in specialized stores, *erboristerie* (natural remedies shops), and pharmacies.

SUN/ELEMENTS/EXTREME WEATHER EXPOSURE Do not underestimate the sun when you visit archaeological areas such as Pompeii and Herculaneum in the summer, as heat stroke is not impossible. Always use sunscreen and a hat and carry an adequate water supply.

WHAT TO DO IF YOU GET SICK AWAY FROM HOME

You'll find English-speaking doctors in most hospitals and pharmacies. Medical staff is generally well trained. The largest hospitals in the region are in Naples, but reputable hospitals, excellent private clinics, and smaller facilities exist in more remote places. We have listed the best hospital or local medical facility under "Fast Facts" for each destination in each chapter.

For travel abroad, you may have to pay all medical costs upfront and be reimbursed later. Medicare and Medicaid do not provide coverage for medical costs outside the U.S. Before leaving home, find out what medical services your health insurance covers. To protect yourself, consider buying medical travel insurance (see "Insurance," in chapter 12).

Very few health insurance plans pay for medical evacuation back to the U.S. (which can cost $10,000 and up). A number of companies offer medical evacuation services anywhere in the world. If you're ever hospitalized more than 150 miles from home, **MedjetAssist** (© **800/527-7478;** www.medjetassistance.com) will pick you up and fly you to the hospital of your choice virtually anywhere in the world in a medically equipped and staffed aircraft 24 hours a day, 7 days a week.

Annual memberships are $225 for an individual, $350 for a family; you can also purchase short-term memberships.

U.K. nationals will need a **European Health Insurance Card (EHIC)** to receive free or reduced-cost health benefits during a visit to a European Economic Area (EEA) country (European Union countries plus Iceland, Liechtenstein, and Norway) or Switzerland. The European Health Insurance Card replaces the E111 form, which is no longer valid. For advice, ask at your local post office or see www.dh.gov.uk/travellers.

If you suffer from a chronic illness, consult your doctor before your departure. Pack **prescription medications** in your carry-on luggage, and carry them in their original containers, with pharmacy labels—otherwise they won't make it through security. Carry generic names of prescription medicines, in case a local pharmacist is unfamiliar with the brand.

We list additional **emergency numbers** in chapter 12.

6 SAFETY

Campania is generally safe, though one of the biggest risks in the area is road accidents (see "By Car" under "Getting Around," p. 46). Always be vigilant, particularly as a **pedestrian,** when crossing the street or walking in a narrow street with no sidewalk. Look very carefully before proceeding, even if you have a green light and are using a pedestrian crossing.

The **crime rate** in Campania is generally low, and usually does not concern tourists. Most petty crimes are concentrated in certain areas, such as near Naples's Stazione Centrale and in the poverty-stricken neighborhoods of the city's suburbs. Stay away from the narrow streets of Naples's historic district and from poor

neighborhoods after dark. The countryside is quite safe and tranquil.

The most common menace for the average tourist, especially in Naples, is the plague of **pickpockets** and car thieves. Pickpockets are active in all crowded places, particularly tourist areas. Note that they are sometimes dressed in elegant attire, and often work in pairs or groups, using various techniques, from distraction routines to razor blades to cut the bottom of your bag. Even savvy travelers must be vigilant.

The city center is also where most **car thefts** occur, although vehicles are always at risk, except in the most remote rural areas. Never leave valuables inside your car, never travel with your doors unlocked, and always park in a garage with an attendant. Be careful when traveling on highways at night, as robbery scams involve fake breakdowns being staged and good Samaritans who stopped to help being robbed. Instead of stopping, call the police from your mobile; they'll send a car.

A good idea is to make photocopies of your **important documents:** tickets, passport, credit cards, and IDs. Make sure you keep them in a different pocket or bag than the originals. Also, if you rent a car, make sure there is no rental sticker on the car that could make you a target (tourists often have expensive gear, such as cameras and electronic devices). Also, make sure no luggage or other items are visible inside the car, such as in the back seat. Do not open your trunk and display the contents in the parking spot where you're planning to leave your car unguarded: Get what you need from your luggage ahead of time.

We have heard a few reports from other areas in Italy of **robberies** performed by individuals who befriend travelers at stations, airports, and bars, and then take advantage of their lower level of vigilance: Choose your friends carefully.

One further concern is **ATM skimming.** Attached to legitimate bank ATMs usually located in tourist areas, electronic devices can capture your credit card information and record your PIN through a pin-hole camera. Always make sure the ATM you are planning to use does not look as if it has been tampered with, and cover the keypad with one hand as you enter your PIN.

Italian law is generally fair; but if you commit a crime, the law will be enforced. Do not drink and drive, do not traffic or carry illegal drugs, do not engage in illicit sexual activities, do not litter, and do not exhibit loud and drunken behavior. If you are driving, respect the **rules of the road** (p. 51). Also note that if you make any kind of purchase, from a cafe, to a meal in a restaurant, to a handbag, the vendor is required by law to give you an official receipt and you are required to keep it with you for a few hundred yards after coming out of the shop.

7 SPECIALIZED TRAVEL RESOURCES

In addition to the destination-specific resources listed below, please visit Frommers.com for additional travel resources.

GAY & LESBIAN TRAVELERS

Since 1861, Campania and Italy have had liberal legislation regarding homosexuality. Ischia and Capri have long been gay meccas, and you'll find a somewhat active gay life in Naples. Still, open displays of same-sex affection are sometimes frowned upon in the highly Catholic country (despite the fact that people in Campania are very physical, and men and women alike embrace when saying hello and goodbye).

ARCI Gay (www.arcigay.it) is the country's leading gay organization, with branches throughout Campania. Naples's section is Circolo Antinoo, Vico San Geronimo 17, Naples (© **081-5528815**). Another major organization is **Gay.it** (www.gay.it), which maintains a search engine (http://guida.gay.it) for gay-friendly bars, restaurants, and the like, and a specialized tour operator **Gayfriendlyitaly.com** (www.gayfriendlyitaly.com).

Gay publications include *Pride,* a free national monthly, available at most gay venues; and *Babilonia,* which is available at most large newsstands.

The International Gay and Lesbian Travel Association (IGLTA; © **800/448-8550** or 954/776-2626; www.iglta.org) is the trade association for the gay and lesbian travel industry and offers an online

HOTEL ★★★★
POSEIDON
POSITANO

Via Pasitea, 148,
84017 POSITANO (SA) Italy
Tel. + 39 089 811111 Pbx
Fax + 39 089 875833
internet: www.hotelposeidonpositano.it
e-mail:info@hotelposeidonpositano.it

"CUMPA' COSIMO"

La Sirenuse

directory of gay- and lesbian-friendly travel businesses and tour operators.

Many agencies offer tours and travel itineraries specifically for gay and lesbian travelers. **Above and Beyond Tours** (℃ 800/397-2681; www.abovebeyond tours.com) is an Australia-based gay tour specialist. San Francisco–based **Now, Voyager** (℃ 800/255-6951; www.now voyager.com) offers worldwide trips and cruises, and **Olivia** (℃ 800/631-6277; www.olivia.com) offers lesbian cruises and resort vacations.

Gay.com (℃ 800/929-2268 or 415/644-8044; www.gay.com) is an excellent online successor to the popular *Out & About* print magazine (membership is required). It provides regularly updated information about gay-owned, gay-oriented, and gay-friendly lodging, dining, sightseeing, nightlife, and shopping establishments in every major destination worldwide. British travelers should click on the "Travel" link at **www.uk.gay.com** for advice and gay-friendly trip ideas (membership is required). The Canadian website **GayTraveler** (www.gaytraveler.ca) offers ideas and advice for gay travel all over the world. **Outtraveler.com** is another good online resource.

The following travel guides are available at many bookstores, or you can order them from any online bookseller: *Spartacus International Gay Guide, 35th Edition* (Bruno Gmünder Verlag; www.spartacusworld.com/gayguide) and *Odysseus: The International Gay Travel Planner, 17th Edition*; and the *Damron* guides (www.damron.com), with separate, annual books for gays and lesbians.

TRAVELERS WITH DISABILITIES

Laws in Campania and in Italy have compelled train stations, airports, hotels, and most restaurants to follow a stricter set of regulations for **wheelchair accessibility** to restrooms, ticket counters, and the like.

Museums and other attractions have conformed to the regulations, which mimic many of those presently in effect in the United States. Always call ahead to check on accessibility in hotels, restaurants, and sights you want to visit.

Local resources include **Accessible Italy** (www.accessibleitaly.com), a nonprofit association based in San Marino (the ministate in central Italy), which offers specialized tours and assistance for organizing your own vacation, including rental of equipment and lists of accessible accommodations and other services.

Other organizations that offer a vast range of resources and assistance to travelers with disabilities include **MossRehab** (℃ 800/CALL-MOSS [225-5667]; www.mossresourcenet.org), the **American Foundation for the Blind** (AFB; ℃ 800/232-5463; www.afb.org), and **SATH** (Society for Accessible Travel & Hospitality; ℃ 212/447-7284; www.sath.org). **AirAmbulanceCard.com** is now partnered with SATH and allows you to preselect top-notch hospitals in case of an emergency.

Access-Able Travel Source (℃ 303/232-2979; www.access-able.com) offers a comprehensive database on travel agents from around the world with experience in accessible travel, destination-specific access information, and links to such resources as service animals, equipment rentals, and access guides.

Many travel agencies offer customized tours and itineraries for travelers with disabilities. Among them are **Flying Wheels Travel** (℃ 507/451-5005; www.flying wheelstravel.com); and **Accessible Journeys** (℃ 800/846-4537 or 610/521-0339; www.disabilitytravel.com).

Flying with Disability (www.flying-with-disability.org) is a comprehensive information source on airplane travel. **Avis Rent a Car** (℃ 888/879-4273) has an "Avis Access" program that offers services for customers with special travel needs.

These include specially outfitted vehicles with swivel seats, spinner knobs, and hand controls; mobility scooter rentals; and accessible bus service. Be sure to reserve well in advance.

Also check out the quarterly magazine *Emerging Horizons* (www.emerging horizons.com), available by subscription ($16.95 per year U.S.; $21.95 outside U.S.).

The "Accessible Travel" link at **Mobility-Advisor.com** (www.mobility-advisor. com) offers a variety of travel resources to persons with disabilities.

British travelers should contact **Holiday Care** (✆ **0845-124-9971** in the U.K. only; www.holidaycare.org.uk) to access a wide range of travel information and resources for elderly people and those with disabilities.

FAMILY TRAVEL

The whole country, especially Southern Italy, is completely welcoming to children. Italians love kids and take theirs with them wherever they go. Hotels, restaurants, and attraction managers will always be most accommodating of your children's special needs, but don't expect special amenities: There will be no playroom, no babysitting program, and no kiddy area with small tables and crayons. Children in Italy partake in their parents' lives: They eat at the same table and from the same menu, though you can obtain half portions *(mezza porzione)* in most restaurants and ask for specially prepared dishes not on the menu. Kids sleep in the same room or suite—though most hoteliers will add a cot to your room for your child, and most have special rooms or suites designed for families with children, but you need to book in advance. Even the largest hotels will offer babysitting only on request, meaning they are not on permanent staff but can be brought in as childcare is needed. Throughout the region, private attractions offer discounts to all children, while in state-run museums, only E.U.

citizens ages 17 and under are admitted free.

Campania is particularly suited for a vacation with children: The ancient sites and castles stimulate children's imagination while the many beaches and resorts are a perfect place for them to vent their energy (though if you have younger children, you might want to avoid the rocky Sorrento peninsula and Capri, where sandy beaches are rare, and favor Ischia and the Cilento, which have the best sandy stretches in the region).

The key to a successful family vacation in Italy lies in some smart planning: Involve your children in both the research and the decision-making process; schedule your visits alternating "adult" attractions with those in which your kids will be interested; and plan to make lots of gelato (ice cream) and pizza breaks. Ice cream here—the *artigianale* variety (see p. 29)—is basically guilt free, as is has much less fat and sugar than its American counterpart, particularly the fruit flavors, which are prepared with fresh fruit. In general, we find that 1 hour is about how long any kid (and many adults) can stand to look at paintings and other artifacts in a museum, no matter how splendid and unique. If you absolutely need to spend several hours in a museum, take turns with another adult in the party, if there is one. Chances are good, however, that a lot of attractions in the region will satisfy both adults and children simultaneously.

Throughout this book we indicate accommodations, restaurants, and attractions that are particularly kid friendly, with a (**Kids**) icon. In chapter 4 we also mapped out an itinerary especially for families.

For additional information on family travel, we recommend **Family Travel Forum** (www.familytravelforum.com), a comprehensive website that offers customized trip planning; the online magazine **Family Travel Network** (www.familytravel network.com), which provides travel tips;

and **TravelWithYourKids.com** (www. travelwithyourkids.com), a comprehensive site written by parents for parents, offering sound advice for long-distance and international travel with children.

WOMEN TRAVELERS

Naples used to be on the black list for women travelers, but conditions have improved enormously after years of refurbishment in the city's historical district. Southern Italians are also much more accustomed to seeing blond visitors. There are, though, some remaining safety issues (see "Safety," p. 55).

However, women chronically attract men's attention and often have to fend off their proffered "friendship." Most often, ignoring remarks, avoiding eye contact, and proceeding on your way as if you hadn't noticed anything is the best approach.

Always dress appropriately. Especially in summer, remember that Italian women are attired more conservatively in urban surroundings than their counterparts in the United States: Reserve your strappy tanks and short shorts for the beach, ladies.

Should you ever perceive a real threat, immediately request assistance from a policeman, a storekeeper, or even a passerby (elderly women are usually perceived as particularly forbidding by young Italian males). In general, avoid seedy neighborhoods where you don't see many women strolling around, and use your common sense. Also women should not walk around alone in sketchy neighborhoods after dark.

If you are a solo traveler, see "Single Travelers," below.

Also check out the award-winning website **Journeywoman** (www.journeywoman.com), a "real life" women's travel-information network where you can sign up for a free e-mail newsletter and get advice on everything from etiquette and

dress to safety. The travel guide *Safety and Security for Women Who Travel,* by Sheila Swan and Peter Laufer (Travelers' Tales Guides), offering common-sense tips on safe travel, was updated in 2004.

For general travel resources for women, go to www.frommers.com/planning.

AFRICAN-AMERICAN TRAVELERS

The people of Naples and its environs are remarkably open-minded. For the most part, Naples is a safe haven for all ethnicities.

SoulOfAmerica.com (www.soulofamerica.com) is a comprehensive website, with travel tips, event and family-reunion postings, and sections on historically black beach resorts and active vacations.

Agencies and organizations that provide resources for black travelers include **Rodgers Travel** (✆ 800/825-1775; www.rodgerstravel.com); the **African American Association of Innkeepers International** (✆ 877/422-5777; www.africanamericaninns.com); and **Henderson Travel & Tours** (✆ 800/327-2309 or 301/650-5700; www.hendersontravel.com), which has specialized in trips to Africa since 1957.

Go Girl: The Black Woman's Guide to Travel & Adventure is a compilation of travel essays by writers including Jill Nelson and Audre Lorde. *The African-American Travel Guide,* by Wayne C. Robinson, was published in 1997, so it may be somewhat dated. The well-done *Pathfinders Magazine* (✆ 877/977-PATH [7284]; www.pathfinderstravel.com) includes articles on a wide range of topics, often related to travel in Italy.

SENIOR TRAVEL

Mention the fact that you're a senior when you first make your travel reservations. Most major airlines and many international chain hotels offer discounts for seniors.

Members of **AARP,** 601 E St. NW, Washington, DC 20049 (© 888/687-2277; www.aarp.org), get discounts on hotels, airfares, and car rentals. AARP offers members a wide range of benefits, including *AARP The Magazine* and a monthly newsletter. Anyone 50 and over can join.

Many reliable agencies and organizations target the 50-plus market. **Grand Circle Travel** (© 800/221-2610 or 617/350-7500; www.gct.com) offers package deals for the 50-plus market, mostly of the tour-bus variety, with free trips thrown in for those who organize groups of 10 or more. **Elderhostel** (© 877/426-8056; www.elderhostel.org) arranges study programs for those ages 55 and over (and a spouse or companion of any age) in the U.S. and in more than 80 countries around the world, including Italy.

Recommended publications offering travel resources and discounts for seniors include the quarterly magazine *Travel 50 & Beyond* (www.travel50andbeyond. com) and the bestselling paperback *Unbelievably Good Deals and Great Adventures That You Absolutely Can't Get Unless You're Over 50, 2007–2008, 17th Edition,* by Joann Rattner Heilman.

Many discounts on admission to museums and attractions in Italy are available only to citizens of the European community because of the lack of reciprocity with the United States and other countries.

STUDENT TRAVEL

Naples and Campania are heaven for students, especially those who are interested in art, antiquity, or music.

The **International Student Travel Confederation** (ISTC; www.istc.org) was formed in 1949 to make travel around the world more affordable for students. Visit its website for comprehensive travel services information and details on how to get an **International Student Identity Card (ISIC),** which qualifies students for substantial savings on rail passes, plane tickets, entrance fees, and more. It also provides students with basic health and life insurance and a 24-hour help line. The card is valid for a maximum of 18 months. You can apply for the card online or in person at **STA Travel** (© 800/781-4040 in North America; www.statravel.com), the biggest student travel agency in the world; visit the website to locate STA Travel offices worldwide. If you're no longer a student but are 25 or under, you can get an **International Youth Travel Card (IYTC)** from STA Travel that entitles you to discounts on airfare, hotel stays, entrance fees, dining, and shopping. **Travel CUTS** (© 800/592-2887; www. travelcuts.com) offers similar services for both Canadians and U.S. residents. Irish students may prefer to turn to **USIT** (© 01/602-1904; www.usit.ie), an Ireland-based specialist in student, youth, and independent travel.

SINGLE TRAVELERS

Solo travelers do not usually have a problem in Campania, as many hotels have single rooms for business travelers. On package vacations, however, single travelers are often hit with a "single supplement" to the base price. To avoid it, you can agree to room with other single travelers or find a compatible roommate before you go, from one of the many roommate-locator agencies.

Whether you are male or female, it is imperative you remain vigilant for shady characters, as solo travelers are easy prey for crooks, who may try to befriend (and then rob) you. If you feel uncomfortable, ask for help; speaking up will often diffuse a potentially dangerous situation.

TravelChums (© 212/787-2621; www.travelchums.com) is an Internet-only travel-companion matching service, hosted by the respected New York–based Shaw Guides travel service.

Many reputable tour companies offer singles-only trips. **Singles Travel International** (© 877/765-6874; www.singles travelintl.com) offers singles-only escorted tours to Southern Italy. **Backroads** (© 800/462-2848; www.backroads.com) offers "Singles + Solos" active-travel trips to destinations worldwide, including Italy.

For more information, check out Eleanor Berman's classic *Traveling Solo: Advice and Ideas for More than 250 Great Vacations, 6th Edition* (Globe Pequot), updated in 2008.

For more information on traveling single, go to www.frommers.com/planning.

8 SUSTAINABLE TOURISM

Responsible tourism is a key conservation element on the Amalfi Coast and surrounding areas. Nature has done its best to protect itself here, with steep cliffs making it really hard for developers, but the resulting beauty attracts so many tourists, both local and international, that the entire region is at serious risk. Overbuilding, forest fires, and overuse of water resources are the region's top problems, together with marine pollution: All of these are exacerbated by the enormous tourist pressure. The dawning of conservation and sustainable tourism in recent years has made the local tourist industry well aware of the fragility of the local environment and committed to protect it, together with the Italian government and the numerous local associations working for its preservation. Water and sewage management plans are active in most hotels and restaurants, and a large number of them buy only local produce and services. Shortsighted developers, backed by organized crime, are still very active though, and constantly try to encroach on protected land, often resorting to arson. We can all make a difference by choosing sustainable resorts and accommodations, and by respecting the local ecosystem.

Naples might hardly be what you picture as an eco-friendly destination, but the rest of the region is actually one of the prime destinations for eco-tourism in Italy.

Campania is home to Italy's second largest national park—the Cilento—and to a large number of parks and nature preserves, including the National Park of Mount Vesuvius, the miniarea of the Valle delle Ferriere in Amalfi, and the marine bioparks of Baia (near Pozzuoli), Procida, Ischia, Punta Campanella (Massa Lubrense), parts of Capri, and of the Cilento coast.

You'll also find a great number of *agriturismi,* working farms that increase their income by turning themselves into small resorts (similar to some ranches in the United States). This movement has been successfully promoted by the Italian government to reduce acquisition of abandoned farms by developers, and to protect natural areas, and has found a perfect home in Campania, where the countryside often offers dramatic natural attractions and close proximity to the seaside. Also, most of the *agriturismi* have embraced the organic movement, adding increased environmental benefit. Operations are controlled through methods such as surprise inspections, and *agriturismi* are strictly regulated by law to prevent exploitation by corporations and developers: In order to obtain the right to call itself an *agriturismo,* the farm must: (a) offer fewer than 30 beds total; and (b) make most of its profits from the agricultural component of the property—in other words, the property has to remain a farm and not become a glorified hotel.

Staying in an *agriturismo* is a great way to contribute to green tourism in Italy; it can also be quite attractive for the special amenities it offers. For more information, see "Tips on Accommodations," on p. 67.

Throughout this book we recommend services that are committed to sustainable tourism. These hotels may have bathroom fixtures that reduce the amount of wasted water, soap dispensers to reduce the number of empty plastic bottles and unused soap that ends up in the garbage, and energy-saving bulbs. They increasingly rely on energy derived from solar or wind power, and they also invite guests to save water by using towels and bed sheets for more than one night. They often have made or are enacting plans for the recycling of gray water, and reduce plastic use by offering fresh, local, and often organic foods rather than industrial prepackaged breakfast goods, and water bottled in recyclable glass bottles.

Several local organizations are good resources: **Associazione Italiana Turismo Responsabile** (www.aitr.org), **Legambiente** (www.legambiente.eu) and its regional section for Campania (www.legambiente.campania.it), **FAI** (Fondo Ambiente Italiano; www.fondoambiente.it), and **WWF Italy** (www.wwf.it). We also recommend a few excellent operators: **Planet Viaggi** (www.planetviaggi.it) organizes enticing eco-tours in Naples and the Cilento, **CTS** (Centro Turismo Studentesco; www.cts.it), and **AMEntelibera** (www.viaggiamentelibera.it). See "Special Interest Trips" below for additional nature-oriented resources.

9 SPECIAL-INTEREST TRIPS & ESCORTED TOURS

SPECIAL-INTEREST TRIPS

Our favorite special-interest tour group in the region is the lively Napoli-based **Rising Incoming Organizer (RIO),** Via Monte di Dio 9, 80132 Napoli (© 081-7644934; www.riorimontitours.com), a family business now in its third generation. It offers a variety of unique, off-the-beaten-path tours that cover all kinds of special interests, from classic art and ceramics—a 12-day tour in Naples, Vietri, the Amalfi Coast, and Cerreto Sannita (near Benevento) that we particularly recommend—to golf, sailing, and culinary adventures, including one featuring Neapolitan pastries.

Another operator we like is the Philadelphia-based **Context Travel** (© 800/691-6036 toll-free in the U.S., or 215/392-0303; www.contexttravel.com), offering tours and excursions guided by docents and experts. The list of available walking tours of Naples is impressive; each tour focuses on one area of interest, such as art, archaeology, architecture, history, theology, city ambience, shopping, or cuisine.

San Diego–based **Cultural Italy** (© 800/380-0014 or 619/822-1099; www.culturalitaly.com) is also a good source for a variety of tours.

ACADEMIC TRIPS & LANGUAGE CLASSES

Our favorite language school in the area is **Sorrento Lingue,** Via S. Francesco 8, 80067 Sorrento (© 081-8075599; www.sorrentolingue.com). It also offers cooking and art classes. Our other favorite is **Centro Italiano,** Vico Santa Maria dell'Aiuto 17, 80134 Napoli (© 081-5524331; www.centroitaliano.it), which also offers excellent seminars on local culture as well as courses on archaeology, ceramics, wine, and yoga.

Both offer high academic value and comparable costs (weekly courses start at about 200€ per person). Another resource is the British-based **LCA** (Language Courses Abroad; www.languagesabroad.co.uk) which organizes language as well as cooking and art classes in the region.

ADVENTURE & WELLNESS TRIPS

The Sorrento peninsula and Amalfi Coast are hikers' heavens, while the Cilento simultaneously offers the best to both hikers and bicycle enthusiasts. A great number of agencies, both local and international, offer hiking and biking trips, but you can also hire local guides to organize your own individual trip (see our suggestions in the destination chapters that follow).

Our favorite locally based organization is **Cycling Cilento Adventure** (© 328-3652736; www.cyclingcilentoadventure.com), based in Cilento National Park. It offers a great—both in number and quality—choice of road bike, mountain bike, and hiking tours, all of which allow you to sample the local cuisine and see the best sights.

An excellent agency is **Country Walkers** (© 800/464-9255 or 802/244-1387; www.countrywalkers.com); based in Vermont, it organizes great walking tours with highly experienced local guides, from a more laid-back tour of Capri and the Amalfi Coast, to a more taxing hike of the Amalfi Coast.

Another excellent agency is the U.K.-based **Sherpa Expeditions** (© 20-8577-2717; www.sherpa-walking-holidays.co.uk), offering several guided and self-guided walking tours in Campania, both on the Amalfi Coast and in Cilento National Park.

La Dolce Vita Wine Tours (© 888/746-0022; www.dolcetours.com) organizes easier walking tours, including one that covers Capri, Mount Vesuvius, and

Pompeii, as well as some of the best vineyards in the region.

Breakaway Adventures (© 800/567-6286; www.breakaway-adventures.com) organizes cycling and walking tours in the Sorrento peninsula and Amalfi Coast as well as in the Cilento.

The region is also a major wellness destination, with the local volcanic activity creating endless natural spa opportunities. The island of Ischia and Castellamare di Stabia are where you'll find the world-renown resorts. We have highlighted the best spas for each destination throughout this book.

FOOD & WINE TRIPS

As home to some of the best culinary traditions in Italy, Campania offers a number of food-oriented tours. Our personal favorites are those offered by the **Sorrento Cooking School** (© 081-8783255; www.sorrentocookingschool.com), whose program includes a large variety of choices both in length (from daily excursions to longer tours lasting up to 8 days) and content (from cooking classes and wine tours to gastronomic and cultural explorations).

We also like the Italian cooking school of **Mami Camilla,** Via cocumella 06, Sant'Agnello di Sorrento (© 081-8782067; www.mamicamilla.com).

Other excellent classes are organized by **Sorrento Lingue** and **Centro Italiano** (see "Academic Trips & Language Classes," above).

Specializing in culinary vacations, **Epiculinary** (© 888/380-9010; www.epiculinary.com) hosts a large variety of Italian classes and tours, several of which are in the Sorrento and Amalfi Coast areas.

Chicago-based **International Kitchen** (© 800/945-8606; www.theinternationalkitchen.com) is one of the best companies devoted to culinary tours, and its program includes several destinations on the Amalfi Coast, such as the delightful

Oasi Olympia Relais in Sant'Agata sui due Golfi, between Sorrento and Positano.

With its "taste your travel" slogan, Italy-based **Pagine di Gusto** (© 0461-829964; www.paginedigusto.com) organizes several discovery tours of Campania, highlighting its art, food, and wines.

Another good resource is **Gourmet Traveler** (www.gourmetravel.com), offering specialized tours of the Amalfi Coast.

· As for wine, our favorite tour operator is the Benevento-based **Savour the Sannio** (© 0823-953663; www.savourthesannio. com), operated by Barbara and Federico. They organize delectable tours of the local wineries as well as excellent cooking classes and cultural excursions.

VOLUNTEER & WORKING TRIPS

Legambiente and **FAI** (p. 62) regularly organize working vacations during which you volunteer on a specific conservation project, paying only your basic lodging expenses. Another good resource is **Worldwide Opportunities on Organic Farms** (www.wwoof.org), which organizes volunteer work on organic farms.

ESCORTED GENERAL INTEREST TOURS

Escorted tours are structured group tours with a group leader. The price usually includes everything from airfare to hotels, meals, tours, admission to attractions, and local transportation. Among the major companies, we recommend **Italiatour** (© 800/845-3365; fax 212/765-2183; www.italiatour.com); the prices and quality are very competitive, and it is the only company that offers exclusive tours of Campania. (Some tours merely pause in the region as part of Italy-wide itineraries.)

We also recommend the Boston-based **Bella Vista Tours** (© 877/723-0802 toll-free outside Massachusetts, or 617/723-0802; www.bellavistatours.com), which

offers a completely customizable tour of the Amalfi Coast; and Albany-based **Celtic Tours** (© 800/833-4373 or 518/862-0042; www.celtictours.com) offering a good tour of Sorrento and the Amalfi Coast.

We also recommend **Perillo Tours** (© 800/431-1515; www.perillotours. com), family operated for three generations—perhaps you've seen the TV commercials that feature the "King of Italy," Mario Perillo, or the ones that feature his son, Steve—and **Trafalgar Tours** (© 800/854-0103; www.trafalgartours.com), one of Europe's largest tour operators, offering affordable guided tours with lodgings in unpretentious hotels. Leading competitors to the previous two companies are **Globus+Cosmos Tours** (© 800/338-7092; www.globusandcosmos.com), offering first-class escorted coach tours as well as budget tours, and **Insight Vacations** (© 800/582-8380; www.insight vacations.com), which books superior, first-class, fully escorted motorcoach tours. Among smaller companies, Connecticut-based **Tour Italy Now** (© 800/955-4418; www.touritalynow.com) offers a variety of tours to the Amalfi Coast and Campania.

Abercrombie & Kent (© 800/323-7308 in the U.S., or 020-7730-9600 in the U.K.; www.abercrombiekent.com) offers luxurious premium packages. Your overnight stays will be in meticulously restored castles and exquisite villas. The oldest travel agency in Britain, **Cox & Kings** (© 020-7873-5000; www.coxand kings.co.uk), specializes in unusual, if pricey, holidays, focusing on special interests, such as gardens or religion. The company is noted for its focus on tours of an ecological and environmental interest.

For more information on escorted general-interest tours, including questions to ask before booking your trip, see www.frommers.com/planning.

To call Italy:

1. Dial the international access code: 011 from the U.S.; 00 from the U.K., Ireland, and New Zealand; or 0011 from Australia.
2. Dial the country code for Italy: 39.
3. Dial the local area code and then the number. Telephone numbers in Italy can have any number of digits depending on the location and the type of telephone line, which can be very confusing to foreigners. The amount of numbers can range from five (for special switchboards of hospitals and other public services, such as the railroad info line of Trenitalia, ✆ **892021** for example) to a maximum of 10 (for some land lines and all cellular lines). Telephone numbers always include the area code, which can have two or three digits. Area codes begin with 0, for land lines, or 3, for cellular lines; and you always need to dial the 0.

To make international calls: To make international calls from Italy, first dial 00 and then the country code (U.S. or Canada 1, U.K. 44, Ireland 353, Australia 61, New Zealand 64). Next, dial the area code and number. For example, if you wanted to call the British Embassy in Washington, D.C., you would dial 00-1-202-588-7800.

For directory assistance: Dial ✆ **1240.**

For operator assistance: Dial ✆ **170;** the service is available only from 7am to midnight.

Toll-free numbers: Numbers beginning with 800 or 888 within Italy are toll-free, but calling a 1-800 number in the States from Italy is not toll-free: It costs the same as an overseas call.

Local pay phones in Italy require prepaid telephone cards, called *carta telefonica,* which you can buy at a tobacconist (*tabacchi,* marked by a sign with a white T on a black background), bar, or newsstand. The local Telecom card is available for 5€ or 10€, and gives you unlimited call time within Italy for 1 month. The card has a perforated corner that you need to tear off before inserting it into the phone slot. If you are using coins, a local call in Italy costs .10€.

To make international calls you need to purchase an international prepaid card, which varies depending on which country you will be calling the most. The cards are sold at tobacconists and some bars and newsstands. They usually allow from 200 to 700 minutes call time for 5€. You need to scratch the back to reveal the secret code and dial it after the access code indicated on the card; then dial the number you want to call.

More convenient but not necessarily cheaper is to have: (1) your own calling card linked to your home phone, or (2) a prepaid calling card that you pay monthly by credit card; both are good options. Some calling cards offer a toll-free access number in Italy, while others do not; the first kind is obviously more convenient. When calling from a public phone booth, you sometimes need to put in money or a *carta telefonica* just to obtain the dial tone, even if you are using a prepaid card; you may be charged only for a local call or not at all. Check with your calling-card provider before leaving on your trip.

You can also make collect calls directly by calling the operator (see above) or through a telephone provider in your country. For **AT&T,** dial ✆ **800-1724444;** for **MCI,** dial ✆ **800-905825;** and for **Sprint,** dial ✆ **800-172405** or 800-172406.

Remember that calling from a hotel is convenient but usually very expensive.

MOBILE PHONES

If you have a dual-band or triband GSM phone, it will work in Italy and all over Europe. The bandwidth used in Europe for GSM phones is 900–1800 hertz. Just call your wireless operator and ask for "international roaming" to be activated on your account. Unfortunately, charges can be high—anywhere from $1 to $5 per minute.

You can enjoy much cheaper rates by renting or buying an Italian **SIM card.** You might need to have your phone unlocked by your provider at home so that it will function with any SIM card and network. You can buy an Italian prepaid SIM card, called *scheda pre-pagata*, in mobile phone shops, which exist in most towns throughout Italy. Major networks that have excellent local coverage in the region are Telecom Italia (TIM), Vodafone, Wind, and H3G. The SIM is encoded with the phone number that will be yours for the time of your stay. The scheda pre-pagata costs 25€, 50€, 80€, 100€, or 150€.

The other option is to rent a phone with the bandwidth used in Europe and a local SIM card. A number of companies offer mobile phones for rent, and you may also be able to add a phone to your car rental.

Renting before you go has the advantage that you know your phone number in advance and can communicate it to your friends and family. The disadvantage is that the phones are not necessarily set with an Italian SIM card, in which case you may have to pay some roaming charges.

North Americans can rent a mobile before leaving home from **Context Travel** (www.contexttravel.com). The company will ship the phone to you in the U.S. 10 days before your departure (you'll then ship it back to them in Philadelphia). You can also have a phone shipped to you in Italy. Incoming calls are free.

Easyline (© **800-010600** toll-free within Italy) also delivers phones for free in Italy. The company will issue you your phone number before you leave for your trip. Other useful resources are **InTouch USA** (© **800/872-7626;** www.intouch global.com) or **RoadPost** (© **888/290-1606** or 905/272-5665; www.roadpost. com). InTouch will also, for free, advise you on whether your existing phone will work overseas; simply call © **703/222-7161** between 9am and 4pm EST, or go to **http://intouchglobal.com/travel.htm**.

INTERNET & E-MAIL

An increasing number of hotels and resorts in the region are going **Wi-Fi,** becoming "hotspots" that offer free high-speed Wi-Fi access or charge a small fee for usage. If you are planning to carry your laptop, check **www.jiwire.com** and their Wi-Fi Finder, the world's largest directory of public wireless hotspots.

For dial-up access, most medium- and upper-range hotels in the region offer dataports in the room unless they offer Wi-Fi.

Note: Italy uses 220V electricity and round-pronged plugs: See "Electricity" on p. 318. Always bring a **connection kit** of the right power and phone adapters, a spare phone cord, and a spare Ethernet network cable—or find out whether your hotel supplies them to guests. Most phone plugs in hotels and private homes throughout Italy have been upgraded to the standard phone jack used on computers, but some of the old ones with three round prongs are still in use. You can easily buy an adaptor at any local hardware store if your hotel doesn't have one for you.

If you are not planning to bring your laptop, a number of hotels in the area offer Internet access for their clients, usually free of charge, or they'll know how to direct you to the closest paying Internet Point in town: You'll find one everywhere but the most remote location. For a directory of cybercafes in the region check **www.cybercaptive.com** and **www.cyber cafe.com**.

On the Amalfi Coast, the climate is mild, so hotels are structured to maximize outdoor enjoyment, with guest rooms opening onto patios, balconies, terraces, and gardens. Carpeting is the exception, while a tiled floor—often with hand-decorated tiles from the local industry—is the rule. Some of the local cultural idiosyncrasies (such as lack of amenities and small bathrooms) can be less charming; they become more and more apparent as you go down in the level and price of accommodations.

In general, hotels tend to have fewer amenities, particularly in urban areas, than their same-level counterparts in the U.S. and Britain. Swimming pools are a rare luxury in town, though outdoor summer-only pools are more common in seaside and some mountain resort destinations. Fitness clubs and gyms are becoming more widespread, but only in top-tier hotels. Spas are routinely offered only in luxury hotels; you'll find some in more moderate hotels, but only in thermal destinations. In-room dining is offered only in the most expensive hotels and rarely on a 24-hour basis. Moderate hotels may not have a restaurant at all, just a breakfast service which they may even cater from the nearby bar. Only the cheapest accommodations don't have TVs, but more expensive hotels may offer satellite TV (necessary for programs in English). Air-conditioning is far from standard, but the climate is so nearly perfect—warm and breezy—that you will rarely need it.

Also, because buildings are old—sometimes centuries old—elevators tend to be small and rarely fully accessible to the mobility challenged: Steps tend to be ubiquitous. Rooms also tend to be smaller than, say, in the U.S. or Britain, but the biggest difference is in the bathrooms, which tend to be tiny, rarely featuring a bathtub (shower only), with fixtures that look old-fashioned even if they are in perfect working order.

So, if you are planning to spend a lot of time in your room—having drinks with friends and romantic dinners—and in the hotel, lounging in the public areas, the spa, the swimming pool, and the hotel's restaurants and bars, you should consider only the most luxurious hotels. Only there will you find the level of amenities you are seeking. If instead you want to spend most of your time exploring your destination, using your hotel as a sleeping base, then you should definitely consider moderate hotels, because, while their extra amenities are basic, you'll get spacious—sometimes even luxurious—rooms with modern bathrooms.

If all you really want is a good bed, then you can consider inexpensive hotels, where the room's decor will be simpler but accommodation will always include all the basic amenities (comfortable and scrupulously clean bed and bathroom, telephone, and local TV).

Hotels with restaurants often offer a meal plan to go with the room. You can usually choose among B&B service (breakfast only), half-board (breakfast and either lunch or dinner), and full board (breakfast, lunch, and dinner). Some smaller establishments make a meal plan mandatory during the month of August, when many of these same hotels may enforce a minimum-stay requirement of 3 or 7 days.

Most hotels in the region are private—often family-run—properties, yet you will also find a few hotels run by some major chains: In addition to **Best Western** (www.bestwestern.com), **Hilton** (www.hilton.com), **Holiday Inn** (www.holiday-inn.com), and **Starwood Hotels**—including Sheraton, Four Points, Le Meridien, Westin, St. Regis, and Luxury Collection—(www.starwoodhotels.com), you'll find the

Italian chain **NH/Jolly Hotels** (www.jolly hotels.it), catering to business as well as family travelers. You'll also find the French chain **Sofitel** (www.sofitel.com), which offers somewhat simpler accommodations and caters mostly to families, and the European **Accor Hotels** (www.accorhotels.com) with its moderately priced Novotel and its more elegant Mercure hotels.

Because most hotels in the area are private, often family-run businesses—including some of the most famous luxury hotels such as the San Pietro in Positano—you'll do much better checking an Italy-based search engine such as **Venere Net** (www. venere.com). Other sites to check out are **Italyhotels** (www.italyhotelink.com), **ITWG.com** (www.italyhotels.com), **Welcome to Italy** (www.wel.it), **Europa Hotels** (www.europa-hotels.com), and **Italy Hotels** (www.hotels-in-italy.com).

Also, always check the hotel's website directly, as these often list the same rates as some supposed discount agencies, but without the extra fee, or even unique online deals.

Remember: It's always a good idea to **get a confirmation number,** record the name of the representative with whom you spoke, and **make a printout** of any online booking transaction.

AGRITURISMO (FARM STAYS)

Another option—a favorite with Italians—is *agriturismo:* staying on a working farm or former farm somewhere in the countryside (see "Sustainable Tourism," p. 61). Your lodging usually includes breakfast and at least one other meal (your choice of dinner or lunch), prepared with ingredients produced on the farm or by nearby local farms. Among the rapidly multiplying online agencies, the best are **Agriturist.it** (www.agriturist.it) and **Agriturismo.it** (www.agriturismo.it). Accommodations are usually pretty posh, and

range from palatial (for example, on famous wine-producing estates) to country-inn style. They all usually offer such amenities as swimming pools and outdoor activities. However, some *agriturismi* offer only basic accommodations: You'll be satisfied only if you are really after the barn experience. Rates are usually proportional to what is provided.

RENTING A VILLA

This option used to be available only in Tuscany, but the Amalfi Coast is rapidly catching up. The appeal of the arrangement for a tourist is obvious, and the number of properties for rent has been on the increase.

Many good agencies specialize in stays on the Amalfi Coast. We like the **Right Vacation Rental** (www.therightvacation rental.com), offering apartment, farmhouse, and cottage stays of 2 weeks or more; it is a subsidiary of **Idyll Untours** (© **888-868-6871;** www.untours.com) and donates part of its profits to provide low-interest loans to underprivileged entrepreneurs around the world. Others we like for their portfolio and commitment are **Doorways LTD** (© **800/261-4460** or 610/520-0806; www.villavacations. com), **Rent Villas** (© **800/726-6702** or 805/641-1650; fax 805/641-1630; www. rentvillas.com), **Europe at Cost** (© **800/ 322-3876;** www.europeatcost.com), the **Parker Company, Ltd.** (© **800/280-2811** or 781/596-8282; fax 781/596-3125; www.theparkercompany.com), **Villas and Apartments Abroad, Ltd.** (© **800/433-3020** or 212/213-6435; www.ideal-villas.com), and **Villas International** (© **800/221-2260** or 415/499-9490; www.villasintl.com), all U.S. based.

In the U.K., contact **Cottages to Castles** (© **1622-775-217;** www.cottagesto castles.com). There's also an Australia-based **Cottages & Castles** (© **03-9889-3350;** www.cottagesandcastles.com.au).

ITALIAN BED & BREAKFASTS

Bed and breakfasts (B&Bs) are becoming increasingly common in the region and provide a good alternative to hotels. The best Web portals are **www.bedand breakfast.it**, with the largest portfolio, followed by **www.bbitalia.it**. We also recommend the Naples-based agency **Rent a Bed-Napoli e Campania,** Vico San Carlo alle Mortelle 14, 80132 Napoli (© **081-417721;** mobile 392-3174864; www.rentabed.it). In each destination chapter throughout this book we recommend local options.

4

Suggested Campania & the Amalfi Coast Itineraries

Campania's offerings can be explored a number of ways. Public transportation in the region is good, so you can easily move about from one destination to the other by train or bus. Exploring the countryside, though, will require a car, which you can rent in any city or large town for just the time you need it—with the rocketing car theft rates in Campania (and the parking woes in the coastal towns), having a car is more of a liability than a commodity. Another possibility is renting a car with a driver, an increasingly popular option, particularly for exploring the Sorrento peninsula and the famous Amalfi Drive.

While Naples is usually a port of entry to the region—it is the largest city, and is served by an international airport and harbor—we recommend you keep your exploration of this bustling city for last: Naples can be overwhelming, literally bursting with life and noise, and you'll appreciate it a lot more if you ease yourself slowly into this special cultural universe by starting your visit in smaller towns. Plus, with so much to see in Naples, you might never get to explore the rest of the region. The itineraries below take in all our favorite destinations; you can mix and match them depending on your particular interests and the amount of time you have.

1 CAMPANIA & THE AMALFI COAST IN 1 WEEK

One week is not long to visit the entire Amalfi Coast region, but you'll certainly be able to get a good idea of its key attractions. Because your time is short, you'll have to pare your exploration to the essentials. You'll miss a lot of the pleasurable lingering, which is so suitable to this region, but you'll have enough time to plunge right into the most phenomenal sights.

You can do a lot of this itinerary by public transportation (including ferries), but you might want to have a car for days 2 and 3, while exploring the region's southern area.

Days ❶ & ❷: Sorrento & the Amalfi Coast

Fly into Naples's Capodichino Airport and get yourself directly to **Sorrento** (there's bus as well as limo service from the airport, or you can rent a car, if you feel more daring). Once there, allow yourself a day

of relaxation to recover from jet lag. Stroll the **lungomare,** do some swimming, and, if you are more ambitious, catch a concert in the evening. The best—if you plan in advance to get tickets—are those offered in the cloister of San Francesco (see "Campania Calendar of Events," in chapter 3).

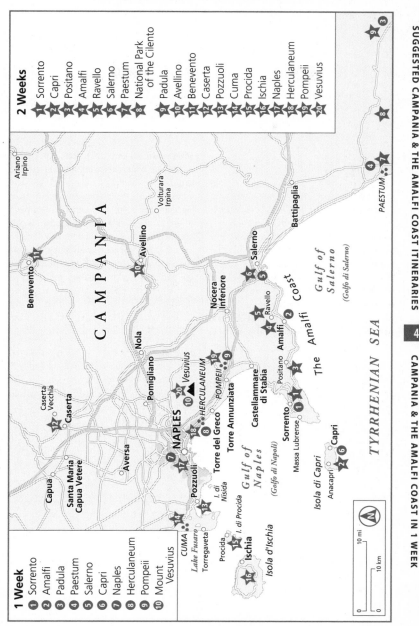

2 Weeks

1 Sorrento
2 Capri
3 Positano
4 Amalfi
5 Ravello
6 Salerno
7 Paestum
8 National Park of the Cilento
9 Padula
10 Avellino
11 Benevento
12 Caserta
13 Pozzuoli
14 Cuma
15 Procida
16 Ischia
17 Naples
18 Herculaneum
19 Pompeii
20 Vesuvius

1 Week

1 Sorrento
2 Amalfi
3 Padula
4 Paestum
5 Salerno
6 Capri
7 Naples
8 Herculaneum
9 Pompeii
10 Mount Vesuvius

On Day 2, get an early start and explore the **Sorrento peninsula** and **Amalfi Coast.** (Hiring a limo is the best option, as your driver will double as guide.) Hike, swim, visit the splendid **Amalfi cathedral** (don't miss the interior). You might even have time for some of the smaller towns off the beaten track. Have dinner at one of our favorite restaurants in the area: **Relais Blu, San Pietro, Faro di Capo d'Orso, Taverna del Capitano, Olimpia Relais,** or **Don Alfonso 1890**—on this stretch of coast, you'll find the region's best gourmet haunts, as well as those with the best views. See chapters 7 and 8.

Day ❸: Padula, Paestum & Salerno

In the morning, go to **Certosa di Padula** (you can use public transportation, but you'll have to keep a strict timetable; it is best to rent or hire a car) and devote a few hours to this architectural marvel. In the afternoon, drive or take a bus to **Paestum** to visit the stunning temples at sunset—on the way, you'll cross through Cilento National Park. Spend the night in **Salerno** (where you can relinquish your car if you rented one), and have dinner in the **medieval town.** See chapter 10.

Day ❹: Salerno & Capri

After an early stroll through **Salerno,** enjoying its splendid **lungomare,** take a ferry to **Capri,** where you can spend the rest of the day shopping and seeing the sights. Stay overnight—this is especially important in summer—to get the full flavor of this mythical island after most of the crowds have gone back to the mainland). See chapter 9.

Days ❺ & ❻: Naples

The next morning, catch one of the frequent ferry or hydrofoil services to **Naples.** At this point you'll be ready for the big city and its vast artistic riches. Start your visit with the **Maschio Angioino,** not far from the harbor. You might have time for a short visit to both **Palazzo Reale** and the **Museo Nazionale di Capodimonte** before you call it a day. Proceed to the **lungomare** to enjoy the panoramic views of **Borgo Marinari** over a well-deserved dinner.

On Day 6, take the **walking tour of SpaccaNapoli** (p. 124), and have a pizza lunch in one of the nearby historical pizzerie to round out your Old Naples experience. Spend the afternoon at the **Museo Archeologico Nazionale** in preparation for your last day. See chapter 5.

Day ❼: Herculaneum, Pompeii & Mount Vesuvius

For a relaxing, quiet excursion, catch a train on the Circumvesuviana railroad to **Herculaneum;** or go to **Pompeii,** if you like grandiose stretches of excavations. Both sites offer enormous amounts to see—covering both in 1 day is impossible, and we don't recommend trying. Use the other half of your day to climb **Mount Vesuvius,** the burning heart of Campania, and visit one of the ancient Roman villas there. See chapter 6.

2 CAMPANIA & THE AMALFI COAST IN 2 WEEKS

Two weeks is an ideal amount of time to explore this culturally and naturally rich region. You'll be able to see some of the best artistic treasures in Italy, but you can also relax and enjoy the sea, coastline, and mountains. We have organized this itinerary so that you can choose whether to rent a car or to use public transportation. If you decide not to rent a car, you can skip the countryside and concentrate on the main destinations, which are all

well connected by public transportation. Should you change your mind, you can always
hire a car with a driver for a day or two, or rent a car in any big town.

Day ❶: Sorrento

Fly into Naples and take either the bus or a limo service to **Sorrento** (you could rent a car at the airport, but you won't need one until Day 3). Recover from jet lag while relaxing in this splendid resort town: Take in the sights, do some shopping, have a swim. See chapter 5.

Day ❷: Capri

Take a ferry to **Capri,** where you'll spend the night: You'll have a full day to explore this unique island, hike, swim, sunbathe, and shop. See chapter 9.

Days ❸ & ❹: The Sorrento Peninsula & the Amalfi Coast

Take a morning ferry to **Positano,** where you'll visit the town and pick up your car (you can also use public transportation for your exploration, but you'll have to keep a stricter schedule). Spend days 3 and 4 taking in **Amalfi, Ravello,** and the lesser-known towns both along the coast and in the interior. See chapters 7 and 8.

Day ❺: Salerno & Paestum

Arrive in **Salerno** in the morning. This town makes a good base for your explorations: Plan to spend 2 nights here.

After a stroll along the **lungomare,** head for the **medieval town** to visit the splendid **cathedral** and have lunch. In the afternoon, arrive in **Paestum,** with its unique temples: Be sure to stay until sunset to enjoy the views. See chapter 10.

Day ❻: Padula & the Cilento

Hire a car to explore the **Park of the Cilento** and its memorable coast in the morning. Then make your way to the **Certosa di Padula** for an afternoon visit, crossing through the imposing Cilento massif, with its eerie caves and soaring peaks. You could rely solely on public transportation here, but you'll have to keep to a strict timetable. See chapter 10.

Days ❼ & ❽: Avellino & Benevento

Dedicate days 7 and 8 to **Avellino** and **Benevento.** These two towns are each the capital of a sub-region rich in cultural, natural, and artistic heritage. You could easily dedicate a few days to each; but if you're on a strict schedule, you'll have to satisfy yourself with the highlights. Having a car will allow you to make the most of it, and you can add a quick tour of the countryside. We recommend that you make time for a visit to the little town of **Sant'Angelo dei Lombardi,** with its castle and famous abbey. Spend Day 8 in **Benevento,** taking in the town's attractions. See chapter 11.

Day ❾: Caserta & Surroundings

Leave early in the morning for **Caserta** and start with a visit to the awesome **Reggia** and its gardens. We suggest you also visit the **Cathedral of Casertavecchia** and the **Belvedere di San Leucio,** maybe taking in a concert there if you are visiting during the season and have planned in advance for tickets. See chapter 11.

Day ❿: Pozzuoli, Cuma & the Phlegrean Fields

Arrive in the morning in the splendid Bay of **Pozzuoli,** home to treasures from antiquity and views beloved by Neapolitans. Spend the day visiting the **Parco Archeologico Subacqueo di Baia** and the **Acropolis of Cuma.** (See chapter 6.) In the evening, catch a ferry from Pozzuoli to have dinner on the island of **Procida,** where you can spend the night. See chapter 9.

Day ⓫: Ischia

From Pozzuoli (or Procida), catch a ferry to **Ischia.** On the island, hire a local taxi to take you on a tour, or use the excellent public bus system. Then spend a few hours in **Giardini Poseidon**—our favorite outdoor spa on the island—or pick one of the indoor ones we recommend. Then head for the beach: **Spiaggia di Citara** and **Lido dei Maronti** are the best on the island. For dinner, sample the local cuisine and wines. See chapter 9.

Days ⑫ & ⑬: Naples
In the early morning, catch a ferry to **Naples;** arrive in its famous harbor under the towering shadow of Mount Vesuvius

before the sun rises too high, and enjoy the scene in its best light. To see the city, follow days 5 and 6 of our "Campania & the Amalfi Coast in 1 Week" itinerary, above.

Day ⑭: Herculaneum, Pompeii & Mount Vesuvius
Follow Day 7 of our itinerary for "Campania & the Amalfi Coast in 1 Week."

3 CAMPANIA & THE AMALFI COAST FOR FAMILIES

If you had any concerns before starting out on this vacation with your kids, they'll melt away as soon as you arrive in this warm and welcoming region. Depending on the attention span and specific interests of your family members, you might have to cut out some artistic attractions, but you'll be more than rewarded with outdoor activities. This itinerary minimizes boring car trips and, instead, relies on ferries—usually more fun for children—to explore the seaside offerings of this region.

Days ❶ & ❷: Ischia
From Naples's Capodichino Airport, take a taxi to Mergellina Harbor where you can catch the ferry to **Ischia.** With lots of water activities and beautiful sandy beaches (instead of the rocky ones on Capri and the Sorrento peninsula), this lesser-known island is more geared to families than its more famous sibling. You'll have your choice of hotels, which are beautiful but less expensive and stuffy than the ones in the region's more glamorous destinations. Pack a picnic lunch and enjoy the views before descending to the beach—**Spiaggia di Citara** and **Lido dei Maronti** are the best on the island. Treat yourself and the kids to some ice cream while strolling along the seaside promenades. See chapter 9.

Day ❸: Capri
Make an early start and catch a ferry to Capri. Spend the rest of the day and night on this mythical island, enjoying its rocky beaches and hiking trails. Climb the **Fenician Staircase** and take a boat tour of the

island (much better than waiting in line for the Blue Grotto, if you're there in high season). See chapter 9.

Day ❹: Salerno & Paestum
Catch a ferry to **Salerno** early enough for a leisurely morning: Stroll along the splendid **lungomare** and pay a visit to the noteworthy **cathedral** before having lunch in the **medieval district.** Then catch one of the frequent buses to **Paestum,** where you'll spend the night in one of its seaside hotels. The afternoon is beach time: You can go swimming, if the weather's nice, and then pay a sunset visit to the ancient Greek temples (or save your visit for early the next morning). See chapter 10.

Day ❺: The Amalfi Coast
Hire a car with a driver for a tour of the **Amalfi Coast:** You'll eliminate parking headaches and make the most of your day. You'll want to allot more time to swimming, ice-cream sampling, and hiking than to visiting churches and driving; still, don't miss the splendid **Amalfi cathedral**

① Ischia   ④ Paestum   ⑦ Herculaneum
② Capri   ⑤ Amalfi   ⑧ Pompeii
③ Salerno   ⑥ Naples   ⑨ Vesuvius

(see chapter 8). Have the car drop you in Naples for the night.

Days ⑥ & ⑦: Naples

Follow days 5 and 6 of our itinerary for "Campania & the Amalfi Coast in 1 Week," but don't try too hard to pack everything in. Concentrate on the many mighty castles—**Castel Nuovo, Castel dell'Ovo, Castello di Sant'Elmo**—and the church of **San Lorenzo Maggiore,** where you can explore several layers of excavations: Most kids should find this exciting. Also, do not miss a pizza lunch at the historical **Pizzeria Di Matteo.** (These are individual pizzas; order one each plus a deep-fried one for the table, to share as

appetizer.) Make sure you take your children on a funicular ride as well, and have dinner in the Vomero area. If you have little ones along, visit the playground in the Villa Comunale on the lungomare. (This was greatly appreciated by our own little guy—so much so that we now have to squeeze in an hour there every day we are in Naples.) See chapter 5.

Day ⑧: Herculaneum, Pompeii & Mount Vesuvius

Follow Day 7 of our itinerary for "Campania & the Amalfi Coast in 1 Week." The casts of dead bodies in the museum in **Herculaneum** might be just the thing if your teenagers and preteens are like some we know, but they may disturb younger children. **Pompeii** is a larger and more comprehensive site, yet might be more tiring for younger children. Definitely hire a guide to explore **Mount Vesuvius:**

Descending into the crater will thrill older kids, while the nature trails on the north slope of the volcano are fun for all ages. See chapter 6.

4 NATURAL WONDERS

If you think Campania is museums, churches, and archaeological areas, you'll miss out on its great attractions not made by human hands. This region offers manifold opportunities to combine culture with outdoor activities and superb natural sights. The itinerary below is designed for a week, but you can shorten or lengthen it at your leisure to accommodate your other plans. Driving a car allows the greatest freedom.

Days ❶ to ❷: Vico Equense & the Sorrento Peninsula

Start with one of the lesser-known resorts on the Sorrento peninsula, **Vico Equense,** where you can spend the night and have your first encounter with the sea at **Marina di Equa**—the best beach in town—which is dominated by a powerful 17th-century tower. (If you don't have a car, take the Sorrento-bound bus from Capodichino Airport to Vico Equense.)

Reserve the afternoon for a beautiful hike through the peninsula, taking the moderately challenging footpath from Sorrento toward **Punta Sant'Elia;** this scenic point overlooks the islets of Li Galli in the Bay of Salerno, which have made Positano famous. See chapter 7.

On Day 2, continue on to the tip of the peninsula and the beach of **Punta del Capo.** Beloved by the locals, it is located near the ruins of a Roman villa. Nearby, a small pool of water enclosed by rocks is known as the Bath of Queen Giovanna.

In the afternoon, hire a boat from Marina del Cantone to reach the Bay of Ieranto and its marine preserve. You will be rewarded with magical surroundings—when the light is just right toward the end of the day, the boats appear to float in midair. Overnight in Marina del Cantone. See chapter 7.

Day ❸: The Amalfi Coast

Get an early start for your ride along the historic **Amalfi Drive.** Stop for a swim (or have a rowboat take you) into the Grotta dello Smeraldo, in the village of **Conca dei Marini.** Continue with a hike from **Furore** down to **Furore Marina,** the deep fjord graced by a small beach, over the ancient footpath. You can then hike the Sentiero degli Dei or the Via degli Incanti, and finish your day visiting the natural preserve of Capo d'Orso. From here, walk to the 11th-century monastery and have dinner at the lighthouse. Overnight in Salerno. See chapter 8.

Day ❹: Capri

Take an early morning ferry or hydrofoil to **Capri,** where you'll spend the night. Use the day to explore the island, taking the chairlift up to the top of **Monte Solaro** and descending the famous **Scala Fenicia** into town. End your day with a swim at the **Bagni di Tiberio,** near the ruins of one of Emperor Tiberius's notorious pleasure palaces. See chapter 9.

Days ❺ & ❻: The Cilento & Paestum

Hop on a ferry early in the morning and rejoin your car in **Salerno.** Head for the **National Park of the Cilento,** starting with the beautiful coast where you can

① Vico Equense
② Punta del Capo
③ Conca dei
  Marini
④ Furore
⑤ Capri
⑥ National Park of
  the Cilento
⑦ Paestum
⑧ Mount Vesuvius
⑨ Oplontis
⑩ Boscoreale

Benevento

Mondragone Capua
Caserta
Vecchia
Santa Maria
Capua Vetere Caserta

C A M P A N I A

Aversa
LITERNUM Nola Avellino
Lake Patria Pomigliano
Licola Mare Volturara
CUMA Irpina
NAPLES
Lake Fusaro Pozzuoli
Torregaveta Baia HERCULANEUM BOSCOREALE
Procida I. di Torre del Greco OPLONTIS Nocera
Nisida Torre Annunziata POMPEII Inferiore
I. di Procida Gulf of Castellammare
Ischia Naples di Stabia
Vico Salerno
Isola d'Ischia (Golfo di Napoli) Equense
Conca dei Ravello
Sorrento Positano Marina Amalfi
Massa Lubrense Furore Coast Battipaglia
Isola di Capri Punta del The Amalfi Gulf of
Anacapri Capri Capo Salerno
(Golfo di Salerno)

0 10 mi
0 10 km
N T Y R R H E N I A N S E A PAESTUM

enjoy a variety of watersports, including diving and water-skiing. The best beach is **Baia della Calanca,** in Marina di Camerota. Don't forget the interior, though. Schedule a visit to the **Grottoes of Castelcivita** or **Grottoes of Pertosa** for fantastic spelunking (nothing demanding athleticism or ropes), as well as a hike on **Monte Cervati,** the highest peak of the Cilento massif; another excellent hike is **Monte Alburno.**

Make sure you reserve the afternoon of Day 6 for **Paestum,** to visit its temples,

walk its walls, and swim from one of the best beaches in Italy. See chapter 10.

Day ⑦: Mount Vesuvius & Ancient Roman Villas

For your last day, head toward Naples's **Mount Vesuvius** area. Start your visit with **Oplontis** and **Boscoreale**—two excellent sites for exploring ancient Roman ruins— and then take your leave of the region with a hike to the crater of Naples's volcano. What could be more appropriate than ending your trip with a blast? See chapter 5.

Naples

Much has been written on Naples ("Napule," in local parlance), but nothing can render the multifaceted reality of this city better than a visit—or actually several visits. The third Italian city by size, Naples *is* a big city (with the world's worst traffic outside of Cairo); but once you get past the initial grit, you'll find treasures galore, equaling and often surpassing many more-popular destinations in Italy.

The first adjective that comes to mind to define it is "ebullient." You'll feel this energy everywhere—in the traffic, the noise, the music, the performing arts, and in the people's deep love for and pride in their city and in their fervent religiosity. Above all, you'll pick up on a sense of enthusiasm for what the city has to offer, from romantic evening walks along the shore to magnificent views over the Bay with Mount Vesuvius in the background to the beauty of Piazza del Plebiscito, Castel Nuovo, and Castel dell'Ovo. And, of course, this being Italy, Neapolitans are proud of their food, especially the fresh seafood; local tomatoes, which make excellent fresh sauces; and the pizza they invented.

The second adjective that describes Naples is "welcoming." Neapolitans reach out to visitors and relish others' enjoyment of their beloved city. Maybe that is the most truly fascinating thing about Naples:

It has incredible architectural and artistic attractions, natural beauty, and fantastic food and wines, but ultimately, when you fall in love with the city, you'll do so because of its humanity. When you walk the streets of Naples, you'll understand that its underlying character hasn't changed much in 2 millennia. It takes a certain kind of people, surely, to live in the shadow of a very dangerous volcano, century after century, and to find it beautiful.

This appreciation should not make you less careful with your belongings: Police work has been effective in reducing crime and making the tourist areas safer than ever, but Naples is legendary for its pickpockets and other petty criminals. Large parts of Naples are very poor and as plagued as any such place by drugs and thievery. Though depressed areas of Naples are well in the outskirts, even the most experienced travelers should always keep a careful eye on their belongings.

If you get past the noise, you can relax and discover a city that many visitors over the centuries have described in justly heavenly terms. The city's artistic and historical riches are more accessible today after refurbishment of the historic center in the 1990s.

Allow at least 2 full days for this city, with its matchless museums, culinary delights, and amazing churches.

1 ESSENTIALS

GETTING THERE

BY PLANE Naples's airport, **Aeroporto Capodichino** (𝄢 **081-7896259;** www.gesac. it), is only about 7km (4 miles) from the city center. It is a small but well-organized airport, receiving flights from many Italian and European cities, as well as a few intercontinental flights. See "Getting There & Around," in chapter 3, for more information on

airlines that service Capodichino. From the airport, you can easily take a taxi into town 79
(make sure it is an official taxi, white with the Naples municipal logo and a taxi sign on
the roof); the flat rate for the 15-minute trip is 19€ plus gratuity. Many hotels offer a
limousine service, but it is more costly, at about 35€.

If you don't have much luggage, the convenient ANM bus (© **800-639525;** www.
anm.it) is a viable option (a one-way ticket is 3€). The bus runs to Piazza Municipio in
the town center (it stops across from the Teatro Mercadante), with an intermediary stop
in Piazza Garibaldi (by the post office at Corso Novara). Buses run every 30 minutes
from the airport (Mon–Fri 6:30am–11:39pm; Sat–Sun 6:30am–11:50pm) and from
Piazza Municipio (Mon–Fri 6am–12:12am; Sat–Sun 6am–midnight).

BY TRAIN   Naples is on the main southern rail corridor and is served by frequent and
fast service from most Italian and European cities and towns. EuroStar trains (marked
ES) make very limited stops, InterCity trains (IC) make limited stops, and AltaVelocità
(AV) trains are high-speed express trains. Regular trains take between 2 and 2½ hours
between Rome and Naples, while the AV train takes only 87 minutes, making it by far
the best method of transport between the two cities and to destinations farther north.
The fare is about 25€ one way. Contact **Trenitalia** (© **892021;** www.trenitalia.it) for
reservations, fares, and information.

The city has several train stations: **Stazione Centrale** (© **081-5543188**), on Piazza
Garibaldi, northeast of the city's historical center, is the main railway station for most
long-distance trains from all over Italy and Europe. Nearby is the **Stazione Circumvesuviana Napoli-Porta Nolana** (© **800-053939;** www.vesuviana.it), on Corso Garibaldi,
off Piazza Garibaldi. This is the starting point for commuter lines serving the Vesuvian
and coastal area south of Naples, including trains to Sorrento, Pompei, and Ercolano
(trains also stop at Napoli Garibaldi, under Naples's Stazione Centrale, which is more
convenient by public transportation). The **Stazione Cumana Montesanto** (© **081-
7354111;** www.sepsa.it), in Via Montesanto, off Via Tarsia (west of Via Toledo), receives
commuter trains from the Campi Flegrei, including Cuma, Pozzuoli, and Baia. Some
long-distance trains also stop at the **Stazione Mergellina** (© **081-7612102**), on Piazza
Piedigrotta, to the west of Naples's historical center. This station is convenient for transfers to the **ferry** (Terminal Aliscafi). Taxis, subways, and buses connect all these stations
with the town center and other destinations nearby (see "Getting Around," below). *Note:*
If you are approached by "taxi" drivers—actually gypsy taxis—in the train station, ignore
them: They charge outrageous rates and are a source of Naples's bad rap for dishonesty.

BY BOAT   Arriving into the Bay of Naples by boat is an unforgettable experience and
the best introduction to the city. The major port of central Italy, Naples's **Stazione Marittima** (just off Via Cristoforo Colombo, steps from the Castel Nuovo) receives both cruise
ships and regular ferry service from many destinations in Italy, including Ischia, Capri,
Sicily (Messina, Siracusa Catania, Palermo, and the Aeolian Islands), and Sardinia
(Cagliari). Hydrofoil service (suspended in winter) operates mostly from Mergellina's
nearby **Terminal Aliscafi,** with frequent and fast runs to Capri, Ischia, Procida, Sorrento,
Positano, Amalfi, Salerno, and Sicily (Milazzo and the Aeolian Islands). See "By Boat,"
p. 45 for a list of companies.

BY CAR   Car theft—even from guarded parking lots—fierce traffic, and the local passion for speed make driving in Naples a real hassle. Still, arriving or leaving the city by
car is not horribly difficult: Major highways connect the city to most other destinations
in Italy. From the north, take autostrada A1 MILANO ROMA NAPOLI, whereas from the
south take autostrada A3 REGGIO CALABRIA SALERNO NAPOLI. If you are not returning

your rental car, you can leave it at your own risk in one of the large and well-posted public parking lots at the city's entrance. The most convenient is the **Parcheggio Brin,** at the Via Brin corner of Via Volta (℗ **081-7632855;** .30€ per hr.). Most hotels offer parking which is usually expensive and secure, but driving to your hotel is a challenge best left to those who know the city, with its narrow and labyrinthine streets, pedestrian areas, and one-way streets. Unless you have very precise and up-to-date driving directions or an excellent and recent driving map of Naples (one that marks every street and its driving direction), do not attempt it.

VISITOR INFORMATION

Naples's Provincial Tourist Office, **EPT,** Piazza dei Martiri 58, by Riviera di Chiaia (℗ 081-4107211; www.eptnapoli.info; bus no. 152; Mon–Fri 9am–2pm), maintains tourist booths in the Stazione Centrale (℗ **081-268799;** Metro: Piazza Garibaldi; Mon–Sat 9am–7pm) and at the Stazione Mergellina, Piazza Piedigrotta 1 (℗ **081-7612102;** Metro: Mergellina; Mon–Sat 9am–7pm). They provide basic advice, but **AASCT** (℗ 081-2525711; www.inaples.it), has far better information and material. They maintain three excellent tourist information points: **Via San Carlo 9,** off Piazza del Plebiscito (℗ **081-402394**); **Piazza del Gesù** (℗ 081-5512701); and **Via Santa Lucia 107,** near Castel dell'Ovo (℗ **081-1457475**), all open Monday to Saturday (9am–1:30pm and 2:30–7pm).

Another excellent resource is the organization **Museo Aperto Napoli** (℗ **081-5636062;** www.museoapertonapoli.it), which maintains a cultural center offering free information and guided tours (with a live guide or an audioguide in six languages) of the historical center. It's at Via Pietro Colletta 85 and is open daily 10am to 6pm; the center also houses a cafe, bookshop, and small exhibit space selling crafts.

CITY LAYOUT

A crescent-shaped city resting along the shores of a bay, Naples extends vertically up the steep hills that surround it. Proceeding from west to east, you will find **Posillipo;** then **Mergellina, Chiaia, Santa Lucia;** the **historical center,** with the **Quartieri Spagnoli** along its western side and the **Stazione Marittima** on its southern side; then **Piazza Garibaldi,** with the **Stazione Centrale** and **Stazione Circumvesuviana;** and finally, a number of industrial and poorer neighborhoods.

Above Chiaia and the historical center lies the **Vomero;** farther east is **Capodimonte.** The historical center is the fat part of the crescent, crossed north–south by three major avenues: **Via Toledo, Via Medina,** and **Via Agostino Depretis.** These are crossed west–east by the continuous **Via Armando Diaz–Via G.Sanfelice–Corso Umberto I** and by the continuous Via Benedetto Croce–Via San Biagio dei Librai, also known as **Spaccanapoli,** both leading to **Piazza Garibaldi** and the **Stazione Centrale.**

THE NEIGHBORHOODS IN BRIEF

In this section, we give you a short description of each of Naples's central neighborhoods—including its major monuments—to give you some idea of what each is like and where you might want to stay.

Posillipo ★ This residential neighborhood is graced by a number of dramatic villas perched on rocky cliffs over the sea, as well as a few restaurants offering great food and fantastic views.

Mergellina ★ Situated well to the west of the historical center, this residential neighborhood is served by its own train and hydrofoil stations. It lies near Naples's pleasant marina: The small harbor is lined with restaurants and cafes, where Neapolitans come for dinner by the sea and a romantic promenade.

Chiaia ★★ Charming and elegant, this neighborhood is graced by the public park **Villa Comunale.** The hillside area has elegant villas and a couple of hotels and restaurants, which enjoy dramatic views over the Bay. The shore area along Riviera di Chiaia is famous for its upscale shopping and restaurants, where Neapolitan nightlife congregates. The historical center and its monuments are a short ride away on public transportation, but it is also possible to walk.

Santa Lucia ★★★ Once a village by the sea and retaining some of that character, this neighborhood is separated from the historical center by steep Monte Echia. It is probably Naples's most famous neighborhood and a favorite with visitors for its unique charm and splendid views. **Via Partenope**—the promenade created in the 19th century by filling in part of the harbor—overlooks the Bay and **Castel dell'Ovo** and is lined with elegant hotels and restaurants. **Borgo Marinari,** under Castel dell'Ovo, is another popular nighttime spot. Behind the major hotels, you'll find a less-explored neighborhood, with grocery shops and cafes frequented by locals.

Quartieri Spagnoli North of **Piazza del Plebiscito**—the monumental heart of the city—this neighborhood of closely knit narrow streets lies on the western side of **Via Toledo** (called "Via Roma" by Neapolitans). Prior to the 1990s, this area was considered quite

dangerous, but the blocks around Via Toledo have experienced an urban renewal, with small hotels and quite a few nice restaurants sprouting up. This budget-friendly area is a perfect base for cost-conscious visitors as it is walking distance from most of Naples's major attractions. The streets farther out, however, still show the original grunginess and are not the best place for your romantic evening stroll.

Historical Center Locally known as the *Decumani,* this is Naples's heart, extending from the **Castel Nuovo** and the **Stazione Marittima** by the sea to the **Museo Archeologico Nazionale** to the north, the **Quartieri Spagnoli** to the west, and **Castel Capuano** to the east. Many of the city's political and administrative offices as well as the University of Naples are here—along with the cascade of small restaurants, bars, and clubs fostered by such institutions. You'll find all of Naples represented here, from the most elegant palaces to pockets of unbelievable grittiness. Many of Naples's major historical and religious attractions are located here, making it a perfect location for visitors. Most of the hotels here are small and housed in historical buildings, but larger and more modern hotels line Via Medina and the parallel Via Agostino Depretis, at the southern edge of this area.

Piazza Garibaldi Across from Naples's main rail station, Stazione Centrale, this location is definitely less than glamorous (some of the area, behind the station and away from the main avenues, is positively grungy, with decaying buildings and cheap street vendors lining the narrow lanes, and the undescript streets by the harbor are dire). It also feels—and *is*—unsafe at night. A number of top-notch hotels catering to businesspeople have opened here, though, and charge a fraction of the price you would pay in Santa Lucia or Chiaia for a similar level of comfort. The neighborhood is very well connected through public transportation to all major tourist destinations both within and outside the city (train station, Metro station, Circumvesuviana rail station—the one to Pompeii and Sorrento—are only steps away). The historical center's eastern edge along **Castel Capuano** is within walking distance, past a somewhat unsavory belt around the train station (take a taxi after dark). You'll also be near a full range of convenience shopping, from groceries to clothing stores, and a number of good restaurants are in the area. That said, we nevertheless find it too remote.

Vomero ★ This is the dwelling place of the *Napoli bene* (the city's middle and upper classes), where residents enjoy fresher air and some spectacular views. A quiet and residential neighborhood, Vomero is mostly composed of elegant 19th- and early-20th-century buildings, with good shopping and a few restaurants, plus three famous attractions: the **Castel Sant'Elmo, Certosa SanMartino,** and **Villa Floridiana.**

Capodimonte A middle-class and blue-collar residential neighborhood, this is a good choice in summer, when the air is cooler up in the hills. This is also a good base if you plan to spend a lot of your time in the giant **Museo di Capodimonte** and the wonderful public park that surrounds it. There are plenty of local grocery shops and bars, but only a few hotels and restaurants.

GETTING AROUND

Walking is the best way to explore the historical heart of Naples. Public transportation works well when you need to travel greater distances and if you want to take in some local color, although at rush hour there might be too much of the latter on the major subway and bus lines. If you have to travel during those hours, take the electric buses that serve the city center and are rarely crowded—or take a taxi.

On Foot Naples is a beautiful city to discover on foot; its attractions are close together and the sea is always in the background. While the free city map offered by the tourist office is perfectly sufficient for your general orientation, we recommend you purchase a more detailed map with a *stradario* (alphabetical list of streets), if you are planning more extensive explorations (see "Fast Facts," below).

By Public Transportation When you're tired of walking, the best way to get around Naples is its extensive network of public transportation: Buses, trams, subway, and funiculars provide fast transportation to major hubs. **Bus** lines take you everywhere: The R lines (R1, R2, R3, R4) are fast lines with frequent service that stop at major tourist attractions; the electric minibuses (marked E) serve the historic district; C lines serve

Heads Up

Always beware of pickpockets and purse snatchers in Naples; they favor crowded places, such as public transportation and such busy streets as Via Toledo. At night, avoid badly lit and solitary places, because mugging is not completely uncommon.

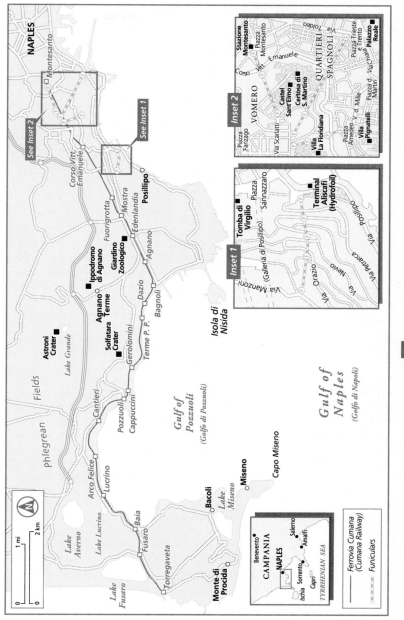

NAPLES

5

ESSENTIALS

Inset 2

Stazione Montesanto
Piazza Montesanto
Corso Vitt. Emanuele
Via Toledo
Piazza Trieste e Trento
QUARTIERI SPAGNOLI
Palazzo Reale
VOMERO
Castel Sant'Elmo
Certosa di S. Martino
Via Chiaia
Piazza d. Martiri
Piazza Fanzago
Via Scarlatti
V. d. Mille
Villa La Floridiana
Piazza Amedeo
Villa Pignatelli

Inset 1

Tomba di Virgilio
Piazza Sannazzaro
Terminal Aliscafi (Hydrofoil)
Via Manzoni
(Galleria di Posillipo)
Via Nevio
Via Orazio
Via Petrarca
Via Posillipo

NAPLES
Montesanto
See Inset 2
Corso Vitt. Emanuele
Fuorigrotta
Mostra
Edenlandia
Agnano
See Inset 1
Posillipo
Ippodromo di Agnano
Giardino Zoologico
Agnano Terme
Dazio
Bagnoli
Solfatara Crater
Gerolomini
Terme P. P.
Astroni Crater
Lake Grande
Cantieri
Pozzuoli
Cappuccini
Isola di Nisida
Phlegrean Fields
Arco Felice
Lucrino
Bacoli
Lake Miseno
Miseno
Capo Miseno
Lake Averno
Lake Lucrino
Baia
Fusaro
Lake Fusaro
Torregaveta
Monte di Procida

Gulf of Pozzuoli
(Golfo di Pozzuoli)

Gulf of Naples
(Golfo di Napoli)

CAMPANIA
Benevento
NAPLES
Salerno
Amalfi
Sorrento
Ischia
Capri
TYRRHENIAN SEA

—— Ferrovia Cumana (Cumana Railway)
✕✕✕✕ Funiculars

N

0   1 mi
0   2 km

Taxi Rates in Naples

Because the municipality has not raised official taxi rates since 2002, most drivers will ask a certain percentage increase, and it is common practice to grant it, provided it is reasonable. The minimum cost of a ride is 4.50€. The meter starts at 3€ on Monday to Saturday from 7am to 10pm; otherwise, the meter starts at 5.50€. It adds .05€ every 65 meters (213 ft.) or every 10 seconds when waiting or stopped in traffic. Extra charges are .50€ per piece of luggage in the trunk, 1€ for a radio-taxi call (as opposed to you going to a taxi stand), 2.60€ for a ride to the airport, and 3.10€ for a ride from the airport. There are also a number of flat rates, including the following (a card with the complete list is inside each official taxi):

Piazza Municipio to Museo Capodimonte	9.50€
Stazione Centrale to Aliscafi Mergellina	13€
Stazione Centrale to Molo Beverello	9.50€
Stazione Centrale to Hotels in Santa Lucia or Chiaia	9.50€
to destinations on Corso Vittorio Emanuele	20€

central Naples, while numbered lines go to the suburbs and are less frequent. All buses operate daily from 5:30am; R lines till midnight, E and some other lines till 11pm. Some lines stop at 8:30pm. A few lines are actually **tramways,** with dedicated tracks, but because of vehicular traffic, these can be as slow as the regular buses. The few *linee notturne* (night lines) start around midnight and run every hour.

Dear to the hearts of Neapolitans is the *funicolare,* a cable railway tunneled through rock to reach the cliffs surrounding the Bay. Three funiculars reach the Vomero: **Montesanto** (at Metro station Montesanto; daily 7am–10pm), **Chiaia** (from Piazza Amedeo; daily 7am–10pm), and **Centrale** (from Via Toledo, off Piazza Trieste e Trento; Mon–Tues 6:30am–10pm and Wed–Sun 6:30am–12:30am). **Mergellina** also has a funicular, from Via Mergellina by the harbor up to Via Manzoni (daily 7am–10pm). Also important for negotiating the city are the public elevators and escalators: The *ascensore* (elevator) tucked away in Via Acton, at the corner of Palazzo Reale, ascends to Piazza Plebiscito. On the Vomero, several escalators climb the steepest slopes.

The **Metropolitana** (subway) has two lines, line 1 from Piazza Dante to the Vomero and beyond (daily 6am–11pm) and line 2 from Pozzuoli to Piazza Garibaldi and beyond (daily 5:30am–11pm). You can also use the urban section of the **Cumana** railroad from Montesanto, which is convenient to Mergellina and other coastal locations north of the city center (daily 5am–11pm).

Naples's **Transportation Authority** (© **081-5513109;** www.unicocampania.it) provides information on all the above and maintains an information booth on Piazza Garibaldi, where you can get an excellent public transportation map. Public transportation tickets are valid on the entire network (see "The Unico Travel Pass," p. 48) and are sold at tobacconists and at some bars and newsstands. A *biglietto* (ticket) for the city costs 1.10€ and is valid for 90 minutes; a *giornaliero* (day pass) is valid until midnight (the cost is 3.10€ Mon-Sat and 2.60€ for Sun). The **Artecard** (p. 110) also includes a public transportation pass.

By Taxi Taxis are an excellent, relatively inexpensive way to get around the city. If you've heard that they're dishonest, these stories originate with people who have not visited Naples in the past decade or two or who have fallen prey to gypsy cabs. Today, taxis are very reliable and strictly regulated. Official taxis are painted white and marked by the *Comune di Napoli* (Naples municipality). Inside, on the back of the front seat, you'll find a sign listing official flat rates to the seaports, central hotels, and major attractions—although it might be an old sign; refer to "Taxi Rates in Naples," above for current established rates. Also, don't fret if your driver doesn't use the meter—*not* using the meter is legal for all rides that have established flat rates. As elsewhere in Italy, taxis do not cruise but are found at the many taxi stands around town, or, for an extra 1€ surcharge, can be called by phone. Restaurants and hotels will do this for you, but a list of numbers is provided in "Fast Facts," below. Some of the main taxi stands operating 24 hours are **Piazza Amedeo 8, Piazza Carità** (near Via Cesare Battisti), **Piazza Cavour, Piazza Dante** (by Via Bellini), **Piazza Garibaldi** (by the statue), **Piazza Municipio** (at Via De Pretis), **Teatro San Carlo, Via Santa Lucia** (at corner of Via Nazario Sauro), **Piazza Vanvitelli** (by Via Scarlatti), and **Piazza Vittoria** (by the entrance to Villa Comunale). Other taxi stands close between 2 and 6am or between 11:30pm and 6am.

Naples also has a water taxi that offers private and public service, **Taxi del Mare** (✆ **081-8773600;** www.taxidelmare.it).

(*Fast Facts*) **Naples**

American Express **Every Tours** travel agency on Piazza del Municipio 5 (✆ **081-5518564;** bus no. R2 or R3 to Piazza del Municipio) handles American Express business. It is open Monday through Friday from 9:30am to 1pm and 3:30 to 7pm and Saturday 9:30am to 1pm.

Banks Most banks are located in the city center and near the major hotels and have **ATMs** outside their doors. **BNL** (Banca Nazionale del Lavoro; ✆ **081-7991111**) offers the PLUS network you'll likely need for your ATM card. Its several locations in Naples include Via Toledo 126 and Piazza dei Martiri 23.

Currency Exchange Among the numerous choices in town, the most convenient exchange places are the ones at the airport and around the Stazione Centrale on Piazza Garibaldi (Metro: Piazza Garibaldi). There are four *cambios* (exchanges) on Corso Umberto at nos. 44, 92, 212, and 292 (bus no. R2 to Corso Umberto). Thomas Cook is on Piazza del Municipio (bus no. R2 or R3 to Piazza del Municipio).

Doctors **Guardia Medica Specialistica** (✆ **081-431111**) is on call 24 hours a day. Consulates maintain a list of English-speaking doctors.

Embassies & Consulates See chapter 12.

Emergencies Call ✆ **113** or **112** for the **police.** For an **ambulance,** call ✆ **118;** for the **fire department** call ✆ **115;** for **first aid** (*pronto soccorso*), call ✆ **081-7520696.**

Hospital **Ospedale Fatebenefratelli,** the central hospital, is at Via Manzoni 220 (✆ **081-7697220**).

Internet Access The three locations of **Internet Point** ((C) **081-4976090** or 081-19568227) are conveniently located and offer ADSL connection at 1€ for 30 minutes: They are Vico Tre Re a Toledo 59/a (off Via Toledo to the left coming from Piazza Trieste e Trento, across from the Banco di Napoli); Via Montecalvario 9 (also off Via Toledo to the left, a few streets farther up); and Via Francesco Sav Correra 245 (3 blocks north and then left from Piazza Dante).

Laundry/Dry Cleaning Self-service laundromats are rare in Naples; your best bet is a *tintoria* (dry cleaner) or a *lavanderia* (dry cleaner and laundry service). A few good and central businesses are **Lavanderia Tintoria** at Via San Tommaso d'Aquino 43 ((C) **081-5511895**), **Lavanderia Helvetia** (Via San Mattia 1; (C) **081-415635**), and the *lavanderia* at Salita Sant'Anna di Palazzo 4 ((C) **081-407222**).

Mail The **Central Post Office (Ufficio Postale)** is at Piazza Matteotti ((C) **081-5511456**; bus no. R3 to Piazza Matteotti).

Maps You can buy a good map with a *stradario* (street directory) of Naples at any newspaper stand in town (most carry the reliable **Pianta Generale** by N. Vincitorio); if you prefer something smaller, buy the excellent, foldable, credit card–size **Mini-City**, sold at museum shops in town (try the shop at Palazzo Reale).

Newspapers & Magazines Foreign newspapers and magazines are sold at train station kiosks and near the American consulate. Do not miss *QuiNapoli,* the dashing free monthly (bilingual Italian/English) prepared by the city tourist office, which lists all the latest events as well as opening hours of monuments and museums. (It's also online at www.inaples.it.)

Pharmacies There are several pharmacies open weekday nights and taking turns on weekend nights. A good one is located in the Stazione Centrale (Piazza Garibaldi 11; (C) **081-5548894**; Metro: Piazza Garibaldi).

Police Call (C) **113** for emergencies or (C) **112**.

Safety Pickpocketing and car thefts are fairly common throughout Naples. In dark alleys and outside the city center, getting mugged is possible, particularly at night. Steer clear of the area behind the Stazione Centrale at dark, when it gets particularly seedy. The poorest suburbs in the outskirts of Naples to the east and southeast are where crime rates tend to be highest, but these are removed from the major tourist areas.

Smoking Thanks to a 2005 law, smoking is not allowed in public areas, including cafes and restaurants. It remains very common, however, and you will find that separate smoking areas are often available.

Taxis For pickups, call **Radio Taxi Napoli** ((C) 081-444444, 081-5555555, or 081-5564444; www.consorziotaxinapoli.it); **Cooperativa Partenopea** ((C) 081-5606666, 081-5515151, or 081-5560202); **Radio Taxi La 570** ((C) 081-5707070; www.la570.it); or **Consortaxi** ((C) 081-202020).

Toilets Public bathrooms are basically nonexistent outside museums and major attractions. Your best bet is to use those in bars and cafes; they are reserved for clients, though, so you'll have to buy at least a coffee or a glass of mineral water.

Weather Watch the news, or check out http://meteo.tiscali.it.

2 WHERE TO STAY

SANTA LUCIA

Very Expensive

Grand Hotel Santa Lucia ★   Next door to the more luxurious Grand Hotel Vesuvio (below), this historic hotel offers an old-fashioned atmosphere mixed with elegant decor. The professional service is impeccable, and the public spaces are grand—if a bit dusty and worn in places—graced by curving staircases, marble floors, and Murano chandeliers. Guest rooms are good size, with wood or carpet floors, period or reproduction furniture, marble bathrooms, and great views over the Castel dell'Ovo and the Bay. Most rooms have balconies to take in the view—they're too small for a table and chairs, though. The buffet breakfast is excellent and the hotel's restaurant is elegant. The one drawback is the lack of amenities for a hotel of this level.

Via Partenope 46 (off Via Santa Lucia by Castel dell'Ovo), 80121 Napoli. ℂ **081-7640666.** Fax 081-7648580. www.santalucia.it. 96 units. 295€–410€ double, from 650€ suite. Extra bed 60€. Children 2 and under stay free in parent's room. Internet specials available. AE, DC, MC, V. Parking 25€. Bus: 152, 140, or C25. **Amenities:** Restaurant; bar; concierge; Internet in lobby (free); room service. *In room:* A/C, TV/VCR/DVD, minibar Wi-Fi (free).

Grand Hotel Vesuvio ★★ **Kids**   This elegant hotel is admittedly the best in Naples, even though we find it overpriced. Exquisite service and accommodations compensate for a more austere, and thereby less romantic, atmosphere. Even the standard doubles are very roomy (all with large marble bathrooms and Jacuzzi tubs), and come furnished with special details such as linen sheets and extra-firm mattresses. Superior rooms and suites have large balconies from which you can enjoy some of the best views in Naples over Borgo Marinari or Mount Vesuvius. The breakfast buffet—served in a delightful bright room with a view of the harbor—is superb, including several kinds of freshly squeezed juice, fresh fruit, bacon, and eggs, along with oven-fresh Neapolitan pastries, local cheeses and cold cuts, and several breads. At presstime, one of the hotel's two restaurants, the **Caruso Roof Garden,** famous for its cuisine and splendid views, was closed for renovation; a reopening date was not yet scheduled.

Via Partenope 45 (off Via Santa Lucia by Castel dell'Ovo), 80121 Napoli. ℂ **081-7640044.** Fax 081-7644483. www.vesuvio.it. 161 units. 450€–460€ double; from 750€ suite. Rates include buffet breakfast. Children 2 and under stay free in parent's room. Internet specials available. AE, DC, MC, V. Parking 25€. Bus: 152, 140, or C25. **Amenities:** 2 restaurants; bar; babysitting; concierge; fitness center & spa, pool (for a fee); room service; smoke-free rooms. *In room:* A/C, TV/VCR/DVD, minibar, Wi-Fi.

Hotel Excelsior **Kids**   Fronting the bay on Via Partenope, this Starwood property has more moderate prices and less glamour than its neighbors listed here, but shares the gorgeous views and offers a splendid roof garden. It also has a partnership with the Grand Hotel Vesuvio (above) and the Majestic Hotel (below), which gives its guests access (for a fee) to the Vesuvio's famed spa. The rooms are good size and tastefully decorated, with marble bathrooms and linen sheets, as well as all the amenities you expect at this level (and price); however, everything comes in a slightly smaller scale than at the Vesuvio, the Grand Hotel Santa Lucia, and the Royal Continental.

Via Partenope 48 (off Via Santa Lucia, by Castel dell'Ovo), 80121 Napoli. ℂ **081-7640111.** Fax 081-7649743. www.excelsior.it. 121 units. 360€ double, from 650€ suite. Rates include buffet breakfast. Children 2 and under stay free in parent's room. AE, DC, MC, V. Parking 23€. Bus: 152, 140, or C25. **Amenities:** Restaurant; bar; babysitting; concierge; health club; room service; smoke-free rooms. *In room:* A/C, TV/VCR/DVD, minibar.

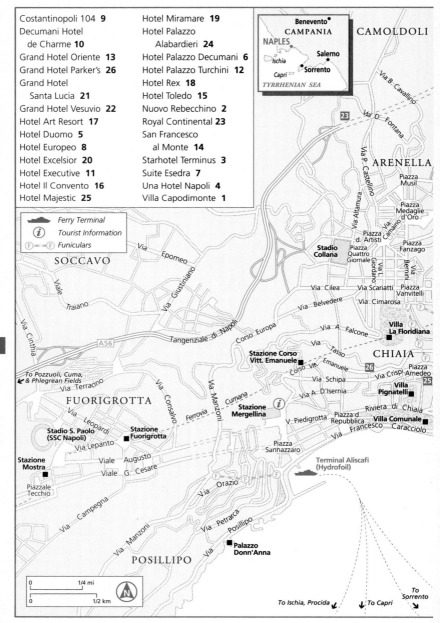

Costantinopoli 104 **9**

Decumani Hotel
de Charme **10**

Grand Hotel Oriente **13**

Grand Hotel Parker's **26**

Grand Hotel
Santa Lucia **21**

Grand Hotel Vesuvio **22**

Hotel Art Resort **17**

Hotel Duomo **5**

Hotel Europeo **8**

Hotel Excelsior **20**

Hotel Executive **11**

Hotel Il Convento **16**

Hotel Majestic **25**

Hotel Miramare **19**

Hotel Palazzo
Alabardieri **24**

Hotel Palazzo Decumani **6**

Hotel Palazzo Turchini **12**

Hotel Rex **18**

Hotel Toledo **15**

Nuovo Rebecchino **2**

Royal Continental **23**

San Francesco
al Monte **14**

Starhotel Terminus **3**

Suite Esedra **7**

Una Hotel Napoli **4**

Villa Capodimonte **1**

Ferry Terminal

(i) Tourist Information

(F) ⊶ (F) Funiculars

Royal Continental ★ Born from the renovation of two connected buildings, this is a new and welcome addition to Via Partenope, only a few doors down from its three more famous siblings above. It might lack the architectural charm or stately elegance of some of the older hotels, but the clean lines and modernity of the well-appointed accommodations and the swimming pool on the rooftop successfully compensate for it. Standard rooms are spacious and full of light, and open onto a private balcony, although they lack the splendid views of the superior rooms, some of them with nice hardwood flooring. The four executive rooms each have a delightful large private terrace. All rooms have spacious marble bathrooms, some of them shower only, and a few have Jacuzzi tubs.

Via Partenope 38 (off Via Santa Lucia), 80121 Napoli. ✆ **081-2452068.** Fax 081-7644616. www.royal continental.it. 400 units. 226€–266€ double; 256€ junior suite; from 296€ suite. 1 child 2 and under stays free in parent's room. Internet specials available. Parking 20€. Bus: 152, 140, or C25. Dogs accepted. **Amenities:** Restaurant; bar; babysitting; concierge; fitness center; pool; room service. *In room:* A/C, TV, minibar, Wi-Fi.

Moderate

Hotel Miramare ★ ⟨**Value**⟩ On the waterfront overlooking Castel dell'Ovo, this small, elegant hotel offers excellent value and warm service. Originally a private villa built in 1914, it briefly housed the American consulate before opening as a hotel in 1944. The public areas are still decorated in Liberty style, but guest rooms have been renovated, each with its own whimsical assortment of furniture. The attentive family management is reflected in such little touches as cool linen sheets in the summer. The rooms overlooking the sea have splendid views, and all those above the mezzanine level are graced by private balconies. We recommend the deluxe rooms, which are oversize, with large balconies, and have bathrooms with tub and shower—others have only a shower. In clement weather, breakfast is served on the roof terrace overlooking the Bay. You'll get special treatment at the restaurants run by the owner's brothers: **La Cantinella** (p. 101), **La Piazzetta, Il Posto Accanto, Rosolino,** and **Putipù.** They all feature Neapolitan cuisine and pizza, and some double as nightclubs.

Via Nazario Sauro 24 (off Via Santa Lucia, by Castel dell'Ovo), 80132 Napoli. ✆ **081-7647589.** Fax 081-7640775. www.hotelmiramare.com. 18 units. High season 230€–299€ double; low season 145€–220€ double. Rates include buffet breakfast. Children 5 and under stay free in parent's room. Weekend and Internet specials available. AE, DC, MC, V. Parking 25€ in nearby garage. Bus: 152, C25, or 140. **Amenities:** Bar; airport pickup (40€); babysitting; concierge; Internet in lobby (free); room service. *In room:* A/C, TV/ VCR (free videos in lobby), minibar.

Inexpensive

Hotel Rex ⟨**Kids**⟩ ⟨**Value**⟩ This hotel is a steal: In a 19th-century palace by the most famous harborside area of Naples, only steps from the top-notch hotels of Via Partenope (see above), it offers spacious accommodations at moderate prices. Word has gotten out about this family-run spot, and it's very popular, especially with groups; so you must reserve well in advance. Guest rooms are simply but carefully decorated; some come with views over the harbor or Mount Vesuvio, and some come with private balconies. Bathrooms are modern and roomy. A simple continental breakfast, served in your room, is included in the rates. Up to two extra beds can be added to a room for the same price.

Via Palepoli 12 (off Via Santa Lucia, by Castel dell'Ovo), 80132 Napoli. ✆ **081-7649389.** Fax 081-7649227. www.hotel-rex.it. 34 units. 150€ double. Rates include continental breakfast. Children 3 and under stay free in parent's room. Internet specials available. AE, DC, MC, V. Parking 25€ in nearby garage. Bus: 152, C25, or 140. **Amenities:** Bar; babysitting; concierge. *In room:* A/C, TV, minibar.

Expensive

Grand Hotel Parker's ★   A landmark building of the Liberty (Italian Art Nouveau) style, this glorious villa still features most of its original architectural details and statuary—it served as the Allied headquarters during World War II. The public spaces are splendid and definitely worth a visit, even if you are not staying in the hotel. The commodious guest rooms fronting the Bay share the same spectacular views as the public spaces and are decorated with elegant period furniture (different floors are decorated in various styles—Louis XIV, Empire, and so on). Suites are truly elegant duplex apartments on two levels. The back rooms, however, are unremarkable and overlook the garage. The spa is world class, with such treatments as hydrotherapy, inhalation therapy, and Turkish baths. **George's** (p. 100), on the roof, is considered by many, including us, to be the best restaurant in Naples—although for everyday dining, we generally prefer a more down-to-earth atmosphere. The bar has a separate cigar room.

Corso Vittorio Emanuele 135 (up the cliff from Riviera di Chiaia), 80121 Napoli. © **081-7612474.** Fax 081-663527. www.grandhotelparkers.com. 81 units. 255€–360€ double; from 450€ suite. Rates include buffet breakfast. Children 1 and under stay free in parent's room. Internet specials available. AE, DC, MC, V. Parking 21€–23€. Bus: C24 or C27 to Via Tasso-Corso Vittorio Emanuele II. Metro: Piazza Amedeo. **Amenities:** Restaurant; bar; babysitting; concierge; health club; room service; smoke-free rooms; spa. *In room:* A/C, TV/VCR/DVD, fax, minibar.

Moderate

Hotel Majestic   Popular with Italian businesspeople and well-to-do travelers, this hotel is located at the end of the elegant shopping strip in the lower part of Chiaia and offers upscale accommodations. The large guest rooms are decorated with low-key elegance, sporting hardwood floors, streamlined modern furniture, and marble bathrooms. Many of the rooms afford great views of the Bay. **La Giara,** the hotel's restaurant, is quite good.

Largo Vasto a Chiaia 68 (off Riviera di Chiaia), 80121 Napoli. © **081-416500.** Fax 081-410145. www.majestic.it. 250€–280€ double; from 420€ suite. Rates include buffet breakfast. Children 2 and under stay free in parent's room. Internet specials available. AE, DC, MC, V. Parking 23€. Metro: Piazza Amedeo. **Amenities:** Restaurant; bar; babysitting; concierge; room service. *In room:* A/C, TV/VCR, minibar.

Hotel Palazzo Alabardieri ★   This is one of our favorite hotels in Naples for location and style. In an elegant palace created in 1870 in the ancient cloister of the convent of Santa Caterina a Chiaia, it opened in 2004, after a careful restoration that respected the building's history. Sleek marble floors in the public areas contrast the warm hardwood floors in the guest rooms, which are furnished with period furniture and color coordinated in earth tones and pastel colors. The junior suites are especially pleasant, with stylish furnishings and designer accents. All units come with good-size marble bathrooms.

Via Alabardieri 38 (off Riviera di Chiaia), 80121 Napoli. © **081-415278.** Fax 081-19722010. www.palazzoalabardieri.it. 33 units. 190€–220€ double; 320€ junior suite. Rates include buffet breakfast. Children 2 and under stay free in parent's room. Children ages 3–11 stay in parent's room for 20€ each. Internet specials available. AE, DC, MC, V. Parking 30€. Metro: Piazza Amedeo. **Amenities:** Bar; babysitting; concierge; room service. *In room:* A/C, TV, Internet, minibar.

San Francesco al Monte   You cannot beat the atmosphere of this elegant hotel inside an ex-Franciscan convent, nor the location on the slope of the hill overlooking

Riviera di Chiaia. The views are quite spectacular, particularly from the terrace (often booked for wedding receptions) with its restaurant and heart-shaped swimming pool. All the tastefully furnished guest rooms (some shower only) open onto the Bay; they are good size, with tiled floors, and lots of wood. Some are highlighted with original architectural details, such as an arched doorway or a rounded window. The hotel's restaurant, Terrazza dei Barbanti, is good if a bit overpriced, and affords matchless views over the Bay.

Corso Vittorio Emanuele 328 (up the cliff from Riviera di Chiaia), 80135 Napoli. © 081-4239111. Fax 081-2512485. www.sanfrancescoalmonte.it. 45 units. 245€–295€ double; 350€ suite. Rates include buffet breakfast. AE, DC, MC, V. Parking 25€. Metro: Piazza Amedeo. **Am**enities: Restaurant; bar; babysitting; pool; room service; smoke-free rooms. *In room:* A/C, TV/DVD, Internet, minibar.

PIAZZA DEL PLEBISCITO
Expensive
Hotel Art Resort Galleria Umberto ★   Smack in the heart of the city, in one of the city's historic landmarks, this hotel is steps from many Naples attractions. The hotel occupies the upper floors of the Galleria Umberto I (p. 121), which explains the somewhat pricier rates, and its charming hidden entrance inside the gallery and up an early-20th-century elevator. The hotel is lavishly decorated in an eclectic style, mixing baroque and Liberty elements, and each of its rooms is dedicated to an artist, from Klee to van Gogh. Rooms with interior windows that open onto the gallery can be a bit dark, while those facing the street are a bit noisy; but the quality of the furnishings and decor—with four-poster beds, elegant marble floors, and state-of-the-art bathrooms—compensate for it.

Galleria Umberto I 83 (off Via Toledo), 80132 Napoli. © 081-4976224. Fax 081-4104114. www.artresort galleriaumberto.it. 16 units. 240€–300€ double; 280€–400€ junior suite. Rates include buffet breakfast. Children 2 and under stay free in parent's room. Internet specials available. AE, DC, MC, V. Parking 25€ in nearby garage. Bus: R2 to Piazza Municipio. **Amenities:** Babysitting; concierge. *In room:* A/C, TV/VCR, minibar, Wi-Fi.

QUARTIERI SPAGNOLI
Moderate
Hotel Il Convento ★ (Kids)   Family-run, this hotel offers very pleasant accommodations at moderate prices in the heart of Naples. Housed in a 17th-century *palazzo*, it has been carefully restored. Guest rooms are decorated with pastel-colored plaster walls that highlight varying architectural details, such as wooden beams in some rooms and arches in others; the two junior suites on the top floor enjoy delightful private roof gardens, while each of the two very nicely appointed family rooms has a loft bedroom. All have modern bathrooms and are furnished with quality modern furniture in dark wood. Breakfast is served in two small breakfast rooms; the buffet includes breads and jams, fruit, cold cuts, and cheese. Guests have access to the sauna facility at the Hotel Executive (see below) and can check their e-mail in the reception area.

Via Speranzella 137/a (2 short blocks west of Via Toledo/Via Roma), 80134 Napoli. © 081-403977. Fax 081-400332. www.hotelilconvento.com. 14 units. 180€ double; 210€ junior suite; 240€ quad. Rates include buffet breakfast. Children 2 and under stay free in parent's room. Internet and family specials available. AE, DC, MC, V. Parking 22€ in nearby garage. Pets allowed. Bus: R2 to Piazza Municipio. **Amenities:** Bar; concierge; fitness room & sauna; room service. *In room:* A/C, satellite TV/VCR, minibar.

Inexpensive

Hotel Toledo (Finds) This small picturesque hotel is on a narrow side street off Via Toledo. Sharing the same convenient location as the Hotel Il Convento (above), it is less charming than its neighbor, but makes up for it with lower rates and good service. Guest rooms are good size and clean, with adequate if uninspired furnishings, and modern, tiled bathrooms (shower only). The hotel also has excellent amenities for this price level, including a pleasant roof garden and free Internet for guests.

Via Montecalvario 15 (off west side of Via Toledo/Via Roma), 80134 Napoli. (C) **081-406800.** Fax 081-406871. www.hoteltoledo.net. 35 units. 100€ double; 120€ suite. Rates include buffet breakfast. Children 2 and under stay free in parent's room. Internet specials available. AE, MC, V. Parking 22€ in nearby garage. Bus: R2 to Piazza Municipio. **Amenities:** Restaurant; bar; fitness room. *In room:* A/C, TV, minibar, Wi-Fi.

CITTA ANTICA

Expensive

Hotel Palazzo Turchini This centrally located hotel offers modern accommodations inside the shell of a 17th-century palace, once part of an orphanage specializing in musical studies. Guest rooms have been redone using state-of-the-art technology to completely soundproof them; all have hardwood floors and are furnished with a stylish mix of modern and period furniture. The marble bathrooms are good size, some with showers and others with Jacuzzi bathtubs. The executive doubles are larger and brighter than the "classics," which mostly open onto light shafts and the narrow street. Some executive doubles come with small private terraces, and others come with lounge areas. Some rooms are available for those with limited mobility. Breakfast is served on the roof terrace in clement weather.

Via Medina 21, off Piazza Municipio, 80132 Napoli. (C) **081-5510606.** Fax 081-5521473. www.palazzo turchini.it. 27 units. 260€–300€ double; 340€ suite. Rates include buffet breakfast. Internet specials available. Children 10 and under stay free in parent's room. AE, DC, MC, V. Parking 25€ in nearby garage. Bus: C57, E3, or R3 to Via Medina. **Amenities:** Bar; concierge; room service. *In room:* A/C, TV, Internet (for a fee), minibar.

Moderate

Costantinopoli 104 ★ (Finds) In the heart of the historical center, this charming small hotel is in a 19th-century Italian Art Nouveau palace that belonged to a marquis. Behind the gates is a harbor of peace and luxury from the city's noise and grit. Public spaces have the atmosphere of a private palatial home, from the living room with a fireplace to the private courtyard with palm trees, chaise longues, and a bean-shaped swimming pool. Some guest rooms open onto the terrace where breakfast is served in fair weather, and others have private balconies. All are medium size and individually decorated with modern furnishings and hardwood floors or hand-painted tiles. Suites have Jacuzzi tubs. Room service shows excellent attention to detail, with homemade liquors and ice cream and a fabulous breakfast.

Via Santa Maria di Costantinopoli 104 (off Piazza Bellini), 80134 Napoli. (C) **081-5571035.** Fax 081-5571051. www.costantinopoli104.com. 19 units. 220€ double; 250€ suite. Rates include buffet breakfast. AE, DC, MC, V. Parking 25€. Metro: Piazza Dante. **Am**enities: Babysitting; concierge; Internet (free); pool; room service; smoke-free rooms. *In room:* A/C, TV, Internet, minibar.

Decumani Hotel de Charme (Finds) The palatial home of the last bishop of the Bourbon kingdom, Cardinal Sisto Riario Sforza, was recently renovated as an elegant and moderately priced hotel. The good-size rooms (some shower only) are furnished with period furniture and a few antiques, and many feature original architectural details and decorations.

Via San Giovanni Maggiore Pignatelli 15 (off Via Benedetto Croce, btw. Via Santa Chiara and Via Mezzo-cannone), 80134 Napoli. © **081-5518188.** Fax 081-5518188. www.decumani.it. 22 units. 124€–144€ double. MC, V. Rates includes breakfast. Children 3 and under stay free in parent's room. Children 12 and under 12€. Internet specials available. AE, MC, V. Parking 20€ in nearby garage. Metro: Piazza Dante. *In room:* A/C, TV, minibar, Wi-Fi (free).

Grand Hotel Oriente   At the southern edge of the historic district, this modern hotel belongs to the same owners as the Grand Hotel Santa Lucia (p. 87), and offers a less pricey but convenient location in the heart of Naples with good amenities. Popular among business travelers, its guest rooms are spacious and pleasantly furnished, all with carpeting and good-size modern bathrooms. Those on the higher floors have balconies with good views of Mount Vesuvius and the Gulf. The excellent **restaurant** is popular for its Neapolitan cuisine, and the bar is a good place to hang out.

Via Armando Diaz 44 (btw. Via Toledo and Via Medina), 80134 Napoli. © **081-5512133.** Fax 081-5514915. www.naples-hotel-oriente-turinhotels.com. 131 units. 200€–210€ double; 280€ suite. Rates include buffet breakfast. Internet specials available. Children 12 and under stay free in parent's room. AE, DC, MC, V. Parking 22€. Bus: C25, E2, or R2 to Via Toledo; C57, E3, or R3 to Via Medina. **Amenities:** Restaurant; bar; babysitting; concierge; room service. *In room:* A/C, TV/VCR, Internet, minibar.

Hotel Executive ⟨**Value**⟩   This comfortable hotel enjoys an excellent location in central Naples and offers a lot for its price, making it a good address for both moderately oriented business travelers and tourists. Guest rooms are nicely appointed, with tiled floors, tasteful modern furniture, and good-size, modern bathrooms (shower only). The one available suite is definitely "executive" level, with two balconies as well as a Jacuzzi tub. The hotel also offers a sizeable sauna and a delightful roof garden, where breakfast is served in good weather.

Via del Cerriglio 10 (btw. Via Monteoliveto and Piazza G. Bovio [Corso Umberto]), 80134 Napoli. © **081-5520611.** Fax 081-5520611. http://executive.hotelsinnapoli.com. 19 units. 110€–120€ double; 205€ suite. Rates include buffet breakfast. Internet specials available. Children 2 and under stay free in parent's room. AE, DC, MC, V. Parking 22€. Bus: CS, CD, or C25 to Via San Felice. Pets accepted. **Amenities:** Bar; concierge; sauna. *In room:* A/C, TV, minibar.

Hotel Palazzo Decumani ★   A welcome addition to the local scene, this elegant hotel is in the heart of Naples, steps from the historic district's attractions. Its restoration successfully complements the original architecture of the palazzo with sophisticated contemporary furnishings. Guest rooms are spacious and bright, with state-of-the-art comforts, including elegant marble bathrooms.

Piazza Giustino Fortunato 8 (btw. Vico San Severino and Via Duomo, off Via San Biagio dei Librai), 80100 Napoli. © **081-4201379.** Fax 081-7901540. www.palazzodecumani.com. 28 units. 140€–200€ double; 230€ junior suite. MC, V. Rates include buffet breakfast. Internet and seasonal specials available. Parking 22€. Metro: Piazza Dante. **Amenities:** Bar; smoke-free rooms; Wi-Fi. *In room:* A/C, TV, Internet, minibar.

Inexpensive

Hotel Europeo/Europeo Flowers ⟨**Value**⟩   It is difficult to find nicer budget-friendly accommodations in Naples. In the heart of the historical center, this modest hotel (technically two) offers good-size rooms that are adequate and tastefully appointed. The catch? It doesn't have public spaces, and it is on the upper floors (fourth and fifth) of a residential building. Yet, if you can do without a breakfast room and a lounge, the only drawback is that you'll need a small reserve of .10€ coins to operate the elevator. The Europeo Flowers has the largest rooms, which can accommodate up to four persons.

Via Mezzocannone 109 and 109/c (btw. Corso Umberto and Via San Biagio dei Librai), 80134 Napoli. ℭ **081-5517254.** Fax 081-5518787. www.sea-hotels.com. 17 units. 105€ double; 110€ triple; 114€–130€ quad. Internet specials available. Children 6 and under stay free in parent's room. AE, DC, MC, V. Parking 22€ in nearby garage. Pets accepted. Metro: Piazza Dante. **Amenities:** Concierge; Wi-Fi (free). *In room:* A/C, TV, minibar (in some).

Hotel Duomo ⟨**Value**⟩ With an excellent location on the first floor of a building a short distance from the Duomo, this family-run budget hotel offers basic but pleasant rooms in central Naples. The rooms are good-size, scrupulously clean, and surprisingly quiet— but a bit dark, as they all open on side streets or the inner courtyard. Don't expect a lot of amenities: There is no A/C, only ceiling fans, and the bathrooms have showers only. On the plus side, the front desk is open 24 hours.

Via Duomo 228 (off Piazza Nicola Amore), Naples 80138. ℭ **081-265988.** www.hotelduomonapoli.it. 10 units. 65€ double; 85€ triple; 95€ quad. MC, V. No parking. Bus: R2 to Piazza Nicola Amore. **Amenities:** Internet in lobby (for a fee). *In room:* Ceiling fans, TV.

Suite Esedra ⟨**Value**⟩ This pleasant small hotel offers moderately priced rooms in the heart of Naples. Housed in an aristocratic palace that has been completely restored, bedrooms are tastefully furnished, with excellent care to details; some have sweet little balconies. Of the two suites, one of them offers a fantastic private terrace equipped with a small pool. Breakfast is served in a pleasant common room.

Via Arnaldo Cantani 12 (btw. Via Nuova Marina and Corso Umberto), 80134 Napoli. ℭ **081-5537087.** Fax 081-5537087. www.esedra.hotelsinnapoli.com. 17 units. 95€–105€ double. Rates include buffet break- fast. Internet specials available. Children 5 and under stay free in parent's room. AE, DC, MC, V. Parking 22€ in nearby garage. Metro: Piazza Dante. **Amenities:** Bar; concierge; health club. *In room:* A/C, TV, minibar.

PIAZZA GARIBALDI
Moderate

Starhotel Terminus ⟨**Kids**⟩ A member of the Italian Starhotel group, this hotel offers elegant accommodations with full amenities and excellent service. The commodious guest rooms are stylishly furnished, with warm wood, modern furniture, tasteful carpet- ing and fabrics, and elegant bathrooms. The "executive" doubles have extras such as trouser presses, a second TV in the bathroom, a cutting-edge CD/cassette system, and a complimentary tea/coffee/hot chocolate tray. The panoramic restaurant and bar on the roof garden have become quite a hit with Neapolitan socialites (see "Naples After Dark," later in this chapter).

Piazza Garibaldi 91 (beside Stazione Centrale), 80142 Napoli. ℭ **081-7793111.** Fax 081-206689. terminus. na@starhotels.it. 171 units. 160€–210€ double; 290€ junior suite; 340€ suite. Rates include buffet break- fast. Internet specials available. Children 11 and under stay free in parent's room. AE, DC, MC, V. Free parking in garage. Metro: Garibaldi. Pets accepted. **Amenities:** Restaurant; bar; babysitting; concierge; fitness room; room service. *In room:* A/C, TV, minibar, Wi-Fi.

Una Hotel Napoli ★ A welcome addition to Naples's accommodations roster, this recently opened hotel is in an elegant 19th-century palazzo, located by Stazione Centrale and near the Circumvesuviana rail station. Its pleasant public spaces include a trendy panoramic roof terrace, featuring both bar and restaurant. The spacious guest rooms are stylish, with a streamlined modern design and neutral-colored decor. The good-size bathrooms are ultramodern.

Piazza Garibaldi 9 (opposite Stazione Centrale), 80142 Napoli. (C) **081-5636901.** Fax 081-5636972. www. unahotels.it. 89 units. 160€–240€ double; 400€ suite. Rates include buffet breakfast. Internet specials available. AE, DC, MC, V. Free parking in garage. Metro: Garibaldi. **Amenities:** Restaurant; bar; concierge; room service. *In room:* A/C, TV, minibar, Wi-Fi.

Inexpensive

Nuovo Rebecchino ⟨**Value**⟩ A few steps from Stazione Centrale and within walking distance of the ancient city, this hotel offers pleasant accommodations at reasonable rates. One of the oldest hotels in Naples, it was restored to its original beauty in 2004. The ample guest rooms have an elegantly classic style, with carpeting and modern features. Bathrooms are good size, and a number of the rooms have Jacuzzi tubs.

Corso Garibaldi 356 (off Piazza Garibaldi and Stazione Centrale to the north), 80142 Napoli. (C) **081-5535327.** Fax 081-268026. www.nuovorebecchino.it. 58 units. 95€–105€ double; 110€ triple; 120€ quad. Rates include buffet breakfast. Children 12 and under stay free in parent's room. AE, DC, MC, V. Parking 22€ in nearby garage. Metro: Garibaldi. **Amenities:** Restaurant; bar; babysitting; concierge; room service. *In room:* A/C, TV, minibar, Wi-Fi (free).

CAPODIMONTE

Moderate

Villa Capodimonte ★ This 1995 hotel is just steps from the Royal Park of Capodimonte and is surrounded by its own park with splendid views. Family run, it offers personalized and welcoming service, and a variety of public spaces where you can enjoy some downtime. Guest rooms are large and nicely appointed, with classic furniture and wooden floors; each is basically a junior suite opening onto either the garden or a terrace. Many enjoy vistas of Mount Vesuvius and the Gulf.

Via Moiariello 66 (off Via S. Antonio, opposite the south gate of the Park of the Museo Nazionale di Capodimonte), 80131 Napoli. (C) **081-459000.** Fax 081-299344. www.villacapodimonte.it. 57 units. 175€–200€ double; 215€ triple; 260€ quad. Rates include buffet breakfast. Internet specials available. Children 5 and under stay free in parent's room. AE, DC, MC, V. Free parking. Bus: C66 or 24 to Via Ponti Rossi. Pets accepted. **Amenities:** Restaurant; bar; babysitting; concierge; room service. *In room:* A/C, TV, minibar.

3 WHERE TO DINE

Neapolitans love to eat and love their traditions: Seafood and pizza dominate the scene (see p. 24 for an introduction to local cuisine and wines, and p. 331 for a glossary of menu terms), yet many traditional local dishes are vegetarian or meat based. In addition to our suggestions below, consider also some of the **hotel dining** recommended above, and see "Naples After Dark" on p. 129 for *enoteche* (wine bars offering food).

POSILLIPO

Expensive

Giuseppone a Mare ★ NEAPOLITAN/SEAFOOD   Going on 200 years of service, this restaurant is right on the seashore and commands a beautiful view of the Bay looking back toward Napoli. The menu is large—two pages are devoted solely to pasta—but the specialties are fish and seafood, which can be cooked to order (priced by the kg). We recommend the delicious *polpi Giuseppone* (squid in a tomato and black olive sauce) and the exceptional *fusilli della Baia* (with swordfish and pumpkin served in a crunchy cheese crust). The space is bright and airy, with an antique majolica floor in lemon hues. Toward **97** the back wall, you can see how the building was literally hewn out of the looming cliff above it. During warm months, you can dine on the terrace outside.

Via Ferdinando Russo 13. (C) 081-5756002 or 081-7691384. Reservations recommended. Secondi 8€–15€. AE, DC, MC, V. Tues–Sat 10:30am–3:30pm and 8–11:30pm; Sun 10:30am–5:30pm. Closed 2 weeks in Aug. Bus: C3 to Mergellina (end of line), and then 140.

Rosiello (Finds) NEAPOLITAN/SEAFOOD   This elegant restaurant is beloved not only for the quality of its cuisine, but also for the exceptional sea views from its terrace. Locals will line up for an outdoor table from spring to fall, so reserve in advance. You will delight in the excellent dishes such as risotto alla pescatora (with seafood) and scialatielli con melanzane e provola (fresh pasta with local cheese and eggplant), as well as the perfectly fried calamari and the pezzogna all'acquapazza (fish in a light tomato broth).

Via Santo Strato 10. (C) 081-7691288. Reservations recommended. Secondi 14€–20€. AE, DC, MC, V. Thurs–Tues 12:30–3pm and 8–11:30pm. Closed 2 weeks each in Jan and Aug. Bus: C3 to Mergellina (end of line), and then 140.

Moderate
Ristorante La Fazenda NEAPOLITAN/SEAFOOD   With a beautiful view over the Bay and an informal atmosphere, La Fazenda pleases both locals and visitors. La Fazenda is famous for its fish specialties, and we loved their *pasta alle vongole* (with clams) and fresh grilled seafood. The terrace here is popular in summer (don't try to go then without a reservation).

Via Mare Chiaro 58/a. (C) 081-5757420. Reservations recommended. Secondi 12€–18€. AE, DC, MC, V. Mon 7:30–11:30pm; Tues–Sat 12:30–4pm and 7:30–11:30pm; Sun 12:30–4pm. Closed 1 week in Aug. Bus: C3 to Mergellina (end of line), and then 140.

MERGELLINA
Moderate
Ciro a Mergellina ★ NEAPOLITAN/PIZZA/SEAFOOD   This historic restaurant is a favorite destination for tourists and locals alike, who come for the seafood—sautéed mussels and small clams, pasta dishes, and excellent pizza made with *mozzarella di bufala* (buffalo mozzarella)—and for the excellent service. We also love the seafood salad appetizer, *spaghetti alle vongole* (with baby clams), *pasta all'aragosta* (with lobster), and *spigola fritta* (deep-fried sea bass). The wonderful, homemade ice cream comes in a variety of flavors.

Via Mergellina 18. (C) 081-681780. www.ciroamergellina.it. Reservations recommended. Secondi 8€–18€. Tues–Sun 11:30am–11:30pm. AE, DC, MC, V. Bus: 140. Metro: Mergellina. Tram: 1.

Sbrescia (Finds) NEAPOLITAN/PIZZA   This is a real local hangout, where Neapolitans of all ages come to enjoy the view of the nearby Bay and the classic cuisine. The menu varies, but when you're in luck, this is a great place to taste Naples's traditional specialty, *sartù* (a baked rice dish filled with baby meatballs, cheese, and other ingredients). You'll find many other classics of Neapolitan cuisine, among them the well-prepared *fritto misto* (deep-fried seafood). There is also a wood-fired oven where excellent pizza is prepared.

Rampe Sant'Antonio 109. (C) 081-669140. Reservations recommended. Secondi 6€–14€. AE, MC, V. Tues–Sun 12:30–3:30pm and 8–11pm. Bus: C3 to Mergellina (end of line), and then 140.

NAPLES

5

WHERE TO DINE

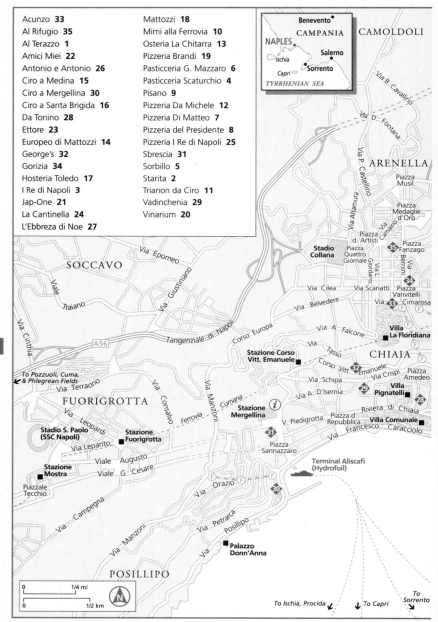

Acunzo **33**
Al Rifugio **35**
Al Terazzo **1**
Amici Miei **22**
Antonio e Antonio **26**
Ciro a Medina **15**
Ciro a Mergellina **30**
Ciro a Santa Brigida **16**
Da Tonino **28**
Ettore **23**
Europeo di Mattozzi **14**
George's **32**
Gorizia **34**
Hosteria Toledo **17**
I Re di Napoli **3**
Jap-One **21**
La Cantinella **24**
L'Ebbreza di Noe **27**

Mattozzi **18**
Mimi alla Ferrovia **10**
Osteria La Chitarra **13**
Pizzeria Brandi **19**
Pasticceria G. Mazzaro **6**
Pasticceria Scaturchio **4**
Pisano **9**
Pizzeria Da Michele **12**
Pizzeria Di Matteo **7**
Pizzeria del Presidente **8**
Pizzeria I Re di Napoli **25**
Sbrescia **31**
Sorbillo **5**
Starita **2**
Trianon da Ciro **11**
Vadinchenia **29**
Vinarium **20**

Benevento
CAMPANIA   CAMOLDOLI
NAPLES
Ischia   Salerno
Capri   Sorrento
TYRRHENIAN SEA

ARENELLA

Piazza
Musil

Piazza
Medaglie
d'Oro

Piazza
d. Artisti   Piazza
Fanzago

Stadio   Piazza
Collana   Quattro
              Giornate

Via Cilea   Via Scariatti   Piazza
                                  Vanvitelli
                         Piazza
                         Cimarosa

Via Belvedere

Via A. Falcone   Villa
                    La Floridiana

Via Tasso

SOCCAVO

Via Epomeo

Via Giustiniano

Tangenziale di Napoli   Corso Europa

Stazione Corso
Vitt. Emanuele   Corso Vitt. Emanuele   CHIAIA

To Pozzuoli, Cuma,
& Phlegrean Fields   Piazza
Via Terracino   Amedeo
              Via Schipa   Via Crispi
                         Via A. D'Isernia   Villa
FUORIGROTTA   Pignatelli

Stazione
Mergellina   Riviera di Chiaia

V. Piedigrotta   Piazza d.   Villa Comunale
                    Repubblica
Stadio S. Paolo   Via Francesco Caracciolo
(SSC Napoli)   Stazione
                    Fuorigrotta
Via Lepanto   Piazza
                    Sannazzaro
Stazione
Mostra   Viale Augusto   Terminal Aliscafi
              Viale G. Cesare   (Hydrofoil)
Piazzale
Tecchio   Via Orazio

Via Campegna   Via Petrarca
                  Posillipo

              Palazzo
              Donn'Anna

POSILLIPO

0   1/4 mi
0   1/2 km
N

To Ischia, Procida   To Capri   To Sorrento

Expensive

George's ★★ NEAPOLITAN   A temple of good taste, located on the top floor of Grand Hotel Parker's, this place has a view second to none. You can watch the sun set on the Gulf as your taste buds are pampered by Chef Baciòt's preparations. He likes to revisit the ancient dishes of Neapolitan tradition, removing a bit of fat and adding a lot of imagination. The menu is seasonal and might include *pizzelle foglia* (eggless homemade leaves of pasta with sautéed garden vegetables), *pezzogna arrosto in guazzetto di tartufi* (local fish in a light sauce with truffles), and *costolette d'agnello con le melanzane* (lamb with eggplants). In addition to its regular menu, George's serves a "de light" menu, in line with the therapies proposed in the hotel's spa and based on the principles of Marc Messegué, the herbal specialist; it's detoxifying yet extremely satisfying. The wine list is extensive, including a large variety of Campanian and Italian wines (no foreign wines, not even French, which apparently is why this restaurant has no Michelin rating).

Corso Vittorio Emanuele 135. ℂ **081-7612474.** www.grandhotelparkers.com. Reservations required. Secondi 22€–30€. AE, DC, MC, V. Daily 12:30–2:30pm and 8–10:30pm. Bus: C24 or C27 to Via Tasso-Corso Vittorio Emanuele II. Metro: Piazza Amedeo.

Moderate

Amici Miei (Finds) ITALIAN/NEAPOLITAN   If you are tired of seafood, this restaurant, located on the hill between Chiaia and the Quartieri Spagnoli, is for you. The menu focuses on meat—as in goose, lamb, pork—as well as on vegetarian choices. We recommend the homemade *fusilli alle melanzane* (with eggplant), the *pappardelle al sugo di agnello* (fresh large noodles with a lamb sauce), and the *costine e salsicce alla brace* (chargrilled lamb ribs and sausages), but anything on the seasonal menu is good. Just try not to fill up on the tasty homemade bread before your meal.

Via Monte di Dio 77. ℂ **081-7646063.** www.ristoranteamicimiei.com. Reservations required. Secondi 12€–13€. AE, DC, MC, V. Tues–Sat 12:30–3:30pm and 7:30–11:30pm; Sun 12:30–3:30pm. Closed July–Aug. Tram: 1 to Piazza dei Martiri.

Jap-One (Finds) SUSHI   This trendy sushi bar, hidden away at the end of a winding narrow alley under the cliff of Monte di Dio (taking a cab is the best way to find it), feels more New York than Napoli with its überstylish decor. But thanks to the care and warm personality of owner Roberto Goretti, the atmosphere is friendly and relaxed, with cool jazz in the background and chefs preparing food at the sushi bar in view of the diners. Although the restaurant is Japanese, it has that irrepressible Neapolitan flair, seen in the use of local fish—for example the *maki di astice* (local lobster maki), or the *coccio sashimi* (sashimi of coccio, a local fish), depending on the day's catch.

Via Santa Maria Cappella Vecchia 30/i (off Piazza dei Martiri). ℂ **081-7646667.** Reservations required. Secondi 14€–36€. AE, DC, MC, V. Tues–Sat 8:30–11pm. Tram: 1 to Piazza dei Martiri.

Inexpensive

Da Tonino (Value) NEAPOLITAN   One of the real traditional osteria left in Naples, Da Tonino has been run by the same family for over a century, and is consistently loved by locals—and now tourists. The interior is rustic and the menu small, but the atmosphere friendly and authentic. You can't go wrong with anything on the menu featuring hearty dishes from the local tradition, like the winning *ragù*. The restaurant features a small but excellent wine list.

Via Santa Teresa A Chiaia 47. ℰ **081-421533.** Reservations accepted only for large parties. Secondi 8€–16€. **101**
No credit cards. Mon–Thurs 12:30–3:30pm; Fri–Sat 12:30–3:30pm and 8–11:30pm. Metro: Amedeo.

Vadinchenia (Finds) MODERN CAMPANIAN   This restaurant, beloved by local connoisseurs, offers excellent food and professional service in a welcoming setting. The menu is
large, including many unusual and surprisingly delicious offerings, such as the ricotta farcita
(stuffed ricotta cheese) appetizer, the paccheri alici e pecorino (fresh large pasta with sardines
and pecorino cheese), and the *calamaro ripieno di verdure e salsiccia* (squid stuffed with greens
and sausage). The menu is well complemented by the moderately priced wine list.

Via Pontano 21 (off Corso Vittorio Emanuele). ℰ **081-660265.** Reservations required. Secondi 8€–14€.
AE, DC, MC, V. Mon–Sat 12:30–3pm and 7:30–11:30pm; Sun 12:30–3pm. Closed Aug and Dec 25. Bus: C24
or C27 to Via Tasso-Corso Vittorio Emanuele II. Metro: Piazza Amedeo.

SANTA LUCIA
Expensive
La Cantinella ★ NEAPOLITAN/SEAFOOD   A well-established address in Naples,
this local favorite is always bursting with chic clientele. The stylish old-fashioned nightclub atmosphere doubles with top-quality—and mostly strictly traditional—Neapolitan
food. The choice of *antipasti* is good and savory. You can follow it with *pappardelle sotto
il cielo di Napoli* (homemade pasta with zucchini, prawns, and green tomatoes) or *tubetti
con le cozze* (short pasta with mussels). For your secondo, the *frittura* (deep-fried seafood)
is a winner. Do not skip dessert—all are deliciously homemade (such as the superb souf-
flé, if you have the patience to wait). The attached club features live music and a similar
menu. The wine list is huge at both spots.

Via Cuma 42. ℰ **081-7648684.** www.lacantinella.it. Reservations required. Secondi 19€–30€. AE, DC, MC, V.
Mon–Sat 12:30–3:30pm and 7:30pm–midnight. Closed 1 week in Jan and 3 weeks in Aug. Bus: 152, C25, or 140.

Moderate
Antonio e Antonio PIZZA/NEAPOLITAN   Located on the beautiful lungomare
(oceanfront), this restaurant is popular with locals, many of whom come for its youthful
atmosphere. The two Antonios who created this restaurant grew up and were trained in
two of Naples's most famous, historic restaurants, Zi Teresa and Giuseppone a Mare. The
open kitchen zips out 40 types of pizza and all the great Neapolitan classics, including
fusilli di pasta fresca ai pomodorini del Vesuvio (with cherry tomatoes from Mount Vesuvius, an especially tasty variety) and *polipetti affogati in cassuola* (squid cooked in an
earthware pot with tomatoes and herbs). Appetizers and side dishes are served buffet
style. A second location in Chiaia is located on the slopes of the Vomero, at Via Francesco
Crispi 89 (ℰ **081-682528** or 081-682438).

Via Partenope 24. ℰ **081-2451987.** Reservations recommended. Secondi 6€–17€. AE, DC, MC, V. Wed–
Mon 12:30–3:30pm and 7:30–11:30pm. Bus: 152, C25, or 140.

Inexpensive
Ettore (Value) NEAPOLITAN/PIZZA   This unpretentious and untrendy restaurant is
a real neighborhood place. It's so popular with locals, in fact, that you might want to
come early to get a seat. The menu is simple but varies often, according to the season.
They make excellent pizza, and their specialty is *pagnottiello*—calzone filled with mozzarella, ricotta, and prosciutto.

Via Santa Lucia 56. ℰ **081-7640498.** Reservations recommended. Secondi 6€–15€. AE, DC, MC, V. Mon–
Sat 12:30–3:30pm and 7:30–11pm. Bus: 152, C25, or 140.

NAPLES

5

WHERE TO DINE

Pizzeria I Re di Napoli PIZZA/NEAPOLITAN   Not to be confused with the restaurant I Re di Napoli (p. 104), this good casual address on the lungomare is popular among the younger set. The menu features not only pizza and appetizers, but also a choice of *primi* secondo (mostly meat, depending on the market offerings), and *contorni* (side dishes). The dining rooms—a second one is up a spiral staircase—are warm and welcoming, and there are tables outside under umbrellas.

Via Partenope 29. 𝒞 **081-7647775.** Secondi 8€–15€. AE, MC, V. Daily noon–1am. Closed Dec 25. Bus: 152, C25, or 140.

QUARTIERI SPAGNOLI
Inexpensive
Hosteria Toledo NEAPOLITAN   A picturesque restaurant, Hosteria Toledo serves tasty but not too expensive meals in a lively atmosphere. It's been serving traditional Neapolitan food to locals and visitors since 1951, and people keep coming, for the great pasta—*alle cozze e vongole* (mussels and clams)—and main courses—*polipo in guazzetto* (squid in a tomato sauce), *arrosto di maiale* (pork roast), and *salsicce* (sausages) are highly recommended. If you have room left after those entrees, try one of the luscious desserts, which often include such great classics as *babà* (a sort of brioche with rum) and *pastiera* (a creamy sort of thick pie).

Vico Giardinetto a Toledo 78. 𝒞 **081-421257.** www.hosteriatoledo.it. Secondi 8€–15€. AE, DC, MC, V. Tues 12:30–3pm; Wed–Mon 12:30–3pm and 7:30–11pm. Bus: R2 or R3 to Piazza Trieste e Trento. Coming from Piazza Trieste e Trento, it's off Via Toledo to the left, across from the Banco di Napoli.

Pizzeria Brandi ★ (**Kids**) NEAPOLITAN/PIZZA   Continuously—and successfully—operated since 1780, this restaurant is a must visit. Back in 1889, the *pizzaiolo* (pizza chef) was so renowned for his pizza that he was invited to prepare it for the royal family who had never tasted it. He created a pizza with mozzarella, basil, and tomatoes—the colors of the newly unified country's flag—and named his creation *pizza alla margherita* in honor of the first queen of Italy, Margherita di Savoia. The queen accepted the offering, and the pizza became an instant favorite throughout the country. The restaurant succeeds in being good and authentic in spite of the streams of tourists now mixed in along the locals. The pizza is superb. Try the *alla Totò*, a deep-fried pizza somewhat like a calzone; but for many, it is only an appetizer. If you have a hard time choosing, we recommend one of the tasting menus. Children are welcomed with highchairs, child-size pizzas, and infinite patience from the staff.

Salita Sant'Anna di Palazzo 1 (at the corner with Via Chiaja). 𝒞 **081-416928.** www.brandi.it. Reservations recommended. Secondi 7€–18€; tasting menus 34€–60€. AE, DC, MC, V. Daily 12:30–3:30pm and 7:30pm–midnight. Bus: R2 or R3 to Piazza Trieste e Trento.

CITTA ANTICA
Expensive
Europeo di Mattozzi ★ NEAPOLITAN/PIZZA/SEAFOOD   This landmark of Neapolitan dining is consistently very rewarding. The chef/owner creates a welcoming atmosphere and offers a winning interpretation of traditional dishes. Among the *primi*, you can have a very tasty *zuppa di cannellini e cozze* (bean and mussel soup) or *pasta e patate con provola* (pasta and potatoes with melted local cheese); for a secondo, you could try *ricciola all' acquapazza* (a local fish in a light tomato and herb broth) or *stoccafisso alla pizzaiola* (dried codfish in a tomato, garlic, and oregano sauce). Pizza is also on the menu

The Best Neapolitan Pizza in the Historic District

Forget all you have ever known about this cheesy treat and open your mind to the experience of pizza in Naples, so different from what we call pizza in the rest of the world. Here is the lowdown on the absolute best Naples pizzerie, where the decor is minimal or nonexistent, and an individual pizza costs between 3€ and 8€:

- **Mattozzi,** Piazza Carità 2 (℗ **081-5524322;** closed Fri), is one of the oldest pizzerie in Naples, using strictly local ingredients, from the regional flour and the tomatoes of Mount Vesuvius, to the *fiordilatte* from the Lattari Mountains on the Sorrento peninsula, and the *mozzarella di bufala*.
- **Pizzeria Da Michele,** Via Sersale 1, off Via Forcella (℗ **081-5539204;** www.damichele.net; closed Sun), is where you'll find the best pizza in Naples, according to many locals. In business since 1888, it serves only two varieties: *margherita* or marinara, basically with or without cheese. Come early; it is usually quite crowded.
- **Pizzaiolo del Presidente,** Via Tribunali 120 (℗ **081-210903;** closed Sun), was opened in 2000 by Ernesto Cacialli, the former *pizzaiolo* (pizza chef) of Di Matteo (below). He is the one who personally served Bill Clinton in 1994—apparently convincing the president to try his special *margherita* pizza—and has named his pizzeria after that event. Do not miss the *margherita* or the *pizza fritta*.
- **Pizzeria Di Matteo,** Via dei Tribunali 94, at Vico Giganti (℗ **081-455262;** closed Sun), is another historical establishment serving excellent classic pizza and specializing in the to-die-for *pizza fritta,* a delicacy of fluffy thin dough filled with a mix of ham, tomatoes, and local cheese—provola, ricotta, and mozzarella—which you can split as an appetizer or eat on your own. President Clinton ate here during the G7 Summit in 1994.
- **Sorbillo,** Via Tribunali 32 (℗ **081-446643;** closed Sun), provides a somewhat more formal setting and an equally—if not superior—quality of pizza. Open since 1935, it specializes in pizza made exclusively with local high-quality ingredients: the *fiordilatte* from Agerola on the Sorrento peninsula, the local extra-virgin olive oil, and the oregano from Frattamaggiore, which is best savored on the simple marinara. The other house specialty is the pizza with olives, capers, Vesuvian tomatoes, and provola (local cheese).
- **Starita,** Via Materdei 27 (℗ **081-5441485;** closed Mon), is a pleasant, small pizzeria run by one of the best pizzaioli in the city. It is popular for the unique quality of its dough and famous for its *pizza fritta* as well as its *pizza coi fiori di zucca* (with zucchini flowers), which is available only in summer.
- **Trianon da Ciro,** Via Pietro Colletta 42 (℗ **081-5539426;** open daily), is an extremely popular pizzeria, where you'll have to compete for a table with the students of the nearby university and the many local aficionados who come to savor the exceptional *pizza con salsiccia e friarelli* (with sausages and broccoli) and *pizza con pomodorini e mozzarella di bufala* (with Vesuvian tomatoes and buffalo mozzarella).

and is very well prepared, as are the desserts, including hometown favorites such as *babà* and *pastiera*.

Via Marchese Campodisola 4. ℂ **081-5521323**. www.europeomattozzi.it. Reservations required. Secondi 12€–18€. AE, DC, MC, V. Mon–Wed noon–3:30pm; Thurs–Sat noon–3:30pm and 7:30–11pm. Closed 2 weeks in Aug. Bus: R2 or R3 to Piazza Trieste e Trento.

Moderate

Ciro a Medina NEAPOLITAN/PIZZA   It is easy to mistake this large, glitzy, and centrally located restaurant for a tourist trap, particularly since it was redone in 2007, with vividly painted frescoes of the Amalfi Coast. However, this is one of Naples's most popular addresses among locals, who come to enjoy the cheerful atmosphere. It serves excellent pizza and a large array of traditional dishes: *scialatielli ai frutti di mare* (handmade pasta with seafood), *fusilli melanzane e ricotta affumicata* (with sauteed eggplant and smoked ricotta), *costolette* (lamb or pork cutlets), and delightful vegetarian side dishes.

Via Medina 19. ℂ **081-5515355**. www.ciroamedina.it. Reservations recommended Sat–Sun. Secondi 7€–14€. AE, DC, MC, V. Daily noon–3pm and 7pm–midnight. Closed for lunch Dec 24 and all day Dec 25. Bus: R2.

Ciro a Santa Brigida ★ NEAPOLITAN   A traditional restaurant with a formal— but absolutely not stuffy—atmosphere and very professional service, Ciro a Santa Brigida is one of the most famous, and most typical, Neapolitan restaurants around. The restaurant was opened in 1932 by the father of the current owner/managers at Via Foria, and transferred here by his children. Since then, Santa Brigida has become a gastronomical institution, serving cuisine in a warm atmosphere laden with traditional decor. Popular with locals for its *fritto* (deep-fried dishes including meat cutlets and seafood), and for side dishes such as hard-to-find traditional vegetables, it also serves good pizza and excellent desserts. Of the traditional Neapolitan specialties on hand, try *rigatoni ricotta e polpettine* (with baby meatballs) and *polpi alla Luciana* (squid cooked in a pocket with tomato and herbs). Counted among the restaurant's famous and faithful customers are the writer Pirandello, the artist De Filippo, and the actors Gassman and Totò.

Via Santa Brigida 71 (off Via Toledo). ℂ **081-5524072**. Reservations required. Secondi 8€–16€. AE, DC, MC, V. Mon–Sat noon–3:30pm and 7–11:30pm. Bus: R2 or R3 to Piazza Trieste e Trento.

Inexpensive

I Re di Napoli PIZZA   This is a simple restaurant offering good food at inexpensive prices. Their specialty is pizza, which they prepare in a traditional brick oven. They have a small menu of other dishes and a substantial buffet of appetizers/side dishes, including wonderful *involtini di melanzane* (eggplant filled with mozzarella and basil, then rolledup and fried) and *peperonata* (sautéed sweet peppers)—perfect for a light meal.

Piazza Dante 16. ℂ **081-423013**. Reservations recommended Sat–Sun. Secondi 5€–9€. AE, DC, MC, V. Daily 11:30am–1am. Bus: R4, 24, CS, or 201. Metro: Piazza Dante.

Osteria La Chitarra NEAPOLITAN   An immediate success since its opening in the 1990s, this restaurant dishes up traditional food prepared with local and strictly seasonal ingredients—which means a menu that varies weekly according to the market finds. We loved the *paccheri lardiati* (homemade noodles with pork tidbits), the authentic lasagna, and the *baccalà con i ceci* (salted cod with chickpeas), as well as the excellent *risotto alla pescatora* (with seafood).

Rampe San Giovanni Maggiore 1bis. ℂ **081-5529103**. www.osterialachitarra.it. Reservations recommended Sat–Sun. Secondi 10€–16€. AE, DC, MC, V. Mon noon–3pm; Tues–Sat noon–3pm and 7pm–midnight. Closed 2 weeks in Aug. Metro: Dante.

For Your Sweet Tooth

Naples is famous for its desserts, which include such world-famous specialties as *babà*, *sfogliatelle*, and *pastiera* (see chapter 13, p. 331). To taste those and many others, head to the **Pasticceria Scaturchio** ★★, Piazza San Domenico Maggiore 19 (✆ **081-5516944**). This historic pastry and coffee shop opened in 1903 and has been a favorite with locals ever since. Locals come for a pick-me-up (there's nothing better than a *sfogliatella* as a midmorning or midafternoon snack), or to buy dessert to take to their hosts and family for dinner. Besides the excellent pastries, a chocolate candy developed here made the shop famous: the *Ministeriale*, a medallion of dark chocolate with a liqueur cream filling. **Pasticceria Attanasio,** Vico Ferrovia 2 (✆ **081-285675;** www.sfogliatellecalde.com; closed Mon) is another renowned spot to sample *sfogliatella* in Naples.

Caffetteria Pasticceria Gelateria G. Mazzaro ★ Palazzo Spinelli, Via Tribunali 359 (✆ **081-459248;** www.pasticceriamazzaro.it; daily 7am–midnight), makes scrumptious pastries and also excellent gelato in many flavors.

Pisano (Value) (Finds) NEAPOLITAN/SEAFOOD   Hidden behind the Duomo, this pleasant family-run restaurant serves well-prepared dishes from the local culinary tradition. The menu is large and includes both surf and turf. We recommend the scialatielli ai frutti di mare (fresh pasta with seafood) and the linguine al coccio (with local fish), as well as the spigola all'acquapazza (sea bass in a light tomato herbed broth) and the roasted sausages.

Piazzetta Crocelle ai Mannesi 1. ✆ **081-5548325.** Reservations recommended Sat–Sun. Secondi 6€–12€. AE, DC, MC, V. Mon–Sat noon–3pm and 7:30–10:30pm. Bus: R2.

PIAZZA GARIBALDI
Moderate
Mimì alla Ferrovia ★ (Finds) NEAPOLITAN   This is another of Naples's historical landmark restaurants. Its recent face-lift has not diminished its popularity with locals, nor changed its cuisine, which remains true to Neapolitan tradition. The chef prepares excellent renditions of local favorites, varying according to the season. Depending on the time of year, you'll probably find *scialatielli ai frutti di mare* (eggless homemade pasta with seafood), *polipo alla Luciana* (squid cooked in a pocket with tomato and herbs), *in guazzetto* (squid in a light tomato sauce), and *sartù* (rice with baby meatballs and cheese). Not surprisingly, the desserts are those of the Neapolitan tradition—*babà* and *pastiera*.

Via Alfonso d'Aragona 21. ✆ **081-5538525.** Reservations recommended Sat–Sun. Secondi 8€–15€. AE, DC, MC, V. Mon–Sat noon–3pm and 7:30–10:30pm. Metro: Piazza Garibaldi.

VOMERO
Inexpensive
Acunzo ★ PIZZA   This authentic neighborhood restaurant is often crowded with locals eating pizza with a variety of toppings—the 40-some different choices include *pizza con i fusilli* (with fusilli seasoned with tomatoes, peas, bacon, and mushrooms). Purists may prefer the typical Neapolitan dishes, such as *friarelli* (sautéed broccoli),

superb eggplant Parmigiana (Parmesan), and *zuppa di fagioli* (cannellini-bean soup). If you are not planning a visit to Sorrento, try the *gnocchi alla Sorrentina* (potato dumplings with tomato sauce and mozzarella)—it is superb.

Via Domenico Cimarosa 60 (off Via Lorenzo Bernini to the south). (C) **081-5785362.** Reservations recommended for dinner. Secondi 6€–16€. AE, DC, MC, V. Mon–Sat 12:30–4pm and 6:30pm–midnight. Funicular: Vomero. Metro: Vanvitelli.

Al Rifugio ★ (**Finds**) NEAPOLITAN   You shouldn't find many tourists at this restaurant, although it is a well-known local favorite. The atmosphere is simple, even rustic (you enter through a wine shop), but the hearty food is heavenly. The seafood is well prepared, but the reason to come here is for the steaks (a rarity in Naples); choose between local, Tuscan, and Argentine meat. The braciola (thin beef cutlets filled with herbs, pine nuts, and raisins) is a true homage to tradition, as is the homemade pasta. A platter of local cheese and cured meat accompanied by a good glass of red wine is a perfect light meal, and the desserts are homemade and scrumptious. A simple lunch menu is available for 10€ (Mon–Sat).

Via San Gennaro ad Antignano 119 (off Via Gian Lorenzo Bernini to the north). (C) **081-2292213.** Reservations recommended for dinner. Secondi 8€–18€. AE, DC, MC, V. Wed–Mon 12:30–4pm and 7pm–11:30am. Funicular: Vomero. Metro: Vanvitelli.

Gorizia ★ (**Finds**) NEAPOLITAN/PIZZA   This excellent pizzeria was started in 1916 by the grandfather of the current owners (brothers Salvatore and Antonio). True to local tradition, the two brothers are convinced the secret is in the crust and don't believe pizza needs to be dressed up with fancy toppings to be good. According to them, the crust has to be puffy but not gummy, with a slightly crunchy edge. Once you taste the result, you can only agree. Pizza's not the only thing on the menu, however: They offer a small daily menu that always includes one soup and a few choices of antipasto, primo, secondo, and contorno. We recommend the pasta with artichokes, olives, and tomatoes, as well as *pasta e ceci* (a thick soup made of garbanzo beans). The delicious escarole is stuffed with bread crumbs, olives, pinoli nuts, and raisins. This is a popular place for business lunches, and it helps to have a reservation in the evening.

Via Bernini 31 (off Piazza Vanvitelli). (C) **081-5782248.** Reservations recommended for dinner. Secondi 6€–18€. AE, DC, MC, V. Tues–Sun 12:30–4pm and 6pm–1am. Funicular: Vomero. Metro: Vanvitelli.

CAPODIMONTE

Inexpensive

Al Terrazzo NEAPOLITAN/PIZZA   This large, simple neighborhood restaurant has been around since 1945 and is a convenient stop before or after visiting the Museo Capodimonte. It makes excellent pizza—try the *Antica Capri* (with smoked provola and fresh tomatoes)—and has a large menu including specialties such as *scialatielli ai frutti di mare* (eggless fresh pasta with seafood). The restaurant prides itself on its large buffet of *antipasti* and side dishes, offering 50 choices daily. During clement weather, you can dine on the terrace, which is on the second floor and above the traffic and street noise.

Viale Colli Aminei 99 (off Via Capodimonte). (C) **081-7414400** or 081-7414680. Secondi 6€–12€. AE, DC, MC, V. Daily 11am–3:30pm and 6:30–11pm, later on Fri and Sat. Bus: R4.

4 EXPLORING NAPLES

For those willing to see beyond the noise and urban grit, Naples reveals itself as a city of fun, surprise, and wonder that is particularly loved by art lovers and history buffs.

We suggest purchasing an **Artecard** (see "Campania Artecard," below) before starting your exploration of the region. The **City Sightseeing** hop-on-and-off tour is another good idea, particularly if your time is limited (see "Guided Tours," p. 123).

ROYAL NAPLES: PALACES & CASTLES

Castel Capuano (**Kids**) A fortress built by Guglielmo I d'Altavilla in the 12th century and restored in the 13th century by Carlo d'Angió, this castle was transformed into a royal residence by the Aragona dynasty in 1484. In 1540, Don Pedro di Toledo, the viceroy of Naples, decided to change the residence to the seat of tribunals, a function it has maintained to this day. Less dramatic than the other fortresses in Naples, Castel Capuano takes its name from the nearby gate, Porta Capuana, once at the head of the main road leading to Capua. Inside the courtyard, the medieval structure is visible. You can visit some of the decorated halls and the Cappella Sommaria, with its 16th-century frescoes.

Via Concezio Muzy (off Via dei Tribunali). Free admission. Daily 9am–6pm. Metro: Piazza Garibaldi.

Castel dell'Ovo ★ (**Kids**) Built over the small island where the first Greek colony was created in the 9th century B.C., this castle is one of Naples's most famous sites; its profile graces most pictures of the Bay. According to legend, its name, "Castle of the Egg," refers to the magic egg that the classic poet Virgil—the author of the *Aeneid* and a reputed magician—placed under the foundations to protect it. The fortress evolved from the villa of the Roman Lucullus (a celebrated gourmand), which was fortified in the Middle Ages and transformed into a castle by Frederick II. Enlarged and strengthened between the 16th and the 18th centuries, it remained a royal residence until the 20th century. Part of the castle now houses the Museum of Ethno-Prehistory, which is open only for special exhibits. The rest of the castle offers the *Sala delle Colonne* (**Hall of the Columns**) ★, and the **Loggiato** ★—both architectural masterpieces, and great views from two towers, **Torre Maestra** and **Torre Normanna.** The castle occupies only part of the island, which is connected to the shore in front of the Santa Lucia neighborhood. Around it are the picturesque alleys and fishermen's houses of the **Borgo dei Marinari** ★—many of which have been transformed into restaurants.

Borgo Marinari (off Via Partenope). ✆ 081-2400055. Free admission. Mon–Sat 8am–6pm; Sun 8am–2pm. Bus: 152, C25, 140, or E5 to Via Santa Lucia.

Castel Nuovo, aka Maschio Angioino & Museo Civico ★ (**Kids**) An imposing fortress dominating the Bay only steps from the shore, this castle was created by the French architect Pierre d'Angicourt in the 13th century for the new king, Carlo I d'Angió. The first king of the Angevin dynasty, he wanted a more suitable residence than Castel dell'Ovo and Castel Capuano—both used by previous sovereigns. Started in 1279 and finished in 1282, Castel Nuovo was enlarged in the 15th century by Alfonso I d'Aragona, first king of the Aragonese dynasty. The castle has five towers: del Beverello (overlooking the harbor), di San Giorgio, di Mezzo, di Guardia, and dell'Oro (note its tufa stone structure)—and a facade (facing inland) graced by the grandiose **Triumphal Arch of Alfonso I of Aragona** ★, a splendid example of early Renaissance architecture.

Cappella del
 Monte di Pieta **17**
Cappella Sansevero **9**
Castel Capuano **14**
Castel dell'Ovo **25**
Castel Nuovo **20**
Castel Sant'Elmo **27**
Catacombe
 di San Gennaro **1**
Certosa di San Martino **26**
Chiesa del Gesù Nuovo **5**
Chiesa dei Girolamini **15**
Chiesa di Monteoliveto **4**
Complesso Monumentale
 di Santa Chiara **6**
Duomo **12**
Fontana del Nettuno **19**
Galleria Umberto I **21**

Museo Archeologico
 Nazionale **3**
Museo Nazionale
 di Capodimonte **2**
Palazzo Reale **23**
Paleontology, Mineralogy
 & Zoology Museums **18**
Piazza del Plebiscito **24**
San Domenico Maggiore **8**
San Giovanni
 a Carbonara **13**
San Gregorio Armeno **10**
San Lorenzo Maggiore **16**
San Paolo Maggiore **11**
Sant'Angelo a Nilo **7**
Teatro San Carlo **22**
Villa Comunale **29**
Villa La Floridiana **28**

Ferry Terminal
Tourist Information
Funiculars

CAMOLDOLI
Via B. Cavallino
Via D. Fontana
Via P. Castellino
ARENELLA
Via Altamura
Piazza Musil
Piazza Medaglie d'Oro
Via L. Caldieri
Via Bernini
Piazza d. Artisti
Piazza Fanzago
Stadio Collana
Piazza Quattro Giornate
Via L. Giordano
Via Cilea   Via Scariatti   Piazza Vanvitelli
Via Belvedere   Via Cimarosa
Via A. Falcone
Via Tasso
CHIAIA
28
Corso Europa
Tangenziale di Napoli
Stazione Corso Vitt. Emanuele
Corso Vitt. Emanuele   Piazza Amedeo
Via Crispi
A56
Via Cinthia
To Pozzuoli, Cuma, & Phlegrean Fields
Via Terracino
Via Consalvo
Via Manzoni
Cumana
Ferrovia
Stazione Mergellina
Via Schipa
Via A. D'Isernia
V. Piedigrotta
Piazza d. Repubblica
Riviera di Chiaia
Villa Pignatelli
29
FUORIGROTTA
Via Leopardi
Stazione Fuorigrotta
Stadio S. Paolo (SSC Napoli)
Via Lepanto
Piazza Sannazzaro
Via Francesco Caracciolo
Stazione Mostra
Viale Augusto
Viale G. Cesare
Via Orazio
Terminal Aliscafi (Hydrofoil)
Piazzale Tecchio
Via Campegna
Via Petrarca
Via Posillipo
Via Manzoni
Palazzo Donn'Anna
POSILLIPO

SOCCAVO
Via Epomeo
Via Giustiniano

BENEVENTO
CAMPANIA
NAPLES
Salerno
Ischia
Capri
Sorrento
TYRRHENIAN SEA

0   1/4 mi
0   1/2 km
N

To Ischia, Procida   To Capri   To Sorrento

(Value) Campania Artecard

The **Artecard** (© **800-600601** or 06-39967650; www.campaniartecard.it) gives you discounted admission to a great number of attractions, free access to public transportation, and discounts to a number of participating businesses. The pass now comes in 11 different versions (12€–30€). All grant admission to the first two or three attractions you visit from the list below and a 50% discount on all the rest, plus a 10% to 25% discount on several other museums and attractions, and free access to all public transportation—including regional trains and special buses—during the validity of the card. A youth card is offered but only to citizens of the European Union and other countries with reciprocity rights. There is also a version that is valid for a year.

The sites that qualify for free or 50% admission (depending on the type of card you choose) are:

Naples's Museo Archeologico Nazionale, Museo Nazionale di Capodimonte, Certosa and Museo Di San Martino, Castel Sant'Elmo, Museo Civico di Castelnuovo, Museo Duca di Martina (Villa Floridiana), Museo Pignatelli Cortes, Museo Diocesano, Museo del Tesoro di San Gennaro, MADRE, Palazzo Reale, and Città Della Scienza; **Campi Flegrei's** Flavian Amphitheatre, Serapeum, archaeological areas of Baia, Museo Archeologico di Baia, Cuma, and Rione Terra; **Mount Vesuvius's** archaeological areas of Pompeii, Herculaneum, Paestum, Stabia, Velia, Oplontis, and Boscoreale; **Capua's** Mitreo, Anfiteatro Campano, Museo dei Gladiatori, and Museo Archeologico dell'Antica Capua; **Caserta's** Belvedere di San Leucio and Reggia; **Cilento's** Certosa di Padula and Museo del Santuario di Hera Argiva; and **Sorrento's** Museo.

The list of sites and businesses offering discounts between 10% and 25% is too long to print here, but we have noted them throughout the book. The card is for sale online (see above), as well as at all participating sites and museums, at the Campania Artecard stands at Capodichino Airport and the Napoli Cantrale train station, and some major hotels.

Across from the entrance in the courtyard and up a 15th-century staircase is the magnificent **Sala dei Baroni** ★★, an architectural masterpiece. The monumental room is an enormous cube, 27m (89 ft.) wide and 28m (92 ft.) high, with a star-shaped vaulted ceiling originally decorated by Giotto in the 14th century. (His frescoes and most of the sculptures were lost in a fire in 1919.)

Today the castle houses the *Museo Civico* (**Civic Museum**) ★, holding a rich collection of artworks from the castle itself and other important monuments in Naples. Part of the museum's exhibit is inside the **Cappella Palatina** ★, the only surviving part of the Angevin castle. The chapel's facade opens onto the courtyard and is graced with a beautiful 15th-century carved **portal** and a **rose window** ★. Built in 1307, the chapel was completely decorated by Giotto, but only a few fragments remain. Inside you'll see a fine selection of 14th- and 15th-century sculptures, including a **Tabernacle** ★★ by Domenico Gagini (a pupil of Donatello and Brunelleschi), depicting a Madonna with

Child, and two **Madonna with Child** ★ sculptures by Francesco Laurana—one from the portal of this chapel and the second from a nearby church. In the vestibule on the second floor, you'll find a **bronze door** ★ with a cannonball hole: It is the original 15th-century door of the castle, which was taken as war booty by the French in 1496 and later returned. In the other rooms, you'll find a collection of 16th- and 17th-century paintings, including works by Luca Giordano and Francesco Solimena. On the third floor is an interesting collection of paintings dating from the 18th to the 20th centuries.

Piazza Municipio. ⒸⒸ **081-7955877** or 081-4201241. Admission 5€. Mon–Sat 9am–7pm. Ticket booth closes 1 hr. earlier. Bus: R1, R2, R3, R4, E2, E3, C25, C57, 24, or 152.

Castel Sant'Elmo Ⓚⓘⓓⓢ Atop Vomero hill, near the Certosa di San Martino (p. 116), this majestic star-shaped structure, with its six points and several moats, is visible from everywhere in the city. It was originally built by the Angevins in 1329 and called Belforte, then was remade into the present fortress by Viceroy Pedro Toledo in the 16th century. Used as a prison during the Masaniello revolution in 1799, it recently has been restored and now houses special exhibits. You can visit the prisons and the terraces, which offer great views over Naples and the Bay.

Via Tito Angelini 20 (down from Piazza Vanvitelli). Ⓒ **081-2294401.** Admission 3€; free with admission to the Certosa di San Martino; additional fee for special exhibits. Wed–Mon 8:30am–6:30pm. Ticket booth closes 1 hr. earlier. Closed Jan 1 and Dec 25. Bus: C28, C31 or C36 to Piazza Vanvitelli. Funicular: Centrale to Piazza Fuga or Montesanto to Morghen. Metro: Vanvitelli, and then bus V1 to Piazzale San Martino.

Palazzo Reale ★ This imposing palace was designed by Domenico Fontana and built in 2 years, from 1600 to 1602, for the Spanish king Filippo III. Ironically, he never made it to Naples, and the castle was used by later kings who enlarged it in the 18th century. Luigi Vanvitelli worked on the **facade** ★, closing some of the arches to strengthen the walls and creating niches that were filled in 1888 by Umberto I, king of Italy, with eight statues of Neapolitan kings. Badly damaged by U.S. bombing during World War II, the building has since been completely restored. A guided tour gives you a full appreciation of the sprawling place. The **Royal Apartment** ★ occupies one half of the palace, and is still furnished with the original furniture plus a number of masterpieces taken from Neapolitan churches that have closed. From the elegant *Cortile d'Onore* **(Court of Honor)** the double ramp of the main staircase leads to the first floor and the **Teatrino di Corte,** the private "home theater" of the royal family. Continuing through, you enter the semipublic rooms, including the **Throne Room.** Beyond the corner begins the **Private Appartment,** where the kings lived until 1837, when a fire obliged them to move upstairs. Its rooms open onto the manicured elevated gardens, with beautiful views over the Gulf. With colored marble, tapestries, frescoes, and 19th-century furniture, the rooms are quite splendid, especially the beautifully furnished *Studio del Re* **(King's Study),** where you can admire a **desk** and two *secretaires* ★ made for Napoleon Bonaparte by Adam Weisweiler. The magnificent **Hall of Hercules** ★, the ballroom, is hung with Neapolitan tapestries and decorated with some beautiful Sèvres vases. The chapel, **Cappella Palatina,** is worth a visit for its carved wooden **doors** ★ dating from the 16th century; its beautiful baroque **marble altar** ★ by Dionisio Lazzari, with inlays of lapis lazuli, agate, amethyst, and gilt; and the splendid 18th-century *Presepio del Banco di Napoli* **(Nativity Scene of the Bank of Naples)** ★★.

The other half of the palace contains the reception wing: the **Appartamento delle Feste** ★, with elegant rooms dedicated to public celebrations and festivities. It is now, together with the second floor, occupied by the **Biblioteca Nazionale di Vittorio**

NAPLES

EXPLORING NAPLES

Emanuele III, the library that was originally established by Charles de Bourbon. The library is one of the best in the south, with about two million volumes (including 32,950 manuscripts, 4,563 incunabula, and 1,752 papyrus manuscripts from Herculaneum).

Piazza del Plebiscito 1. (℃) 081-5808111. www.palazzorealenapoli.it. Admission 4€; courtyard and gardens free. Guided tour by reservation 4€ (2.50€ with Artecard). Thurs–Tues 9am–7pm. Ticket booth closes 1 hr. earlier. Bus: R2 or R3 to Piazza Trieste e Trento.

Villa La Floridiana & Museo Nazionale della Ceramica Duca di Martina ★★
Surrounded by a magnificent park, this museum was once the 18th-century *casale* (country house) of Lucia Migliaccio, duchess of Floridia and second wife of Ferdinand II di Borbone. It now houses the **Museo Nazionale della Ceramica Duca di Martina** ★, a rich collection of ceramics. The core of the museum is the private collection of Duc Placido De Sangro di Martina who, through his travels in Europe, collected precious objects not only in majolica and porcelain, but also glass, ivory, and coral. The collection was then expanded with objects from other museums in Naples. The star of the show is the collection of *porcellane di Capodimonte* (Capodimonte porcelain) ★, the most important collection in the world of this kind, with works from 1743 to 1759 by important artists such as Giuseppe Gricci; and the collection of **Japanese and Chinese porcelain** ★, including precious Ming and Edo dynasty pieces. Decorating the walls are **sketches** by great Neapolitan artists of the 18th century, including Francesco Solimena, Domenico Antonio Vaccaro, and Corrado Giaquinto.

Note: Visits to the museum are only possible with an official guide, and you need to make a reservation. Even if you are not interested in ceramics, the villa is well worth a stop both for its architecture and for the splendid views over the whole bay.

Via Cimarosa 77. (℃) 081-5788418. Admission 2.50€. Wed–Mon 8:30am–2pm; ticket booth closes 1 hr. earlier. Closed Jan 1 and Dec 25. Guided tour 9:30am, 11am, and 12:30pm. Bus: C28, C32, or C36. Funicular: Chiaia to Cimarosa. Metro: Vanvitelli.

GREAT MUSEUMS

MADRE (Museo d'Arte Contemporanea Donnaregina) This modern museum has recently opened after a major renovation of the historical **Palazzo Regina,** in the heart of the historical district. The rich collection of the museum comes both from the city's endowment, bestowed in recent decades, and from permanent loans from private collectors. Some of the world's best contemporary artists are represented, including Horn, Kapoor, and Lewitt, as well as a number of Italian artists such as Fabro, Clemente, and Serra. In addition to the permanent collection, the MADRE houses noteworthy temporary exhibits (check with the tourist office for current events). From the Cortile della Caffetteria, also called Cortile Banco dei Pegni, you can now access **Santa Maria di Donnaregina Vecchia,** a beautiful Gothic church that holds a monument to Queen Maria d'Ungheria carved by Tino da Camaino.

Via Settembrini 79 (btw. Via Duomo and Via Carbonara). (℃) 081-19313016. www.museomadre.it. Admission Wed–Sun 7€; Mon free. Mon and Wed–Fri 10am–9pm; Sat–Sun 10am–midnight. Bus E1. Metro: Cavour.

Museo Archeologico Nazionale ★★★ **(Kids)** This 16th-century palace was remodeled in the 17th century to house the National Archaeological Museum of Naples. According to the fashion of the time, precious antiquities were embedded in the building as decoration: The marble statues on the **facade** were found during early excavations of Pompeii; the mosaics embedded in many of the **floors** are originals from the ancient Roman villas excavated in the 17th century. The whole collection is jaw dropping and very extensive; even children will love the Egyptian section, and teens will be fascinated by the amazing precious Gemme collection and reconstruction of entire rooms from Pompeii (see below).

The original core of the museum is the Farnese Collection, which was moved here in 1777 and enriched with treasures found during the archaeological excavations of Pompeii, Herculaneum, Stabia, and the rest of the region. The first-floor galleries here hold a superb collection of Roman sculptures, illustrating the integration of Hellenic principles into Roman art, and including such masterpieces as the ***Doriforo* (Spear Bearer)** ★★ from Pompeii, a unique, complete copy of the famous 5th-century-B.C. bronze statue by the Greek sculptor Policleto (in the Galleria dei Grandi Maestri, section 2). Other great masterpieces on display in the Farnese Collection include the superb ***Ercole Farnese*** ★★, a Hercules copied from a 4th-century-B.C. bronze by Greek sculptor Lisippo (found in the Terme di Caracalla in Rome, this sculpture had enormous influence on Renaissance artists); and the exceptional ***Toro Romano*** or ***Toro Farnese*** ★★, one of the largest existing sculpture groups from antiquity. Standing over 4m (13 ft.) high, the *Toro Farnese* is a copy of a Greek original from the 2nd century B.C., representing the torment of the queen of Beotia as she is tied to a bull. Also part of the Farnese Collection are the three rooms of the **Gemme della Collezione Farnese** ★★, a matchless collection of precious objects (over 2,000 pieces), including the unique ***tazza farnese*** ★★ created in Alexandria in the 2nd century B.C.: Carved from a single piece of agate into the shape of a drinking cup, it is one of the largest cameos ever created.

From the first floor, you can also access the **Epigraphic Collection** (inscriptions) ★— the most important epigraphic collection in the world that pertains to ancient Roman and Greek civilizations—and the **Egyptian Collection** ★, holding artifacts from 2700 B.C. up to the Ptolemaic-Roman period of the 2nd and 1st centuries B.C.

On the mezzanine level, besides the reorganized **Numismatic Collection** ★, with over 200,000 coins and medals from antiquity, you'll find the richest **mosaic collection** ★★★ in the world, with pieces spanning from the 2nd century B.C. to the 1st century A.D. Among the many works of art here is the magnificent ***Alexander the Great Defeating Darius of Persia*** ★★★, a huge mosaic covering 20sq. m (215 sq. ft.), which was found in the Casa del Fauno in Pompeii.

More ancient Roman mosaics line the floors of the second level, where you'll find the beautiful **Meridiana Hall** ★ and the complete findings from the several Roman towns and villas destroyed by the eruption of Mount Vesuvius in A.D. 79. The collection of ancient Roman **paintings** ★★★ covers the period from the 1st century B.C. to the 1st century A.D. *Note:* If you have time for only one section of the museum, make it this one: Entire rooms have been reconstructed from villas in Pompeii, Herculaneum, Boscoreale, Boscotrecase, and other locations. Our single favorite room is number 77, with its **landscapes** and a portrait of the girl **Saffo.** (At presstime, the frescoes of this room were under restoration and only visible on selected days, so call ahead.) Don't miss the room dedicated to the Herculaneum's **Villa dei Papiri** ★★. Further collections here include precious objects—silver, ivory, pottery, and glass—as well as weaponry and a scale reconstruction of Pompeii. Also on this floor, are unique findings from the Naples area's prehistoric through Etruscan and Greek periods.

We recommend the helpful audioguides. You may also make a reservation for a guided tour of the Roman erotica (famous since Goethe's day) in the **Gabinetto Segreto (Secret Room)** ★★. The collection documents the acceptance of sexuality in everyday Roman life until Christians demonized it as the embodiment of paganism.

Piazza Museo 19 (off Via Pessina [Via Toledo]). © **081-4422149.** www.marketplace.it/museo.nazionale. Admission 10€. Audioguide and guided tours 4€ (2.50€ with Artecard) in Italian or English (90 min.). Wed–Mon 9am–7:30pm. Ticket booth closes 90 min. earlier. Closed Jan 1 and Dec 25. Bus R1, R2, or 24 to Via Pessina, or E1 to Via Costantinopoli. Metro: Museo or Cavour.

Museo Nazionale di Capodimonte ★★★ In the middle of a magnificent park that once was a hunting preserve for the Bourbon kings, this museum was created by Carlo III di Borbone in 1743 to house his mother's art collection (she was Elisabetta Farnese, and had her own share of the family's art endowment). Also on the grounds, the king founded the Capodimonte workshops in 1739 in his endeavor to develop a local high-end industry. The workshops produced artistic ceramics following a unique technique and style that made them famous around the world. The laboratories slowed down considerably in 1759, when the king left Naples to become king of Spain, but his son Ferdinando kept it going until 1805.

While the wooded park—still called *bosco reale* (royal woods) by locals—is a pleasant destination for a stroll (locals love to come here for family outings, especially on weekends), the museum is a prime destination for art lovers. In addition to its own huge collection, the museum hosts stellar annual exhibits. *Note:* You'll have to book your tickets well in advance if you are planning your visit during this yearly series of events.

While the **19th-Century Gallery,** on the mezzanine level, includes a number of interesting paintings, if this is your first visit, we recommend you head for the **Farnese Gallery** ★★, on the second floor, which features the stars of the collection, with several paintings by some of the best Italian artists—**Tiziano, Raffaello, Masaccio, Botticelli, Perugino, Luca Signorelli, Sandro Botticelli, Correggio, Giovanni Bellini, Mantegna, Parmigianino, Guido Reni, Caravaggio**—and by a number of the best artists from the Flemish school, such as **Pieter Bruegel the Elder** and **Van Dyck.** Besides paintings, the gallery holds sculptures and precious tapestries. Smaller but also worth a visit is the **Borgia Collection** ★, also on the second floor. It contains many precious Renaissance **ivory** and **enamel** pieces.

The **Royal Apartments** ★ take up much of the second floor. In the **Porcelain Gallery** ★, you'll find a number of unique pieces, with objects and dinner plates from all the royal palaces of Naples, including *bisquits* (a firing process) of **Sèvres** and **Vienna,** and porcelains of **Meissen** and, of course, the famous **Capodimonte** ceramics created in the local workshops. Nearby is the **De Ciccio Collection** with more porcelain, but also paintings and precious objects. **The Armory** has interesting pieces, but is overshadowed by the famous **Salottino di Porcellana** ★★, a small room completely inlaid with porcelain, made for Maria Amalia in the 18th century for the royal palace of Portici.

A **gallery** ★ dedicated to "Painting in Naples from the 13th to the 19th Centuries" occupies the third floor, and provides a unique overview of artists who worked in Naples. It includes works by **Sodoma, Vasari, Tiziano, Caravaggio,** and **Luca Giordano;** here you can also admire the seven beautiful 16th-century **tapestries** ★ from the **d'Avalos Collection,** and also the picture collection including work by **Ribera** and **Luca Giordano.** The contemporary art collection extends from the third to the fourth floor, with works by Alberto Burri, Jannis Kounellis, Andy Warhol, and Enzo Cucchi, among others. On the fourth floor you can also find a **Photography Collection** and the **Galleria dell'Ottocento** focusing on painters of the 19th century (Neapolitans, but also other Italians and foreigners).

Note: The special exhibits at this museum are hugely popular; reserve your tickets in advance.

reservations from Italy, or 06-39967050 from mobiles and from abroad. www.museo-capodimonte.it.
Admission 7.50€; 6.50€ after 2pm. Audioguide (70 min.) 4€ (2.50€ with Artecard). Thurs–Tues 8:30am–
7:30pm. Ticket booth closes 1 hr. earlier. Closed Jan 1 and Dec 25. Bus: R4, R24, 137, 160, 161, or 178.

RELIGIOUS NAPLES: CHURCHES & MONASTERIES

Perhaps the most religious city in Italy, Naples rivals Rome when it comes to the number
and beauty of its churches. It is impossible to list them all, although we wanted to; we
cover only the best.

Cappella del Monte di Pietà (Finds)   The sober 16th-century palace of the Monte di
Pietà hides one of Naples's art treasures: a perfectly preserved and richly decorated 16th-
century chapel. Opening onto the palazzo's courtyard, the chapel is decorated by important artists of the 16th and 17th centuries. On the facade are two **sculptures** by Pietro
Bernini, father of the famous Lorenzo. Inside the church, the **ceiling** bears a beautiful
fresco depicting scenes from the life of Jesus by Belisario Corenzio. Farther on, you can
visit the adjoining rooms, in particular the **sacristy** ★ at the beginning, and the **Sala
delle Cantoniere** ★ at the end, perfectly preserved in 17th-century style, down to the
furnishings and floors. ***Note:*** For a visit, you need to ask the *custode* (keeper), at the Pio
Monte di Pietà.

Via Biagio dei Librai 114. ☎ **081-5807111.** Free admission. Sat 9am–7pm; Sun and holidays 9am–2pm.
Bus: C57, R2. Metro: Dante.

Museo Cappella Sansevero ★ (Kids)   In the 18th century, Prince Raimondo di
Sangro of Sansevero remodeled this funerary chapel—built in the 16th century for his
family—and lavishly decorated it with sculptures. Among those are some particularly
renowned works, starting with Giuseppe Sanmartino's *Cristo Velato* (**Veiled Christ**) ★,
created by the Neapolitan sculptor in 1753, and still with the original patina. The challenge of depicting veiled figures in stone seems to have obsessed the prince: Other sculptures here are the *Disinganno,* a technical virtuoso by Queirolo showing a standing
figure of a man disentangling himself from a net; and *Pudicizia,* a masterpiece by Cor-
radini showing a veiled naked woman. The prince—a student of science, an inventor,
and an alchemist—achieved fame as a master of the occult, and the decoration of the
chapel has contributed to this reputation. The most striking (and weird) objects here are
two actual human bodies conserved in the crypt, whose circulatory systems are perfectly
preserved after 2 centuries. The chapel is also used for art exhibits and concerts—call for
schedules.

Via Francesco De Sanctis 19 (south of Via dei Tribunali, 1 block east of Via Mezzocannone). ☎ **081-
5518470.** www.museosansevero.it. Admission 6€; 1€ discount with Artecard. Mon and Wed–Sat 10am–
6pm; Sun 10am–1:30pm. Last admission 20 min. before closing. Closed May 1 and Easter Monday. Bus:
R1, R2, or R3. Metro: Dante.

Catacombe di San Gennaro (Catacombs of St. Gennaro) ★ (Kids)   These catacombs, attached to the church of San Gennaro Extra Moenia, are the most important in
southern Italy, prized for both the length of the period they were in continued use—from
the emergence of Christianity until the 10th century—and the well-preserved **fresco
cycles** ★ that decorate their corridors and chapels—spanning from the 2nd to the 10th
centuries. Organized on two levels, its broad corridors and halls distinguish it from the
narrower Roman catacombs. Among the most interesting things here is the **Cripta dei
Vescovi** ★, a bishop burial chamber magnificently decorated with mosaics dating from
the 5th century. The lower level holds the **Basilica di Sant'Agrippino** *ipogea* ("ipogean,"

or subterranean) where St. Agrippino, the 3rd-century bishop of Naples, is buried. Also nearby is the **Cubicolo di San Gennaro,** with the tomb of the patron saint of Naples, whose remains were moved here in the 5th century.

Via Capodimonte 13. ✆ **081-7411071.** Admission 3€. By guided tour only. Tues–Sun on the hour 9am–noon; in summer also 2 and 3pm. Bus: 24 or R4 to Via Capodimonte, and then down an alley alongside the church Madre del Buon Consiglio.

Certosa e Museo Nazionale di San Martino (Carthusian Monastery and National Museum of St. Martin) ★   Originally built in 1325 and redone in the 17th century, this great monastery has been restored to all its original beauty. Entering from the courtyard, you first come to the **church** ★, a masterpiece of baroque decoration, from the marble **floor** to the various works of art by artists such as Jusepe de Ribera (various paintings), Giuseppe Sanmartino (sculptures), and Battistello Caracciolo (frescoes). Do not overlook the marble **transenna** of the presbytery, decorated with precious stones (lapis lazuli and agate), and the **Cappella del Tesoro** ★, with a rich altar made of the same materials; beautiful **frescoes** by Luca Giordano—including the *Trionfo di Giuditta*—decorate the ceiling. You can also view the *Deposizione* by Jusepe de Ribera. You can then continue to the **Chiostro Grande** ★★. The **Quarto del Priore** ★★—the elegant apartment used for the reception of important personalities—contains a number of masterpieces, including a *Madonna col Bambino e San Giovannino* by Pietro Bernini. The monastery also houses the **Museo Nazionale di San Martino,** which has several sections. One of our favorites is the ***presepi*** section (or **manger scenes**) ★, off the Chiostro dei Procuratori. Some of the scenes are unbelievably complex, such as the *presepio* (Nativity scene) **Cuciniello,** created in 1879 with a collection of 18th-century figures and accessories. Other sections include the **Images and Memories of Naples exhibit** ★★, on the first and second floors, displaying paintings, sculpture, porcelain, and precious objects, and the **Collezione Rotondo** ★, with paintings and bronze sculpures by Neapolitan artists of the 19th century. In the Gothic **cellars** of the monastery, you will find sections dedicated to sculpture and epigraphy. On the second floor is the library that houses the **Prints and Drawings Collection,** with over 8,000 pieces.

Largo San Martino 8. ✆ **081-5781769.** Admission 6€. Thurs–Tues 8:30am–7:30pm; ticket booth closes 90 min. earlier. Closed Jan 1 and Dec 25. Metro: Vanvitelli and then bus V1 to Piazzale San Martino. Bus: C28, C31, or C36 to Piazza Vanvitelli. Funicular: Centrale to Piazza Fuga or Montesanto to Morghen.

Chiesa and Quadreria dei Girolamini ★ (Finds)   Rarely visited, this church and its attached convent hide a great collection of artwork by some prominent Italian Renaissance artists. The church was built between the end of the 16th century and the beginning of the 17th. Among the masterpieces you'll find inside are: in the counterfacade, a **fresco** by Luca Giordano; in the first chapel to the right, *Sant'Alessandro Moribondo* by Pietro da Cortona; in the transept, **frescoes** by Francesco Solimena and **statues** by Pietro Bernini; and over the altar in the sacristy, the painting *San Giovanni Battista,* by Guido Reni.

In the annexed **Casa dei Padri dell'Oratorio** (entrance on Via Duomo 142), you can visit the beautiful **Chiostro Maggiore** ★ and the **Quadreria dei Girolamini** ★★, a rich collection of paintings donated to the convent and including notable artists such as Cavalier d'Arpino, Sermoneta, Guido Reni, and Jusepe de Ribera. You can also visit the splendid **library** ★, with its beautiful halls, especially the **Sala Grande.**

Chiesa: Via dei Tribunali. ✆ **081-292316.** Free admission. Mon–Sat 9am–1pm and 4–7pm; Sun 9am–1pm. **Quadreria:** Via Duomo 142. ✆ **081-449139.** www.girolamini.it. Free admission. Mon–Sat 9am–12:30pm. Closed holidays and Aug. Bus: R1, R2, R3, or R4. Metro: Dante.

Chiesa del Gesù Nuovo ★   Built by Jesuits in 1470, this church transformed Palazzo Sanseverino, the palace of the Prince of Salerno. Its striking facade in the rare technique *bugnato a punta di diamante* (ashlar work) was preserved from the palazzo's original facade, while a baroque portal was created to englobe the original Renaissance portal. The church's interior is majestic, featuring stucco, frescoes, and marble decorations by some of Naples's best artists from the 16th century to the beginning of the 19th. Among the masterpieces are the impressive **fresco** ★ by Francesco Solimena, called the *Expulsion of Eliodorus from the Temple,* and the rich decorations in the left transept, including a beautiful **altar** ★ and **statues** ★ of Jeremiah and David by Cosimo Fanzago. The **oratory** is usually closed, but you can request entry from the *custode* (keeper) of the Liceo at number 1 of Piazza del Gesù.

On the piazza outside the church, you'll find one of Naples's several baroque spires, the **Guglia dell'Immacolata,** a tall pile of statues and reliefs. Typically Neapolitan, this kind of religious monument is modeled after processional objects—part float, part conglomeration of statues and figures—built for religious celebrations from baroque times until the 1950s. This particular spire was created in 1750 by Matteo Bottighero and Francesco Pagano to celebrate one of the major points of the Jesuits' teachings; it depicts Jesuit saints and the story of Mary.

Piazza del Gesù (off Via Toledo on Via Benedetto Croce). ℂ **081-5518613** or 081-5578151. Free admission. Daily 7am–12:30pm and 4–7:30pm. Bus: R1, R2, R3, or R4. Metro: Dante.

Chiesa di Santa Maria di Monteoliveto (aka Sant'Anna dei Lombardi) ★★
Built in 1411, the Chiesa di Monteoliveto is not large but, as this was one of the favorite churches of the Aragonese royal family, is chock-full of art. The church opens onto a pretty square graced by the **Fontana di Monteoliveto.** The most beautiful baroque fountain in Naples, it was built for Don Pedro de Aragona in 1699, based on a design by Cosimo Fanzago: It is a grandiose celebration of royal authority, with white marble eagles and lions crowned by the bronze statue of Carlo II d'Asburgo.

In the atrium, behind the church's elegant facade in *piperno* (a unique colorful stone that was carved in underground quarries in the Naples area), is the tomb of the architect Domenico Fontana. Inside the church are three superb Renaissance chapels: **Cappella Correale** ★ to the right of the entrance, with an altar by Benedetto da Maiano and the *San Cristoforo* over the altar by Francesco Solimena; **Cappella Piccolomini** ★ to the left of the entrance—an almost perfect replica of the more well-known Chapel of the Cardinal of Portugal in the Florentine San Miniato al Monte church, graced by the tomb of Maria d'Aragona by Antonio Rossellino and Benedetto da Maiano; and **Cappella Tolosa** ★, also to the left, attributed to Giuliano da Maiano and decorated in the styles of Brunelleschi and della Robbia. This last chapel is a triumph of sculpture, and gives a good overview of 15th- and 16th-century Neapolitan sculpture. From the right of the presbytery you can access the old **sacristy** ★ with its vaulted ceilings frescoed by Giorgio Vasari. Its walls, decorated with wood inlays depicting classical panoramas, musical instruments, and other scenes, were created by Giovanni da Verona between 1506 and 1510.

Piazza Monteoliveto 44 (off Via Monteoliveto, 1 block east of Via Toledo/Via Roma). ℂ **081-5513333.** Free admission. Mon–Fri 9am–noon; Sat 9am–noon and 5:30–6:30pm. Bus: R1, R2, R3, or R4. Metro: Dante.

Complesso Museale di Santa Chiara (Museum Complex of St. Clare) ★★
The most famous basilica in Naples, this church was built in 1310 by King Roberto I d'Angió as the burial church for the Angevin dynasty. In the 18th century, it was lavishly

decorated by the best artists of the time, but bombings in 1943 destroyed much of the art. A subsequent restoration in 1953 brought it back to its original Gothic structure. A large rose window decorates the facade, flanked by a majestic bell tower that dominates the neighborhood (its lower part is 14th century).

The interior is simple but monumental in size, with 10 chapels opening onto the central nave. It contains many royal tombs, including the grandiose **tomb of Roberto d'Angió** ★, a magnificent example of Tuscan-style Renaissance sculpture. From the sacristy you can access the *Coro delle Clarisse* **(Choir of the Clares)** ★, with its beautiful 14th-century marble portal. The nuns sat in the *coro* during Mass, protected from the public; only fragments remain, sadly, of Giotto's frescoes that decorated its walls. After your visit to the basilica, walk behind the church and enter the door to the right: It leads to the unique **Chiostro delle Clarisse** ★★, the monastery's main cloister. Strikingly decorated with bright majolica tiles in the mid–18th century, it is considered a masterpiece of Neapolitan art. The spaces adjacent to the cloister house a museum, the **Museo dell'Opera di Santa Chiara,** dedicated to the history of the monastery and attached basilica. It exhibits sculptures and reliefs by local artists, including the beautiful *Crucifiction* and the *Visitation,* both by Tino di Camaino; it also gives access to the excavations of thermal baths from the 1st or 2nd century A.D.

Church: Via Santa Chiara 49 (off Via Benedetto Croce). ✆ **081-5526280.** Free admission. Mon and Wed–Sat 7:30am–1pm and 4:30–8pm. **Cloister & Museum:** Via Benedetto Croce 16. ✆ **081-7971256.** www.monasterodisantachiara.eu. Admission 5€. Mon and Wed–Sat 9:30am–5:30pm; Sun 10am–2:30pm. Bus: R1, R2, R3, or R4. Metro: Dante.

Duomo (Cattedrale di Santa Maria Assunta) ★★★ A monumental construction, graced inside by 110 ancient granite columns which support its Latin cross structure, the Duomo was begun by King Carlo I d'Angió in the 13th century and finished by his successor Roberto d'Angió in 1313. The grandiose interior of the cathedral is lavishly decorated. Among the most precious artwork is the painting *Assunta* by **Perugino,** located on the right side of the transept. Several chapels open from both naves and the transept; the most splendid is the Gothic **Cappella Capece Minutolo** ★★, with its beautiful 13th-century frescoes and mosaic floor. To the right of the presbytery is another Gothic chapel of great beauty, the **Cappella Tocco** ★. You'll also want to descend downstairs to access the **Succorpo** or **Cappella Carafa** ★, one of the most elegant Renaissance architectural structures ever created, in the style of **Bramante.**

From the right nave, the third chapel to the right is the monumental **Cappella di San Gennaro** ★★, dedicated to the patron saint of Naples. Richly decorated with precious marbles, gold leaf, frescoes, and artworks, it is considered by art historians as the highest achievement of Neapolitan baroque. The fresco cycle around the dome, illustrating the life of San Gennaro, is by **Domenichino,** while the oil painting over copper, depicting San Genarro, is by Jusepe de Ribera—the rich frame of gilded bronze and lapis lazuli is by Onofrio D'Alessio. The famous reliquaries containing the skull and the blood of San Gennaro—which is said to miraculously liquefy each September 19 (Feast Day of San Gennaro) as well as the first Sunday in May and December 16—are inside a safe over the main altar; they are exposed to the public only on the dates of the miraculous event: for 1 week in May, 1 week in September, and on the 16th of December.

From the left nave, the third chapel entrance to the left gives access to **Santa Restituta** ★★, the oldest basilica in Naples and the city's Duomo until the new one was finished in the 14th century. Built in the 4th century by Emperor Constantine, it is a very atmospheric church in spite of the many changes it underwent—its facade and atrium were demolished when it was annexed to the Duomo, while its apse was redecorated in baroque style in the 17th century; also, to strengthen its structure, the two outermost of its original five naves were closed into chapels. We love the sixth chapel on the left, with its luminous 14th-century **mosaic** by Lello da Orvieto and two beautiful 13th-century reliefs. Also, make sure not to miss the **Baptistery of San Giovanni in Fonte** ★★, which you can access from an entrance at the end of the right nave. Founded in the 4th century, it is the world's oldest Western baptistery. Its cupola is decorated with beautiful **mosaics** from the 5th century (unfortunately, some of them are damaged). From the end of the left nave, you can access the archaeological excavations under the Duomo, which date back to Greek times.

Adjacent to the Duomo is the entrance to the *Museo del Tesoro di San Gennaro* **(Museum of the Treasure of San Gennaro)** ★. The holdings here are exceptional in quality and quantity: The amount of the treasure is so great that the museum rotates its exhibits annually over a multiple-year cycle. An additional reason to visit is that the museum gives access to the Duomo's **sacristy** ★★, beautifully decorated with **frescoes** by Luca Giordano and paintings by **Domenichino.** In the sacristy, you can also arrange an appointment to visit Santa Restituta and the Cappella Minutolo if you find them closed.

Cathedral: Via Duomo 147. ✆ **081-449097.** Free admission. Mon–Sat 8am–12:30pm and 4:30–7pm; Sun and holidays 8:30am–1pm and 5–7pm. **Excavations:** Mon–Fri 9am–noon and 4:30–7pm; Sat–Sun and holidays 9am–12:30pm. **Museum:** Via Duomo 149. ✆ **081-421609.** www.museosangennaro.com. Admission 6€. Tues–Sat 9:30am–5pm; Sun and holidays 9am–2pm. Bus: E1 to Via Duomo. Metro: Cavour.

San Domenico Maggiore ★★ Opening onto one of Naples's most beautiful squares—graced by the **Guglia San Domenico,** a marble spire erected between 1658 and 1737 in gratitude for the end of that century's plague—this church actually offers its back to the public: Its facade, following an Angevin tradition, is only visible from the inner courtyard. Built by Carlo II d'Angiò between 1283 and 1324, San Domenico Maggiore encloses the older church of **San Michele Arcangelo a Morfisa,** which is still accessible from the transept. Inside both are innumerable works of art, including many **Renaissance monumental tombs** graced by sculptures and carvings, as well as 14th-century **frescoes** and 15th- and 16th-century **paintings.** The main **altar** is a beautiful work of marble inlay from the 16th century.

Piazza San Domenico Maggiore (off Via San Biagio dei Librai). ✆ **081-449097** or 081-459298. Free admission. Daily 9am–noon and 5–7pm. Metro: Piazza Cavour.

San Giovanni a Carbonara ★ (Finds) Built in 1343 with the annex convent, this church was used by the Angevin dynasty to bury their last members. It is one of Naples's

Impressions

It would be rash to say that the whole population of Naples is always in the street, for if you look into the shops or cafes, or, I dare say, the houses, you will find them quite full. . . . Then there is the expansive temperament, which if it were shut up would probably be much more explosive than it is now. As it is, it vents itself in volleyed detonations and scattered shots, which language can give no sense of. For the true sense of it you must go to Naples, and then you will never lose the sense of it.

—William Dean Howells, *Naples and Her Joyful Noise,* 1908

undiscovered jewels, which is not surprising, considering that it's rather difficult to find. First, you'll need to climb a scenic staircase leading to the baroque Consolazione a Carbonara church, and continue farther up until you reach three portals. Admire the central one—the Gothic entrance to the Cappella Santa Monica—and take the portal to the left. This will lead you into a terraced courtyard, and there you will finally find the entrance to San Giovanni, which you can access from its 15th-century lateral portal. Inside the church are several important works of art, including, in the apse—flat, not rounded as is usual—the **Monumental Tomb of King Ladislao,** a 15th-century masterpiece by several Tuscan artists. Behind the monument is the circular **Cappella Caracciolo del Sole,** with a majolica floor and beautiful **frescoes** from the 15th century, very handsome but less harmonious than the other circular chapel in this church—**Cappella Caracciolo di Vico.** This chapel, located to the left of the presbytery, is an architectural tour de force from the beginning of the 16th century, graced by a beautifully carved 16th-century altar. At the end of the courtyard, an entrance gives access to yet another chapel: the **Cappella Seripando,** with *Crucifiction* by Vasari.

Via San Giovanni a Carbonara 5 (5 short blocks east of the Duomo). ℭ **081-295873.** Free admission. Mon–Sat 8am–noon and 4:30–8:30pm; Sun 8am–2pm. Metro: Piazza Cavour.

San Gregorio Armeno Giving its name to the street famous for its manger artists and vendors (see "Shopping for Local Crafts," p. 127), this church and its adjoining monastery are little visited. Yet they are well worth a visit to admire the bell tower and the richly decorated interior. Dating from the 8th century, the church's interior was redone in 1580, with lavish use of gold leaf and artwork by famous masters of the time: The exceptional **wooden ceiling** ★ was carved and painted by Teodoro d'Errico, while the **frescoes** ★ in the counterfacade are by Luca Giordano. You should also visit the pretty **cloister** ★ of the attached monastery (through the entrance outside the church, beyond the bell tower), beautifully preserved and graced by a marble **fountain** depicting Jesus meeting the good Samaritan.

Via San Gregorio Armeno 44 (btw. Via San Biagio dei librai and Via dei Tribunali, 3 short blocks west of Via Duomo). Free admission. Daily 9:30am–noon. Metro: Piazza Cavour.

San Lorenzo Maggiore ★★ (Kids) The most beautiful of Naples's medieval churches, San Lorenzo is famous for its literary past—here Giovanni Boccaccio met his Fiammetta in 1334, and the attached convent hosted Francesco Petrarca for a period. Originally a basilica from the 6th century A.D., the church was rebuilt in 1270 by Carlo I d'Angiò and his successor in Gothic style; its facade is baroque as the original was partially destroyed by an earthquake. The interior is airy and holds innumerable works of art, including 13th- and 14th-century **frescoes,** as well as beautiful **altars** and monumental tombs. From the baroque cloister you can visit the Chapter Hall and the refectory of the monastery, built in the 13th century. From the 14th-century cloister, enter the **Greek and Roman excavations** ★, where you'll see a slice of the city's layers of construction, from the Roman Macellum—the city market dating from the 1st century A.D.—complete with merchant stalls, to a paleochristian basilica, to a medieval building to, finally, the existing buildings. Children usually love the underground visit. The best pieces from the excavations are displayed in the **museum,** which also features a collection of historical ceremonial religious attire and a collection of 18th-century *presepio* (Nativity scene) figures. *Note:* At presstime, the museum is still being organized and is only partially accessible.

www.sanlorenzomaggiorenapoli.it. Free admission. Mon–Sat 8am–noon and 5–7pm. **Excavations:** 𝄐 081-2110860. Admission 4€. Mon–Sat 9:30am–5:30pm; Sun and holidays 9:30am–1:30pm. Metro: Piazza Cavour.

San Paolo Maggiore ★   Founded between the 8th and 9th centuries A.D. over a preexisting Roman Temple of the Dioscuri—two of its columns remain on the facade—San Paolo Maggiore was completely redone in the 16th century. The interior was decorated by many important artists of the 17th and 18th century, but the standouts here are the statue *Angelo Custode* by Domenico Antonio Vaccaro to the left of the central nave; the **frescoes** in the sacristy—considered the best work of Francesco Solimena; and the **Cappella Firrao** to the left of the presbytery, one of the most beautiful baroque chapels in Naples.

Via San Paolo (off Via dei Tribunali, opposite Piazza San Gaetano). 𝄐 **081-454048.** Free admission. Daily 8am–noon and 5–7pm. Metro: Piazza Cavour.

Sant'Angelo a Nilo   Built in 1385 for the Brancaccio family and redone in the 18th century, this church merits a visit for its **Funerary Monument of Cardinal Rinaldo Brancaccio** ★★. This monument to the church's founder was created in Pisa by **Donatello** and **Michelozzo** between 1426 and 1427, and shipped by sea to Naples. Very modern for its time, the work merges Gothic and Renaissance elements. The two portals to the right of the presbytery, one from the 14th and the other from the 16th century, are also noteworthy.

The Church of Sant'Angelo a Nilo gets its name from the Greek-Roman **Statue of the Egyptian god Nile** in the small square near the church. Originally carved for merchants from Alexandria who worked in the area, the statue was lost for centuries and was found again in the 15th century. In typical Neapolitan spirit, the statue of the river god, with his babies representing the river tributaries, was interpreted as a representation of motherly Naples, nourishing its children; hence the nickname still in use today among the locals—*cuorp'e Napule* or "body of Naples." The statue's head was a 17th-century addition.

Piazzetta Nilo (off Via Benedetto Croce). Free admission. Mon–Sat 8:30am–1pm and 4:45–7pm; Sun 8:30am–1pm. Bus: E1 or R2. Metro: Piazza Cavour.

PUBLIC NAPLES

Fontana del Nettuno   Naples's most beautiful fountain has a unique history of mobility. Originally built for Viceroy Enrico Guzman, count of Olivares, it was located in front of the Arsenal for 30 years. In 1622, the Duca d'Alba had it moved to the Piazza del Palazzo Reale. In 1637, it was moved again in front of the Castel dell'Ovo. A few years later, worried that it was dangerously positioned (open to attacks from the sea), city authorities moved it "temporarily" to Piazza delle Corregge. It stayed there until the beginning of the 20th century, when it was moved again to its present—and maybe permanent—position.

Piazza G. Bovio (off Via Medina). Bus: C57, E3, or R3.

Galleria Umberto I   This gallery is an elegant glass-and-iron covered passage following a Greek cross shape, with each of its four arms opening onto a street on one end and meeting at a rotunda, covered with a cupola, on the other. Built at the end of the 19th century—20 years after its larger Milanese counterpart—this is a splendid Liberty-style (Italian Art Nouveau) construction with obvious Parisian inspiration. Inside, the galleria is lined with elegant shops and cafes.

The Best Gelato in Naples

The following list of our favorite gelato is not complete without a mention of **Gelateria G. Mazzaro** (p. 105). For more info on Italian gelato, see p. 29.

- **Chalet da Ciro,** Via Caracciolo, in Mergellina (✆ **081-669928;** closed Wed), is known for its superlative *nocciola* (hazelnut flavor).
- **Fantasia Gelati,** Via Toledo 381 (✆ **081-5511212**), is located with another branch on Piazza Vanvitelli, in Vomero.
- **Gelateria La Scimmia,** Piazza Carità 4, off Via Toledo (✆ **081-5520272**), prepares its gelato from scratch with fresh fruits. This is the original parlor, better than the branch at Piazzetta Nilo, off Via Benedetto Croce.
- **Gelateria Otranto,** Via Scarlatti 78, off Piazza Vanvitelli (✆ **081-5587498;** closed Wed) is our favorite in the Vomero neighborhood.
- **Gran Bar Riviera,** Riviera di Chiaia 181 (✆ **081-665026**), is popular particularly among the evening crowds.
- **Polo Nord,** Via Pietro Colletta 41 (✆ **081-205431;** closed Sun) is not too touristy, but is also convenient to the Duomo.
- **Bilancione,** Via Posillipo, off Piazza San Luigi, Posillipo (✆ **081-7691923**), has views over the Bay that rival the gelato.

You'll find a second Liberty-era gallery in town, **Galleria del Principe di Napoli** (off Piazza Cavour to the right; Metro Piazza Cavour), which is virtually unknown, probably because of its location outside the most touristy area of Via Toledo.

4 entrances: To the right off Via Toledo as you come from Piazza del Plebiscito, Via Giuseppe Verdi, Via Santa Brigida, and Via San Carlo. Bus: R2 or R3 to Piazza Trieste e Trento.

Piazza del Plebiscito ★★ This is the most beautiful piazza in Naples, defined by the majestic colonnade of **San Francesco di Paola**—an 1817 church built in full neoclassical style and inspired by the Roman Pantheon—and the elegant neoclassical facade of the Royal Palace. In the square are two equestrian statues, one of **Carlo III** by Antonio Canova and one of **Ferdinando I** (only the horse is by Canova). The square is fittingly called the "salotto" (living room) by Neapolitans, as it has been completely closed to traffic and locals use it as a gathering place. Nearby is Piazza Trieste e Trento, with the Fontana del Carciofo, and the start of Via Toledo (Neapolitans call this Via Roma), an extremely popular promenade and shopping street.

Off Piazza Trieste e Trento (btw. Via Chiaia and Via C. Console). Bus: R2 or R3 to Piazza Trieste e Trento.

Teatro San Carlo ★ Built for Carlo Borbone by Antonio Medrano, the Teatro San Carlo is among Europe's most beautiful opera houses and one of the most famous. A neoclassical jewel with an ornate gilded interior, the San Carlo was the first opera theater in the world; it was inaugurated on November 4, 1737. The facade was added in 1812 by Antonio Piccolini, who rebuilt the interior after a fire destroyed it in 1816. The theater hall, which holds 1,470 seats, is considered to have even better acoustics than Milan's famous La Scala, and such artists as Donizetti, Rossin, and Verdi produced and directed masterpieces here. You can appreciate its architecture and decoration by taking the guided tour (in Italian or English) or come for a performance (see "Naples After Dark," later in this chapter) and see the building in its full glory.

Via San Carlo 93. (C) **081-400300** or 081-7972111; 081-7972331 tickets; 081-5534565 guided tours res- ervations. www.teatrosancarlo.it. Guided tours 5€. Ticket hours: Tues–Sat 10am–1pm and 4:30–6:30pm; Sun 10am–1pm. Tours: Thurs–Mon 9am–5:30pm; Tues–Wed by advance reservation only. Bus: R2 or R3 to Via San Carlo.

Villa Comunale ★ **Kids**   Created in 1780 according to a design by Luigi Vanvitelli, as the private Royal Promenade for King Ferdinando IV Bourbon, this park was later transformed by the king into a public garden. The park is a baroque creation graced by statues, fountains—including the beloved **Fontana delle Paperelle** ("fountain of the ducks")—and several elegant buildings such as **Casina Pompeiana, Chiosco della Musica,** and **Stazione Zoologica** with Europe's oldest **aquarium,** specializing in the study of local marine life. The Villa Comunale also hosts an antiques market ((C) **081-7612541;** usually on the 3rd and 4th weekends of each month, 8:30am-1pm), which is very popular. You can find excellent souvenirs as well as more important pieces. If you have young children, we also recommend the merry-go-round and children playground located in the southeast corner of the park; it might not be up with the best in the U.S. but still is very welcome by the younger ones. It is not so unpleasant for parents as well, who can sit and look at the seaside promenade.

Park: Piazza Vittoria. (C) **081-7611131.** Daily 7am–midnight. **Aquarium:** (C) **081-5833111** or 081-2452099. Admission free. Tues–Sun 9am–5pm. Bus: C82 or R2.

THE KID ZONE

Throughout this book, look for the "kids" icon to indicate that an attraction is kid friendly. The **CitySightseeing** open-top bus tours, and the fascinating **Napoli Sotterranea** (below and p. 124) and the University of Naples museums ((C) **081-2537587;** www.musei.unina.it), are great for the younger set. The university's *Museo di Paleontologia* **(Paleonthology Museum),** Largo San Marcellino 10 ((C) **081-2537516**), contains a large fossil collection, with splendid fish fossils from local digs, and even a carnivorous dinosaur. For some cool rocks and minerals from around the globe, the *Museo di Mineralogia* **(Mineralogy Museum),** Via Mezzocannone 8 ((C) **081-2535163**), has a unique section on Vesuvian minerals as well as a real gold nugget, a diamond from South Africa, meteorites, and beautiful crystals. Animal lovers will enjoy the *Museo di Zoologia* **(Zoology Museum),** Via Mezzocannone 8 ((C) **081-2535164**). Admission is 2.50€ for one museum (1.50€ kids), 3.50€ for two museums (2€ kids), or 4.50€ for all of them (3€ kids; Tues–Wed and Fri 9am–1:30pm, Mon and Thurs 9am–1:30pm and 3–5pm, Sat–Sun and holidays 9am–1pm; bus R2 to Corso Umberto-Mezzocannone). See "Family Travel," p. 58 for more tips.

GUIDED TOURS

CitySightseeing Napoli ((C) **081-5517279;** www.napoli.city-sightseeing.it) offers hop-on-hop-off double-decker bus tours of the city. Buses depart from Piazza Municipio/ Parco Castello and run with varying frequency to all major attractions. Tickets are valid for 24 hours on all lines and can be purchased onboard for 22€ for adults, 11€ for children ages 6 to 15; and 66€ for a family (2 adults and 3 children 18 and under). You'll get a 10% discount with your Artecard (p. 110).

   MAN-Museo Aperto Napoli ((C) **081-5636062;** www.museoapertonapoli.it) is the cultural organization serving Naples's historic district. It is based in a large cultural and information center (Via Pietro Colletta 85, to the right of Castel Capuano, at the eastern edge of the historic district; daily 10am–6pm) where you'll find a knowledgeable and kind multilingual staff, a multimedia center with information on the historic district, exhibits on the area, as well as a cafe offering typical local products, a bookshop, a small space with crafts for sale, and, luckily, bathrooms. The center offers all kinds of services useful to the tourist, from maps and information on the historic district, to umbrellas on loan and excellent guided tours: Choose among four self-guided audio tours or walking tours with a live guide; all tours are offered in six languages.

Napoli Sotterranea (✆ 081-296944; www.lanapolisotterranea.it), or "Naples Underground," organizes guided tours of the city's abandoned aqueduct tunnels. The tunnels date back some 5,000 years and feature ancient Greek and Roman artifacts—in particularly a recently uncovered Greek theater—as well as more modern sites, such as the galleries used as hideouts during World War II. The tour lasts about 2 hours and meets at Piazza San Gaetano 68, off Via dei Tribunali, 3 blocks west of Via Duomo (bus R1, R4, 24, CS, C57, or 201 to Dante, E1 to Via Duomo; Metro: Dante). Especially popular among older children and teens, the tours cost 9.30€ (10% off with Artecard) and usually take place Thursday at 9pm; Saturday at 10am, noon, and 6pm; and Sunday and holidays at 10am, 11am, noon, and 6pm (call to confirm).

For more classic city tours, the agency **Every Tours,** Piazza del Municipio 5 (✆ 081-5518564), works for American Express in Naples; it organizes tours of the city as well as day excursions to Vesuvio and other sights. It's open Monday through Friday from 9am to 1:30pm and 3:30 to 7pm and Saturday from 9am to 1pm. Another good agency is **NapoliVision** (✆ 081-5595130; www.napolivision.it), offering guided tours of Naples, Pompei, and Capri starting at 30€ per person (20% discount with Artecard).

5 SPACCANAPOLI: A WALKING TOUR IN THE VERY HEART OF NAPLES

If you have only 1 afternoon in Naples, you should dedicate it to SpaccaNapoli, the succession of streets that divides Naples's historic district into two equal halves (*spacca* means "cracks"). The oldest part of town, it dates back to Greek and Roman times and has been the city's heart ever since. Along SpaccaNapoli and its cross streets, you will find Naples's most interesting artistic and cultural highlights, including the city's best churches, as well as notable small shops and traditional craftsmakers.

START:	Piazza del Gesù.
FINISH:	Duomo.
TIME:	2 hours for the walk, but you could turn it into a day-long tour with all the interior visits.
BEST TIMES:	Tuesday to Saturday 9am to 1pm and 4 to 7pm, when most of the churches and museums are open.
WORST TIMES:	Evening, when everything is closed. Sunday morning, because many churches cannot be visited during Mass. Monday, when some of the museums are closed. Lunchtime is also tricky, because only some of the attractions are open during that time.

❶ Piazza del Gesù

This pleasant piazza is defined by the **Guglia dell'Addolorata** at its center. One of Naples's typical baroque spires, this particular one was created by the Jesuits to commemorate their principles and was placed in front of their church, the **Chiesa del Gesù.** Its striking facade was once that of Palazzo Sanseverino, sold to the Jesuits in the 15th century and preserved when

Map legend:
1. Piazza del Gesù
2. Complesso Monumentale di Santa Chiara
3. Palazzo Filomarino
4. Piazza San Domenico Maggiore
 Pasticceria Scaturchio
5. Cappella Sansevero
6. Piazzetta Nilo
7. Cappella del Monte di Pietà
8. Chiesa di San Severino e San Sossio
9. Via San Gregorio Armeno
10. Piazza San Gaetano
 Pasticceria G. Mazzaro & Pizzeria Di Matteo
11. Chiesa and Quadreria dei Girolamini
12. Duomo

the church was built. Inside, you'll find several noteworthy works of art, including a **fresco** by Solimena.

Cross the piazza to the beginning of Via Benedetto Croce. A few steps farther up to the right is the:

2 Complesso Monumentale di Santa Chiara

This huge religious complex includes a church, a monastery, and a museum. The church itself contains some beautiful **monumental tombs** and the **Choir of the Clares,** but if your time is tight, walk along the church's outer wall and take the entrance to the right, leading to **the Clares' Cloister,** a majolica masterpiece that shouldn't be missed.

Return to Via Benedetto Croce and continue on to no. 12 at your left. It is:

3 Palazzo Filomarino

This palazzo is one of the oldest in Naples, built in the 14th century and redone in the 16th. You can go through its portal and peek at its monumental **internal court,** dating from the 16th century. Here lived and died the Italian 20th-century historian and philosopher Benedetto Croce, after whom the street is named.

Return to Via Benedetto Croce and continue on, passing a number of other elegant palazzi, until you reach:

4 Piazza San Domenico Maggiore

This is one of the most beautiful squares in Naples, graced in the center by the

Guglia di San Domenico, another of Naples's spires. This one was built between 1658 and 1737, in thanks for the end of a plague that struck in 1656. It is lined by beautiful palazzi; we recommend you peek into no. 17, the 18th-century **Palazzo di Sangro di Casacalenda,** finished by Vanvitelli and with a beautiful inner court; and no. 3, the 15th-century **Palazzo Petrucci,** with its striking original portal and loggias. Also in the square is **San Domenico Maggiore:** The artwork in this church is exceptional, including 14th-century **frescoes** and spectacular 16th-century **sculptures.**

> ☕ **TAKE A BREAK**
> Whether you need a break or not, you should stop at **Pasticceria Scaturchio,** Piazza San Domenico Maggiore 19 (☏ **081-5516944**), a historical pastry and coffee shop right on the square across from the church. Here you can enjoy excellent coffee and sample wonderful pastries, or try their *Ministeriale,* a medallion of dark chocolate with a liqueur cream filling.

Go back toward the church and walk along its side on Vicolo San Domenico. Take the first right, to Via Francesco de Sanctis. At no. 19 you will find the:

⑤ Museo Cappella Sansevero

This private chapel is decorated with some of the best Neapolitan sculptures from the 17th and 18th centuries. It is imbued with the spirit of its decorator, the mysterious alchemist and scientist Prince Raimondo di Sangro (see p. 115).

Walk back to Piazza San Domenico Maggiore, and continuing east on Via Benedetto Croce you'll find yourself in the:

⑥ Piazzetta Nilo

This piazza was named after the Hellenistic Egyptian statue of the Nile that graces one of its corners. Believed in medieval times to depict a mother with her children, the statue was adopted as an image of the city of Naples, hence its name in

local parlance—*cuorp'e Napule,* or "body of Naples." You'll also find the **Sant'Angelo a Nilo** church here, with its monumental tomb of Cardinal Brancaccio, designed and partly sculpted by **Donatello.**

Continue on Via Benedetto Croce, which turns into Via San Biagio dei Librai, named after the bookstores that traditionally have lined this street. At no. 114, to your right, is the:

⑦ Cappella del Monte di Pietà

This small chapel is a beautiful example of 16th-century art, perfect in style and richly decorated. Its sacristy and adjoining rooms are in perfectly preserved 18th-century style, down to the floors and furnishings.

Take the alley on the right before the Cappella Vicolo Santi Severino e Sossio and follow it to the entrance, to your left, of the:

⑧ Chiesa dei Santi Severino e Sossio (with Adjoining Monastery and State Archives)

This church is part of a large religious complex, the monastery of Saints Severino and Sossio, which is one of the oldest and richest monasteries of Naples. Both the church and the monastery are beautifully decorated with 16th-, 17th-, and 18th-century art. The monastery today houses the **State Archives** (entrance on Piazzetta Grande Archivio; ☏ **081-563811**), and it is open to the public. Visitors can see its 16th-century cloisters and beautifully frescoed rooms.

Return to Via San Biagio dei Librai and continue on to:

⑨ Via San Gregorio Armeno

This is one of Naples's most famous streets, known for the many artist workshops and merchants, specializing in *presepio* works (Nativity scenes; see "Shopping for Local Crafts," p. 127). On this lively street (hold on to your wallet and other precious belongings in the crowds), you'll find the **Church and Convent of San Gregorio Armeno,** with its beautifully preserved cloister and stunning artwork.

Continue on to the end of Via San Gregorio Armeno and turn right onto Via dei Tribunali to arrive at:

⑩ Piazza San Gaetano

This piazza is home to two of Naples's major churches, **San Lorenzo Maggiore** (to your right) and **San Paolo Maggiore** (to your left). Both are rich in art and history and well worth a visit (see the review for each, earlier in this chapter). In San Lorenzo Maggiore, you can descend into an archaeological excavation going back to the Greek layer of town, ancient Neapolis.

TAKE A BREAK
Caffetteria Pasticceria Gelateria G. Mazzaro, Palazzo Spinelli, Via Tribunali 359 (℃ **081-459248;** www. pasticceriamazzaro.it) is a valiant competitor of Pasticceria Scaturchio (above). In addition to excellent coffee and pastries, this shop makes some of the best gelato in town, in a variety of flavors.

Continue on Via dei Tribunali to Piazza dei Girolamini, opening to your left. Here is the:

⑪ Chiesa and Quadreria dei Girolamini

This church and attached monastery hold a treasure trove of artwork by great artists, including Luca Giordano, Pietro da Cortona, Francesco Solimena, Guido Reni, and Cavalier d'Arpino.

Return to Via dei Tribunali and continue on it until you reach Via del Duomo, where you'll make a left. To your right is the entrance to the:

⑫ Duomo

Monumental in scope, this church actually houses two other churches, the paleochristian **Santa Restituta**—known as Naples Duomo until the 14th century—and the 17th-century **Real Cappella del Tesoro di San Gennaro,** considered the most richly decorated chapel in Naples. The museum attached to the church is also well worth a visit.

TAKE A BREAK
Via dei Tribunali is home to some of the best pizzerie in Naples: If you're hankering for something substantial, head back along this street to **Pizzaiolo del Presidente,** Via Tribunali 120 (℃ **081-210903;** closed Sun); **Pizzeria Di Matteo,** Via dei Tribunali 94 (℃ **081-455262;** closed Sun); or, farther along, **Sorbillo,** Via Tribunali 32 (℃ **081-446643;** closed Sun). They all prepare excellent pizza (see "The Best Neapolitan Pizza in the Historic District," p. 103).

---

6 SHOPPING FOR LOCAL CRAFTS

Naples is a great source for Italian designer clothes and accessories, as well as for antiques and crafts. You have to know your stuff, though, because Naples is where counterfeit goods were invented back in the 17th or 18th century. It is a good idea to stay away from fakes altogether, even if the price seems right. You risk heavy fines at customs on your way home, as most countries are cracking down on such purchases as a way to protect brand identity.

Opening hours for stores are generally Monday to Saturday from 10:30am to 1pm and from 4 to 7:30pm.

Riviera di Chiaia, Via Calabritto, Via dei Mille, Via Filangeri, Via Poerio, and Piazza dei Martiri in **Chiaia** are where to go for the big-name **Italian fashion,** such as Valentino, Versace, Prada, and, of course, Salvatore Ferragamo—a Naples native (the latter four are on and around Piazza dei Martiri). The area is also great for exploring the many smaller boutiques and stores that mostly sell accessories and clothing.

The Presepio

Although the tradition of Nativity scenes—called *presepio* in Italy—dates back to the 13th century, the art form really reached its peak in the 18th and 19th centuries when the aristocracy competed to acquire figurines for their mangers, modeled by the famous sculptors of the time. All the great names of sculpture participated in this game, creating the terra-cotta parts of the figurines (usually the head and limbs). These were then mounted on mannequins of wire and *stoppa* (fiber) by craftsmen, and richly dressed with precious silk clothes embroidered with gold. Skilled sculptors, goldsmiths, tailors, and scenographers created everything from the figures to the complicated settings—grottoes, buildings, rivers, and ponds—combining their crafts into the first examples of multimedia art. Only the wealthier aristocrats could purchase such works of art, and all others had to make do with copies produced by Nativity craftsmen.

The *presepio* tradition is still alive today, and Neapolitan mangers go beyond typical Nativity representations to depict current historical and political happenings. Among the figures you'll find on sale are such recognizable characters as Princess Diana, Mother Teresa of Calcutta, and even Versace. **Via San Gregorio Armeno,** near the Duomo, is where most of the historic workshops, along with several merchants, are located. The artisans who have carried on their crafts from father to son have organized into a guild that protects their traditions, but only a few of them have survived the times. In the shops along this street, you'll find everything from characters and rocks, to grottoes and miniature street lamps. At the back of the few authentic laboratories, you'll also find figurines carefully crafted in different sizes, from amazingly precise half-inch miniatures to life-size figures to realistic scenes. While commercial mangers come in a variety of prices, the real thing is rather expensive, and few customers can afford the real thing: A medium-size hand-painted and handcrafted terra-cotta shepherd can cost as much as 300€.

In the vicinity are old-time local favorites, such as **Marinella,** Via Riviera di Chiaia 287 (© **081-7644214**), famous for classic and colorful ties; **Aldo Tramontano,** Via Chiaia 149 (© **081-414837**), for his handbags; and **Mario Talarico,** Vico Due Porte a Toledo 4/b (© **081-401979**), for his umbrellas. You'll also find some of the most reputable **antiques** dealers, such as **Regency House,** Via D. Morelli 36 (© **081-7643640**), and **Navarra,** Piazza dei Martiri (© **081-7643595**), but also **Maurizio Brandi,** Via Domenico Morelli 9 (© **081-7643882**).

Every third Saturday and Sunday of each month from 8am to 2pm (except in Aug), a *fiera antiquaria* (antiques fair; © **081-621951**) is held in the Villa Comunale di Napoli on Viale Dohrn.

In the **Vomero,** the best shopping is centered on Via Scarlatti.

For more casual shopping and some specialty stores, try strolling the popular **Via Toledo/Via Roma** in the Quartieri Spagnoli/historical center. Here you will find the historic chocolate factory **Gay-Odin,** Via Toledo 214 and Via Toledo 427 (© **081/417-** 843; www.gay-odin.it). The area is also home to the elegant shops of the **Galleria Umberto I,** such as **Ascione 1855** (© **081-421111**) and its **cameo** workshop, where you can observe the delicate process of carving agate and coral, and also purchase unique jewelry.

The best place to shop for crafts is the historic district. Head for **Via San Gregorio Armeno** ★★ if you are looking for *presepio.* The most reputable workshops are **Gambardella Pastori,** Via San Gregorio Armeno 40 (© **081-5517107**); **Giuseppe Ferrigno,** Via San Gregorio Armeno 8 (© **081-5523148**); and **Amendola,** Via San Gregorio Armeno 51 (© **081-5514899**). Via San Biagio dei Librai is lined with interesting shops selling paper goods and jewelry. Good addresses for antique prints and books are **Libreria Colonnese,** Via San Pietro a Majella 32 (© **081-459858**); **Dante e Descartes,** Via Mezzocannone 75 (© **081-5516771**; www.dantedescartes.it); and **Libreria Internazionale Treves,** Piazza Plebiscito (© **081-415211**).

7 NAPLES AFTER DARK

A warm southern city, Naples is best experienced outdoors. Neapolitans know this, and they enjoy spending their evenings on the terraces of the city's many popular cafes. One of the best is **Gran Caffè Gambrinus,** Via Chiaia 1, in Piazza Trento e Trieste (© **081-417582** or 081-414133). It's the oldest cafe in Naples, and its original Liberty-style interior was decorated by Antonio Curri in the 1860s. Another very popular spot is **La Caffetteria,** Piazza dei Martiri 25 (© **081-7644243**), frequented by local elegant crowds who come here for evening aperitifs.

OPERA   If you have the time, see a performance at **Teatro San Carlo,** Via San Carlo 98/f (© **081-7972412** or 081-7972331; fax 081-400902; www.teatrosancarlo.it), a world-class venue with a consistently high-level program. Performances take place Tuesday through Sunday, December through June. Tickets run between 45€ and 100€; you'll get a 10% discount with an Artecard (p. 110).

Another historic theater we recommend is **Teatro Mercadante,** Piazza Municipio 1 (© **081-5513396**), which always has a prestigious program. Tickets are around 50€, depending on the performance; you'll get a 10% discount with an Artecard (p. 110).

MUSIC   If you love music, Naples is the place to be. At any given time, the city is alive with concerts spanning from the classics to the most avant-garde. If classical music is your preference, besides the concerts at **Teatro San Carlo** (see above), the **Centro di Musica Antica Pietà dei Turchini,** Via Santa Caterina da Siena 38 (© **081-402395**; www.turchini.it), is one of the best venues in town; ticket prices depend on the performance, and you'll get a 25% discount with your Artecard (p. 110). Another excellent venue is the **Associazione Alessandro Scarlatti,** Piazza dei Martiri 58 (© **081-406011**; www.associazionescarlatti.it), which also organizes a successful concert series at Castel Sant'Elmo; tickets prices range from 15€ to 25€, with a 20% discount given to those with an Artecard (p. 110). For immersion in Neapolitan traditional music, the best address in town is the **Trianon, Teatro della Canzone Napoletana,** Piazza Vincenzo Calenda 9 (© **081-2440411**; www.teatrotrianon.it); the concert season usually starts in April, with performances Thursday through Sunday, but check the theater for changes in the programs. Ticket prices depend on seat and performance, but you'll get a 10% discount with the Artecard (p. 110).

Side margin: NAPLES 5 NAPLES AFTER DARK

ENOTECHE   The taste for good wine has been increasing, and Naples counts a growing number of excellent *enoteche*. This unique Italian venue merges the wine store and wine bar, often doubling as a restaurant. Following the popular Italian adage, never drink on an empty stomach, *enoteche* offer a small menu of high-quality local specialties. We recommend the quiet **Berevino,** Via Sebastiano 62 (✆ **081-290313;** closed Mon), as well as Barrique, Piazzetta Ascensione 9 (✆ **081-662721;** closed Mon), where you can sample the best local wines and a large choice of grappa and rhums while delighting in scrumptious small dishes from the weekly menu. The elegant and trendy **L'Ebrezza di Noè,** Vico Vetriera 9 (✆ **081-400104;** daily 7:30pm–12:30am), serves a simple menu of cured meats, cheeses, and appetizers to accompany the wide selection of wines from its excellent cellar. Its specialty is the discovery of unusual and lesser-known wines and vintages of great quality; don't be afraid to ask for guidance from the experienced staff. **Vinarium,** Vico Cappella Vecchia 7 (✆ **081-7644114;** Mon–Fri 10:30am–4:30pm; Mon–Sat 7pm–2:30am), is also popular but less upscale. It serves a more rounded menu to accompany the large choice of Campania's best D.O.C. wines (see "And Some Vino To Wash It All Down," p. 30) as well as other wines from farther afield. A specially priced selection of wines is introduced each day. Cantina di Triunfo, Via Riviera di Chiaia 64 (✆ **081-668101;** Tues–Sat 10am–7:30pm wine store; Mon–Sat 7:30pm–midnight wine bar cum restaurant), offers a limited but excellent menu to accompany its large choice of wines. **Enoteca Belledonne,** Vico Belledonne a Chiaia 18 (✆ **081-403162;** closed Sun) has a large choice of wines and snacks.

BARS, DISCOS & CLUBS   Naples is a port, a cosmopolitan city, and a university town all in one, so its lively nighttime scene is eclectic. Trendy bars and cafes stay open until at least until 2am every day of the week, while clubs stay open even later—usually until 4 or 5am—but often only from Thursday to Saturday. Bars and cafes usually don't charge covers, but clubs may charge a cover of about 14€.

Good places to grab a drink range from **Conoco Club,** Via Nilo 33 (✆ **081-5517784**), a pub with a good beer selection and a relaxed atmosphere, to the sleek and exotic recently reopened **Miami Bar Club,** Via Morghen 68C (✆ **081-2298332**). The historic **Velvet Zone** (aka "Velvet"), Via Cisterna dell'Olio 11 (✆ **339-6700234;** Fri–Sun 10am–4am) is a good place to dance.

For jazz, head to **Riot,** Via San Biagio 38 (✆ **081-5523231**), which has a young ambience; for live Neapolitan bands, check out **Vibes Café,** Via San Giovanni Maggiore Pignatelli 10 (✆ **081-5513984**), where you can dance inside or outside on the terrace in summer. Another good place for live music is **Il Re Nudo,** Via Manzoni 126 (✆ **081-7146272**), where you can hear anything from jazz to South American groups. **Rising South,** Via San Sebastiano 19 (✆ **081-447001**) and **Kestè,** Largo San Giovanni Maggiore 26 (✆ **081-5513984**) are favored by younger crowds (20s and early 30s).

An elegant nightclub worth checking out is **Chez Moi,** Via del Parco Margherita 13 (✆ **081-407526**), in the Riviera di Chiaia. Nearby **La Mela,** Via dei Mille (✆ **081-4010270**), is not bad either; neither is **Tongue,** Via Manzoni 202 (✆ **081-7690888**) in Posillipo, a club with a good mix of gays and lesbians as well as a straight clientele.

For a more specifically gay-men-only spot, head for **Bar B,** Via Giovanni Manna, off Via Duomo (✆ **081-287681**), a famous gay sauna—with Turkish and Finnish spas on three levels, and with two bars and five dark rooms—that turns into a disco on Thursday and Saturday nights; music ranges from Latin to techno. For a mixed/gay-male scene, check out **Sputnik Club** at Via Santa Teresa degli Scalzi 154 bis (✆ **081-19813222**).

Pompeii, Herculaneum, Vesuvius & the Campi Flegrei

Many sites identified in ancient mythology are in the volcanic areas near Naples, Mount Vesuvius, and the Phlegrean Fields—where bubbling springs and hot mud conjure images of the underworld. Once a paradise on Earth, these areas are now suburbs of Naples, complete with pockets of squalor. Yet, their standout natural and archaeological attractions cannot be overlooked.

The area's rich archaeological remains are a paramount reason to come, from the fascinating ruins of Cuma—the first Greek colony in Italy—to the underwater archaeological park of Baia. In Campi Flegrei is Lake Fusaro; Solfatara has its volcanic hot mud and sulfur springs; the promontory of Capo Miseno affords views of the delightful bay; and Lake Averno is the mythical entrance to the Kingdom of the Dead.

And what would Naples's skyline be like without Mount Vesuvius? You'll discover the love-fear relationship Neapolitans have with their volcano when you climb its slopes and taste its marvelous *Lacrima Christi* wine. The region is home to some of the world's most renowned ancient ruins—Pompeii and Herculaneum—as well as some lesser-known ones like the Roman villa of Oplonti (a UNESCO World Heritage Site).

Mount Vesuvius had been dormant for centuries when the great explosion of A.D. 79 occurred. At the time of the eruption, it seems that nobody knew it was a volcano, and its slopes—sought after for the fertile soil—were heavily inhabited. Towns, villages, and estates were covered by lava or ash during the eruption, causing thousands of deaths and immense economic loss. Pompeii was the first of the lost towns to be excavated—the discovery dates from the 16th century. Recently, modern archaeologists have unveiled many other sites that were not spoiled by illegal digs over the years.

Herculaneum is striking because of how well the houses have been preserved. Rarely visited by foreign tourists, the grandiose Roman villa of Oplontis is still decorated with magnificent frescoes, and we also recommend the smaller villas of Boscoreale and Boscotrecase.

All of the destinations we describe in this chapter make an easy day trip from Naples, but if you are not planning to visit the city itself, it is a good idea to stay in the area, which offers less-pricey accommodations than Naples. We give options for Campi Flegrei and Vesuvius–Herculaneum, Pompeii, and nearby Torre del Greco, or, a bit farther down the coast, Castellammare di Stabia (see chapter 7).

1 HERCULANEUM ★★

9.5km (6 miles) SE of Naples

The volcanic mud that covered Herculaneum during the A.D. 79 Mount Vesuvius eruption that killed most of the town's estimated 5,000 inhabitants quickly hardened to a
semirock material, protecting the structures underneath but also making archaeological
excavations much slower than at other sites. Herculaneum was discovered in 1709, and
although excavations started shortly after and proceeded alongside those in Pompeii, the
uncovered area here is much smaller than that of the more famous sibling site. Also,
unlike at Pompeii, much of the ancient town lies under the modern one, making excavation even more difficult. The findings, though, are stunning.

Although many questions about Herculaneum remain to be answered, researchers tell
us that this town was about a third of the size of Pompeii and had a different urban
makeup. A glitzy seaside resort for wealthy Romans, Herculaneum had little commercial
and industrial activity. Most of the town was composed of elegant villas—many even
more richly decorated than those of Pompeii—and some apartment blocks for poor
laborers, while the middle-class of merchants and artisans, which was so largely represented in Pompeii, was almost completely absent here. The town was also a harbor, with
moderate activity.

ESSENTIALS

GETTING THERE   You can access Herculaneum via the **Circumvesuviana railway**
(© **800-053939** toll-free within Italy; www.vesuviana.it), with lines between Naples,
Sorrento, and Poggiomarino/Sarno. From Naples, trains stop at **Ercolano Scavi,** and the
20-minute ride costs 1.80€. From Sorrento, the 47-minute ride costs 1.90€ (for more
information on fares, see "The Unico Travel Pass," p. 48). Outside the station, you can
then get a shuttle bus to the archaeological site or grab a taxi.

You can also take a **taxi** from Naples (the official flat rate for a round-trip to Herculaneum is 70€, and includes a 2-hr. wait at the ruins), or a **car service** from any location.
For recommended taxi and car service companies, see "Getting Around," in chapter 3.

If you are based in Naples, another excellent option is to sign up for a guided tour
from Naples (see chapter 5, p. 123).

We do not recommend driving, as modern Ercolano lies in the poorer outskirts of
Naples, with terrible traffic, difficult parking, and questionable safety (your car is at
certain risk, and you don't want to leave it unattended). If you really need to use your
car, Ercolano lies along busy coastal route SS 18, which links Naples to Torre del Greco
and Pompeii. From autostrada A3, take the ERCOLANO-PORTICI exit and follow the brown
signs for the archaeological area, or *scavi*.

Stretch Your Euros

If you are planning an extensive visit to the Vesuvian archaeological sites, save on
admission prices by purchasing the **Biglietto Unico (Vesuvian area cumulative
ticket)** which grants access to all the archaeological sites—Herculaneum, Pompeii, Oplontis, Stabiae, and Boscoreale—for 20€ and is valid for 3 days.

EXPLORING HERCULANEUM

The archaeological area is in the heart of the modern town of Ercolano, a relatively depressed and not exactly tourist-friendly suburb of Naples. The town is perfectly safe during the day, particularly by the archaeological area, but rather ugly. If you are up for a little exploring, though, you might also want to visit the showroom of a local talented artist, a maker of **cameos,** named **Biagio Piscopo.** He is located at Corso Resina 318 (© **081-7322736**), conveniently near the archaeological site. The difficult art of cameo making was first developed in nearby Torre del Greco (see "Cameo Making," below), and the beautiful jewels produced here are exported all over the globe.

The town is struggling to reverse a relatively recent downturn, dating back only about a century. Before—and since—Roman times, Ercolano had been a posh resort for Naples's patricians, who built their summer villas at the foot of Mount Vesuvius, to enjoy the cooler weather. The some 122 mansions, built during the 18th century by members of the Bourbon court, made up the so-called **Miglio d'Oro,** the Golden Mile. Abandoned after Ercolano became an impoverished suburb of modern Naples, some of the villas have been restored under the supervision of the association **Ente Ville Vesuviane**

(*C* 081-7322134; www.villevesuviane.net). Museo Diffuso is a self-guided visit to three villas, the starting point being **Villa Campolieto,** where you pick up the audioguide. Grand Tour is a longer circuit with five main stops, also starting from Villa Campolieto (*C* **081-3625121** for reservations; villadelleginestre@villevesuviane.net). In July, the restored villas are the stage for the **Festival Ville Vesuviane,** featuring concerts—classical, jazz, and pop—and dance.

Herculaneum Archeological Area ★★★ Smaller and easier to visit than Pompeii, Herculaneum may appear at first to also be less impressive. You'll be quickly pervaded by the eerie sensation that, far from being a place of dusty ruins, the town was abandoned only a short time ago, instead of nearly 2,000 years in the past. Part of this feeling of entering a ghost town stems from the fact that many of the houses still have their upper floors. The volcanic mud that enveloped the site allowed for the unusual preservation of wood, from housing structures to room furnishings, allowing archaeologists to learn an incredible amount about the daily life and building techniques in Roman times.

The excavated area stretches from Herculaneum's **Decumanus Maximus** (the town's main street) to the shore; the rest of the Roman town away from the water remains inaccessible beneath the buildings of modern Ercolano. The archaeological area is in continuous evolution as ongoing excavations lead to new discoveries. For instance, a boat was found near the shore in the 1990s: It was still filled with the corpses of victims caught in frantic postures of escape.

The highlights of a visit should definitely include the *Collegio degli Augustali* (**College of the Augustali**) ★★, with its marble floor and wall paintings; the custodian's room has also been preserved, together with the bed where a man's corpse was found, presumably killed in his sleep. We also recommend a tour of the elegantly decorated **Thermal Baths,** and the **Palestra,** a monumental sports arena for competition and training. Among the private homes, the most interesting are the *Casa del Tramezzo di Legno* (**House of the Wooden Partition**), with its perfectly preserved facade, and the *Casa dei Cervi* (**House of the Stags**), the most elegant ruin in the excavated area, with terraces overlooking the sea and top-quality decorations. The *Casa a Graticcio* (**House of the Latticework**) is particularly fascinating because it's one of the very few examples of lower-class housing that has emerged from antiquity (usually only grand public buildings and the solidly constructed villas of the wealthy have survived); notice the partitions, cheaply made of interwoven cane and plaster. Another interesting house is the *Casa del Mosaico di Nettuno e Anfitrite* (**House of the Neptune and Anfitritis Mosaic**) and the annexed shop, still with merchandise on the counter and goods in the cabinets.

Elegant villas dotted what was the western seashore of Herculaneum, and one of the most famous is **Villa dei Papiri** ★★, so-called because of it's library room chock-full of **papyrus rolls** (there were about 1,000). They are now preserved in the Biblioteca Nazionale Vittorio Emanuele III in the Palazzo Reale (see chapter 5). The villa also yielded a treasure trove of elegant sculptures, now in the collection of the Museo Archeologico Nazionale in Naples (see chapter 5). *Note:* Tours of the villa have been suspended since late 2007 for ongoing excavation. No reopening date had been announced at presstime.

The newly opened **maritime pavilion** contains the remains of a Roman boat that was found in front of Herculaneum and painstakingly restored, plus other discoveries from the harbor.

Corso Resina, Ercolano. *C* **081-8575347.** www.pompeiisites.org. Admission 11€ or free w/Artecard (p. 110). Nov–Mar daily 8:30am–5pm; Apr–Oct daily 8:30am–7:30pm. Last admission 90 min. earlier. Closed Jan 1, May 1, and Dec 25.

Decumanus Maxim

Bicentenary
House

Insula
VII

House of
the Double
Colonnade

Insula
VI

Insula
V

Insula
Orientalis
II

House of
the Great
Portal

Pistrinum

Decumanus   Inferiore

House of
the Alcove

Insula
II

Insula
III

Insula
IV

Insula
Orientalis
I

House
of
Argus

House of
the Inn

Old Harbor

Entrance

Benevento
CAMPANIA
NAPLES   Herculaneum
Ischia   Salerno
Capri   Sorrento
TYRRHENIAN SEA

Casa a Graticcio
  (House of the Latticework) **4**
Casa dei Cervi
  (House of the Stags) **6**
Casa dell'Atrio a Mosaico
  (House of the Mosaic Atrium) **5**

Casa del Tramezzo di Legno
  (House of the Wooden Partition) **3**
Collegio degli Augustali **1**
Palestra **8**
Terme (Baths) **2**
Terme Suburbane (Suburban Baths) **7**

MAV-Museo Archeologico Virtuale (Kids The installation at the brand-new Virtual
Archeological Museum—in a larger complex that contains a media library and spaces for
special exhibits—has over 30 visual segments recreating various aspects of life in Herculaneum and the other archaeological sites of the Vesuvian area.

Via IV Novembre (the street opposite the main entrance to the Herculaneum Archeological Area), Ercolano. (C) **081-19806511.** www.museomav.com. Admission 7€; 1.50€ discount with Artecard. Tues–Sun
9am–5pm.

WHERE TO STAY

You really don't want to spend more time in Ercolano than is necessary; and if you want
to sleep in the area, we recommend heading for nearby **Torre del Greco,** a modern

seaside resort a couple miles south of Ercolano (both towns are about 9.5km/6 miles southeast of Naples), with hotels and restaurants that cater both to tourists and business travelers who are attracted by the seaside and the flourishing craft of cameo making. By public transportation the town is two stops beyond the Ercolano Scavi station on the **Circumvesuviana railway** (✆ **800-053939;** www.vesuviana.it); take either the Sorrento or the Poggiomarino line (see "Getting There," above). **Taxis** also wait outside the train station. By **car,** take the SS 18 toward Torre del Greco and Pompeii, or, from the autostrada A3, take the exit marked TORRE DEL GRECO NORD or TORRE DEL GRECO SUD.

Expensive

Miglio D'Oro Park Hotel ★ (Kids)   This restored villa was one of the patrician summer residences of the Miglio d'Oro (see "Exploring Herculaneum," above), hence the name of the hotel. On the main road that runs parallel to autostrada A3, it is a short distance south of the archaeological area. The place is rather grand and is often booked for weddings and events. Guest rooms have a contemporary decor and are spacious and full of light, with state-of-the-art details, including Jacuzzi bathtubs. The grounds are beautiful and have a small pond.

Corso Resina 296, 80056 Ercolano. ✆ **081-7399999.** Fax 081-7777049. www.migliodoroparkhotel.it. 53 units. 180€–200€ double; 330€ junior suite; 370€ suite. Rates include buffet breakfast. Children 2 and under stay free in parent's room. AE, DC, MC, V. Free parking. Train: Btw. Circumvesuviana stops Ercolano-Scavi (Piazzale Circumvesuviana, off Via 4 Novembre) and Ercolano-Miglio D'Oro (Via Doglie). **Amenities:** 3 restaurants; bar; concierge; room service. *In room:* A/C, TV, minibar, Wi-Fi (for a fee).

Moderate

Hotel Marad   In a quiet area outside town, this hotel enjoys a great panoramic position on the slope of Vesuvius. It is a relaxing place to take a break from visiting the ruins, with a pleasant garden and a swimming pool. Rooms are quiet and well-appointed, with quality furniture, tiled or carpeted floors, and modern bathrooms. All rooms have a private balcony. Guests have access to a spa and gym nearby.

Via Benedetto Croce 20 (off Via Gugliemo Marconi, north of autostrada A3), 80059 Torre del Greco. ✆ **081-8492168.** Fax 081-8828716. www.marad.it. 74 units. 110€–140€ double. Rates include buffet breakfast. Children 2 and under stay free in parent's room. AE, DC, MC, V. Free parking. Train: Circumvesuviana stop Torre del Greco. **Amenities:** 2 restaurants; bar; babysitting; concierge; pool; room service. *In room:* A/C, TV, minibar, Wi-Fi.

Sakura ★ (Kids)   Also on the slopes of Vesuvius, affording cooler air during the summer, this hotel offers accommodations of a similar quality to the more sober Marad, but is farther from the Circumvesuviana train stop. The spacious guest rooms are individually decorated in an Asian theme, with a mix of classic and contemporary furniture, hardwood floors, and state-of-the-art bathrooms with Jacuzzi tubs. The discounted transfers from Naples's rail station and airport are a plus.

Via Enrico De Nicola 26, 80059 Torre del Greco. ✆ **081-8493144.** Fax 081-8491122. www.hotelsakura.it. 80 units. 150€ double; 195€ triple or junior suite; 225€ quad. Rates include buffet breakfast. Children 5 and under stay free in parent's room. Internet specials available. AE, DC, MC, V. Free parking. Train: Circumvesuviana stop Torre del Greco. **Amenities:** Restaurant; 2 bars; airport transfers (10€); babysitting; concierge; pool; room service; train transfers (7€). *In room:* A/C, TV, minibar.

Inexpensive

Hotel Restaurant Holidays   This modern family-run hotel caters mostly to Italian tourists and is a good budget option. It offers basic but welcoming accommodations in

Cameo Making

Coral jewelry and cameos have a long history in Torre del Greco. [...] has been a traditional activity since antiquity, when the art of the [...] invented. Lost during the Middle Ages, the craft boomed in the 1[...] when local artisans took inspiration from the jewelry of the excav[...] peii and Herculaneum. In 1879, the *Scuola di Incisione del Corallo* (School of Coral Carving) opened, giving further impulse to the development of the industry. Today, the school is called the **Istituto Statale per l'Arte del Corallo e l'Oreficeria** and maintains its own museum, the **Museo del Corallo** ★★, Piazza Palomba (✆ **081-8811360**), where you can admire a fairly large collection from the 18th century onward. Also in town is the privately held—it belongs to one of the historical cameo factories—**Museo Liverino del Corallo e dei Cammei** ★★, Via Montedoro 61 (✆ **081-8811225**), which displays over 3,000 pieces from the 16th century on.

Although the local coral beds are practically exhausted, cameo making still flourishes today, thanks to the use of corals and shells from the Pacific Ocean. About 90% of all coral fished around the world makes its way to this little town on the Italian coast, and the jewelry produced here is exported all over the world. Among the many cameo workshops in the area, some of the most reputable congregate around Via Ettore de Nicola. At no. 1 is **Giovanni Apa** (✆ **081-8811155**); no. 25 is **Antonino del Gatto** (✆ **081-8814191**); **Baldo Liguoro** (✆ **081-8812600**) inhabits no. 35; and **Vincenzo Ricevuto** (✆ **081-8814976**) occupies no. 38. Other noteworthy workshops are **Fratelli De Simone,** Via Roma 4 (✆ **081-8829368**), **B.&E. Mazza,** Via Tironi 14 (✆ **081-8812665**), and **Giuseppe Pepere,** Via Friuli 11 (✆ **081-8834888**).

a seaside location, only steps from the beach. Guest rooms are spacious and nicely appointed, with tiled floors, comfortable furnishings, and updated bathrooms (shower only). Only the best rooms—with sea views or private terraces—have air-conditioning and a minibar. The **restaurant** specializes in local cuisine and regional wines, and enjoys great views over the bay.

Via Litoranea 154 (off Via Santa Maria La Bruna), 80059 Torre del Greco. ✆ **081-8832170.** Fax 081-8836591. www.holidayshotel.it. 38 units. 75€–100€ double; 95€–115€ triple; 100€–130€ quad. Rates include breakfast. Children under 2 stay free in parent's room. Family specials available. AE, DC, MC, V. Free parking. Train: Btw. Circumvesuviana stop Via Monaci and Villa delle Ginestre. **Amenities:** Restaurant; bar. *In room:* A/C (in some), TV, minibar (in some).

WHERE TO DINE

Ercolano itself does not offer significant dining, although just outside the entrance to the site are a few options. On the main road are snack bars and grocery shops. You can get a real meal—and an excellent one—in nearby Torre del Greco (see "Where to Stay," above). Torre del Greco is popular among Italians who come to sample the excellent local cuisine, famous for its fresh seafood dishes, and partake of the local D.O.C. wines. The whole stretch of the main seashore road is lined with restaurants large and small, some simple shacks and others more upscale. Lots of others are hidden away on the inner the town also has an array of excellent pizzerie; we recommend **Pizzeria la** ★, Via Nazionale 678 (© **081-8832431;** Circumvesuviana train to Villa delle nestre), which makes delicious Neapolitan pizza and has a private garden.

Expensive

Ristorante Pernice Salvatore ★ NEAPOLITAN/SEAFOOD   A bit more upscale than Gaetano a Mare or Chiarina A'Mmare (below), this restaurant offers dining both indoors and on its open-air terrace. The menu is seasonal and market based, but usually on offer is their delicious version of *acqua pazza* (light herbed broth) and *pesce al sale* (daily catch baked in a bed of salt). Two of the most outstanding first courses are *risotto alla pescatora* (with seafood) and *scialatielli ai frutti di mare* (fresh pasta with shellfish).

Via Ruggiero 45, Torre del Greco. © **081-8832297.** Reservations recommended Sat–Sun. Secondi 16€– 28€. AE, DC, MC, V. Daily noon–3pm and 7:30–11pm. Train: Circumvesuviana stop Via del Monte, but better by taxi.

Moderate

Chiarina A'Mmare ★★ NEAPOLITAN/SEAFOOD   Our favorite in town, and a local institution since 1898, this restaurant, on weekends, is very crowded with locals who crave seafood. Right on the harbor—the view is exceptional—it specializes in seafood, which is always extremely fresh. The seasonal menu always includes traditional specialties, of which we'd recommend *spaghetti zucchine e cozze* (with mussels and zucchini), *calamarata* (ring-shaped pasta with calamari), *sauté di frutti di mare* (sauteed mussels and clams), and *pesce all'acquapazza* (fish cooked in a light tomato broth).

Via Calastro, Torre del Greco. © **081-8812067.** Reservations recommended Sat–Sun. Secondi 14€–22€. AE, DC, MC, V. Thurs–Tues 12:30–3:30pm and 7:30–10:30pm. Closed Dec 20–Jan 5. Train: Circumvesuviana stop Torre del Greco.

Gaetano a Mare (Kids) NEAPOLITAN/SEAFOOD   This is one of the town's best-established restaurants, favored by locals who love to come here on weekends for traditional cuisine and good wine (while the children play in the restaurant's playground). The menu is seasonal and based on market selection, but you'll usually find an excellent *frittura* (medley of deep-fried seafood) and delicious *pasta alle cozze* (with sautéed mussels). Catches of the day are prepared according to your choice, *all'acquapazza* (poached with an herb broth), baked, or grilled.

Via Litoranea 5, Torre del Greco. © **081-8831558.** Reservations recommended Sat–Sun. Secondi 12€– 22€. No credit cards. Sat–Thurs noon–3pm and 7:30–11pm. Train Circumvesuviana stop Santa Maria La Bruna, but better by taxi.

2 POMPEII ★★★

27km (17 miles) SE of Naples

Pompeii is Italy's most famous archaeological site and with good reason: With an excavated area of 44 hectares (109 acres), Pompeii is unique in the world. No other ancient town has been brought to light so completely. Discovered by chance during excavations for a canal in the 16th century, the ruins of Pompeii were not recognized for what they were until further explorations in the 18th century. Scientific excavations started only at the end of the 19th century, but continued steadily until most of the ancient town was uncovered and are still ongoing today. Based on calculations of the city walls—only

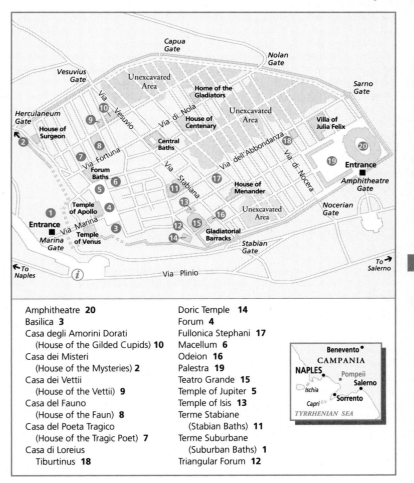

Amphitheatre **20**
Basilica **3**
Casa degli Amorini Dorati
  (House of the Gilded Cupids) **10**
Casa dei Misteri
  (House of the Mysteries) **2**
Casa dei Vettii
  (House of the Vettii) **9**
Casa del Fauno
  (House of the Faun) **8**
Casa del Poeta Tragico
  (House of the Tragic Poet) **7**
Casa di Loreius
  Tiburtinus **18**

Doric Temple **14**
Forum **4**
Fullonica Stephani **17**
Macellum **6**
Odeion **16**
Palestra **19**
Teatro Grande **15**
Temple of Jupiter **5**
Temple of Isis **13**
Terme Stabiane
  (Stabian Baths) **11**
Terme Suburbane
  (Suburban Baths) **1**
Triangular Forum **12**

partly excavated—Pompeii covered an area of 66 hectares (163 acres). Originally an Etruscan and then a Sannite town, it was colonized by the Romans in 80 B.C. At the time of the eruption, experts estimate the town had about 35,000 inhabitants.

GETTING THERE   Served by three train stations, Pompei is easily accessible by public transportation. A few **FS-Trenitalia trains** (© **892021** in Italy; www.trenitalia.it) stop in **Pompei FS rail station** in the center of town, but service is much more frequent on the **Circumvesuviana railway** (© **800-053939;** www.vesuviana.it) between Naples, Sorrento, and Poggiomarino/Sarno. On the Sorrento line, get off at **Pompei–Villa dei Misteri,** only a few yards from the Porta Marina entrance to the archaeological area. If you take the Poggiomarino line, get off at **Pompei-Santuario,** in the center of Pompei, only steps from the sanctuary and a couple hundred yards from the Piazza Anfiteatro entrance to the site. The ride from Naples takes 45 minutes and costs 2.40€; from Sorrento it's 30 minutes and 1.90€ (for more information on public transportation fares, see "The Unico Travel Pass," p. 48).

Taking a **taxi** from Naples is a good alternative (the official flat rate for a round-trip to Pompei is 90€, and includes a 2-hr. wait at the ruins), or take a **car service** from any location (see "Getting Around" in chapter 3).

From Naples, you can also sign up for a guided tour (p. 123).

By **car,** take the autostrada A3 and exit at POMPEI OVEST or POMPEI EST. Follow the brown signs for POMPEI SCAVI.

EXPLORING POMPEI

In recent decades, the city of Pompei was very depressed—run-down by cheap sprawl, slums, and the resultant petty crime. The town has experienced successful urban renewal, however, and visitors now can enjoy its other attractions. The **Santuario della Madonna del Rosario,** Piazza Bartolo Longo 1 (ℂ 081-8577111; www.santuario.it; Mon–Sat 6:15am–7:30pm; Sun and holidays 5:45am–8:30pm), is one of Italy's major religious centers dedicated to the Madonna, and a pilgrimage destination for Catholics worldwide. Built in the 19th century, the richly decorated sanctuary is well worth a visit. The attached buildings house a school and the offices of a number of important charities.

The archaeological area is, of course, the main attraction in Pompei. Come prepared, as the site is huge and a visit here is quite demanding in both time and energy. Bring comfortable shoes, a hat, sunscreen, and plenty of water. We also recommend taking a **guided tour** or, at least, purchasing the official guidebook, complete with itineraries and photographs, for sale at the bookstore located just beyond the ticket booth. Guidebooks are available in various languages, including English. The **Ufficio Scavi** (ℂ 081-8575347; www.pompeiisites.org) sometimes offers thematic guided tours that are fascinating: Each focuses on one aspect of the town's life. Some are seasonal, as the **Vendemmia (Grape Harvest),** where you can visit the vineyards that produce an excellent red wine (the Villa dei Misteri label) using 2,000-year-old techniques. You can reserve these as well as guided tours of specific buildings and houses at ℂ 081-8616405, or online at www.arethusa.net.

Excavations of Pompeii (Scavi) ★★★   In Roman times, Pompeii was an important industrial and commercial town, with a complex layered society, that is reflected in the urban structures on view today. Besides elegant villas belonging to the richer citizens, there were blocks of more modest housing, as well as shops, restaurants, hotels, and public buildings. The eruption covered Pompeii with volcanic ash and pumice stone, a

---

Antiquity Online

You can now purchase admission tickets to all the archaeological sites **online** at **www.pompei.napoli.com** (via a third party called **Lauro**). The procedure is simple: You pay by credit card and then print your tickets. *Note:* You need to be certain of the date of your visit: The tickets sold online are valid only for the date you choose and are nonrefundable.

much lighter material than in Herculaneum; therefore, the survivors of the disaster were able to retrieve some of their possessions, leaving less behind than in other locations. This also made it easier for the site to be excavated—and, unfortunately looted—in more recent centuries. In the 19th and early 20th century, precious mosaics and frescoes were carefully detached and placed on display in museums; but the contemporary approach is to leave everything *in situ* to depict the town as it must have been.

Surrounded by walls, the city was much closer to the sea than it is now, as the water has receded substantially since the days of the eruption. Pompeii had three centers of civic life: the **Forum;** the **Triangular Forum** with the **Theater District;** and the complex with the **Amphitheatre** and the **Palestra.** The rest of town was residential and commercial. Streets were lined with small shops and taverns, and the walls were covered with red writing advertising the candidates to the local elections. You'll also see black charcoal graffiti, and painted signs for bars and shops. All these are still visible in the area of the so-called **Nuovi Scavi** (still bearing the name that was given to this area in 1911) to the southeast of town.

The **Forum** is a large rectangular open space covering over 17,400sq. m. (58,000 sq. ft.) and surrounded by a portico on three sides. On the fourth is the **Temple of Jupiter,** from the 2nd century B.C., built over a high foundation. The Forum was decorated with bronze and marble statues of important citizens, but the niches stand empty because their objects were removed after the tragedy in A.D. 79. On the Forum was the **Macellum,** the covered food market. Opposite the market was the **Basilica,** the largest building in town, which housed the meeting hall and tribunal.

The **Triangular Forum** is another large area that was once surrounded by a portico. In the middle are the ruins of the **Doric Temple** from the 6th century B.C. This was the heart of the **Theater District,** with the beautiful **Teatro Grande** ★ from the 2nd century B.C., which could hold an audience of 5,000. Farther on is the **Odeion,** or Small Theater, from the 1st century B.C., for music and mime shows, which could hold 1,000 spectators. Nearby is the **Temple of Isis** ★, one of the best-conserved temples to this goddess to survive from antiquity. Also nearby is the *Terme Stabiane* **(Stabian Baths)** ★, one of the town's four **public baths,** with well-preserved mosaic, painting, and marble works.

From the Forum, you can take **Via dell'Abbondanza,** the town's main commercial street, lined with shops of all kinds and leading to the southeast of town, the most recently excavated area. One of the most curious shops is the *Fullonica Stephani* **(Stephen's Dry-Cleaning);** the shop is on the ground floor and the owner's apartment on the second. Farther on is the **Casa di Loreius Tiburtinus,** with an elegant internal **loggia** ★ bordering a long pool and decorated with small marble statues; at the end is the **Triclinium,** with two beautiful **paintings** ★★. At the end of the road to the right is the complex with the **Palestra,** where sports events were held, with a grandiose swimming pool and surrounded by plane trees (you can see the plaster casts of the stumps). Farther on is the **Amphitheatre,** the oldest Roman amphitheater in the world, built in 80 B.C., with seating for 1,000 people.

Among the other famous private houses here is the elegant *Casa dei Vettii* **(House of the Vettii),** with its magnificent paintings belonging to two rich merchants; they had just redecorated after the damages caused by the earthquake in A.D. 62, so all of the paintings were in excellent shape. The magnificent frescoed *Triclinium* **(Dining Room)** ★★ features figures and *amorini* (cupids) on Pompeiian red-and-black backgrounds. Nearby is the *Casa del Fauno* **(House of the Faun),** the largest of private homes—it takes up an entire block. The finest decorative pieces of this once-exquisite mansion are now in the

Museo Nazionale Archeologico in Naples. Also renowned (though again, most of its paintings have been moved to Naples's museums), is the ***Casa del Poeta Tragico*** **(House of the Tragic Poet),** with its famous *cave canem* (Beware of Dog) mosaic by the entrance. The gilded cupids that ornately decorated one of the rooms of ***Casa degli Amorini Dorati*** **(House of the Gilded Cupids)** ★ (by guided tour only) are also in the Museo Nazionale Archeologico in Naples, but many of the frescoes and marble decorations remain.

On the edge of town, along Via Villa dei Misteri, was Pompeii's fourth thermal establishment, **Terme Suburbane** ★★ (by guided tour only). These privately owned thermal baths were opened to the public in 2002 after lengthy restoration. Much looted over the centuries, they were the newest of the bath establishments in Pompeii and the most unusual. Contrary to traditional Roman custom, the baths are "mixed," for both men and women. The interior holds beautiful **frescoes** and **mosaic** decorations, including some of erotic content: One even shows a homosexual scene between women, uncommon in Roman iconography.

Outside Pompeii's walls the excavations continue along Via dei Sepolcri, a road lined with funerary monuments that leads outside the city walls toward the Porto Ercolano, Pompeii's harbor (about a 1km/half-mile walk). The ***Villa dei Misteri*** **(House of the Mysteries)** ★★ is a suburban estate famous for its paintings illustrating the three styles of Pompeiian paintings. Its most famous is the large **fresco** on the wall of what was probably a *triclynium* (dining room), depicting several figures participating in a ceremony thought to be related to the cult of Dionysus (Bacchus).

Tip: Guided tours are offered daily free of charge, with advance reservation (📞 081-8616405; www.arethusa.net). If you are signing up for more than one tour, keep in mind that it might take more than 30 minutes to walk between sites.

Porta Marina, Via Villa dei Misteri, Pompei (secondary entrance at Piazza Anfiteatro, Pompei). 📞 081-8575347. www.pompeiisites.org. Admission 11€ or free w/Artecard (p. 110). Nov 1–Mar 31 daily 8:30am–5pm; Apr 1–Oct 31 daily 8:30am–7:30pm. Last admission 90 min. earlier. Closed Jan 1, May 1, and Dec 25.

Virtual Pompei (**Kids**) This exhibit allows you to check out a reconstruction of the ancient town to see how it might have looked before the eruption. In addition to showing 3-D films, demonstrations of ancient Roman craft-making are given by live artists. The presentations are only organized for groups, and you can join existing groups by reserving in advance.

Via Plinio 105 (91m/300 ft. from the entrance to the archaeological area of Porta Marina), Pompei. 📞/fax 081-8610500. www.virtualpompei.it. Admission 8€ by reservation only.

WHERE TO STAY

The once sketchy town of Pompei has notably improved, and quite a few nice hotels are convenient to the archaeological area. You should still be careful, though, and avoid night strolls along deserted streets.

Moderate

Hotel Forum ★ (**Kids**) More elegant than the other options reviewed here, this family-run hotel is quite close to the excavations and convenient to the Santuario as well. Guest rooms are individually decorated, some with tiled floors, others with wooden floors; all have modern quality furnishings and good-size bathrooms (some with shower only). Some rooms open onto the garden, and suites afford panoramic views over the excavations or

Vesuvius, and have Jacuzzi tubs in their bathrooms. The largest rooms, which can accom- **143**
modate up to five guests, are good for families.

Via Roma 99, 80045 Pompei. *C* **081-8501170.** Fax 081-8506132. www.hotelforum.it. 36 units. 120€
double; 170€ junior suite. Rates include buffet breakfast. Children 2 and under stay free in parent's room.
AE, DC, MC, V. Free parking. **Amenities:** Bar; Internet in lobby (free). *In room:* A/C, TV, minibar.

Inexpensive
Hotel Iside   This good budget hotel offers basic, clean, and quiet accommodations in
the center of town, only 183m (600 ft.) from the Piazza Anfiteatro entrance to the *scavi*.
Guest rooms are plain but spacious and open either onto a private balcony or onto the
hotel's pleasant citrus garden. Some have quite nice views over the ruins or Vesuvius.
Bathrooms are good-size (some are shower only).

Via Minutella 27, 80045 Pompei. *C*/fax: **081-8598863.** www.hoteliside.it. 18 units. 90€ double. Rate
includes buffet breakfast. Children 2 and under stay free in parent's room. AE, DC, MC, V. Free parking.
Pets accepted. **Amenities:** Bar. *In room:* A/C, TV.

Hotel Diana (**Kids**)   This small family-run hotel is really welcoming, thanks to the
efforts of the charming hosts. Guest rooms are well-appointed and pleasantly decorated,
with all the expected amenities; yet some can also be a bit noisy. It is quite comparable
to the Iside (see above)—comfortable rooms, friendly service, pleasant garden—and
slightly less convenient to the ruins yet closer to the town center and right by the FS train
station.

Vicolo Sant'Abbondio 12 (off Via Sacra, by the FS train station), 80045 Pompei. *C*/fax: **081-8631264.**
www.pompeihotel.com. 10 units. 105€ double; 125€ triple; 145€ quad. Rates include buffet breakfast.
Children 2 and under stay free in parent's room. AE, DC, MC, V. Free parking. Pets accepted. **Amenities:**
Bar; babysitting; concierge; room service; smoke-free rooms. *In room:* A/C, Internet, TV.

Hotel Villa dei Misteri (**Kids**)   This old-fashioned family-run hotel has the advantage
of being right by the main entrance to the excavations. Built in the 1930s, it has a certain
charm and is an excellent choice if you don't need some amenities. Guest rooms are spacious and well-appointed, with modern quality furnishings and tiled floors; some have
private balconies. Some overlook the amphora-shaped pool, while others have street
views. If you want a room with A/C (for an additional 9€ charge), you must book well
in advance. The staff is extremely accommodating, and the pool and good restaurant are
great pluses, particularly if you have children.

Via Villa dei Misteri 11, 80045 Pompei. *C* **081-8613593.** Fax 081-8622983. www.villadeimisteri.it. 40
units. 75€ double; 97€ triple. Half- and full-board plans available. Children 2 and under stay free in parent's room; 10% discount for children 12 and under. DC, MC, V. Free parking. **Amenities:** Restaurant; bar;
pool. *In room:* A/C (in some, 9€ fee), TV (in some), Wi-Fi.

WHERE TO DINE
Most establishments in Pompei are tourist joints catering to large groups of visitors from
around the world. The following restaurants have their share of tourist groups but are
also favored by locals for their high-quality food.

Il Principe ★★ NEAPOLITAN/ANCIENT ROMAN   With a dining room that
strives for a modern version of Pompei's luxury, this is the best restaurant in the area and
a perfect conclusion to a day spent visiting the ruins. Right in the center of town, it
provides excellent food, a lively atmosphere, and outdoor dining. The talented chef and
owner is a real epicurean; the seasonal menu includes a choice of tasty ancient Roman
recipes, such as the *lagane al garum* (homemade egg-free pasta with an anchovy-paste

sauce). More modern choices include excellent *spaghetti alle vongole* (with baby clams) and delicious *maccheroni* with zucchini and prawns. The recent addition of a lounge bar with music makes it even better.

Piazza Bartolo Longo. (C) **081-8505566.** www.ilprincipe.com. Reservations recommended. Secondi 15€–24€. AE, DC, MC, V. Tues–Sat 12:30–3pm and 8–11pm; Sun 12:30–3pm.

Ristorante President ★ NEAPOLITAN   This is the most upscale place to eat in the area, offering gourmet food and great service. In addition to the wine list you'll be offered a water list, a beer list, a cheese list, and a honey and dried-fruit list, as well as the usual dessert menu. The food is seasonal and focuses on seafood, with such appetizers as smoked swordfish or tuna and, delicious pasta dishes such as the *scialatielli allo scorfano* (homemade flat pasta with scorpion-fish). The secondi, which come with a vegetable side dish—unusual for Italy, but most welcome—include a large choice of fish masterfully prepared au gratin, baked in a salt crust, or simply baked. We also recommend the tasting menus (call or check the website for a schedule of events), that explore the regional cuisine, from the modern to the ancient Roman (35€–55€ with wine pairings). Desserts are excellent and strictly homemade.

Piazza Schettino 12 (parking at back entrance, Via San Giuseppe 16). (C) **081-8507245.** www.ristorante president.it. Reservations recommended Sat–Sun. Secondi 12€–25€. AE, DC, MC, V. Tues–Sat noon–3pm and 7:30–11:30pm; Sun noon–3pm. Closed 2 weeks in Aug and 3 days for Christmas.

3 OPLONTIS ★

20km (12 miles) SE of Naples

Not far from **Torre Annunziata**—the coastal town famous for its flour mills and its pasta industry—is one of the more recently excavated archaeological areas on the slopes of Mount Vesuvius. Much remains to be done here, but what has already been uncovered is quite spectacular. The size of the site is much more manageable than Pompeii or even Herculaneum, making it a good choice for those desiring a brief archaeological visit.

ESSENTIALS

GETTING THERE   You can easily get to Oplontis using the **Circumvesuviana railway** ((C) **800-053939** toll-free within Italy; www.vesuviana.it) running between Naples, Sorrento, and Poggiomarino/Sarno; get off at **Torre Annunziata-Oplonti Villa di Poppea** (a few stops after Ercolano Scavi). The 20- or 35-minute ride (depending on the train) from Naples costs 1.80€, from Sorrento 1.90€ for a 30-minute ride. (for more information on public transportation fares, see "The Unico Travel Pass," p. 48)

By car, take the autostrada A3 Napoli-Salerno and exit at TORRE ANNUNZIATA SUD. Then follow the brown signs for SCAVI DI OPLONTI.

Impressions

Live in danger. Build your cities on the slopes of Vesuvius.

—Friedrich Nietzsche (1844–1900)

As of the 1st century B.C., Oplontis was already an elegant residential suburb of nearby Pompeii The überrich had their countryside villas here, and the very name might come from the Latin *opulentia,* or opulence. Discovered in the 18th century, the site was not excavated until the 1960s. Only the ruin of one extraordinary villa is currently open to the public, yet it is well worth the visit.

Villa di Poppea ★★ This is the largest ancient Roman suburban villa ever discovered. It was declared a UNESCO World Heritage Site because of the unique quality of its frescoes. It was certainly a villa belonging to the imperial family, and scientists believe it was the property of the famous Poppea Sabina, the second wife of Emperor Nero: An amphora bearing the name of her freedman and a vase bearing her mark were found on the villa's grounds, thus giving evidence justifying the claim. The villa is enormous, with a large portico opening onto a garden with a huge pool surrounded by statues, and innumerable rooms, passages, and cubicles, including a still-recognizable kitchen.

The greatest feature is the villa's absolutely superb decorations: Frescoes, stucco work, and mosaics have been left *in situ,* unlike in Pompeii or Herculaneum where, except in the latest excavations, they were removed to museums. Most of the interior was lavishly painted and many of the frescoes are still in very good repair, closely recalling the more well-known frescoes in the Villa dei Misteri of Pompeii and in the Museo Archeologico Nazionale of Naples.

The villa also yielded a treasure trove of high-quality statuary—a very rich collection, second only to what was found in the Villa dei Papiri in Herculaneum (see "Herculaneum Archeological Area," earlier in this chapter)—but, oddly, it was found tucked away in a storeroom. Actually, the entire villa was devoid of signs of daily life, leading the experts to believe that it was being restored at the moment of the eruption—maybe as a consequence of the preceding earthquake of A.D. 62.

Via Sepolcri 12, Torre Annunziata. (© 081-8621755. www.pompeiisites.org. Admission 5.50€ includes same-day entry to Boscoreale and Stabiae; or free with purchase of Artecard. Nov–Mar daily 8:30am–5pm; Apr–Oct daily 8:30am–7:30pm. Last admission 90 min. earlier. Closed Jan 1, May 1, and Dec 25.

4 BOSCOREALE

31km (19 miles) SE of Naples

In ancient Roman times, this agricultural center for wine, wheat, and olive oil on the slopes of Mount Vesuvius was part of the northern suburbs of Pompeii. Boscoreale today still has farms and vineyards (the adjacent Boscotrecase is famous for the production of Lacrimae Cristi, the amber-colored D.O.C. Vesuvian wine). Over 30 Roman villas have been found in Boscoreale to date, but only one has been completely excavated.

ESSENTIALS

GETTING THERE **Circumvesuviana trains** ((© 800-053939; www.vesuviana.it) run between Naples and Poggiomarino/Sarno, and stop at **Boscoreale.** The 25-minute ride from Naples costs 2.10€, and it is a 40-minute ride from Sorrento, because you need to change at Torre Annunziata (1.90€). From the station, take a taxi or switch to the local bus to Villa Regina. By **car,** take the autostrada A3 and exit at TORRE ANNUNZIATA; follow the brown signs for COMUNI VESUVIANI and BOSCOREALE. *Note:* For more information on public transportation fares, see "The Unico Travel Pass," p. 48.

Sweet Stop

If you have a sweet tooth, like us, you'll love the local specialty, the *zandraglia*. Sold at pastry shops in the area, this traditional treat is a large sweet cookie shaped like a butterfly. Dedicated to the pastry, the *Sagra della Zandraglia* is a fair that's held on the second Sunday of July. For the best *zandraglia*, head for **Vaiano**, with one shop near the excavations at Via Cirillo Emanuele 163 (✆ **081-5374372**), and the other at Via Marra (✆ **081-8593732**).

EXPLORING THE ARCHAEOLOGICAL AREA

Excavations in this area started at the end of the 19th century and were mostly performed by local landowners for the sole purpose of gathering valuable art. Once the objects were extracted and the frescoes detached, the villas were buried again. Most of the finds from these early excavations are on display in various museums around the world, including Paris's Louvre and the Metropolitan Museum in New York. Of some 30 villas discovered in the area, one, the **Villa della Pisanella**, yielded a real treasure: over 1,000 gold coins, some jewelry, and a complete set of silverware, including richly decorated cups and pitchers. Most of this treasure is now in the Louvre.

Modern excavations are ongoing, and archaeologists have learned a great deal about ancient Roman life. Farms were typically organized around a rural villa, with richly decorated apartments for the rare visits of the landlord, and larger quarters for the workmen and slaves.

Adjacent to the antiquarium (below), **Villa Regina** is the only local villa that was completely excavated and with the aid of modern technology. Discovered in the 1970s, the villa is modest in size, but reflects the typical structure of Roman rural villas, with an elegant residential space for the owner and a farm producing wine and grains. The villa is now a sort of living museum: Vineyards have been replanted with historical accuracy, and the ancient *torcularium* (the room for pressing grapes) and the cellar, which had a capacity of 10,000 liters (over 2,600 gal.), have been replicated.

Antiquarium Nazionale Uomo e Ambiente nel Territorio Vesuviano Kids Most of the recent finds from the local sites have been collected in this museum and divided into two sections. The first is dedicated to the running of a Roman farm, with exhibits on the techniques and objects related to agriculture and husbandry; the second focuses on architecture and, specifically, how these farming villas were structured differently than other Roman villas on the coast, which were solely dedicated to leisure.

Via Settetermini 15, Località Villaregina, Boscoreale. ✆ **081-5368796**. www.pompeiisites.org. Admission 5.50€ includes same-day admission to Villa Regina, Oplonti, and Stabiae; or free w/Artecard. Nov–Mar daily 8:30am–6:30pm; Apr–Oct daily 8:30am–7:30pm. Last admission 90 min. earlier. Closed Jan 1, May 1, and Dec. 25.

5 VESUVIUS

One of the most romantic volcanoes in the world, Vesuvius is also one of the most dangerous; yet, people continue to live on its fertile slopes, as they have since antiquity (and since the last eruption in 1944).

Treading Lightly on Mount Vesuvius

Stand at the bottom of the great market-place of Pompeii, and look up at the silent streets . . . over the broken houses with their inmost sanctuaries open to the day, away to Mount Vesuvius, bright and snowy in the peaceful distance; and lose all count of time, and heed of other things, in the strange and melancholy sensation of seeing the Destroyed and the Destroyer making this quiet picture in the sun.

—Charles Dickens, *Pictures from Italy*

A volcano that has struck terror in Campania, the towering, pitch-black **Mount Vesuvius** looms menacingly over the Bay of Naples. August 24, A.D. 79, is the infamous date when Vesuvius burst forth and buried Pompeii, Herculaneum, and Stabiae under ash and volcanic mud. Vesuvius has erupted periodically ever since (thousands were killed in 1631): The last major spouting of lava occurred in the 20th century (it blew off the ring of its crater in 1906). The last spectacular eruption was on March 31, 1944. The approach to Vesuvius is dramatic, with the terrain growing foreboding as you near the top. Along the way, you'll see villas rising on its slopes, and vineyards—the grapes produce an amber-colored wine known as Lacrimae Christi (Tears of Christ); the citizens of ancient Pompeii enjoyed wine from here, as excavations have revealed. Closer to the summit, the soil becomes puce colored and an occasional wildflower appears.

It might sound like a dubious invitation, but it's possible to visit the rim of the crater's mouth. As you look down into its smoldering core, you might recall that Spartacus, a century before the eruption that buried Pompeii, hid in the hollow of the crater, which was then covered with vines.

Named Vesvinum or Vesuvinum after its vineyards, which were famous for their excellent wine even centuries ago, Vesuvius was first known to erupt in A.D. 79. Other eruptions followed in 202, 472, 512, 1139, and 1306. The long period of quiet lulled everybody again until 1631, when an eruption caused great destruction. The following eruptions in 1794—nicely timed for Goethe's visit, when a guide hauled him up through the poisonous smoke to look into the crater—1871, 1906, and 1944—were lesser calamities. The most recent signs of activity were in 1999—some puffs of smoke, ju keep everybody on their toes.

GETTING THERE

The **Circumvesuviana railway** (© **800-053939** toll-free within Italy it) goes from Naples, Sorrento, and Poggiomarino/Sarno to Vesuviu make a stop at **Ercolano Scavi,** and the 20-minute ride costs 1. tion on public transportation fares, see "The Unico Travel Pa the 47-minute ride costs 1.90€. Once at the station, you Vesuvius or a **taxi** (confirm the price before getting i

A good alternative is taking a taxi from Naple transport and 2-hr. wait), or a **car service** fro chapter 3).

From Naples, another excellent option is a guided tour (see chapter 5, p. 123).

Ercolano Station is also where you'll meet your group, if you have signed up for one of the specialty tours organized by **La Porta del Vesuvio** (© 081-274200; www.laporta delvesuvio.it; 9am–1:30pm), offering excursions from walks along nature trails on the slopes, to scenic night tours of the crater.

Note: All transportation gets you only as far as the park entrance at 1,017m (3,337 ft.) in altitude; the trails are not wheelchair accessible.

WHAT TO SEE & DO

The only volcano still active in continental Europe, Mount Vesuvius is part of **Parco Nazionale del Vesuvio** (© 081-7710911; www.parconazionaledelvesuvio.it). The entrance to the park is at an altitude of 1,000m (3,281 ft.). Of its nine trails, the most popular is *Gran Cono* (path number 5), ascending to the **crater** ★. Admission is by guided tour only (6.50€ adults, 4.50€ ages 8–17, free for children 7 and under). Tours are led by a volcanologist and are offered throughout the day (no reservation necessary). The climb traverses hardened lava to the rim, 170m (558 ft.) above the park entrance, and 1,170m (3,839 ft.) above sea level. The trail affords great views of the crater itself and the whole Gulf of Naples. The park is open daily (Nov–Mar 9am–3pm; Apr–May 9am–5:30pm; June–Aug 9am–6:30pm; Sept–Oct 9am–5pm). *Note:* The trail to the crater closes in extreme weather.

Below the park entrance, at 608m (1,995 ft.) is the **Observatory** (© 081-5832111; www.ov.ingv.it): Established in 1841 to monitor Mount Vesuvius's activity, it is the oldest and one of the best volcanology research centers in the world. You can visit its rich scientific library and **Geological Museum** ★, Via Osservatorio 14 (© 081-6108483), which holds a vast collection of minerals and scientific instruments from the 18th century onward (Sat–Sun 10am–2pm; closed Jan 1 and 6, Easter and Easter Monday, Aug 1–31, Dec 8, 24–26, and 31; free admission).

6 THE PHLEGREAN FIELDS ★

18km (11 miles) W of Naples

...est is a land of hills, craters, lagoons, ... the proximity of Naples tarnished ...shed as a national park in 1993 to ... side, urban sprawl could not take ...nd the islands of Ischia and Procida ... on Earth.

...use of its boiling mud craters, this ...s for its warm and hot springs, its ...t to light many ruins and archae-...s amphitheater and temples; Baia ...ybilla Cave and Greek ruins.

...icearchia, founded in 530 B.C.; it ...nt Roman harbor favored by the

...t to

...www.vesuviana.
...From Naples, lines
...0€ (for more informa-
...ss," p. 48). From Sorrento,
...can then get a **shuttle bus** to
...flat rate of 90€ includes round-trip
...any location (see "Getting Around," in

Rim of Campanian Ignimbrite Caldera (3400 BC)
Fault Lines
Craters

Benevento
Phlegrean Fields CAMPANIA
NAPLES
Ischia Sorrento Salerno
Capri Amalfi
TYRRHENIAN SEA

Quarto Plain
Quarto
Licola Mare
Monte Ruscello
SS7
Senga Crater
Pianura
Piana Campana
Pisani Crater
Pianura Plain
Monte Sant'Angelo
Gauro
Cigliano Crater
Astroni Crater
CUMA
ARCO FELICE
Monte Barbaro
L. Grande
A56
Lake Averno
Monte Nuovo
Arco Felice
Agnano
Agnano Crater
L. Lucrino
La Starza (Marine Terrace)
Solfatara Crater
Lake Fusaro
Pozzuoli
Fuorigrotta Plain
Fusaro
Baia
Bagnoli
Posillipo
Torregaveta
Fondi di Baia Crater
Gulf of Pozzuoli
(Golfo di Pozzuoli)
Lake Miseno
Bacoli
Monte di Procida
Isola di Nisida
Punta Cavallo
Miseno
Capo Miseno

0   2 mi
0   3 km

POMPEII, HERCULANEUM, VESUVIUS

6

THE PHLEGREAN FIELDS

Roman emperors over Partenope (Naples), which had maintained closer allegiance to Greece. The town was destroyed by the barbarian Alaric in A.D. 410, but the acropolis, on a tufa-stone promontory protruding over the sea, continued to be inhabited, and Pozzuoli slowly developed around it. Because the town is just a few kilometers from Naples, you'd expect it to be downright suburban, but it maintains a life of its own—even though many of its residents commute to Naples for work each day. The town boasts unique monuments from its past as well as sweeping views over the sea and the islands of Ischia and Procida in one direction, and the island of Nisita (linked to the mainland by a causeway) on the other.

VISITOR INFORMATION   The **tourist office,** Via Campi Flegrei 3, 80078 Napoli (℡ 081-5262419; www.infocampiflegrei.it), dispenses information on Pozzuoli, the Phlegrean Fields region, and the province of Naples and its islands.

GETTING THERE   Pozzuoli is very well connected by public transportation to Naples and the islands, particularly to Ischia and Procida (see chapter 9). The most scenic way to arrive in Pozzuoli is by **city bus:** No. 152 starts in Piazza Garibaldi near Naples's Stazione Centrale and traverses the whole city, following the shoreline to the center of Pozzuoli—picturesque, but slow. Less scenic but faster is the **Metro** (line 2) or the **Cumana Railroad** (℡ 800-001616), starting from Piazza Montesanto.

In summer, another option is the commuter ferry run by **Metrò del Mare** (℡ 199-446644; www.metrodelmare.com). Water taxi service is by **Taxi del Mare** (℡ 081-8773600; www.taxidelmare.it).

GETTING AROUND   Taxis (℡ 081-5265800) operate from a stand in Piazza della Repubblica. You can also use the **buses** operated by **Consorzio Trasporti Pubblici** (℡ 081-5265321; www.ctpn.it) and **SEPSA** (℡ 800-001616; www.sepsa.it), with several lines connecting the train and Metro stations to the harbor and other parts of the Phlegrean Fields.

WHAT TO SEE & DO   The modern town tightly encloses Pozzuoli's monuments of antiquity. The original Greek Acropolis, **Rione Terra** ★, Largo Sedile di Porta (℡ 848-800288, 06-39967050, or 081-1930578), was the first inhabited area of Pozzuoli. Near the harbor, it has been progressively subsiding under the sea, so much so that it had to be abandoned in the 1970s. A large, ongoing excavation and restoration campaign, begun in 1993, has uncovered a virtually untouched Roman town—sort of an underground Pompeii. Along the main *Decumano* (the central avenue running east–west) and some minor streets, are shops, *osterie* (taverns), a *pistrinum* (mill), and the *ergastula* (slaves' cells) with some drawings by prisoners still visible on the walls. The site is open to the public, by guided tour only, during certain periods of the year (admission 4€); call before your visit. Sculptures and other important objects from this site are on display in the Museo Archeologico dei Campi Felgrei in Baia (p. 153).

Not far from the harbor, at Via Roma 10, is the entrance to the **Serapeo** ★, the ruins of the ancient Roman town market. The large structure, built in the 1st century A.D., was lined with porticos where shops and taverns operated. At its center are the remains of a temple, much spoiled during the centuries (its alabaster columns, for instance, were used to decorate the Royal Palace in Caserta; see chapter 11). Named after the Egyptian god Serapis because of the statue found here during its excavation, this ruin has been used to study the geological phenomenon of bradyseism (in which large tracts of land slowly subside beneath sea level, while others rise up); you can see little holes in the marble of the columns where they were submerged in water. A bit farther inland, at Via Terracciano 75, is the **Anfiteatro Neroniano/Flavio** ★. Started by Roman emperor Nero and finished by Emperor Vespasiano, it is in the upper part of town, where the roads to Cuma, Pozzuoli, and Naples converged in Roman times. This was the third largest amphitheater after the Colosseo and the Anfiteatro Campano in Capua (see chapter 11). Admission for both sites is 4€; it includes the Museo Archeologico dei Campi Flegrei, Parco Archeologica di Baia, and Scavi di Cuma, and is valid 2 days. (Wed-Mon 9am–4pm, last admission 3pm; closed Jan 1, May 1, Dec 25). The theater, which could accommodate more than 20,000 spectators, is used today for special musical events; check with the local tourist office for information.

6

SOLFATARA ★

Lesser known and less romanticized than Vesuvius—and also way less dangerous—this largest volcano of the Phlegrean Fields is still an impressive sight. The active volcano was a favorite stop during the Grand Tour (the educational trip through Europe for 19th-century aristocrats), and it is one of the few places in the area that has not been touched by urban sprawl—and for good reason! Today, as 2 centuries ago, the varied **volcanic phenomena** include bubbling hot mud, foul-smelling sulfurous hot water, and steam issuing from fissures in the soil. It is a very interesting visit for grown-ups and children alike.

GETTING THERE   The park is 10km (6¼ miles) from Naples. The easiest means of travel is the Metro (line 2) to **Pozzuoli-Solfatara** station, which is only about 732m (2,400 ft.) from the entrance to the park. You can walk the distance or catch the local P9 bus from outside the Metro station. City bus 152 from Naples to Pozzuoli also stops at Solfatara. You can also walk the 1.6km (1 mile)—a 20-minute trek uphill from Pozzuoli. A taxi from Naples is a flat rate of 40€ one way to Solfatara.

WHAT TO SEE & DO   The site is a nature preserve covering an expanse of 33 hectares (81 acres), with large wooded areas where a number of rare birds, plants, and small animals have found refuge. At the entrance, Via Solfatara 161 (© **081-5262341;** www. solfatara.it), pick up the nature trail that leads to the points of interest in the park; the whole thing takes about 45 minutes to 1 hour. The best spots are the Fangaia, with its huge bubbling mud holes, and the Bocca Grande, Solfatara's main crater. Because Solfatara is the epicenter of the Phlegrean Fields' volcanic area, the ancients believed this was the residence of the god Vulcanus. Nearby are the Stufe (Italian for stoves): A number of small caves constantly filled by hot steam. During antiquity, they were used as natural saunas. Entry fees are 6€ for adults, 4.50€ for children 4 to 9, and free for children 3 and under; Artecard holders receive a 20% discount. The preserve is open daily from 8:30am to 1 hour before sunset.

BAIA ★★

On the coastal stretch that bounds the Gulf of Pozzuoli to the west, the fishing town of **Baia** maintains something of its picturesque past, with pastel-colored buildings opening onto a small harbor. Ancient Roman Baia was a flourishing seaside resort adjacent to the large harbor Portus Julius. Due to the geological phenomenon of bradyseism, much of the ancient structures have been preserved underwater, creating a unique submarine archaeological area.

Getting There

Baia is well connected to Pozzuoli public transportation (see "Getting Around," p. 150). Or take a taxi, either from Pozzuoli's Metro station (agree on the price beforehand) or from Naples, where taxis offer a flat rate of 85€ for a round-trip to the archaeological area of Baia and Solfatara with a 3-hour wait.

What to See & Do

The most unique attraction here is obviously the **Parco Archeologico Subacqueo ★**, Harbor of Baia (© **081-8688923;** www.baiasommersa.it), the submerged archaeological site. The ruins are only a few feet below the surface, and the visit is an eerie and magical experience, however you choose to go about viewing it. Many of the structures have been excavated and in places roped off and labeled for visitors coming by **guided scuba tour** (only summer and fall) or by **boat** equipped with a submerged video camera or clear bottom. Visits are possible only during good weather (Mid-Mar to mid-Nov Tues–Sun 9:30am–1:30pm and 3:30–7:30pm); boats depart from the dock in Baia's harbor, and the tour costs 35€, inclusive of admission, insurance, and boat transport. For about the same cost, you can enjoy the ruins from underwater, by booking a guided snorkeling or scuba tour either directly with the park or by contacting one of the local authorized diving centers: **Blue Point** (© **081-8704444**) or **Cardone Sub** (© **081-8706886**).

The unsubmerged part of Baia reserves some quite exceptional ruins. **Parco Monumentale ★**, Via Bellavista (© **081-5233797;** free admission; daily 9am to 1 hr. before sunset; last entrance 1 hr. before closing time; closed Jan 1, May 1, and Dec 25) is a huge archaeological area covering 14 hectares (34 acres) of "historical landscape" on which excavations are ongoing. Walk among the ruins of imperial residences and elegant villas now shaded by pine trees and enjoy the views. **Parco Archeologico Terme di Baia ★★**, whose main entrance is at Via Sella di Baia 22 (© **081-8687592;** admission 4€, includes Anfiteatro Flavio and Serapeo in Pozzuoli, Museo Archeologico in Baia, and

Scavi di Cuma, and is valid 2 days; Tues–Sun 9am to 1 hr. before sunset; last entrance 1 hr. before closing time; closed Jan 1, May 1, and Dec 25), features the ruins of the Imperial Palace and the **thermal baths.** These were the most celebrated of ancient Roman baths, beloved by the VIPs of ancient Rome both for the therapeutic properties of their waters and for the matchless scenery. Built by Emperor Ottaviano between 27 B.C. and A.D. 14, the baths took advantage of local, natural hot springs and were hydraulically engineered to be fed by gravity only. The shifting ground, though, altered the original construction, and little water reaches the baths today. We recommend starting with the Parco Monumentale and taking the scenic **footpath** ★, which starts from the **Esedra** (the park's main square) and connects with a secondary entrance to the Parco Archeologico (no ticket sales).

Don't miss the **Museo Archeologico dei Campi Flegrei** ★★★, Via Castello 39 (𝄇 **081-5233797** or 848-8002884), whose rich endowment is second only to the National Archaeological Museum of Naples. The museum is in the scenic **Castello Aragonese,** the castle overlooking the harbor from a small promontory. Built in 1442 by Alfonso d'Aragona, it is worth a visit in itself, if nothing else for the view. Inside is a superb collection, including entire rooms that were carefully excavated from local ancient Roman villas and reconstructed here, such as the **Sacello degli Augustali** ★★ and the famous **Ninfeo di Punta Epitaffio** ★★★ (a ninfeo is an ancient Roman porch enclosed with columns—this one was found underwater) from the excavations of Baia and Miseno, and the **Ninfeo of Emperor Claudius.** Admission is 4€ and includes entrance to Anfiteatro Flavio and Serapeo in Pozzuoli, Zona Archeologica in Baia, and Scavi di Cuma (valid 2 days). Hours are Tuesday to Sunday from 9am to 8pm, but the ticket booth closes 1 hour earlier (museum closed Jan 1, May 1, and Dec 25).

Baia is also a good base for exploring the bay; you can rent a boat from the **Associazione Barcaioli di Baia** (𝄇 **081-8701222**), or join an organized boat excursion with **Peppe Navigazione del Golfo** (𝄇 **333-8877883**) or with the ferry company **Alilauro** (𝄇 **081-7611004** or 081-4972293; www.alilauro.it). All the above companies are located along the dock in the harbor.

Last but not least, you can enjoy a bit of relaxation ancient-roman style in the **spa Terme Stufe di Nerone,** Via Stufe di Nerone 45, Bacoli (𝄇 **081-8688006;** www.terme stufedinerone.it), where there are have two operating natural saunas. Hours vary, so call before your visit.

CUMA ★★

Easily overlooked, this special little place is where the ancient Greeks founded their first stable colony in the western Mediterranean, giving birth to what would become Magna Grecia. The peninsula today is a trifle more built-up, but enough remains for one to imagine Cuma high atop a promontory, dominating the Phlegrean Fields peninsula, and overlooking what at the time was a green expanse of land interspersed with volcanic lakes and surrounded by the sea on both sides. The city of Cuma proved to be the most important Greek colony on this coast, keeping the Etruscans and later the Romans at bay (see chapter 2 for more history).

Getting There

Although local **SEPSA** buses are available from Pozzuoli and the nearby **Fusaro** stop of the Cumana train line (𝄇 **800-001616** or 081-7354311; www.sepsa.it), a **taxi** from Pozzuoli is a more comfortable option (see "Getting Around," p. 150).

The entrance to the archaeological area, **Scavi di Cuma** (② 081-8543060), is at Via Monte di Cuma 3. The site has several ruins. On the **Acropolis** ★ are two **temples**—one to **Apollo** and the other to **Jupiter**—which served as churches from the Middle Ages; beyond the **fortified walls** is the **Necropolis** and an **amphitheater** dating from the late 2nd century B.C. Nearby is Cuma's most intriguing and atmospheric site, the mysterious *Antro della Sibilla* (**Sibylla's cave**) ★★. According to one interpretation, this is where the famous priestess to the god Apollo received her supplicants. Whatever the truth, the majestic proportions of the tunnel and the engineering feat of its construction are admirable. The terrace outside the cave provides a splendid **view** ★★ over the harbor of Cuma, which is in itself reason enough for a visit. Admission to the *scavi* is 4€ and includes entry to Anfiteatro Flavio and Serapeo in Pozzuoli, Museo Archeologico and Zona Archeologica in Baia, and is valid 2 days (daily 9am to 1 hr. before sunset; last admission 1 hr. before closing time; closed Jan 1, May 1, and Dec 25).

As you leave the excavations, notice the imposing arch the local road passes under: Named **Arco Felice** by locals, it dates from the 1st century A.D., when the mountain was cut and a viaduct was built for the passage of the Domitian Road, an immense engineering feat realized under Emperor Domitian. Also nearby is **Lake Averno:** Described by classic poet Virgil in the *Aeneid* as the entrance to the underworld, this volcanic lake is strangely dark and quiet. Its name is ancient Greek for "no birds," and it is believed that volcanic vapors might have kept the animals away. Despite its dark fame, in 37 B.C. Marco Agrippa had it connected via channel to the nearby lagoon Lucrino for use as a Roman shipyard. On the eastern shore are the remains of a large **thermal bath complex,** known as Tempio di Apollo.

The largest of the volcanic lakes is **Lake Fusaro** ★, a short distance farther to the south. It was known to the ancients as *Acherusia Palus,* or the Infernal Swamp. In 1782, quite indifferent to the ancients beliefs, Ferdinando IV Bourbon had architect Carlo Vanvitelli (son of the famous Luigi) build a hunting and fishing lodge, the **Casina Reale** ★ (Via Fusaro, Bacoli), on a little island in the lake. At presstime, volunteer-run visits were offered only on Sunday from 10am to 1pm (② 081-8687635; admission 1€).

Where to Stay

The hotels in this area are generally not quality, however, staying locally is a good alternative to booking a more-expensive—and logistically less-convenient—hotel in Naples, particularly if you are planning a full day of sightseeing followed by a visit to Ischia or Procida (see chapter 9).

Cala Moresca ★   On the cliffs of Capo Miseno, this pleasant and welcoming hotel offers comfortable accommodations and lots of extras, such as an outdoor swimming pool, a playground, a country trail, and outdoor activities such as tennis and squash. A path descends to a large shelf of rock on a secluded cove from which swimmers plunge into the blue sea. Guest rooms are large and bright, with simple modern furnishings, tiled floors, and good-size bathrooms. Most rooms have private balconies overlooking the sea. There are also studios and one-bedroom serviced apartments that rent for a minimum of 3 days during high season and 1 week the rest of the year, for similar rates as the hotel's doubles. The onsite **restaurant** is a great place for a very good and moderately priced meal.

Via Faro, 44 80070 Bacoli. © **081-5235595.** Fax 081-5235557. www.calamoresca.it. 27 units. 135€–160€ **155**
double. Rates include buffet breakfast. Children 2 and under stay free in parent's room. AE, DC, MC, V. Free
parking. Closed Dec 24–26. **Amenities:** Restaurant; bar; babysitting; pool; tennis court; room service. *In
room:* A/C, TV, minibar.

Hotel Ristorante il Gabbiano   The pluses at this hotel are the courtesy shuttle (to
local destinations, otherwise, discounted taxi rates are offered), the good **restaurant,** and
the welcoming service. The amiable management does its best to compensate for a not-
so-glamorous location in town near busy roads (it also has soundproof windows). The
hotel is not by the water but enjoys good sea views from some rooms. All rooms are spacious, full of light, and classically decorated with period furniture. Bathrooms are modern and good-size.

Via Cicerone 21, Baia. © **081-8687969.** Fax 081-8040255. www.ilgabbianohotel.com. 23 units. 170€
double; 185€ triple; 250€ junior suite. Rates include buffet breakfast. Half- and full-board available. Children 3 and under stay free in parent's room; children 12 and under 50% discount. AE, DC, MC, V. Free
parking. Closed Dec 24–26. **Amenities:** Restaurant; bar; babysitting; Internet (free); room service.
In room: A/C, TV, minibar.

Villa Giulia (Finds)   The delightful host has tastefully restored this ancient farmhouse,
creating a haven of beauty in the mist of unsightly new construction (happily invisible
from the premises). The homey B&B offers only five units, ranging in size from studios
to huge one-bedroom accommodations, each complete with kitchen and its own patio
or garden. The large garden is full of flowers in fair weather, and the good-size pool is
another bonus. The week-long cooking classes that focus on pizza and other Neapolitan
specialties are fun and well organized.

Via Cuma Licola 178, 80072 Pozzuoli. © **081-8540163.** Fax 081-8044356. www.villagiulia.info. 5 units.
110€–130€ double; 150€ triple. Rates include buffet breakfast. Children 2 and under stay free in parent's
room. AE, DC, MC, V. Free parking. **Amenities:** Restaurant; pool. *In room:* TV.

Where to Dine

In addition to the following restaurants, also consider the restaurants in the hotels we list
above and the local farms that operate as *agriturismo:* One we like for the quality of the
food and the hospitality is **Il Casolare di Tobia,** Via Selvatico 12, off Via Castello, Contrada Coste Fondi di Baia, 80070 Bacoli (© **081-5235193;** fax 081-3048034; www.
datobia.it; reservations recommended), in a valley that is actually an extinct crater. **Il
Cetrangolo,** Via Faro 62, Miseno (© **081-5232688** or 081-5235595) offers excellent
food at moderate prices and great views to boot.

Moderate

Arturo al Fusaro ★ (Finds) NEAPOLITAN   This excellent restaurant offers traditional local cuisine in a pleasant atmosphere, and at reasonable prices. The specialty is
seafood, which is extremely fresh and served up in appetizers, pasta and rice dishes, and
main courses. You might want to sample the flawless *risotto ai frutti di mare* (with seafood); *vermicelli cozze e vongole* (with mussels and clams); or one of the catches of the day
prepared *all'acqua pazza* (in light herbed broth), grilled with herbs, or baked over a bed
of potatoes.

Via Cuma 322, Bacoli. © **081-8543130.** Reservations recommended Sat–Sun. Secondi 7€–14€. AE, DC,
MC, V. Daily noon–3pm and 7–10:30pm.

Bobò ★ NEAPOLITAN   Along the harbor in Pozzuoli, this is an excellent choice for a
seafood dinner by the shore. The cuisine is traditional but prepared with high-quality, fresh

Great Gelato Breaks

For the best gelato in the area, head to Via Napoli in Pozzuoli. Among the many bars and *gelaterie* lining the street, our favorites are **Anema e Cono,** Corso Umberto I 59 (☏ **081-5263254**), and **Sneezy,** Corso Umberto I 165 (☏ **081-5264777**).

ingredients, and infused with a spark of creativity. We recommend the homemade fresh fusilli with zucchini, baby clams, and *pecorino di fossa* (aged sheep cheese) or the excellent grilled fish. The tasting menu for 50€ is the way to go if you have a hearty appetite.

Lungomare Cristoforo Colombo 20, Pozzuoli. ☏ **081-5262034.** www.ristorantebobo.it. Reservations recommended. Secondi 15€–24€. AE, DC, MC, V. Mon and Wed–Fri 12:30–2pm and 7:30–11pm; Sat 7:30–11pm; Sun 12:30–2pm.

Cagi Di Ludovico Avallone ★ NEAPOLITAN   This is a good address in Pozzuoli for meat as well as seafood. All dishes are prepared traditionally, with good local ingredients. We are partial to *spaghetti alle vongole* (with clams), but the *fusilli al ragù* (with Neapolitan meat sauce) is also excellent; for secondo, we recommend the *fettina alla pizzaiola* (beef in a tomato and oregano sauce).

Via Nicola Fasano 6, Pozzuoli. ☏ **081-5268255.** Reservations recommended Sat–Sun. Secondi 12€–18€. AE, DC, MC, V. Tues–Sat noon–3pm and 7:30–11pm; Sun noon–3pm.

Inexpensive

Abraxas Osteria & Wine Bar NEAPOLITAN   Popular with the younger crowd and the Anglo-American community from the nearby NATO base, this trendy restaurant offers good cuisine, pleasant views, and a great garden for outdoor dining. It is also active at organizing wine tastings and other special culinary and cultural events. We particularly appreciated the great attention to the wine list, with many little-known but excellent local choices (such as the very good house wine), and to the ever-changing menu, merging creativity with a love for the hearty products of this region. If they are on the menu, do not miss the *crespelle* (thin savory crepes/pancakes with a cheese and walnuts sauce) or the *coniglio in porchetta* (roasted boneless rabbit). The chef also prepares a great grilled steak and, in winter, superb sausage-based dishes, such as the *verza con salsicce e castagne* (savoy cabbage with sausages and chestnuts) and polenta, served grilled with sausages or with sauce.

Via Scalandrone 15, Lucrino. ☏ **081-854-9347.** www.abraxasosteria.it. Reservations recommended Sat–Sun. Secondi 10€–15€. AE, DC, MC, V. Wed–Sat 7:30–11pm; Sun noon–3pm and 7:30–11pm.

Garibaldi NEAPOLITAN/SEAFOOD   This seaside place makes for an excellent stop after a visit to the museum or the archaeological area of Baia. It takes advantage of its prime location by specializing in seafood—simply prepared, but using fresh ingredients and traditional recipes. *Fusilli ai frutti di mare* (with seafood) is a perfect way to begin the meal, but you shouldn't miss out on the secondo: excellent *polpi in guazzetto* (squid in a tomato sauce), as well as some of the most flavorful grilled fish in the area.

Via Spiaggia di Bacoli 36, Bacoli. ☏ **081-5234368.** Reservations recommended Sat–Sun. Secondi 8€–16€. AE, DC, MC, V. Tues–Sun noon–3pm and 7–11pm.

Il Tucano PIZZA It's a bit touristy, yes, but excellent pizza and traditional specialties make this restaurant worth a visit. The heir of the historical Trattoria Miramare, which occupied this spot since 1929, Il Tucano makes a real effort to honor the old trattoria's menu and to offer a wide selection of local wines. It also serves up a large variety of pizzas—including the exceptional *quattro formaggi e gamberetti* (four cheese and shrimp). The slices are served "by the foot": you ask for a length, and they cut it and charge you accordingly.

Via Molo di Baia, Baia. (𝒞 **081-8545046.** Pizza 3€–8€. MC, V. Tues–Sun noon–midnight.

POMPEII, HERCULANEUM, VESUVIUS

6

THE PHLEGREAN FIELDS

7

The Land of Sirens: Sorrento & Its Peninsula

The unique beauty of Sorrento's coast has inspired many myths: This, for instance, is where the Sirens are said to have waylaid travelers with their irresistible song, as happened to Ulysses in Homer's *Odyssey*.

Today, the pull of the sea and imposing rock-bound coast remain as strong as in Homer's day, attracting legions of visitors. Indeed, it is unlikely that you will feel alone here, especially if you come during the summer months. Sorrento's charms are not tarnished by the crowds, though, as the town is only made merrier by the bustle. You will also always find many off-the-beaten-path attractions along this peninsula, which is simply one of the most beautiful in the Mediterranean.

A rocky point of land jutting into the sea and dominated by the high mountains of Monti Lattari, the Sorrentine peninsula stretches for about 20km (12 miles). It is a finger of land pointing to Capri—which is only 5km (3 miles) away at Punta Campanella, the closest point—and dividing the Gulf of Naples from the Gulf of Salerno. Visitors come here to hike rugged paths, discover towers and rural villages,

explore ancient ruins, and sample a cuisine rich with locally produced ingredients, including cheeses and cured meats so good that they don't make it to the rest of the mainland.

The gateway to the Sorrento peninsula is **Castellammare di Stabia,** a modern town and thermal resort built over the ancient Roman settlement of Stabiae. **Sorrento** is the main town of the peninsula, about midway to the tip on the northern shore, opening onto the Gulf of Naples. On the mountains above Sorrento and on the cliffs beyond are many villages connected by winding—and often bumpy—narrow local roads, which remain undiscovered precisely because of their inaccessibility.

On the other side of the mountains is a very authentic and little-explored stretch of coast. Harsh and rocky, it is the continuation of the famous Amalfi Coast—which starts at Positano (see chapter 8)—and of the Sorrentine peninsula's southern shore. Even in the midst of celebrated attractions and hordes of tourists, you'll find yourself only a stone's throw from quieter byways and hidden pleasures.

1 CASTELLAMMARE DI STABIA ★

33km (20 miles) SE of Naples

If you have a taste for restful and leisurely sightseeing, then the town of Castellammare di Stabia is the place for you. Opening like a fan onto the Bay of Naples, the town enjoys a beautiful location between beaches and hills. It is blessed with several natural springs—28 of them, each with its own therapeutic characteristics—that have made Castellammare a popular resort since antiquity. It was then called Stabiae; and Cicero, among other prominent Romans, used to spend his vacations here, until the eruption of

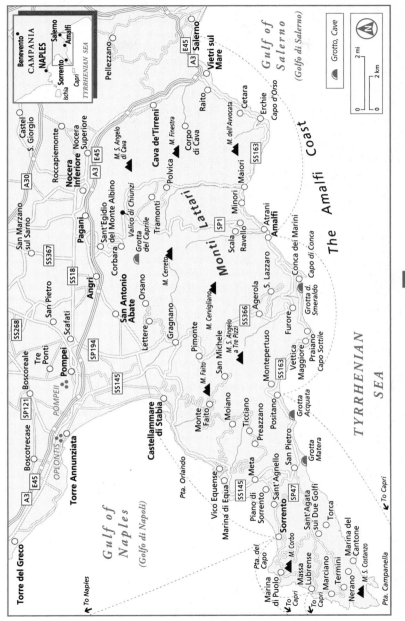

A.D. 79 obliterated the town. The settlement was reborn after the disaster, but its inhabitants were forced to take refuge in the mountains to escape from the incursions of Goths and Longobards.

In the 9th century, the citizens build Castrum a Mare, the castle that lent the town its modern name. The Angevin dynasty later surrounded the town with walls, enlarged its harbor, and built the Royal Palace for the king's vacations. The Bourbons subsequently created a prosperous shipyard that fueled the development of the town. Today, it remains one of the most important shipyards in Italy.

ESSENTIALS

GETTING THERE & AROUND The **bus** is a good option, with **SITA** (☎ 081-5522176; www.sitabus.it) offering service from Naples, Sorrento, and **Curreri Viaggi** (☎ 081-8015420; www.curreriviaggi.it) offering regular departures from Naples's Capodichino Airport as well as from Rome (respectively for 10€ and 16€). You can also easily arrive by **train:** The **Circumvesuviana** (☎ 800-053939; www.vesuviana.it) railroad from Naples and nearby towns offers frequent service and makes four stops in town; the ride takes 35 minutes from Naples and costs 2.40€ (for more information on public transportation fares, see "The Unico Travel Pass," p. 48). You can also use the **FS** national rail service (☎ 892021 in Italy; www.trenitalia.it); trains arrive at Castellammare FS station on Piazza Giacomo Matteotti.

From Naples or another seaside location, **ferries** provide the most scenic method of travel to Castellammare: **Metro del Mare** (☎ 199-600700; www.metrodelmare.com) runs from Pozzuoli, Naples, and Sorrento (service is suspended in winter). Other companies offering seasonal service are **Alilauro** (☎ 081-4972238; www.alilauro.it), **LMP** (☎ 081-5513236; www.consorziolmp.it), and **NLG** (☎ 081-5527209; www.navlib.it). By **car,** take autostrada A3 to the exit for CASTELLAMMARE DI STABIA; once on SS 145, follow the CASTELLAMMARE DI STABIA signs directly into town.

Buses and trains are the best way to get around the area; in town, there are local buses, but **taxis** are more convenient. As elsewhere in Italy, drivers wait at taxi stands, at Piazza Matteotti (☎ 081-8706251) and Piazza Unità d'Italia (☎ 081-8710577).

VISITOR INFORMATION The **tourist office,** Piazza Matteotti 34, 80053 Castellammare di Stabia (☎ 081-8711334t), provides information on all things Castellammare, from spas to archaeology. You'll find a **pharmacy** (☎ 081-8701077) at Via Plinio il Vecchio 62. The **hospital,** Ospedale San Leonardo (☎ 081-8729111), is on Viale Europa. Dial ☎ 118 for an **ambulance** and ☎ 113 or 112 for the **police.** The **post office,** Piazza Giovanni XXIII 4 (☎ 081-8711449), is open Monday to Saturday from 8am to 2pm. For your banking needs, **Banco San Paolo** (☎ 081-8713501) is at Corso Vittorio Emanuele 76.

EXPLORING THE TOWN

In addition to its excavated ancient Roman villas, **Scavi di Stabia,** Castellammare prides itself on a number of other worthy attractions. In addition to the archaeological area, we highly recommend an excursion up **Monte Faito** ★, the tall mountain (1,100m/3,609 ft. high) looming over Castellammare and the sea: You'll enjoy unrivaled views over the Gulf of Naples. Although you can drive, we'd much rather take the *funivia* **(funicular)** from the center of town (Piazza Stazione Circumvesuviana). It runs every half-hour, and the round-trip fare is 7€. You can return via funivia, or hike down (consider about an hour for the descent; inquire at the tourist office for more information).

DINING ◆
Giovanni di Pozzano **1**
Osteria da Mena **5**
Tolino dal 1816 **2**
Trattoria O' Pignatiello **4**

ACCOMMODATIONS ■
GH La Medusa **6**
Hotel dei Congressi **7**
Hotel Stabia **3**

Nuove Terme Stabiane ★, Viale delle Terme 3, on the slopes of Monte Faito (© **081-391311;** www.termedistabia.com), is a state-of-the-art thermal spa near **Villa Quisisana,** the historic royal summer palace. Downtown, **Villa Comunale,** off Piazza Giovanni XXIII, near the Stazione Circumvesuviana (free admission; open from sunrise to sunset) is a public garden that opens onto the Gulf of Naples. Not to be missed is the elegant **Cassa Armonica** (bandstand)—a Liberty masterpiece created by Eugenio Cosenza in 1901. The **castle** above the town is private and cannot be visited; nor can you tour the **Villa Quisiana,** the residence of Bourbon royals, which is being renovated to house multimedia exhibits on the Vesuvian area, as well as the local archaeological collection.

Scavi di Stabia ★ This archaeological area contains the remains of Stabiae, the ancient Roman resort town destroyed in the same eruption as the more famous Pompeii and Herculaneum. Little of the town itself has been excavated, but some of the elegant *villae di otium* (pleasure residences) were uncovered in the 18th century; much of the art that was found is on display in the National Archaeological Museum of Naples. Further excavations in the 1950s uncovered more artifacts that were left *in situ.* A superb example of an ancient Roman patrician villa, the **Villa di Arianna** ★, Via Piana di Varano (from town, take Viale Europa and turn left onto SS 366 toward Gragnano, and then immediately left again onto Via Piana di Varano), takes its name from a painting found inside: a beautiful **fresco** depicting the mythological Ariadne as she is discovered sleeping by Dyonisius.

In a dramatic location, the villa was designed to take maximum advantage of the views over the sea and Mount Faito. Though partly ransacked in the 18th century after its discovery, the villa retains much of its decorative elements: Of particular beauty are the frescos in the summer *triclinium* (**dining room**)—the one of Ariadne described above and another depicting Ganimede taken by an eagle up to Jupiter—and the room decorated with diagonal stripes of delicately **painted tiles**—only a few remain as many have been removed (some can be seen at the archaeological museum in Naples). You should also visit **Villa di San Marco** ★, Via Passeggiata Archeologica, a very impressive patrician villa (in spite of damage suffered in the 1980 earthquake). Built in the 1st century B.C. as the residence of a rich family, it was later enlarged in the 1st century A.D. and became quite palatial, with porticos, halls, and private thermal baths (in three temperatures: *calidarium, tepidarium,* and *frigidarium*), all decorated with stucco, paintings, and frescoes.

Within walking distance, you'll find the ***Grotta di San Biagio*** (**St. Biagio's Grotto**), a tufa-stone quarry—used in Roman times for the construction of the villas in Stabiae—that was transformed into a paleochristian oratory in the 5th to 6th centuries A.D. The first bishops of Stabiae are buried here, making it one of the oldest known Christian burial sites. It is decorated with well-preserved frescoes and paintings that date from the 5th to 6th centuries and from the 9th to 10th centuries A.D., except for three frescoes by the entrance, which are from the 14th century.

Via Passeggiata Archeologica (follow directions for Varano, also for Grand Hotel La Medusa). ℂ **081-8575347**. www.pompeiisites.org. Admission 5.50€, includes same-day admission to Boscoreale and Oplonti. Artecard discount available (p. 110); 3-day cumulative ticket (includes Herculaneum, Pompeii, Oplontis, Stabiae, and Boscoreale) 20€. Train: Circumvesuviana to Via Nocera stop, then switch to bus 1 rosso. Nov–Mar daily 8:30am–6:30pm; Apr–Oct daily 8:30am–7:30pm. Last admission 90 min. earlier. Closed Jan 1, May 1, and Dec 25.

WHERE TO STAY

Castellammare is a good jumping-off point for visits to the archaeological areas of Vesuvius, including Pompeii and Herculaneum. It's better than the more crowded and expensive suburbs of Naples, and your money goes farther than in the region's capital, nearby Vico Equense, or glitzy Sorrento.

Expensive

Crowne Plaza Stabiae Sorrento Coast ★ **(Kids)**   Inside a refurbished cement factory in Pozzano, south of town, this seaside hotel is large but charming. Amenities include access to a private beach—small but one of the rare stretches of sand in the area—and a spa that is the pride of the hotel, with 13 treatment rooms, five hydro baths, a Jacuzzi, a solarium, a sauna, fitness facilities, and specially tailored health and beauty programs. Guest rooms are spacious and full of light, although only the better rooms enjoy the best sea views. Some open onto a private terrace, and "family rooms" are actually two-bedroom units with separate bathrooms. All bathrooms have tub/shower combinations.

Strada Statale Sorrentina (SS 145, km 11), Pozzano, 80053 Castellammare di Stabia. ℂ **081-3946700**. Fax 081-3946770. www.crowneplazasorrento.com. 150 units. 220€–280€ double; from 400€ suite. Rates include buffet breakfast. Internet specials available. AE, DC, MC, V. Free parking. **Amenities:** Restaurant; bar; concierge; pool; room service; spa. *In room:* A/C, TV, minibar, Wi-Fi (for a fee).

Grand Hotel La Medusa ★★ This luxury hotel has the best setting in town: In a beautifully restored 19th-century villa surrounded by a splendid park and terraced garden, it is simply picture perfect and oh so romantic. It is convenient to the archaeological area, albeit farther from the center of town and the shore. The hotel features plush public spaces and salons, and elegantly appointed guest rooms, which are decorated with a sophisticated mix of classic and modern furnishings, beautiful tiled floors, and Oriental carpets, as well as fine linens and fabrics. Bathrooms are a good size (some with shower only), and the best rooms have Jacuzzi tubs and views over the Gulf of Naples. We recommend upgrading to a superior or a deluxe room, as the "traditional" ones are a bit dark.

Via Passeggiata Archeologica 5, 80053 Castellammare di Stabia. ℂ **081-8723383.** Fax 081-8717009. www.lamedusahotel.com. 52 units. High season 190€–280€ double; 300€ suite. Rates include buffet breakfast. Internet specials available. AE, DC, MC, V. Free parking. **Amenities:** Restaurant; 2 bars; concierge; pool; outdoor tennis courts; room service. *In room:* A/C, TV, minibar.

Moderate

Hotel dei Congressi ★ (**Kids**) This highly service-oriented establishment is conveniently located across from the Nuove Terme Stabiane and a short distance from the archaeological area. In a more modern building than La Medusa, the hotel offers spacious public spaces, including a large swimming pool and a pleasant terrace garden. Guest rooms are large and bright, each with a private balcony large enough for a table and chairs. The furnishings are tasteful, and rooms have tiled floors and ample modern bathrooms. The best rooms share superb panoramic views with the terraced swimming pool. The triple and quad rooms are a plus for families or small groups.

Viale Puglia 45, 80053 Castellammare di Stabia. ℂ/fax **081-8722277.** www.hoteldeicongressi.it. 84 units. 150€–250€ double. Rates include buffet breakfast. Children 2 and under stay free in parent's room. AE, DC, MC, V. Free parking. **Amenities:** Restaurant; bar; concierge; pool; room service. *In room:* A/C, TV, minibar.

Hotel Stabia ★ (**Finds**) Serving guests since 1876 and offering professional service and fine accommodations, this fetchingly pink hotel is the best of Castellammare's historic establishments. Built in the 19th century along the downtown seaside promenade, the hotel was carefully restored to preserve its neoclassical style. Both common spaces and guest rooms have been redecorated, but many of the original furnishings have been incorporated into the design, inspiring a sense of peaceful elegance. Guest rooms are spacious, with tiled floors and neoclassical furnishings; many rooms have their own small balconies or terraces sharing views of Monte Faito or—the best rooms—of the Gulf of Naples and Ischia.

Corso Vittorio Emanuele 101, 80053 Castellammare di Stabia. ℂ **081-8722577.** Fax 081-8722105. www. hotelstabia.com. 97 units. 200€ double. Rate includes buffet breakfast. AE, DC, MC, V. Free parking. **Amenities:** Restaurant; bar; room service. *In room:* A/C, TV, Internet, minibar.

WHERE TO DINE
Moderate

Giovanni di Pozzano ★ (**Finds**) SORRENTINE/SEAFOOD   Adored by locals, this traditional restaurant offers dining rooms and outdoor terraces invigorated by live music on weekend evenings. The menu changes with the season, but fresh homemade pasta and seafood are particularly well prepared year-round. We highly recommend the *cavatelli alle vongole* (with clams) and the *pezzogna al sale* (local fish baked in a salt crust).

Via Vecchia Pozzano 40. ℂ **081-8026101.** Reservations recommended Sat–Sun. Secondi 12€–18€. AE, DC, MC, V. Wed–Mon noon–3pm and 7:30–11pm.

Tolino dal 1816 ★★ SORRENTINE/PIZZA   This historic restaurant has not lost its touch over the years. Locals and visitors alike come to enjoy the indoor and outdoor dining as well as the pleasant piano bar. The cuisine is traditional, with a focus on seafood, but you'll also find vegetarian and meat choices on the menu. We recommend the *linguine con le zucchine* (with zucchini) and the great *impepata di cozze* (steamed mussels with white pepper). The pizza is also very good.

Corso Vittorio Emanuele 13. ℂ **081-8711607.** Reservations recommended. Secondi 12€–21€. AE, DC, MC, V. Wed–Mon 12:30–3:30pm and 8–11:30pm.

Inexpensive

Osteria da Mena ★ (Finds) SORRENTINE   This little osteria offers well-prepared local specialties in a relaxed atmosphere. The homemade pasta is very good—when in luck, you'll find excellent *scialatielli ai frutti di mare* (thick spaghetti with basil and shellfish)—and the *frittura* (deep-fried medley of seafood) is crisp and juicy. Meat often graces the seasonal menu, including excellent *pollo arrosto* (roasted chicken) and tender *arrosto di maiale* (pork roast).

Via Pietro Carrese 32. ℂ **081-8713048.** Reservations recommended. Secondi 10€–18€. No credit cards. Daily noon–3pm and 7:30–11pm.

Trattoria O'Pignatiello ★ (Finds) SORRENTINE/SEAFOOD   This authentic local hangout is excellent for simple and traditional food, prepared with local ingredients. Family run, it always offers a well-rounded choice of dishes, though it prides itself on the seafood specialties. Usually on the menu is the *insalata di polipo* (octopus salad), which we highly recommend as an appetizer, followed by the delicious *spaghetti ai frutti di mare* (with seafood). The grilled blue fish and the grilled meats are also excellent. The lunch menu, including a pasta dish and a secondo, is a steal at 10€.

Via Alcide De Gasperi 207. ℂ **081-8715100.** Reservations recommended. Secondi 8€–15€. AE, DC, MC, V. Daily noon–3pm and 7:30–11pm. Closed Dec 24–Jan 6.

2 VICO EQUENSE ★

42 km (26 miles) SE of Naples

Smaller and less elegant then Sorrento, Vico Equense is far less visited by foreign tourists. On a tufa-stone platform overlooking the sea, the town's charm and personality are not lost on Italian tourists, who seek it out especially in August.

ESSENTIALS

GETTING THERE   You can easily reach Vico Equense by **train,** via the **Circumvesuviana Railway** (ℂ 800-053939; www.vesuviana.it), or by **bus,** via **SITA** (ℂ 081-5522176; www.sitabus.it) service from Naples, Sorrento, and the Amalfi Coast. **Curreri Viaggi** (ℂ 081-8015420; www.curreriviaggi.it) offers service from Naples's Capodichino Airport as well as from Rome (respectively for 10€ and 16€).

If you are coming by **car,** from the autostrada A1, switch to the A3, and take the exit CASTELLAMMARE DI STABIA. Follow the signs for VICO EQUENSE and SORRENTO to SS 145, the coastal road that leads to Vico Equense.

GETTING AROUND   Vico is not a large town and everything is pretty much within **walking** distance, including the beaches and mountain trails. You can also call a **taxi** at ℂ **081-8015405,** or go to the taxi stand on Piazza Umberto I.

The **tourist office** (© 081-8015752; fax 081-8799351;
www.vicoturismo.it) is at Via San Ciro 16 and maintains an information stand at Piazza
Umberto I 19. The **hospital** (© 081-8015465) is on Via D. Caccioppoli. You'll find a
pharmacy (© 081-8015525) on Via Roma 18 and another on Corso Filangieri, as well as
several **banks,** including a Banco di Napoli (© 081-8015915). For first aid, the hospital,
or an ambulance, dial © 081-8729103. You can call the **police** at © 113 and the **fire
department** at © 115. The **post office** (© 081-8016811) is at Via San Ciro 57.

EXPLORING THE TOWN

Excavations in the ancient town of Vico Equense have found remains dating to the 6th
century B.C., proving the existence of Oscan, Etruscan, and Greek occupants (evidenced
by the **Necropolis** of Via Nicotera). Named *Aequa* during Roman times, the town survived the eruption of A.D. 79 and flourished until it was destroyed by the Goths in 553.
It was then reestablished as "Vico Equense" by the Angevins in the 12th century. To
discover the delightful medieval buildings of Vico Equense, start from the main square,
Piazza Umberto I, take **Via Filangieri,** and turn right onto **Via Monsignor Natale.**

This street is the heart of the medieval town and its buildings shelter delightful medieval courtyards, such as the splendid one at no. 3. Continuing on, you can enjoy the great
view from **Largo dei Tigli,** and, retracing your steps to Vescovado, visit the **Chiesa
dell'Annunziata,** Via Cattedrale (daily 8am–12:30pm and 3:30–7pm), a 14th-century
church partially redone in the 17th century after the 1688 earthquake. In the upper town
is a 13th-century **castle,** renovated and enlarged in later centuries, and thermal springs
feed the local **spas.**

Scrajo Terme ★   A thermal spa created in the 19th century, this is the best place in
town to "take the waters." The old-fashioned jewel is a short distance from town, off SS
145 on a cliff overlooking the beach, and offers a wide range of treatments and therapies
(fees start at 24€). The public spaces overlook the shore in a cascade of terraces, and the
spa has a delightful ambience. Swim at the private beach where the sulfur spring flows
into the sea, creating a mineral mix with unique healing properties. The charming **restaurant** on the premises is housed in a Liberty-style (Italian Art Nouveau) hall, with a
bar and attached terrace affording beautiful views over the sea. The spa also offers seven
bright and well-furnished guest rooms (150€–220€ double, including breakfast and
access to the spa).

Via Luigi Serio 10 (SS 145), Località Scrajo, 80069 Vico Equense. © 081-8015731. www.scrajoterme.it.
AE, DC, MC, V. Daily 8am–8pm; restaurant till 10pm.

STAYING ACTIVE

Vico offers many opportunities to explore the area's natural attractions, and enjoying the
sea and the mountains is one of the best things to do in town. Across from the Municipio
in the center of town, you can take **Via Castello Marina,** the steep old footpath that,
descending through olive groves, will lead you to **Vico Marina.** There you will find small
beaches hidden inside picturesque coves. One of the nicest is **Marina di Equa,** west of
a defensive tower built in the 17th century.

Another great hike—but one that requires you to be moderately fit and is best accomplished with a good trail map (available from the tourist office in town)—is the old
footpath to **Positano.** Although the area has been inhabited for thousands of years, SS
163, the Amalfi Drive, dates only from 1840; before then, the footpaths were the only
means of travel and communication on the peninsula. For centuries, residents trekked

over mountain paths and commuted by boat to points along the coast. Walking the succession of trails to Positano will require about 3½ hours. Follow the directions for Ticciano until you reach the **bridge over the Milo;** there, on your left, you'll find a dirt road to the pass of **Santa Maria al Castello** (altitude 685m/2,247 ft.). Just before the church, to your left, is the connection to *Sentiero degli Dei* **(Trail of Gods)** toward Nocelle. Instead, turn left at the dirt track directly across from the church; this is the trail that leads to Positano. When you reach the fork, the western spur climbs to Monte Comune (altitude 877m/2,877 ft.), with its sweeping views; the eastern branch begins the descent to Positano. Along this trail are several tricky passages around points of rock, so look carefully at your map.

The many *agriturismi* (farmhouses) are great places to have lunch and to experience daily agricultural activities; you can also arrange an overnight stay. One of our favorites is **Coop-Agrituristica La Ginestra,** Via Tessa 2, Santa Maria di Castello (© **081-8023211;** www.laginestra.org; 80€ double, including breakfast), a beekeeping farm that makes delicious organic honey. Another *agriturismo* is **Masseria Astapiana Villa Giusso,** Via Camaldoli 51, 80069 Vico Equense (©/fax **081-8024392** or 081-403797; www.astapiana.com). A historic patrician farm building, it dates from the 17th century, and many of the original frescoes have been preserved. Surrounded by parkland, it has a museum, offers organized tours and cooking classes, and serves dinner. It also has a few simply appointed rooms for rent (100€–120€ double).

WHERE TO STAY

Hotels in Vico command dramatic views and are perfectly fine for a night, but are not ideal for extended stays. Families in particular might do better at **Scrajo Terme** (p. 165) or the two *agriturismi* mentioned above.

Expensive

Grand Hotel Angiolieri   Outside Vico Equense in the village of Seiano, this grand villa was built in the 18th century on the ruins of an ancient Roman patrician residence said to have belonged to Cicero. The restoration added a few questionable details but, on the whole, the place is elegant and the views superb. Guest rooms are not large—particularly the basic ones: It's definitely worth upgrading—but they are attractive, with a complementary mix of contemporary furniture and classic details. Bathrooms are nicely styled with bright mosaic tiles (some with shower or bathtub only). Pricier rooms enjoy sea views; some of these units, and all the suites, have private terraces or balconies. The swimming pool is a plus, and the gourmet restaurant **L'Accanto** serves beautiful food from a breathtaking terrace.

Via Santa Maria Vecchia 2, 80066 Seiano di Vico Equense. © **081-8029161.** Fax 081-8028558. www.grandhotelangiolieri.it. 40 units. 310€ double; 490€ junior suite. Rates include buffet breakfast. Children 2 and under stay free in parent's room. AE, DC, MC, V. Parking 15€. **Amenities:** Restaurant; pool. *In room:* A/C, TV, Internet, minibar.

Hotel Capo La Gala   In the cliffs among olive groves and lemon-tree terraces overlooking the sea, this hotel enjoys a rare quiet not far from town. Guest rooms are bright and tastefully decorated with streamlined modern furniture and local hand-painted tiles; each has its own private balcony and great views. The outdoor swimming pool is filled from a natural spring of sulfur thermal water (the smell takes some getting used to, but it is oh so good for your skin), or you can use the facilities at the rocky beach on the Tyrrenian Sea. Management might require a minimum stay of 3 nights during the months of July and August.

Via Luigi Serio 8 (1km/.6 mile before Vico coming from Castellammare), Scrajo Terme 80069 Vico Equense.
© 081-8015758. Fax 081-8798747. www.capolagala.com. 18 units. 350€–550€ double. Rates include buffet breakfast and rental of beach facilities. Internet specials available. AE, DC, MC, V. Free parking. Closed Nov–Mar. **Amenities:** Restaurant; pool; room service. *In room:* A/C, TV/DVD, minibar, Wi-Fi.

Moderate

Hotel Aequa (Finds) This hotel has been serving its guests in the heart of town by the medieval area since the 1940s, and its old-fashioned charm has only been enhanced by the renovations. The property is perched on the cliffs overlooking the sea and affords excellent views: We love gazing at Mount Vesuvius from under the glorious wisteria on the terrace. Guest rooms are spacious and well-appointed with hardwood floors and classic furnishings; bathrooms are modern and good-size.

Via Filangeri 46, 80069 Vico Equense. © 081-8015331. Fax 081-8015071. www.aequahotel.it. 70 units. 120€–145€ double. Rates include buffet breakfast. Children 2 and under stay free in parent's room. AE, DC, MC, V. Parking 12€. **Amenities:** Restaurant; bar; pool. *In room:* A/C, TV, minibar.

WHERE TO DINE

In addition to the following restaurants, good local food is available at the hotels and *agriturismi* above. Great for a picnic, **La Tradizione** ★★★, Via Raffaele Bosco 969, Seiano di Vico Equense (© 081-8028437; www.latradizione.com; Tues-Sun 9am–2pm and 4:30–9pm) sells wine, olive oil, delicious bread, and local mozzarella (which can be braided and studded with olives and prosciutto), as well as preserves and crispy *taralli* (Italian cookies). You'll find superb gelato at **Da Gabriele** ★★, Corso Umberto I 5 (© 081-8798744).

Expensive

Ristorante Torre del Saracino ★★★ MODERN SORRENTINE This is a special and justly renowned restaurant, where the food is truly extraordinary and the service just perfect. Hitting the right note between elegance and country, the warm hospitality of Chef Gennaro Esposito remains unmatched. The recent renovations have not affected the quality and, if anything, have made the restaurant even more welcoming. The menu includes popular traditional mainstays as well as the imaginative creations of this talented chef. We highly recommend the delectable *ravioli di pesce ripieni di verdure* (with fish and vegetables), the dish that made this restaurant famous. We also recommend the two tasting menus (80€ and 100€), which are the best way to experience the culinary spirit of the chef. Whatever you do, leave room for the unique homemade desserts, such as the *babà al rhum con crema pasticcera e fragoline di bosco* (rum cake with cream and local wild strawberries).

Via Torretta 9, Marina d'Equa. © 081-8028555. www.torredelsaracino.it. Secondi 15€–35€. AE, DC, MC, V. Tues-Sat 12:30–3:30pm and 7:30–11:30pm; Sun 12:30–3:30pm.

Moderate

Nonna Rosa ★★★ (Finds) MODERN SORRENTINE Tucked away on the road that ascends Monte Faito from the center of town, this restaurant in a 17th-century house is a well-kept local secret. The countryside elegance of the small dining room provides a comfortable background for the excellent food that includes a few interesting seafood dishes; we recommend the *pasta e ceci con le seppioline* (chickpea and pasta soup with baby squid) if it is on the menu—and the lamb roast, or the filet mignon with walnuts and local provolone.

Via Privata Bonea 4 (off Via Raffaele Bosco, Pietrapiano), Vico Equense. © **081-8799055.** www. osterianonnarosa.it. Reservations recommended. Secondi 15€–22€. Tasting menus 65€ and 75€. AE, DC, MC, V. Tues–Sun 7:30–11pm.

Inexpensive

Da Gigino Pizza a Metro, L'Università della Pizza ★★★ PIZZA   At the opposite end of the spectrum from the Torre (above), this eatery is a virtual temple to pizza. In the 1950s, Gigino Dell'Amura baked a pizza that was so long a visiting journalist termed it "pizza a metro," or pizza by the meter. The specialty pizza—perfectly seasoned and with a unique, crispy dough—quickly began to attract admirers; today, Dell'Amura's five sons maintain the tradition in their cavernous restaurant. A meter (about 3 ft.) of pizza is a good serving for five people, and the price depends on the toppings. This place not only serves the best Italian pizza in the world—really!—but it also offers delightful appetizers, such as *frittelle di alghe* (seaweed fritters), a local specialty.

Via Giovanni Nicotera 15, Vico Equense. © **081-8798426** or 081-8798309. www.pizzametro.it. Reservations not accepted. Pizza from 7€. No credit cards. Daily 12:30–3:30pm and 7pm–midnight.

3 SORRENTO ★★★

39km (20 miles) SE of Naples

Emperor Augustus and his successor, Tiberius, were two of Sorrento's early devotees. In later years, the town became a favorite destination for artists and writers, as well as tourists. Although the presence of crowds may dull some of its magic at times, Sorrento's charming cobblestone streets, alluring *lungomare* (seafront promenade), colorful and fragrant flowers, matchless vistas, and lively cultural scene keep getting our high votes.

ESSENTIALS

GETTING THERE   Sorrento is connected to most other destinations in the region by the **Circumvesuviana** railway (© **800-053939;** www.vesuviana.it), and the ride takes about 50 minutes from Naples. **SITA** (© **081-5522176;** www.sitabus.it) offers frequent **bus** service to Sorrento from Naples, Amalfi, Positano, and Salerno. **Curreri Viaggi** (© **081-8015420;** www.curreriviaggi.it) maintains routes from Naples's Capodichino Airport, as well as from Rome and Naples, with stops in Castellammare di Stabia, Vico Equense, Meta, Piano di Sorrento, and Sant'Agnello. The ride to Sorrento from Naples takes about 1 hour and costs 10€; from Rome it is about 3½ hours and costs 16€ (for more information on fares, see "The Unico Travel Pass," p. 48). **Marozzi** (© **06-44249519;** www.marozzivt.it) has daily connections from Rome to Sorrento with stops in Naples, Pompeii, Castellammare di Stabia, and Vico Equense.

In summer, ferries and hydrofoils are a pleasant way to travel. **LMP-Linee Marittime Partenopee** (© **081-55513236;** www.consorziolmp.it), **NLG-Navigazione Libera del Golfo** (© **081-5527209;** www.navlib.it), and **Linee Lauro** (© **081-5522838;** www. alilauro.it) make daily runs to and from Naples, Ischia, and Capri. **Caremar** (© **081-5513882;** www.caremar.it) also serves Capri; and **Volaviamare** (© **081-4972211;** www. volaviamare.it) makes runs from Amalfi and Positano. **Metrò del Mare,** at the Marina Piccola downtown (© **199-446644;** www.metrodelmare.com), is a summer-only commuter ferry serving the whole coast between Salerno and Bacoli.

Taxis offer a flat rate of 100€ to Sorrento from Naples, and **car service** can be arranged in advance with **2golfi,** Via Deserto 30/e, 80064 Sant'Agata sui due Golfi (🕾 **339-8307748** or 339-3494479; www.duegolficarservice.com). **Curreri Viaggi** (above) offers a **shuttle service** (80€ for the first three passengers, 10€ each additional passenger).

By **car,** take the exit for CASTELLAMMARE DI STABIA off autostrada A3, and then follow signs for VICO EQUENSE, META DI SORRENTO, and SORRENTO; these will lead you to route SS 145, the Sorrento peninsula's coastal road.

GETTING AROUND   The **Circumvesuviana** railway (see "Getting There," above) is convenient, as are **ferries** to harbors along the coast (see "Getting There," above). Another option is to **rent a boat** (see "Staying Active," p. 172) or join a **tour group** (see "Tours," p. 172).

Taxi stands are at the harbor (🕾 **081-8783527**), on Piazza Tasso (🕾 **081-8782204**), and in the adjacent village of Sant'Agnello (🕾 **081-8781428**).

Car-rental companies in town include **De Martino,** Via Parsano 8 (🕾 **081 8782801;** www.autoservizidemartino.com), which also provides car service and rents boats and motor scooters. You can rent a motor scooter at **Penisola Rent,** Corso Italia 257 (🕾 **081-8774664;** www.penisolarent.com), which also rents cars; and at **Sorrento Car Service/ Rent a Scooter,** Corso Italia 210 (🕾 **081-8781386;** www.sorrento.it). For **bicycle rental,** head to **Reaction Retail,** Viale Nizza 58 (🕾 **081-8770613;** www.emporiobici.com).

VISITOR INFORMATION   The **AASCT tourist office** (🕾 **081-8074033;** fax 081-8773397; www.sorrentotourism.com) is at Via Luigi De Maio 35, off Piazza Tasso. It's open Monday to Saturday from 9am to 6pm; in July and August it's also open Sunday from 9am to 12:30pm. Besides a good city map, it carries copies of the excellent free magazine *Sorrentum.*

FAST FACTS   You'll find a **pharmacy** (🕾 **081-8781226**) on Corso Italia 131. The **hospital** (🕾 **081-5331111**) is on Corso Italia 1. For an **ambulance,** dial 🕾 **118.** You can call the **police** at 🕾 **112,** 113, or 081-8075311; and you can reach the **fire department** at 🕾 **115.** You will find several **ATMs** in town; one is at the **Deutsche Bank,** Piazza Angelina Lauro 22. The **post office** (🕾 **081-8781495**) is at Corso Italia 210; it's open Monday to Friday from 8am to 6pm and Saturday from 8am to 12:30pm. For **Internet access,** go to **Sorrento info,** Via Tasso 19 (🕾 **081-8074000**).

EXPLORING THE TOWN

Sorrento has ancient Greek, Etruscan, and Oscan beginnings, and was colonized by the Romans in the 1st century B.C., when it became a valued resort for the affluent. But the town's history is checkered, to say the least; this jewel by the sea has been fought over many times. After the fall of the empire, it was taken by the Goths, and then reconquered by the Byzantines in A.D. 552. It remained part of the Byzantine Duchy of Naples until the 10th century. Having been conquered by the Prince of Salerno at the beginning of the 11th century, it succeeded in gaining its independence as a Duchy in 1067, and remained so until conquest by the Normans in 1133; it then passed into the hands of the Angevins. Saracen incursions and rivalry between the nearby towns of Vico Equense and Massa Lubrense made life difficult in Sorrento—and there was worse to come. The town was completely destroyed by Barbary pirates on the nights of June 12 and 13, 1558. Still, the town was immediately rebuilt, this time with numerous defensive towers along the surrounding coast and a new set of walls.

We love strolling through the heart of Sorrento, where some medieval buildings are still intact. From the west side of **Piazza Tasso**, start off on **Via Pietà**; at number 14 you'll find **Palazzo Veniero,** with its facade of typical 13th-century decorations, similar to wood marquetry. At number 24 is **ex-Palazzo Correale** with its original 14th-century portal and two windows. A few steps away, we recommend a visit to the beautiful 15th-century **Duomo,** the Cathedral of San Filippo and San Giacomo, Corso Italia 1 (✆ **081-8782248;** daily 8am–noon and 4–8pm), with its striking Romanesque facade graced by a fresco over the portal. The stubby bell tower to the right is particularly interesting, graced by a majolica clock, and four antique columns at its base; only three of its five levels are original (the two top ones were later additions). Inside the Duomo, you can admire 14th- and 15th-century bas-reliefs and a wooden choir decorated with superb intarsia.

Sorrento is famous for its historical craft of marquetry and wood inlay. We suggest a stop at the **Museo Bottega della Tarsia Lignea** ★, Via San Nicola 28, 2 blocks from Corso Italia (✆ **081-8771942;** admission 8€; Mon–Sat 10am–1pm and 3–6pm; closed national holidays), where you can admire an intriguing collection of 19th-century marquetry furniture in addition to the beautiful frescoes that decorate the 18th-century **Palazzo Pomaranci Santomasi,** which houses the museum.

Continuing on our stroll through medieval Sorrento, you'll come to Piazzetta Padre Reginaldo Giuliani, off Via San Cesareo, where you can take in the elegant and very well-preserved 15th-century *palazzo* **Sedile Dominova.** Nearby is Sorrento's second-most important church, **Basilica di Sant'Antonino,** Piazza Sant'Antonino, off Via Luigi de Maio. Built in the 11th century over a preexisting oratory dedicated to Saint Anthony, it was later redone in the present baroque style, but the interior retains some 15th-century decorations.

Walking back toward the seafront promenade, you will come upon the 18th-century church of **San Francesco,** Piazza Francesco Saverio Gargiulo, off Via San Francesco (daily 8am–1pm and 2–7pm); hidden inside is the splendid 14th-century **cloister** ★★, famous for its concerts and art shows. Contact the tourist center (p. 169) for details. Across from the church is the entrance to **Villa Comunale,** which has a panoramic terrace and is a perfect spot for a quiet rest. From here, you can take the steep ramps descending to **Marina Piccola,** one of Sorrento's harbors. The town's other harbor is **Marina Grande,** which is lined with restaurants and seaside establishments.

Another interesting attraction is the **Museo Correale di Terranova,** Via Correale 48 (✆ **081-8781846;** admission 6€; Wed–Mon 9:30am–1:30pm except national holidays; additional hours Sat 8:15–10:45pm July–Sept), once the home of the brothers Alfredo and Pompeo Correale, counts of Terranova—an old aristocratic family of Sorrento—who donated their villa and private collections to the public. The place gives a unique overview of decorative art from the 16th to the 19th centuries: Stocked with its original furnishings, it houses some excellent Flemish paintings, a collection of Italian and foreign porcelain from reputedly the best 17th- and 18th-century manufacturers, and a number of unusual clocks.

The streets leading to this museum are part of the package: **Via Correale** ★★, starting off Piazza Tasso, is one of the few streets that preserves the flavor of 19th-century Sorrento. We encourage you to continue beyond the museum until you reach the little town of **Sant'Agnello,** with its stately villas built in the past century or two and many elegant hotels.

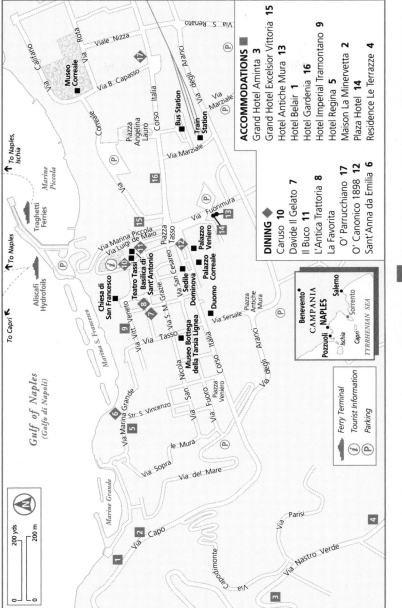

ACCOMMODATIONS ■

Grand Hotel Aminta **3**
Grand Hotel Excelsior Vittoria **15**
Hotel Antiche Mura **13**
Hotel Belair **1**
Hotel Gardenia **16**
Hotel Imperial Tramontano **9**
Hotel Regina **5**
Maison La Minervetta **2**
Plaza Hotel **14**
Residence Le Terrazze **4**

DINING ◆

Caruso **10**
Davide Il Gelato **7**
Il Buco **11**
L'Antica Trattoria **8**
La Favorita
O' Parrucchiano **17**
O' Canonico 1898 **12**
Sant'Anna da Emilia **6**

Benevento
CAMPANIA NAPLES Salerno
Sorrento
Pozzuoli Ischia Capri TYRRHENIAN SEA

🛥 Ferry Terminal
ⓘ Tourist Information
Ⓟ Parking

TOURS   You can rent a car service with a driver (p. 169), but the open-top buses of **Sorrento City Sightseeing,** Via degli Aranci 172, 80067 Sorrento (*©* **081-8774707;** www.sorrento.city-sightseeing.it), are a good option if your time is limited. Departures are from Piazza De Curtis (stazione Circumvesuviana) for the seven-stop hop-on-and-off loop through Massa Lubrense, Termini, Sant'Agata sui Due Golfi, and Sorrento. Tickets are valid for 6 hours and cost 15€ for adults, 7.50€ for children 5 to 15 (children 4 and under are free), and 45€ for a family (two adults and up to three children). The new route to Positano has three departures from Sorrento in the morning and three returns from Positano in the afternoon (round-trip 12€ for adults and 6€ for children).

   Marine Club (*©* **081-8772621;** www.marineclub.it) offers two daily minicruises: One takes in Ischia and Procida, and the other the Sorrentine and Amalfi coasts (with a swimming break in Capri), both with 1- or 2-hour stops at each attraction. The cost is 35€ per person, and the roundtrip takes a full day.

STAYING ACTIVE

Most visitors come to Sorrento for the cultural activities, but those in the know also take advantage of the many opportunities to enjoy the great outdoors. You'll soon realize though that the ruggedness that makes this stretch of coast so beautiful can be a serious obstacle to your physical enjoyment of the shimmering sea: While rocky points and cliffs are part of the visual charm, swimming from them isn't easy. Most of the major hotels in town have worked this out by building their own floating docks that are equipped with umbrellas and lounge chairs—usually connected by elevator to the top of the cliff and the hotel. The only small stretch of pebbly beach is at **Marina Grande,** but it isn't the perfect swimming spot. For real sand, you need to venture east out of town to the small **Marinella Beach,** or farther away to **Vico Equense** (p. 164).

   Nautica Sic Sic, Via Marina Piccola 43 (*©* **081-8072283** or 081-8785606; www. nauticasicsic.com; closed Nov–Apr), is a good place to rent boats; they go for 20€ and up, depending on the size and type. The shop also organizes cruises and offers certified diving courses. Another reputable vendor is **Tony's Beach,** Marina Grande (*©* **081-8785606**).

   A half-hour away by boat (or a longer trip on foot, from a trail starting from the Calata Capo di Sorrento, off Via Capo) *Bagno della Regina Giovanna* **(Queen Giovanna's Bath)** at **Punta del Capo** ★ is our favorite local swimming spot: A small pool of water enclosed by rocks, it was once the private harbor of an ancient Roman villa—**Villa of Pollio Felice**—the ruins of which you can visit at the top of the cliff. Another pleasant boat ride is the one to the *Grotta delle Sirene* **(Grotto of the Sirens),** which is east of Marina Piccola and past Sant'Agnello. In the grotto, the water takes on surprising hues— as if by the charm of magical sea creatures—but it's really based on the ever-changing light.

   Hiking is also high on our list, and the great number of trails, most of which are well maintained and marked, offer treks for people of all skill levels. We recommend using a good trail map; the best is *Carta dei Sentieri* published by C.A.I., the Club Alpino Italiano and for sale at libraries and some newsstands in town. It covers the **Monti Lattari, Penisola Sorrentina,** and **Costiera Amalfitana,** and costs 10€. One of the most beautiful hikes is the one to **Punta Sant'Elia** ★★★, starting from Piazza Sant'Agnello in Sant'Agnello; the trail ends at a rocky point across the peninsula overlooking the little islands of Li Galli, along the Amalfi Coast in the Gulf of Salerno. To reach the trail, take Via Bonaventura Gargiulo up to **Trasaella,** at an altitude of 196m (643 ft.), and then

---

(Moments)   Taking a Cooking Class

If you want to replicate the local cuisine, sign up for a cooking class at the **Sorrento Cooking School,** Viale dei Pini 52 (𝓒 **081-8783555;** www.sorrentocooking
school.com). Classes last 3 hours and end with lunch or dinner, at which you eat
what you prepared (or what the chef has, in the worst case), and drink local wine.
Prices run about 120€. For more to do in and around Sorrento, see "Special-
Interest Trips," p. 62.

---

continue toward **Colli di Fontanelle** at an altitude of 343m (1,125 ft.). From the center
of this village and across Via Belvedere begins the trail to Punta Sant'Elia.

It is also possible to hire a professional guide; we recommend **Giovanni Visetti**
(𝓒 **081-8089613;** www.giovis.com), an expert on this coast and its hinterlands, who
organizes guided hikes of varying difficulty and cost.

WHERE TO STAY

This mecca of international tourism offers myriad choices, but be prepared to shell out
if you want to be in Sorrento proper. Sant'Agnello, adjacent to Sorrento to the east, is
slightly cheaper.

Expensive

Grand Hotel Excelsior Vittoria ★★★ **(Kids)**   On the estate of an impressive villa
and surrounded by a park right in the heart of town, this is one of the best hotels in the
world. Welcoming guests since 1834, it has been run by the same family since its opening. Service is exquisite and individualized; the elegant public spaces and terraces—still
with the original 19th-century furnishings—are perfect places to enjoy a drink. The huge
guest rooms are elegant abodes that are finely decorated and furnished with many
antiques—and all the modern comforts. The refined bathrooms are marble clad. Most of
the rooms open onto a private balcony or terrace, and the best have views over the Gulf
of Naples (the others over the delightful orange-tree garden). From the hotel, elevators
take guests to the private beach-pier off Marina Piccola. In a splendid setting overlooking
the gulf, Terrazza Bosquet offers the most romantic gourmet dining in Sorrento.

Piazza Tasso 34, 80067 Sorrento. 𝓒 **081-8777111.** Fax 081-8771206. www.exvitt.it. 105 units. 400€–610€
double; from 660€ suite. Rates include buffet breakfast. Children 3 and under stay free in parent's room.
Internet and family specials available. AE, DC, MC, V. Free parking. **Amenities:** 2 restaurants; bar; babysitting; concierge; pool; room service; spa. *In room:* A/C, TV, minibar, Wi-Fi (free).

Moderate

Grand Hotel Aminta ★ **(Kids)**   In a dominant position above the town (3km/2 miles
away by free shuttle service), this modern hotel more than compensates for the distance
with breathtaking views, professional service, and good amenities. Public spaces are welcoming, with plenty of arches and curving architectural lines. The hotel's annex is the
completely renovated 18th-century Villa Aminta with a few additional rooms a hundred
meters away from the main building via a garden path. Guest rooms are all bright
and tastefully decorated with modern furniture. Some are more spacious, but all have
modern and scrupulously clean bathrooms; many have balconies affording great views.

The **restaurant** has a magnificent terrace where live music and dancing are often scheduled on summer evenings.

Via Nastro Verde 23, 80067 Sorrento. ℂ **081-8781821.** Fax 081-8781822. www.aminta.it. 81 units. 200€–350€ double; 450€ junior suite. Rates include buffet breakfast. Internet specials available. Children 2 and under stay free in parent's room. AE, DC, MC, V. Free parking. **Amenities:** Restaurant; bar; babysitting; concierge; pool; smoke-free rooms. *In room:* A/C, TV, minibar, Wi-Fi (free).

Hotel Antiche Mura ★ In the heart of town—one of its entrances is on Piazza Tasso—this hotel is in an elegant Italian Art Nouveau–style palazzo built on top of the town's defensive walls, hence, its name. Restoration in keeping with the Belle Epoque spirit of the historic hotel has brought the sophisticated public spaces back to splendor. Guest rooms are bright, decorated with Vietri-tile floors and Sorrentine marquetry furniture. "Comfort" rooms are spacious, and all rooms are equipped with state-of-the-art bathrooms with tub and special hydromassage showers.

Via Fuorimura 7 (entrance on Piazza Tasso), 80067 Sorrento. ℂ **081-8073523.** Fax 081-8071323. www.hotelantichemura.com. 46 units. 300€ double; 400€–430€ suite. Rates include buffet breakfast. Internet specials available. Children 2 and under stay free in parent's room. AE, DC, MC, V. Parking 10€. **Amenities:** Bar; concierge; pool; Wi-Fi (free). *In room:* A/C, TV, minibar.

Hotel Imperial Tramontano ★ (**Kids**) Another of Sorrento's historic hotels, the Tramontano enjoys a dramatic position on a cliff overlooking the sea, a short distance from the center of town. Surrounded by a beautiful garden, the hotel offers the luxury of a patrician abode, with elegant public spaces and top-notch amenities. The spacious guest rooms are furnished with antiques and are bright and welcoming. Some of the rooms have private balconies and sea views. Guests have access to the hotel's private beach via elevator—or a hair-raising series of steps originally built by ancient Romans. The hotel's **restaurant** is one of the best in the area and music events are regularly staged on the **terrace.**

Via Vittorio Veneto 1, 80067 Sorrento. ℂ **081-8782588.** Fax 081-8072344. www.hoteltramontano.it. 116 units. 230€–330€ double; from 390€ suite. Rates include buffet breakfast. Family specials available. Children 3 and under stay free in parent's room. AE, MC, V. Free parking. Closed Jan–Feb. **Amenities:** Restaurant; bar; concierge; pool; room service. *In room:* A/C, TV, minibar.

Hotel Belair ★ Suspended between sky and sea, this little hotel's charm and matchless views compensate for its location outside the center of town. Built on the cliff overlooking Marina Grande, the hotel is connected to the shore by a picturesque set of stairs carved into the rock. Each of the guest rooms is different in shape and individually decorated, with a small sea-view balcony or terrace. Most rooms are spacious and all are bright and pleasantly decorated, with ceramic floors and quality classic furniture. Bathrooms are good-size and very clean.

Via Capo 29, 80067 Sorrento. ℂ **081-8071622.** Fax 081-8071467. www.belair.it. 49 units. 320€–360€ double; from 490€ suite. Rates include buffet breakfast. Internet specials available. Children 3 and under stay free in parent's room. AE, DC, MC, V. Free parking. Closed Nov–Mar. **Amenities:** Bar; concierge; pool. *In room:* A/C, TV, Internet, minibar.

Maison La Minervetta ★ Originally a restaurant in the 1950s, this hotel enjoys a peerless position on the cliff overlooking Marina Grande. Ownership was recently restored to the original hoteliers, who have transformed it into a boutique hotel. Stepping inside is a breath of fresh air from the more typical accommodations of this stretch of coast. The alluring interior design successfully marries hypermodern style—almost Scandinavian in flavor—with bold Mediterranean colors and details. Guest rooms are very different from each other, but all are blessed with huge picture windows; the best enjoy private sun terraces with Jacuzzi pools. Artwork from around the world highlights public spaces, while the pine floors in the guest rooms add warmth. We love the modern bathrooms decorated with hand-painted tiles.

Via Capo 25, 80067 Sorrento. ℭ **081-8774455.** Fax 081-8784601. www.laminervetta.com. 12 units. 300€–350€ double. Rates include buffet breakfast. Internet specials available. Children 2 and under stay free in parent's room. AE, DC, MC, V. Free parking. Closed 1 week in Jan. **Amenities:** Concierge. *In room:* A/C, TV, minibar.

Plaza Hotel ★★ The Plaza is better than ever after a "green" overhaul that added natural and renewable materials, thermal insulation, energy and water conserving equipment, and biodegradable cleaning substances. We love their ecofriendly philosophy, but also the central location in town and competent service. Guest rooms are modern and streamlined, with contemporary details. Bright and welcoming, some open onto private balconies. Bathrooms are good-size, with contemporary hardware (some with shower only). Guests get discounted access to a nearby beach (10€, including changing room and lounger).

Via Fuorimura 3, 80067 Sorrento. ℭ 081-8782831. Fax: 081-8073942. www.plazasorrento.com. 65 units. 190€–260€ double. Rates include buffet breakfast. Internet specials available. Children 2 and under stay free in parent's room. AE, DC, MC, V. Parking 10€. **Amenities:** 2 bars; concierge; pool; room service. *In room:* A/C, TV, minibar, Wi-Fi (for a fee).

Inexpensive

Hotel Gardenia (Kids) At the edge of town toward Sant'Agnello and away from the sea, this family-run hotel offers moderately priced accommodations. Guest rooms are large and simply but comfortably appointed, with modern furniture and tiled floors; all rooms have private balconies. The hotel also prides itself on its Olympic-size swimming pool and a fitness club. The pool and the possibility of triples and quads make it a good choice for budget-oriented families. Because the Gardenia is on the main street in town, it can get a bit noisy, particularly if you like keeping your windows open; although Corso Italia is closed to automobile traffic in summer from 7pm to 7am and again from 10am to 1pm.

Corso Italia 258, 80067 Sant'Agnello. ℭ **081-8772365.** Fax 081-8074486. www.hotelgardenia.com. 30 units. 110€–140€ double; 160€ triple; 180€ quad. Rates include buffet breakfast. Children 2 and under stay free in parent's room. AE, DC, MC, V. Free parking. Closed Jan to mid-Feb. **Amenities:** Restaurant; bar; pool; outdoor tennis court; Wi-Fi. *In room:* A/C, TV, minibar.

Relais Villa Savarese (Finds) The perfect place to enjoy Sorrento as a 19th-century nobleman might have, this B&B/boutique hotel is in a former patrician villa complete with garden and pool. The location along the road that leads out of Sorrento into adjacent Sant'Agnello is pleasant and quiet. Guest rooms are spacious and well-appointed. Bathrooms are good-size and modern (some with shower only).

Corso M. Crawford 59, 80065 Sant'Agnello. ℭ 081-5324920. Fax: 081-5324920. www.relaisvillasavarese. com. 10 units. 150€–180€ double; 210€ junior suite. Rates include buffet breakfast. Internet specials available. AE, DC, MC, V. Parking 15€. Closed Nov–Mar. **Amenities:** Bar; concierge; fitness center (for a fee); Internet; pool; smoke-free rooms. *In room:* A/C, TV, minibar.

Residence Le Terrazze (Kids) This pleasant hotel in a panoramic position high above Sorrento is convenient to town as well as to the best beaches and attractions. Family-run and immaculately kept, it offers moderately priced miniapartments in various sizes, all with kitchenette—a good solution for families. The whitewashed rooms are plain but bright, with no-frill tiled floors, rattan or pine furniture, and good-size bathrooms with all the essentials. The new swimming pool is a great addition.

Via Nastro Verde 98, 80067 Sorrento. ℂ **081-8780906.** Fax 081-8085204. www.residenceleterrazze.it. 16 units. 110€–140€ double; 170€ triple; 200€ quad. Rates include buffet breakfast. Internet specials available. Children 2 and under stay free in parent's room. AE, DC, MC, V. Free parking. Closed Jan 8–Feb. **Amenities:** Concierge; pool. *In room:* A/C, TV, kitchenette.

WHERE TO DINE

While the **Excelsior Victoria** and the **Imperial Tramontano** (both reviewed above) offer the most exclusive dining experiences—sure to inspire future memories, with superb food served on terraces overlooking the sea—the town's waterside and main streets are lined with many other great restaurants big and small, traditional and modern.

Expensive

Il Buco ★★ CREATIVE SORRENTINE   In the wine cellar of an ancient convent near the ancient city gate, this restaurant offers a menu of fine, imaginative cuisine that changes daily according to the market. Only the best of local ingredients make their way to the kitchen, and you won't be disappointed. We loved the *mezzanelle con ragù di pesce in bianco* (pasta in a delicate seafood sauce flavored with black olives and wild fennel), and the *agnellodi paese al timo* (tender lamb served with rosemary roasted potatoes and savoy cabbage). The *piatti unici* is a one-course meal for two, such as a perfect florentine steak or a superb fish stew. The house red is a standout and the outdoor terrace is delightful in summer.

2d Rampa Marina Piccola 5 (off Piazza Sant'Antonino). ℂ **081-8782354.** www.ilbucoristorante.it. Reservations recommended. Secondi 20€–40€; tasting menus 75€–85€; prix-fixe menu 45€–65€. AE, DC, MC, V. Thurs–Tues 12:30–3:30pm and 7:30–11:30pm. Closed Jan.

L'Antica Trattoria ★ SORRENTINE   This picturesque restaurant—complete with master mandolin player—has served excellent food for 8 decades. The dining rooms are cozy, but we adore the outdoor terrace, where you can dine under the arbor vines. The chef's sophisticated recipes explore the combination of local produce, seafood, and wines. Fixed-price menus allow you to choose three courses for 59€ or four courses for 69€; or you can opt for the set-price tasting menu (80€, including wine). The menu is seasonal but always includes delicious homemade ravioli—maybe flavored with local cheese and tomatoes, or with seafood and local citrus fruits—and elegantly presented meat and fish dishes, such as *bronzino con scarola, capperi, olive, e slasa di alici* (with escarole, olives, capers, and anchovy sauce).

Via Padre Reginaldo Giuliani 33. ℂ **081-8071082.** www.lanticatrattoria.com. Reservations recommended. Secondi 21€–40€. AE, MC, V. Nov–Mar 30 Tues–Sun noon–3:30pm and 7–11:30pm; Mar 31–Oct daily noon–3:30pm and 7–11:30pm. Closed Jan 15–Feb.

Moderate

Caruso ★ SORRENTINE   A local institution, this upscale restaurant doubles as a museum dedicated to Enrico Caruso, the famous Italian tenor who so loved Sorrento. The excellent menu offers gourmet renditions of traditional recipes. The seasonal cuisine includes such delicious meals as *ravioli all'aragosta* (with lobster), *ravioli con salsa di melanzane* (with an eggplant sauce), *lasagne ai frutti di mare* (with seafood), and *risotto zucchine e gamberi* (with shrimp and zucchini).

Via Sant'Antonino 12. ℂ **081-8073156.** www.ristorantemuseocaruso.com. Reservations recommended. Secondi 16€–32€. AE, DC, MC, V. Daily noon–midnight.

A Gelato to Remember

The absolute best gelato parlor in the whole area—and maybe in the whole country—is **Davide Il gelato** ★★, Via Padre Reginaldo Giuliani 39 (© 081-8072092; closed Wed in winter), producing divine homemade gelato made with typical regional fruits and specialties. Among the 60 flavors (more or less, depending on the day), we favor the sweet and deliciously creamy *noci di Sorrento* (Sorrento walnuts), the rich *cioccolato con canditi* (dark chocolate cream studded with candied oranges), the sinful *rhum babà* (rum-flavored cream with bits of soft cake), and the heavenly *delizia al limone* (a delectable lemon cream). You'll definitely have to return, at least once (or twice, or three times . . .) to sample them all.

La Favorita O'Parrucchiano SORRENTINE   In the center of town, this venerable restaurant—in operation since 1868—boasts picturesque dining spaces, including outdoor seating in a beautiful garden. It claims to have invented cannelloni (tubes of fresh pasta filled with meat and baked with tomato sauce and cheese), and whether that assertion is true or not, the dish is very well prepared. However, the setting and the friendly service tend to be better than the quality of the cooking, and, it's popular more for its atmosphere than its cuisine.

Corso Italia 71. © **081-8781321.** Reservations recommended for dinner. Secondi 8.50€–14€. MC, V. Nov 15–Mar 15 Thurs–Tues noon–3:30pm and 7–11:30pm; Mar 16–Nov 14 daily noon–3:30pm and 7–11:30pm.

O'Canonico 1898 ★ (Value) SORRENTINE   This historic restaurant on Sorrento's main square has successfully maintained its quality despite its well-trafficked location. Canonico offers professional service and a well-prepared traditional cuisine that incorporates only the freshest ingredients. We recommend the excellent *pappardelle ai frutti di mare* (fresh broad noodles with seafood) and the perfect *pezzogna in crosta* (local fish baked in a salt crust). The wine list is extensive.

Piazza Tasso 5. © **081-8783277.** Reservations recommended Sat–Sun. Secondi 18€–28€. AE, DC, MC, V. Daily noon–3:30pm and 7–11:30pm (closed Tues Oct–Apr).

Inexpensive
Sant'Anna da Emilia ★ (Kids) SORRENTINE   This moderately priced trattoria is our favorite, offering informal dining in an ancient boat shed in Marina Grande, complete with an outdoor terrace on a wooden pier. It is mobbed in summer, so be prepared to wait if you want to taste the great homestyle cuisine that varies daily with the market offerings. Simplicity is the key to success here, and we promise you won't taste a better caprese (mozzarella and fresh tomato salad) or *spaghetti alle cozze* (with mussels). We also recommend the *gnocchi alla Sorrentina* (Sorrento-style potato dumplings) and *fritto misto* (deep-fried calamari and fish) accompanied by the best *patatine fritte* (french fries). The house wine is excellent.

Via Marina Grande 62. © **081-8072720.** Reservations not accepted. Secondi 8.50€–14€. No credit cards. Daily noon–3:30pm and 7:30–11:30pm (closed Tues in winter). Closed Nov.

Via San Cesareo is Sorrento's main shopping street. Specialty shopping includes the bounty from local farms and groves—lemons and lemon products, walnuts, D.O.P. olive oil, and Penisola Sorrentina D.O.C. wine (some experts call it "the Beaujolais of Campania")—and the slowly disappearing local crafts: lace and embroideries, and wood intarsia and marquetry furniture.

For fresh ricotta formed in traditional handmade baskets and a sample of local products, head to one of **Apreda's** two locations: Via Tasso 6 (✆ **081-8782351**) or Via del Mare 20 (✆ **081-8074059**). You can find excellent *limoncello* and other specialties at **Sapori & Colori,** Via San Cesareo 26 and 57 (✆ **081-8784278** or 081-8773552), and **Luigia Gargiulo,** Corso Italia 48 (✆ **081-8781081**) sells lovely, intricate embroideries. **Gargiulo & Jannuzzi,** Piazza Tasso 1 (✆ **081-8781041**), offers the best wood intarsia; you can visit the workshops for a demonstration of this ancient technique that follows centuries-old patterns. At the weekly **street market,** vendors sell everything from crockery to swimming suits (Tues morning, parking lot on Via San Renato).

SORRENTO AFTER DARK

The narrow streets of Sorrento's *centro storico* are alive with cafes, clubs, and restaurants, which become positively crowded during the sweet nights of summer. Locals as well as newcomers love sitting on the terrace of the **Fauno Bar,** Piazza Tasso 13 (✆ **081-8781135;** www.faunobar.it; closed Nov), for an *aperitivo* (aperitif) and people-watching till late into the evening. Other popular venues for pre- and postdinner drinks are, of course, the romantic terraces of the many historic hotels (p. 176).

Spring and summer are a special time in Sorrento, as music festivals and other musical programs are staged in venues throughout town. Some of the most popular are the concerts at the **Albergo Cocumella,** Via Cocumella 7, Sant'Agnello (✆ **081-8782933;** www.cocumella.com), and those at the **cloister of San Francesco,** Piazza Francesco Saverio Gargiulo. Contact the tourist office (p. 169) for a schedule of events, including those staged at many restaurants and taverns in town.

For dancing and more lively entertainment for a more mature clientele (40s and up), head to Piazza Tasso and the nightclub **Fauno Notte Club** (✆ **081-8781021;** www.faunonotte.it; cover 23€). It also offers a colorful **Tarantella Show,** the frenetic traditional folk dance, between stretches of DJ music (Mar–Oct; daily 9–11pm). **Li'Ly,** Via Fuorimura 47 (✆ **081-8773236,** www.lilysorrento.it), is a classic disco lounge attracting younger crowds.

Sorrento Musical is a revue of Neapolitan songs hosted by **Teatro Tasso,** Piazza Sant'Antonino (✆ **081-8075525;** www.teatrotasso.com; tickets about 21€ depending on show; Mar–Oct Mon–Sat 9:30pm). Live music (a changing menu of pop, folk, jazz, etc.) can also be heard at **Circolo dei Forestieri,** Via Luigi de Maio 35 (✆ **081-8773012;** closed Nov–Feb).

For more leisurely entertainment (à la drinks with some background music), we love the laid-back atmosphere at **Chantecler,** Via Santa Maria della Pietà 38 (✆ **081-8075868;** www.chanteclers.com); there's some dancing on weekends, and always some food. Other choices are **Chaplin's Video Pub,** Corso Italia 18 (✆ **081-8072551**) and the **English Inn,** Corso Italia 55 (✆ **081-8074357**); located across from each other, both stock a good selection of beers and maintain a lively atmosphere—sometimes even too lively on summer weekends. Depending on the season, the crowd can be a mix of nationalities.

4 BEYOND SORRENTO: MASSA LUBRENSE & SANT'AGATA SUI DUE GOLFI

60km (38 miles) S of Naples

Much less traveled, the tip of the Sorrentine peninsula is also the most authentic. Villages—sometimes little more than handfuls of houses—dot the rocky coast and cliffs, and you'll find peace and quiet even in the middle of the summer season. Such a surprising feat has been accomplished via mundane means: terrible roads and transportation. The train stops in Sorrento, and the main loop road (SS 145) passes through Sant'Agata sui due Golfi, but bypasses Massa Lubrense completely, swerving back toward the coast on the other side of the peninsula to rejoin SS 163, the famous Amalfi Drive. The result is a little-visited, though ruggedly beautiful corner that feels more remote than it is. You can easily visit the whole area in 1 day; yet, once you have arrived, you'll hardly want to leave.

ESSENTIALS

GETTING THERE & AROUND   **Sorrento** is the gateway to the rest of the peninsula (see "Getting There," p. 168). Although **SITA's** (© 081-5522176; www.sitabus.it) **bus** service from Sorrento is frequent and efficient, we feel that, unless you have unlimited time, renting a **scooter** or a **car**—or even better, a **taxi** or **limousine** with a driver—is a lot more functional: You'll be able to see more, have a flexible schedule, and your driver will double as a guide. Distances are short, hence charges remain quite reasonable (consider about 45€ per hour for two people, with special discounts for longer periods). You can rent a car from the major operators listed in chapter 3 (p. 46) or from a number of local vendors (p. 169).

Another option is renting a small launch from one of the many boatyards, or hiring one of their captains to guide you; or you may sign up for one of their organized excursions. We recommend Peppe, and his beautiful boat, *La Granseola,* Marina del Cantone (© 081-8081027, c/o Ristorante Le Sirene; mobile 338-9542573; www.lagranseola.com). Other reliable providers are **Coop Marina della Lobra,** Marina della Lobra (© 081-8089380; www.marinalobra.com); **Cooperativa S. Antonio,** Marina del Cantone (© 081-8081638; cooperativasantonio@libero.it); and **Nautica 'O Masticiello,** Marina del Cantone (© 081-8081443, 081-8082006, or 339-3142791; www.masticiello.com).

VISITOR INFORMATION   Your best source of local information is the small **Proloco tourist office,** Viale Filangeri 11, Massa Lubrense (© 081-5339021; www.prolocomassalubrense.com). You'll find a **pharmacy** (© 081-8789081) at Via Palma 16, Massa Lubrense. The **hospital** is in Sorrento (p. 169). For an **ambulance,** dial © 118. You can call the **police** at © 113 or 112, and you can reach the **fire department** at © 115. You'll find a **post office** (© 081-8789045) in Massa Lubrense at Via Massa Turro 13 and another in Sant'Agata sui due Golfi at Corso Sant'Agata 32 (© 081-8780162). There is a **Banco di Napoli** (© 081-8089687) at number 15 on Viale Filangeri in Massa Lubrense, and a **Deutsche Bank** (© 081-8089530) at number 26.

EXPLORING THE AREA

Massa Lubrense was once an important town and a powerful rival to Sorrento for dominance over this coast. Situations have changed, and Massa is now just one of the small villages that dot this rocky point. The diminished political importance of this area has not deprived it of its unique beauty, though, and Italian tourists in the know come to enjoy the cliffs and the increased sense of solitude the environment affords.

Among the villages, **Massa Lubrense** prides itself on its church, **Santa Maria delle Grazie** (Piazza Vescovado), which was built in 1512 and redone in the 18th century. In the transept and presbytery you'll find nice examples of the original **majolica floor** ★, but the real attraction here is the fantastic **view** ★★ over Capri that you can enjoy from the terrace to the right of the church. Below the church is **Marina della Lobra** ★, a picturesque fishing hamlet with a little harbor—and also one of the peninsula's rare stretches of sand. The sanctuary here—**Santa Maria della Lobra**—was built in the 16th century over a Roman temple, probably dedicated to Minerva. Inside you can see the original 17th-century, wood-carved **ceiling** and the 18th-century **majolica floor.**

From Santa Maria delle Grazie, follow the sign toward **Annunziata;** the road leads to the old Massa Lubrense, established in the 10th century and destroyed by the Angevins in the 1300s. Here you'll find the church of the **Santissima Annunziata,** the original cathedral of Massa, redone in the 17th century. Nearby are the ruins of the castle—only one tower is standing—which was built in 1389. From the **Belvedere,** weather permitting, you can enjoy an extraordinary **panorama** ★★ that encompasses the whole Gulf of Naples.

Farther on toward the tip of the Sorrentine peninsula is the village of **Nerano,** perched atop a cliff at 166m (544 ft.). Below the village is the fishing hamlet of **Marina del Cantone** ★ with its lovely beach where locals keep their boats. Nearby **Termini** is another small town built on a natural terrace overlooking Capri. From Termini, drive down the local road to **Punta Campanella,** on the tip of the Sorrento peninsula, with its famous lighthouse (see "Staying Active," below).

Finally, you will reach **Sant'Agata sui Due Golfi** ★★: One of the region's largest villages, it benefits from its matchless position overlooking the two gulfs—of Naples and of Salerno—hence its name. The village is focused around **Santa Maria delle Grazie,** a 17th-century church that boasts a beautiful **altar** of colored marble and semiprecious stones. Follow the signs toward **Deserto** ★, once a Carmelite hermitage and now a Benedictine monastery. At an altitude of 456m (1,496 ft.), it affords a spectacular **circular panorama** ★★★ over the Campanian coast, stretching all the way from Ischia to Punta Licosa, south of Paestum. The monastery is open to visitors October to March (8:30am–12:30pm and 2:30–4:30pm) and April to September (8:30am–12:30pm and 4–8pm).

From Sant'Agata, you can also head toward **Torca,** a village only a few minutes away, perched at 352m (1,155 ft.) above sea level. From the village, take in the beautiful view over Li Galli, Positano's small archipelago.

A SPECIAL TOUR

In addition to the recommended tours of the area (p. 172), the **Due Golfi Train Tour** ★ (© **333-3323189;** www.duegolfitraintour.com) is a gastronomic ride on a small train that will delight children and adult foodies alike. The train departs from the Agip of Sant'Agata sui Due Golfi gas station and loops through Massa Lubrense's scenic hamlets, stopping at local farms for tastings of mozzarella, jams, and other local specialties. Departures are daily at 10am, with an additional ride at 4pm on Tuesday and Thursday from October to April and also at 6:30pm from May to September. The cost is 20€ for adults and 10€ for children.

You can do some swimming from the **beach** at **Marina del Cantone,** but to really enjoy the sea, **renting a boat** (with or without driver) is a must: It allows you to discover small beaches, inlets, and hidden bays otherwise inaccessible from the high cliffs (see "Getting There & Around," above). The seashore here is a marine park, **Area Marina Protetta di Punta Campanella** (① **081-8089877;** www.puntacampanella.org), extending all the way from Punta del Capo, near Sorrento, to Punta Germano, near Positano.

Our favorite excursion is the one to the **Bay of Ieranto** ★★★, a lovely cove with a magical atmosphere. Well-known to the ancient Greeks who named it Hyeros Anthos, meaning "Sacred Flower," this bay was declared a protected area in 1984 and, as a result, it remains a completely untouched haven. Cut into the cliff, the cove of clear water ends in a beach, Marina del Cantone, where a few boats are usually moored. In the afternoon, oblique sunlight creates the odd illusion that the water has disappeared and the boats are suspended in thin air, a phenomenon we love to watch.

Arriving by boat to this lovely cove is a striking and marvelous experience. Rent a boat—with or without a driver—and dedicate about a half-day for the excursion. From the beach, hug the coast heading southwest till you see the large Y-shaped promontory called Sedia del Diavolo, meaning "Devil's Chair," a particularly appropriate name when you see it during a flaming sunset. As you pass the first arm of the Y, with the medieval watchtower **Torre di Montalto,** there is a pretty little cove, which is an introduction to the more spectacular bay that awaits you farther along. Once you pass the second arm of the Y, the Bay of Ieranto opens like a fan in front of your bow and is closed to the west by Punta Campanella (below). Beyond, starts the Gulf of Naples.

If you are moderately fit, we highly recommend hiking the local **footpaths** for breathtaking views. The area offers 22 marked and maintained hiking trails, for a total length of 110km (68 miles). One of the best hikes is the one to **Punta Campanella** ★, much more impressive than the drive there (see "Exploring the Area," above). From the village of Termini, take the small sloping street to the right of the central square: This road slowly descends to the hamlet of Cercito, and then continues down the **Vallone della Cala di Mitigliano.** This beautiful valley is filled with olive groves and typical vegetation (called *macchia mediterranea*), including scented *mirto,* a plant that is quite rare nowadays. The trail then crosses a plateau with large boulders and the ruins of **Torre di Namonte,** a medieval watchtower. Past the tower, the trail begins a steep descent toward the sea as the beautiful profile of Capri looms into view. You'll get clear views of Capri, with Monte Tiberio, Monte Solaro, and the Faraglioni, only 5km (3 miles) away. A modern lighthouse guards this dangerous cape and its waters, made treacherous by the many rocks in the Capri Narrows.

On the last part of the trail, you'll actually be treading the ancient **Via Minerva,** the original road that led to the Greek temple dedicated to Athena (called Minerva by the Romans). To be visible to all passing ships, the temple was positioned near the lighthouse. The olive groves in this area go back thousands of years and were originally planted by the Greeks: Believing that olive oil was a gift from Athena, the goddess of wisdom—we tend to agree with that—they brought gifts of olive oil to her temple.

Punta Campanella takes its name from the bell on **Torre Minerva,** the watchtower—built in 1335 and redone in 1566—that warned of pirate incursions (*campanella* means "small bell"). Near the tower are the remains of a Roman villa. From a cliff to the east of the tower, you can look down into the wild, but sheltered, Bay of Ieranto. The trail goes from 300m (984 ft.) down almost to sea level; count on spending about 45 minutes for

Impressions

And lo! the Siren shores like mists arise.
Sunk were at once the winds; the air above,
And waves below, at once forgot to move;
Some demon calm'd the air and smooth'd the deep,
Hush'd the loud winds, and charm'd the waves to sleep.
Now every sail we furl, each oar we ply;
Lash'd by the stroke, the frothy waters fly . . .
—Homer, *The Odyssey*, book XII, lines 97–101,
translation Alexander Pope, 1616

the descent and a bit more for the ascent. If you like a challenge, you could take the alternate trail to Punta Campanella: Starting from Termini, you first climb up **Mount San Costanzo,** at 497m (1,630 ft.) above sea level, before descending to the point. It is even more picturesque, but quite a bit longer and a lot more strenuous (allow about 3 hr. for this trail).

Another of our favorite hikes is the trail to the **Bay of Ieranto.** The terrain is quite steep at times and can be moderately challenging. The best time to go is early afternoon to have a chance to experience the water phenomenon we describe above. From Nerano, take the street at the right-hand side of the village, past the last cluster of houses. This street connects to a trail on the slopes of **Monte San Costanzo,** the westernmost peak of the **Monti Lattari.** The trail descends through *macchia mediterranea* and eventually descends the cliffs overlooking the sea, affording spectacular views. Budget a little over an hour each way.

One last hike we greatly recommend is the one down to **Fiordo di Crapolla** and its beach. From the village of Torca (see "Exploring the Area," above), take Via Pedara, which eventually turns into a dirt path. The trail descends a steep slope among olive groves and old farmhouses, and then among the rocks of a narrow crack in the cliff. As you descend on the western side of the cliff, you will see the ruins of the 12th-century abbey of San Pietro. Once at the bottom, you'll find a small beach; the blue water beyond the cove is broken by many rocks—the very ones, it is said, where the Sirens wrecked the ships of innocent mariners. By the beach, you can also see the ruins of a patrician Roman villa, where the ancient town of Capreolae (today Crapolla) was built. Figure on spending about 30 minutes on the descent.

WHERE TO STAY & DINE

Massa Lubrense is one of the most sought-after dining destinations in all of Italy, with a high density of Michelin-starred venues. As an old Italian saying goes, "Pancia fatti capanna," or "Tummy, become as large as a hut." However, you shouldn't miss out on simpler fare, such as the delicious bread made by **Antico Panificio Gargiulo,** Via Rivo a Casa 8 (off Via Roma), Massa Lubrense, studded with your choice of salami, local walnuts, olives, or sweet peppers. It is accompanied by your choice of local cheese: *treccia, scamorza,* or the delicious *triavulilli,* and the small *caciocavallo farcito* (pear shaped cheese studded or filled with sun-dried tomatoes, butter, olives, or ham).

Some of the best purveyors are **Caseificio Cordiale,** Via Campi 30 (off Corso Sant'Agata), Sant'Agata sui Due Golfi (© **081-8080888**); **Caseificio Savarese,** Via IV Novembre 19/a, Massa Lubrense (© **081-8789825**); and **Caseificio Valestra,** Via Bozzaotra 13, Monticchio (© **081-8780119**).

You'll find a good choice of other local products, including olive oil, cured meats, dried fruits, and spirits, at **Da Ferdinando,** Corso Sant'Agata 53, Sant'Agata sui Due Golfi (© **081-8780196**), or at **Don Alfonso 1890,** Sant'Agata sui Due Golfi (© **081-8780026;** see below).

Very Expensive

Don Alfonso 1890 ★★★ CREATIVE SORRENTINE   Reputed to be the best restaurant in southern Italy—with two Michelin stars—Don Alfonso does indeed offer superb food, location, and service. The elegant dining rooms in this historical residence in the heart of town overlook a delightful garden, and the ambience is welcoming and refreshing. The owners, Livia and Alfonso Iaccarino, also started an organic farm, **Azienda Agricola Le Peracciole** on Punta Campanella, which sources their perfect ingredients. Choose one of the two tasting menus: One features more creative dishes, while the other revisits local classics. The seasonal a la carte menu may include *pesce spada ai ceci e al timo* (swordfish with thyme and chickpeas) or *salame di cinghiale affumicato all'alloro* (smoked boar salami with bay leaves). The roasted chicken—free-range, organically fed, and seasoned with fresh herbs—is exquisite. Ask to visit the century-old cellar. ***Note:*** In summer, a less formal lunch is served by the outdoor pool.

Don Alfonso has finally opened its planned **cooking school.** Taking a class here is an extravagant treat, though it may be worthwhile only to his most dedicated fans, or to very serious cooks.

Above the restaurant is the **Don Alfonso 1890 Relais,** with garden, outdoor pool, library, bar, private parking, and nine delightfully appointed suites (one is actually an apartment). These are decorated with hardwood floors and elegant classic furnishings, including many antiques (300€ junior suite; 500€ suite, including top-notch breakfast).

Corso Sant'Agata 11, Sant'Agata sui Due Golfi. © **081-8780026.** Fax 081-5330226. www.donalfonso. com. Reservations required. Children 5 and under not allowed at dinner. Secondi 28€–36€; tasting menu 90€–150€. AE, DC, MC, V. Wed–Sun 12:30–2:30pm and 8–10:30pm (June–Sept also Tues 8–10:30pm).

Expensive

Oasi Olimpia Relais ★★ SORRENTINE   This excellent restaurant is in a former aristocratic villa a short distance from the center of Sant'Agata. You can take full advantage of the splendid grounds in summer, when meals are served in the delightful outdoor arbor terrace covered with wisteria. Otherwise, the elegant dining room provides the perfect background for a romantic dinner. The cuisine is traditional and—while not attempting to rival Don Alfonso's haute cuisine (above)—definitely deserves a mention of honor. The seasonal menu is based on local produce and fish, and we are fans of the delicate *risotto agli agrumi di Sorrento* (with local citrus) and the tasteful *calamarata* (medley of pasta and squid with fresh tomatoes). The wine list is short but top-notch. ***Note:*** Lunch is a less-formal affair with a simpler menu (it is served by the pool in summer).

The **cooking classes** are definitely the best in the area; they are offered year-round and very well run. Classes are not extravagantly priced, and the program is solid, though some of the cooking programs are "informal" and rather tentatively scheduled, so you'll need to remain flexible.

The Olimpia also offers 11 elegantly appointed **rooms:** though less formal than at Don Alfonso's (above), they are more airy and bright, with beautiful sea views; three apartments are also available in nearby cottages. All guests can enjoy the outdoor swimming pool, courtesy van to the hotel's private beach, tennis courts, and Wi-Fi (320€ double, including buffet breakfast).

Via Deserto 26, Sant'Agata sui Due Golfi. ✆ 081-8080560. www.oasiolimpiarelais.it. Reservations recommended. Secondi 15€–38€. AE, DC, MC, V. Sat–Thurs noon–3pm and 7:30–10:30pm.

Quattro Passi ★ CREATIVE SORRENTINE From the charming garden terrace among lemon trees and bougainvillea to the somewhat more formal dining room with arched doorways and hand-painted ceramic floors, what you experience here is the soul of the Mediterranean: Its colors and touches of exuberance are all matched by professional service and excellent food, which earned a Michelin star. The sophisticated appetizers might include the likes of *totano ripieno di provola con cozza gratinata e tortino di patate* (stuffed squid and mussel au gratin with potato torte). Among the *primi* are *pappardelle fave piselli e formaggio* (large fresh pasta with peas, fresh fava beans, and cheese shavings); and the secondi include such intriguing choices as *rose di sogliola con capperi pomodorini e patate* (rosettes of sole with capers, cherry tomatoes, and potatoes). The homemade bread is served with citrus- or herb-flavored butter. For dessert, try the local specialty, *delizie al limone* (puff pastry filled with lemon cream), or one of the more creative choices, such as the superb chocolate torte with coffee-flavored ice-cream cake and orange sauce.

Under the restaurant is the **Quattro Passi Relais,** with five large guest rooms opening on the garden. Appointed with sober country elegance, rooms include all the usual comforts, such as A/C and spacious tiled bathrooms (200€ double, including breakfast).

Via Amerigo Vespucci 13, Marina del Cantone, Massa Lubrense. ✆ **081-8082800.** Fax 081-8081271. www.ristorantequattropassi.com. Reservations recommended Sat–Sun. Secondi 21€–42€. AE, MC, V. Thurs–Mon 12:30–3:30pm and 7:30–11pm, Tues 12:30–3:30pm; June 15–Sept 15 daily 12:30–3:30pm and 7:30–11pm. Closed Dec–Feb.

Relais Blu Belvedere ★★ (Finds) CREATIVE SORRENTINE This recently opened restaurant-cum-hotel is on the road to Massa Lubrense, a short distance from Sorrento (the bus stops nearby). What was once a private villa has been transformed into a strikingly stylish hotel. The views from the terrace opening onto the sea are absolutely breathtaking—Capri feels so close you could touch it—and we highly recommend a visit, if only for drinks at sunset. The warm welcome of Chef Antonino Acampora will make your visit even more special. The chef has worked with some of the greatest— Heinz Beck and Alain Ducasse for instance—and offers a seasonal menu based on the best ingredients this stretch of coast has to offer. You can also choose a la carte: The updated *pezzogna all'acqua pazza* (local fish in a tomato and herb broth) is a delight as is the lamb with local herbs. *Note:* The **cooking classes** start in 2010; check the website for more information.

The 11 **guest rooms,** all with sea views, are in keeping with the decor: elegant contemporary furnishings, picture windows, fine linens, state-of-the-art bathrooms, and private gardens and terraces (310€ double; 360€–410€ suite).

Via Roncato 60, Termini, 80061 Massa Lubrense. ✆ **081-8789552.** Fax 081-8789304. www.relaisblu.com. Reservations recommended. Secondi 30€; 10-course tasting menu 95€. AE, DC, MC, V. Daily noon– 3:30pm and 7–11:30pm. Closed Nov 5–Mar 20.

Taverna del Capitano ★★★ CREATIVE SORRENTINE   Our favorite on the peninsula, this Michelin-starred restaurant is a refuge of Mediterranean simplicity and top-notch food. On the best beach in the area, it offers wonderful cuisine, homemade with respect for local produce and seafood. Of the three tasting and a la carte menus, all seasonal, you might find *insalata di aragosta con verdure* (lobster and fresh vegetable salad), *zuppa di gamberi e cicorie selvatiche* (shrimp and dandelion soup), or *pesce alla salsa di agrumi* (fish in citrus sauce). The wine list is short but has an excellent selection of regional and national wines.

The Caputo family also offers hospitality in the **Locanda del Capitano.** The 15 **guest rooms** (160€–230€ double, including breakfast) above the restaurant are nicely appointed with a nautical feeling. The best overlook the sea, and all have private terraces.

Piazza delle Sirene 10, Marina del Cantone, 80061 Massa Lubrense. ✆ **081-8081028.** Fax 081-8081892. www.tavernadelcapitano.it. Reservations recommended Sat–Sun. Secondi 14€–28€; tasting menus 65€–85€. AE, DC, MC, V. Oct–Apr Tues 7:30–10:30pm, Wed–Sun 12:30–3:30pm and 7:30–10:30pm; May–Sept Tues–Sun 12:30–3:30pm and 7:30–10:30pm. Closed 6 weeks Jan–Feb.

Moderate

Antico Francischiello ★ SORRENTINE   This is one of the region's historical restaurants—it celebrated its centenary in 2009—and its fame has not abated. Now run by the third generation of Gargiulos, it remains a local favorite. The food is traditional: No attempts at nouvelle cuisine with skimpy portions here—and you'll find all the local specialties prepared with practiced skill. We like the seafood tasting menu because it allows you to try a large variety of dishes: Our favorites are *cozze gratinate* (mussels au gratin), *gnocchetti verdi all'astice* (green potato dumplings with lobster), and *zuppa di pesce* (fish stew). For smaller appetites, the rich buffet of *antipasti* is enough to suffice as a light meal. The renovated dining premises are a perfect setting for a meal, and if you are here by sunset, an *aperitivo* on the terrace is an absolute must.

Across the street, the management's **Hotel Villa Pina,** Via Partenope 40, offers simple, well-appointed rooms that are welcoming and scrupulously clean (100€ double).

Via Partenope 27, 80061 Massa Lubrense. ✆ **081-5339780.** Fax 081-5342963. www.francischiello.com. Reservations recommended Sat–Sun. Secondi 18€–38€. AE, MC, V. Daily noon–3:30pm and 7–11:30pm (closed Wed in winter).

Conca del Sogno ★ **Finds** SORRENTINE/SEAFOOD   This restaurant is a standout not only for the good food but also for its setting atop a rocky beach: The little cove is known locally as "dream cove," which, by the way, is the name of the restaurant. From Marina del Cantone, a few-minutes ride in a motor dinghy will get you to the restaurant, which caters mostly to the owners of the private sailboats and motor yachts anchored in the little bay. Meals are served throughout the day, with a menu based—you guessed—on seafood, as well as on local cheeses and produce. We highly recommend the tasty *gamberetti di Crapolla saltati con sale e pepe* (local shrimp sautéed with salt and pepper) and the perfect grilled catch of the day. Everything is simple and delicious, including the homemade desserts.

Baia di Recommone, Nerano. ✆ **081-8081036.** Reservations recommended Sat–Sun. Secondi 12€–21€. AE, MC, V. Daily noon–3pm and 7:30–11pm. Closed Nov–Mar.

Lo Scoglio da Tommaso ★ **Finds** SORRENTINE   Opened in 1958 by the De Simone family, this restaurant is now run by the third generation, with young Tommaso in the kitchen. Everything on the menu is made from local ingredients produced by regional farms or caught by local fishermen. We recommend the delectable and simple *spaghetti con le zucchine* (with zucchini), the fancy *linguine all'aragosta* (with local lobster) and, if it is on the menu—and if you don't mind a bit of work—the excellent *zuppa di pesce* (soupy stew with whole fish). We also recommend the homemade desserts.

There are 14 **guest rooms** (230€ double, including breakfast) that are well-appointed and welcoming, all opening onto a private balcony. The establishment also offers moorings with launch service, beach chairs and umbrellas, and boat rental.

Piazze delle Sirene 15, Località Marina del Cantone, Massa Lubrense. (C) **081-8081026.** www.restaurant loscoglio.com. Reservations recommended. Secondi 12€–28€. AE, DC, MC, V. Daily noon–3pm and 7:30–10:30pm.

Riccardo di Francischiello CREATIVE SORRENTINE   Run by Riccardo, the second son of the elder Francischiello, this restaurant is the legitimate heir of the neighboring **Antico Francischiello** (above), and the food—such as the *frutti di mare* (shellfish), ravioli, and *acquapazza* (a light broth that is flavored with fresh herbs and tomato, and used to poach fish), all prepared according to traditional recipes—is indeed very good. We feel the lighter bill and the pleasant dining spaces—decorated with Vietri ceramics and the adjacent covered terrace, both overlooking the sea—compensate for the less-imaginative and more-casual food presentation.

The 32 rooms in the attached **Hotel Bellavista** (140€–180€ double) enjoy a wonderfully scenic position on the cliffs—the sunset views, with Capri in the foreground, are amazing. Amenities include a swimming pool on a garden terrace overlooking the sea, a new spa with an attached gym, and boat and mountain bike rentals.

Via Partenope 26, 80061 Massa Lubrense. (C) **081-8789181.** Fax 081-8089341. www.francischiello.it. Reservations recommended Sat–Sun. Secondi 12€–25€. AE, MC, V. Daily noon–3:30pm and 7–11:30pm (closed Tues Oct–Mar).

Inexpensive

Lo Stuzzichino (Kids) (Finds) SORRENTINE   This down-to-earth restaurant is a welcome relief to the area's Michelin-starred restaurants: The atmosphere is informal, and children can play by the pleasant outdoor terrace. The whole family can delight in the seasonal menu based on the best locally produced ingredients. We loved the *antipasto della casa,* which includes the *fritto misto Napoletano* (Neapolitan deep-fried rice balls, stuffed ravioli, and mozzarella); the *cannelloni alla Sorrentina* (stuffed pasta baked with mozzarella and tomato); as well as the masterfully prepared *scialatielli ai frutti di mare* (traditional fresh pasta with seafood) and the perfect *frittura di calamari e gamberi* (deep-fried medley of squid and shrimp). If it is on the menu, do taste the delicious *torta di ricotta e pere* (torte with sweet ricotta and pears), a family recipe from your host's grandmother.

Via Deserto 1, Sant'Agata sui Due Golfi. (C) **081-5330010.** www.ristorantelostuzzichino.it. Reservations recommended Sat–Sun. Secondi 9€–20€. AE, MC, V. Thurs–Tues noon–3:30pm and 7:30–11pm (daily July–Aug). Closed Jan 25–Feb 20.

The Amalfi Coast

Celebrated by 19th-century tourists as the most gorgeous stretch of coast in the world, the beauty of the Amalfi Coast was already well-known during antiquity, and its fame has not abated in modern days. It is a magical landscape of cultivated cliffs hanging over a beautiful sea, interspersed with villages that literally appear to have grown from the underlying rocks; here and there, where the mouth of a stream has created a natural harbor, a larger town has developed around this favorable nook—Such is the case in the namesake town of Amalfi, the queen of the Costiera. The valley of its river allowed for the development of paper mills that produced paper for much of Europe during the Middle Ages and well into the Renaissance, while its harbor became the shipyard that fueled Amalfi's political and commercial power.

The Amalfi Coast's unique views and plunging cliffs have inspired the works of many famous artists, from Giovanni Boccaccio to Richard Wagner, while the small towns and hamlets have been the refuge of many others, including Henrik Ibsen, Pablo Picasso, Rudolf Nureyev, and, more recently, Gore Vidal.

The most famous destination in Campania, the Amalfi Coast will enchant you with its dramatic coastline and picturesque villages. From **Vietri sul Mare** to the east—a town famous for its ceramics and majolica—to Piano di Sorrento to the west, the (sometimes harrowing) Amalfi Drive is home to leading resort towns (even though they're not exactly undiscovered): sophisticated **Ravello** (high above the sea), glitzy **Positano** (right on the water), and historic **Amalfi** (also on the sea). We also recommend going off the beaten path to explore lesser-known towns, all with a rich history and impressive views of the coast. East of Amalfi, you will find the fishing harbor of **Cetara;** the coastal villages of **Maiori, Minori,** and **Atrani;** and the inland (and, hence, upward) villages of **Scala** and **Tramonti;** west of Amalfi are the charming seaside villages of **Conca dei Marini, Praiano,** and **Vettica Maggiore** and the mountain villages of **Agerola** and **Furore.**

The Amalfi Coast is one of the most visited seaside destinations in the world, particularly during spring and summer, when each hamlet and village along this coast becomes the stage for art and cultural events, and the sweet evening air is pervaded by the scent of citrus flowers. In winter, everything is much quieter, as many places close down and the sea gets too chilly to swim in. You may have the place all to yourself in these colder months, but you'll miss much of the spirit it shows when in full bloom.

One word about transportation: Public transit is well developed here and is a way to make your vacation in this protected area slightly more ecofriendly.

See p. 35 for a map of the Amalfi Coast.

1 POSITANO ★★★

17km (10 miles) W of Amalfi; 51km (101 miles) W of Salerno; 56km (35 miles) SE of Naples

Hugging a semivertical rock formation, Positano is the quintessence of picturesque. Once one of the most exclusive retreats in Italy, this seaside resort has been thoroughly "discovered" but retains its character. Its unique mix of seascapes, colors, art, and cultural life has fascinated many famous artists, from Picasso and Klee to Toscanini, Bernstein, and Steinbeck. Today, it is a favorite destination of tourists and fashionistas, coming to buy what has become known as "Positano Fashion" from the local designer showrooms and elegant boutiques, and partaking of the cultural life.

ESSENTIALS

GETTING THERE   The **bus** is the best and fastest option, with **SITA** (© 081-5522176; www.sitabus.it) offering frequent service from Naples, Sorrento, Amalfi, Vietri, and Salerno (for information on fares, see "The Unico Travel Pass," p. 48). For the best views, get a seat on the right side of the bus when you are traveling from Sorrento and the left side from Vietri, Amalfi, and Salerno.

In fair weather, April through September, Positano is also well served by **ferry** and hydrofoils: **Metrò del Mare** (© 199-446644; www.metrodelmare.com) offers regular service to Positano from Naples, Sorrento, Amalfi, Salerno, and other harbors along the coast; fares vary depending on the distance, from 9€ from Amalfi to 16€ from Pozzuoli. Amalfi-based **Cooperativa Sant'Andrea** (© 089-873190; www.coopsantandrea.it) offers regular service from Amalfi, Capri, Minori, Salerno, and Sorrento, as well as special cruises and excursions; fares range from 6€ from Amalfi to 16€ from Capri. **Lucibello** (© 089-975032 or 089-811164; www.lucibello.it) offers regular service to and from Capri for 17€. **Alicost** (© 089/811986; www.lauroweb.com/alicost.htm) maintains regular *aliscafo* (hydrofoil) and *motonave* (motorboat) service from Capri and Ischia to Positano; fares are 20€ from Capri and 26€ from Ischia (you must reserve at least 24 hr. in advance).

Travelmar (© 081-7041911; www.travelmar.it) maintains routes to Positano from Salerno, and **LMP** (© 081-5513236; www.consorziolmp.it) offers regular hydrofoil and boat service between Positano, Capri, and Sorrento. Prices range between 10€ and 18€ for both companies.

From Naples or its airport, **taxis** offer a flat rate of 120€ to Positano. **Car services** (see "Getting Around," p. 47) also offer transfers from Naples's Capodichino Airport or train station. Alternatively, **Curreri Viaggi** (© 081-8015420; www.curreriviaggi.it) offers a shuttle service from Capodichino for 150€ for one to three passengers and 12€ for each additional passenger.

If you are traveling by **train** (© 892021 in Italy; www.trenitalia.it), the closest station is **Vietri sul Mare,** on the local line between **Naples** (where you'll change trains if you are coming from the north) and **Salerno** (if you are coming from the south).

By car, take autostrada A3 toward NAPOLI-SALERNO to the exit for VIETRI SUL MARE. Follow the signs for VIETRI, MAIORI, AMALFI, and POSITANO; they will lead you to the famed SS 163, the coastal road that meanders from Salerno to Positano and a bit beyond. You can also reach SS 163 from Castellammare di Stabia, Piana di Sorrento, Vico Equense, and Sorrento heading east and following signs for POSITANO and AMALFI. *Note:* Because of the solid traffic here in summer, local authorities have occasionally limited car access to SS 163; check with the tourist office and your hotel before making your plans.

GETTING AROUND   The simplest and cheapest way to move between villages along this coast is the **bus: SITA** (see "Getting There," above) offers regular service from Positano and its hub in Amalfi. In Positano, the orange town **buses** make the loop of Viale Pasitea, Via Cristoforo Colombo, and Via G. Marconi (SS 163), stopping several times

Map Legend:

- Ferry Terminal
- ⓘ Tourist Information
- Ⓟ Parking
- ➹ Beach
- ⊞ Steps

ACCOMMODATIONS ■
Casa Albertina **4**
Casa Maresca **2**
Covo dei Saraceni **6**
Hotel Bougainville **11**
Hotel Buca di Bacco **7**
Hotel Le Sirenuse **10**

Hotel Savoia **12**
Hotel Villa Franca **1**
La Fenice **16**
La Rosa deVenti **3**
La Tavolozza **14**
Palazzo Murat **13**
Villa Rosa **9**

DINING ◆
Da Vincenzo **5**
La Cambusa **8**
Il Grottino
Azzurro **15**

Inset map: Benevento, CAMPANIA, NAPLES, Salerno, Sorrento, Capri, Positano, TYRRHENIAN SEA

Chiesa Nuova, Chiesa di Santa Caterina, FORNILLO **3**, Belvedere dello Schiaccone, Spiaggia Fornillo, Torre Trasita, Santa Maria Assunta, Spiaggia Grande, Torre Sponda, PARLATI

0 200 yds
0 200 m

To Capri, Sorrento, Ischia & Naples
To Amalfi, Salerno & Minori

TYRRHENIAN SEA

along the way. They run every half-hour, saving your tired knees from some of the town's endless steps. You can purchase the 1€ ticket onboard.

Ferries are a convenient alternative to slogging along the local road (see "Getting There," p. 168). You can also hire a **boat,** with or without a captain, to take you to secluded beaches (see "Staying Active," p. 207). A **boat service** links Marina Grande to Fornillo during the summer, with departures every half-hour (about 5€).

To reach other towns and villages, hiring a **taxi** ℂ **089-875230** or a **car service** with a chauffeur makes sense, especially if you plan to stay here only a day or two; plus, an experienced local driver can double as a guide. We list specific companies in "Getting Around by Limousine/Car Service" in chapter 3 (p. 50) as well as in "Getting to Sorrento" and "Getting Around Sorrento" in chapter 7 (p. 168).

Renting a **car** is an option we don't recommend, especially in summer, but you can do so from major national and international companies (see "Fast Facts," p. 326) as well as from **Rent a Car,** Viale Pasitea (ℂ **089-811777**), or one of the companies in Sorrento (see chapter 7). You can rent a motor scooter at **Positano Rent a Scooter,** Viale Pasitea 99 (ℂ **089-8122077**) for about 40€ per day at the height of summer.

VISITOR INFORMATION   The **AAST tourist office** (✆ **089-875067;** www.azienda turismopositano.it) is at Via del Saracino 4, 84017 Positano. It is open Monday to Saturday 8:30am to 2pm, with additional hours (3:30–8pm) in July and August.

FAST FACTS   You'll find a **pharmacy** (✆ **089-875863**) on Viale Pasitea. For the closest hospital, see "Fast Facts," p. 263; for an **ambulance,** dial ✆ **118.** You can call the **police** at ✆ **113** or 112. The **post office** (✆ **089-875142**) is at Via G. Marconi 320 (SS 163), at the corner with Viale Pasitea; it is open Monday to Saturday 8am to 2pm. You will find several banks with **ATMs,** including **Banco di Napoli,** Piazza dei Mulini 18 (✆ **089-8122367**). The **exchange office** (✆ **089-875864**) is in Piazza dei Mulini. You can get Internet access at **Dimensione Servizi,** Via San Sebastiano 8 (✆ **089-811993**).

SPECIAL EVENTS   **Summer Music** is an international chamber music festival that takes place from the end of August to the beginning of September every year (2007 marked its 40th anniversary). The **Festival of the Assunta** is a lively event held August 14 and 15, when the violent attack of the Saracens and the Madonna's miraculous intervention are reenacted, accompanied by much noise and fanfare by Positanese of all ages. The histrionics include a fake fire and colorful historic costumes.

EXPLORING THE TOWN

Positano remains as picturesque as ever in spite of the crowds. It is not a destination for the faint of heart, though, with steep ramps of stairs serving as walkways. The typical pastel-colored houses—cubes with domed roofs and porticoes or loggias overlooking the sea—poke from the overflowing green of gardens and citrus groves. *Tip:* Wearing comfortable shoes without heels is a must here; otherwise, climbing the steep alleys and many steps will be an ordeal.

The heart of town is **Marina Grande,** the beach where fishermen used to haul up their boats. At its western end is the pier where ferries arrive and depart. From Marina Grande starts **Via Positanesi d'America** ★★—a cliffside pedestrian promenade, and the only flat street in Positano—which stretches along the shore past the cape of **Torre Trasita** to the smaller beach of **Fornillo.** Not far from Marina Grande is the **Collegiata di Santa Maria Assunta** ★★, Piazza Flavio Gioia (✆ **089-875480;** daily 8am–noon and 4–7pm), founded in the 13th century and later decorated with a gorgeous majolica dome. Inside, you will find the famous *tavola* of the *Madonna Nera* (Black Madonna), an icon in 13th-century Byzantine style. The church is at the center of the **Festival of the Assunta** (see "Special Events," above).

In our opinion, though, the best churches of Positano are the lesser-known ones. The small **Chiesa di Nuova,** Via Chiesa Nuova, was restored in the 18th century, and has a striking colored **tile floor** ★★, one of the most beautiful in an area known for its colorful tile work. The **Chiesa di Santa Caterina** ★★, Via Pasitea, built for the local Porcelli family, is another small architectural masterpiece in neo-Gothic style, with an elegant bell tower. Just west of Positano on SS 163 is the renowned **Belvedere dello Schiaccone** ★★★, the best lookout on Amalfi Drive. At 200m (656 ft.) above sea level, it overlooks the archipelago of Li Galli and Capo Sottile over a palm and citrus grove, with the splendid Monte Sant'Angelo a Tre Pizzi in the background.

BEACHES & BOATING

Positano is blessed with four delightful **beaches** besides the central **Spiaggia Grande** by the marina: **Fornillo** ★ (linked by boat service from the marina) to the west of town and

La Porta, Ciumicello, and Arienzo to the east. The sand is rather gray and pebbly, but the views are idyllic and the sea is clear and refreshing. You can rent a chair and umbrella at the reserved areas for about 18€ per day, or use the free but crowded public beach. Another beach, **Laurito** ★, is also a bit out of town, but you can easily reach it with the boat service offered by the restaurant Le Sirene (see "Where to Dine," later in this chapter), which also rents chairs and umbrellas.

For a quieter swim, locals like to take a boat to one of the small coves accessible only by sea. You can **rent a boat** at Spiaggia Grande for between 15€ and 35€ per hour, depending on the kind of boat and the duration of the rental. One popular destination is the archipelago of *Li Galli* **(The Roosters)** ★★, the four small islands visible to the west of Marina Grande. Named Gallo Lungo, Castelluccio, Gallo dei Briganti, and La Rotonda, these are the islands where—according to Homer—the Sirens lived. Indeed, the other name of the archipelago is Sirenuse, from the Latin *Sirenusae,* meaning Sirens. According to legend, these creatures attracted mariners with their enchanted songs, causing their ships to crash into the rocks. In Greek mythology, sirens were represented as birds with human faces and the bodies of fish (hence the name Li Galli, "The Roosters"). Once you skirt past the Sirens and arrive safely on Gallo Lungo, you'll spot a watchtower and the remains of a Roman villa; the archipelago is the site of the house where Rudolf Nureyev spent the last years of his life.

HIKING & TREKKING ★★

Hiking the local trails is one of the best ways to enjoy the area's incomparable natural beauty as well as its historic and artistic monuments. Continuations of the town's own steep streets, trails start right on the community outskirts. Most are historic footpaths that were the only land passage before SS 163 was opened in 1840. Still used for bringing animals to pasture, most are well maintained and well marked. If you are a serious hiker, we recommend the map published by the CAI (Club Alpino Italiano), *Monti Lattari Penisola Sorrentina, Costiera Amalfitana: Carta dei sentieri,* sold for 10€ at the best newsstands and bookstores in Ravello, Amalfi, and Tramonti (inquire in Positano, but they often run out). **Comunità Montana Penisola Amalfitana,** Via Municipio, 84010 Tramonti (*©* **089-876354** or 089-876547), also has guides and trail information. **Giovanni Visetti** (*©* **081-8089613;** www.giovis.com) is an experienced local guide who organizes some of the best treks on the peninsula.

Trails are steep and progress can be hampered by rocks and gravel: To tackle most of the paths you need to be moderately fit and have basic equipment: good shoes, a backpack, a good supply of water (especially in the summer), and a jacket for the rain and cold (all times of year).

A somewhat demanding hike is the path to **Santa Maria di Castello** ★★ (marked no. 33 on the CAI map), with its spectacular natural terrace overlooking Positano. This town straddles the pass between the Sorrento and Positano sides of the peninsula, and it is basically straight up from Positano, through Corvo. You can also cheat and drive yourself to Santa Maria di Castello (the road approaches from Vico Equense, on the Sorrento side of the peninsula, see chapter 7). An easier hike is the ascent 400m (1,312 ft.) to **Montepertuso** ★. This is the first part of the **trek** ★★, which winds through terraces of citrus groves between Positano and Amalfi. The going is relatively easy in this direction, but the best views are on the more demanding ascent from Amalfi (see "Staying Active," p. 207). Another scenic trail is the climb to **Nocelle** ★★, at an altitude of 443m (1,453 ft.). In this little paradise, where cars are not allowed, you can have an excellent

THE AMALFI COAST

8

POSITANO

lunch (or dinner) at **Ristorante Santa Croce** (make reservations in advance by calling ℂ **089-875319**). The trail starts from SS 163, between Arienzo and Laurito, about 3km (1¾ miles) east of town. From Montepertuso and Nocelle you can continue on the **Sentiero degli Dei** (See "Staying Active," p. 199).

WHERE TO STAY

As you would expect of such a world-renowned resort town, you'll find a large range of accommodations, with relatively high rates. In addition to the hotels we review here, see **Pupetto** ★ and **Le Sirene** ★, in "Where to Dine," later in this chapter. If you'd like to stay in the vertical countryside above town, and provided you are adequately fit, we recommend the *agriturismo* **Rifugio degli Dei** ★, Via Arienzo 43 (ℂ **339-8390809;** fax 089-811279; www.rifugiodeglidei.it), up some 250 stairs and 183m (600 ft.) of footpath; the staff will carry your luggage up from SS 163.

Very Expensive

Hotel Le Sirenuse ★★   This huge red-and-white 18th-century villa with terraced floors overlooking the bay is a picturesque sight—you may have seen it featured in the film *Only You* with Marisa Tomei and Robert Downey, Jr. Just above the harbor, it was the residence of the Marchesi Sersale family until 1951, and the public spaces are palatial. Guest rooms are large and bright, with vaulted ceilings, antiques, hand-painted tile floors, and fine fabrics; all have private terraces and luxurious bathrooms. Most rooms have priceless views of the bay. The hotel's swimming pool is perched on a terrace, and a state-of-the-art health club with an attached Aveda spa offers further relaxation. The buffet breakfast here is lavish, and the **restaurant La Sponda** (closed 3 weeks in Mar and 3 weeks in Nov; reservations are required) is highly recommended for meals. Children 6 and under are not accepted in the hotel from May 1 through September 30, or at the restaurant for dinner.

Via Cristoforo Colombo 30, 84017 Positano. ℂ **089-875066.** Fax 089-811798. www.sirenuse.it. 63 units. 500€–890€ double; from 1,260€ suite. Rates include buffet breakfast. AE, DC, MC, V. Parking 35€. **Amenities:** Restaurant; 2 bars; concierge; health club; pool; room service; spa. *In room:* A/C, TV, minibar.

Il San Pietro di Positano ★★★   Affording luxurious accommodations and exceptionally professional service in a wonderful location just outside Positano by Laurito Beach, this family-run member of the Relais & Châteaux group is *the* place to stay on the Amalfi Coast. Elegant public areas have French windows opening onto the garden and the sea; spacious guest rooms have antiques, tiled floors, pink-marble bathrooms, and private terraces; some have huge picture windows. The hotel's private beach is accessible by elevator, and there's a splendid panoramic swimming pool, tennis court, and a state-of-the-art fitness center with a wonderful spa. *Note:* The hotel welcomes children only age 10 and above.

The Michelin-rated **Il San Pietro** is a unique restaurant for the postcard views, cozy terrace, garden, and exceptional food: Chef Alois Vanlangenacker uses local ingredients—mostly from the hotel's own farm—to create sophisticated yet simple concoctions such as the *pollo ruspante in crosta di agrumi* (free-range chicken in a citrus crust). The restaurant is closed November through March; reservations are required as well as formal dress for dinner. Guests can also enjoy the new beachside restaurant **Carlino.**

Via Laurito 2, 84017 Positano. ℂ **800/735-2478** in the U.S., or 089-875455. Fax 089-811449. www.ilsan pietro.it. 60 units. 550€–630€ double; from 760€ suite. Rates include breakfast. 3 nights minimum stay in high season (May–Oct 18). AE, DC, MC, V. Free parking. Closed Nov–Mar. **Amenities:** Restaurants; bar; concierge; health club; pool; room service; sauna; spa; tennis court. *In room:* A/C, TV, minibar.

Expensive

Covo dei Saraceni ★ Named after the fisherman's house that was used as the Saracens's hideout (see "Festival of the Assunta," p. 190), this establishment offers peaceful and alluring accommodations right on the marina, away from the hubbub. Guest rooms are large and bright, with comfortable furnishings, terra-cotta floors, and lovely private balconies or terraces with great views. The seawater swimming pool on the fifth-floor terrace and the restaurant, **Savino,** are added incentives.

Via Regina Giovanna 5, 84017 Positano. ℂ **089-875400.** Fax 089-875878. www.covodeisaraceni.it. 58 units. 296€ double; from 400€ junior suite. Rates include buffet breakfast. Children 2 and under stay free in parent's room. AE, DC, MC, V. Parking 25€. Closed mid-Oct to Mar. **Amenities:** Restaurant; 2 bars; concierge; pool; room service. *In room:* A/C, TV, minibar.

Palazzo Murat ★ This 18th-century baroque palace near the marina is said to have been built for Gioacchino Murat, Napoleon's brother-in-law and later king of Naples. The five more-expensive guest rooms in the historical part of the palace are decorated with antiques and original furnishings; the ones in the new wings are also very nicely appointed. All units have good-size bathrooms, and most rooms have ocean views. The rich buffet breakfast is served in the delightful garden when weather permits; in August and September this is the site of chamber music concerts. The hotel's restaurant **Al Palazzo** offers alfresco dining in a charming setting.

Via dei Mulini 23, 84017 Positano. ℂ **089-875177.** Fax 089-811419. www.palazzomurat.it. 30 units. 220€–475€ double. Rates include buffet breakfast. Children 2 and under stay free in parent's room. AE, DC, MC, V. Parking 25€ nearby. Closed Jan to week before Easter. **Amenities:** Restaurant; concierge; room service. *In room:* A/C, TV, minibar.

Villa Franca (Finds) ★ This delightful family-run hotel overlooking the sea is one of Positano's lesser-known, distinctive hotels. The common areas are decorated with reproduction artwork and fine tiles to evoke a neoclassical feeling. The motif continues in the elegant, comfortable guest rooms, all of which are decorated in Mediterranean style, with bright artistic tiled floors and bathrooms; private balconies overlook the sea. The roof terrace has a 360-degree view over the town and a swimming pool with a solarium. An additional 10 rooms are in the less-inspired annex (the cheaper "standard" rooms are likely to be here; inquire when you book). The hotel's restaurant serves good food in a romantic setting. Another nice feature is the free shuttle bus to the center of Positano.

Via Pasitea 318, 84017 Positano. ℂ **089-875655.** Fax 089-875735. www.villafrancahotel.it. 38 units. 210€–410€ double. Rates include buffet breakfast. Children 2 and under stay free in parent's room. AE, DC, MC, V. Parking 21€. Closed Nov–Mar. **Amenities:** Restaurant; bar; concierge; health club; pool; room service; spa. *In room:* A/C, TV, minibar.

Moderate

Casa Albertina ★★ (Kids) This small, family-run hotel in the upper part of Positano offers attentive service and great views. The famous Sicilian writer Luigi Pirandello had his usual abode in one of the beautiful guest rooms, and the rooms here do make you want to settle in. Each is individually decorated, with carefully chosen furniture and a simple, monochromatic theme; French doors open onto private balconies (with water views). When the weather's nice, breakfast is served on the terra-cotta tiled terrace. In the high season, rates include half-board (breakfast and dinner).

Via della Tavolozza 3, 84017 Positano. ℂ **089-875143.** Fax 089-811540. www.casalbertina.it. 20 units. 170€–240€ double. Rates include breakfast. Children 2 and under stay free in parent's room. AE, DC, MC, V. Parking 20€–40€ nearby. **Amenities:** Restaurant; bar; concierge; room service. *In room:* A/C, TV, minibar.

Myth or Reality: The Truth About the Amalfi Coast Drive

Is the Amalfi Coast Drive as hair-raising as they say? More to the point: "Is driving the best way to enjoy the views?" And the answer is no, not for the driver. One of the world's most famous drives, the stretch of road between Vietri sul Mare and Positano is only 36km (22 miles). While the technical difficulty of the drive is moderate (easier than the road to Hana in Maui, let's say, but more difficult than the Pacific Coast Highway), traffic and the aggressive Neapolitan driving style can turn it into a headache for even the most-experienced driver—and into a complete nightmare if you generally drive on spacious freeways in flat or gentle terrain. Luckily, alternatives—car service, bus, taxi, and ferry—are well developed; see p. 47. On the other hand, if you want to explore this area in depth within a limited time period, having your own car with driver will provide you with more flexibility.

Hotel Buca di Bacco   Centrally positioned on the Marina Grande—a great choice if you don't mind a bit of noise—this excellent hotel boasts beautiful rooms that are all large and well furnished. Most have balconies facing the sea, and six superior rooms have full seafront terraces. The less-expensive guest rooms in the annexed buildings enjoy similar levels of comfort. The hotel's restaurant, **La Pergola,** is extremely popular, as is the less-pricey snack bar.

Via Rampa Teglia 4, 84017 Positano. © **089-875699.** Fax 089-875731. www.bucadibacco.it. 54 units. 300€–435€ double. Rates include buffet breakfast. AE, DC, MC, V. No parking. Closed 2 weeks in winter. **Amenities:** Restaurant; bar; babysitting; concierge; room service; Wi-Fi. *In room:* A/C, TV, minibar.

Inexpensive

Hotel Bougainville (Finds)   This family-run hotel is quite small, having only 14 units, but it's a good choice if you don't mind sacrificing amenities for location—it sits in the heart of Positano only steps from the beach. Rates are very reasonable. Some of the rear-facing guest rooms open onto flowery private terraces, where you can have breakfast in good weather; other rooms overlook the village, and few of the standard doubles have only a miniscule window (make sure you don't get one of those). All are decorated with simple but quality modern furniture and pastel-colored tiled floors, and have good-size bathrooms (some with shower only).

Via Cristoforo Colombo 25, 84017 Positano. © **089-875047.** Fax 089-811150. www.bougainville.it. 14 units. 120€–170€ double. AE, V. No parking. Closed Nov to mid-Mar. **Amenities:** Bar. *In room:* A/C, TV, minibar, Wi-Fi.

Hotel Savoia ★★   Nestled in the heart of Positano, this quiet, well-run hotel is just steps away from shops and the beach. Guest units are spacious, bright, and comfortably furnished (think good beds and roomy cabinets), with tiled floors and good-size modern bathrooms. Some of the rooms have sea views, while others overlook the village; bathrooms are good-size (some with shower only) and those in the best rooms have sauna showers or Jacuzzi tubs. This place has been run by the D'Aiello family since 1936, and prides itself on courteous service.

Via Cristoforo Colombo 73, 84017 Positano. © **089-875003.** Fax 089-811844. www.savoiapositano.it. 42 units. 140€–220€ double; 270€ suite. Rates include buffet breakfast. AE, DC, MC, V. Parking 25€ nearby. **Amenities:** Bar; babysitting; concierge; room service. *In room:* A/C, TV, minibar.

Staying at a B&B

Given the huge demand for moderately priced rooms in Positano (under 200€ on average, btw. 130€–260€ depending on the season and the quality of the room), B&Bs have flourished. Our favorites are **La Tavolozza**, Via Cristoforo Colombo 10 (© **089-875040**); **Villa Rosa**, Via C. Colombo 127 (© **089-811955**; www.villarosapositano.it); **La Rosa dei Venti**, Via Fornillo 40 (© **089-875252**; www.larosadeiventi.net); **Casa Maresca**, Via Lepanto 17 (© **089-875679**; www.casamaresca.it); **Casa Soriano**, Via Pasitea (© **089-875494**); and **La Fenice**, Via Marconi 4, Chetrara (© **089-875513**; www.bbfenice.com).

WHERE TO DINE

The best and most elegant dining in Positano is at the town's top hotels: **Il San Pietro** and **La Sponda** at **Le Sirenuse**. Recommendations for casual dining are below.

Expensive

La Cambusa AMALFITAN/SEAFOOD   Baldo and Luigi created this restaurant in 1970 vowing to serve traditionally prepared fish of the highest quality, and they have kept their promise. Only the freshest fish—brought in every morning by local fishermen—is prepared with techniques designed to bring out the natural flavors. Try *penne con gamberetti e rughetta* (with shrimp and arugula); or our favorite, *spaghetti con le cozze di scoglio* (with sautéed mussels and local cherry tomatoes). For the secondo, pick your fish from the display and have it prepared grilled or *all'acqua pazza* (with an herb broth).

Piazza Amerigo Vespucci 4, near Spiaggia Grande. © **089-875432**. www.lacambusapositano.com. Reservations recommended. Secondi 16€–28€. AE, DC, MC, V. Daily noon–3pm and 7:30–11pm.

Moderate

Da Adolfo ★ AMALFITAN/SEAFOOD   You might like the challenge of reaching this picturesque beach restaurant from SS 163 via the flight of 450 rugged steps. If not, a free water-shuttle service for the restaurant's guests is available at Marina Grande (daily 10am and 1pm, return 4–7pm; later on Sat nights in July and Aug), you'll recognize the boat by the red fish symbol. The restaurant has a laid-back atmosphere, and the menu includes many simple local dishes. The signature dish is mozzarella *alla brace* (grilled on fresh lemon leaves) and a truly special *zuppa di cozze* (mussel stew), but we also recommend the tasty *grigliata di pesce* (medley of fresh grilled seafood). Da Adolfo also offers **beach facilities** with changing rooms, showers, and chair-and-umbrella rentals (8€ for both per day).

Via Spiaggia di Laurito 40. © **089-875022**. www.daadolfo.com. Reservations recommended. Secondi 12€–18€. No credit cards. Daily noon–3pm; July–Aug also Sat 8pm–midnight. Closed Oct–May.

Da Vincenzo ★★ AMALFITAN   In the small stone dining rooms of this family-run restaurant, you'll find great down-home local dishes. The menu changes regularly but you will always find *antipasti di mare* (a variety of tasty seafood appetizers) and scrumptious *panzerotti* (deep-fried square ravioli filled with ham and cheese). Other specialties are *panzerottini Margaret* (small square ricotta ravioli in a fresh basil and local cherry-tomato sauce), and *peperoni ripieni* (sweet peppers stuffed with olives, herbs, and cheese).

Viale Pasitea 172. © **089-875128**. www.davincenzo.it. Reservations recommended. Secondi 14€–18€. No credit cards. Tues 7:30–10pm; Wed–Mon 12:30–3pm and 7:30–10pm. Closed Nov–Feb.

Donna Rosa ★★ AMALFITAN   In the green outskirts of Positano, this is where locals come to eat homemade pasta and excellent seafood prepared by two sisters and served—in the good season—on a charming terrace overlooking the sea. The menu surprises with a choice of turf and surf: Our favorites were the *salsicce alla griglia* (grilled local sausages), the *agnello arrosto* (roasted lamb), and the excellent *scialatielli zucchine e vongole* (eggless pasta with clams and zucchini).

Via Montepertuso 97. © **089-811806.** Reservations recommended. Secondi 12€–21€. AE, DC, MC, V. Aug and Oct–May Wed–Mon 12:30–2:30pm and 7:30–10:30pm; June–July and Sept Wed–Sun 12:30–2:30pm; June–Sept daily 7:30–10:30pm. Closed 11 weeks btw. Jan and Mar.

Hotel Ristorante Le Sirene ★ AMALFITAN/SEAFOOD   This popular restaurant is right on the beach in Laurito, about 2km (1¼ miles) from the center of Positano. The restaurant's boat service will pick you up from Marina Grande, a much better option than navigating the several hundred steps down from SS 163. A competitor of Da Adolfo (above), it offers a less casual setting and similarly good food. The menu focuses on seafood, such as the *scialatielli allo scoglio* (local fresh pasta with seafood), but also offers such well-prepared local dishes as *mozzarella alla brace* (grilled on fresh lemon leaves). Above the restaurant are eight simply but nicely appointed **guest rooms** (165€–190€ double, including breakfast, beach chairs, and umbrella).

Via Spiaggia di Laurito 24. © **089-875490.** Fax 089-875353. www.lesirenepositano.com. Secondi 12€–18€. No credit cards. Daily 12:30–3pm and 7:30–10pm. Closed Oct–May 20.

Il Ritrovo (Finds) AMALFITAN/PIZZA   High above Positano, this pleasant restaurant offers a great escape from the crowds, high prices, and summer heat below. The restaurant has a cool arbor-covered terrace with magnificent views, and a seasonal menu focused on meat and vegetables from the family farm. Both the *grigliata mista* (grilled meat medley) and the free-range chicken baked with herbs are excellent, as is homemade pasta such as ravioli or tagliatelle. The SITA bus stop from Positano is nearby, or you can call the restaurant for free pickup. Chef Salvatore also offers well-organized **cooking classes** year-round.

Via Montepertuso 77. © **089-812005** or 089-875453. www.ilritrovo.com. Reservations recommended. Secondi 10€–14€; set-price menu 30€–40€. AE, DC, MC, V. Thurs–Tues 12:30–3pm and 7:30–10pm; daily in summer 12:30–3pm and 7:30–10pm. Closed Jan.

Pupetto ★ (Kids) AMALFITAN/PIZZA   Right on the beach at Fornillo, this historic restaurant cannot be reached by car (an elevator will take you down from the parking lot off SS 163), but is a moderately short walk away from Marina Grande along a seaside path. A 1950s vibe has been preserved, with the colorful and informal dining terrace and down-to-earth menu. The food is good, and your kids can run around on the beach outside (where you can rent umbrellas and chairs). We recommend the excellent *spaghetti alle vongole* (with fresh clams) and the *fritto misto* (deep-fried seafood medley). *Note:* Pizza is served only for dinner. Above the restaurant are 34 large **guest rooms** with basic amenities (180€–220€ double, including breakfast; parking 15€).

Via Fornillo 37, Spiaggia di Fornillo, 84017 Positano. © **089-875087.** Fax 089-811517. www.hotel pupetto.it. 34 units. Secondi 12€–22€. AE, DC, MC, V. Daily 12:30–3pm and 7:30–10pm. Closed Nov–Mar.

Inexpensive

Il Grottino Azzurro (Finds) AMALFITAN/WINERY   This historic wine cellar has been a favorite with visitors and locals for decades. It offers a simple array of well-prepared traditional dishes, centered—for a welcome change—on meat, fresh homemade pasta, and wine. Locals come for delicious cannelloni (tubes of fresh pasta filled with meat and baked with cheese and tomato sauce), Parmigiana (eggplant Parmesan), and succulent roasted chicken. Obviously, you'll find a good number of local and regional vintages to quaff.

Via Guglielmo Marconi 158 (SS 163). ℂ **089-875466.** Reservations recommended. Secondi 10€–16€. No credit cards. Thurs–Tues 12:30–3pm and 7:30–10pm (also Wed in summer).

SHOPPING ★★

Positano's main drag for shopping is Via dei Mulini, but you'll find all kinds of small shops and boutiques along the town's steep streets, many of them offering what is known around the world as "Positano Fashion." The small tailoring boutiques of the 1960s, where dresses or trousers were made to order, have evolved into a highly specialized craft. Modern local designers create a unique style of colorful garments that are the embodiment of Positano's Mediterranean sensibility. Wonderful summer clothes and beachwear—swimsuits are a specialty—as well as more dressy items await you in the elegant boutiques, most of which line Viale Pasitea. **Sartoria Maria Lampo,** Viale Pasitea 12 (ℂ 089-875021; www.marialampo.it), is one of the remaining original boutiques and is keeping up its reputation. Other favorites are **Pepito's,** Viale Pasitea 15 (ℂ **089-875446;** www.pepitos-fashion.com); **Nadir,** Viale Pasitea 44 (ℂ **089-875975**); **La Bottega di Brunella,** Via dei Mulini 21 (ℂ **089-875812**), and Viale Pasitea 76 (ℂ **089-875228**); and **La Tartana,** Via della Tartana (ℂ **089-875645**).

The town is also famous for its handmade sandals. Some of the artisan shops will make them for you while you wait. Try **D'Antonio,** Via Trara Genoino 13 (ℂ **089-811824**); **Dattilo,** Via Rampa Teglia 19 (ℂ **089-811440**); or **Safari,** Via della Taratana 2 (ℂ **089-811440;** www.safaripositano.com).

Positano has a number of high-quality antiques shops, such as **Cose Antiche,** Via Cristoforo Colombo 21 (ℂ **089-811811;** www.coseantichepositano.it), and **Le Myricae,** Via Cristoforo Colombo 27 (ℂ **089-875882**), with its splendid collection of Art Deco jewelry.

POSITANO AFTER DARK

During the sweet summer nights, Positano's bars are packed with locals and visitors having *aperitivo* and indulging in people-watching. If you are in the mood for luxury, have drinks on the delightful terrace at the hotel **Le Sirenuse** (see "Hotel Le Sirenuse," earlier in this chapter); for less-formal entertainment, a perfect spot is **L'Incanto,** Via Marina 4 (ℂ **089-811177**), not far from the sea at Spiaggia Grande, and so is popular **Chez Black,** Via del Brigantino 19 (ℂ **089-875036**) nearby. On the beach of Spiaggia Grande is the historic **La Buca di Bacco,** Via del Brigantino 35 (ℂ **089-811461;** www.buca positano.it), which started as a tavern and a nightclub that was the meeting place for the local *dolce vita* back when Positano was an exclusive resort for VIPs; it is poised for a new era of glory. The bar in front is a perfect place for a coffee or a *granita,* while the tavern below has evolved into a pleasant late-night wine bar–cum–art gallery and Internet cafe. At **Conwinum,** Via Rampa Teglia 12 (ℂ **089-811461**), a trendy local crowd comes to listen to live jazz on summer weekends and to sip at the good vintages.

Another hot spot is **Caffe Positano,** Viale Pasitea 182 (ℂ **089-875082**), a bar with live music on the terrace over the marina (they also make excellent coffee). Popular among locals, **Internazionale,** Via Marconi 306, by Chiesa Nuova (ℂ **089-875434**), has a good wine selection and yummy pastries. If you have a sweet tooth, you will definitely like **La Zagara,** Via dei Mulini 8 (ℂ **089-875964;** www.lazagara.com), where locals come after dinner to enjoy excellent homemade ice cream and *granite* in various flavors—try the melon—in a marvelous garden of citrus trees. Its famous pastry shop serves *torta positanese* (a local cake made with almonds), *delizie al limone* (lemon cream puffs), and *Bavarese* (a pastry filled with wild strawberries and whipped cream).

Music on the Rocks, Via Grotto dell'Incanto 51 (℡ **089-875874;** www.musicon therocks.it), is a two-level dance club including **Le Terrazze,** with food and a piano bar; the disco below, inside a grotto by the beach, has the same owners as Chez Black. The club is open Friday and Saturday nights in May and September, and daily June through August (closed Oct–Apr).

2 PRAIANO & VETTICA MAGGIORE

6.5km (4 miles) E of Positano; 9km (5 miles) W of Amalfi

Only a short distance from Positano, Praiano offer a less "international" version of the Costiera Amalfitana: You will share your stay mostly with locals and other Italian visitors, as most foreign tourists instead beeline for the more famous destinations.

ESSENTIALS

GETTING THERE & AROUND   Praiano is the first village you encounter east of Positano and is easily reached from Positano, Amalfi, or Sorrento by **SITA bus, taxi** or **car service,** or **rental car** or scooter (see "Getting Around," p. 188, 204, and 169). **La Sibilla,** Via Umberto I, Praiano (℡ **089-874365;** www.lasibilla.org), offers **water taxi** service to and from Marina di Praia from Amalfi, Atrani, Capri, and Positano (about 65€ per hr.); it also offers boat rental, and daily excursions to Capri, the Emerald Grotto (p. 222), and Furore. **Benvenuto Limos,** Via Roma 54, Praiano (℡ **334-3078342;** www.benvenutolimos.com), is the local car service. **Taxi** service is provided by **Umberto Benvenuto,** Via Roma (℡ **089-874024**), and **Gennaro Rispoli,** Via G. Capriglione (℡ **089-874370**).

VISITOR INFORMATION   Praiano's **tourist office** (℡ **089-874557;** www.praiano. org) is at Via G. Capriglione.

FAST FACTS   You'll find a **pharmacy** (℡ **089-874846**) on Via Capriglione 142 (SS 163). For the nearest hospital see "Fast Facts," p. 263; for an **ambulance,** dial ℡ **118.** You can call the **police** at ℡ **113** or 112. The **post office** (℡ **089-874086**) is on Via Capriglione 80 (SS 163). You'll find an **ATM** by the tourist office (see "Visitor Information," above); the nearest bank is in Positano.

EXPLORING THE TOWN

The preferred residence of the Amalfi doges—who loved the beautiful views over Positano, Amalfi, and the Faraglioni of Capri—Praiano is still popular among Italians for the same reason. The twin villages of Praiano and Vettica Maggiore, to the west, occupy the two faces of the promontory known as Capo Sottile. With a graceful profusion of porticos and domes, the **medieval village** is 120m (394 ft.) above sea level on the slopes of Monte Sant'Angelo. Strolling along the steep streets you'll encounter the church of **San Gennaro**—technically in Vettica Maggiore—crowned by a beautiful oval dome tiled with colored majolica. Its 18th-century majolica floor was recreated in 1966 according to the original design. The **view** from the church square is superb.

Twin towns, twin harbors: East of town is the picturesque **Marina di Praia** ★★, with its small pebbly beach and clear waters, where you can rent chairs and umbrellas. West of town is the more secluded **Spiaggia della Gavitella** ★, a cove that is only accessible by boat or by footpath. The footpath starts from the Church of San Gennaro (above), off to the right from Via Masa; it also crosses SS 163, down across from the tourist office.

From the beach of Marina di Praia **Via Torremare** is a scenic footpath carved along the cliff. Go left to the natural grotto housing the nightclub L'Africana (see "Praiana After Dark," below), or head right up to the medieval watchtower **Torre Asciola** (aka Torre a Mare, or tower by the sea), housing the studio of local artist **Sandulli,** a painter and sculptor. *Note:* The footpath is generally easy but becomes dangerously slippery in bad weather, when the sea has been known to wash people off the path to their possible death below.

From the trail to Spiaggia della Gavitella a long flight of steps leads to the medieval tower **Torre di Grado.** The walk is particularly romantic at sunset or in the moonlight.

For more serious **hiking,** Praiano is one of the gateways to the Amalfi Coast's most famous trail, *Sentiero degli Dei* (**Trail of the Gods**) ★★★. A ridge trail, it runs high above the sea between Nocella and Bomerano and affords magnificent views of the entire coast. The Sentiero is actually a section of the longer **Via degli Incanti,** the Trail of Charms ★★, which runs between Amalfi and Positano (see "Staying Active," p. 207). As you walk westward from Praiano, you'll enjoy the best views. The ascent takes you first to Colle Serra and on to San Domenico, where you will start the ridge trail to Nocella and Montepertuso, before heading down to Positano. The trail is moderately difficult and requires some preparation, but it is—as its name suggests—a divine trail.

In Marina di Praia you can also **rent boats** and sign up for excursions with **La Sibilla** ★ (see "Getting Around," earlier in this chapter).

WHERE TO STAY
Expensive

Casa Angelina ★★   This new boutique hotel is in a starchy white structure overlooking the cliff and affording excellent views. Guest rooms—bright and sparsely decorated with contemporary, streamlined furniture and tiled floors—often open to private terraces and balconies with loungers or chairs. Bathrooms are good-size and modern, many with large windows overlooking the sea (some with shower only). The best rooms have large terraces with great views and even larger bathrooms. If you don't mind being separated from the main hotel and its services, we recommend the four "Eaudesea" suites with kitchenettes, inside restored fishing sheds on the Spiaggia della Gavitella. The outdoor pool has current-making engines and an elevator connects to the private beach below, with umbrellas and chairs reserved for the hotel's guests. On-site is the gourmet restaurant **Un Piano nel Cielo** (p. 201).

Via Gennaro Capriglione 147 (SS 163), 84010 Praiano. © **089-8131333.** Fax 089-874266. www.casangelina. com. 39 units. 270€–450€ double; 750€ suite. Children 12 and under welcome only during low season. AE, DC, MC, V. Parking 25€. **Amenities:** Restaurant; bar; gym; 2 pools; room service; spa. *In room:* A/C, TV, Internet, minibar.

Moderate

Grand Hotel Tritone (**Kids**)   Off SS 163, a short distance west of Praiano, this hotel offers gorgeous views and quiet accommodations. The old-fashioned elegance creates a welcoming and warm atmosphere. Built over a high cliff, with an elevator to the private beach below, it has a terrace garden with a lemon grove. The seawater pool is a great spot, and the hotel even has a picturesque chapel built in a grotto. Guest rooms are well-appointed and pleasantly furnished, many with private balconies, sea views, and good-size bathrooms (some with shower only). The 12 suites are gorgeous, each with its own private terrace overlooking the water. The hotel's restaurant, **La Cala delle Lampare,** is good.

Via Campo 5 (off SS 163, 2km/1¼ miles) west of Praiano), 84010 Praiano. ℂ **089-874333.** Fax 089-813024. www.tritone.it or www.hoteltritonepraiano.com. 62 units. 210€–240€ double; 280€ triple; from 320€ suite. Rates include buffet breakfast. Children 3 and under stay free in parent's room. AE, DC, MC, V. Free parking. **Amenities:** Restaurant; bar; pool. *In room:* A/C, TV, minibar.

Hotel Onda Verde   Perched on a cliff, this personal, friendly hotel has several buildings connected by flights of steps. Guest rooms vary in shape and style but are uniform in amenities and service, although some are more conveniently located than others. They are tasteful and well-appointed, with modern furniture, tiled floors, and good-size bathrooms (some with shower only); each unit has its own panoramic small terrace. Via more steps, you can descend to the "beach"—a few chairs on the rocks—from which you can swim into the sea.

Via Terramare 3, Marina di Praia, 84010 Praiano. ℂ **089-874143.** Fax 089-8131049. www.ondaverde.it. 25 units. 210€–230€ double; 250€–270€ triple; 260€–280€ quad. Rates include buffet breakfast. Children 2 and under stay free in parent's room. AE, DC, MC, V. Free parking. Closed Nov–Mar. **Amenities:** Restaurant; bar; Wi-Fi. *In room:* A/C, TV, minibar.

Hotel Tramonto D'oro (Kids)   The name of this family-run hotel means "Golden Sunset," and the end-of-day views are indeed superb. Right off SS 163, it is convenient to the SITA bus, and the warm service and good amenities—including a swimming pool on the terrace, a gym, and free shuttle to the beach—make it a popular choice, often for groups. Guest rooms are spacious and individually decorated, with modern light woods and tiled floors. Bathrooms are good-size (some with shower only). We recommend upgrading to the best rooms, which offer wonderful sea views and are filled with light. The hotel's **restaurant,** with a panoramic terrace affording spectacular views, serves lip-smacking food (closed Nov–Feb).

Via Gennaro Capriglione 119 (SS 163), 84010 Praiano. ℂ **089-874955.** Fax 089-874670. www.tramonto doro.it. 40 units. 180€–280€ double; 250€–340€ triple; 280€–370€ quad. Rates include buffet breakfast. Children 3 and under stay free in parent's room. AE, DC, MC, V. Free parking. **Amenities:** Restaurant; bar; concierge; gym; pool; sauna. *In room:* A/C, TV, minibar.

Inexpensive

Hotel Margherita ★ (Kids) (Finds)   This family-run hotel offers high-standard accommodations at moderate prices. The swimming pool and panoramic terraces are nice places to lounge, and the beach is only a few minutes away. Guest units are comfortable and well-appointed, with tiled floors, traditional painted furniture, and good-size bathrooms (some with shower only). Each opens onto a private balcony, some overlooking the lemon grove but the best overlooking the sea. The hotel's **restaurant** prepares excellent local cuisine.

Via Umberto I 70 (off Via Roma [SS 163]), 84010 Praiano. ℂ **089-874628.** www.hotelmargherita.info. 28 units. 110€–150€ double; 160€ triple; 180€ quad. Rates include breakfast. Children 2 and under stay free in parent's room. AE, DC, MC, V. Free parking. **Amenities:** Restaurant; bar; pool; room service; smoke-free rooms. *In room:* A/C, TV, Internet, minibar.

Il Pino   This family-run hotel is prized by locals for the sea views from its pleasant terrace, and for the good food in its moderately priced **restaurant,** with a menu of enticing local favorites. Above the restaurant, guest rooms are large, bright, and simply furnished but welcoming, with sea views, tiled floors, and comfortable-size bathrooms (some with shower only). Each room opens onto a private terrace with a view of the Mediterranean.

Via Gennaro Capriglione 13 (SS 163), 84010 Praiano. (*C*/fax **089-874389.** www.hotelilpino.it. 16 units. 160€ double; 180€ triple; 200€ quad. Rates include breakfast. Children 2 and under stay free in parent's room. Closed Nov–Mar. AE, DC, MC, V. Free parking. **Amenities:** Restaurant; bar. *In room:* A/C, TV.

WHERE TO DINE

In addition to the excellent choices below, we recommend the hotel restaurants of **Il Pino, Margherita,** and **Tramonto d'Oro,** as well as the restaurant **La Cala delle Lampare,** in the Grand Hotel Tritone (see "Where to Stay," above).

Expensive

Un Piano nel Cielo CREATIVE AMALFITAN   Your experience at this gourmet restaurant in the hotel Casa Angelina is enhanced by the minimalist setting—in line with the contemporary design of the hotel—and the splendid views from both the indoor dining room and the terrace. The seasonal menu is based on traditional foods, revisited by the creative chef, with such dishes as spinach and *astice* (local lobster), ravioli with a sea truffle sauce, or *raviolini di rana pescatrice in salsa di vongole e broccoletti* (small fish ravioli in a sauce of clams and broccoli rabe). Desserts, such as the warm chocolate torte with red pepper and pistachio sauce, are delicate and enticing.

Via Gennaro Capriglione 147 (SS 163). (*C*) **089-8131333.** www.unpianonelcielo.it. Reservations recommended. Secondi 18€–28€. AE, DC, MC, V. Thurs–Tues 12:30–3pm and 7:30–11pm (also Wed in summer).

Inexpensive

La Brace ★★ AMALFITAN/PIZZA   In the perfect location to enjoy the beautiful scenery, this is our favorite restaurant in Praiano. The food is excellent and moderately priced, and the hosts are delightful. The seasonal menu includes many simple home-cooked dishes, based on the market offering of seafood, meat, and veggies. The homemade pastas are to die for—try the *fusilli con provola, melanzane, e basilico* (with provola cheese, sauted eggplant, and fresh basil)—and so is the tasty grilled fish. The desserts are strictly homemade and deliciously traditional. In the evening pizza is also served.

Via Gennaro Capriglione 146 (SS 163). (*C*) **089-874226.** Reservations recommended. Secondi 9€–14€. AE, DC, MC, V. Thurs–Tues 12:30–3pm and 7:30–11pm (also Wed Apr–Sept).

SHOPPING

Do you have a musician in the family? You might not have thought of purchasing a musical instrument while on your vacation, but once you've visited this artisans' workshop, you might change your mind. At **Bottega Scala** ★★, Via Roma 57 (*C* **089-874894;** www.liuteriascala.com), the *liutai* (stringed instruments maker) Pasquale and Leonardo Scala create instruments using ancient techniques. Many of their clients are famous Italian musicians—one is Pino Daniele. They specialize in classic guitars and ancient instruments, from medieval to baroque.

PRAIANO AFTER DARK

For a good evening out and a historic pilgrimage, we suggest a visit to **L'Africana** ★★, off SS 163 in Vettica Maggiore, and take the elevator down (*C* **089-874042**). This popular nightclub was a mythical hangout during the *anni ruggenti* (roaring years) of the 1960s, when it was the destination of choice of VIPs and their trendy friends. In a grotto right above the lapping sea, it has experienced a second coming and is again a lively scene. Don't be surprised if fishermen pull their nets up from the sea just beyond the edge of the dance floor; their fresh catch is what's on tomorrow's menus in town. The club is open Friday and Saturday nights May and September, and daily June through August (closed Oct–Apr).

3 AMALFI

34km (21 miles) W of Salerno; 61km (38 miles) SE of Naples

Amalfi, the queen of the Costiera, has origins dating to the 6th century, when it was a small harbor that slowly gained importance under the Byzantine Empire. It finally declared its independence in A.D. 839, and its perfect strategic location—opening onto a natural harbor at the mouth of a valley rich in water, yet protected by the forbidding Monti Lattari from the incursions of both Turks and Normans—allowed Amalfi to develop into a florishing city-state. Its river valley allowed for the development of mills that produced paper for much of Europe during the Middle Ages and well into the Renaissance, while its harbor became the shipyard that fueled Amalfi's political and commercial power. It became Italy's first maritime republic, before either Pisa or Venice, and for 2 centuries it was a maritime power to be reckoned with. The small republic was rich and cosmopolitan, and its coins were widely used across the Mediterranean, from the Greek Empire to Africa to the Longobard territories. Amalfi also dominated the markets in spices, perfumes, silk, and valuable carpets.

Visitors marvel that a town so small and picturesque could reach such prominence, and indeed Amalfi's toehold among the cliffs eventually became a liability; the limited size of its land area and comparable lack of military power obliged Amalfi to accept Norman rule in 1073. Pisa, which had developed into a powerful maritime republic itself in the meantime, then sacked Amalfi in 1135; and, in 1143, a terrible seaquake destroyed large parts of the harbor, including the fortifications and the shipyards. The Amalfi of old was completely annihilated 5 years later, when the plague struck in 1348. Afterward, Amalfi became a pretty fishing village, until it was rediscovered as a tourist destination by 19th-century travelers.

ESSENTIALS

GETTING THERE   The **bus** is an easy option, with **SITA** (© 081-5522176; www.sitabus.it) offering frequent service from Naples, Sorrento, Positano, Vietri, and Salerno (for more information on fares, see "The Unico Travel Pass," p. 48). For the best views, remember to sit on the right side of the bus when traveling from Sorrento and the left side from Vietri and Salerno. Amalfi is the largest harbor in the area after Salerno and is well served by **ferries** and hydrofoils: **Metrò del Mare** (© 199-446644; www.metrodelmare.com) offers regular service from Naples, Sorrento, Positano, Salerno, and other harbors along the coast. Fares vary depending on the distance, from 9€ from Positano to 18€ from Pozzuoli. Amalfi-based **Cooperativa Sant'Andrea** (© 089-873190; www.coopsantandrea.it) offers regular service from Capri, Minori, Positano, Salerno, and Sorrento, as well as special cruises and excursions; fares vary with the distance, from 6€ to about 16€.

DINING ◆
Da Gemma **8**
La Caravella **4**
Lido Azzurro **3**
Pasticceria Pansa **13**
Ristorante Eolo **14**
Trattoria San Giuseppe **7**

ACCOMMODATIONS ■
Hotel Floridiana **10**
Hotel La Bussola **2**
Hotel Lidomare **5**
Hotel Marina Riviera **14**
Hotel Miramalfi **1**
Residenza del Duca **9**

ATTRACTIONS ●
Arsenale Marinaro **6**
Duomo **11**
Museo Civico and
Palazzo di Città **12**

LMP (℗ **081-5513236;** www.consorziolmp.it) maintains *aliscafo* (hydrofoil) and *motonave* (ferry) service between Amalfi and Capri. **Travelmar** (℗ **081-7041911;** www. travelmar.it) makes runs between Salerno, Amalfi, Minori, Maiori, and Positano during the summer. Fares are 10€ to 18€ for both companies.

From the Naples Capodichino Airport, **taxis** offer a flat rate of 130€ to Amalfi. **Car services** (see "Getting Around," below) also offer transfers from Naples's airport or train station. Alternatively, private company **Curreri Viaggi** (℗ **081-8015420;** www.curreri viaggi.it) offers a shuttle service from the airport for 150€ for one to three passengers and 12€ for each additional passenger.

By **train** (℗ **892021** in Italy; www.trenitalia.it), the closest station is **Vietri sul Mare,** on the local line between **Naples** (where you'll change trains, if you are coming from the north) and **Salerno** (if you are coming from the south). Faster, though, is to get off in Salerno and take a SITA bus or a taxi directly to Amalfi.

By car, take the autostrada A3 toward NAPOLI-SALERNO to the exit for VIETRI SUL MARE, then follow the signs for VIETRI, AMALFI; they will lead you to the famed SS 163 that hugs the Amalfi Coast. You can also reach SS 163 from Castellammare di Stabia, Piana di

Sorrento, Vico Equense, and Sorrento, heading east and following signs for POSITANO and AMALFI—scenic but longer. *Note:* Because of the solid traffic here in summer, local authorities occasionally limit car access to SS 163; check with the tourist office and your hotel before making plans.

GETTING AROUND   The boat companies mentioned above offer transfers to nearby harbors. The **SITA terminal** on Piazza Flavio Gioia (© **089-871009**) is the hub for all the local **bus lines.** Adjacent to the terminal is the **taxi stand** (© **089-872239**).

VISITOR INFORMATION   The **tourist office** (© **089-871107**; www.amalfitourist office.it) is in Palazzo di Città, Corso delle Repubbliche Marinare 19, 84011 Amalfi. In winter, it is open Monday to Friday 8am to 1:30pm and Saturday 8am to noon; in summer, it's also open Monday to Friday 3 to 5pm.

FAST FACTS   You'll find a **pharmacy** at Piazza dei Dogi (© **089-871063**) and another at Via L. d'Amalfi (© **089-871045**). The closest **hospital** is in Salerno (see "Fast Facts," p. 263); for an **ambulance,** dial © **118.** The **police** can be reached at © **113** or 112. The **post office** (© **089-872996**) is at Via delle Repubbliche Marinare, next to the tourist office, and is open Monday to Saturday 8am to 2pm. Next door, you will find a Deutsche Bank **ATM. Amalfi Servizi Express,** Piazza dei Dogi 8 (© **089-873447;** www. amalfiservizi.it), has Internet access.

SPECIAL EVENTS   On the first Sunday of June, the **Historic Regatta of the Maritime Republics** is held, with turns being taken by each of the four historical towns—Genova, Pisa, Venice, and Amalfi. Amalfi's turn was in 2009 and will come again in 2013. Civic pride and thousand-year-old rivalries are at stake, and the boat races are run with pomp, athleticism, and great seriousness. The spectacular, colorful event is accompanied by parades and musical performances.

EXPLORING THE TOWN

Full of mementos of its glorious past and decorated with gardens—olive, orange, and lemon trees, the groves sloping all the way to the sea—Amalfi is a jewel of a small town. Its central square, **Piazza Flavio Gioia,** commemorates the inventor of the compass (or, at least, the man who perfected it for marine use), according to local legend. Indeed, Amalfi's mariners were the first in Europe to use the properties of magnetism for navigation, starting back in the 12th century; they provided material for the first nautical charts of the Middle Ages.

The medieval heart of Amalfi stretches from **Piazza Duomo** along **Via Genova** and **Via Capuano,** with typical covered porticos and narrow streets. To get its flavor, stroll under the Supportico Sant'Andrea Apostolo till you reach Largo Filippo Augustariccio. There, through a characteristic Arab-style trilobate arch, you can enter another covered passage, Campo de Cinnamellis—the seat, in medieval times, of Amalfi's spice market.

Fun Facts   **Amalfi by the Book**

Amalfi is best known to English readers from John Webster's masterpiece, *The Duchess of Malfi* (1623). This bloody tale of love, lust, and murder captures the scandalous side of Renaissance court life; what's more, it may actually be true. The original source is the **Novelle** of the Dominican priest Matteo Bandello (1485–1561), who served several courts and no doubt knew whereof he spoke.

Be sure to visit the **Convento di San Francesco**—now Hotel Luna Convento (later in this chapter). Its 16th-century watchtower over the cape to the east of town is an annex of the hotel. Here you can visit the well-conserved 13th-century cloister and the attached church.

Arsenale Marinaro   Here at the Republic of Amalfi's shipyard, citizens built the vessels that maintained power over the Mediterranean in the Middle Ages. Established in the 11th century, the shipyard was restored in the 13th century, and at its height, it could build galleys up to 40m (131 ft.) long. Only half of the building remains today—the other half, which reached into the sea, was destroyed by a series of storms in the 14th century. You can still admire the building's beautiful architecture, such as its pointed arches and cross vaults resting over stone pillars. Between the Arsenale and the Porta della Marina is a tile panel depicting Amalfi's commercial empire in the Middle Ages; it was created by the artist Renato Rossi in the 1950s.

Via Matteo Camera (off Piazza Flavio Gioia). Free admission. Easter–Sept 9am–8pm.

Duomo ★★   This superb example of Arabo-Norman architecture dates to the 9th century, when the Republic of Amalfi was just gaining success. The majestic facade is decorated with a mosaic of gold leaf and majolica, with a magnificent 11th-century **bronze door** ★ made in Constantinople. The lovely Romanesque bell tower was finished in 1276. The Duomo was enlarged between the 16th and 18th centuries, when it was also given a baroque interior, including the majestic, imposing staircase leading to a beautiful atrium in black-and-white marble. It was renovated in 1891 and further restored in 1929, with respect for the 13th-century structures.

To the left of the Duomo is the breathtakingly beautiful cloister, the **Chiostro del Paradiso** ★★★, dating from 1266. The cloister, in Arab-Sicilian style, is decorated with interlaced arches over double columns and was originally built as the cemetery for the city's religious and political elite. The site now holds a small museum with ancient Roman and medieval artifacts. Among the best pieces are the **Roman sarcophagus of Ottavio Rufo** ★, richly carved with bas-reliefs, and two other sarcophagi. From the cloister, enter the **Chiesa del Crocifisso,** the original cathedral of Amalfi dating from the 10th century, where other artworks are preserved. July through September, concerts are held in the cloister on Friday nights (see "Amalfi After Dark," later in this chapter).

From the right nave of this church you can descend to the **Crypt,** the repository for the remains of the apostle St. Andrew, the protector saint of Amalfi. The crypt was built in the 13th century, when the remains of the saint were brought back from the 4th Crusade; it was redecorated in 1719. Over the main altar is the beautiful bronze **Statue of Sant'Andrea** by Michelangelo Naccherino.

Piazza del Duomo, 84011 Amalfi. **Duomo:** ☏ **089-871059.** Free admission. Nov–Feb daily 10am–1pm and 2:30–4:30pm; Mar and Oct daily 9:30am–5:15pm; Apr–June daily 9am–7pm; July–Sept daily 9am–9pm. **Museum and cloister:** ☏ **089-871324.** Admission 3€. June–Oct daily 9:30am–7pm; Nov–May daily 9:30am–5:15pm.

Museo Civico & Palazzo di Città   The Palazzo di Città is Amalfi's Town Hall. On its southern wall hangs a famous **Pannello in ceramica** ★, a majolica panel relating key moments in Amalfi's history. Created in the 1970s by artist Diodoro Cossa, it is made of two large colored tiles, which you can read from left to right. In the Town Hall, the **museum** is interesting mostly for local history buffs. It contains, however, at least one very important piece: the *Tabula Amalphitana,* the original maritime code written around the 11th century to regulate maritime traffic in the Mediterranean (this was

Amalfi & the Industry of Papermaking

Amalfi is believed to be the first European location where paper as we know it today was made. The process was discovered by the Arabs and perfected in the Arab town of El-Marubig, where the original name *bambagina* referred to the special kind of paper that became known as *paper of Amalfi,* made from recycled cotton, linen, and hemp cloths. The process was then exported to Amalfi through the close commercial relationship the republic had with the Arab world. Considered less durable than parchment, paper was still forbidden in 1250 for public use, but the industry developed rapidly and Amalfi sold its paper far and wide throughout the Middle Ages and the Renaissance. Paper continued to be made by hand till the 18th century, when machines were finally introduced; at that time there were 16 paper mills in the area, 10 of which are still active today. The cloths (or rags) were reduced to a poultice in large vats and then strained in forms marked with the symbol of the paper mill. The paper was then pressed between layers of woolen felt to extract excess water, air dried, and finally "ironed." Even if it was considered inferior to parchment or vellum, this paper was of high quality: The oldest sheets still in existence date from the 13th and 14th centuries. The *bambagina* of Amalfi is still highly appreciated by many—for example, the Vatican uses Amalfi paper for its correspondence.

If you wish to visit one of the working mills, **Cartiera Amatruda,** Via Marino del Giudice, (© **089-871315**) is still run by the original family, who welcomes visitors and will give you a tour of their facilities. **Antonio Cavaliere,** Via Fiume, (© **089-871954**), one of the descendants of the ancient master papermakers, is another, smaller option. Antonio's specialty is paper with real dried flowers as filigree, ideal for very special letters.

Both shops produce paper of an almost forgotten quality, made completely by hand, which is sold to the most exclusive paper shops in Italy, Europe, and the U.S. The water for this craft still comes from the covered river that crosses town and was the key resource in the development of Amalfi's paper industry. Both workshops are open regular business hours.

enforced till at least the 16th century). The artifact was redeemed from Austria in 1929 and brought back to Amalfi. Also interesting are the original pastel drawings for the Duomo's mosaics by Domenico Morelli.

Piazza Municipio. © **089-8736211.** www.comune.amalfi.sa.it. Free admission. Mon–Fri 8am–1pm.

Museo della Carta (Museum of Paper) This museum is the perfect place to learn more about the history of the local paper industry. In one of the abandoned paper mills, this working museum has a great collection of original tools and machines. It also maintains a library with over 3,000 texts on the origins of paper and a gift shop.

Palazzo Pagliara, Via delle Cartiere 24. © **089-8304561.** www.museodellacarta.it. Admission 3.40€. Nov–Feb Tues–Sun 10am–3:30pm; Mar–Oct daily 10am–6:30pm.

City Sightseeing Sorrento, Via degli Aranci 172, 80067 Sorrento (*C* **081-8774707;** www. sorrento.city-sightseeing.it), has partnered with SITA to offer tours on open-deck buses on two different routes: one along the coast to Minori and Maiori and one inland to Ravello. Buses depart hourly from Piazza Flavio Gioia in Amalfi (one ride 3€; day pass, valid for four rides on the Amalfi-Maiori line and one round-trip on the Ravello-Amalfi line, 10€).

STAYING ACTIVE

Amalfi used to have large **beaches,** but sea erosion and landslides have reduced the beach to two narrow strips on either side of the harbor. Most hotels on the waterfront have small private beaches carved out of the cliffs. For a larger beach, take the footpath to Atrani, an easy 15-minute stroll eastward.

From the harbor at **Marina Grande** you can rent **boats**—with or without captain—to explore the nooks and crannies of the coast. **Cooperativa Sant'Andrea** (*C* **089-873190;** www.coopsantandrea.it) offers regular service to the beaches of Duoglio and Santa Croce, only a few minutes away from Molo Pennello; boats leave every 30 minutes between 9am and 5pm. It also serves **Grotta dello Smeraldo** ★★ in Conca dei Marini (p. 222), leaving every hour between 9:30am and 3:30pm (10€ round-trip).

Amalfi is a great starting point for a number of beautiful **hikes.** The most popular is the pleasant and easy walk along **Valle dei Mulini (Valley of the Mills)** ★, which is the valley of the Torrente Canneto, Amalfi's small river. This valley has been declared a World Heritage Site by UNESCO, precisely because of its unique environment. Head up Via Genova from Piazza del Duomo where the street turns into a picturesque trail that leads to the area known as the **Mulino Rovinato (Ruined Mill),** about 1 hour away. The namesake flour mills were put out of business by the development of the pasta industry farther north, where the conditions were more favorable. In contrast, the paper mills continued to prosper, and some are still active today. Continuing up, you'll reach the more demanding trail through the **Vallone delle Ferriere** ★★. The going is good but quite steep as you near the ancient *ferriere* (iron mills), with their imposing walls partly hidden by growth. Already extant in the Middle Ages, they were active until the 19th century. Those in good shape can climb even farther up to the waterfalls; the ascent is short but steep. Allow 6 hours for the round-trip on the 12km (7.5-mile) trail.

Less demanding and highly rewarding is the famous *Via degli Incanti* **(Trail of Charms)** ★★ that connects Amalfi to Positano. The trail is indeed bewitching, wending through the cultivated terraces and citrus groves of the Amalfi countryside. The hike is moderate, with some taxing passages, but, due to its length, most people choose to do only a section of it, or do the whole trip over several days. The best views are heading west, though the footing will be a bit more hazardous. From the Valle dei Mulini above, take the trail to the left, climbing through the outskirts of town to Pogerola. Continuing up and left, you'll reach San Lazzaro. From here, the path procedes to Bomerano, where you'll join the section of the trek called **Sentiero degli Dei** ★★★ (see "Staying Active," p. 199). You'll then continue to Montepertuso, then down to Positano (see "Staying Active," p. 199).

WHERE TO STAY
Very Expensive
Hotel Santa Caterina ★★★   This is the most luxurious hotel in Amalfi, offering great, family-run service and a superb cliffside location. Guests have access to a private beach, which you can reach by elevator or a winding garden path; the pleasant swimming

pool is filled with seawater and surrounded by a luscious garden and citrus groves. Guest rooms are in the main building and in three annexes. All are large and refined, with antique furnishings, ceramic tiles from Vietri, and luxurious bathrooms (some with shower only). Each opens to a private balcony or terrace with views over the sea. Some of the suites are absolutely fantastic—Follia Amalfitana and Casa dell'Arancio, in particular; they are actually luxurious bungalows immersed in a citrus grove, with a private garden and a small pool. On-site is **Ristorante Santa Caterina** ★★ (p. 210); **Ristorante a Mare** ★ offers a simpler menu (open during the summer months only).

Via Nazionale 9, 84011 Amalfi. ✆ **089-871012.** Fax 089-871351. www.hotelsantacaterina.it. 66 units. 445€–780€ double; from 930€ suite. Rates include buffet breakfast. AE, DC, MC, V. Parking 15€. **Amenities:** 2 restaurants; bar; concierge; gym; pool; room service; spa. *In room:* A/C, TV, Internet, minibar.

Expensive

Hotel Luna Convento ★★   Transformed into a hotel in 1822, the Hotel Luna Convento occupies Amalfi's watchtower dating from 1564, and the ancient Franciscan monastery founded by Saint Francis in 1222, complete with its beautiful original cloister and church. Just 273m (896 ft.) from the town's center, on the promontory protecting Amalfi's harbor, this family-run place counts Henrik Ibsen (who wrote *A Doll's House* here in 1879) among its famous guests. The space remains as artistically inspiring as ever: The hotel is surrounded by a garden, with sun terraces and a large seawater swimming pool carved out of the cliff. There is also a private, rather rocky beach and a highly praised gourmet restaurant, where you have to make reservations long in advance. The watchtower houses a disco and piano bar, as well as another restaurant with fantastic views. Guest rooms vary in size and decor, but all are bright and spacious, with sweeping vistas, commodious tiled bathrooms, and some with private terraces.

Via Pantaleone Comite 33, 84011 Amalfi. ✆ **089-871002.** Fax 089-871333. www.lunahotel.it. 48 units. 280€–310€ double; from 400€ suite. Rates include buffet breakfast. Children 2 and under stay free in parent's room. AE, DC, MC, V. Parking 18€. **Amenities:** 2 restaurants; bar; babysitting; concierge; outdoor pool; room service. *In room:* A/C, TV, hair dryer, minibar.

Hotel Marina Riviera ★ (Kids)   With a great location above Amalfi's easternmost bay, this hotel has both views and proximity to the harbor and historic district. Guest rooms are not large, but are bright and pleasant, with Vietri tiled floors and simple furnishings. All enjoy sea views, and better rooms open onto private balconies or terraces. Bathrooms are good-size (some with shower only). The hotel's restaurant is **Eolo** (p. 210).

Via Pantaleone Comite 19, 84011 Amalfi. ✆ **089-871104.** Fax 089-871024. www.marinariviera.it. 34 units. 270€–350€ double; 410€ triple; 460€ quad; 480€ junior suite; from 580€ suite. Rates include buffet breakfast. AE, DC, MC, V. Closed Nov–Mar. Parking 15€. **Amenities:** Restaurant; bar; babysitting; concierge. *In room:* A/C, TV, Internet, minibar.

Hotel Miramalfi   On a rocky point west of town, this family-run hotel offers attractive rooms and views in every direction. It has its own private beach, as well as a pool, which is accessible by elevator. Guest rooms are welcoming, modern in style, with good-size bathrooms (most with shower only); all have balconies and views overlooking the sea.

Via Salvatore Quasimodo 3, 84011 Amalfi. ✆ **089-871588.** Fax 089-871287. www.miramalfi.it. 49 units. 270€–300€ double; 400€–500€ suite. Rates include breakfast. Children 2 and under stay free in parent's room. AE, DC, MC, V. Parking 15€. **Amenities:** Restaurant; bar; concierge; pool; room service. *In room:* A/C, TV, minibar.

Moderate

Hotel La Bussola ★   We like this welcoming hotel right on the beach by the harbor, with its clean lines and decor, and eco-friendly policies (it's one of the few on the coast to be certified). A great example of industrial architecture, La Bussola is in the former Pastificio Bergamasco, a historic pasta-making factory. A short walk away from the medieval town, it offers pleasant accommodations and kind, professional service. Guest rooms are bright and comfortable, with colorful tiled floors, and modern bathrooms (some with shower only). Most rooms open onto private balconies, with the better rooms enjoying full ocean views. Standard rooms do not have A/C, and only some have balconies and minibars; it is worth paying the extra 10€ to upgrade to a "class A" room or above. The **restaurant** ★ is excellent and focuses on seafood.

Lungomare dei Cavalieri 16, 84011 Amalfi. ✆ **089-871533.** Fax 089-871369. www.labussolahotel.it. 65 units. 130€–200€ double. Rates include buffet breakfast. Children 2 and under stay free in parent's room. AE, DC, MC, V. Parking 10€. **Amenities:** Restaurant; bar; Wi-Fi. *In room:* A/C (in most), TV, minibar (in most).

Residenza del Duca (Finds)   This tiny welcoming hotel is in a lovingly restored 16th-century *palazzo* in the medieval part of town. Each guest room opens onto its own balcony or small terrace, with views either over the sea or of the medieval district, and has its own character, with wooden beams, replicas of the original ceramic tiles, original architectural details, and period furniture.

Via Duca Mastalo II 3, Amalfi. ✆/fax **089-8736365.** www.residencedelduca.it. 5 units. 150€–190€ double; 195€ triple. Rates include buffet breakfast. Children 2 and under stay free in parent's room. AE, MC, V. Parking 16€–20€. *In room:* A/C, TV, hair dryer, minibar.

Inexpensive

Hotel Floridiana (Value)   Only steps from the Duomo and not far from the harbor, this hotel occupies an elegant palazzo dating back to the 12th century. Guest rooms are good-size (particularly the "superior") and welcoming, nicely done with Vietri ceramic tiles and a mix of modern and classic furnishings. Bathrooms are good-size (most with shower only). Breakfast is served in a vaulted hall decorated with original frescoes. The hotel is on a side street only accessible on foot. Its garage is nearby though, and your luggage can be collected at no extra expense.

Via Brancia 1, 84011 Amalfi. ✆ **089-8736373.** Fax 089-873907. www.hotelfloridiana.it. 36 units. 140€–170€ double; 210€ triple; 250€ quad. Rates include buffet breakfast. Children 2 and under stay free in parent's room. AE, DC, MC, V. Free parking. **Amenities:** Restaurant; bar. *In room:* A/C, TV, minibar, Wi-Fi.

Hotel Lidomare (Value)   This small family-run hotel is a good budget choice, offering friendly service in the heart of the historic district, only steps from the Duomo and not far from the beach. In a 13th-century building, guest rooms are pleasant, with bright tiled floors and a mix of modern furniture and antiques. The small bathrooms (some with shower only) are perfectly kept. A room upgrade will get you more space, sea views, and a Jacuzzis tub.

Largo Duchi Piccolomini 9 (off Piazza Duomo), 84011 Amalfi. ✆ **089-871332.** Fax 089-871394. www.lidomare.it. 15 units. 140€ double; 160€ triple; 185€ quad. Rates include breakfast. Children 2 and under stay free in parent's room. AE, MC, V. Parking 15€. *In room:* A/C, TV, minibar, Wi-Fi.

WHERE TO DINE

In addition to the below, we recommend **La Bussola** ★ (above). For desserts and other sweets, do not miss the historic **Pasticceria Pansa** ★★, Piazza Duomo 40 (✆ **089-871065;** www.pasticceriapansa.it; closed Tues.)

La Caravella ★★★ MODERN AMALFITAN   Do not expect sea views in this temple of cuisine, where guests are not to be distracted by such frivolities as a sunset. The successful initiator of the marriage between classic and modern culinary traditions, Chef Antonio Dipino offers a seasonal menu with both elaborate and simple dishes prepared only with the freshest local ingredients. Great attention is paid to service and setting, and you'll be surrounded by sober elegance in the dining hall of this 12th-century palazzo. Go with the tasting menu, or order a la carte: The seaweed fritters are excellent, followed by *tubetti di Gragnano al ragù di zuppa di pesce* (short pasta in a seafood sauce) and a superb *pezzogna* (fresh local fish). Those who prefer meat may favor *ziti di Torre Annunziata ripieni di carne alla Genovese* (pasta tubes filled with beef). The desserts and the wine list are on par with the rest of the menu. To celebrate its 50th year, La Caravella also opened an art gallery nearby the restaurant.

Via Matteo Camera 12. ✆ **089-871029.** www.ristorantelacaravella.it. Reservations required. Secondi 25€–35€; tasting menu 100€. AE, DC, MC, V. Wed–Mon noon–2pm and 7:30–10:30pm (also Tues in Aug). Closed mid-Nov to Dec 25.

Ristorante Santa Caterina ★★ CREATIVE AMALFITAN   This wonderful restaurant has gained international praise and is now competing with the best restaurants on this stretch of coast. In the beautiful Hotel Santa Caterina, it enjoys a glorious setting that well matches the gourmet food: We recommend the delicate *ravioli di zucchine al limone con formaggio fresco di bufala* (zucchini and buffalo ricotta ravioli) as well as the buckwheat tagliatelle with shrimp and eggplant. The excellent meat selection includes great steaks and filet mignon.

Via Nazionale 9. ✆ **089-871012.** Fax 089-871351. www.hotelsantacaterina.it. Reservations required. Secondi 22€–28€. AE, DC, MC, V. Daily 12:30–2:45pm and 7:45–10:30pm.

Moderate

Da Gemma AMALFITAN   Serving customers for over a century, this venerable restaurant has racked up sheaves of reviews attesting to its quality. The atmosphere is upscale but relaxed enough. One of the most famous specialties is *paccheri con gamberetti* (homemade pasta with shrimp). *Zuppa di pesce per due* (fish stew for two) is another winner. Don't forget to try the typical Amalfian side dish known as *ciambotta* (a mix of sautéed potatoes, peppers, and eggplant). Half portions are available for children.

Via Frà Gerardo Sasso 9. ✆ **089-871345.** www.trattoriadagemma.com. Reservations required. Secondi 16€–26€. AE, DC, MC, V. Thurs–Tues 12:30–2:45pm and 7:45–10:30pm (also Wed in summer). Closed mid-Jan to mid-Feb.

Ristorante Eolo ★ CREATIVE AMALFITAN   The welcoming dining room and romantic terrace of the hotel **Marina Riviera's** (p. 208) restaurant is the perfect setting for the gourmet meal that awaits you. The accent is on seafood and the seasonal menu offers innovative dishes based on the local tradition. Portions are small, but the food is delicious. We recommend the *seppie ripiene* (stuffed cuttlefish) as well as the *cannelloni di mare* (homemade pasta filled with seafood).

Via Pantaleone Comite 3. ✆ **089-871241.** www.eoloamalfi.it. Reservations recommended. Secondi 18€–28€. AE, DC, MC, V. Wed–Mon 12:30–3pm and 7:30–10:30pm. Closed 2 weeks in Jan–Feb.

Inexpensive

'a Paranza ★★ AMALFITAN   This simple trattoria is our favorite restaurant in the area. Popular for its well-prepared seafood at moderate prices, it is hidden away off the main

Christmas on the Amalfi Coast

Christmas *(Natale)* is always a special time in Italy, when lights and decorations create a suggestive atmosphere in even the smallest of hamlets. *Natale* on the Amalfi Coast is unique in its own way; the already picturesque villages and towns become truly magical with Christmas illumination, and you will find elaborate *presepi* (Nativity scenes, or creches) everywhere. However, besides the more traditional location inside churches—such as the 10th-century church of **Santa Maria Maggiore,** whose very fine *presepi* dates from its redecoration in the 18th century (Largo S. Maria Maggiore, Amalfi)—*presepi* are placed in fountains and in grottos. Perhaps the most important of these is the one inside **Grotta dello Smeraldo,** in Conca dei Marini (see "Conca dei Marini," p. 222), which receives a procession on December 24, and again on January 6 (Epiphany). Call the visitor center in Amalfi at ☎ **089-871107** for more information.

street of Atrani—the village adjacent to Amalfi to the east—and does not have sea views. The traditional cuisine focuses on the best local ingredients, but standouts are the delicious *scialatielli alla paranza* (homemade pasta with small fish), *polipetti in cassuola* (baby octopus stewed in a terra-cotta pot), or *scampi al limone* (prawns in lemon sauce). Do not miss the homemade desserts. The wine list is short but includes excellent local wines.

Via dei Dogi (at Traversa Dragone), Atrani. ☎ **089-871840.** www.ristoranteparanza.com. Reservations recommended. Secondi 12€–18€. AE, DC, MC, V. Wed–Mon 12:30–3pm and 7:30–10:30pm (also Tues in summer). Closed 2 weeks in Nov–Dec.

Lido Azzurro ★ AMALFITAN   This simple restaurant has a prime spot on the town's seaside promenade and great views from its terrace. The menu includes many kinds of pasta with seafood—*tubetti zucchine, vongole e cozze* (short pasta with clams, mussels and zucchini) is quite good. We recommend the day's fresh fish prepared either baked in a potato crust, or *all'acquapazza* (in a light tomato broth).

Lungomare dei Cavalieri. ☎ **089-871384.** Reservations recommended Sat–Sun. Secondi 15€–22€. AE, DC, MC, V. Tues–Sun 12:30–3pm and 7:30–10:30pm. Closed mid-Jan to mid-Mar.

Trattoria San Giuseppe (Finds AMALFITAN/PIZZA   Hidden away in the medieval part of town, this simple, down-to-earth place is a real local hangout. It's a great alternative to upscale dining, and the traditional meals include a variety of solid pasta dishes. In the evening, you can get excellent pizza—probably the best in town.

Salita Ruggiero II 4. ☎ **089-872640.** Reservations recommended Sat–Sun. Secondi 8€–14€; pizza 7€–11€. No credit cards. Fri–Wed noon–2:30pm and 7:30–10:30pm.

AMALFI AFTER DARK

Summer is entertainment time in Amalfi, when musical events are held throughout town. Among the most striking are the piano and vocal concerts held in the **Chiostro del Paradiso** (Piazza del Duomo, off the Duomo's atrium) July through September on Friday evenings.

The town's other key entertainment is visiting one of its many pleasant cafes to sip an *aperitivo* or enjoy a gelato. On Piazza Duomo, try **Bar Francese,** Piazza Duomo 20 elegant seating and excellent pastries. Overlooking the sea is ~~so~~ Repubbliche Marinare (📞 **089-857874**), a standout for **...alvo,** Piazza Duomo 22 (📞 **089-871655**; closed Jan–Mar) ...on this coast—try the *mandorla candita* (candied almond) ...iazza Duomo 40 (📞 **089-871065**; closed Tues) has been ...e 1830.

4 RAVELLO

6km (3¾ miles) NE of Amalfi; 29km (18 miles) W of Salerno; 66km (41 miles) SE of Naples

High up in the mountains, Ravello is a terrace over the sea, overlooking the villages of Minori and Maiori. The focal point of the short stretch of coast between Maiori and Amalfi, it has been the refuge of VIPs since Positano lost some of its glamour to the tourist invasion that began in the 1980s. Although tourists invade Ravello, too—Gore Vidal's decision to sell his villa here may have been the signal to the jet set that it is no longer cool—the lay of the land ensures that the town remains an attractive retreat.

ESSENTIALS

GETTING THERE The **bus** is the best option, with **SITA** (📞 **081-5522176**; www.sitabus.it) offering frequent service from Amalfi (see "Getting Around," p. 204).

Taxi service from Naples's Capodichino Airport costs a fixed 135€. **Curreri Viaggi** (📞 **081-8015420**; www.curreriviaggi.it) offers a shuttle from the airport for 150€ for one to three passengers and 12€ for each additional passenger.

By **train** (📞 **892021** in Italy; www.trenitalia.it), the closest station is **Vietri sul Mare,** on the local line between **Naples** (where you'll change trains if you are coming from the north) and **Salerno** (if you are coming from the south). Your best bet is to alight in Salerno and take a SITA bus or a taxi directly to Ravello.

In summer, another option is taking a ferry. The nearest harbors are Salerno and Amalfi; transfer to Ravello from there (see "Getting There," p. 262 and 202).

By car, take autostrada A3 to NAPOLI-SALERNO to the exit VIETRI SUL MARE; then follow signs for VIETRI, AMALFI to the SS 163. Follow signs for RAVELLO up the narrow curvy road. *Note:* Because of summer traffic, car access to SS 163 is occasionally limited; contact the tourist office before setting out.

GETTING AROUND The town is largely **pedestrian,** with steep, narrow lanes and flights of stairs. All cars must stop at the large public parking lot not far from the Duomo. **Taxis** are available at stands on Piazza Duomo, Gradillo, San Giovanni del Toro, and Castiglione, or by calling 📞 **089-857917.**

VISITOR INFORMATION The **AAST tourist office,** Via Roma 18, 84010 Ravello (📞 **089-857096**; www.ravellotime.it), is open October to April, Monday to Saturday from 9am to 6pm and May to September Monday to Saturday 9am to 8pm.

FAST FACTS You'll find a **pharmacy** (📞 **089-857189**) on Via Boccaccio, off Piazza Duomo. The closest **hospital** is in Salerno (see "Fast Facts," p. 263). For an **ambulance,** dial 📞 **118.** Call the **police** at 📞 **113** or 112. The **post office,** Via Boccaccio 15, off Piazza Vescovado (📞 **089-8586611**), is open Monday to Saturday 8am to 2pm. You'll find **Banca Monte Paschi di Siena** at Piazza Duomo 6 (📞 **089-857120**), and **Banca della Campania** at Via Roma 15 (📞 **089-857872**)—both with **ATMs.**

ACCOMMODATIONS ■
Hotel Caruso **4**
Hotel Giordano **3**
Hotel Graal **7**
Hotel Parsifal **9**
Hotel Rufolo **2**
Palazzo Sasso **8**

LACCO

SS373

Benevento
CAMPANIA
NAPLES
Ischia   Ravello   Salerno
Capri   Sorrento
TYRRHENIAN SEA

ⓘ Tourist Information
Ⓟ Parking
⚬⚬⚬ Steps

Belvedere
Chiesa di
S. Giovanni
del Toro
Belvedere
Principessa
di Piemonte

← To Amalfi
S. Maria
a Gradillo

Via S. Giovanni del Toro

Via
Wagner

To Salerno →

Piazza
Vescovado   Piazza
Ⓟ   Duomo   Duomo
Museo del
Corallo

Villa
Rufolo

S. Pietro
a Costa

S. Maria
d. Grazie
Chiesa
dell'Annunziata

Convento di
S. Francesco

0 ——— 300 ft
0 ——— 100 m

Monastero
di S. Chiara

Via del Fusco

DINING ◆
Al Ristoro del Moro **7**
Cumpa' Cosimo **5**
Da Salvatore **11**
Figli di Papa' **6**
Ristorante Pizzeria Vittoria **10**
Ristorante Villa Maria **1**
Rossellinis **8**

To Amalfi
Villa
Cimbrone
Santuario
Ss. Cosma
e Damiano

THE AMALFI COAST

SPECIAL EVENTS The internationally famous **Festival di Ravello** (
or 334-6264222; www.ravellofestival.com) focuses on classical musi
occasion for other events, including jazz, dance, and visual arts. It is
well in advance) not only for the big names it attracts, but also
tings. Performances are held at Piazza Duomo, Villa Rufolo, a
other venues. The festival is organized into several series, i
Wagneriano—classical music concerts held in July in
and the unique **Concerti dell'Aurora,** a group of co
at 4am), to welcome the day in music. The festi
depend on the event, and though some events
cost anywhere between 15€ and 130€.

Music continues before and after th
March through October. You can fin
Fondazione Ravello (© 089-858
cert Society** (© 089-858149;

According to local legend, Ravello was founded in the 5th to 6th centuries A.D. by Roman patricians fleeing barbarians who were ransacking Rome. The small town flourished in the Middle Ages, when it became part of the Republic of Amalfi. It was then the elected residence of some of the wealthiest merchant families of the republic, who created the numerous palaces that adorn this small town (many transformed into hotels today) and decorated the churches with works of high art. Often overlooked, the beautiful Romanesque church of **Santa Maria a Gradillo** ★★, dating from the 12th century, is the first architecturally noteworthy site you will see upon entering Ravello.

The heart of town is **Piazza del Vescovado,** a terrace overlooking the valley of the Dragone, and the adjacent Piazza del Duomo. Taking Via Emanuele Filiberto, you will reach **Via San Giovanni del Toro** ★★, which has some of the most beautiful medieval palaces of Ravello, including the 11th-century **Casa Tolla,** today housing the **Municipio.** Crossing the **Belvedere Principessa di Piemonte,** you'll reach **Palazzo Sasso** (today Albergo Palumbo) and **Palazzo d'Afflitto** (now the Albergo Caruso Belvedere). You will arrive at **Piazza Fontana,** with its 13th-century **Convent of Sant'Augostino,** today transformed into the Hotel Parsifal.

Chiesa di San Giovanni del Toro ★★ This 12th-century church, restored in 1715 after earthquake damage and again in the 1990s, is one of the most beautiful religious buildings in Ravello. The slender bell tower in Arab-Sicilian style rises beside a facade graced by a triple portal. A steep staircase descends on the right, allowing a view of the three high apses, each crowned by a dome and decorated with intertwined arcs. The interior is decorated with 13th- and 14th-century frescoes, mosaics, majolica, stucco work, and bas-reliefs. Particularly beautiful is the 12th-century **pergamo** ★ by Alfano da ... well as the 14th-century frescoes in the crypt's apse. The church is usually ... request a visit at Via San Giovanni del Toro 50.

... Visit by request (inquire at Via San Giovanni del Toro 50, daily 9:30am ... ...raged.

RAVELLO

... the patron saint of Ravello, this cathe-
... Built in 1087 by the Rufolo
... the 18th century. The
... arch's **bronze**
... nstantinople.
... zantine influ-
... apse; in the
... from 1130,
... is the richly
... y Niccolò di
... **Pantaleone,**
... Nicomedia on
... essel) miracu-
... lo blood leaks
... an admire the
... gaida Rufolo),
... , including the

© 08-3422
... but ... so an
... very po ... serve
... for the m ... t set-
... nd Villa Cir ... among
... luding the F ... usicale
... the garden of V ... tarting
... ncerts held at day ... , prices
... l runs July throug ... ers can
... ave free admission, ... o **Con-**
... festival with concerts ... heduled
... information on these ot ... tacting
... 560; www.fondazioneravello
... www.ravelloarts.org).

Museo del Corallo   Created in 1986, this small museum has a wonderful collection
of precious objects made of coral, including cameos, totaling over 600 pieces. Located on
the premises of the workshop **Camo,** which specialize in this traditional art (see "Cameo
Making," p. 137), the collection stretches from ancient Roman pieces all the way to the
19th century. Particularly beautiful are the 16th-century **Crucifix** on a crystal cross and a
Madonna from 1532. Be sure to note the 3rd-century-A.D. Roman amphora with a coral
formation inside it and a beautiful set of 14 cherub heads from the 18th to 19th centuries.
Piazza Duomo 9. © **089-857461.** www.museodelcorallo.com. Free admission. Mon–Sat 9:30am–noon
and 3–5:30pm.

Villa Cimbrone ★   This privately owned villa is home to the splendid **Belvedere
Cimbrone ★★★**, a terrace famed for its awe-inspiring panorama. Between the sculptures that decorate the balustrade, you can look from Atrani and the whole Gulf of
Salerno down to the plain of Paestum and distant Punta Licosa. The body of the villa
itself dates from the 14th and 15th centuries, but was largely rebuilt in 1904 by its new
owner, an eccentric English lord named William Beckett, with somewhat disharmonious
results. The **gardens ★★**, though, are absolutely lovely. Call ahead for a guided tour,
and ring the bell at the entrance. The villa accepts overnighters in some of the **guest
rooms** and diners in its small but delicious **restaurant,** for dinner only. *Note:* In the
upper part of town, the villa is accessible only by foot; and the path is rather steep.
Via Santa Chiara 26. © **089-858072,** or 089-857459 for reservations. Fax 089-857777. www.villa
cimbrone.it. Admission 6€ adults, 4€ children. Daily 9am–sunset; last admission 30 min. earlier.

Villa Rufolo ★★   In the center of town, to the right of the Duomo, this beautiful
villa was built between 1270 and 1280 for the prominent Rufolo family, then passed on
to the Gonfalone e Muscettola family in the 15th century. It was bought in 1851 by the
Scotsman Francis Devile Reid, who partially restructured it. A public building since
1975, the villa and its beautiful **gardens ★** can be visited, at a spectacular 340m (1,115
ft.) above sea level. The original architecture shows much Arab influence, especially in
the detail of intertwined arches, which recurs in the **Entrance Hall** and in the beautiful
courtyard. The three-story main building at the end of a tree-lined alley opens to a marvelous **Inner Court.** Across from the entrance is the famous **Terrace ★**, which was
renamed Terrazza Wagner in memory of the German composer who wrote the Klingsor
Garden scene in the second act of *Parsifal* here. Today, the garden is the setting for the
Concerti Wagneriani, a summer festival of classical music.
Piazza Vescovado. © **089-857621.** www.villarufolo.it. Admission 5€. Summer daily 9am–8pm; winter
daily 9am–sunset; last admission 15 min. earlier.

STAYING ACTIVE

What Ravello lacks in beaches, it compensates for in trails. The two **walks** we suggest
below are quite easy, allowing you to return by bus or taxi, but the ambitious might
undertake a complete loop of the two.

The **Monastero di San Nicola** makes for a pleasant and easy hike. From the center of
Ravello, take the road to Chiunzi for 1km (.5 mile) toward the hamlet of Sambuco,
320m (1,050 ft.) above sea level (you can also get to this point by car). Descending from
here a few steps to your right, you can reach the trail that climbs to the Monastery of

Saint Nicholas at an altitude of 486m (1,594 ft.). Plan on about 2 hours for the 9km (5.8-mile) hike. It is then possible to descend to Minori—or to Maiori if you prefer—in about a half-hour. Hiking the reverse route (starting from Minori or Maiori) is more demanding, but you can do it by taking the small road that connects Maiori with Minori and passes behind the Collegiata to reach the path that climbs gently toward the monastery. The trail becomes progressively steeper and more scenic until you reach the top. Figure on spending about 1 hour for the ascent from Maiori or Minori to the monastery.

Another scenic hike in the area is the one to Minori. From the center of Ravello, take another footpath—a charming mix of steps and hidden alleys—which descends all the way to Minori and the sea. Start from the alley to the left of Villa Rufolo, marked by a small fountain, at an altitude of 350m (1,148 ft.). You will pass by the small 13th-century Annunziata church and by San Pietro church before reaching the hamlet of **Torello,** with its Addolorata Church and graceful bell tower in Arab-Sicilian style. The picturesque trail continues through olive trees down to **Minori.** The hike down takes a half-hour; double that for the ascent.

WHERE TO STAY

For a luxury address in town, provided you don't mind the 10-minute climb on foot from the closest car drop off (a porter will carry your luggage), **Villa Cimbrone** ★★ (see "Villa Cimbrone," above) accepts overnight guests in its 19 elegantly appointed rooms (410€–660€ double, from 780€ suite; all rates include breakfast). For more modest accommodations, we recommend the few rooms offered by **Da Salvatore** and by **Palazzo della Marra** (see "Where to Dine," below).

Very Expensive

Hotel Caruso ★★ **Kids**   In the splendid 11th-century Palazzo D'Afflitto, this state-of-the-art hotel affords a unique and exclusive experience. Guest rooms are palatial and welcoming, with baldaquin beds, heavenly linens, and large bathrooms. Most have sea views and open to private balconies, terraces, or small gardens. The hotel's facilities are crowned by a breathtaking outdoor infinity pool; we also recommend asking for a guided tour of the gardens. Guests enjoy access to two golf courses and a tennis court, though you do have to pay a fee. PlayStations, toys, and kids' bathrobes and slippers are available upon request.

Piazza San Giovanni del Toro 2, 84010 Ravello. ℭ **089-858801.** Fax 089-858806. www.hotelcaruso.com. 48 units. 780€–1,010€ double; from 1,370€ suite. Rates include American buffet breakfast. Children 11 and under stay free in parent's room. AE, DC, MC, V. Parking 20€. Closed Nov–Mar. **Amenities:** 2 restaurants; 2 bars; babysitting; concierge; gym; pool; room service; spa. *In room:* A/C, TV/DVD, minibar, Wi-Fi.

Expensive

Palazzo Sasso ★★★   In a 12th-century patrician palace, this opulent hotel enjoys a splendid location between plunging cliffs and steep mountainside. One of the best hotels in the world, it is *the* place to stay in Ravello. Guest rooms are luxuriously appointed with real antiques and handmade Vietri ceramic floors. Some afford gorgeous views—the best are from room numbers 1, 201, 204, and 301, and suite 304. Some of the suites are as big as a good-size apartment, and even the lower-priced rooms are spacious (a few have no view). Bathrooms are done up in marble, with large tubs. A free shuttle takes guests to Villa Sasso, a facility including the casual restaurant **Sasso,** an outdoor pool, and a "beach"—a seaside terrace with chairs and umbrellas. The hotel prides itself on its excellent restaurants (see "Rossellinis," p. 218).

Via San Giovanni del Toro 28, 84010 Ravello. ☎ **089-818181.** Fax 089-858900. www.palazzosasso.com.
44 units. 360€–710€ double; from 930€ suite. Rates include buffet breakfast. Children 2 and under stay
free in parent's room. AE, DC, MC, V. Parking 34€. Closed mid-Oct to Mar. **Amenities:** Restaurant; bar;
concierge; gym; Jacuzzi; pool; room service; spa. *In room:* A/C, TV, Internet, minibar.

Moderate

Hotel Rufolo ★   In the heart of Ravello, this family-run hotel overlooks the gardens
of Villa Rufolo. In a modern building decorated in a traditional style, this hotel offers
comfortable accommodations and friendly service. The views from the terrace gardens,
the restaurant terrace, and the sun decks are superb. Guest rooms are spacious and attractive, with tiled Vietri floors and classic furnishings. Bathrooms are good-size and well
maintained (some with shower only). Better rooms open onto private balconies and
enjoy gorgeous views, while others overlook the town or garden. The hotel's restaurant,
Sigilgaida ★, serves tasty cuisine prepared with produce from the hotel's organic gardens
and select local ingredients (closed Jan–Feb).

Via San Francesco 1, 84010 Ravello. ☎ **089-857133.** Fax 089-857935. www.hotelrufolo.it. 30 units.
290€–350€ double; 550€ junior suite. Rates include buffet breakfast. Children 2 and under stay free in
parent's room. AE, DC, MC, V. Free parking. Closed Dec 22–28. **Amenities:** Restaurant; bar; babysitting;
concierge; gym; pool; spa. *In room:* A/C, TV, minibar.

Inexpensive

Hotel Giordano   Not far from Villa Rufolo, guest rooms at this newly renovated,
family-run hotel are on average a bit smaller than at the Rufolo, but some are very spacious—the largest are good options for families and have private small terraces. The large
swimming pool in the garden is very pleasant, and free use of the hotel's garage near
Ravello's main square is included (porters collect your luggage). Guests enjoy access to
the splendid gardens of **Villa Eva** and special rates at **Villa Maria ★** (see "Where to
Dine," p. 218).

Via Trinita 14, 84010 Ravello. ☎ **089-857170.** Fax 089-857071. www.giordanohotel.it. 30 units. 185€–
245€ double; 300€ triple; 355€ quad; 360€ junior suite. Rates include breakfast. Children 2 and under stay
free in parent's room. AE, DC, MC, V. Free parking. **Amenities:** Bar; concierge; pool. *In room:* A/C, TV,
minibar.

Hotel Graal ⓥ**Value**   This small hotel offers great accommodations in a scenic location,
is moderately priced for such a fashionable part of town, and abides to the prerequisites
of sustainable hospitality, including water and energy saving, and waste management.
Public areas are a bit faded, but guest rooms are bright and modern, with good-size
bathrooms (some with showers only) and balconies with sea views. The hotel's restaurant,
Al Ristoro del Moro ★ (p. 218), offers a nice setting, well-prepared food, and uses
excellent ingredients, but hotel guests who choose half- or full-board eat in a separate
dining room.

Via della Repubblica 8, 84010 Ravello. ☎ **089-857222.** Fax 089-857551. www.hotelgraal.it. 42 units.
180€–220€ double; 250€–300€ junior suite. Rates include breakfast. Children 2 and under stay free in
parent's room. AE, DC, MC, V. Parking 11€. **Amenities:** Restaurant; bar; babysitting; concierge; pool; room
service; Wi-Fi. *In room:* A/C, TV, minibar.

Hotel Parsifal ⓕ**Finds**   In the northern part of town, this former 13th-century convent
is a good budget option, with charming architectural details throughout. Guest rooms
vary in size and shape—some with nice views over the sea; all are pleasantly done with
bright Vietri tiled floors, whitewashed walls, and good-size bathrooms (some with shower
only). The hotel's **restaurant ★** is very good.

Via Gioacchino D'Anna 5, 84010 Ravello. 📞 **089-857144.** www.hotelparsifal.com. 17 units. 135€–155€ double; 200€ junior suite. Rates include buffet breakfast. Children 2 and under stay free in parent's room. AE, DC, MC, V. Parking 15€. **Amenities:** Restaurant; bar; concierge; Wi-Fi. *In room:* A/C (in some), TV.

WHERE TO DINE

In addition to the restaurants below, we recommend the **Parsifal** ★ in the hotel of the same name, the **Sigilgaida** ★ in the Hotel Rufolo, and, for a special experience, the restaurant at **Villa Cimbrone** ★★ (p. 215).

Expensive

Rossellinis ★★★ CREATIVE AMALFITAN   Elegance and impeccable service are the background for a sophisticated menu and perfect dining experience at this highly praised gourmet destination that boasts two Michelin stars. Talented chef Pino Lavarra creates delicious meals from local ingredients best showcased in his tasting menu. Dishes might include delectable *ravioli di totano gigante ripieni di granchio e zucchine* (squid ravioli filled with crab meat and zucchini) and *merluzzo in crosta d'olive di Gaeta* (Mediterranean cod encrusted with local olives).

Via San Giovanni del Toro 28 (in the Palazzo Sasso, p. 216). 📞 **089-818181.** Fax 089-858900. www.palazzo sasso.com. Reservations required. Secondi 28€–32€; tasting menu 115€. AE, DC, MC, V. Daily 7:30–11pm. Closed Nov–Mar.

Moderate

Al Ristoro del Moro ★ AMALFITAN   On the premises of the Hotel Graal (p. 217), the terrace at this popular restaurant affords superb views but is open only in warm weather (usually Apr or May to Sept or Oct). The menu is well-rounded, with excellent seafood dishes and a good selection of meat. We like the *scialatielli ai frutti di mare* (homemade pasta with seafood) and the ravioli, as well as the tasty *tagliata* (steak). Save room for dessert.

Via della Repubblica 8. 📞 **089-857901.** www.alristorodelmoro.it. Reservations recommended. Secondi 15€–22€. AE, DC, MC, V. Daily 12:30–3pm and 7:30–10pm.

Ristorante Villa Maria ★   In the hotel of the same name, this restaurant features a delightful arbor terrace with breathtaking views. Enjoy delicious variations of original family recipes prepared with ingredients from the hotel's own organic gardens: the *scialatielli,* lasagna, ravioli, and cannelloni are all great, and we also recommend the *grigliata mista* (grilled fish or meats). The restaurant offers cooking classes, too.

Via Santa Chiara 2. 📞 **089-857255.** Fax 089-857071. www.villamaria.it. Reservations recommended. Secondi 16€–22€. AE, DC, MC, V. Daily 12:30–3pm and 7:30–10pm.

Inexpensive

Cumpà Cosimo Ⓚⁱᵈˢ AMALFITAN/PIZZA   Once a simple winery, this place has blossomed into a popular restaurant, favored by locals. Family run since it opened in 1929—the second generation is still at the helm—it serves generous portions of homemade traditional dishes. The seasonal menu always includes mouthwatering homemade pasta—we love the cannelloni (pasta tubes filled with meat or fish and baked with sauce)—and succulent secondo—you might find *zuppa di pesce* (fish stew) and a fine *fritto misto* (deep-fried medley of seafood), or roasted lamb with herbs. Pizza is served in the evening. The staff is particularly accommodating to the needs of little ones and allows half-portions.

Via Roma 44. 📞 **089-857156.** Reservations recommended. Secondi 11€–18€. AE, DC, MC, V. Tues–Sun 12:30–3pm and 7:30–11pm (also Mon Mar–Nov).

Da Salvatore ★ AMALFITAN   This simple restaurant offers local cuisine in a striking setting—the views are superb both from the dining room and the garden terrace, which is open for alfresco dining in warm weather. The style and atmosphere are relaxed, with simple tables and chairs. In addition to the scrumptious homemade breads, savor fish or meat from among the traditional dishes, which include *gnoccoloni al pomodoro e basilico* (potato dumplings with fresh tomatoes and basil), grilled fish, and roasted veal. The restaurant has six **guest rooms** for rent.

Via della Repubblica 2. (℃ **089-857227**. www.salvatoreravello.com. Reservations recommended. Secondi 12€–18€. AE, V. Tues–Sun 12:30–3pm and 7:30–11pm (also Mon Apr–Oct).

Figli di Papà (Finds)   In the historic 13th-century Palazzo della Marra, this pleasant restaurant serves hearty cuisine with a creative twist. We recommend the *crespolini* (thin pancakes filled with seafood or meat in a creamy sauce) and the *grigliata* (medley of grilled meat or fish). The tourist menu for 15€ is an excellent deal. The management also maintains 10 simply furnished **guest rooms** (100€ double) on a B&B basis (Via della Marra 3; www.palazzodellamarra.com).

Via della Marra 7, 84010 Ravello. (℃ **089-858302**. www.ristorantefiglidipapa.it. Reservations recommended. Secondi 12€–18€. AE, DC, MC, V. Daily 12:30–3pm and 7:30–10pm.

Ristorante Pizzeria Vittoria (Finds) AMALFITAN/PIZZA   This family-run restaurant is a good choice for a moderately priced meal. The dining room is welcoming and the service is prompt. The wood-oven pizza is top-notch and the menu includes many tasty choices such as *spaghetti alle vongole* (with clams) and the excellent *pesce alla griglia* (whole grilled fish of your choice).

Via dei Rufolo 3. (℃ **089-857947**. www.ristorantepizzeriavittoria.it. Reservations recommended Sat–Sun. Secondi 8€–16€. AE, DC, MC, V. Wed–Mon 12:30–3pm and 7:30–11pm (also Tues Apr–Oct).

RAVELLO AFTER DARK

Most locals spend their nights sipping an *aperitivo*—or nibbling on sweets—at one of the town's cafes. The activity can take on a theatrical air when the weather is nice and people-watching is at its prime. At the **Bar Calce,** Via Roma 2, next to the Duomo ((℃ **089-857152**), people gather for the excellent pastries and homemade ice cream. **Caffè San Domingo,** Piazza Duomo ((℃ **089-857142**) has been run by the same family since 1929 and is famous for its *babà* (sponge cake) and *dolcezze al limone* (traditional lemon pastries).

SIDE TRIPS: SCALA & TRAMONTI

Little known by most tourists, the environs of Ravello offer dramatic mountain and sea views as well as unspoiled rural retreats.

Scala, only 2.5km (1½ miles) from Ravello, was a fortified town protecting the Amalfi Maritime Republic. Its two castles—one guarding inland approaches, the other overlooking the sea—were connected by walls that enclosed the town completely, and are now in ruins. The 12th-century **Duomo,** Piazza Municipio 5 ((℃ **089-857397**; daily 8am–1pm and 6–7pm), features a **crypt** ★ with a 14th-century **funerary monument** ★★ for Marinella Rufolo, erected by her husband Antonio Coppola. Of the smaller surrounding hamlets, each a small replica of Scala's defensive structure, **Minuto** is our pick: Only 1km (a half-mile) south of Scala, it's interesting **Chiesa della Santissima Annunziata** ★★ was probably Scala's original cathedral. Built between the 11th and 12th centuries, it's one of the best examples of Romanesque architecture on the whole Amalfi Coast (and the view alone is worth a stop). Be sure to visit the **crypt,** where you will find **12th-century frescoes** ★★, including a Christ Pantocraor that accurately represents

Limoncello & Other Rosoli

The typical liqueur of the Costeria, *limoncello* is the most famous of the *rosoli*—sweet liqueurs crafted from fruits and herbs—made in the region. The rarest are *finocchietto* (wild fennel), *lauro* (bay leaf), *mirto* (myrtle), *nocello* (walnut), *nanassino* (prickly pear), the exotic *mandarino* (mandarin), and *fragolino* (wild strawberry).

Limoncello is probably the most versatile *rosolio*. You will find local versions—and endless claims of paternity—from Vico Equense on the Sorrento peninsula all the way to Vietri and beyond, to the islands of Ischia, Capri, and Procida. The liqueur's actual origin is probably the area of Maiori, Amalfi, and Vietri—although Sorrento has good foundations for its claim.

Almost every family in Campania has its own recipe, passed on for centuries. True *limoncello* is made from *sfusato di Amalfi*, a particular lemon that has obtained the mark D.O.P. (the stamp of controlled origin for produce, similar to D.O.C. for wine). The Amalfi lemon is large, long, and light in color, with a sweet and very flavorful aroma and taste, almost no seeds, and a very thick skin.

Limoncello is sold in pretty, hard-to-resist bottles. If you plan to buy a few bottles as gifts, don't forget to give the recipient tips on how to drink it. Always served very cold, the drink can be sipped as a digestive after a meal. It also makes an excellent lemon-flavored long drink—dilute with tonic water or seltzer. Some like it as a cocktail with a small quantity of champagne or prosecco. To make *granita*—dilute the *limoncello* with simple syrup and freeze it, stirring occasionally.

You can buy these liqueurs from various specialty stores, the most reputed of which is **Limunciel,** Corso Vittorio Emanuele 9, Minori (℃ **089-877393**). This shop was also among the first to commercialize the local *rosolio,* which it makes in small batches according to a generations-old recipe. Another excellent shop is **Profumi della Costiera,** Via Trinita 37, Ravello (℃ **089-858167;** www.profumidellacostiera.it).

Byzantine style. *Note:* The church is open only for Mass on Sunday (9:30–10:30am), but can be visited upon request (ask at the parish house on Via Ficuciello).

About 10km (6 miles) farther inland of Scala, is **Tramonti,** a fertile agricultural area *intra montes,* or "between the mountains" which comprises 13 historic *casali* (farms), each graced by its own small church. This area is famous today for its D.O.C. wine, and for **concierto,** a bittersweet digestive liquor concocted in the 17th century by the nuns of the local convent, using nine different mountain herbs and spices. The convent, **Regio Conservatorio dei Santi Giuseppe e Teresa,** Località Pucara (℃ **339-1746893**), is open to visitors, and still makes the drink—which makes an excellent souvenir. We also recommend the drive to **Valico di Chiunzi,** the high pass in the mountains once guarded by a powerful castle, now reduced to a single tower. At an altitude of 656m (2,152 ft.), it affords a spectacular **panorama** ★★★ of the plain of Pompeii and Mount Vesuvius.

If you'd like to explore the area on horseback, sign up for a pleasant **horse ride and guided excursion** in the countryside at one of the horse farms in Scala; the best are **Carmusina,** Via Casa Romana (☎ 089-857904), and **La Piccola California,** Via Sento (☎ **089-858042**). Alternatively, the best **hike** in the area is from **Campidoglio di Scala**—one of the bourgs connected to Scala, at an altitude of 470m (1,542 ft.). The first part is a ridge trail, extremely scenic and not very arduous. You can make the walk more challenging by descending all the way to Amalfi. Along the way you will find, on your left, the ruins of the 12th-century church of Sant'Eustachio. The trail continues through a natural rock formation in the form of an amphitheater, showing the ruins of ancient fortifications, called Castello. About halfway through the descent, you will reach the waterfalls at the top of the Vallone delle Ferriere of Amalfi (see "Staying Active," p. 207). If you want, you can then walk down along the Vallone and reach Amalfi through the Valle dei Mulini. Figure on spending about 2 hours to get to the waterfall and an additional 2 hours to get to Amalfi.

Where to Stay & Dine

To have a full experience of the countryside here, we recommend staying in an *agriturismo;* we like **Azienda Agrituristica Le Chiancolelle,** Via Valico di Chiunzi, Località Campinola, 84010 Tramonti (☎ **089-876339;** 5 units), and **Azienda Agrituristica Mare e Monti,** Via Trugnano 3, Località Campinola, 84010 Tramonti (☎ **089-876665;** www.agriturismomaremonti.it; 2 units). The area also boasts several excellent restaurants.

Da Lorenzo ★★ (Finds) AMALFITAN   We love this countryside restaurant, with a great outdoor dining area overlooking the valley, Ravello, and the sea. The cuisine is simple and traditional, with homemade dishes based on fish in summer and meat in winter. The bread is made in a wood-burning oven that also turns out excellent pizza in the evening. Some of the best dishes are *scialatielli ai frutti di mare* (fresh pasta with shellfish), *pappardelle con il coccio* (wide noodles with fish), *grigliata di gamberoni* (perfectly grilled large shrimp), *scamorza alla brace* (grilled local cheese), and a selection of cured meats.

Via Frà G. Sasso, Santa Maria, Scala. ☎ 089-858290. www.trattoriadalorenzo.com. Reservations recommended. Secondi 15€–21€. AE, DC, MC, V. Winter Sat–Sun noon–2:30pm and 7:30–10:30pm; summer daily noon–2:30pm and 7:30–10:30pm.

Da Nino (Finds) AMALFITAN/PIZZA   Affectionately called "Ninuccio" (little Nino) by the locals, this trattoria offers a warm welcome and delicious specialties, made in large part with ingredients from the owners' farm. For an appetizer, taste the superb salamis and *sottoli* (vegetables preserved in olive oil) with homemade bread and local mozzarella. Follow this with a secondo of pasta or the whole-wheat pizza—the one with veggies *(con le verdure)* is particularly savory.

Via Pucara 39, Tramonti. ☎ 089-876184. Reservations recommended Sat–Sun. Secondi 8€–15€. No credit cards. Wed–Mon noon–3pm and 7:30–10pm (also Tues in summer).

La Violetta (Finds) AMALFITAN   The views are gorgeous and the food is divine at this simple, honest restaurant. The hearty menu includes lots of salamis produced on the farm here, as well as homemade pasta and gnocchi. The *risotto ai chiodini* (with local wild mushrooms) bursts with flavor; and the grilled meats are superb. A good local red wine is also served.

Via Valico di Chiunzi, Tramonti. ☎ 089-876384. Reservations recommended Sat–Sun. Secondi 12€–18€. No credit cards. Tues–Sun 12:30–3pm and 7:30–11pm (also Mon in summer).

While the three pearls of the Amalfi Coast—Positano, Ravello, and Amalfi—are the undisputed stars of the area, lesser-known and often more-authentic towns can be found along the coast and farther inland. Those on the coast can also provide a good base as an alternative to the more crowded communities, provided you don't require loads of amenities.

CONCA DEI MARINI
5km (3 miles) W of Amalfi

Little more than a hamlet, Conca is rarely visited, in spite of being right on the main road between Positano and Amalfi; most visitors usually limit themselves to the **Emerald Grotto** (see "Exploring the Town," below).

Essentials
GETTING THERE & AROUND   Conca is on SS 163 between Positano and Amalfi. Take a **SITA bus** from Amalfi or Positano or a **taxi** or a **car** (see "Getting Around," p. 204 and 188).

VISITOR INFORMATION   You can get **tourist information** at the municipal office: Casa Comunale (© **089-831301**).

FAST FACTS   The closest **pharmacy** and **bank** are in Amalfi, the nearest **hospital** in Salerno (see "Fast Facts," p. 263). For an **ambulance,** dial © **118.** You can call the **police** at © **113** or 112. The **post office** (© **089-831286**) is on Piazza Olmo 3, off SS 163.

Exploring the Town
Conca is on a hill overlooking a picturesque cove and a tiny beach, **Marina di Conca,** where a few boats are moored. This quiet hamlet was once an important commercial stronghold for the Amalfi Republic. Its small harbor had boat building and commercial facilities that made it richer than neighboring Amalfi, until raiders destroyed the town in 1543. The view from the Church of **San Pancrazio** (Salita San Pancrazio) is splendid, and the 14th-century **Convento di Santa Rosa** (where nuns invented the famous *sfogliatella* of the same name, see "Sfogliatella di Santa Rosa," below), off Via Roma (above SS 163), makes for a pleasant excursion. In summer, the convent's church, Santa Maria di Grado, hosts chamber music concerts held by the **Ravello Concert Society** (© **089-858149;** www.ravelloarts.org).

Discovered in 1932, the **Grotta dello Smeraldo (Emerald Grotto)** ★★ is a beautiful underwater grotto that shines with a unique blue-green light when the sun is high and the sea calm. Less famous than Capri's Blue Grotto, it is still impressive, at 30m (98 ft.) long by 60m (197 ft.) wide, with stalactites, stalagmites, and an underwater ceramic manger that was submerged in 1956. It is accessible by boat from the tiny beach, by swimming, on foot down a long series of steps from SS 163, or via the elevator by the Conca Azzurra hotel and the SITA bus stop (Positano-Amalfi line) on SS 163. Excursions are also offered from Amalfi and Praiano. The grotto is open daily, weather permitting, November to February from 9am to 4pm and March to October from 9am to 7pm. Admission is 6€ and includes the rowboat ride from the beach or elevator (***Note:*** You're not expected to tip the oarman unless he goes especially out of his way to accommodate you.).

Hotel II Belvedere   This beautiful hotel is in a cliffside 19th-century villa only minutes from the Emerald Grotto. Public spaces include a pretty seawater pool overlooking a rocky private beach. The bright, large guest rooms are comfortably furnished with period furniture or reproductions, and have colorful tile floors. Bathrooms are also nicely tiled, with modern fixtures. Each room has a small terrace (large enough for a table and chairs) with an ocean view.

Via Smeraldo (off SS 163), 84010 Conca dei Marini. ℂ 089-831282. Fax 089-831439. www.belvederehotel. it. 40 units. 210€–240€ double. Rates include buffet breakfast. Children 1 and under stay free in parent's room. AE, DC, MC, V. Free parking. Closed Nov–Mar. **Amenities:** Restaurant; bar; pool. *In room:* A/C, TV.

La Tonnarella ★★ AMALFITAN   On the beach at Marina di Conca, this is one of the most excellent restaurants in the area. Opened in the '50s in what was then a boat shed, it is now best reached from the sea (call for a pickup from the nearest harbor). The menu focuses on seafood—and rightly so—taken straight from the fishing boat to the kitchen, and prepared simply and excellently. The chef is justly proud of his *scialatielli ai frutti di mare* (fresh pasta with seafood and tomatoes), which we suggest following with the traditional dish *totani alle patate* (squid and potatoes), or a delicious *pezzogna all'acquapazza* (fish in herbed broth). The vegetarian *grigliate* (grilled plate) is excellent.

Via Marina 1, Borgo Marinaro, Conca dei Marini. ℂ **089-831939.** www.ristorantelatonnarella.it. Reservations required. Secondi 15€–25€. AE, DC, MC, V. Daily 12:30–3pm and 7:30–11pm. Closed Nov–Mar.

FURORE
10.6km (6¹/₂ miles) W of Amalfi

On the cliff over Conca dei Marini and SS 163, this rural community was completely unknown to the public until recently, when its wine obtained the D.O.C. label.

Essentials
GETTING THERE & AROUND   In addition to hopping on the **SITA bus** from Amalfi, you can come by **taxi** or **car** from Amalfi or Positano (see "Getting Around," p. 204 and 188). If you are **driving,** take the sharp turn off SS 163 on SS 366 at Conca dei Marini (btw. Positano and Amalfi).

VISITOR INFORMATION   Visitors can obtain **tourist information** at the municipal office, Via Mola 39 (ℂ **089-874100**).

FAST FACTS   The **pharmacy** (ℂ 089-831109) is at Via Mola 35. The nearest **hospital** is in Salerno (see "Fast Facts," p. 263). For an **ambulance,** dial ℂ **118.** You can call

THE AMALFI COAST

8

OFF THE BEATEN PATH

Sfogliatella di Santa Rosa

In the 17th century, the nuns at **Convento di Santa Rosa** replaced the traditional ricotta-cheese filling of a Neapolitan *sfogliatella* pastry with a delicate pastry cream and a spoonful of *amarene*—candied sour cherries in syrup—a change that met with immediate success. Today you can taste this delicious creation in local pastry shops such as **Pasticceria Pansa** in Amalfi (p. 209) and in Conca dei Marini in August during the festival dedicated to it, **Sagra della Sfogliatella di Santa Rosa.**

the **police** at $©$ **113** or 112. You'll find the **post office** ($©$ **089-874129**) at Via Mola 33. For **banks,** head to Agerola and Amalfi.

Exploring the Town

Furore is more a sparsely built rural area than a proper village, and little would justify a visit here if it weren't for the local wine and good food. A visit to the local winery, **Cantine Gran Furor,** Via Lama 14 ($©$ **089-874489**), is pretty informal, but the wine is great. **Hikers** will enjoy the scenic *Sentiero della Volpe Pescatrice* (**Fishing Fox Trail**) ★ (about 45 min.) that leads from Contrada Sant'Elia down to **Furore Marina,** the small beach at the bottom of the narrow cove—a fjord, really—where the local peasant fishermen keep their boats. The long steep trail was the regular village path (no. 17 on the CAI map; p. 191) that cut down the rocky walls of the fjord created by the brook that still flows at the bottom (*furore* means rage and refers to how the sea rises in the fjord during storms). You can also reach the cove by boat, from one of the harbors nearby.

Where to Stay & Dine

Antica Hostaria di Bacco ★★   Surrounded by vineyards and views, this historic address is now a foodie destination. Founded in 1930 and expertly run by the third generation of Ferraiolis, it also offers comfortable accommodations and kind service. The menu is a delightful journey through superb renditions of local recipes long forgotten elsewhere on the coast. Do try the *ferrazzuoli alla nannarella* (a type of fresh pasta handmade using a small iron tool and seasoned with a mix of grape tomatoes, smoked sword fish, raisins, red pepper, and arugula) and the *frittura* (deep-fried seafood). The simple guest rooms are bright, with Wi-Fi and private terraces (100€ double).

Via G.B. Lama 9, 84010 Furore. $©$ **089-830360.** Fax 089-830352. www.baccofurore.it. Reservations required. Secondi 15€–25€. AE, DC, MC, V. Sat–Thurs 12:30–3pm and 7:30–11pm (also Fri June–Sept).

Furore Inn Resort ★★   This luxury spa-hotel is a striking whitewashed structure with dramatic sea views that are pleasantly equaled by the elegant interior. The panoramic rooms all feature Vietri tiled floors and classic furnishings; the best open onto private terraces, but all are equipped with an elegant tiled bathroom (some with shower only). The pool is great, and the spa offers a wide range of beauty treatments and massages. Of the two restaurants, **La Volpe Pescatrice** is renowned for its creative Amalfitan fare and the beautiful views from its terrace, while the **Italian Touch** offers modern Italian cuisine in a more formal atmosphere. They both offer tasting menus: 60€ and 70€ at La Volpe, and 75€ and 90€ at the Touch.

Via dell'Amore 1, Contrada Sant'Elia, 84010 Furore. $©$ **089-8304711.** Fax 089-8304777. www.furoreinn. it. 22 units. 360€–460€ double; from 550€ suite. AE, DC, MC, V. Free parking. Closed Nov–Mar. **Amenities:** 2 restaurants; bar; concierge; pool; room service; spa; outdoor tennis court. *In room:* A/C, TV, minibar.

AGEROLA ★

14.5km (9 miles) W of Amalfi

A sparse rural area on a high plateau in the Monti Lattari range, Agerola is famous for its beauty and its cows' and sheep's milk for which the mountains were named (*latte* means milk). The region's best cheese comes from Agerola's farms—indeed, some of the most excellent cheese in the country is made here. Completely bypassed by most, this rural area offers visitors beauty and autenthicity.

GETTING THERE & AROUND   In addition to the **SITA bus** from Amalfi, you can come by **taxi** or **car** from Amalfi or Positano (see "Getting Around," p. 204 and 188). If you are **driving,** take the sharp turn off SS 163 on SS 366 at Conca dei Marini, and continue about 4km (2½ miles) farther up the cliff past Furore.

VISITOR INFORMATION   The **Proloco tourist office** (© **089-8791064**) is on Viale della Vittoria.

FAST FACTS   A **pharmacy** (© **081-8791085**) is at Via Armando Diaz 14. The closest **hospital** is in Salerno (see "Fast Facts," p. 263). For an **ambulance,** dial © **118.** You can call the **police** at © **113** or 112. You'll find **post offices** at Via Roma 1 (© **081-8731573**) and at Via Ponte 1 (© **081-8731266**). There are two **banks:** Banco di Napoli, Piazza Capasso 3 (© **081-8740323**), and Banca Intesa, Via Roma 16 (© **081-8740511**).

Exploring the Town

A collection of farming hamlets, Agerola has its administrative center in **Pianillo.** The most scenic of Agerola's bourgs is **San Lazzaro** where, past the church to the left, you will find the **Punta,** a natural terrace offering dramatic **views** ★★ over the sea. Via the road to the right of the church, more awesome panoramas open from the terrace by the former **Castle Avitabile** (Colonia Montana), and from the ruins of **Castel Lauritano** ★★★. The whole area offers unending **hiking** opportunities, including the demanding but extremely scenic 5-hour hike to the **Vallone delle Ferriere** waterfall, starting from San Lazzaro.

Visit a cheese shop to sample *fiordilatte, caciocavallo,* and *scamorze.* Among the best are **Caseificio Agerolina,** Via Tutti I Santi 6 (© **089-8731022**); **Caseificio Belfiore,** Via Belvedere 35 (© **089-8791338**); **Caseificio Fior di Agerola,** Via Galli 74 (© **089-8791339**); and **La Montanina,** Via Carlo Poerio 30 bis (© **089-8731022**).

Where to Stay & Dine

Don't expect luxury, but a few acceptable hotels offer simple accommodations, such as **Albergo Ristorante Risorgimento,** Via Antonio Coppola 32, Località San Lazzaro, 84051 Agerola (©/fax **081-8025072**; www.hotelrisorgimento.it; 90€ double), a welcoming historic hotel (established 1878) with an attached restaurant serving good pizza and a number of local specialties. Better still is a meal at one of the local *agriturismi:* The best are **Il Castagno,** Via Radicosa 39 (© **081-8025164**); **Mare e Monti,** Via Santa Lucia 24 and Traversa San Lazzaro 1 (© **081-8025226**); and **Zi' Carmine,** Via Fontana 59 (© **081-8025032**). Call ahead for reservations.

MINORI

3km (2 miles) east of Amalfi

This tiny harbor at the mouth of a small stream—the Reginna Minor—enjoys the largest beaches on the Costiera after Maiori (p. 228) and hides a few little-known art treasures.

Essentials

GETTING THERE & AROUND   Minori is on SS 163, between Amalfi and Vietri, west of Maiori. In addition to the **bus** from Amalfi, you can take a **taxi** or **car** from Amalfi or Positano (see "Getting Around," p. 204 and 188). The town is small enough to explore **on foot,** but you can get a **taxi** at the harbor (or call © **089-877435**). To explore by sea, you can **rent motorboats and sailboats** at **Noleggio,** Via Nazionale 5 (✆ **335-5443010;** www.amalficharter.it).

VISITOR INFORMATION The **tourist office** (✆ **089-877087** or 089-877607; www. proloco.minori.sa.it) is on Piazza Cantilena.

FAST FACTS The **pharmacy** (✆ **089-877200**) is on Corso Vittorio Emanuele, but the closest **hospital** is in Salerno (see "Fast Facts," p. 263). For an **ambulance,** dial ✆ **118.** For the **police,** call ✆ **113** or 112. The **post office** (✆ **089-853549**) is on Via Pergola. Several banks have **ATMs,** including **Banco di Napoli,** Corso Vittoria Emanuele 29 (✆ **089-877150**).

SPECIAL EVENTS A number of festivals and events take place in summer. The much-acclaimed **summer music festival** enlivens the town's cultural scene, and the Associazione Musical Costiera Amlfitana hosts the annual **Jazz on the Coast** (✆ **338-4076618;** www. jazzonthecoast.it) festival in July. Contact the tourist office for a full schedule of events.

Exploring the Town

Famous for its sandy beach, Minori is a picturesque little town gloriously nestled between blue seas and citrus groves. The village, with its small harbor on a beautiful cove, was the arsenal for the medieval Republic of Amalfi. A few steps from the harbor is the **Basilica of Santa Trofimena.** Built in the 11th century, the cathedral was completely redone in the 19th century; its original crypt (restored in the 17th century) houses the remains of Saint Trofimena, Amalfi's protector saint. If you walk along the left side of the basilica and go right up the steps, you will reach the wonderful 12th-century **Campanile** ★; it is the sole remnant of the church of Santa Annunziata, and its original inlay decorations are still well-preserved.

Following the canal along the road from the beach, you will come to **Villa Romana,** aka **Villa Marittima** ★, Via Capo di Piazza 28 (✆ **089-852893;** Mon–Sat 9am to 1 hr. before sunset), a patrician villa dating from the 1st century A.D. It was discovered in 1932 but was not excavated until the 1950s. The villa was built on two floors around a vast courtyard graced by a pool and surrounded by a portico. One side of the portico opens onto the beautiful ninfeo, a hall richly decorated with frescoes and stucco work. Also of architectural interest are the perfectly preserved thermal baths. The **Antiquarium** contains a collection of artifacts and frescoes from this and nearby excavations.

Where to Stay

Hoel Santa Lucia (**Kids**) This modern hotel offers comfortable accommodations on the outskirts west of town. Guest rooms are modern, with no-nonsense furnishings, good-size bathrooms (shower only), and private balconies (in some). Good options for families, quads rent for a reasonable 165€. Guests enjoy special rates at the nearby beach. The hotel's **restaurant** is good and moderately priced.

Via Nazionale 44, 84010 Minori. ✆ **089-853636.** Fax 089-877142. www.hotelsantalucia.it. 35 units. 124€ double. Rates include buffet breakfast. Children 2 and under stay free in parent's room. AE, DC, MC, V. Parking 18€. Closed Nov–Mar. **Amenities:** Restaurant; bar; room service; smoke-free rooms. *In room:* A/C, TV, minibar, Wi-Fi.

Hotel Villa Romana ★ The best hotel in town, the welcoming Villa Romana offers spacious and pleasantly furnished guest rooms, with whitewashed walls, woodwork, and tile. Bathrooms are modern and good-size (some with shower only). The swimming pool **227** with solarium is a plus.

Corso Vittorio Emanuele 90, 84010 Minori. ✆ **089-877237.** Fax 089-877302. www.hotelvillaromana.it. 50 units. 160€ double. Rates include buffet breakfast. Children 2 and under stay free in parent's room. AE, DC, MC, V. Free parking. **Amenities:** Restaurant; bar; pool; room service. *In room:* A/C, TV, minibar.

Where to Dine

Minori is a little culinary heaven that is proud of its specialties, both savory and sweet. In the former category are *sarchiapone* (squash filled with ground meat and ricotta and cooked in a tomato sauce) and *'ndunderi* (fresh homemade dumplings made of spelt flour and fresh cheese, served with olive oil, cheese, local herbs, and often chopped walnuts). The latter category is best represented by the mouth-watering *sospiri,* aka *Zizz'e monache;* the first name translates as "sighs," and the second as "nuns' breasts"—the sacred and profane names for the delicious dome-shaped pastries filled with lemon cream. You can taste *sospiri* and additional wonderful pastries at **Pasticceria De Riso,** Piazza Cantilena 1 (✆ **089-877396;** www.deriso.it), one of the best pastry shops in Italy.

Il Giardiniello ★ AMALFITAN/PIZZA   Good food and a cozy atmosphere mark this restaurant that is especially charming in nice weather, when you can dine in the lemon grove. The menu focuses on seafood—from a splendid *laganelle alla marinara* (fresh eggless pasta with squid, shrimp, arugula, and cherry tomatoes), a rich *riso al nero di seppia* (rice with squid ink), to the satisfying *alici impanate con la provola* (fresh anchovies deep-fried with cheese). In the evening, pizzas are offered and very good ones at that.

Corso Vittorio Emanuele 17. ✆ **089-877050.** www.ristorantegiardiniello.com. Reservations recommended. Secondi 11€–18€. AE, DC, MC, V. Thurs–Tues 12:30–2:30pm and 7:30–10:30pm (also Wed Jun–Sept). Closed Nov–Jan.

La Botte (Finds AMALFITAN/PIZZA   In a former church near the Villa Romana's archaeological site, the rustic decor of this popular restaurant is a picturesque setting for a hearty meal. The arbor terrace is delightful in summer. The cuisine ranges from the classic *scialatielli ai frutti di mare* (fresh homemade pasta with shellfish) to such venturesome choices as *ravioli con aragosta e crema d'asparagi* (lobster ravioli with cream of asparagus). Chef Mastro Pantaleone makes his own pasta, such as the delightful pumpkin ravioli, which is served with provola cheese, tomatoes, and porcini mushrooms. In the evening, the menu includes a whopping 36 kinds of pizza.

Via S. M. Vetrano 15. ✆ **089-877893.** Reservations recommended Sat–Sun. Secondi 6€–16€. DC, MC, V. Wed–Mon 12:30–3pm and 7:30–11pm (also Tues in summer). Closed 3 weeks in Jan.

L'Arsenale ★ CREATIVE AMALFITAN   Founded in 1992 by the three Proto brothers, this small restaurant—it has a few tables under a portico outside—is a moderate, more-than-just-reliable choice. A large variety of *antipasti* is complemented by tasty and rich homemade pasta, such as *tortelli con crostacei e porcini* (large ravioli with shellfish and porcini mushrooms) and *quadroni di carne con burro e salvia* (meat ravioli in sage and butter). To the joy of many, the menu includes excellent meat options, so when it comes to the secondo you might try the lamb or rabbit for a change of pace from the Costeria's omnipresent fish.

Via San Giovanni a Mare 20. ✆ **089-851418.** Reservations recommended. Secondi 15€–21€. AE, DC, MC, V. Fri–Wed 12:30–3pm and 7:30–11pm. Closed 3 weeks Jan–Feb.

6km (4 miles) east of Amalfi on SS 163

Maiori opens onto one of the largest beaches of the whole Costiera and, consequently, one of the most developed. The area is popular among Italians as a seaside resort, but few foreign tourists come this way. While it might lack the unique charm of Positano and Ravello, Maiori enjoys the same beautiful sea and its own distinctive character.

Essentials

GETTING THERE & AROUND   Maiori is on SS 163 between Amalfi and Vietri, a short distance east of Minori. In addition to the **bus** from Amalfi, you can grab a **taxi** or a **car** from Amalfi or Positano (see "Getting Around," p. 204 and 188). The town is walkable, but you can find a **taxi** (© **089-877897**) on Piazza San Giacomo, by the harbor.

VISITOR INFORMATION   Azienda Autonoma di Soggiorno e Turismo (© 089-877452; www.aziendaturismo-maiori.it) provides **tourist information** at Corso Reginna 73.

FAST FACTS   You'll find **pharmacies** at Via Santa Tecla (© **089-877063**) and Corso Reginna (© **089-877052**). The nearest **hospital** is in Salerno (see "Fast Facts," p. 263). For an **ambulance,** dial © **118.** You can call the **police** at © **113** or 112. The **post office** (© **089-877095**) is at Via Orti. Banks with **ATMs** include **Banco di Napoli** (© **089-877043**) on Lungomare Amendola, and **Deutsche Bank** (© **089-853433**) on Corso Reginna.

Exploring the Town

In the Middle Ages, Maiori was an important town, surrounded by walls and defended by towers and castles, with elegant palaces and buildings along the covered-over Reginna Maior river. Much as in Amalfi, the river ran under the main street, but a disastrous flood in 1954 took out the road, collapsing all the adjacent buildings and destroying the medieval town. It was rebuilt with nondescript modern buildings, but if you venture out of the center, you'll discover some narrow medieval streets spared by the flood. Dominating the village from atop 108 steps is a memento of Maiori's glorious past, the **Collegiata di Santa Maria a Mare,** Corso Reginna (© **328-7639925**). Built in the 12th century, this church is graced by a large majolica cupola, a richly carved wooden ceiling dating from the 16th century, and, in the crypt, the original majolica floor from the same period. Adjacent to the church, the **Museo d'Arte Sacra Don Clemente Confalone** houses valuable art from the church's past.

The wide **seaside promenade** is a pleasant place to enjoy excellent views all the way to the diminutive rocky harbor to the west of town. The **beach** below gets rather crowded in summer and is the usual Italian affair, with establishments renting out chairs, umbrellas, and **boats**—motor or oars—with which explore the coast. You can also rent boats at the harbor. One easy **boat excursion** ★★ is to follow the beach east past the Norman Tower. In the cliff below is a grotto, whose dubious attraction is a sulfur-smelling mineral spring; but farther on is a secluded crescent of beach and, beyond that, the partially underwater entrance to **Grotta Pannone.**

An area to explore on foot is the promontory of **Capo d'Orso** ★★, east of town. Covering 500 hectares (1,235 acres), with an average altitude of 70m (230 ft.), the protected natural area extends all the way to Torrente Bonea and is perhaps the most scenic stretch of the whole Amalfi Coast. The underlying limestone promontory has been eroded by the sea, and stones poke through the blanket of *macchia mediterranea,* creating a unique dolomitic landscape. A **scenic trail** ★ leads from SS 163 to the **lighthouse** and the entrance to the preserve. Past the lighthouse to the right is **Abbazia di Santa Maria de Olearia** ★, off SS 163/Via Diego Tajani (© 089-877452; daily 5–7:30pm). Locally known as the Catacombe di Badia, this incredible place was completely carved from the cliff's rocky face. Begun in the 10th century as a shrine to Santa Maria de Olearia, it was soon surrounded by a few cliff dwellings, which were then transformed into a monastery in the 11th century. The main chapel has a vaulted ceiling and an apse, both decorated with 11th-century fresco work; underneath is the crypt, where well-preserved frescoes depict the Virgin Mary and two saints.

Where to Stay

Hotel San Francesco   This well-designed modern hotel is in a quiet location a short distance from the sea, near the harbor and the center of town, and is surrounded by a garden. Guest rooms are spacious and pleasantly furnished with hardwood, wrought iron, tiled floors, and private balconies affording superior views. Bathrooms are modern, but not large, and the hotel is scrupulously clean. Guests enjoy beach rights on the hotel's beach, and the formal **restaurant** has a pleasant garden and serves local cuisine, with an emphasis on seafood.

Via Santa Tecla 54, 84010 Maiori. ©/fax **089-877070.** www.hotel-sanfrancesco.it. 44 units. 160€–180€ double. Rates include buffet breakfast. Children 2 and under stay free in parent's room. AE, DC, MC, V. Free parking. Pets accepted. **Amenities:** Restaurant; bar; room service. *In room:* A/C, TV, minibar.

Reginna Palace Hotel ★   This desirable hotel is the perfect base for a leisurely vacation. Management favors week-long bookings, but shorter stays are accommodated depending on availability. An elegant property right in the heart of Maiori, it is surrounded by a luxurious garden. The noteworthy swimming pool is filled with seawater. Guest rooms are spacious and furnished in contemporary style with fine fabrics and artistically tiled floors and bathrooms. A number of the rooms have ocean views, and some have private balconies. Guests enjoy access to the hotel's beach (14€ for an umbrella and one chair per day), only 46m (150 ft.) away; and the elegant on-site **restaurant** has a lovely outdoor terrace for dining on fair summer nights.

Via Cristoforo Colombo 1, 84010 Maiori. © **089-877183.** Fax 089-851200. www.hotelreginna.it. 67 units. 190€–230€ double. Rates include buffet breakfast. Children 2 and under stay free in parent's room. Internet specials available. Minimum 2-week stay around Aug 15. AE, DC, MC, V. Parking 18€. Closed Nov–Mar. **Amenities:** Restaurant; 2 bars; pool; room service. *In room:* A/C, TV, minibar.

Where to Dine

Maiori has lots of good restaurants, starting with those in the hotels we recommend above.

Faro di Capo d'Orso ★★ MODERN AMALFITAN   In an elegant glassed-in dining room, with spectacular views over Capri and Ravello, this restaurant is a special place you'll want to visit again and again, both for the haute cuisine and the magical atmosphere. The chef loves the bounty of his region and takes the utmost care in combining ingredients. The menu changes with the seasons, the market, and his inspiration, with lots of raw or rare fresh seafood. Among the innovative offerings you might find are *totanetti di paranza farciti di gamberetti bianchi* (local squid stuffed with white shrimp), or *linguine con ragù di calamaretti, pomodorini, prezzemolo e ricci di mare* (pasta with squid, cherry tomatoes, and sea urchins). The desserts are equally elaborate, and the wine list includes the very best of the local vineyards.

Via Diego Tajani 48 (off Capo d'Orso). © **089-877022.** www.capodorso.org. Reservations recommended. Secondi 20€–30€; tasting menus 60€ and 120€. AE, DC, MC, V. Thurs–Mon 12:30–3pm and 7:30–11pm (also Wed in summer). Closed 2 weeks in Jan.

Mammato (Value) AMALFITAN   On the shorefront, this relaxed, no-frills restaurant is popular among locals who come to eat seafood prepared according to the region's traditional recipes. Among the noteworthy classics of that cuisine are *scialatielli ai frutti di mare* (homemade pasta with basil and seafood), and *frittura* (deep-fried calamari and small fish).

Lungomare Amendola. © **089-877036.** www.ristorantemammato.it. Reservations recommended. Secondi 12€–18€. AE, DC, MC, V. Wed–Mon 1–3:30pm and 8–11:30pm (also Tues in summer). Closed 2 weeks in Nov.

CETARA ★
6km (3³/₄ miles) west of Vietri; 15km (9¹/₃ miles) east of Amalfi on SS 163

Off the beaten path for most foreign tourists, Cetara is a picturesque village with a still-active—if controversial—fishing tradition. It is a great place for relaxing on the beach or for a meal by the sea.

Essentials
GETTING THERE & AROUND   In addition to the **SITA bus** from Salerno and Amalfi, you can come by **taxi** or **car** (see "Getting Around," p. 262 and 204). If you are **driving,** take SS 163 past Vietri; Cetara is the next town. The town is small and you'll be able to travel **on foot.**

VISITOR INFORMATION   The **Proloco tourist office** (© **089-261593;** www.proloco cetara.it) is at Corso Garibaldi 15.

FAST FACTS   You'll find a **pharmacy** (© 089-261082) at Corso Umberto 43. The closest **hospital** is in Salerno (see "Fast Facts," p. 263). For an **ambulance,** dial © **118.** To reach the **police,** call © **113** or 112. The **post office** (© 089-261065) is at Corso Federici, and a bank (© **089-261313**) with an **ATM** is at Corso Garibaldi 41.

Exploring the Town
An important fishing harbor since Roman times—Cetara actually derives its name from the Latin *cetaria* (tuna fishery)—this still is the main fishing harbor in the area and very authentic. The town's *tonnare* (tuna-fishing facilities) were big complexes built mostly over the sea. Tuna was trapped in huge netting channels out at sea and brought to underwater cages. From there, the fish were pushed into a seawater pool, where they were processed. Today, most catches happen at sea, with massive trawlers and often with the help of planes that scour the Mediterranean for the red tuna.

This is definitely an industry, not a sport, and we don't endorse unsustainable practices, no matter how traditional. Recent research shows that the tuna collected are actually young tuna that have not yet reached full maturity, which in turn contributes to the depletion of the species. Yet locals proudly defend their traditional fleet, the only one left in the Tyrrenian Sea, as well as their traditional cuisine.

Locals celebrate in July with the **Sagra del Tonno (Tuna Festival),** when preserved tuna and other local delicacies are sold in town; the festival also features music and other scheduled events. Contact the **Proloco tourist office** (above) for more information.

The rest of the year, the key attraction is the **San Pietro** church, with its bright majolica cupola and 13th-century bell tower. We recommend a stroll around the back streets of the village, rarely visited by tourists.

The best beach in the area is **Marina di Erchie,** technically in Maiori. It's past the next village, only 2km (1¼ miles) west of Cetara. If you don't want to venture that far, check out the small beaches by Cetara's harbor.

Where to Stay

Hotel Cetus ★ (Value) (Kids) In a spectacular panoramic location (on a cliff) just outside town, this is a great hotel (although being the only one in the village gives it a decided advantage). Guest rooms are larger than average, comfortable, and bright, and have colorful tiled floors and bathrooms, and scenic views. The Cetus is particularly welcoming to children; it has its own sandy cove with umbrellas and chairs for its guests, along with a playground. Of the on-site restaurants—both upscale—**Il Gabbiano** offers excellent, traditional food; and Falalella serves up gourmet international cuisine.

Corso Umberto I 1, 84010 Cetara. ✆/fax **089-261388.** 43 units. High season 260€ double; low season 130€ double. Rates include breakfast. Children 2 and under stay free in parent's room. AE, MC, V. Free parking. **Amenities:** Restaurant; bar; babysitting; concierge; room service. *In room:* A/C, TV, hair dryer, minibar.

Where to Dine

Cetara's secret has spread from nearby Salerno to the rest of Italy, and gourmets come to partake of the local cuisine based on the freshest seafood just brought in from the harbor. Anchovies are the specialty here—be they roasted, grilled, deep-fried, or dressed with local herbs. You can buy fresh fish and preserved anchovies at **Pescheria Battista Delfino,** Via Umberto I 78 (✆ **089-261069**), or at **Pescheria San Pietro,** Via Umberto I 72 (✆ **089-261147**).

Acquapazza ★ AMALFITAN This small and trendy trattoria not far from the harbor is a good place to try the local fish and experience high cuisine without spending a fortune. It prepares a wonderful array of *antipasti,* including *tortino di melanzane e alici* (fresh anchovy and eggplant torte), marinated tuna, and *carpaccio di pesce* (raw fish in a citrus sauce), and a number of tasty pasta dishes, such as *tubetti al ragù di pesce* (short pasta with a seafood and tomato sauce). For a secondo, you can pick your fish from the daily catch display and have it prepared as you choose.

Corso Garibaldi 38. ✆ **089-261606.** www.acquapazza.it. Reservations recommended Sat–Sun. Secondi 16€–21€. AE, DC, MC, V. Tues–Sun 12:30–3pm and 7:30–11pm.

Ristorante Pizzeria Al Convento ★ (Kids) AMALFITAN/PIZZA The perfect place to satisfy the whole family, this welcoming restaurant offers delicious local specialties as well as tasty *pizza al metro* (pizza by the yard) in the tradition of Vico Equense (p. 164; *Note:* The pizza is excellent but is served only at dinnertime.). The frescoed dining hall is a great setting for a meal, but so is the outdoor arbor terrace. The menu is centered on seafood, and particularly on anchovies, the local fish. Try the classic *spaghetti alla colatura di alici* (seasoned with anchovies), and the *totani e patate* (calamari with potatoes). **Cooking class** are offered, where you start at the market and are guided all the way through to the presentation of the finished meal.

Piazza S. Francesco 15. ✆ **089-261039.** www.alconvento.net. Reservations recommended. Secondi 12€–18€; tasting menu 30€. AE, DC, MC, V. Thurs–Tues noon–2:30pm and 7–10:30pm (also Wed May 15–Sept 30).

San Pietro ★ AMALFITAN This elegant yet pleasantly down-to-earth and reasonably priced restaurant has a small dining room and a few tables under an arbor, where you can enjoy a most satisfying meal. In addition to the perfectly prepared dishes that uphold the local tradition—such as *vermicelli con colatura di alici* (with anchovy essence) and fried anchovies—

we recommend the innovative dishes that might include *riso con sconcigli* (rice with fresh seafood and seaweed) or *pezzogna allo sfusato di Amalfi* (fish with local lemon sauce).

Piazza San Francesco 2. ℂ **089-261091**. www.sanpietroristorante.it. Reservations recommended. Secondi 15€–19€. AE, DC, MC, V. Wed–Mon noon–2:30pm and 7–10:30pm (also Tues in summer). Closed 2 weeks in Jan–Feb.

VIETRI SUL MARE ★★

5km (3 miles) west of Salerno on SS 163

The gateway to the Amalfi Coast, Vietri is a small working town with a well-established traditional craft industry. Vietri's main street, with its famous ceramic shops, gets a lot of tourist attention; but it usually makes for a hit-and-run shopping excursion, which leaves the area otherwise undisturbed. Vietri is also well worth a visit for its scenic seashore.

Essentials

GETTING THERE & AROUND In addition to the **SITA bus** from Salerno and Amalfi, you can use a **taxi** or a **car** (see "Getting Around," p. 262 and 204). If you are **driving,** take SS 163 north, and Vietri is the first town. Once there, you'll be able to get around **on foot.**

VISITOR INFORMATION The **Proloco tourist office** (ℂ **089-211285**) is in the Municipal Building on Piazza Matteotti.

FAST FACTS You'll find a **pharmacy** (ℂ **089-210181**) at Corso Umberto 12. The closest **hospital** is in Salerno (see "Fast Facts," p. 263). For an **ambulance,** dial ℂ **118.** You can reach the **police** at ℂ **113** or 112. The **post office** (ℂ **089-211897**) is at Via Giuseppe Mazzini 38. **Banks** with **ATMs** include **Banco di Napoli,** Via Giuseppe Mazzini 30 (ℂ **089-763154**), and **Banca della Campania,** Via Giuseppe Mazzini 13 (ℂ **089-762467**).

Exploring the Town

The heart of town is Via Madonna degli Angeli, closed to car traffic and lined with shops selling local ceramics (below). No visit is complete without a stop at the **Duomo** ★, the church dedicated to **San Giovanni Battista,** with its cupola adorned with painted majolica. The **panorama** ★ from the square in front of the church is one of the prettiest of the coastal towns. Inside, in addition to some excellent 17th-century ceramics, is the impressive carved and gilded 18th-century ceiling and artwork that includes a 16th-century polyptych of the Virgin Mary and an 11th-century crucifix.

The most famous of the ceramic shops is **Ceramica Artistica Solimene Vincenzo** ★, Via Madonna degli Angeli 7 (ℂ **089-210243;** www.solimene.com), one of Vietri's historic workshops. Besides visiting the showroom and buying contemporary ceramics, admire the building itself—a beautiful example of organic architecture from the 1930s by Paolo Soleri, who went on to work in the U.S. with Frank Lloyd Wright.

From Piazza Matteotti in the center of town, descend Via Costabile about 1km (a half-mile) to arrive at the beach of **Marina di Vietri** ★, dominated by a watchtower that was transformed into a villa; across its surrounding park is a small, more secluded beach, but it becomes crowded and dirty at the height of summer.

Shopping

Famous for their quality and vivid colors, the local ceramics make for a perfect souvenir for yourself or a gift for someone at home. The town feels like an open-air showroom, with walls along the main streets literally lined with beautiful tableware, ceramics of all kinds, and shelves burgeoning with variously shaped bowls and vases. After an initial pass-through, you'll begin to see stylistic differences and be able to spot individual artists, each characterized by a proprietary pattern and color palette. Most artists sell directly from their premises in town, on in the nearby suburb of Molina, due north past the train station along Via Enrico De Marinis. In town, some of the showrooms belong to individual artists, while other boutiques sell pieces from a variety of artists. Some of them specialize by technique, depending whether the terra cotta is thrown or pressed (the latter uses a mold).

Recommended studios of long-standing include **Ceramiche Artistiche Pinto,** Corso Umberto I 27 (© **089-210271**); **Vietritaly,** Corso Umberto I 45 (© **089-211122;** www.vietritaly.it); **Solimene Ceramica,** Via Case Sparse, Fontana Vecchia (© **089-210188;** www.solimeneceramica.com); **Tortora & Giordano,** Via Travertino 17 (© **089-211894**); and **Antonio D'Acunto,** Via Enrico De Marinis 33, Molina Di Vietri Sul Mare (© **089-211143**). For pressed terra cotta we also recommend **Cotto Artistico Vietrese,** Via Travertino 17 (© **089-211894**); **Alfonso Fasano,** Via E. De Marinis 45, Molina Di Vietri Sul Mare (© **089-211598**); and **Giuseppe Landi,** Via Chellavanna 51, Molina Di Vietri Sul Mare (© **089-211819**), whereas for thrown terra cotta, try **Il Vasaio Vietrese Di Apicella Benvenuto,** Via D. Taiani 110 (© **340-5294062**). We are very fond of the little goats that are the trademark of **D'Amore,** Via De Marinis 64; they have been imitated by many, so look for his signature on each piece. Most shops will ship your purchases home for you, but ask before buying.

RAITO: AN EXCURSION IN THE INTERIOR

Along the road that heads out of town and inland, we discovered **Raito** ★, a picturesque little village of whitewashed houses and gardens that enjoy excellent views of the bay. The highlights here are the 16th-century church **Madonna delle Grazie** ★, with a chapel decorated by Luca Giordano, and the historic **Villa Guariglia** ★, surrounded by a park. In the scenic Torretta Belvedere is the **Museo della Ceramica,** Via Nuova Raito (© **089-211835;** free admission; Tues–Sun 9am–1pm and 2–8pm). Created in 1981, the museum's collection retraces the history of the local ceramic production and includes a number of masterworks from religious art and everyday items to the "German period," with works created or inspired by the wave of foreign (mainly German) artists who came to Vietri between 1929 and 1947. On most evenings during the summer season, Villa Guariglia is the enchanting setting for classical music **concerts;** call the tourist information office in Vietri (p. 232) for information on the program. To reach Raito, take SP 75 off SS 163; it's about 2km (1¼ miles) west of Vietri. Only 1km (a half-mile) farther on is the little hamlet of **Albori,** with its 16th-century church, **Santa Margherita ad Albori,** and prime sea views.

Where to Stay & Dine

Hotel Raito ★ This modern luxury resort hotel enjoys a superior position high on the cliffs in the village of Raito, west of Vietri. Guest rooms are spacious and comfortable, with modern, stylish furnishings; most offer breathtaking views and balconies. The newly added Seiren wing offers exclusive decor and service, including free Wi-Fi and daily fruit and spumante. All units have good-size (and new) bathrooms. Guests can ride the free hotel shuttle down to the private beach or just take it easy and enjoy the pools and the spa. The hotel's **restaurants** serve a range of traditional and international cuisine.

Via Nuova Raito 9, Frazione Raito, 84010 Vietri sul Mare. © **089-210033.** Fax 089-211434. 77 units. 300€–550€ double; from 700€ suite. Rates include buffet breakfast. Internet specials available. AE, DC, MC, V. Free parking. **Amenities:** 3 restaurants; bar; babysitting; concierge; pool (for a fee); room service; spa (for a fee). *In room:* A/C, TV, Internet, minibar.

The Jewels of the Gulf of Naples: The Islands of Capri, Ischia & Procida

Much of the splendor of this part of Italy comes from the islands that define the Gulf of Naples: Ischia and Procida as the organic extension of Capo Miseno in the Phlegrean Fields, and Capri as the natural continuation of Punta Campanella at the tip of the Sorrento peninsula. Each with its own character, these three islands have enjoyed completely different fortunes as far as tourism is concerned. Capri, the most well-known, has been a lively resort since antiquity, famous for the debauches of Emperor Tiberius. Ischia, also known to the ancient world, was noted for its spas, and has traditionally remained a place for relaxation. Procida was and still is a small fisherman's haunt, where locals continue to make their living from the sea and tourists are comparatively rare.

Of the three, Capri is the most sought after (it's particularly famous for its Blue Grotto), but it remains a must see, even if you have to brave huge crowds.

Because of their proximity to the mainland, each of these islands makes a good day trip. Even Ischia, the largest of the three, can be enjoyed in a day: You can arrive early in the morning, check in at one of the spas—we love the ones with scenic outdoor facilities—and leave after a gourmet dinner. Of course, after darkness falls and the last ferryboats have gone, the islands become a romantic haven for visitors who choose to stay the night.

1 ISCHIA: ISOLA VERDE & ISLAND OF ETERNAL YOUTH ★★★

42km (26 miles) NW of Naples; 20km (13 miles) W of Pozzuoli

When the Greeks arrived on this coast more than 2,500 years ago, they first landed in Ischia. They felt that Ischia was a perfect base from which to dominate the mainland. Yet they quickly changed their minds and moved to nearby Cuma, by modern Pozzuoli (see chapter 6), because of Ischia's very active volcano, which erupted violently and repeatedly throughout the 14th century. Only then did the island's population start growing, laying the base for the development of the spa industry we see today. The first thermal establishment opened in Casamicciola Terme in 1604, destination of the upper crust of society. Today Ischia is where savvy travelers come for fabulous spa vacations: The inactive volcano—788m-high (2,585-ft.) Monte Epomeo—feeds the mineral hot springs and therapeutic muds that are used by the more than 150 spas on the island. Yet the atmosphere still remains quieter than on Capri, partly because of Ischia's larger size, but also because its large beaches are an attraction to families, whose presence helps deter partiers and preserves its calm and bucolic character.

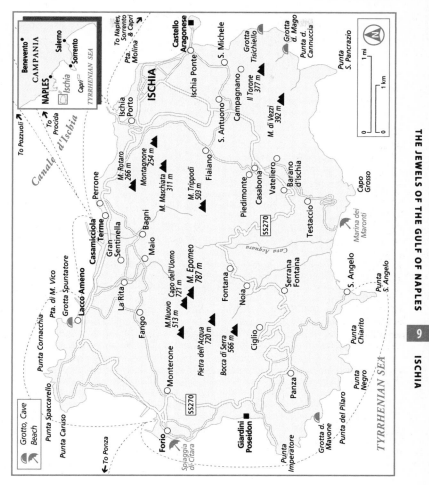

ESSENTIALS

GETTING THERE Ischia's three main harbors—Ischia Porto (the largest), Forio, and Casamicciola—are very well connected to the mainland, with most ferries leaving from Pozzuoli and Naples's two harbors of Mergellina Terminal Aliscafi and Stazione Marittima. Both ferry and hydrofoil service is frequent in summer but slows down during the winter, when some of the hydrofoil lines are suspended because of rough seas. **Medmar** (*℃* 081-3334411; www.medmargroup.it), **Caremar** (*℃* 081-5513882; www.caremar.it), and **SNAV** (*℃* 081-4285555 or 081-4285500; www.snav.it) offer regular service from Napoli, Pozzuoli, and Procida to Ischia Porto and Casamicciola. **Alilauro** (*℃* 081-4972238;

www.alilauro.it) runs hydrofoils from Naples (Mergellina and Molo Beverello) to Ischia Porto and to Forio; **NLG-Navigazione Libera del Golfo** (✆ **081-5527209;** www.navlib.it) operates from Salerno to Ischia; **Alicost** (✆ **089-234892;** www.lauroweb.com/alicost.htm) offers connections from Salerno, Capri, Amalfi, and Positano to Ischia Porto. *Note:* During high season, car access to the island is restricted and the number of car slots is limited; if you are planning to bring your car, check with the transport company and make your reservations well in advance.

GETTING AROUND Ischia is quite large and hilly, and you will need some form of transportation. Public transportation is good, with a well-organized **bus** system with SEPSA (✆ **081-991828**) and Pegaso (✆ **081-908581**). One line circles the island toward the right (*circolare destra* marked CD), and one toward the left (*circolare sinistra,* marked CS), plus a number of other lines crisscrossing the island among its major destinations. Tickets cost 1.20€ and are valid for 90 minutes; a daily pass costs 4€; they are for sale at bars, tobacconists, and news kiosks. You can get a printout of the bus schedule from the tourist office (see "Visitor Information," below).

More expensive, **taxis** wait at stands strategically located around the island, including: Piazza Antica Reggia (✆ **081-984998**), Piazza degli Eroi (✆ **081-992550**), and Piazzetta San Girolamo (✆ **081-993720**) in **Ischia Porto;** Piazza Marina (✆ **081-994800**), Porto (✆ **081-900369**), and Piazza Bagni (✆ **081-900234**) in Casamicciola; Porto (✆ **081-994310**) and Piazza Girardi (✆ **081-995183**) in Lacco Ameno; Forio (✆ **081-997085,** 081-997450, 081-997367, or 081-997482); and Piazzetta S. Angelo (✆ **081-99899**) in Serrara Fontana. Some of the taxis are picturesque three-wheelers— *motorette*—but they are rapidly disappearing. A 10€ minimum charge applies in the small town of Ischia (it's pretty much a flat rate), while drivers use the meter for trips outside town.

You can **rent motor scooters, bicycles,** and **cars** on the island from a number of agencies, including **Ischia,** Via Alfredo de Luca 61 (✆ **081-992444**), and **Island Center,** Via V. Di Meglio 161 (✆ **081-902525**).

For **boat** rental, contact **Futurnautica,** Via Porto 86 (✆ **081-993699**), or **Nautica Effe,** Via Iasolino 110 (✆ **081-993185**) in Ischia town.

VISITOR INFORMATION The **AACST tourist office** (✆ **081-5074231;** fax 081-5074230; www.infoischiaprocida.it) is at Corso Vittoria Colonna 116, 80077 Ischia; at its **information booth** at Via Sogliuzzo 72, Ischia Porto, you'll find free maps of the island as well as information and brochures. In addition, the **Proloco** (✆ **081-4972293;** www.prolocoischia.it) maintains an information booth at Piazza Antica Reggia 11, Ischia Porto, and organizes guided tours.

FAST FACTS You'll find **pharmacies** in each of the main villages on the island, including in Ischia, at Via Alfredo De Luca 117 (✆ **081-3331275**) and Via Michele Mazzella 143 (✆ **081-985089**); in Lacco Ameno, at Corso Rizzoli 77 (✆ **081-900224**); and in Casamicciola Terme, at Piazza Marina 1 (✆ **081-994060**). The **hospital** (✆ **081-994044** or 081-5079111) is in Lacco Ameno, on Via Fundera, and the **medical center** (✆ **081-998989**) is on Via Cava delle Pezze, Forio. For an **ambulance,** dial ✆ **081-996405** or 081-995495. You can call the **police** at ✆ **113** or 112. The main **post office** (✆ **081-992180;** Mon–Sat 8am–2pm) is at Via Sogliuzzo, on the corner of Via Pontano. You will find several banks with **ATMs,** including a **Banco di Napoli** (✆ **081-993480**), at Via Iasolino 26, Ischia Porto.

In May, the island hosts **Ipomea,** an international exposition of rare temperate-zone plants that is held on the exclusive grounds of the **Parco Termale del Negombo** (✆ **081-986152;** www.negombo.it).

The **Festival of Sant'Anna** on July 26 is celebrated with evocative displays by the Aragonese Castle. The festival originated from the adoration of Saint Ann, the mother of Mary, who is believed to protect pregnant women. Originally, locals would sail to the small bay of Cartaromana with candles on their bows to honor the saint. Slowly, this tradition developed into the spectacular **Festa del Mare,** in which a procession of boats and floats crosses the water, and the castle and harbor are illuminated. If you are in the area around this time, be sure not to miss this memorable sight.

Summer is also the height of the musical season at **La Mortella** (✆ **081-986220;** www.lamortella.it), the seat of the William Walton Foundation. Besides the concerts, the foundation also hosts a yearly music and opera workshop. An additional musical event is the **Ischia Jazz Festival** (www.ischiajazz.eu or www.circuitojazz.it), which usually takes place over 5 days in the beginning of September.

EXPLORING THE ISLAND

Ischia is the largest of Campania's islands, covering about 46sq. km (18 sq. miles). Its velvety slopes, green with pine woods and vineyards, have earned it the nickname **Isola Verde (Emerald Isle),** while its fame as a healthy retreat has earned it another nickname, **Island of Eternal Youth,** for its peaceful atmosphere and its spas. These are fueled by the widespread volcanic activity still occurring on the island, although its volcano, Mount Epomeo, has long been dormant. Hot springs, mineral-water springs, and steam and hot-mud holes dot the island's slopes.

The largest town on the island is **Ischia** ★★, on the island's northeastern corner. The majority of activity is concentrated in **Ischia Porto,** around the main harbor (*porto* means harbor), and **Ischia Ponte** (*ponte* means bridge), by the bridge to the island promontory that flanks a small natural harbor. In between runs the pleasant promenade of Via Roma and Corso Vittoria Colonna—*il corso* in local parlance—stretching about 2km (1¼ miles). The promontory, with its small natural harbor, was the site of the original settlement, fortified by a castle as far back as the 5th century B.C. The **castle** ★★, Piazzale Aragonese, Ischia Ponte (✆ **081-992834;** www.castellodischia.it; 10€ adults, 6€ youth 9–19; free for children 8 and under; winter 10am–4:30pm, summer 9am–7pm) on the promontory today was built by the **Aragonese** over the ruins of earlier fortifications. We encourage you to climb up for a visit (though you can take an elevator), as it is quite scenic and picturesque. The last eruption of Mount Epomeo, in 1301, destroyed most of the village that had grown around the small natural harbor. The population resettled, but closer to the castle and bridge.

Ischia Porto, the other, now larger, part of town was founded by the Bourbons on a whim. When they took over the island in the 18th century, all that was there was a scenic volcanic lake (originally a volcano crater) and a few villas. The new kings fell in love with a villa-cum-spa built by a doctor, Francesco Buonocore, and decided to establish their residence there. They transformed the villa overlooking the lake into a small palace— what happened to the doctor is unknown; maybe he graciously donated his home to their majesties—the **Casina Reale Borbonica,** which today houses a military spa (not open to the public). They also cut a channel into the outer shore of the lake, transforming it into a large harbor. Inaugurated in 1854, it has been the island's major port ever since, and a lively town has developed around it, with many nice bars and a few restaurants.

A short distance away from Ischia (6.5km/4 miles) on the north shore, you'll find the small village of **Casamicciola Terme** ★, with its scenic harbor and **marina** (although, being right on the main road, its charm is a bit spoiled by the traffic), and **Villa Ibsen,** where the famous Norwegian writer wrote *Peer Gynt.* Founded in the 16th century to take advantage of the area's thermo-mineral springs, Casamicciola Terme is where the first modern spa was opened on the island in 1604. The village, though, suffered a reversal of fortunes when it was destroyed by the earthquake of 1883. It was immediately rebuilt, but closer to the shore, in its current position by the marina. The remains of the original town are in the inland hamlet of **Bagni,** with the island's oldest spas opening onto its main square, and the village of **Majo,** farther up the slope.

Adjacent to Casamicciola, 8km (5 miles) west of Ischia Porto, is the picturesque **Lacco Ameno** ★★, famous for its mushroom-shaped rock a few yards from the sandy shore. The ancient Greeks established their first settlement on this coast; although, daunted by the frequent—at that time—earthquakes and eruptions, they never developed a colony. An unassuming fishing harbor until the 1950s, it was then shaken out of its sleep by Italian publisher Angelo Rizzoli. He built his villa on the promontory of Monte Vico, overlooking the village to the west, and decided to invest in the area and transform it into an exclusive resort. His plan was successful and the promontory has become the most exclusive spa destination in Italy, offering many luxurious hotels and villas. **Villa Arbusto,** Angelo Rizzoli's own summer home, is today a museum—**Museo Civico Archeologico di Pithecusae** ★ (✆ 081-900356; admission 3€; Tues–Sun 9:30am–1pm and 4–8pm)—displaying the findings of local archaeological excavation. It is worth a visit, if only to admire the famous **Coppa di Nestore:** Dating from 725 b.c., it bears one of the oldest known Greek inscriptions, which, appropriately, celebrates the wine of Ischia. Nearby is an important Catholic pilgrimage site, the **Sanctuary of Santa Restituta** (✆ 081-980706 or 081-980538; daily 10am–1pm and 4–7pm), with its attached **archaeological excavations** and **museum.** The original church was created in the 4th or 5th century a.d. by adapting an ancient Roman water cistern, and later restructured.

On the west side of the Monte Vico promontory are the lovely **gardens of Villa La Mortella** ★★, Via F. Calise 39, 80075 Forio (✆ **081-986220;** www.lamortella.it). Covering 2 hectares (5 acres), the gardens were created by the Argentinean wife of William Walton, who collected many rare botanical species. Admission is 10€ for adults, 8€ for children 8 to 12, 6€ for children 5 to 7, and free for children 4 and under (Apr 1–Nov 15 Tues, Thurs, and Sat–Sun 9am–7pm; ticket booth closes 30 min. earlier).

On the western coast of the island, 13km (8 miles) west of Ischia Porto, is the lively town of **Forio,** with its wealth of bars and beaches. Popular among Naples residents, it is usually bypassed by foreign tourists. A favorite retreat of writers and musicians for centuries, Forio is also appreciated by those who come to enjoy the locally produced wine and its watchtower, **Il Torrione.** The tower was built in the 16th century to defend the town from the Saracen attacks, was once a prison, and now houses a small **museum**

(Fun Facts **Flower Power**

Ischia's unusual volcanic characteristics have produced more than spa-perfect conditions. The fertile soil and unique subtropical climate have been so favorable to flowering plants and shrubs that you can find on the island 50% of the entire European patrimony of flower species, a number of them indigenous to Ischia.

(© **081-3332934**) of the work of local poet and sculptor Giovanni Maltese. **La Colombaia,** Via F. Calise 130, 80075 Forio (© **081-3332147**) is the historic villa of Italian film director Luchino Visconti; it houses a film school and a small **museum** (Mon–Sat 9:30am–12:30pm and 3:30–6:30pm).

The southern half of Ischia is more agricultural, with only one town on the southern shore: the tiny fishing harbor of **Sant'Angelo** ★★, 11km (7 miles) south of Ischia Porto. Shaded by a tall promontory jutting into the sea and connected to the shore by a sandy isthmus (100m/328 ft. long) that is closed to vehicles, it is one of Ischia's most picturesque sights. Far from the hype of the high-priced spa resorts, it is quite exclusive and secluded. The other villages on this part of the island are nestled on the steep slopes of the mountain, overlooking the sea. **Serrara Fontana** ★★ (9.5km/6 miles southwest of Ischia Porto) is a tiny hamlet centered on a lookout terrace affording spectacular views.

STAYING ACTIVE

Ischia's shore alternates between rugged cliffs and sandy stretches, to the delight of sunbathers and swimmers. The island's beautiful **beaches** are all the more special because they are a commodity almost completely lacking in the Bay of Naples and the Amalfi

Coast. The town of Ischia has a beach—or rather several small ones, with the best being the **Spiaggia dei Pescatori,** where local fishermen beach their boats, a short distance west of the Aragonese Castle. You can do way better, though. The island's most beautiful beach is **Spiaggia dei Maronti** ★★★, stretching for about 2km (1¼ miles) east of the village of Sant'Angelo, straight down the cliff from **Barano d'Ischia** (4km/2½ miles south of Ischia Porto). These long stretches of sand are scenic but crowded in the summer. The **Spiaggia di Cartaromana** ★★, down from the village of San Michele on the east coast of the island, is on a slightly more secluded cove. North of Forio is the **Spiaggia di San Francesco** ★, overlooked by the promontory of Monte Vico, while south of Forio is the scenic **Spiaggia di Citara** ★★, which used to be the island's largest and most beautiful sandy beach. Though much diminished by erosion, it is still nice and is quite popular for the hot mineral springs that flow out to sea at its southern edge; these springs are the same ones that are used by the spa Giardini Poseidon (see "Spas & Thermo-Mineral Treatments," below). We also highly recommend **renting a boat** from one of the harbors and visiting those coves that are accessible only by sea.

If you are not into swimming or relaxation, you can visit the countryside, which is dotted with **vineyards** producing well-known—and excellent—D.O.C. wines. You could combine the sampling with some interesting **hikes** up the slopes of Mount Epomeo. We recommend you procure the diminutive brochure from the tourist office in Ischia, titled *Lizard Trails,* which has descriptions and maps of the island's best trails.

SPAS & THERMO-MINERAL TREATMENTS

What attracts most visitors to Ischia are the island's many **spas,** offering a variety of **thermo-mineral health and beauty treatments.** With over 56 different mineral springs on the island—not to mention the hot-mud, hot-sands, and numerous steam holes—Ischia is spa paradise. These natural resources, scattered across the island's slopes and beaches, have been harnessed by over 150 spa operators.

A number of the island's modern facilities operate as day parks and are perfect for a visit; many hotels also have their own spas and will offer package stays including meals and basic spa services, such as the use of the thermo-mineral pools. Even if you are not particularly interested in spa treatments, the outdoor spa parks are a unique and relaxing experience. *Note:* Many establishments specialize in medical treatments, in which even beauty care and stress relief are tackled from a scientific rather than a pampering viewpoint. In any case, remember to pack some old swimsuit, possibly dark colored, as the high mineral content of some waters will stain the fabric, or leave a sulfurous smell that is near impossible to remove.

Located between Ischia Porto and Casamicciola, **Parco Termale Castiglione** ★★ is a state-of-the-art facility offering thermo-mineral waters and mud treatments in a mix of indoor and open-air facilities. The scenic outdoor pools range in temperature from 82°F to 104°F (28°C–40°C). On the promontory of Monte Vico near Lacco Ameno, you'll find **Parco Termale Negombo** ★★ (✆ **081-986152;** www.negombo.it), nestled in the island's most picturesque cove, **Lido di San Montano.** Here you can enjoy magnificent gardens, a secluded beach, and elegant thermal pools. South of Forio, on the pretty Bay of Citara, is **Parco Termale Giardini Poseidon** ★★★, Via Giovanni Mazzella Citara, Forio d'Ischia (✆ **081-907122** or 081-907420), an open-air facility with 22 pools (both relaxing and curative), a large private beach, and several restaurants. Finally, to the east of Sant'Angelo, you'll find the **Parco Termale Giardini Aphrodite-Apollon (✆ 081-999219**), an indoor-outdoor facility with lovely grounds and pools that is part of the Park Hotel Miramare (see "Where to Stay," below).

The D.O.C. Wines of Ischia

Ischia's vineyards produce wines that have been increasingly appreciated by connoisseurs; three even earned the D.O.C. label—a government recognition reserved only for those superior wines from specific areas that answer to severe requirements of consistently good quality and characteristics. The winning wines are the red Monte Epomeo, the Ischia (red and white), and the white Biancolella. Wine enthusiasts around the world have to thank the Greeks for this bounty, for it was they who recognized the local potential and planted the varieties of grape still used today to produce the area's wines.

For a more traditional spa experience, we recommend the state-of-the-art **Ischia Thermal Center** ★★, Via delle Terme 15, Ischia (℃ **081-984376;** www.ischiathermalcenter. it), offering a wide range of health and beauty treatments. We also recommend the four historical spas of **Casamicciola Terme**—Terme Manzi, Belliazzi, Elisabetta, and Lucibello—opening onto the famous **Piazza Bagni** in the hamlet of Bagni. For an even more exclusive experience, head to the **Terme della Regina Isabella** ★★ (see "Where to Stay," below), a hotel and thermal resort in **Lacco Ameno.** This is one of the most elegant spas on the island.

WHERE TO STAY
Very Expensive
Hotel Regina Isabella ★★ (Kids) Set in a beautiful location, with views over the village and harbor, this prestigious historic hotel offers fine accommodations, a state-of-the-art thermal spa (above), and a private cove. The public spaces are palatial, with many original furnishings, and the extra amenities will make your stay idyllic. The large guest rooms are decorated with a mix of contemporary and antique, with hand-painted ceramic floors and luxurious bathrooms. Many rooms have private balconies, opening onto views of the sea or the gardens. The hotel's private cove is equipped with floating chairs, suitable for lounging.

Piazza Santa Restituta 1, 80076 Lacco Ameno d'Ischia. ℃ **081-994322.** Fax 081-990190. www.regina isabella.it. 128 units 560€–760€ double; from 980€ suite. Rates include buffet breakfast. Children 2 and under stay free in parent's room. Internet specials available. AE, DC, MC, V. Free parking. Closed Nov–Mar, but open 1 week over the New Year. **Amenities:** 2 restaurants; 2 bars; babysitting; children's programs during school holidays; concierge; pool; room service; spa; tennis courts; Wi-Fi. *In room:* A/C, TV, minibar.

Mezzatorre Resort & Spa ★★ On the promontory of Monte Vico near Lacco Ameno, this is the best hotel on the island. Atop its own rocky point looking straight down to the sea and surrounded by a 3-hectare (7-acre) wooded park, the hotel is built around a 15th-century watchtower that now houses some of the more requested guest rooms (directly connected to the spa by elevator). All guest rooms are spacious and individually decorated in a tasteful mix of Mediterranean and contemporary style, with geometric-design tiled floors, quality furnishings, and warm-colored fabrics. All are equipped with state-of-the-art bathrooms, many with Jacuzzi tubs. Many rooms enjoy private terraces or gardens, and a number of them have splendid sea views. The saltwater pool on a cliffside terrace is fantastic, and guests can walk down a footpath to the rocky beach.

Via Mezzatorre, 80075 Forio d'Ischia. ✆ **081-986111.** Fax 081-986015. www.mezzatorre.it. 60 units. 440€–560€ double; from 700€ suite. Rates include buffet breakfast. Children 1 and under stay free in parent's room. AE, DC, MC, V. Free parking. Closed Nov–Apr. **Amenities:** 2 restaurants; bar; babysitting; concierge; health club; pool; outdoor tennis courts; room service; spa. *In room:* A/C, TV, minibar.

Expensive

Grand Hotel Excelsior ★ With a perfect location in the town of Ischia— convenient to both Ischia Ponte and Ischia Porto—this hotel offers top-notch service and amenities, such as its own private beach. Posh public spaces—a pool with a view, elegant lounges, a spa with a beauty center—are complemented by beautiful guest rooms. The commodious rooms are furnished with great taste and attention to detail and are deco- rated with wrought-iron bedsteads, hand-painted tile floors, and designer-tiled bath- rooms; each room has a private patio-terrace. It is definitely worth paying extra for a room with a view. *Note:* The hotel only offers half-board, which means that breakfast and dinner are included in your nightly rate.

Via E. Gianturco 19, 80077 Ischia. ✆ **081-991522.** Fax 081-984100. www.excelsiorischia.it. 76 units. 360€–470€ double; from 520€ suite. Rates include buffet breakfast and dinner. Children 1 and under stay free in parent's room. AE, DC, MC, V. Closed mid-Oct to mid-Apr. **Amenities:** Restaurant; bar; concierge; health club; pool; room service; spa; Wi-Fi. *In room:* A/C, TV, minibar.

Park Hotel Miramare Old-fashioned in style but not in spirit, this hotel is in the small village of Sant'Angelo. Opened in 1923 and run by the same family ever since, its real strength is the attached spa, **Aphrodite-Apollon** ★, which includes 12 different pools, extensive treatments and fitness programs, and a private beach. A portion of it is reserved only for nudists, one of the only such beach areas on the island. Guest rooms are bright and comfortable, furnished in an old-fashioned seaside style, with wicker and wrought-iron furniture plus antiques and quality reproductions. Bathrooms are modern (some with shower only), and all the rooms open onto private balconies or terraces over- looking the sea. The hotel also has a few rooms in two houses nearby; guests there have access to the hotel's facilities (192€-214€ double).

Via Comandante Magdalena 29, 80070 Sant'Angelo d'Ischia. ✆ **081-999219.** Fax 081-999325. www. hotelmiramare.it. 50 units. 260€–414€ double; from 650€ suite. Rates include buffet breakfast. AE, DC, MC, V. Closed Nov 11–Apr 6. **Amenities:** 2 restaurants; bar; babysitting; children's program; concierge; spa; Wi-Fi. *In room:* A/C, TV, hair dryer, minibar.

Moderate

Floridiana Terme (Finds) This centrally located yet quiet hotel is in the pedestrian area near the harbor. In an elegant former villa surrounded by greenery, it is only a short walk from the sea. Guest rooms are large, bright, and nicely appointed, with quality furnish- ings, colorful tiled floors, and good-size bathrooms. All the rooms open onto their own private balcony or terrace, and some have sea views. *Note:* The hotel only offers half- board, which means that breakfast and dinner are included in your nightly rate.

Corso Vittoria Colonna 153, 80070 Ischia. ✆ **081-991014.** Fax 081-981014. www.hotelfloridianaischia. com. 64 units. 252€–262€ double. Rates include buffet breakfast and dinner. Children 1 and under stay free in parent's room. AE, DC, MC, V. Closed Nov–Mar. **Amenities:** Restaurant; bar; babysitting; concierge; health club; pool; room service; spa. *In room:* A/C, TV, minibar.

Hotel Casa Celestino (Value) We like this unassuming hotel that is built vertically, hugging the cliff above the pedestrian promenade and overlooking the pretty harbor. Guest rooms are large and bright, decorated in modern Mediterranean style, with simple

furnishings, colorful ceramic-tiled floors, and coordinated fabrics in bold, tasteful colors.
Guests appreciate the tiled bathrooms and private terraces (complete with table and chairs), as well as the superb sea views.

Via Chiaia di Rose, 80070 Sant'Angelo d'Ischia. ℂ **081-999213.** Fax 081-999805. www.casacelestino.it. 20 units. 220€ double; 250€ junior suite; 280€ suite. Rates include buffet breakfast. Children 2 and under stay free in parent's room. AE, DC, MC, V. Closed Nov–Mar. **Amenities:** Restaurant; bar; Internet; room service; access to spa. In room: A/C, TV, minibar.

Inexpensive

Albergo Il Monastero ★ (Finds In a former monastery inside Ischia's Aragonese Castle (p. 237), this is the island's most picturesque hotel. The atmosphere is unique, the reception warm and welcoming, and the views are quite superb. Guest rooms are spacious—especially considering they were monk cells—and are decorated with stylish sobriety, from the whitewashed walls and tiled floors to the solid dark wood or wicker furniture. The bathrooms are small but fully tiled, with a tasteful design (some are downright tiny, with space for only showerheads and a drain in the tile below). A few rooms boast small but delightful private terraces, while others open onto a common terrace. Note: The hotel is only accessible on foot.

Castello Aragonese. ℂ **081-992435.** Fax 081-991849. www.albergoilmonastero.it. 13 units. 120€–160€ double. AE, DC, MC, V. Closed Nov–Mar. **Amenities:** Restaurant; concierge. In room: A/C.

WHERE TO DINE

Ischia offers a lively dining scene, especially in the neighborhood of **Ischia Ponte** with its many restaurants and bars, and the exclusive **Via Porto**—called Rive Droite by the locals—lined with elegant nightclubs and restaurants.

Expensive

Melograno ★★ CREATIVE ISCHITAN/SEAFOOD We love this restaurant, tucked away from the main streets of Forio. Elegant and welcoming, it offers delightful outdoor dining in a pleasant garden, and truly interesting and delicious cuisine that has received a Michelin star. Two tasting menus are available, and an a la carte menu—centered on seafood—changes with the market and the whims of the talented chef, Libera Iovine. We highly recommend the *mezzi paccheri al ragù bianco di scoglio* (local pasta with a seafood sauce and shrimp and squid) and the *guazzetto di scorfano di fondale con crema di patate* (a moist fish with black olives, capers, and a potato puree). Do not miss the local cheese selection and the creatively delicious desserts.

Via G. Mazzella 110, Forio. ℂ **081-998450.** www.ilmelogranoischia.it. Reservations recommended. Secondi 22€–35€; prix-fixe menus 60€ and 75€. AE, DC, MC, V. Nov–Jan Tues–Wed 7:30–11pm, Thurs–Sun noon–3:30pm and 7:30–11pm; Mar–Sept Mon noon–3:30pm, Tues–Sun noon–3:30pm and 7:30–11pm; Oct Tues–Sun noon–3:30pm and 7:30–11pm. Closed Jan 7–Mar 15.

Umberto a Mare ★★ CAMPANIAN/SEAFOOD This historic restaurant that has been drawing diners for decades is still going strong. The beautiful terrace—which affords a matchless panorama and is so romantic at sunset—combines with the gourmet cuisine for a perfect dinner. The menu is large and changes daily with the market offerings, with a strong focus on seafood. From the copious choices of *antipasti* we loved the *insalatina di mare* (seafood salad) and the *tartare di palamito al profumo d'arancia* (tartar of local fish with citrus). We recommend you follow it with the delicious *pennette* *all'aragosta e agli asparagi* (short penne with lobster and asparagus) or with the catch of the day, which varies in preparation from classic grilled or *all'acqua pazza* (in a light herb broth), to the more imaginative.

Via Soccorso 2, Forio. © **081-997171**. www.umbertoamare.it. Reservations recommended. Secondi 25€–36€; prix-fixe menus 60€ and 70€. AE, DC, MC, V. Mon–Thurs 7:30–11pm; Fri–Sun noon–3:30pm and 7:30–11pm. Closed Jan–Mar.

Moderate

Alberto ★ ISCHITANO/SEAFOOD   This traditional restaurant, with a veranda right on the beach promenade between the harbor and the Aragonese Castle (p. 237), is an excellent spot for sampling this coast's freshest seafood. The menu is small and focuses on local specialties as interpreted by the chef. We highly recommend the *marinata mista* appetizer, a medley of fish marinated in a tangy and delicate citrus sauce, to be followed by the superb *linguine alle vongole* (with clams) and the delicious *pesce all'Alberto*, oven-baked fish with potatoes, olives, and capers. The wine list offers an ample choice of local wines.

Via Cristoforo Colombo, Ischia Porto. © **081-981259**. www.albertoischia.it. Reservations recommended. Secondi 22€–35€; tasting menu 65€. AE, DC, MC, V. Daily noon–3pm and 7–11pm. Closed Nov–Mar except 1 week over the New Year.

Damiano ★ ISCHITANO/SEAFOOD   A favorite among locals and visitors who love to come for a romantic dinner, this restaurant is in the outskirts of town, on the steep slope of the mountain. It offers equally tantalizing views and food, with a menu centered on seafood. The dishes change with the market, but we recommend the *linguine con le cozze* (with mussels) and the superb grilled catch of the day. Do absolutely leave room for the fantastic homemade desserts.

Via delle Vigne 30 (in the upper part of town), Ischia Porto. © **081-983032**. Reservations recommended. Secondi 15€–28€. DC, MC, V. Daily 8–11pm. Apr–June and Sept–Oct also Sat–Sun 1–3pm and 8–11pm. Closed Nov–Mar.

Trattoria da Peppina ★ (Finds ISCHITANO/PIZZA   Popular among locals in the off-season, this restaurant is a great choice for traditional Ischitan food, with a menu featuring local vegetable and meat dishes. We recommend starting with the tasty *bruschette* (slice of grilled peasant bread) seasoned with a choice of beans, smoked sausage, and mushrooms, followed by *ravioloni in salsa di noce* (in walnut sauce). The *grigliata di carne alla brace* (mix of grilled meats) is superb, as is the *coniglio all'Ischitana* (rabbit cooked with tomatoes and herbs in a terra-cotta casserole).

Via Montecorvo 42, Forio. © **081-998312**. www.trattoriadapeppina.it. Reservations recommended. Secondi 11€–20€. AE, DC, MC, V. Mar–May and Oct–Dec Thurs–Tues 7pm–midnight; June and Sept daily 7pm–midnight; July–Aug Mon–Sat 7pm–midnight, Sun noon–3:30pm and 7pm–midnight.

Inexpensive

Pirozzi ★ (Kids ISCHITAN/PIZZA/SEAFOOD   Conveniently located on the main promenade to the Aragonese Castle (p. 237), this pleasant restaurant offers a nice veranda with sea views and no-nonsense local cuisine at moderate prices. The excellent pizza, offered only in the evening, is popular with children (but is so good you might want it too). Among the more elaborate offerings on the menu, the *risotto alla pescatora* (seafood) and the tasty grilled fish are top notch.

Via Seminario 51, Ischia Ponte. © **081-983217**. Reservations recommended for dinner. Secondi 7€–14€. AE, DC, MC, V. Daily noon–3pm and 7pm–midnight. Closed Wed Nov–Mar.

Trattoria il Focolare ★ (Finds) CAMPANIAN   This restaurant offers a welcome **245** break from the fare at other restaurants along this coast, with a focus on the turf rather than the surf. The hearty seasonal menu offers masterfully prepared dishes from the local tradition, such as the excellent *tagliata* (steak) or the *tagliatelle al ragu di cinghiale* (with wild boar ragout). We highly recommend the *coniglio all'Ischitana* (a local rabbit dish), which is a specialty of the chef, but you need to reserve it in advance. The desserts are also good, including Neapolitan favorites such as *pastiera* (pie filled with ricotta and orange peels).

Via Cretajo al Crocefisso 3, Barano d'Ischia. (€) **081-902944.** www.trattoriailfocolare.it. Reservations recommended. Secondi 8€–15€. AE, MC, V. Mon–Tues and Thurs 7:30–11:30pm; Fri–Sun 12:30–3pm and 7:30–11:30pm.

Zelluso ★ (Finds) (Kids) ISCHITANPIZZA/SEAFOOD   Hidden away from the marina on a back street, this is a good place to partake of some local culture. Popular with locals and tourists alike, it is often crowded, and you'll have to factor in a wait, even if you made reservations. The pizza, offered only in the evening, is one of the best you'll ever have and is a great favorite among children. Of the traditional seafood offerings, we recommend the well-prepared *sautee di cozze* (sautéed mussels) followed by the *linguine alle vongole* (with clams), and *fritto misto* (medley of deep fried squid and small fish).

Via Parodi 41, Casamicciola Terme. (€) **081-994423.** Reservations recommended for dinner. Secondi 10€–14€. AE, DC, MC, V. Summer daily noon–3pm and 7pm–midnight; winter closed 1 day per week (day varies, so call ahead).

ISCHIA AFTER DARK

The sweet Ischitan nights are best spent outdoors, enjoying a bit of people-watching from the terraces of the many cafes strategically located on the most picturesque seaside promenades and panoramic outlooks. The elegant cafes around the harbor in Ischia are perfect for *aperitivo,* but we also like the unassuming **Da Lilly,** a shack on the rocks, with a simple terrace overlooking the **Spiaggia dei Pescatori** (p. 240) in Ischia Ponte. **La Floreana** ((€) **081-999570**), at the belvedere of Serrara Fontana, is perfect for a sunset *aperitivo* (there is also a simple restaurant). Other pleasant cafes line the seaside promenade of Forio and Lacco Ameno; we enjoy **Bar Franco,** Via Roma 94, Lacco Ameno ((€) **081-980880**), where you can sit at the pleasant outdoor terrace facing the beach or simply sample their excellent ice cream. We are rather partial to ice cream and highly recommend those made at **De Maio,** Piazza Antica Reggia 9, Ischia Porto ((€) **081-991870**), the best ice-cream parlor on the island; claiming 80 years of experience, the shop makes wonderful creamy flavors. A few doors away is **Da Ciccio,** Via Porto 1, Ischia Porto (no phone), which makes more creative flavors by adding in nuts, chocolate bits, and so on.

We recommend the **concerts**—including classical and jazz—organized by the William Walton Foundation in the lovely gardens of **Villa La Mortella,** Via F. Calise no. 35, 80075 Forio Isola d'Ischia ((€) **081-986220;** www.lamortella.it). The season runs from April to November; concert tickets include admission to the garden and are 15€ for adults and 12€ for children 8 to 12. If you are lucky enough to be on the island for the **Ischia Jazz Festival** (www.ischiajazz.eu) in September, make advance reservations for the scheduled concerts, which usually include some famous international names.

2 ROMANTIC & UNSPOILED PROCIDA ★★

32km (20 miles) NW of Naples; 12km (8 miles) W of Pozzuoli; 7.8km (5 miles) W of Ischia

Small and exclusive Procida is an island where the most fortunate VIPs have their hideaway villas overlooking one of the most beautiful bays in the world. Not well-known to foreigners, Procida is popular among local tourists, who often come just for the day or for dinner.

Procida's landscape is dotted with pretty houses in tones of pink and yellow, contrasting with the green of citrus groves and gardens. Beyond the private residences, you'll find beaches and restaurants catering to various levels of taste and budget. And you won't find yourself competing with the kinds of crowds that can envelop Capri.

ESSENTIALS

GETTING THERE & AROUND   Procida is easily reached from Pozzuoli and Naples: **Medmar** (✆ 081-3334411; www.medmargroup.it), **Caremar** (✆ 081-5513882; www.caremar.it), and **SNAV** (✆ 081-4285555 or 081-4285500; www.snav.it) offer ferry and hydrofoil service from Napoli, Pozzuoli, and Ischia.

Given Procida's diminutive size (see "Exploring Procida," below), the best way to see the island is definitely **on foot**, or by **bicycle** (which you can rent at most hotels)—although cars are plentiful, and traffic jams are a regular occurrence, especially in summer. You can also take one of the four **public bus** lines run by **SEPSA** (✆ 081-5429965). All of the buses start from Marina Grande; tickets are 1€ per ride. **Taxi stands** are at each of the three marinas and at the ferry terminal; or you can call one for pickup (✆ 081-8968785).

VISITOR INFORMATION   The **AACST** (✆ 081-8101968; www.infoischiaprocida.it) maintains a small **tourist office** on Via Marina Grande near the ferry dock. It is open May to September, Monday to Saturday from 9:30am to 1pm and 3:30 to 6pm; the rest of the year it's only open mornings. Additional information is available from **Proloco**, Via Vittorio Emanuele 173 (✆ 081-8109628; www.procida.net). The nearby travel agency **Graziella,** Via Roma 117 (✆ 081-8969191; www.isoladiprocida.it), is another good resource for help with hotel reservations and boat rentals.

FAST FACTS   You'll find a **pharmacy** (✆ 081-8968101) on Piazza dei Martiri 1, Madonna delle Grazie. The nearest **hospital** is in Ischia (see "Fast Facts," p. 236); the **First Aid** medical center (✆ 081-8969660) is at Via Vittorio Emanuele 191; to call an **ambulance** dial ✆ 118. The **police** can be reached at ✆ 113 or 112. For the main **post office** (✆ 081-8967001; Mon–Sat 8am–2pm) visit Via Liberta. Banks with **ATMs** include the **Banco di Napoli** (✆ 081-8967035) at Via Vittorio Emanuele 158.

EXPLORING PROCIDA

The island is basically one whole village, interspersed with citrus groves and gardens and the occasional vineyard, developing northeast–southwest along one main street. The distance from Marina Grande—with the ferry terminal—on the northeastern tip of the island to Marina di Chiaiolella, all the way to the opposite end, is only about 3km (1¾ miles). Several side streets radiate from this main artery. Jutting from the southwestern tip, a bridge connects Procida to the little island of Vivara.

Marina Grande, or Marina di Sancio Cattolico, is the major harbor of the island, and the location of the ferry terminal. A few steps away, along the main street, **Via Principe Umberto,** is **Piazza dei Martiri,** the village's main square. From it you can climb to **Torre Murata,** the highest point of the island, fortified by 16th-century walls. This is where Procida's rulers had their residences, and where you can enjoy some of the most magnificent views of the island and its surroundings. As you climb, you will find a **belvedere** ★ affording good views of the Marina della Corricella; farther up beyond the Piazza d'Armi, you enter the **medieval citadel** of **Terra Casata** ★★ and its belvedere, with a magnificent view over the Gulf of Naples. On the square is the island's main church, **San Michele Arcangelo,** originally from the 11th century but redone in later times.

From Piazza dei Martiri, it is a short walk to **Marina della Corricella** ★★, a picturesque and charming fishing harbor originally established in the 17th century. Its colorful houses and narrow streets surround the small port.

If you continue toward the southwestern tip of the island, you should not miss the detour to the left for **Punta Pizzaco** ★★★, from where you can enjoy one of the best views on the whole island.

Farther on, you'll finally reach **Marina di Chiaiolella** ★★ at the southwestern tip of the island. This crescent-shaped harbor was once the crater of a volcano and now is a pleasant marina, lined with little restaurants and bars. The harbor is dominated by the mountainous, tiny island of **Vivara,** today a wildlife refuge run by the World Wildlife Federation connected to Procida by a bridge—the world's longest Tibetan-style foot bridge, measuring 362m (1,188 ft.).

We also highly recommend signing up for a **boat excursion** ★★ around the island. You can rent a boat, with or without driver, from any of the three harbors on the island: Marina Grande, Marina della Corricella, and Marina di Chiaiolella. You'll spend about 25€ for a 2-hour trip with a boat and driver.

WHERE TO STAY

In addition to the hotels reviewed below, we also recommend staying at **Crescenzo** (see "Where to Dine," below).

Moderate

La Casa sul Mare (Finds)   Housed in a typical 18th-century building at the foot of Terra Murata (the historic *borgo* or village of Procida), this small hotel offers high-quality accommodations with beautiful views over the Marina della Corricella. The elegant guest rooms are furnished with taste, with beautiful tiled floors, wrought-iron bed frames, and good-size bathrooms. Each opens onto its own private terrace with a beautiful view over the sea.

Salita Castello 13. ℰ/fax **081-8968799.** www.lacasasulmare.it. 10 units. 170€ double. Rate includes buffet breakfast. Children 1 and under stay free in parent's room. AE, DC, MC, V. **Amenities:** Bar; bike rental; concierge; Internet. *In room:* A/C, TV, minibar.

Inexpensive

Hotel Celeste   This pleasant, family-run hotel near the Marina di Chiaiolella is a traditional structure where guest rooms open onto the outdoors. Some have private terraces, but others open onto the veranda, the inner courtyard, or the terrace/garden. All are simply furnished with tiled floors and small outdoor spaces with a table and chairs. The service is warm and welcoming; Signora Concetta and her family give you individual attention. The view from the terraces and the solarium is nice. *Note:* In August, all guests must pay an additional 20€ half-board fee, which entitles you to lunch or dinner. Continental breakfast is included in all rates, and pets are welcome.

Via Rivoli 6, 80079 Procida. ℂ **081-8967488.** Fax 081-8967670. www.hotelceleste.it. 34 units. 130€ double; 170€ triple; 200€ quad. Rates include buffet breakfast. In Aug half-board (20€/person) mandatory. AE, DC, MC, V. Closed Oct–Mar. **Amenities:** Restaurant; bar; bike rental. *In room:* A/C, TV, minibar (in some).

WHERE TO DINE
Moderate

La Conchiglia ★ Kids ISCHITANO   Somewhat more formal in atmosphere and more elegant in decor than Caracalè (below), this is a good restaurant in the classic mold, near the beach in Chiaia. It serves dishes prepared according to tradition and seasonal seafood choices. Our favorites are the *linguine all'aragosta* (with local lobster) and the *spiedini di mazzancolle* (prawn skewers), but we also recommend the grilled catches of the day.

Via Pizzaco, Discesa Chiaia. ℂ **081-8967602.** Reservations recommended. Secondi 12€–23€. AE, DC, MC, V. Daily 12:30–3pm and 7:30–11pm. Closed Nov–Mar.

Lo Scarabeo ★ ISCHITANO   This excellent restaurant in the heart of town offers a pleasant atmosphere, particularly if you sit under the delightful lemon arbor in good weather. The menu is seasonal and changes with market offerings, but has a bent toward seafood. We recommend the *spaghetti alle vongole* (with clams) followed by *totani ripieni* (stuffed squid), should they be available when you visit, and, of course, the *insalata di limoni* (seasoned lemons), a local specialty.

Via Salette 10. ℂ **081-8969918.** Reservations recommended. Secondi 10€–18€. AE, DC, MC, V. Tues–Sun 1–3pm and 7:30–11pm. Closed Nov–Dec 20.

Inexpensive

Caracalè ISCHITANO   This picturesque restaurant offers traditional cuisine and a lively atmosphere. The food is well prepared and gratifying and includes many local specialties, most focusing on seafood, but vegetarian and meat choices are also available. We loved the *risotto ai frutti di mare* (with seafood) and the catch of the day, *all'acqua pazza*.

Via Marina Corricella 62. ℂ **081-8969191.** Reservations recommended. Secondi 7€–12€. AE, DC, MC, V. Daily noon–3pm and 7–11pm.

Ristorante Lido di Vivara ★ Kids ISCHITANO   This popular restaurant is by the beach, meaning you can sit down for a meal after enjoying a swim, or let your children run around after the meal. Overlooking the bay, it is moderate in price offering a small menu that changes daily, always focusing on seafood. Specialties include *spaghetti con le cozze* (with mussels) and *polipo in cassuola* (stewed octopus).

Via Cristoforo Colombo 12, Chiaiolella Beach. ℂ **081-8967143.** Reservations recommended. Secondi 6€–15€. AE, MC, V. Daily 12:30–2:30pm and 7:30–10:30pm. Closed Nov–Apr.

3 CAPRI, THE FARAGLIONI & THE BLUE GROTTO ★★★

33km (21 miles) SW of Naples

Italy's most famous island, Capri (pronounced *cap*-ry, not ca-*pree*) is a dramatic rugged mountain soaring out of the sea at the tip of the Sorrento peninsula. A haunt for eccentric characters since antiquity (Roman emperor Tiberius had his villa of pleasures, the

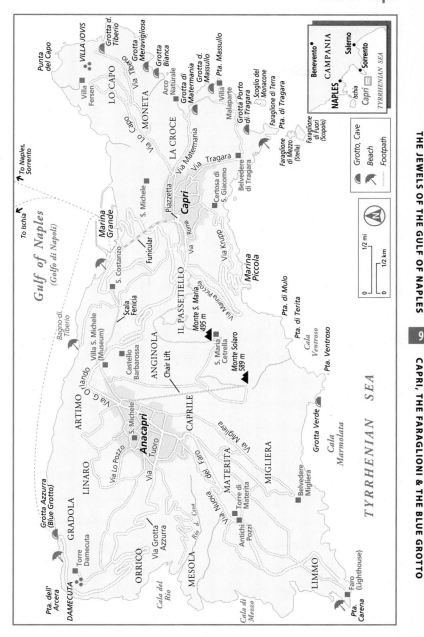

Punta del Capo

VILLA JOVIS

Grotta d. Tiberio

Grotta Meravigliosa

VILLA Villa Fersen

LO CAPO

Grotta Bianca

Via Tiberio

MONETA

Arco Naturale

Grotta di Matermania

Grotta d. Massullo

Pta. Massullo

Via Lo Capo

LA CROCE

Villa Malaparte

Scoglio del Monacone

Grotta Porto di Tragara

Faraglione di Terra

Faraglione di Tragara

Via Matermania

Via Tragara

Faraglione di Mezzo (Stella)

Faraglione di Fuori (Scopolo)

To Naples, Sorrento

Gulf of Naples
(Golfo di Napoli)

To Ischia

Marina Grande

S. Michele

Piazzetta

Capri

Certosa di S. Giacomo

Belvedere di Tragara

S. Costanzo

Funicular

Via Roma

Via Krupp

Bagno di Tiberio

Scala Fenicia

IL PASSETIELLO

Monte S. Maria 495 m

Marina Piccola

Pta. di Mulo

Villa S. Michele (Museum)

Castello Barbarossa

ANGINOLA

Chair Lift

S. Maria Cetrella

Monte Solaro 589 m

Pta. di Terita

Cala Ventroso

Pta. Ventroso

ARTIMO

Via G. O...lando

CAPRILE

S. Michele

Anacapri

Via Tuoro

Via Migliera

Grotta Verde

Cala Marmolata

LINARO

Via Lo Pozzo

MATERITA

MIGLIERA

Belvedere Migliera

Grotta Azzurra (Blue Grotto)

GRADOLA

Via Nuova

Torre di Materita

Antichi Pozzi

Rio d. Casa

DAMECUTA

Pta. dell' Arcera

Torre Damecuta

Via Grotta Azzurra

ORRICO

MESOLA

Cala del Rio

LIMMO

Faro (Lighthouse)

Cala di Mezzo

Pta. Carena

TYRRHENIAN SEA

Grotto, Cave
Beach
Footpath

Benevento

NAPLES

Ischia

Capri

CAMPANIA

Salerno

Sorrento

TYRRHENIAN SEA

0   1/2 mi
0   1/2 km

Villa Jovis, here), Capri has been a favorite retreat of artists, movie stars, and other VIPs in modern times. The island is indeed spectacular, with postcard-worthy soaring cliffs, surrounded by a deep-blue sea. Besides being a choice resort for VIPs and wannabes, it is also a popular gay destination. Positively overcrowded with day visitors during the summer and early fall, Capri gives its best if you stay overnight. You can come in the off-season—Christmastime is popular with Italians—but you will find many businesses shuttered. Even then, don't expect seclusion; Capri is a very busy place.

ESSENTIALS

GETTING THERE   Just as all roads lead to Rome, ferries (*aliscafo* [hydrofoil] or *moto-nave* [motorboat]) leave for Capri from almost every harbor in Campania. Prices range from 9€ to 15€ (by regular ferry) or 15€ to 18€ (by hydrofoil) depending on the season and distance. **Caremar** (✆ 081-5513882; www.caremar.it) runs ferries to Capri from Naples and from Sorrento. **NLG-Navigazione Libera del Golfo** (✆ 081-5527209; www.navlib.it) runs to Capri from Naples, Sorrento, and Castellammare di Stabia. **Alicost** (✆ 089/234-892; www.lauroweb.com/alicost.htm) and **Alilauro** (✆ 081-4972238; www.alilauro.it) connect Capri to Salerno, Positano, Amalfi, and Ischia. **SNAV** (✆ 081-4285555 or 081-4285500; www.snav.it) runs hydrofoils and catamarans to Capri from Mergellina and Naples (Molo Beverello). **Travelmar** (✆ 081-7041911; www.travelmar.it) maintains regular service from Salerno. **LMP** (✆ 081-5513236; www.consorziolmp.it) has regular hydrofoil and boat service from Positano and Sorrento. **Volaviamare** (✆ 081-4972211; www.volaviamare.it) has fast boats between Naples, Sorrento, Amalfi, Positano, Salerno, Ischia, and Capri. During the summer, **Metrò del Mare** (✆ 199-446644; www.metrodelmare.com) makes daily runs to Capri; Amalfi-based **Cooperativa Sant'Andrea** (✆ 089-873190; www.coopsantandrea.it) offers scheduled service from Amalfi, Capri, Minori, Salerno, and Sorrento; Positano-based **Lucibello** (✆ 089-975032 or 089-811164; www.lucibello.it) makes runs to and from Capri. **Blue Cruises** (✆ 081-4972222; www.blucruises.it) and **Capitan Morgan** (✆ 081-985080; www.capitanmorgan.it) offer minicruises to Capri from Ischia. Not cheap but convenient, **Taxi del Mare** (✆ 081-8773600; www.taxidelmare.it) plies the waters within the Naples and Salerno bays (about 600€ from Naples to Capri). From the harbor, you can take a **taxi** or the **funicular** up to town (see "Getting Around," below). *Note:* You'll do best to hire a **porter** *(facchino)* for the climb from the ferry landing to your hotel; the flat rate of 10€ per piece of luggage is well worth it. The service is perfectly trustworthy, so just leave your luggage and head to your hotel. If you like, you can save money by lugging your bags to the funicular or taxi and up into town, where the porters charge only 4€ per piece to the hotels not accessible by car.

GETTING AROUND   Capri gets its name from the ancient Greek *kapriae,* meaning "island of the wild goats." Indeed, only goats can tread these steep slopes and cliffs with ease. Today modern roads—including a short stretch of "highway"—allow for easy transfers, but the price to pay is traffic and congestion, especially in summer. The island is large—the ancient footpaths and trails are walkable, provided you are as fit as a goat—but most of us rely on public transportation. *Note:* Even when using public transportation, you'll still want to wear comfortable shoes. The *funicolare* (funicular), run by **SIPPIC** (✆ 081-8370420), is the picturesque means of transportation between the harbor of Marina Grande—where the ferry and hydrofoil landings are—and the town of Capri, where it arrives in the heart of town, off Piazza Umberto I. Funiculars leave about every 15 minutes for the 5-minute ride, and you need to purchase tickets in advance at

South Winds

A visit to Capri is a perfect occasion to read Scottish writer Norman Douglas's witty novel *South Wind* (1917), part homage to the island and part satire on its eclectic (and even mad) inhabitants.

the ticket booth by the ferry landing. **Taxis** wait by the harbors and at the main **stands:** Piazza Martiri d'Ungheria, in **Capri** ((C) **081-8370543**), and Piazza Vittoria, in **Anacapri** ((C) **081-8371175**). The minimum rate is 8€, and there are flat rates for a few destinations: 15€ between the harbor at Marina Grande and Capri town; 16€ between Capri and Anacapri; 20€ between the harbor at Marina Grande and Anacapri. The well-run public **bus** system is great but quite crowded in the summer, and destines you for a hair-raising ride along the narrow cliff roads that crisscross the island. **ATC** (part of SIPPIC, above) offers service between Marina Grande, Capri, Marina Piccola, and Anacapri, while **Staiano Autotrasporti** ((C) **081-8372422;** www.staianogroup.it) offers service between Anacapri, Faro (Lighthouse), and Grotta Azzurra. Tickets cost 1.40€ for either the bus or funicular. You can also get a 60-minute ticket for 2.20€, valid for one funicular run and unlimited bus runs during the time limit, or a day pass for 6.90€, valid for two funicular rides and unlimited bus service. You can also rent scooters: The most environmentally friendly is **Rent an Electric Scooter,** Via Roma 68 ((C) **081-8375863**), but there are others, such as **Antonio Alfano,** with two locations: Via Marina Grande 280 ((C) **081-8377941**) and Piazza Barile 26, Anacapri ((C) **081-8373888**). Boat rental, with or without driver, is readily available at the **Marina Grande beach** from **Banana Sport** ((C) **081-8375188**) and **Leomar** ((C) **081-8377181**); at **Marina Piccola** from **Rent a Boat** ((C) **081-8370355**); and from **Sercomar,** Via Cristoforo Colombo 64, Capri ((C) **081-8378781;** www.caprisub.com).

VISITOR INFORMATION   The **AACST** ((C) **081-8375308** or 081-8370424; fax 081-8370918; www.capritourism.com) is at Piazzetta Italo Cerio 11.

FAST FACTS   You'll find several **pharmacies,** including one at Via Roma 45 ((C) **081-8370485**). The **hospital** ((C) **081-8381205**) is at Via Provinciale Anacapri 5; to call an **ambulance** dial (C) **118.** You can call the **police** at (C) **113** or 112. The main **post office** ((C) **081-9785211;** Mon–Sat 8am–2pm) is at Via Roma 50. Several banks have **ATMs,** such as **Banco di Napoli,** Via Vittorio Emanuele 37, Capri ((C) **081-8374311**), as well as its other locations at Via G. Orlandi 150, Anacapri ((C) **081-8382169**) and Via Cristoforo Colombo 78, Marina Grande ((C) **081-8374526**).

GUIDED TOURS   **Capri Time Tours** (www.capritime.com), founded by American ex-pat Rebecca Brooks, offers a variety of tours and classes, both on Capri and the mainland. Two companies offer regularly scheduled cruises: **Gruppo Motoscafisti** ((C) 081-8377714; www.motoscaficapri.com) and **Laser Capri** ((C) **081/8375208**), both departing from Marina Grande. We recommend the cruise around the island, which costs 13€ and 10€ respectively. They also offer a Blue Grotto cruise for 11€ and 10€—which does not include admission or rowboat fees (p. 253)—among other choices.

EXPLORING THE ISLAND

Tourists usually pass through **Marina Grande,** the largest harbor on the island, on their way from the ferry to town and pay little attention to the unassuming hamlet. It is worth exploring though, as it shelters the island's oldest church, **San Costanzo** ★. Dating back to the 5th century, it was enlarged in the 14th century, when its orientation was turned 90 degrees so that the original apse can still be discerned in the right nave. A bit farther to the west are the ruins of the **Palazzo a Mare,** one of the several ancient Roman palaces scattered around the island.

Up the steep slope is the town of **Capri** ★★★, the island's heart. With its narrow streets hiding shops, hotels—many of them among the coast's most glamorous—and a wide variety of restaurants and clubs, this is the island's most picturesque destination. Social life radiates from the famous **Piazzetta** (Piazza Umberto I), a favorite spot for seeing and being seen. We highly recommend a walk through the narrow streets of the old town. Start from the Piazzetta, graced by the 14th-century **Palazzo Cerio,** the best medieval building remaining on the island. It houses the **Museo Ignazio Cerio** (© 081-8376681; admission 2.60€), which has exhibits depicting the island's natural history. Take Via Vittorio Emanuele, the town's main street, past the famous **Grand Quisisana Hotel** (p. 255), which was built in the 19th century as a sanatorium. Make a right on Via Ignazio Cerio, which leads to the **Certosa di San Giacomo** ★ (© 081-8376218; free admission; Tues–Sun 9am–2pm), a religious complex—built in the 14th century and later enlarged—that includes a church, a cloister, and a garden with a belvedere affording great views. Nearby are the **Giardini di Augusto** ★★, the terraced public gardens affording some of the best **scenic vistas** in Capri.

From the town of Capri, you can walk to the ruins of **Villa Jovis** ★★ (Viale Amedeo Maiuri), about 2.4km (1½ miles) from the center of Capri on the northeastern tip of the island. Admission is 2€; it is open daily 9am to sunset. The ticket booth closes 1 hr. before sunset. This is the best preserved of the 12 villas built on the island by various ancient Roman emperors. Augustus laid claim to a few of them, but the depraved Tiberius had one built for each of the most important gods of the Roman pantheon. Villa Jovis is the one dedicated to Jupiter and, here, as in his other abodes on the island, Tiberius pursued illicit pleasures away from the prying eyes of the Roman Senate. This was his main residence on the island, and it covered over 5,853 sq. m (63,001 sq. ft.). Its architectural marvels include the **Loggia Imperiale,** a covered promenade on the edge of the cliff. The views from the villa are, to put it mildly, fit for an emperor of even the most jaded tastes.

From Capri, you can also walk (or take a bus or taxi) to the small harbor of **Marina Piccola** ★★ on the southern shore. This is especially popular for its vantage point, from which you can admire the famous **Faraglioni** ★★★, a collection of spiky, rocky structures that jut out of the sea a short distance from the coast. Gracing most of Capri's picturesque views, they are indeed very impressive.

Linked to Capri through the famous **Scala Fenicia** (see "Staying Active," below), the other town on the island is **Anacapri** ★★, perched on the higher part of the island, and set among hills and vineyards. The **Church of San Michele** is worth a visit for its beautiful **majolica floor** ★. A short distance out of town is **Villa San Michele** ★ (© 081-8371401; www.sanmichele.org). The Swedish doctor and writer Axel Munthe had this built as his home in the 19th century, adapting the ruins of an ancient Roman villa. The gardens are also well worth the visit, if anything, just to enjoy the matchless views from the terrace (admission 5€; Jan–Feb 9am–3:30pm, Mar 9am–4:30pm, Apr 9am–5pm, May–Sept 9am–6pm, Oct 9am–5pm, Nov–Dec 9am–3:30pm).

A great excursion from Anacapri is the ascent up **Monte Solaro** ★★★, Capri's highest peak, rising to an altitude of 589m (1,932 ft.). **Seggiovia Monte Solaro** (© 081-8371428) is a chairlift that departs from Via Caposcuro 10 for the 12-minute trip, and the panorama from the top is worth hours of travel. On a clear day, the matchless views encompass the whole stretch of coast and sea, including Mount Vesuvius and the gulfs of Naples and Salerno. Tickets cost 6€ one-way, 8€ round-trip, free for children 8 and under; hours of operation are March through October 9:30am to sunset, and November through February 10:30am to 3pm.

North of Anacapri (a 50-min. walk or a short ride away) is the island's most famous attraction, the **Grotta Azzurra (Blue Grotto)** ★★. The magical colors of the water and walls of this huge grotto are indeed extraordinary, and writers have rhapsodized about it at length since its so-called discovery by foreign tourists in the 19th century. In fact, the grotto has been charted since antiquity: On its southwestern corner, the Galleria dei Pilastri displays the remains of a small, ancient Roman dock. The grotto is part of what appears to be a vast system of caverns that is only partially explored. Unfortunately, you'll have no chance to explore on your own, especially if you come at the height of the season. During this period, motorboats line up outside the grotto, waiting for the small row-boats—the only vessels allowed inside—to squeeze a few passengers at a time under the grotto's narrow opening (because of rising sea levels the aperture now extends only about

9

Impressions

The creaking and puffing little boat, which had conveyed me only from Sorrento, drew closer beneath the prodigious island—beautiful, horrible and haunted—that does most, of all the happy elements and accidents, towards making the Bay of Naples, for the study of composition, a lesson in the grand style.

—Henry James, *Italian Hours,* 1909

.9m/3 ft. above sea level, and you'll have to lie back in the boat). Because of the long lines, you'll be allowed inside the grotto only for a few minutes. Kids will love the adventure, which conjures up visions of secret expeditions, but adults might find the whole experience wearisome.

The grotto is open daily 9am to 1 hour before sunset; admission is 4€, plus 6.50€ for the rowboat fee. Rowboats depart from the beach at the bottom of the footpath (the trail head is on the main road by the bus stop). The alternative is to sign up for a cruise from Marina Grande (see "Guided Tours," above), but we do not particularly recommend this option, as you'll have to factor in even longer waits and negotiate the switch from the large motorboat to the rowboat—in the open sea, this can be quite tricky, particularly when the waters are not perfectly calm. (It is also the least eco-friendly option.)

STAYING ACTIVE

Capri's marvelous waters afford great swimming, which you can easily do from one of the small but picturesque local **beaches.** Most are organized by paying beach clubs *(stabilimenti balneari),* which will provide you with a changing cabin, towels, and a deck chair for about 15€ per day; they are usually open mid-March to mid-November, 9am to sunset. **Bagni di Tiberio** ★ is a nice, sandy beach on the north side of the island, near the ruins of a Roman villa. The beach is only about 1km (a half-mile) from Marina Grande, but getting there involves a steep and rocky descent that can be arduous on the return leg. We recommend going by boat instead—you can get passage there and back for 6€ from Marina Grande.

You'll find two more nice beaches in Marina Piccola, on the southern side of the island. To the east of the village is **Marina di Pennaulo,** and to the west is **Marina di Mulo;** both were a favorite haunt of the 1950s and 1960s jet set. The only **other beaches** on the island are a small one by the Blue Grotto (Via Grotta Azzurra), one by the Faro (lighthouse), and one by the Faraglioni (Via Tragara).

We also recommend a **boat tour of the island** ★★★. You can hire a private boat, with or without a mariner, from both Marina Grande and Marina Piccola (see "Getting Around," p. 250), or board a tour.

Even if you are only moderately fit, do not miss the opportunity to **hike** Capri's cliffs and soak in the beauty of its trails—a great escape from the swarming crowds. Before setting out, stop at the tourist office (see "Visitor Information," above), which has a map of the paths. One of the easiest treks is the short trail from **Capri to Marina Piccola** ★. From Via Roma in town, turn left onto Via Mulo; a series of steps and a dirt path will lead you down to the harbor through cultivated fields and gardens.

A more demanding hike is the *Scala Fenicia* (Fenician Staircase) ★★, which descends—or climbs, for the most intrepid—from **Anacapri to Capri.** Built by the

Greeks in the 8th century B.C., it was the only access to the sea or to the village of Anacapri until 1877, when the current road was built. The steep path—basically a long
staircase with 881 steps—rewards the daring with superb views. Another hike we recommend is the descent from **Mount Solaro** ★★ (p. 252), on a clearly marked dirt path
(after taking the chairlift to the top).

WHERE TO STAY

As a rule of thumb, accommodations in Anacapri tend to be cheaper than those in
glitzier Capri town. However, if you want to enjoy the nightlife, you'll end up taking cabs
from Capri, which can diminish your overall savings.

Very Expensive

Grand Hotel Quisisana ★★★ This luxury hotel offers splendid accommodations
and top-notch service. More old-fashioned than the island's other top hotel, the stylish
Capri Palace, in Anacapri, it is right in the heart of the action, yet well insulated from
the hubbub. Built in the 19th century as an exclusive sanatorium (the name *qui si sana*
means "here we heal"), it quickly changed into a hotel catering to those in need of pampering. Guest rooms are big and bright, opening onto wide arcades, and decorated with
stylish period furniture. The large bathrooms are outfitted in marble or with designer
tiles. Most of the rooms overlook the garden and pool—a few have views of the town—
but only the more expensive suites claim the superb views you can otherwise enjoy from
the hotel terraces. Even if you don't stay here, come for a drink at one of the elegant bars
on the premises. We also recommend the hotel's restaurants, particularly the elegant
Quisi ★★, perfect for a gourmet candlelight dinner (tasting menu 110€; secondi
36€-42€; daily 7:30-11pm).

Via Camerelle 2, 80073 Capri. ✆ **081-8370788.** Fax 081-8376080. www.quisisana.com. 148 units.
320€-550€ double; from 800€ suite. Rates include buffet breakfast. Children 3 and under stay free in
parent's room. AE, DC, MC, V. Closed Nov–Easter. **Amenities:** 3 restaurants; 3 bars; babysitting; concierge;
health club; pool; room service; spa; outdoor tennis courts. *In room:* A/C, TV, minibar.

Expensive

Hotel Punta Tragara ★★ Standing high on a cliff overlooking one of the best
panoramas in Capri, this hotel is in a quiet location slightly away from the heart of things
in Capri. Originally a luxurious private villa, it was designed by one of the greatest architects of the 20th century, Le Corbusier. Guest rooms have large windows and open
onto private terraces, balconies, or small patios. They feature elegant modern furnishings,

---

Impressions

Know'st thou the land where the pale citrons grow,
The golden fruits in darker foliage glow?
Soft blows the wind that breathes from that blue sky!
Still stands the myrtle and the laurel high!
Know'st thou it well that land, beloved Friend?
Thither with thee, O, thither would I wend!

—Johann Wolfgang von Goethe, *Mignon Song*
(trans. Samuel Taylor Coleridge), c. 1760

spacious bathrooms (some with shower only), and a restful ambience. The **restaurant** is worth a detour, even if you're not a guest.

Via Tragara 57, 80073 Capri. ☎ **081-8370844.** Fax 081-8377790. www.hoteltragara.com. 45 units. 520€–780€ double; from 920€ suite. Rates include buffet breakfast. Children 2 and under stay free in parent's room. Internet specials available. AE, DC, MC, V. Closed Nov–Easter. **Amenities:** Restaurant; bar; concierge; gym; pool; room service; spa. *In room:* A/C, TV, minibar.

Hotel Scalinatella ★   This sophisticated hotel enjoys a unique setting overlooking Capri's Faraglioni (p. 252) and offers a pleasant atmosphere and luxury accommodations. Guest rooms are spacious and bright, with pretty tiled floors, high-quality furnishings, and comfortable bathrooms (some with shower only). Most rooms open onto private terraces; the more expensive rooms and the junior suites enjoy views over the sea.

Via Tragara 8, 80073 Capri. ☎ **081-8370633.** Fax 081-8378291. www.scalinatella.com. 45 units. 430€–560€ double; 700€ junior suite. Rates include buffet breakfast. Children 2 and under stay free in parent's room. AE, DC, MC, V. Closed Nov–Mar. **Amenities:** Restaurant; concierge; gym; pool; room service; outdoor tennis court. *In room:* A/C, TV, minibar.

JK Place Capri ★★   Great attention to detail, elegance, and beautiful views have made a winner of this hotel, in spite of its less-than-desirable location on the main road from the harbor up to Capri and Anacapri. Guest rooms are spacious and welcoming, decorated with a perfect mix of stylish elegance and comfort. The best rooms have sea views and are roomy and light filled. Bathrooms are large (some with shower only). The hotel's **kitchen** serves excellent meals on the terrace or in the bar lounge.

Via Marina Grande 255 (up from the harbor), 80073 Capri. ☎ **081-8384111.** Fax 081-8376150. www.jkcapri.com. 22 units. 700€–900€ double; from 1,000€ suite. Rates include buffet breakfast. Internet specials available. AE, DC, MC, V. Closed Nov–Mar. **Amenities:** Restaurant service; bar; concierge; gym; pool; room service; spa. *In room:* A/C, TV, Internet, minibar.

Moderate

Luna Hotel ★   This upscale modern hotel enjoys a choice cliff-top location and offers luxurious accommodations and attentive service. Guest rooms are quiet and elegantly furnished with a mixture of pieces and styles. Bathrooms are spacious and tiled (some with shower only). Most rooms have private terraces overlooking the cliffs or the hotel's beautiful gardens. The formal **restaurant** is very good and has a lovely setting.

Viale Matteotti 3, 80073 Capri. ☎ **081-8370433.** Fax 081-8377459. www.lunahotel.com. 54 units. 290€–460€ double; 560€ suite. Rates include breakfast. Children 2 and under stay free in parent's room. AE, DC, MC, V. Closed mid-Oct to Easter. **Amenities:** Restaurant; bar; concierge; pool. *In room:* A/C, TV, minibar.

Villa Brunella (Finds)   Set in a panoramic position, this was a private villa until 1963, when it was transformed into its current incarnation as a pleasant family-run hotel. Guest rooms have a welcoming atmosphere and each double has its own flowered terrace or balcony with a sea view. Bathrooms are modest in size but come decorated with modern fixtures and designer tiles. Guests have access to the beach club at Marina Piccola. The hotel's restaurant **Terrazza Brunella ★** is excellent for its food, setting, and elegant service.

Via Tragara 24, 80073 Capri. ☎ **081-8370122.** Fax 081-8370430. www.villabrunella.it. 20 units. 250€–360€ double; 460€ junior suite. Rates include buffet breakfast. AE, DC, MC, V. Closed Nov–Apr. **Amenities:** Restaurant; bar; pool; room service. *In room:* A/C, TV, minibar.

Canasta   Recently redone, this small budget hotel is not too far from the center of Capri. Guest rooms are not huge, but are nice and clean in their simplicity, with colorful tiled floors, wrought-iron beds, and whitewashed walls. Bathrooms are adequate, modern, and scrupulously clean. The pool is larger then the Carmencita's (below).

Via Campo di Teste 6, 80073 Capri. *©* **081-8370561.** Fax 081-8376675. www.hotel-canasta.com. 16 units. 170€–230€ double. Rates include buffet breakfast. Children 2 and under stay free in parent's room. AE, DC, MC, V. Closed 1 week for Christmas. **Amenities:** Pool. *In room:* A/C, TV, minibar.

Hotel Carmencita   This small hotel is a good budget choice in an expensive destination. Located in the modern part of Anacapri, it opens onto a private garden with a pool and offers comfortable and quiet accommodations at moderate rates. Guest rooms are spacious and nicely furnished—a bit dated but clean—with tiled floors and private balconies. The swimming pool is small but is a plus in this price category.

Viale T. De Tommaso 4, 80071 Capri. *©* **081-8371360.** Fax 081-8373009. www.carmencitacapri.com. 20 units. 136€–146[eu double; 160€ triple. Children 2 and under stay free in parent's room. AE, DC, MC, V. Closed Nov–Mar. **Amenities:** Bar; babysitting; concierge; Internet; pool. *In room:* A/C, TV.

WHERE TO DINE

In addition to the restaurants we recommend in this section, **Quisi** ★★, in the **Grand Hotel Quisisana** (above), is special enough for a very romantic or celebratory occasion. Some of our favorite hotels above also offer remarkable—and less pricey—dining experiences, particularly **Punta Tragara, Villa Brunella** ★, and **Luna.**

Expensive

Olivo ★★★ CREATIVE CAPRESE   The Michelin-double-starred restaurant of the Capri Palace Hotel, this is the perfect address for a truly exclusive experience. Stylish and pricey, it affords beauty (hand-blown glasses, silver cutlery, luxurious fabrics and details), perfect service, and gourmet haute cuisine. Considered the best restaurant on the island—and one of the best in all of Campania—it owes its fame to the creative cuisine of German chef Oliver Glowig, who captures the flavor of the local tradition with incredible lightness, as with the wonderful handmade *fusilli allo scorfano* (with local fish). The menu is seasonal and best exemplified by the tasting menus.

Via Capodimonte 2, Anacapri. *©* **081-9780111.** www.capri-palace.com. Reservations recommended. Secondi 35€–46€; tasting menus 150€ and 190€. AE, DC, MC, V. Daily noon–3pm and 7pm–midnight. Closed Nov–Mar.

Moderate

Al Grottino ★ CAPRESE/NEAPOLITAN   Serving seafood and other Neapolitan specialties since 1937, this restaurant was a preferred hangout for VIPs in the 1950s. The food is still good, and you can choose from a variety of traditional Neapolitan comfort food, such as *frittura* (medley of deep-fried seafood) and *mozzarella in carrozza* (deep-fried mozzarella)—prepared in four different ways. Excellent *caprese* specialties are *zuppa di cozze* (bean-and-mussel soup) and *ravioli alla caprese* (with fresh mozzarella and basil).

Via Longano 27, Capri. *©* **081-8370584.** Reservations required for dinner. Secondi 12€–20€. AE, MC, V. Daily noon–3pm and 7pm–midnight. Closed Nov–Mar.

Da Paolino ★★ CAPRESE   Popular among locals, this restaurant serves deliciously simple food under a splendid lemon arbor terrace. The menu is traditional and down-to-earth, with a great array of grilled Mediterranean vegetables seasoned with the best local olive oil, and the freshest seafood. In addition to the great buffet of *antipasti*, we highly recommend the *sauté di cozze e vongole* (shellfish), and the *calamarata* (ring-shaped pasta with calamari).

Via Palazzo a Mare 11, Marina Grande. ✆ 081-8376102. www.paolinocapri.com. Reservations required for dinner. Secondi 18€–32€. AE, DC, MC, V. Daily 7pm–midnight. Closed Nov–Mar.

Il Riccio ★ CAPRESE   Born from the proverbial ashes of the historic Add'o Riccio, this new version of the beach restaurant is signed by the Capri Palace Hotel. The club is the right mix of trendy and casual, with a perfect location steps from the Blue Grotto, and a terrace overlooking the sea. The menu focuses on seafood and traditional dishes: From the classic *caprese* salad to the *linguine all'astice* (with spiny lobster), everything is well prepared with only the freshest ingredients. The secluded solarium carved in the rocks is available for private parties.

Via Gradola 4, Anacapri. ✆ 081-8371380. info@ristoranteilriccio.com. Reservations recommended. Secondi 18€–25€. AE, DC, MC, V. Daily 12:30–3pm and 7:30–11pm. Closed Nov–Mar.

La Savardina ★★ CAPRESE   This historic address continues to lure locals and visitors to its excellent traditional food, hospitable service, and delightful lemon and orange arbor terrace. We love it for the variety of its menu, including many vegetarian and meat-based dishes in addition to the typical seafood favorites. We recommend you start with a simple antipasto of grilled vegetables and local cured meat, followed by the very well-prepared *ravioli alla caprese* (filled with mozzarella), or with the linguine seasoned with capers, cherry tomatoes, and fresh herbs. For secondo, the *coniglio* (rabbit) is excellent, or try the excellent fish *all'acqua pazza*. The *torta caprese* (traditional chocolate and nut torte) is quite good.

Via Lo Capo 8, Capri. ✆ 081-8376300. www.caprilasavardina.com. Reservations recommended. Secondi 12€–18€. AE, DC, MC, V. Mar–May and Sept–Oct Wed–Mon 12:30–3pm and 7:30–11pm; June–Aug daily 12:30–3pm and 7:30–11pm. Closed Nov–Feb.

Pizzeria Aurora ★ CAPRESE/PIZZA   For a trendy see-and-be-seen kind of place, you can't go wrong with this establishment—and the food is good too. Choose from a menu including modern renditions of traditional dishes, such as the excellent pasta with zucchini flowers and parmesan, or the simple *spaghetti al pomodoro* (with cherry tomatoes). Thin and crispy pizza is served in the evening.

Via Fuorlovado 18, Capri. ✆ 081-8370181. www.auroracapri.com. Reservations recommended. Secondi 18€–25€. AE, DC, MC, V. Daily 12:30–3pm and 7:30–11pm. Closed Jan–Mar.

Inexpensive

Grottelle (Finds) CAPRESE   This small restaurant off the beaten path is a great place for sampling the local cuisine. The outdoor terrace is very pleasant during fair weather. The menu is centered on traditional Caprisian cuisine, and we highly recommend the *zuppa di fagioli* (bean soup) as well as the simple but delectable *spaghetti con pomodoro e basilica* (with fresh tomatoes and basil), followed by the perfect *frittura di paranza* (deep-fried seafood). The homemade desserts are very good.

Via Arco Naturale 13, Capri. ✆ 0818375719. Fax 081-8389234. Reservations required for dinner. Secondi 11€–15€. AE, DC, MC, V. Fri–Wed noon–3pm and 7–11pm. Closed Nov–Mar.

La Cisterna (Value) CAPRESE/PIZZA   This small, unpretentious restaurant serves well-prepared traditional dishes at very low prices. The menu varies but portions are always generous; you might find *lasagne verdi* (green lasagna), *zuppa di pesce* (seafood

stew), *frittura* (deep-fried seafood), and the market choice of seafood served charbroiled or
all'acqua pazza (poached in a light herb broth). In the evening, excellent pizza is prepared.

Via Madre Serafina 5, Capri. © **081-8375620.** Reservations required. Secondi 8€–14€; pizza 5€–9€. AE, DC, MC, V. Spring–fall daily noon–3:30pm and 7pm–midnight; winter daily 11:30am–2pm and 6:30–11pm.

La Rondinella (**Finds** CAPRESE/PIZZA   This family-run restaurant is a good choice if you're after relaxation and quiet. In the evening, it prepares many varieties of brick-oven pizza. Otherwise, the regular menu is traditional, and you will find an excellent rendition of *ravioli alla caprese* (mozzarella, fresh tomatoes, and basil); *pezzogna all'acqua pazza* (local fish in a light tomato sauce); and *frittura* (deep-fried seafood medley), which they prepare particularly well. For dessert, local specialties such as *torta caprese* (chocolate and almond cake) are excellent.

Via G. Orlandi 245, Anacapri. © **081-8371223.** Reservations required for dinner. Secondi 11€–16€; pizza 6€–10€. AE, DC, MC, V. Daily noon–3pm and 7–11pm. Closed 2 weeks in Feb.

SHOPPING FOR LOCAL CRAFTS

Dedicated shoppers will lose themselves in Capri's little shops. Many of the island's visitors return just to buy more of the locally made goods, especially the sandals and the jewelry. One of the most famous shopping stops is **Carthusia** ★★, a perfume maker that counts many stars among its customers. Its **laboratory/store,** Viale Matteotti 2d (© **081-8370368;** daily 9:30am–6pm; www.carthusia.com), has been concocting unique perfumes from local herbs and flowers since 1948. There are three outlets on the island: Via Camerelle 10, Capri Town (© **081-8370368**); Via Federico Serena, Capri Town (© **081-8375335**); and Via Axel Munthe 26, Anacapri (© **081-8373668**).

Stylish sandals (handmade, of course) can be found at **Amedeo Canfora** ★, Via Camerelle 3, Capri (© **081-8370487;** www.canfora.com), and at Antonio Viva's **L'Arte del Sandalo Caprese** ★, Via Giuseppe Orlandi 75, Anacapri (© **081-8373583;** www.sandalocaprese.it). Finally, the island has an old jewelry-making tradition. You can admire—and purchase—fine examples at **La Perla Gioielli,** Piazza Umberto I 21 (© **081-8370641**).

CAPRI AFTER DARK

Sweet summer nights are lively in Capri, and the nights are long. The island of VIPs will not let you down, so prepare yourself for a trendy scene, with beautiful people dressing up and convening at the famous **Piazzetta** at nightfall. Fashionistas, take note: To compete with the local beauties, you'll have to learn how to walk on the steep cobblestone streets of Capri in your stilettos! Nightlife here centers on the see-and-be-seen at the elegant and trendy bars and restaurants. The **piano bars** in the **Grand Hotel Quisiana** and in the **Capri Palace** are the most exclusive venues, with prices to match; the newly opened **Rendez Vous,** in the **Grand Hotel Quisiana** (p. 255), is more affordable. For a more relaxed scene, **Anema E Core,** Via Sella Orta 39/a, Capri (© **081-8376461;** www.anemaecore.com), is a lively nightclub with live music; and the **Wine Bar,** Vico San Tommaso 1 (© **081-8370732**), in the historic restaurant **La Capannina,** is a cozy place to have a drink and listen to some music.

Salerno, Paestum, Padula & the Cilento

The largest town in southern Campania, Salerno is the gateway to the Amalfi Coast (see chapter 8), and our favorite less-trafficked destination. The refuge of artists for centuries, it remains mostly undiscovered by modern-day tourists. Yet its wealth of artistic and historic offerings makes it a worthy destination. Salerno prides itself on having Italy's most beautiful seafront promenade and a delightful medieval center—rich in small shops and restaurants—with a superb 11th-century Duomo.

Salerno is also the gateway to the Cilento, one of Italy's best-guarded secrets, completely unknown to foreign tourists and very little known even to Italians. Covering a large section of the southern part of Campania, this national park—the second largest in Italy—contains exciting natural attractions—including two huge caves, small fishing towns, and seaside resorts with fine sand beaches. Cilento was where the ancient Greeks built some of their most important colonies, whose grandeur is still visible in the unique ruins of **Paestum,** home to the best-conserved Greek temple after the Theseion in Athens. Cilento's shore is relatively popular with Italians at the height of summer, and the beautiful coastline has been a bit damaged by sprawl, but the interior is uncharted territory: You'll be far away from the swarms of foreign tourists who usually see the temples of Paestum and move on, completely missing out on the Cilento's wild interior, scenic shores, and, last but not least, wonderful cuisine.

1 SALERNO ★★★

55km (34 miles) SE of Naples

With 150,000 inhabitants, Salerno is a lively modern town at the eastern edge of the Amalfi Coast, with a lovely medieval center, which the lack of crowds makes all the more enjoyable. Its lungomare (seafront promenade) is the most beautiful on this coast. The most important harbor of Campania after Naples, Salerno used to be the capital of the Southern kingdom. An Etruscan and Campanian town founded around the 6th century B.C., Salerno was absorbed into Magna Grecia, the conglomerate of Greek colonies in southern Italy, during the 5th century B.C. After becoming a Roman colony in 194 B.C., it acquired greater importance, as Paestum (a short distance to the south) declined in prestige, and it eventually became an independent principality under the Longobards in the 9th century A.D. Its growth continued in medieval and Renaissance times, when it became an important cultural center, thanks to its renowned medical schools. The principality was then ruled by Normans, Swabians, Angevins, and, finally, the Bourbons. Its political and cultural importance declined when Naples became the capital of the new kingdom. Salerno sank back into the quiet life of a smallish provincial town.

SALERNO, PAESTUM, PADULA & THE CILENTO

10

SALERNO

ATTRACTIONS ●
Chiesa di San Giorgio **5**
Duomo/Cattedrale **9**
Giardino della Minerva **2**
Museo Diocesano **8**

ACCOMMODATIONS ■
Convento San Michele **10**
Hotel Montestella **13**
Hotel Plaza **14**
Villa Avenia **3**

DINING ◆
Al Cenacolo **7**
Il Ristoro degli Angeli **12**
Antica Pizzeria Vicolo
della Neve **4**
Hosteria Il Brigante **6**
Ristorante del Golfo **1**
Trattoria del Padreterno **11**

GETTING THERE Salerno's **airport** is **Pontecagnano** (✆ 0828-354311; www.aero portosalerno.it), 12km (7½ miles) from Salerno, off SS 18 and autostrada A3. It receives daily flights from various European cities and is served by a number of airlines, including Alitalia, AirDolomit, and Lufthansa. **CSTP**'s (below) direct **bus line no. 8** makes five runs daily connecting the airport with Salerno, and then on to Battipaglia, in the Cilento. **Taxi** service is also available (✆ 089-757575). The closest intercontinental airport is **Naples's** Capodichino (p. 78).

Salerno is on the main north–south rail corridor and is well served by **train,** with frequent service from a number of Italian and European cities to its train station (*stazione*) on Piazza Vittorio Veneto. Trains leave Naples every 10 to 30 minutes for the 35-minute ride to Salerno; the fare is about 6€. Contact **Trenitalia** (✆ 892021 in Italy; www.trenitalia.it) for more fares and information.

Slower but far more scenic, the **ferry** is our favorite means of transportation on this coast, especially in the summer, when roads tend to be crowded. Salerno is a major harbor, and ferries arrive here from other ports in the Mediterranean (see "Getting There," in chapter 3). Local ferries connect Salerno to nearby harbors: **DiMaio Lines** (✆ 848-151818 in Italy, or 081-8822220; www.dimaiolines.it) connects with Olbia in Sardinia; **Alicost** (✆ 089/234-892; www.lauroweb.com/alicost.htm) and **Alilauro** (✆ 081-4972238; www.alilauro.it) with Capri, Amalfi, Positano, and Ischia; **Travelmar** (✆ 081-7041911; www.travelmar.it) with Positano, Amalfi, Minori, and Maiori; and **Cooperativa Sant'Andrea** (✆ 089-873190; www.coopsantandrea.it) with Amalfi, Capri, Minori, and Sorrento. Operating only in the summer (Apr–Sept), **Metrò del Mare** (✆ 199-600700; www.metrodelmare.com) offers commuter-style connections with all the harbors along this stretch of coast, from Pozzuoli south, including Naples, Sorrento, Positano, Amalfi, and the Cilento; purchase of a **Terra&Mare ticket** entitles you to the boat transfer plus ground transportation for the 45 minutes before and 45 minutes after the ferry link.

Salerno is also well connected by **SITA** (✆ 089-226604 or 089-405145; www.sitabus. it), which maintains regular **bus service** to Salerno from Naples as well as from the various villages of the Amalfi Coast and the Sorrento peninsula. **CSTP** (✆ 800-016659; toll-free within Italy, or 089-487001; www.cstp.it) services Salerno, Pompeii, Paestum, and the Cilento. The **bus terminal** is in Piazza della Concordia, near the train station. See "The Unico Travel Pass," p. 48, for fare information.

You can also reach Salerno by **car.** Off the autostrada A3, take the exit marked SALERNO, and follow signs for the city center. Once there, follow signs for the **Jolly Hotel** and the **public parking,** where you'll need to leave your car, as the town center is pedestrian only.

GETTING AROUND Although large compared to the compact towns of the Amalfi Coast, Salerno has a compact town center, extending along its waterfront, that can be explored **on foot.** The town's historic district is a pedestrian-only area; it stretches from the train station, on **Piazza Vittorio Veneto,** to Piazza Amendola, at the western edge of the medieval center. **Taxis** are your best bet for destinations outside the historic district; taxis wait at stands near points of major interest, including **Piazza Vittorio Veneto** in front of the railway station (✆ 089-229947); **Piazza Amendola** (✆ 089-229963); and **Piazza XXIV Maggio** (✆ 089-229171); or call **Radiotaxi** directly at ✆ 089-757575. The town has a good **public bus** system run by CSTP (see "Getting There," above); the bus hub is Piazza Vittorio Veneto, across from the rail station. **Bus, train,** and **ferries** (see

Salerno.

You can also **rent a car** at the Pontecagnano airport from **Hertz, Maggiore,** or **Pugliano Travel** (© 0828-351004); more companies have agencies downtown (p. 326).

VISITOR INFORMATION The **AACST tourist office** (© 089-224744; www.azienda turismo.sa.it) is at Via Roma 258. The tourist office for the whole province, including the Cilento, is the **EPT,** Via Velia 15, 84100 Salerno (© 089-230401; www.eptsalerno. it). Another office is on Piazza Vittorio Veneto, at the train station (© 089-614259; www.turismoinsalerno.it), which is open Monday to Saturday from 9am to 2pm and 3 to 8pm (until 7pm in winter).

FAST FACTS You'll find several pharmacies in town, including one at Corso Vittorio Emanuele 223 (© 089-231439), not far from the train station, and one at Via Mercanti 62 (© 089-225142), in the medieval district. The **hospital, San Giovanni di Dio e Ruggiero d'Aragona** (© 089-671111), is on Via San Leonardo. For an **ambulance,** dial © **118.** Dial © **113** or 112 for the police, © **115** for the fire department, and © **116** for Automobile Club of Italy (ACI) road assistance. You will find several **banks** and **ATMs** in Salerno along Corso Vittorio Emanuele, not far from the train station; **Banca Nazionale del Lavoro** is in the train station. The main **post office**—in a majestic building—is at Corso Garibaldi 203 (Mon–Sat 8am–2pm).

SPECIAL EVENTS The **Salerno Film Festival** *Linea d'ombra* (Shadow Line) ★ is a major international event, dedicated to new talents in Europe and focusing on the passage from adolescence to adulthood—the "shadow line" of maturation, a term coined by Joseph Conrad and taken as the festival's motto. The festival (© 089-2753673; fax 089-2571125; www.festivalculturegiovani.it) is an annual, weeklong event that takes place in April. Besides films, it includes a number of interesting musical events. During the **Ravello Music Festival,** concerts are also held in the monastery of Santa Maria della Mercede in Salerno; contact the festival office for a schedule of events (p. 213). In advance of your visit, you can check out what's going on in Salerno at www.salernocity.com (Italian only).

EXPLORING SALERNO

During World War II, Salerno was designated the capital of Allied Italy, and much of the town was destroyed by severe bombing. Only the medieval center and part of the 19th-century waterfront were miraculously spared. The reconstruction and expansion that followed, especially to the southeast and northeast of the seafront, gave the town a more modern look. However, in the 1990s, a renovation campaign brought the old sections of Salerno back to their original splendor, particularly its seafront promenade.

Lined with palm trees and opening onto the seascape of the Costiera Amalfitana and Cilentana, **Lungomare Trieste** ★★ is the most beautiful seafront promenade in the whole region—and one of the best in Italy. At the western end, you'll find the **Villa Comunale** (Piazza Amendola), a pleasant and orderly public garden, adjacent to the **Teatro Verdi** ★ (Piazza Luciani; © 089-662141; daily 8am–2pm and 4–8pm). This historic theater was inaugurated on April 15, 1872, with *Rigoletto,* by Giuseppe Verdi. A recent face-lift has brought the beautiful baroque and neoclassical decorations back to life, including the magnificent hall, with its frescoed ceiling by Domenico Morelli. The theater hosts many important concerts and performances (see "Salerno After Dark," below). The town is dominated by the **Castello di Arechi,** Via Benedetto Croce (© 089-2854533; www.ilcastellodiarechi.it; free admission; Tues-Sun 9am–2pm and 4pm–sunset); originally built by the Byzantines, probably over older fortifications, the castle took on its current mantle under Spanish rule in the 16th century. It now hosts special events, but it's worth a visit just for its view. It can be reached by car, taxi, or on foot—a steep 40-minute climb along a pedestrian ramp.

The medieval heart of Salerno—where most of the town's attractions are concentrated—is a picturesque place for a stroll. From Piazza Amendola you can take the exclusive shopping street **Via di Porta Catena** and follow it to charming **Piazza Sedile del Campo,** the medieval market square, graced by the beautiful *Fontana dei Delfini* **(Fountain of the Dolfins)** ★ and the **Palazzo dei Genovesi** (at no. 3)—today a school—with its grand **portal** ★. Off the piazza, in Via Roteprandi, you'll find the church of **Sant'Andrea de Lama,** one of the oldest medieval buildings in Salerno—note its pretty 12th-century bell tower—and, a few steps farther, the even older church of **Sant'Alfonso,** dating from the 10th century. Inside, admire some recently restored frescoes dating from the Longobard era. Return to **Piazza Sedile del Campo** to access **Via dei Mercanti** ★, Salerno's major shopping street, which dates from medieval times. This is where you'll find some of the best boutiques and most elegant stores in town. Off to the left is the **Vicolo dei Sartori** with the **Palazzo Fruscione** ★, notable for its medieval decorations, including a pretty loggia and intertwined arches. Not far off, on Vicolo Adalberga, is the ancient **Palatine San Pietro a Corte** church ★. Its 11th-century frescoes have survived, and excavations of its layered strata have revealed the structure of an ancient Roman thermal bathhouse. Farther along Via dei Mercanti is the 10th-century **Chiesa del Crocifisso** ★★, Piazza Matteotti 1 (© **089-233716;** daily 9am–noon and 4–7pm), famous for its beautiful 13th-century **frescoes** in the main and right apses of the crypt. One depicts the Crucifixion and the other three saints; this fresco is reproduced in mosaics over the main altar of the church.

Scuola Medica Salernitana **(Salerno Medical School)** was one of the first medical schools in the Western world: Scholars believe it was the medical school that operated in the Greek colony of Velia in the 6th century A.D. and developed in later centuries to attract scholars from all over Europe. Today what is left is a small **museum,** Via dei Mercanti (© **089-241292;** Mon–Sat 9am–1pm and 4–7pm, Sun 9am–1pm), inside the former St. Gregorio church that contains documents and a collection of medical instruments, and the school's **botanical garden, Giardino della Minerva** ★, Via Ferrante Sanseverino 1 (© **089-252423;** www.giardinodellaminerva.it), originally created in the 14th century by one of the school's masters, Matteo Silvatico, in the terraced garden of his house. His *Giardino dei Semplici* **(Garden of Simples)** is considered the first botanic garden in the Western world. The name refers to the few key plants from which most basic remedies were obtained. The garden is open Tuesday through Sunday from 10am to 1pm and 5pm to sunset; admission is 2€.

Chiesa di San Giorgio ★   Built in 1647 over an 8th-century church, this is the most beautiful baroque church in Salerno. An atrium with a carved portal stands in front of the imposing facade, and the interior is typically baroque, with ornate gilded stucco and numerous frescoes and paintings. The fresco cycle depicting the *Passion of Christ* in the cantoria, as well as the *Crucifixion* and *San Benedetto* in the transept, are all by Angelo Solimena. *San Michele* (over the fourth altar to the right) and the frescoes of the large chapel are by Francesco Solimena, and other paintings are by Andrea da Salerno. A beautiful carved wooden pulpit is supported by four lions.

Via Duomo 19. © **089-228918.** Free admission. Daily 9:30am–12:30pm.

Duomo/Cattedrale di San Matteo ★★★   Arguably Italy's most beautiful medieval church, the Duomo was built in 1076 and consecrated in 1085 to house the relics of Saint Matthew the Evangelist. The front portion of the church is the **Sala San Lazzaro,** which is believed to have been the Main Hall of the *Scuola Medica Salernitana* **(Salerno Medical School).** A 17th-century staircase leads to the 11th-century Romanesque portal known as **Porta dei Leoni,** with its finely carved architrave; it leads to the church's elegant **atrium** ★. This is surrounded by a portico decorated with stone and tufa intarsia and is dominated by a splendid Romanesque **bell tower** ★★ (you'll get a better view of the bell tower from Via Roberto Il Giscardo, to the right of the Duomo). From here you can admire the facade of the Duomo, with its beautifully carved **central portal,** closed by two **bronze doors** ★★, which were cast in Constantinople in 1099. In spite of the grave damages caused by the earthquake in 1688, and of the intense 18th-century restoration, the Duomo's interior still holds an amazing quantity of impressive artwork, starting with the two magnificent **ambones** ★★★ in the central nave. The smaller is from the 12th century, while the larger dates from the 1400s and is composed of 12 red and gray granite columns blossoming with birds, figures, and vegetation. On the ambone's facade, note the remarkable mosaic showing a sinner with a snake biting him in the breast, and an eagle digging his talons into the unfortunate sinner's head. The monumental **candleholder** ★ in front of the ambone is also impressive. Adjacent to the ambones is the choir, whose sides and floor are embedded with mosaics from the 12th century. The *Cappella delle Crociate* **(Chapel of the Crusades)** ★★, in the right apse, is where the Crusaders had their weapons blessed before sailing for the Holy Land. Fine 13th-century mosaics and later frescoes cover the walls and ceiling. Conserved under the altar are the remains of Pope Gregorio VII, who died in exile in Salerno in 1085.

Piazza Alfano I. ℂ **089-231387.** Free admission. Daily 7:30am–noon and 4–7pm.

Museo Diocesano ★★   Adjacent to the Duomo is the museum, which contains a large art collection dating to Roman times. One of the most impressive rooms in our opinion is the one that holds the ivory collection, including some amazing carvings. The best is a 12th-century *paliotto* **(altar front)** ★★★, composed of 54 carved scenes by different artists. Note that four frames are missing; one is in the Louvre in Paris, one in Berlin, one in Budapest, and the last in the Met in New York. In the other rooms are several other important pieces, including paintings and bas-reliefs from the 16th century, and paintings by such artists as Andrea Vaccaro, Luca Giordano, Jusepe de Ribera, and Francesco Solimena. The museum also has a collection of illuminated manuscripts from the 13th and 14th centuries.

Largo Plebiscito 12. ℂ **089-239126.** Free admission. Mon–Fri 9am–1pm.

WHERE TO STAY

Yet undiscovered by international tourism, Salerno offers good-value hotel rates, if you don't mind lower standards of amenities (satellite TV to get English-language programs, for example, is basically nonexistent).

Convento San Michele ★   This small hotel is near Salerno's historic university, in the heart of the historic district. Catering to professors and scholars, it is also a great option for those coming to discover the medieval treasures of town. The original monastery housing the hotel has been restructured with taste and respect for the original structures (some dating back to the 11th century) and does not offer a lot of amenities. Yet, guest rooms are spacious and welcoming, with vaulted ceilings, whitewashed walls, tiled floors, and simple furnishings. Bathrooms are functional (some with shower only). The best room in the house has frescoed ceilings and opens onto a private terrace. The wine/lounge bar is popular among the younger set.

Via Bastioni 8, 84122 Salerno. ✆ **089-2854533.** Fax 089-2854981. www.ilconventosanmichele.it. 13 units. 130€ double. Rates include breakfast. AE, DC, MC, V. Limited free parking. **Amenities:** Restaurant; wine bar; concierge. *In room:* A/C, TV, Internet.

Hotel Montestella   This family-run hotel has a very central location in the pedestrian area between the train station and the medieval center. The good-size guest rooms come with comfortable, modern furnishings. The bathrooms are medium size, with new fixtures (some with shower only).

Corso Vittorio Emanuele 156, 84122 Salerno. ✆ **089-225122.** Fax 089-229167. www.hotelmontestella.it. 46 units. 110€ double. Rate includes breakfast. Children 2 and under stay free in parent's room. AE, DC, MC, V. No parking. **Amenities:** Bar; room service. *In room:* A/C, TV, minibar.

Hotel Plaza   This hotel is in a large neoclassical building across from the railway station. Inside, it has been completely modernized, and the decor is modern throughout. The guest rooms are not large; but they are certainly adequate, with simple furnishings, carpeting, and either tubs or showers in the bathrooms.

Piazza Vittorio Veneto 42, 84123 Salerno. ✆ **089-224477.** Fax 089-237311. www.plazasalerno.it. 42 units. 130€ double. Rate includes buffet breakfast. Children 2 and under stay free in parent's room. AE, DC, MC, V. Parking 15€. **Amenities:** Bar. *In room:* A/C, TV, minibar.

Villa Avenia ★ (**Kids**)   This B&B has a very special location in the historic district, inside one of the villas surrounded by terraced gardens that extend from the medieval town up to the Castello di Arechi (p. 263). It pretty much feels like being in a private home, and indeed you are, but the lack of amenities and the simple accommodations are largely compensated for by the silence and the garden—a small oasis with a diminutive animal farm (with a Tibetan goat, a donkey, and a few chickens) that will delight younger children.

Via Porta di Ronca 5, 84100 Salerno. ✆ **089-252281.** Fax 089-555555. www.villaavenia.com. 6 units. 130€ double. Rates include breakfast. AE, DC, MC, V. No parking. **Amenities:** Bar; cafeteria. *In room:* A/C, TV, Internet.

WHERE TO DINE

In addition to the restaurants below, many snack bars and pizzerie are in the historic district, and cater to the local university and the mariners from the nearby port. A local favorite is the historic **Antica Pizzeria Vicolo della Neve,** Vicolo della Neve 24 (✆ **089-225705;** www.vicolodellaneve.it; closed Wed).

Moderate

Al Cenacolo SALERNITAN   Across from the Duomo, this is the best restaurant in Salerno—which might not seem a great achievement in a town that favors cheap eateries, but the food is indeed very good. Owner and chef Pietro Rispoli brings together the best flavors of the region—fresh herbs and vegetables, seafood, local meats, and cheeses—sometimes in new combinations. The menu varies regularly, but you might find *mousse di tonno con composta di pomodori* (tuna mousse with tomato jam), *cavatelli con salsa di zucchine* (a delicious creation of homemade pasta with a sauce of zucchini, lemon peel, anchovies, and local provolone cheese), or *mazzancolle con verdurine grigliate e capperi fritti* (local prawns with grilled garden vegetables and fried capers). The breads and the pastas are exclusively homemade, the wines and cheeses superb.

1–2:30pm and 8–10:45pm; Sun 1–2:30pm. Closed 3 weeks in Aug.

Il Ristoro degli Angeli CREATIVE SALERNITAN/SEAFOOD   Don't let the minimalist decor fool you—the chef is a master who perfects apparently simple dishes. Ingredients for the seasonal menu come from the organic family farm and local seafood vendors. We recommend the perfect *spaghetti pomodoro e mozzarella* (with tomato sauce and mozzarella), as well as the *pasta ai frutti di mare* (with seafood), but the chef's specialty is rice: If it's on the menu, try the *risotto aglianico e cacio* (with local wine and cheese).

Via Francesco Conforti 16. ℭ **089-2960329.** Reservations recommended. Secondi 15€–20€. AE, DC, MC, V. Mon–Sat 1–2:30pm and 8–10:45pm; Sun 1–2:30pm.

Ristorante del Golfo SALERNITAN/SEAFOOD   This is a charming old-fashioned restaurant overlooking the harbor, affording interesting views from its dining rooms and terraces. The menu presents modern interpretations of established dishes. We recommend the nice *risotto ai frutti di mare* (with seafood) or the unusual *ciencioni* (homemade pasta squares in a stew of chickpeas and salted cod), followed by the perfectly prepared grilled catch of the day.

Via Porto 57. ℭ **089-231581.** www.ilristorantedelgolfo.it. Reservations recommended. Secondi 18€–25€. AE, DC, MC, V. Mon–Tues and Thurs–Sat 12:30–2:30pm and 8–10:45pm; Wed 8–10:45pm; Sun 12:30–2:30pm.

Trattoria del Padreterno SEAFOOD   In the historic district's prettiest square, this restaurant's menu changes daily with the offerings of the local fish market. We recommend the *cozze gratinate* (mussels au gratin), the *polpi alla Luciana* (stewed octopus), and the splendid *spaghetti cozze, limone, e basilica* (with mussels, lemon, and fresh basil).

Piazza Gioia 12. ℭ **089-239305.** Reservations recommended. Secondi 16€–22€. AE, DC, MC, V. Wed–Mon 1–2:30pm and 8–10:45pm; Tues 8–10:45pm.

Inexpensive

Hosteria Il Brigante ★ (Finds) SALERNITAN   We love this rustic osteria which is a temple to the local traditional cuisine. The seasonal menu focuses on pasta—the specialty is *spaghetti alici, pinoli, uva passa e pomodorini* (seasoned with anchovies, pine nuts, raisins, and cherry tomatoes)—and a variety of seafood and meat dishes: We recommend the *maiale ubriaco* (roast pork with red wine) or the *calamari e fiori di zucca* (with zucchini flowers).

Via Fratelli Linguiti 4 (behind the Duomo). ℭ **089-226592.** Reservations recommended. Secondi 7€–12€. No credit cards. Tues–Sun 12:30–3pm and 7:30–10pm. Closed 2 weeks in Aug.

SALERNO AFTER DARK

As a university town and a major harbor, Salerno has a lively nightlife and cultural scene, with a large number of clubs, discos, and cafes. Among the places to hang out, we recommend the **Bogart Café,** Via Rafastia 9 (ℭ **089-252288**), which turns into a disco on weekends, and **Fabula,** Via Porto 1 (ℭ **340-1403144**), a popular club that also has live music. **Bar Tekabega,** Via Giovanni da Procida 7 (ℭ **347-0873031**), is a gay-friendly hangout. The **Limelight Club,** Via delle Industrie (ℭ **0828-354171**), hosts live music shows late at night and serves pizza during the day.

For more upscale nightlife, heading the top of the list is **Teatro Verdi,** Largo Luciani (ℭ **089-662141;** www.teatroverdisalerno.it; daily 8am–2pm and 4–8pm), which, true to its namesake, is the venue for Italian opera, but also presents classic or contemporary plays, as well as concerts and dance performances.

2 THE RUINS OF PAESTUM ★

35km (22 miles) S of Salerno; 100km (62 miles) SE of Naples

A short distance south of Salerno, the fabled ruins of Paestum are everything they are reported to be. Enormously evocative, the three Greek temples (in an excellent state of conservation) occupy a grassy plain that really gives off the sense of a vanished, ancient city. Most of the town walls are intact as well. The temples are a magical sight, especially at sunset, and in spring and fall when Paestum's roses—praised since antiquity—are in bloom. The archaeological area can be reached as a day trip in Campania; plan on spending a couple of hours exploring the temples and an hour for the museum, but count on a whole day for a more in-depth exploration.

ESSENTIALS

GETTING THERE   Paestum is well connected by public transportation, with several **trains** stopping at its two train stations: **Capaccio-Roccadaspide** (formerly Capaccio Scalo) and **Paestum,** only 5 minutes from each other. The first is in the village of Capaccio Scalo, closer to the ruins of the Sanctuary of Hera Argiva; the second is near the archaeological area of Paestum (about 1km, or a half-mile). It is a 30-minute trip from Salerno and a 90-minute trip from Naples. Contact **Trenitalia** (© **892021** in Italy; www.trenitalia.it) for fares and information.

Paestum is also an easy **bus** connection from Salerno. **CSTP** (© **800-016659;** toll-free within Italy, or 089-487001; www.cstp.it) has regular service to Paestum from Napoli and Salerno (both line 34), with both lines continuing on to Agropoli and Acciaroli, in the Cilento. **SITA** (© **089-226604** or 089-405145; www.sitabus.it) makes runs from Salerno to Capaccio Scalo; and **Autolinee Giuliano Bus** (© **0974-836185;** www.giulianobus.com) has several lines between Naples, Salerno, and the Cilento, making stops in Paestum and Capaccio Scalo (lines 3, 4, 5, 6, 7, and 10).

By **car,** take autostrada A3, exit at BATTIPAGLIA onto SS 18, and follow the brown signs for Paestum.

GETTING AROUND   If you are just visiting the temples, you will be able to do so on foot. Via Porta Sirena leads from the Paestum train station to Via Magna Grecia, which cuts through the middle of the archaeological site. Should you want to explore farther afield, you can rent a **car** from **Travelcar,** Via Magna Grecia (© **0828-811034;** www.travelcar.it); **Aesse Renault,** on SS 18, Km 97 (© **0828-721226**), or from one of the following companies who also offer **taxi/car service** with a driver: **Leonardo D'Onofrio,** Via Cesare Pavese 27 (© **0828-721107** or 339-3201101); and **Fratelli Di Filippo,** Capaccio Scalo (© **0828-724707**).

VISITOR INFORMATION   **AACST,** Via Magna Grecia 887, 84063 Paestum (© **0828-811016;** fax 0828-722322; www.infopaestum.it), maintains an information point at Via Magna Grecia 151, by the Archeological Museum, not far from the main entrance to the temples (Sept–June Mon–Sat 9am–3pm, Sun 9am–1pm; July–Aug Mon–Sat 9am–7pm, Sun 9am–1pm).

FAST FACTS   You'll find a pharmacy on Via Licinella (© **0828-721190**) and several in Capaccio Scalo, including one on Via Magna Grecia 316 (© **0828-725382**). The closest hospital is in Salerno (see "Fast Facts," p. 263). For an **ambulance,** dial © **118.**

Dial © **113** or 112 for the police, © **115** for the fire department, and © **116** for ACI road assistance. The **post office** (© **0828-811029**) is on Via Licinella; and there is one in Capaccio Scalo, at Via C. Dalla Chiesa (© **0828-725246**). A **bank** (© **0828-811141**) is at Via Licinella 1.

SPECIAL EVENTS   The sixth edition of the occasional **Paestum Balloon Festival** took place in 2009. This is a great opportunity to take some pictures of the balloons taking off from the Greek temples and soaring into the sky. For those fortunate enough to secure a flight, the view on a clear day stretches from the Appenines to Capri and beyond. The event is usually scheduled in the fall; visit **www.mongolfiere.it** for information.

| Campania Artecard Cilento

Artecard offers great advantages (see chapter 5, p. 110), whether you are planning an extensive visit to the whole region or just one city or area of interest. The **Artecard Cilento** costs 13€, is valid for 3 days, and grants access to the archaeological area, the National Archeological Museum of Paestum, the Carthusian Monastery of Padula, the Grotte dell'Angelo in Pertosa, and the excavations of Velia. In addition, it allows you to purchase special guided tours in the Cilento National Park with **CitySightseeing** at discounted rates (see "Guided Tours," below). Reservations are recommended; call (C) **800-600601** toll-free within Italy, or 06-39967650; or visit the website at www.campaniartecard.it.

EXPLORING THE RUINS

The Greeks established the colony of Poseidonia—the name Paestum is ancient Roman—in the 7th century B.C., around the same time that the nearby Sanctuary of Hera Argiva (p. 271) was built. The town flourished for almost 3 centuries but dramatically declined after it was overtaken by the Lucanians, a local mountain people, in the 4th century B.C. Only when the Romans established the colony of Paestum in 273 B.C. did the city revive, quickly growing wealthy from its agricultural and commercial activity. The city lost its supremacy during the Middle Ages, when its inhabitants were forced into the hills by the repeated Saracen attacks and the spread of malaria (caused by the fertile plain's transformation into marshland). The Normans arrived in the 11th century, plundering the temples and other buildings for their statuary. The ruins remained known but undisturbed for centuries until the state road was developed in the 18th century and the first archaeological studies were performed. *Note:* The archaeological area is not huge, but the two temples dedicated to Hera are quite distant from the one dedicated to Athena, and you should be prepared to walk; wear comfortable shoes, and carry water and a hat, particularly if it's hot.

Archaeological Area of Paestum ★★★   The enclosed area contains the three temples and a number of other ruins that were part of the sacred area at the center of the ancient Greek town. All the temples are built facing the east. The **Temple to Hera I** (commonly called **Basilica**) ★★★ is the oldest of the three largest structures, built in 550 B.C. in Doric-Archaic style. The 50 columns of its monumental portico still stand, showing the pot-bellied profile typical of archaic temples, but the roof and the pediment have long ago fallen down. In front is a partially ruined sacrificial altar and, on its side, the square *bothros*—the sacrificial well where the remains were thrown. Based on the rich trove of findings in and around the temple, most experts now believe that the temple and surrounding structures were actually part of a huge complex dedicated to Hera, the goddess of fertility and maternity (the same goddess honored in the Sanctuary of Hera Argiva, p. 271). Indeed, several other smaller religious buildings, all dedicated to Hera, have been discovered nearby. The complex is to the south of the archaeological area, near the secondary entrance.

To the right of the basilica is the so-called **Temple of Neptune** ★★★, although most scholars now believe it was dedicated to Apollo or Zeus. This grandiose building, dating from around 450 B.C., is lined in travertine stone and glows a magical gold color when hit by the sun's rays. It is considered the best Doric temple in the world, with its perfect proportions and a number of architectural tricks—the columns at the corners have an elliptical section instead of round, and the horizontal lines are slightly convex instead of perfectly straight—giving it slender elegance and power at the same time. It is also the best preserved of Paestum's temples, with its roof and pediments mostly intact. At the temple's front are two sacrificial altars; the smaller was added by the Romans in the 3rd century B.C.

The third temple, the **Temple of Athena** (so-called **Temple of Ceres**) ★★, was built at the end of the 6th century B.C. and is the smallest of the three. It was also the center of a small sanctuary, of which only traces remain today. Transformed into a church in medieval times, inside its portico are three Christian tombs. It is on the opposite side of the archaeological area, near the main entrance. In between the two complexes is the **Roman Forum.** One of the oldest known rectangular Roman forums, it is lined with Doric columns, but little remains of the porticos and public buildings that surrounded it. Nearby, at the edge of Via Magna Grecia, is the **Roman Amphitheatre.** From the Forum, the *Via Sacra* **(Sacred Street)** leads to the Temple of Athena, with its Roman pavement laid over the Greek road. The original road continued for about 12km (7½ miles), to connect the Greek town of Poseidonia to the Sanctuary of Hera.

Main entrance Via Magna Grecia 917; secondary entrance Porta della Giustizia (Justice Gate, off Via Nettuno; for ticket holders only). ✆ **0828-811023.** www.infopaestum.it. Admission 4€; free with purchase of the Artecard. Daily 9am–sunset (last admission 60 min. earlier). Closed Jan 1, May 1, and Dec 25.

National Archaeological Museum of Paestum ★★   This museum archives the finds from the excavations: From Paestum, the 6th-century-B.C. **Statue of Zeus ★★** is well worth seeing as is the rich collection of 6th-century-B.C. **vases ★★** with red or black figures. Among the finds from the nearby necropolis, the most interesting are the famous Greek frescoes from the **Diver's Tomb ★,** from the 5th century B.C. Also very interesting are the paintings and objects found in the **Lucanian Tombs,** dating from the 6th to the 3rd centuries B.C. One entire area of the museum is dedicated to the architectural remains from the Sanctuary of Hera Argiva (below), including the complete **frieze ★** of metopes and triglyphs; a number of the metopes are unfinished, which helps shed light on the carving techniques.

Via Magna Grecia 918 (across from the entrance to the temples). ✆ **0828-811023.** Admission 4€; free with purchase of the Artecard. Daily 8:30am to 6:45pm (last admission 45 min. earlier). Closed the 1st and 3rd Mon each month and Jan 1, May 1, and Dec 25.

Sanctuary of Hera Argiva (Heraion)   Near the mouth of the river Sele, which is a protected natural area, these ruins are the remains of what must have been a glorious religious complex. The Heraion (sanctuary to the goddess Hera) was one of the most famous temples of antiquity, described by many ancient writings on Magna Grecia (the conglomerate of Greek colonies in the Mediterranean). Sought by archaeologists since the 18th century, it was discovered by two young archaeologists—Paola Zancani Montuoro and Umberto Zanotti Bianco—in the 20th century. Ruins include the foundation of the main temple, together with parts of the smaller *thesaurus* (treasury), and a portico with outlying buildings. All the decorations—metopes and votive statuettes—are conserved in the National Archaeological Museum of Paestum (above). A short distance away from the ruins, in a restored farmhouse, is the **Museo Narrante del Santuario di Hera Argiva ★.** It houses an excellent multimedia installation describing the discovery of the ruins and the function of the sanctuary. The cult of Hera (Juno, in Latin), which

Impressions

And I myself, were I not even now
Furling my sails, and, nigh the journey's end,
Eager to turn my vessel's prow to shore,
Perchance would sing what careful husbandry
Makes the trim garden smile; of Paestum too,
Whose roses bloom and fade and bloom again.

—Virgil, *Georgics*

was very powerful in antiquity, did not disappear with the advent of Christianity but was actually absorbed into Christians' devotion to the Virgin Mary. In the nearby 11th-century sanctuary of the **Madonna del Granato** (road to Capaccio Vecchia; Aug 15 only), the Madonna holds a pomegranate, the symbol for Hera/Juno.

Ruins: Near the mouth of the river Sele, about 1.5km (1 mile) inland from the sea and 11km (6³/₄ miles) north of Paestum. **Museum:** Masseria Procuriali, Via Barizzo, Foce Sele Capaccio (about 2km/1¹/₄ miles from the ruins and 9km/5¹/₂ miles from Paestum). ℭ **0828-861440.** Free admission. Ruins daily 9am–7pm (July–Sept until 10pm). Museum Tues–Sun 9am–4pm.

STAYING ACTIVE

Usually bypassed by harried tourists, ancient Paestum's defensive **walls** offer the opportunity for a unique walk. The going is relatively easy and affords nice views. The walls completely surrounded the town and are one of the very few complete sets of walls left from antiquity. Originally built by the Greeks, they were restored by the Lucanians and then the Romans. Five meters (18 ft.) thick on average, with several towers, they mark a pentagonal perimeter of 4,750m (15,584 ft.), with four main gates at each of the cardinal directions. In 1828, when the Bourbon government built the Via delle Calabriae—today's Via Magna Grecia—they caused the almost complete destruction of the northern gate (Porta Aurea) and part of the southern walls. The western side is the best preserved. At the monumental western gate, **Porta Marina** ★, you can climb the walls and walk on the patrol paths, enjoying the great views over coast and ruins.

Though famous for its archaeological area, Paestum is also a great seaside destination. **Marina di Paestum** ★ is the place to bask in the sun, with miles of sandy **beaches;** the sea is warm and great for swimming, too.

WHERE TO STAY

In addition to the following hotels, we also recommend staying at **Le Trabe** (p. 274).

Moderate

Savoy Beach Hotel (Kids)   Near the beach and a short distance away from the archaeological area, this modern hotel offers more amenities than the Granaio (below) and somewhat more upscale accommodations. Guest rooms are good-size and comfortable, with classic furnishings and modern bathrooms (some with shower only). Some have carpeting, others wood floors, and others yet are tiled; more expensive units open onto private balconies. Don't expect sea views, as the hotel is surrounded by a garden, with a large swimming pool; the beach is 183m (600 ft.) down the road, and guests have access to the hotel's private facilities there. For a fee, guest can use the health center, including a heated indoor pool, a fitness room, and spa. The restaurant, **Tre Olivi** ★, is a gourmet address.

Via Poseidonia 41, 84063 Paestum. ✆ **0828-720100.** Fax 0828-720807. www.hotelsavoybeach.it. 24 units. 218€–258€ double; from 298€ suite. Rates include buffet breakfast. AE, DC, MC, V. Free parking. **Amenities:** Restaurant; bar; pool; room service; outdoor tennis. *In room:* A/C, TV, Internet, minibar.

Inexpensive

Il Granaio dei Casabella ★ (Kids) You cannot beat this hotel's location, right by the archaeological area in Paestum. It is a charming property, in what originally was a granary (some of the rooms are a bit dark). Tastefully restored, it offers simply decorated guest rooms that are spacious and welcoming, with tiled floors and rustic wooden furniture. Bathrooms are functional and modern (some with shower only). The **restaurant** ★ (p. 274) is excellent.

Via Tavernelle 84 (off Via Magna Grecia), 84063 Paestum. ✆ **0828-721014.** Fax 0828-811893. www. ilgranaiodeicasabella.com. 14 units. 120€ double; 170€ family room (sleeps 4). Rates include breakfast. AE, DC, MC, V. Free parking. Closed Nov–Feb. **Amenities:** Restaurant; bar. *In room:* A/C, TV.

Mandetta (Kids) Charmingly old-fashioned, this budget hotel is right on the beach and only 549m (1,800 ft.) from the archaeological area. In addition to the hotel, this family-run property includes a few cabins (with kitchen and small private patio garden), and an RV park. Guest rooms are not large but are functional, simply decorated, and have tiled floors. The hotel has a private beach and facilities, including activities for kids (for a fee). The family-run **restaurant** ★ offers a solid traditional menu that makes it popular among locals.

Via Torre di Mare 2, 84063 Paestum. ✆ **0828-811118.** Fax 0828-721328. www.mandetta.it. 20 units. 120€ double. Rate includes breakfast. AE, DC, MC, V. Free parking. **Amenities:** Restaurant; bar. *In room:* A/C, TV.

Tenuta Seliano This pleasant *agriturismo* is a good budget choice for those who like the countryside. Set in a 19th-century hamlet, the picturesque buildings have been turned into lodgings with large, comfortable guest rooms with country-style elegance and good taste. A well-groomed garden with a swimming pool and some 91 hectares (225 acres) of land complete the property, part of which is dedicated to raising buffaloes (for mozzarella, of course). The cuisine prepared by Mrs. Bellelli—who also offers classes—completes the service. You can choose to have all your meals at the farm, or only breakfast.

Via Seliano, Borgo Antico (Capaccio Scalo), 84063 Paestum. ✆ **0828-723634.** Fax 0828-724544. www. agriturismoseliano.it. 14 units. 120€ double. Rate includes breakfast. AE, DC, MC, V. Free parking. Closed Nov–Dec 27 and Jan 7–Feb. **Amenities:** Pool. *In room:* A/C (5€ per day), TV.

WHERE TO DINE

We highly recommend a visit to the **Tenuta Vannulo** ★★, Via Galileo Galilei, Contrada Vannulo, Capaccio Scalo (✆ **0828-727894;** www.vannulo.it), the best buffalo farm in Italy (hence, in the world). We confess, we really came here just to taste the gelato ★★★, which is famed to be the best in Italy, and discovered a gourmet paradise. Antonio Palmieri's farm is certified organic, and he justly takes great pride in his operation: You can visit the premises, meet the buffalo, and taste the products, including the best mozzarella you can dream of. The Tenuta also has a few **guest rooms** where you can spend the night.

In addition to the restaurants below, we recommend **Tre Olivi,** in the Savoy Beach Hotel (above).

Moderate

Le Trabe ★★ SALERNITAN   This is a beautiful restaurant, inside an old electrical plant in a lovely setting of gardens and streams. The menu is seasonal and changes often, with dishes reminiscent of the local multicultural tradition (Greek, Roman, French, and so on). You may find *taccozzette gamberi e porcini mantecati al provolone* (homemade pasta with shrimp and porcini mushrooms baked with provolone cheese) or *filetto di cernia all'uva* (grouper filet with grapes), or an excellent ragout. The restaurant also has a few rooms (90€ double, including breakfast) to rent for the night.

Via Capo di Fiume 4, Capaccio Scalo. ✆ **0828-724165.** www.letrabe.it. Reservations recommended. Secondi 15€–24€. AE, DC, MC, V. Daily 12:30–3pm and 7:30–10pm.

Nonna Sceppa ★★ SALERNITAN   This restaurant has grown in popularity and is now one of the best in the region. The menu changes seasonally but always includes well-prepared traditional dishes. Everything is homemade, from the bread and delicious pasta to the delectable mozzarella and the desserts. The summer menu focuses on seafood and may include *rombo al forno con patate* (turbot baked on a bed of potatoes), while the winter menu highlights meat dishes, such as the traditional *tiano di carne* (ragout of sausages, pork ribs, and pork rind). We highly recommend the *spaghetti con l' aragosta* (with spiny lobster) and the classic and masterfully grilled catch of the day. The outdoor terrace is a pleasant incentive during fair weather.

Via Laura 45, Capaccio Scalo. ✆ **0828-851064.** www.nonnasceppa.com. Reservations recommended. Secondi 12€–25€. AE, DC, MC, V. Oct–May Fri–Wed 12:30–3pm and 7:30–10pm; June–Sept daily 12:30–3pm and 7:30–10pm. Closed 3 weeks in Oct.

Ristorante Nettuno ★ SALERNITAN   This picturesque and upscale restaurant is in one of ancient Paestum's preserved gate towers, itself part of a 19th-century farmhouse. It opens onto a charming garden that is highly sought after for weddings. Appropriate to the surroundings, the cuisine is traditional but sophisticated, and the menu includes both meat and fish choices. You'll find *crespoline* (savory crepe stuffed with mozzarella and ham), and excellent pasta dishes, as well as a variety of secondi.

Via Nettuno 2 (by the secondary entrance to the archaeological area), Paestum. ✆ **0828-811028.** www.ristorantenettuno.com. Reservations recommended. Secondi 12€–26€. AE, DC, MC, V. July–Aug daily noon–3:30pm and 8–11:30pm; Sept–June Tues–Sun noon–3:30pm.

Inexpensive

Il Granaio dei Casabella ★ SALERNITAN   Across from the walls of ancient Paestum, this countryside restaurant inside the hotel of the same name (p. 273), offers refined dining and a delightful veranda overlooking an internal garden. You may be surprised by the delicious *granatine di lardo ai frutti di mare* (shellfish fritters); *gnocchi con zucca e gamberi in zimino* (with shrimp, pumpkin, and a spinach-and-herb sauce), or *risotto carciofi e aragosta* (with lobster and artichokes). For something simpler, try the grilled fish.

Via Tavernelle 84 (off Via Magna Grecia), 84063 Paestum. ✆ **0828-721014.** Fax 0828-811893. www.ilgranaiodeicasabella.com. Reservations recommended. Secondi 12€–18€. AE, DC, MC, V. Daily 12:30–3pm and 7:30–10pm.

3 PADULA & CERTOSA DI SAN LORENZO ★★★

98km (59 miles) SE of Salerno

Little known to foreign tourists, the Carthusian Monastery of St. Lorenzo—one of the largest in the world—is prized for its architectural splendor and rich collection of artistic treasures. Off the beaten path in Salerno's hinterlands, this grandiose 16th-century monastery nestles in the slopes of the hill near the little town of Padula. It is an easy day trip from Salerno, Naples, or Paestum.

ESSENTIALS

GETTING THERE & AROUND   **Trenitalia** (𝄐 **892021** in Italy; www.trenitalia.it) offers direct connections from Naples and Salerno to Battipaglia, where you will need to switch to a shuttle bus (that runs on schedule with the trains) to Padula and the monastery. You can also take a **bus** directly from Salerno: **Lamanna** (𝄐 **0975-520426**) and **Curcio Viaggi** (𝄐 **089-254080;** www.curcioviaggi.it) both make runs to Padula from Piazza della Concordia near the train station. Curcio Viaggi also offers direct connection to Padula from Firenze and Siena. From Naples, **Autolinee SLA** (𝄐 **0973-21016;** www.slasrl.it) offers direct service to Padula; **Simet** (𝄐 **0983-520315;** www.simetspa.it) has a daily bus that leaves Piazza Garibaldi (across from Stazione Centrale) at 10am. By **car**, take the exit marked PADULA-BUONABITACOLO off the A3 to SS 19, and follow the signs for PADULA.

Padula is small and can be visited **on foot;** the monastery is at the base of the hill on the edge of town.

VISITOR INFORMATION   The local tourist office is **Associazione Pro Loco Padula,** Via Italo Balbo 45, Padula (𝄐 **0975-778611;** www.prolocopadula.com).

FAST FACTS   You'll find a **pharmacy** (𝄐 **0975-74587**) on Via Nazionale in Padula. The nearest **hospital** (𝄐 **0975-312111**) is in the town of Marsicovetere, a few miles east. For an **ambulance,** dial 𝄐 **118.** Dial 𝄐 **113** or 112 for the **police,** 𝄐 **115** for the **fire department,** and 𝄐 **116** for **ACI road assistance.** You will find a **bank** with an ATM, **Banco di Napoli** (𝄐 **0975-778593**), on Piazza Umberto I 15.

EXPLORING PADULA & THE MONASTERY

Padula is a small hill town, with interesting churches and *palazzi* lining its historic streets. The big attraction here is the Carthusian Monastery.

Certosa di San Lorenzo ★★   Established in 1306, the monastery was enlarged over the centuries, reaching the height of its fame during the Renaissance, when it was one of the richest monasteries in Italy. The huge complex of buildings and courtyards covers an area of 51,500 sq. m (554,341 sq. ft.). It has 320 halls, 52 staircases, 100 fireplaces, 13 courtyards, and 41 fountains. Abandoned in 1866, the Certosa was only recently reopened to the public after extensive restorations, including repair from the earthquake of 1980. It is now the setting for important cultural events and international exhibits, not the least of which is the Ravello Music Festival (p. 213), which schedules a number of concerts on the grounds every year.

Many of the original medieval structures were redecorated in baroque style, making it one of the most important baroque works of art in Italy. The first **cloister ★★**, near the

276 entrance to the monastery, dates from 1561 and is graced by an elegant portico and fountain. The richly decorated church boasts two magnificent wooden **choirs** ★★★ inlaid with intarsia artwork; one, created for the monks, dates from 1503, while the other, designed by Giovanni del Gallo in 1507, was meant for the lay brothers. Near the church is the original cemetery from 1552, now a **cloister.** The later, larger cemetery is in the splendid 17th-century **main cloister** ★★★. Along the two levels of porticos decorated with beautiful carvings are the monks' secluded **"cells"**—miniapartments of three to four rooms with private porticos, small gardens, and even a workshop/studio for some. Note the small opening for delivering food and the aperture that allowed in light, both by the entrance to the cell. You can climb to the upper floor via a beautiful **staircase** in an octagonal tower, where you'll see the **Monk's Promenade** ★ around the cloister and the **Apartments of the Prior** ★★.

The **library** and **reception halls** of the monastery house an **archaeological museum,** which holds a collection of ancient artifacts from the nearby necropolis.

Viale Certosa 1. ⓒ **0975-77745.** www.magnifico.beniculturali.it/certosa.html. Admission 4€; free with purchase of the Artecard. Wed–Mon 9am–8pm. Last admission 1 hr. earlier. Closed Jan 1, Aug 15, and Dec 25.

WHERE TO STAY & DINE

The monastery is an easy excursion from Salerno or nearby towns, but few visitors stay the night. We highly recommend stopping for a meal though: The popular **Taverna Il Lupo** ★★, Via Municipio (ⓒ **0975-778376;** www.tavernaillupo.it; secondi 7€–12€; closed Sun dinner and all day Mon), is a rustic and welcoming trattoria serving traditional local cuisine. If you do want to stay for the night, the best hotels in town are the atmospheric **Villa Cosilinum,** Corso Garibaldi, Località Sant'Eligio, 84034 Padula (ⓒ **0975-778615;** www.villacosilinum.it; 100€ double, including buffet breakfast) and **Grand Hotel Certosa,** Viale Certosa 41, 84034 Padula (ⓒ **0975-77126;** www.certosa.it; 90€ double, including breakfast), each with elegant guest rooms and good **restaurants.**

4 THE NATIONAL PARK OF THE CILENTO

110km (68 miles) S of Naples

The Cilento is Campania's loneliest wilderness, well off the beaten track and one of the least inhabited areas in Italy. The population is concentrated on the beautiful coast, while the comparatively abandoned inland area is crossed by only a few roads. Established as a national park in 1991, this is the second-largest national park in Italy, offering a variety of land- and seascapes, from the mountains of the Alburni—where you'll find some of the most interesting caves in the world—and Monte Cervati, the highest mountain in Campania, to the splendid promontory of Cape Palinuro, so justly praised by Virgil. The Cilento is also rich in archaeological and architectural mementoes of the various civilizations that inhabited the area since prehistoric times.

ESSENTIALS

GETTING THERE For such a remote area, the Cilento is well connected by public transportation, with its major towns connected by train, its major harbors by ferry, and its smaller villages by bus. During the summer, **Metrò del Mare** (ⓒ **199-600700;** www.metrodelmare.com; Apr–Sept) offers **boat service** that connects Agropoli, Acciaroli, Palinuro, and Camerota with Pozzuoli, Naples, Sorrento, Positano, Amalfi, and Salerno.

SALERNO, PAESTUM, PADULA & THE CILENTO

10

THE NATIONAL PARK OF THE CILENTO

Direct **trains** link Naples and Salerno to Agropoli/Castellabate, Pisciotta/Palinuro, and Vallo della Lucania. Contact **Trenitalia** (© 892021 in Italy; www.trenitalia.it) for fares and information.

Each of the towns and villages in the park are also served by **bus** from Naples, Pompeii, Salerno, and Paestum: **CSTP,** Piazza Matteo Luciani 33, Salerno (© **800-016659** toll-free within Italy, or 089-487001; www.cstp.it), runs several lines from Napoli, Pompeii, Paestum, and Salerno to Vallo della Lucania, Agropoli, Santa Maria di Castellabate, Acciaroli, and Pollica. **Curcio Viaggi** (© **089-254080;** www.curcioviaggi.it) offers lines from Rome and Salerno to Sicignano degli Alburni, Scario, and Polla. **SCAT** (© **0974-838415**) connects Salerno and Paestum with Agropoli, Santa Maria di Castellabate, and villages along the coast in between. **Lamanna** (© **0975-520426**) offers service from Salerno to Polla. **Autolinee Giuliano Bus** (© **0974-836185;** www.giulianobus.com) covers Naples and Salerno to Roccadaspide, Agropoli, Vallo della Lucania, and Pioppi. Finally, **SITA** (© **089-226604;** www.sitabus.it) has lines from Salerno to Pertosa and Polla.

By **car,** take autostrada A3 to the exit marked SERRE, turning onto SS 19 toward Serre. Turn right on SS 488 following signs for ROCCA D'ASPIDE into the park.

GETTING AROUND   In spite of good public transportation inside the park, only a **car** will provide the necessary flexibility for extensive exploration of the interior, particularly in the off-season, when connections are less frequent and ferry service is suspended. In addition to the major **car-rental** companies (p. 326), you can rent a car through **Alba Rent Car,** Via Alcide de Gasperi, Agropoli (✆ **0974-828099**); **Smec,** Peppino Manente Comunale 35, Castellabate (✆ **0974-961565**); and **L.T. Trasporti,** Via Colombo 11, Castellabate (✆ **0974-961366;** www.ltgroup.it), which also provides taxi/car service. For **radio taxi,** call ✆ **339-4820303.**

VISITOR INFORMATION   The park's **Visitor Center** (✆ **0974-719911;** www.cilento ediano.it) is on Piazza Santa Caterina 8, 84078 **Vallo della Lucania,** the gateway to the park.

FAST FACTS   You'll find **pharmacies** in each of the major towns and villages in the area, including at Via Roma 6 (✆ **0974-4974**), in Vallo della Lucania, and at Corso Garibaldi 43 (✆ **0974-823054**), in Agropoli. The **hospital** (✆ **0974-827511**) is on Contrada Marrota in Agropoli. For an **ambulance,** dial ✆ **118.** Dial ✆ **113** or 112 for the **police,** ✆ **115** in case of **fire,** and ✆ **116** for **ACI road assistance.** You'll find **banks** with ATMs in all major towns and villages in the park.

GUIDED TOURS   **CitySightseeing** (✆ **081-5517279** in Naples, 0828-720859 or 0828-720114 in Paestum; www.napoli.city-sightseeing.it) offers a series of park tours exclusively for **Artecard** (p. 110) holders. Departures are from Pestum, Agropoli, and a number of other towns in the park, including Acciaroli, and Palinuro. The cost is between 5€ and 10€ depending on the itinerary.

EXPLORING THE PARK

The park was declared part of the Biosphere Preservation program of UNESCO in 1997 for its pristine natural environment, rich in rare plant species, such as the *primula di Palinuro*—a rare dune flower that has been adopted as the symbol of the park—and the wild orchid of San Giovanni a Piro, a Mediterranean orchid (*orchidee spontanee*). The park covers almost 180,000 hectares (444,790 acres), and encompasses two mountain masses—the Alburni to the north and Monte Cervati to the south—and several small towns and villages. Vallo della Lucania, the seat of the park information office, is a good base for discovering the interior and enjoying hiking opportunities.

Archaeological Sites

Beyond a belt of uninteresting modern development, Agropoli's well-preserved **medieval citadel** ★ (about 49km/30 miles south of Salerno) crowns a promontory dominated by a **castle** ★, today partially ruined and overlooking the harbor and the small fishing harbor below. On a clear day, you can see all the way to Punta Campanella and Capri from the castle's walls. We also recommend a stroll along the **seafront promenade** ★.

  Teggiano ★ (100km/62 miles south of Salerno and 14km/8¾ miles north of Padula) also makes for a pleasant excursion. The **Cathedral of Santa Maria Maggiore** has beautiful sculpture, particularly the 13th-century ambone and the 14th-century tomb of Enrico Sanseverino. More art is in the **Museo Diocesano** (✆ **0975-79930;** free admission; Tues-Sun 10am-1pm and 3-6pm), in the 13th-century church of San Pietro. The imposing **castle** ★★ dates back to Norman times; owned by the Macchiaroli family, it is not open to the public. Other villages worth the detour are **Castellabate** (20km/13 miles south of Paestum), with its picturesque 12th-century castle, and **Acciaroli** (80km/50 miles south of Salerno) and the adjacent medieval hamlet of **Pioppi.**

The **archaeological excavations of Velia** ★, 90km (56 miles) south of Salerno (© **0974-971409;** daily 9am–sunset; admission 2€, free with purchase of the Artecard), are near the coastline, on the outskirts of Marina di Ascea. These ruins are lesser known than those at Paestum; they are the remains of the Greek colony of **Elea,** created around 540 B.C. as the seat of the famed Eleatic school of philosophy. Elea had grown into such a beacon of Greek culture by Roman times that even after it fell under the rule of the empire it was allowed the privilege of maintaining Greek as its official language. That is when its name was changed to Velia. The **lower town** features portions of the walls from the 5th and 4th centuries B.C., as well as, around the south gate, houses originally from the same period but modified in Roman times. Also of note are the Roman thermal baths, with beautiful mosaics in the *Frigidarium.* From there you can climb to the famous **Porta Rosa** ★★, on a stretch of the original Greek pavement. In the **Acropolis** (the upper town), you'll find ruins of a theater, an Ionic temple that was partially covered by a Norman castle, and a sanctuary to Poseidon. The northern sections of the city walls are still well-preserved.

Natural Attractions

The best attractions in the park are its **grottoes.** Most superb are the **Grotte dell'Angelo** ★★★ in Pertosa (© **0975-397037;** www.grottedellangelo.sa.it; Mar-Oct daily 9am–7pm, Nov-Feb daily 10am–4pm; three guided tours 10€, 13€, and 16€; free with purchase of the Artecard). Created by the stream that still flows there, the grottoes have parts still underwater. A visit here starts with a ride on a raft across the first cave. The corridors extend for over 3km (2 miles), but the actual walk depends on the length of the tour you choose: the Inferno (60 min.), the Purgatorio (75 min.), or the Paradiso (90 min.). Each subsequent hall contains marvelous formations of shapely stalactites and stalagmites, and some pure crystal formations. The grotto's inhabitants built pile dwellings during the Neolithic period, and more traditional dwellings during the Bronze and early Iron ages. The caves were kept in use during Lucanian and ancient Roman times, and during the Christian era, when they were consecrated in the name of Saint Michael, the 11th-century archangel. Experienced spelunkers can book a tour to less accessible parts of the grottoes, including the active subterranean stream. To reach the grottoes, follow the signs for PERTOSA on SS 19; the parking area is a short distance off the road to the left. *Note:* Thursday and Friday, when school is in session, access to the grottoes is reserved for classes; they open to the public at 2pm.

An interesting complement to a visit to the grottoes is the newly opened **MIdA,** Piazza de Marco, Pertosa (© **0975-397220;** www.fondazionemida.it), a museum dedicated to the local ecosystem with a multimedia exhibit on spelunking (admission 2€, free with purchase of the Artecard; Tues-Sun 10am-1pm, Nov-Mar also 3-6pm and Apr-Oct also 3-7pm).

Ernest Hemingway

The fishing harbor of Acciaroli was the preferred hideaway of Ernest Hemingway, who stayed here several times. Built on a promontory, the village is dominated by a square defense **tower** overlooking the harbor and the pretty 12th-century **church of the Annunziata.** The story goes that Hemingway got the idea for *The Old Man and the Sea* after befriending a local fisherman.

SALERNO, PAESTUM, PADULA & THE CILENTO

10

THE NATIONAL PARK OF THE CILENTO

Caselle in Pittari

Rivers sculpted the limestone mountains of the Cilento into scenic narrow valleys. The partially soluble composition of this rock is also at the origin of geological **sinkholes.** This curious phenomenon occurs when a river suddenly descends underground, only to reemerge several miles away. The most spectacular of all is the sinkhole created by the Bussento River; it is one of the largest known sinkholes. The river disappears near the little town of **Caselle in Pittari** into a huge hole in the ground. The Bussento remains underground for about 6km (3³/₄ miles) until it surfaces a few miles south in the pretty medieval village of **Morigerati** ★ to resume its overland course.

The **Grotte di Castelcivita** ★★ (© **0828-975524;** www.grottedicastelcivita.it; admission 8€, 20% discount with purchase of the Artecard) is an astounding succession of large galleries and natural halls extending for over 5km (3 miles) under the Alburni mountains. Inhabited from Paleolithic times to the Bronze Age, the grottoes are composed of a central section of galleries and halls. Lateral chambers that depart from the main core have been only partially explored. Some halls have beautiful stalactite and stalagmite formations, others, such as the so-called *Tempio* (Temple), have multicolored formations. Remember to bring a jacket: It's chilly even in summer. The grottoes are accessible by guided tour only, with visits starting every 90 minutes (Mar 16-Sept 10:30am–6pm; Oct 1-Mar 15 10:30am–4:30pm). To reach the grottoes, follow SS 488 toward the small town of Controne; the grottoes are a few miles down the road.

Outdoor Activities

The best of the many **hiking trails** in the park ascend Monte Cervati (1,898m/6,227 ft.), and Monte Alburno (1,742m/5,715 ft.). **Monte Alburno** ★★ is nicknamed Mount Panorama for the sweeping views you can enjoy from the top. Climb up one of two trails from **Sicignano degli Alburni,** a town off SS 19 not far from Serre. The first trail climbs directly up to the western peak; the second leads to a fork at 1,400m (4,593 ft.), where one branch heads east and the other west. Allow at least 4 hours for either climb. The region's highest mountain is **Monte Cervati** ★★. Cervati is a dramatic sight, especially in the summer, when its extensive lavender fields are in bloom. You can make the ascent via two different trails, both starting from the town of **Sanza,** on SS 517. Allow about 6 hours for either.

Beaches at the leading resorts are positively crowded in summer. Loudspeakers with music and activities for kids turn what was once an idyllic setting into a noisy affair. So, if you are after a secluded beach, you'll have to rent a boat. **Palinuro** ★ is a fishing and resort harbor set among olive groves in a picturesque bay protected by a promontory, famous for its grottoes in the cliffs. The most beautiful of them, the **Grotta Azzurra** ★★, is far less mobbed than its more famous cousin in Capri, yet it also takes on a wonderful coloration, especially around noon and sunset. You'll find boats with or without crew for rent in the harbor; we recommend **Cooperativa dei Pescatori** (© **0974-931233). Santa Maria di Castellabate** ★ is blessed with two beautiful beaches: The one to the north—the largest—has unusually fine sand, while the smaller one to the south enjoys the proximity of a shady pine grove. The whole stretch of sea here, the **Punta Licosa,** is a

biological protected area and marine park, which affords some interesting **snorkeling**
and **scuba diving. Centro Subaqueo,** Via Marina Castellabate (© 0974-961060), is the
best on the coast for guides and equipment. The little fishing harbor and seaside town of
Marina di Camerota is beloved by locals for its less-developed coastline and variety of
sandy or rocky beaches—such as **Baia della Calanca** ★—as well as its coves, grottoes,
towers, and great scuba diving.

WHERE TO STAY

International tourism is new to this area, and accommodations are quite basic. We tend
to prefer the quality of service—and food—at an eco-friendly *agriturismo.*

In a panoramic position in Palinuro is the **Agriturismo Sant'Agata,** Via Sant'Agata
Nord (© 0974-931716; www.agriturismosantagata.it), offering excellent cuisine, **cooking classes** ★, and simple but tasteful guest rooms. Another address serving excellent
food and wine is **Il Vecchio Casale,** Contrada Vigna, 84070 Vatolla di Perdifumo
(© 0974-845235; fax 0974-821296; www.ilvecchiocasale.it), inland of Castellabate:
The elegant farmhouse dates from the 18th century and has a pleasant swimming
pool. **Principe di Vallescura,** Via Marina Campagna, Località Vallescura, near Pollica
(© 0974-973087; fax 0974-973031; www.principedivallescura.com), affords beautiful
sea views and beach access; and **I Fornari,** Località Fornari 2, 84076 Stella Cilento
(© 0974-909204; fax 0974-909907; www.agriturismoifornari.it), offers upscale accommodations in an atmospheric 18th-century mill and has great amenities, including a pool.

Albergo Santa Caterina   The best hotel in Palinuro, this welcoming hotel is located
right in the heart of town. Housed in an elegant building, it offers pleasant public spaces
and nicely appointed pastel-colored guest rooms, decorated with hand-painted Vietri
tiles. The rooms are not huge, but comfortable and pleasantly decorated; most open onto
private balconies and small terraces. Bathrooms are a bit on the small side but are well
kept (most with shower only). The hotel offers a shuttle to the beach plus a beach
umbrella and chairs for 10€ per day.

Via Indipendenza 53, 84064 Palinuro. © 0974-931019. Fax 0974-938325. www.albergosantacaterina.
com. 20 units. 180€–220€ double. AE, DC, MC, V. Free parking. Closed New Year's Eve and Day. **Amenities:**
Restaurant; bar; concierge. *In room:* A/C, TV, minibar.

Grand Hotel San Pietro   On the beach only steps away from central Palinuro, this
modern hotel compensates in amenities what it lacks in charm compared to the Santa
Caterina (above). Guest rooms are good size, bright and functional, with nicely tiled
bathrooms (most with shower only); most rooms open onto private balconies with sea
views. The panoramic pool is filled with seawater, and the private beach has umbrellas,
chairs, and facilities. The hotel's elegant **restaurant** is very good.

Via Carlo Pisacane, 84064 Palinuro. © 0974-931466. Fax 0974-931919. www.grandhotelsanpietro.com.
20 units. 210€–240€ double; from 270€ suite. AE, DC, MC, V. Free parking. Closed Nov–Mar. **Amenities:**
Restaurant; bar; concierge; pool; spa; Wi-Fi. *In room:* A/C, TV, minibar.

Hotel Antichi Feudi   This hotel, in a recently restored baronial palazzo in Teggiano's
medieval district, offers excellent quality. Guest rooms are large and tastefully, if a bit
sparsely, decorated, some with original tiled floors. Bathrooms are modern and good-size
(some with shower only). The **restaurant** is formal, and the food is good.

Via S. Francesco 2, 84039 Teggiano. © 0975-587329. Fax 0975-587421. www.antichifeudi.com. 12 units.
100€–160€ double. AE, DC, MC, V. Free parking. **Amenities:** Restaurant; bar; concierge. *In room:* A/C, TV,
minibar.

La Colombaia   This small family-run hotel is in a charming hillside villa surrounded by olive groves. It offers quiet and well-appointed accommodations, tastefully furnished with period furniture and tiled floors, and all with sea views; bathrooms are small but well kept (most with shower only). *Note:* A 2-day minimum stay is required.

Via La Vecchia 2, Piano delle Pere, 84043 Agropoli. ℂ/fax **0974-821800**. www.lacolombaiahotel.it. 10 units. 140€ double; 190€ triple; 240€ quad. Rates include breakfast. MC, V. Free parking. Closed Nov–Feb. **Amenities:** Restaurant; bar; pool. *In room:* A/C, TV, minibar, Wi-Fi (for a fee).

WHERE TO DINE

In addition to the following dining opportunities, we suggest eating at the restaurants of the *agriturismi* mentioned in "Where to Stay," above.

Moderate

Da Carmine CILENTAN/SEAFOOD   Right on the beach near Castellabate, this restaurant prides itself on its "Mediterranean diet": All dishes on the menu are low cholesterol, cooked with excellent local olive oil, and include plenty of fresh seasonal vegetables. Of the many seafood dishes, we recommend the *spaghetti alle vongole* (with clams) and the grilled catch of the day. The establishment also has a few tastefully appointed **guest rooms,** most of them with sea views (100€ double with breakfast; 180€ double with half-board, required in Aug).

Via Ogliastro Marina, Ogliastro Marina, 84060 Castellabate. ℂ **0974-963023**. Fax 0974-963900. www.albergodacarmine.it. Reservations recommended Sat–Sun. Secondi 10€–18€. AE, DC, MC, V. Wed–Mon 12:30–3pm and 7:30–10:30pm.

Il Ceppo ★ CILENTAN/SEAFOOD   This local favorite has been a reliable choice for decades. The pleasant atmosphere and friendly professional service matches the quality of the food. The menu focuses on traditional dishes, such as the delicious *tagliolini con gamberi, fiori di zucca e vongole* (fresh pasta with clams, shrimp, and zucchini flowers) and the excellent catch of the day cooked in a salt crust until perfectly moist and savory. Attached to the restaurant is a small modern hotel offering 20 well-furnished, comfortable rooms, a pretty garden, and a shuttle to the beach (90€–100€ double; 115€–130€ triple; prices include breakfast and free parking).

Via Madonna del Carmine 31, 84043 Agropoli. ℂ **0974-843036**. Fax 0974-843234. www.hotelristorante ilceppo.com. Reservations recommended Sat–Sun. Secondi 10€–21€. AE, DC, MC, V. Wed–Mon 12:30–3pm and 7:30–10:30pm (also Tues in Aug). Closed 10 days in Jan.

Inexpensive

Angiolina Value CILENTAN   This historic trattoria is a local institution for its authentic food and moderately priced yet generous portions. Try the house specialty, *spaghetti con le alici* (with local anchovies), followed by the daily catch *all'acquapazza* (cooked in herbed broth) or the splendid *frittura* (fried seafood platter).

Via Passariello 2, Pisciotta. ℂ **0974-973188**. Reservations recommended Sat–Sun. Secondi 10€–12€. AE, DC, MC, V. Mon–Sat 7:30–10:30pm; Sun and holidays 12:30–3pm and 7:30–10:30pm.

La Cantina del Marchese CILENTAN   In the heart of Marina di Camerota, this traditional restaurant specializes in local peasant cuisine, such as the cheese and cured meat antipasto. In summer, waiters dress in traditional clothing, and a tasting menu is available in addition to the regular a la carte options. We recommend the *lagane e ceci* (homemade pasta with chickpeas) and the perfect *tagliatelle* (fettucine), followed by the succulent *capretto al forno* (roasted baby goat) and grilled meats. Definitely leave room for the homemade desserts.

Via del Marchese 13, Marina di Camerota. ℂ **0974-932570.** www.lacantinadelmarchese.com. Reservations recommended Sat–Sun. Secondi 8€–12€; tasting menu 16€ (summer only). AE, DC, MC, V. Oct, Dec–Jan, and Mar–May Fri–Sun 7:30–10:30pm; June–Sept Mon–Sat 7:30–10:30pm, Sun 12:30–3pm and 7:30–10:30pm. Closed Nov and Feb.

La Chioccia d'Oro ★ CILENTAN   This is the place to come for a warm welcome, an enticing menu, and a hearty traditional meal. For a perfect, down-to-earth dining experience, we highly recommend the wonderful homemade pasta, such as the rich lasagna or the *fusilli al ragù* (with meat sauce). The *grigliate* (medley of grilled meat) is splendid. Local specialties are the mushrooms and the tasty *coniglio farcito* (stuffed rabbit). The homemade desserts are good, as is the house wine.

Via Biblio di Novi Velia, Vallo della Lucania. ℂ **0974-70004.** www.chiocciadoro.com. Reservations recommended. Secondi 8€–16€. MC, V. Sat–Thurs 12:30–3pm and 7:30–10pm. Closed 2 weeks in Sept.

La Taverna del Pescatore CILENTAN/SEAFOOD   This popular tavern is where locals come for great seafood and a delightful terrace. The menu includes local specialties as well as a choice of daily dishes that depend on market offerings. If it is available, we highly recommend the splendid *zuppa di pesce* (fish stew); rich with local fresh seafood, it is a meal on its own. The *risotto alla pescatora* (with seafood) is another winner.

Via Lamia, 84062 Castellabate. ℂ **0974-968293.** Reservations recommended. Secondi 11€–18€. MC, V. Apr–June and Sept–Oct Tues–Sun noon–3pm; July–Aug Mon–Fri 7:30–11pm, Sat–Sun 12:30–3pm and 7:30–11pm. Closed Nov–Mar.

La Veranda ⓥ**alue** CILENTAN/SEAFOOD   This is the perfect place to have a great seafood meal without spending a fortune. A short distance from the harbor and the medieval citadel, this convivial restaurant offers a seasonal menu featuring traditional dishes. We loved the *scialatielli ai frutti di mare* (homemade local pasta with seafood) as well as the *ravioloni di ricotta al pesto di rucola* (cheese ravioli with arugula pesto), followed by the perfectly grilled daily catch or the excellent *gamberoni al Fiano* (jumbo shrimp stewed in local Fiano wine).

Via Piave 38, Agropoli. ℂ **0974-822272.** Reservations recommended Sat–Sun. Secondi 8€–16€. AE, DC, MC, V. Sept–June Tues–Sun 1–3pm and 8–10pm; July–Aug Tues–Sun 8–10pm. Closed 1 week at Christmas and 2 weeks in July.

11

Campania's Well-Kept Secrets: Caserta, Benevento & Avellino

International tourism is only starting to come to this region that is little-known even among Italians. Discover simple authentic villages, such as the hill towns of **Irpinia** around **Avellino,** and a few artistic treasures, such as the Royal Palace in **Caserta** (the Reggia, as it is known), the Cathedral of **Capua,** the Roman amphitheater in **Santa Maria** **Capua Vetere,** and **Benevento's** Roman arch.

These attractions probably owe their semiforgotten state to their distance from the main train lines and highways. Close enough to tourists giants such as Naples and the Amalfi Coast, they're easily side stepped; but these quiet, little-visited towns are well worth a trip in themselves.

1 CASERTA

17km (11 miles) NW of Naples

The busy town of Caserta, only a few miles north of Naples, is an agroindustrial center serving its fertile environs. It had its moment of glory in the 18th century, when the new Bourbon king decided to move his capital here from Naples, and Caserta suddenly appeared on international maps. The **palace** he built was explicitly meant to rival Versailles and succeeded in its intent. The king also gave new breath to the local economy, creating a small silk industry in nearby **San Leucio.**

ESSENTIALS

GETTING THERE   Caserta is easily reached by train from Naples. Trains leave Napoli Stazione Centrale every 10 to 20 minutes for the 30-minute trip to Caserta. Contact **Trenitalia** (© 892021 in Italy; www.trenitalia.it) for fares and information. Trains arrive at Caserta's **railway station** in Piazza Giuseppe Garibaldi (© 0823-325479), only a few steps from the Reggia, on the other side of Piazza Carlo III. Caserta is also served by **Metro Campania Nord-Est** (© 800-053939 toll-free in Italy; www.metrocampania nordest.it) from Naples.

By car, from either Rome or Naples, take autostrada A1 to the exit marked CASERTA NORD, and follow the signs for CASERTA CENTRO. Coming into town, you will see signs for SAN LEUCIO, CASERTA VECCHIA, and REGGIA. The Reggia (Royal Palace) is in the center of town; from the Royal Palace head northeast and follow the signs reading CASERTAVEC-CHIA; the medieval town is about 10km (6 miles) up the hill. Head northwest from Piazza Vanvitelli, following the signs for SAN LEUCIO to reach the Belvedere.

GETTING AROUND   Public transportation connects all the major sights. You can use the bus to reach Casertavecchia: Bus 110 leaves from Piazza Garibaldi in front of Caserta

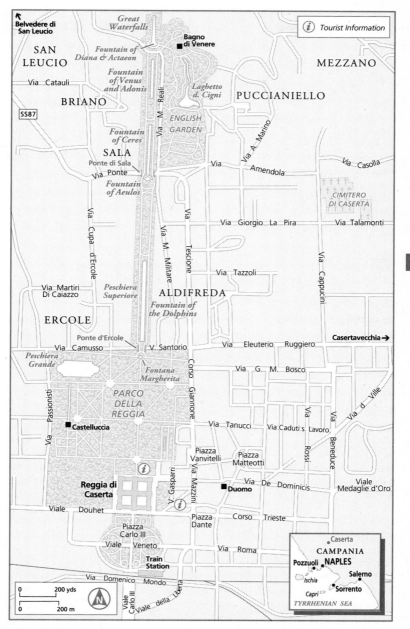

Belvedere di San Leucio

SAN LEUCIO

Great Waterfalls

Bagno di Venere

ⓘ Tourist Information

MEZZANO

Fountain of Diana & Actaeon

Via Catauli

Fountain of Venus and Adonis

BRIANO

Laghetto d. Cigni

PUCCIANIELLO

SS87

Via M. Reali

ENGLISH GARDEN

Via A. Marino

Fountain of Ceres

SALA

Ponte di Sala

Via Ponte

Fountain of Aeulos

Via Cupa d'Ercole

Via

Via M. Militare

Via Tescione

Via Amendola

Via Casolla

CIMITERO DI CASERTA

Via Giorgio La Pira

Via Talamonti

Via Cappucini

Via Tazzoli

Via Martiri Di Caiazzo

Peschiera Superiore

ALDIFREDA

Fountain of the Dolphins

ERCOLE

Ponte d'Ercole

Via Camusso

V. Santorio

Via Eleuterio Ruggiero

Casertavecchia →

Peschiera Grande

Fontana Margherita

Via G. M. Bosco

Via d. Ville

Via Passionisti

PARCO DELLA REGGIA

Corso Giannone

Via Tanucci

Via Caduti s. Lavoro

Via Beneduce

Via Rossi

■ Castelluccia

ⓘ

Reggia di Caserta

ⓘ

V. Gasparri

Via Mazzini

Piazza Vanvitelli

Piazza Matteotti

Via De Dominicis

■ Duomo

Viale Medaglie d'Oro

Viale Douhet

Piazza Carlo III

Piazza Dante

Corso Trieste

Viale Veneto

Via Roma

Train Station

Via Domenico Mondo

Viale Carlo III

Viale della Libertà

0   200 yds
0   200 m

N

Caserta

CAMPANIA

Pozzuoli NAPLES

Ischia

Capri

Salerno

Sorrento

TYRRHENIAN SEA

train station, across from the palace. **Taxis** wait at the stand on Piazza Garibaldi across from the train station (℃ **0823-322400**), and the one on Via Ferrara (℃ **0823-326919**), or you can call them by phone.

VISITOR INFORMATION   The tourist information office for the province, **ETP,** Palazzo Reale, 81100 Caserta (℃ **0823-550011;** fax 0823-326300), maintains an information booth at Corso Trieste 9, at the corner with Piazza Dante and Via Douhet (℃ **0823-321137;** www.eptcaserta.it). It is open Monday to Saturday (9am–7pm).

FAST FACTS   You'll find a **pharmacy,** Corso Trieste 47 (℃ **0823-326147**), not far from the entrance to the Reggia. The *ospedale civile* (**hospital;** ℃ **0823-304964**) is nearby, at Via Tescione Gennaro 1; dial ℃ **118** or 0823-321000 for an **ambulance.** You can call the **police** at ℃ **113** or 112, and the **fire department** at ℃ **115.** The **post office** (℃ **0823-550634**), on Via del Redentore 27, off Via Giuseppe Mazzini, is open Monday to Saturday from 8am to 2pm.

SPECIAL EVENTS   Between the last Monday of August and September 15, **Casertavecchia** hosts a well-established music and art festival, **Settembre al Borgo** (www.casertamusica.com), and the *borgo* comes alive with concerts, theater, and dance.

EXPLORING THE AREA

The modern town itself, heavily ruined during World War II, is uninteresting, but the attractions are mind-boggling. In addition to those highlighted below, we recommend a visit to the 15th-century **Complex of Sant'Agostino** ★, which includes a convent, church, and cloister, as well as several museums, including the Museum of Contemporary Art, the Museum of Traditions, and the newly created **Le Muse** ★. Taking inspiration from Madame Tussauds wax museum in London, this museum offers a unique insight about the local history, presenting the main protagonists in accurate costumes and settings. *Note:* Young children might be disturbed by the lifelike wax figures; please use your own judgment. You'll find the complex on Largo San Sebastiano, off Via Mazzini (℃ **0823-273843;** admission 6€ adults, 4€ children; summer Wed-Mon 9:30am-7:30pm, winter 10am-6pm).

The Reggia (Royal Palace) ★★★

One of the most beautiful royal palaces in the world, the Reggia is a masterpiece of harmonious architecture and decorative arts. (If you experience déjà vu during your visit, it may be because the Reggia was used as a location for *Star Wars: Episode I—The Phantom Menace*). When King Carlo III Bourbon decided to leave Naples, which he considered too open to attacks from the sea, he asked his architect Luigi Vanvitelli to build him a palace that would rival the courts of Paris, London, and Madrid. Vanvitelli dedicated the last 20 years of his life to the construction, for which he used the best materials and workmanship available in the country. The Reggia was finally finished 1 year after the architect's death in 1774, but its interior was not fully completed until 1847. The palace is grandiose, measuring over 45,000 sq. m (484,376 sq. ft.), and divided into four wings, each surrounding a separate courtyard.

Official **guided tours,** led by art historians, are offered on weekends and holidays in winter and daily in summer (℃ **0823-448084** or 0823-277380; www.arethusa.net; admission 5.80€, reservations required); the tours last about 90 minutes. On weekend nights, June through October, *Percorsi di Luce nella Reggia* (**Paths of Light in the Reggia**) ★ (℃ **0823-462078;** www.percorsidiluce.it) uses music, visual, and performing arts to help visitors discover the Reggia, the famous gardens, and the kings who inhabited it. The tours are narrated by art historians and accompanied by light effects, 18th-century music, short performances, and multimedia presentations. Started in 2003, this event is scheduled only a year at a time, and cancellation is always possible due to lack of funds. Make reservations well in advance (18€ adults; free for children 5 and under).

The **horse-carriage tour** of the gardens is relatively short, but very romantic (round-trip 10€ per person). Don't expect it to take you all the way to the top, as the climb is too steep for the horses; the carriages U-turn by the Fountain of Eolus.

Note: A visit to the palace (and even more so the park) involves extensive walking. A shuttle bus is provided between the palace, the Fountain of Diane, and the entrance to the English Gardens; pay and sign up for the bus at the ticket booth. The palace is wheelchair accessible through a private elevator in back of the ticket booth, and golf carts are available for visits to the gardens; call in advance.

You will find a **cafeteria** inside the Reggia, at the end of the main gallery just before the exit to the gardens; it is open during all visiting hours. In summer, you'll find a temporary snack bar at the entrance to the English Gardens.

Royal Palace & Gardens (Reggia di Caserta) ★★★

A visit to the Reggia di Caserta starts in the very scenic main gallery, where the view stretches all the way to the end of the park and to its majestic waterfall. You then climb the splendid main **staircase ★★** to a magnificent octagonal vestibule, decorated with precious marble in various colors. The scale of it is almost stupefying: There are 116 stairs, flanked by niches containing sculptures that allude to the grandeur of the kingdom. We love the two sculpted lions by Pietro Solari and Paolo Persico, which are among the most familiar symbols of the Reggia.

The **Palatine Chapel ★** opens onto the vestibule. Like everything else at the Reggia, it has imposing dimensions (37m/121 ft. long). Inside, over the entrance, you will see the royal box from which the king and queen observed services, while on the main altar you can see the wood model of the ciborium that was never built. Some of the 13 columns defining the gallery still show the damage from the 1943 bombings. Also opening onto the vestibule, to the left of the main staircase, are the **Royal Apartments ★★**. The decorations in the *appartamento nuovo* ("new" apartment) date from the early 19th century, with stuccoes, bas-reliefs, and frescoes. Of the several halls, we like the **Sala di Marte ★**, celebrating military virtues through nine bas-reliefs by Valerio Villareale and a large ceiling fresco by Antonio Galliano depicting mythological scenes from Virgil's *Iliad.* Nearby is the **Throne Room,** which was inaugurated in 1845; it dazzles with gild stucco and 46 medallions depicting all the kings of Naples, from the Norman Roger I to Ferdinand II.

The visit continues through the so-called *appartamento vecchio* ("old" apartment), inaugurated by Ferdinando IV and his wife Maria Carolina of Austria, in 1780. Beautifully furnished and decorated with frescoes, these were the private rooms of the queen and king. First come the "conversation rooms," decorated according to seasonal themes by Antonio Dominici (*Primavera* and *Autunno,* or spring and fall) and Fedele Fischetti (*Estate* and *Inverno*—summer and winter). Spring and summer make up the receiving room and sitting room, respectively, while fall is the dining room, and winter is the smoking room. After these come the bedroom, the king's study, and the queen's parlor. Our favorite furnishings here are the magnificent **Murano glass chandeliers ★★** and the **carved chairs and sofas ★**, masterpieces of neoclassical Italian furniture by Nicola and Pietro Di Fiore. The **paintings** are by **Jakob Philipp Hackert ★**, a court painter who was kept very busy by the Bourbons. Goethe called him an "inveterate hard worker," who not only painted prolifically but also gave drawing lessons to the royal children and delivered lectures. We particularly like his scenes of the kingdom's harbors in the receiving room, as well as the depictions of royal sites in the king's study. Finally, you'll come to the three rooms of the **library**—notice the frescoes in the third room by Friederich Heinrich Függer, said to contain hidden Masonic meanings, a subject which deeply interested the queen—and to an oval hall which contains the magnificent *presepio reale* **(royal Nativity scene)** ★★.

Through a side door from the octagonal vestibule near the main staircase, you can access the permanent exhibit **Terrae Motus** ★, composed of over 70 pieces by Italian and foreign contemporary artists—there is even a piece by Andy Warhol and one by Keith Haring—in reaction to the terrible earthquake that shook Campania in 1980.

At the end of the main gallery on the ground floor is access to the Reggia's magnificent **gardens** ★★★. Covering about 120 hectares (297 acres), the grounds are not only enormous, but simply the most celebrated Italian gardens in the world. The park stretches from the palace to the nearby hills along a central path 3.2km (2 miles) long, graced by a number of fountains, pools, and gardens. A majestic waterfall created by Luigi Vanvitelli cascades from the hills at the end of the park. To fulfill the needs of the palace, he designed an aqueduct to carry water all the way from Monte Taburno, 40km (25 miles) away. The waterfall was the point of arrival of the aqueduct—which he named Caroline Aqueduct after the queen. Today, the water for the fountains is recirculated thanks to pumps, while the aqueduct feeds the town's supply.

Among the fountains depicting mythical events, the most spectacular is the **Fountain of Eolus** ★★, a large construction of grottoes and figures representing the palace of the wind god. Above it and up the hill is a system of **three fountains** ★ feeding into each other, Fountain of Ceres, Fountain of Venus and Adonis, and Fountain of Diana and Atteon. This last is the highest, and we recommend climbing up to it for the superb **view** ★. To the right of this last fountain is the entrance to the **English Garden,** created for Queen Maria Carolina di Borbone by the son of the architect, Carlo Vanvitelli. The Italian architect designed the garden, while English botanist and landscape artist Andrea Graefer created the plant arrangements. Covering over 30 hectares (74 acres), it is a perfect romantic realization, with a lake, a spring, and a small temple, all decorated with ancient Roman statues taken from the ruins of Pompeii. The queen also indulged her infatuation with the Masons here, and the garden is full of hidden symbols and esoteric references. It is accessible only by guided tour.

Viale Douhet. (✆ **0823-277430** or 0823-277111. www.reggiadicaserta.beniculturali.it or www.reggiadi caserta.org. Admission 7€ apts; 3€ gardens; 9€ apts and gardens. Audioguides 4€. Bus shuttle to Diana Fountain 1€. Apts: Wed–Mon 8:30am–7:30pm; last admission 30 min. earlier. Gardens: Wed–Mon 8:30am–sunset; last admission 2 hr. earlier.

Casertavecchia ★★

Overlooking modern Caserta, this medieval *borgo* is one of the best preserved in Italy. It is the original town of Caserta, abandoned when King Carlo III Bourbon built his palace in the valley below and enrolled a large part of the local population to its service. Dominated by a castle that is now in ruins, the village is built around the **cathedral** ★★, Piazza Vescovado (✆ **0823-371318,** free admission, daily 9am–1pm and 3:30–6pm; till 7:30pm in summer), a fine example of Arabo-Norman architectural style. Dedicated to St. Michael, it was built by the Normans in the 12th century, using paleochristian elements as well as material from a nearby temple to Jupiter. The church is built of tufa stone—like the rest of the town—with delicate highlights in white marble: the three portals, the window frames, the decorative columns, and a number of zoomorphic sculptures. The dome is covered by a beautiful *tiburio*—roofed tower—where the Arab influence is readily visible. The octagonal structure has geometric designs in alternate yellow and gray tufa stone, with an ornate intertwining of arches supported by little white columns. Inside you can admire the altar encrusted in mosaic, and the baptismal font from the 4th century. The handsome facade is completed by a 13th-century bell tower, under which passes the main street of the town; it is topped by an octagonal roof and decorated in similar fashion to the cathedral.

Behind the Duomo, on the main street, is the **Chiesetta dell'Annunziata** (daily 9am–1pm and 3:30–6pm; until 7:30pm in summer), a Gothic church built at the end of the 13th century; the portico was added in the 18th century, but behind it you can admire the original facade with the beautiful marble portal. Farther on is the 11th-century **Norman Castle;** most of its original structure—a central core with six towers—is in ruins, but the powerful main tower remains. Do take the time to stroll through the *borgo's* narrow medieval streets, admiring their original paving and the well-preserved medieval decorative details of the buildings and stone archways. Not surprisingly, the town is a favorite dinner destination for locals, who come to enjoy the food, the view, and the atmosphere, especially during warm weather and on weekends.

San Leucio ★★

This hill on the northwest grounds of the Royal Palace is where King Ferdinando IV had his hunting preserve, and where he created a self-sufficient colony as a societal experiment. To make the colony economically independent, the king established a silkworm farm and a weaving factory. Following principles that are quite radical even by today's standards (see "The Radical Philosophy of Gaetano Filangeri," below), Ferdinando and his liberal minister Bernardo Tanucci endowed the colony with completely innovative laws and organization. Education was obligatory and free from the age of 6 up, and only those skilled in their jobs were allowed to marry and have children. There was no distinction between sexes, and every manufacturer had to contribute a portion of its gains to the common fund for people who were unable to work due to poor health or old age. The factory became famous for its precious fabrics, exporting its products far and wide. Today it operates privately, under the Stabilimento Serico De Negri, in which expert artisans keep the tradition alive by weaving damasks, brocades, and other fine fabrics.

Opening onto **Piazza della Seta,** the original colony is very scenic, with ordered rows of houses offering beautiful views over the Reggia and the surroundings. The small **church** preexisted the hamlet and is probably of Longobard origin. The road that leads toward the left from below the steps of the original silk factory on Piazza della Seta climbs to the **Hunting Lodge** of the Aquaviva princes, the original owners of the estate; nearby is the **Vaccheria,** the stables where Ferdinand established the colony's first weaving activity before he built the village.

Casino Reale di Belvedere ★★ This small palace is in a delightful park connected to the Reggia's gardens. The **Royal Apartments ★★** are richly frescoed with **allegoric scenes** painted by Fedele Fischetti; those in the queen's bathroom are by Jakob Philipp Hackert. The view from the **Belvedere ★★** is superb. The **Museo della Seta** has original weaving machinery that is still in working order—you can ask to see one in action—and displays examples of the wonderful original fabrics that were crafted.

Piazza della Seta (off Strada Statale) SS87. (🕿) **800-411515** or 0823-301817. www.realbelvedere.it. Admission 6€. Wed–Mon winter 9:30am–6pm, summer 9:30am–6:30pm. Closed Jan 1, Easter, Aug 15, and Dec 24–25.

The Radical Philosophy of Gaetano Filangeri

Gaetano Filangeri, the mind behind the inventive Bourbon king Ferdinando IV, was an important 18th-century Neapolitan jurist and philosopher. Born near Naples in 1752 as Prince of Arianello, Filangeri was an encyclopedist and a reformer; his work was central to the birth of a liberal movement in southern Italy.

Filangeri's key tenet was his strong belief in public education, which he believed to be the foundation for a happy, healthy, satisfied society. Among his other ideas, he believed that honesty was the primary social virtue, and that merit should be the only distinction among individuals.

Little known to most, his ideas were influential to the elaboration of the U.S. Constitution: Benjamin Franklin was in frequent correspondence with Filangeri during the American Revolution. Having obtained several copies of Filangeri's main work—the six-volume *The Science of Legislation*—he incorporated some of the suggested principles into the U.S. Constitution.

Filangeri's work was cut short by his early death in 1788, and the sixth volume is only an outline. However, the preceding volumes have been translated into English, French, German, and Spanish.

WHERE TO STAY
Moderate

Hotel Europa ★ **Kids**   Only a few steps from the Reggia and the railway station, this hotel offers modern and functional accommodations and good amenities. The large guest rooms have just been remodeled with stylish contemporary furniture and are welcoming and comfortable.

Via Roma 19, 81100 Caserta. ✆ **0823-325400.** Fax 0823-216623. www.hoteleuropacaserta.it. 57 units. 130€ double; 160€ suite. Rates include buffet breakfast. Children 2 and under stay free in parent's room. AE, DC, MC, V. Parking 16€. Closed Dec 31–Jan 1. **Amenities:** Bar; concierge; gym; Internet. *In room:* A/C, TV, Internet, minibar.

Hotel Jolly Caserta   This large old-fashioned hotel in a stately building near Caserta's train station offers comfortable accommodations. Guest rooms are medium-size, with impersonal modern furniture and carpeting. Bathrooms are good-size (some with shower only). The formal **restaurant** is recommended for its well prepared Italian cuisine.

Viale Vittorio Veneto 9, 81100 Caserta. ✆ **0823-325222.** Fax 0823-354522. www.jollyhotelcaserta.it. 107 units. 120€ double. Rate includes buffet breakfast. Children 15 and under stay free in parent's room. AE, DC, MC, V. Free parking. **Amenities:** Restaurant; bar; concierge. *In room:* A/C, TV, minibar.

H2C ★   A welcome addition to the city, this new member of the H2C Italian chain has opened its doors just down the road from the Reggia. Guest rooms are not large but have the clean modern lines that are the signature of this brand; the tiled bathrooms are state-of-the art (most with shower only).

Piazza Vanvitelli 12, 81100 Caserta. ✆ **0823-355520.** Fax 0823-355859. www.h2c.it. 90 units. 160€ double. Rate includes buffet breakfast. Children 2 and under stay free in parent's room. AE, DC, MC, V. Parking 18€ in nearby garage. **Amenities:** Restaurant; bar; concierge; health club; room service; smoke-free rooms; Wi-Fi. *In room:* A/C, TV, Internet, minibar.

Hotel Caserta Antica (**Kids**) On a hillside bordering the old *borgo* of Casertavecchia (about a 15-min. walk), this hotel offers a pleasant countryside location and good amenities, including a generous swimming pool—a real bonus in summer. Bedrooms are adequate and simply decorated, with good-size bathrooms (shower only) and private balconies.

Via Tiglio 41, Casertavecchia, 81100 Caserta. (✆) **0823-371158.** Fax 0823-371333. www.hotelcasertaantica.it. 25 units. 85€ double; 100€ triple; 140€ quad. Rates include breakfast. Children 1 and under stay free in parent's room. AE, DC, MC, V. Free parking. **Amenities:** Restaurant; bar; concierge; pool. *In room:* A/C, TV, Wi-Fi.

WHERE TO DINE
Moderate

Le Colonne ★ CONTEMPORARY CASERTAN Directly across from the Reggia, the key word to describe this popular address in Caserta's dining scene is *elegance*, both in the decor and the presentation of the food. The menu showcases deconstructed traditional dishes prepared with the best organic local ingredients. The house specialty is buffalo, from its meat—perhaps filled with ricotta and served with a traditional vegetable stew—to the famed mozzarella, stuffed with peppers and herbs.

Viale G. Douhet (Via Appia) 7, Caserta. (✆) **0823-467494.** Fax 0823-467988. www.lecolonnemarziale.it. Reservations recommended. Secondi 18€–25€. AE, DC, MC, V. Wed–Mon 12:30–3pm. Closed 2 weeks in Aug.

Inexpensive

Alla Tana del Lupo CASERTAN/PIZZA Popular with the younger set, this atmospheric restaurant a short distance from the medieval *borgo* of Casertavecchia offers solid traditional cuisine, kind service, and respect of the environment (low-consumption electrical bulbs and careful waste recycling). The menu offers an ample choice of both surf and turf, true to the Casertan tradition. We recommend the roasted lamb and the *fusilli ai porcini, provola, e noci* (with porcini mushrooms, smoked local provolone, and walnuts). The pizza is excellent, too.

Via Lupara 1, Casertavecchia. (✆) **0823-371333.** www.allatanadellupo.it. Reservations recommended for dinner. Secondi 8€–14€. AE, DC, MC, V. Daily 12:30–3pm and 7–10:30pm.

Antica Hostaria Massa ★ (**Kids**) CASERTAN/PIZZA This historic restaurant bustles at lunchtime when locals come to enjoy the good food and the pleasant atmosphere (which includes a small arbor patio in summer). The menu ranges from surf to turf and includes a superb pizza and several reinterpretations of traditional dishes. We recommend *pasta alle cozze e vongole* (with mussels and clams), the mouth-watering local sausages, and the splendid *agnello Lauticada* (roasted lamb). There is a tasting menu for 38€ and a kid's tasting menu for 20€ (for your little gourmand).

Via Mazzini 55, Caserta. (✆) **0823-456527.** Fax 0823-214641. www.ristorantemassa.it. Reservations recommended. Secondi 10€–16€. AE, DC, MC, V. Mon–Sat 12:30–3pm and 7–10:30pm; Sun 12:30–3pm. Closed 10 days in Aug.

Antica Locanda ★ CAMPANIAN/CASERTAN This atmospheric restaurant on San Leucio's picturesque main piazza is an outpost of local culinary tradition, offering reliable local dishes as well as a number of regional favorites. They menu includes both seafood and meat dishes, and the house specialty is the risotto, such as the excellent *porcini e provola* (porcini mushrooms and local smoked provolone). We also recommend the excellent *scialatielli ai frutti di mare* (homemade eggless pasta with seafood) and the grilled baby pig.

Piazza della Seta 8, San Leucio. ✆ **0823-305444.** Reservations recommended Sat–Sun. Secondi 10€–16€. AE, DC, MC, V. Daily 12:30–3pm and 7–10:30pm.

Cca' sta' O Masto ★ (**Finds** (**Kids** CASERTAN/PIZZA   This simple, unsophisticated restaurant is a real local hideout, popular for its pizza and delicious dishes from the local peasant tradition. Seafood is served only on weekends, when it is worth coming to taste the perfect *frittura* (deep-fried calamari and shrimp). The rest of the week, we recommend the simple *antipasti*—a sampling of local cheese and cured meats—and the splendid *gnocchi al coccio* (potato dumplings cooked in a terra-cotta dish), as well as the fabulous grilled steak. The 10€ children's menu is appreciated.

Via Sant'Agostino 10, Caserta. ✆ **0823-320042.** Reservations recommended Sat–Sun. Secondi 6€–12€. AE, DC, MC, V. Tues–Sun 12:30–3pm and 7:30–11pm. Closed 2 weeks in Aug.

Da Teresa CASERTAN/PIZZA   This restaurant enjoys a primo location in the medieval *borgo* of Casertavecchia, with a beautiful terrace and a garden offering great views over Caserta and—on clear days—all the way to the sea. The large restaurant includes an indoor dining room and a picturesque inner courtyard. In addition to good-quality pizza, they have an extensive menu of local specialties, such as *misto alla brace* (charbroiled platter of local vegetables, meats, and sausages). The dishes vary daily, but the always-available *menu del ghiottone* (gourmet menu) offers choices such as *cinghiale alla brace* (charbroiled wild boar). The four prix-fixe menus each include a primo, a secondo, a *contorno* (side dish), and a dessert.

Via Torre 6, Casertavecchia. ✆ **0823-371270.** Reservations recommended for dinner. Secondi 8€–16€; prix-fixe menus 15€–25€. AE, DC, MC, V. Thurs–Tues 11:30am–3pm and 7pm–midnight.

2 SANTA MARIA CAPUA VETERE & CAPUA ★★

In the immediate surroundings of Caserta are a few worthwhile archaeological and historic destinations that are untrafficked by international visitors: the ruins of ancient Roman Capua (in the town of **Santa Maria Capua Vetere**) and its fluvial harbor Casilinium (in the town of **Capua**), Capua's **cathedral,** as well as the **Basilica di Sant'Angelo in Formis,** with its magnificent 11th-century frescoes. All of these attractions are easy day trips from Caserta.

SANTA MARIA CAPUA VETERE & ITS AMPHITHEATER ★★

6.5km (4 miles) W of Caserta; 24km (15 miles) NW of Naples.

Now a suburb of modern Caserta, the small town of Santa Maria Capua Vetere is what remains of the glorious Capua, the ancient Roman city that was second only to Rome. Its imposing monuments are proof of the prosperity it reached in ancient times.

Essentials

GETTING THERE   **Trenitalia** (✆ **892021** in Italy; www.trenitalia.it) serves Santa Maria Capua Vetere's **train** station with routes from Rome, Caserta, and Naples. The station is also a stop on the **Metro Campania Nord-Est** line (© **800-053939** toll-free in Italy; www.metrocampanianordest.it) from Naples and Caserta. From Caserta you can also take a **taxi** (see "Getting Around," p. 284). By **car,** exit autostrada A1 at CASERTA NORD and take SS 7 (Via Appia). From Caserta and the Royal Palace, take Viale Douhet west; when it turns into SS 7, follow signs for SANTA MARIA CAPUA VETERE. Two parking lots are off the main road on the left, one behind Piazza San Pietro and another off Via F. Pezzella, which you can access from Corso Garibaldi.

GETTING AROUND   Santa Maria Capua Vetere is small enough to explore **on foot;** its most important attractions are along the ancient Appian Way, which is called Corso Aldo Moro.

VISITOR INFORMATION   The **Pro Loco office** is in the municipal office, Via Albana, Inst. Lucarelli (© **0823-700589;** Mon–Fri 9am–1pm).

FAST FACTS   **Farmacia Salsano** (© **0823-798583**) is the most convenient pharmacy, at Piazza San Francesco 6, not far from the amphitheater. The **hospital, San Giuseppe e Melorio** (© **0823-891111),** is on Via Melorio. For an **ambulance,** dial © **118.** You can call the **police** at © **113** or at 112. The **post office,** Piazza Resistenza 1 (© **0823-818411**), is open Monday to Saturday from 8am to 2pm. You'll find several **banks** with ATMs, including one on Corso Aldo Moro.

EXPLORING THE TOWN

As you walk around town, keep an eye out for archaeological remains that have been incorporated into more modern buildings over the centuries: pieces of column, sculpted busts of gods and goddesses, and capitals. The western entrance to town on the ancient Via Appia was marked *arco di adriano* (**Hadrian's Arch**), a majestic triumphal monument that was actually composed of three arches. Today the marble finish has disappeared and only one arch remains—the southern one—although you can see the three brick pillars that supported the central arch. Farther along, at Corso 210, are the remains of a Roman house, **Casa di Confuleio Sabbio** (discovered by chance during construction in 1955), which dates from the 1st century B.C. It was the home of a freedman, a merchant specializing in the production of *sagum:* the heavy woolen cape worn by soldiers and—in a less-refined version—by slaves and paupers. At the corner of Corso and Via Galatina is the large building that was a prison until only a few decades ago; beneath it are the remains of a **criptoportico,** an ancient Roman covered promenade that is believed to have been part of the *Capitolium,* an ancient Roman temple.

Anfiteatro Campano ★★   Second in size only to the Colosseum in Rome, this Roman amphitheater was probably built around A.D. 3, enlarged in 119 by Emperor Hadrian, and further embellished by Emperor Antoninus Pius. It remains majestic in spite of having been used—like so many Roman buildings in Italy—as a quarry for quality marble and construction materials over the centuries. It was also picked apart in the 9th century onwards during searches for bronze and lead (the building's large stone components were broken apart to get at the heavy metal clamps that held them together). Some of its columns and stones were even used to rebuild the town and the Duomo (see "Duomo," below).

Judging from what remains, though, the amphitheater must have been quite a sight back in those days. Four stories tall, it was completely covered in travertine stone, with marble busts of gods serving as keystones for each of the 240 arches on the lower floors, and full-length statues under the arches of the second and third floors. You can still see the carved keystones over the main entrance (busts of Ceres and Juno). The giant arena has a maximum length of about 170m (558 ft.) and can seat over 60,000 people. The corridors below the arena are relatively well conserved and still show traces of stuccoes and frescoes. This is where the gladiators waited between combats, and where all the scene props were kept. The bestiary—home of the fighting animals—was also here. You can also see the remains of a paleochristian altar and paintings inside one of the small rooms here, which was transformed into a Christian oratory in the 9th century.

The garden in front of the amphitheater has been turned into an open-air museum where you can admire many of the fragments of the original decorations of the amphitheater as well as from other buildings in town. Among the objects on display is a beautiful 2nd-century **mosaic** ★ depicting Nereides and Tritons.

A permanent exhibit dedicated to gladiatorial fights is housed in the *Museo dei Gladiatori* (**Gladiators' Museum**) ★, also in the garden. On display are four complete suits of gladiator armor, and a model reconstruction of the amphitheater. You can also watch a good animation of a gladiator fight. Spartacus, the slave made famous by the

A Twisted History

A bit like the mythical phoenix, Capua started as a small Oscan (one of the local Italic populations) village, and gained importance under the Etruscans—who took power over it in 589 B.C.—and then under the Sannites (the Italic population of the Benevento region), who captured it in 438 B.C. In a fertile location, Capua kept growing rapidly to become, in the words of Roman historian Livy, "the richest and largest town in Italy outside of Rome." The city, though, committed the sin of trying to secede in 211 B.C.; the punishment from Rome was severe: complete annihilation. Only in 89 B.C. did the Romans decide to rebuild a colony here, and the town again grew rapidly to become the second-most significant city in the empire: The Via Appia, or *regina viarum* (queen of all roads), was built to unite Rome and its prosperous neighbor, Capua. This was the first large road the Romans laid (the first "consular" road, as they are still called) and was later extended all the way to Brindisi, the harbor on the eastern Apulian coast, as a commercial highway for trading with Asia. As a major stop on this route, Capua prospered even through the barbarian invasions after the end of the empire, but finally met its match in the Saracens, who, in A.D. 840, destroyed the city, leaving only the Duomo standing. Slowly and yet again, a new village developed from the ruins around the church, and Capua prospered. It had lost its name though, taken by the fleeing population who had reestablished Capua on the Volturno River, over the ruins of the Roman hamlet of Casilinum. So the town was renamed Santa Maria Capua Vetere (*vetere* means "old" in Latin). Its modern-day population is double that of nearby Capua.

1960 Stanley Kubrick film, was a graduate of the gladiator school located near this amphitheater.

Piazza Ottobre (off Piazza Adriano). 𝄢 **0823-798864.** Admission 2.50€ includes Museo Archeologico dell'Antica Capua and Mitreo. Tues–Sun 9am–5:30pm.

Duomo ★★   Dedicated to Santa Maria Maggiore, the core of this church was built in A.D. 432 by Capua's bishop Saint Simmaco over the town's catacombs by the Grotto of Saint Prisco; Arechi II added the two external naves in A.D. 787. When it was restored in 1666, the apse was completely rebuilt. The interior is quite suggestive, with five naves supported by columns topped with Corinthian capitals taken from the nearby amphitheater and Roman temples. It is richly decorated with Renaissance artwork, including a carved **cyborium** ★ located in the chapel at the end of the right-hand nave, and a **wooden choir** ★ in the apse. Our favorite chapels are the ones opening off the left-hand nave—gated **Cappella del Conforto** ★★, with a beautiful altar in colored marble inlay, and **Cappella della Morte** ★, featuring more notable inlay work at the end of the nave.

Via Sirtori 3 (off Piazza Matteotti). 𝄢 **0823-846640.** Free admission. Daily 9am–12:30pm and 4:30–6pm.

Museo Archeologico dell'Antica Capua   In the Torre di Sant'Erasmo—a tower originating before the Longobards—this museum displays a large collection of local archaeological findings ranging from the 10th century B.C. to the 1st century A.D. Behind the museum is the **Mitreo** ★, Vicolo Mitreo (explorable by guided tour only, which is included in price of admission; sign up at the ticket booth of the Anfiteatro Campano), one of the few existing temples dedicated to the god Mithras (worshipped by a Persian cult that diffused in Rome during the 1st century A.D.). Discovered accidentally in 1922, the very well-preserved temple was built between the 2nd and 3rd centuries A.D. Its vaulted ceiling is decorated with a large fresco of Mithras sacrificing a white bull. Above the stalls are remains of frescoes depicting the seven stages of initiation into the cult of Mithras.

Via Roberto D'Angiò 48 (off Corso Aldo Moro [Via Appia]). ✆ **0823-844206.** Admission 2.50€ includes access to Anfiteatro Campano and Mitreo. Tues–Sun 9am–6pm.

CAPUA & ITS CHURCHES ★

11km (6¹⁄₂ miles) W of Caserta; 28km (17 miles) NW of Naples.

A short distance from Caserta, Capua is a sleepy village on a picturesque bend in the Volturno River. Built as a defensive outpost for the bridge and harbor on the river, it still has most of its fortifications intact. The original village was the Roman harbor of Casilinium, which served the nearby town of Capua and guarded the important bridge built by the Romans over the river for the Appian Way (perfectly operational until 1943, when it was bombed by U.S. forces). When ancient Capua was destroyed by the Saracens in A.D. 840, its inhabitants fled here, salvaging all they could from their old town—including the town's name. Repeatedly besieged by various powers until the unification of Italy in 1860, it was the seat of a bishopric and played an important religious role, which is still visible in its many churches.

Essentials

GETTING THERE   Capua's train station has **Trenitalia** (✆ **892021** in Italy; www.trenitalia.it) train service from Caserta and Naples. From Caserta, you can also take a **taxi** (see "Getting Around," p. 284). **By car,** take autostrada A1 to the exit marked CAPUA, which leads to Via Appia. From Caserta, take Viale Douhet past the Reggia and follow it west out of town; follow signs for CAPUA as the road becomes Via Appia and passes through Santa Maria Capua Vetere. The town is to your left after you cross the bridge over the Volturno River. You will find a parking lot off Via Appia at Piazza Umberto I, near the town center.

GETTING AROUND   Capua is small and can easily be explored **on foot.** A stroll along Corso Appio (the original Via Appia), the historic district's main street, will take you past most of the town's attractions. You can grab a **taxi** at the stand by the train station (or call one at ✆ **0823-963142** or 0823-963521).

VISITOR INFORMATION   The Pro Loco **tourist office** (✆ **0823 962729**) is in the municipal building, Piazza dei Giudici 6. Hours are Monday to Friday from 9am to 1pm.

FAST FACTS   You'll find a **pharmacy** (✆ **0823-961224**) at Via Duomo 32. The nearest **hospitals** are in Caserta and Santa Maria Capua Vetere (see "Fast Facts," p. 286 and 293). For **medical aid,** dial ✆ **118.** You can call the **police** at ✆ **113** or 112. The **post office,** Via Pier Delle Vigne 3 (✆ **0823-620511**), is open Monday to Saturday from 8am to 2pm.

SPECIAL EVENTS   During Carnival, Capua is the seat of an important festival, including a grand parade; farcical theater performances, often reflecting on recent political events; and cabaret shows. Always featured is the famous character **Pulcinella** (p. 313), whom Capuans claim as one of their own. (Check with the tourist office in Caserta for a schedule of events.)

EXPLORING THE TOWN

Surrounded by walls and castles, Capua maintains the feeling of an ancient town. Its western gate is by the bridge, and the 15th-century eastern gate—Porta Napoli—is near the ruins of the 11th-century Norman **Castello delle Pietre,** on Via Andreozzi, which still has one of its four original crenellated towers. The facades of many buildings are decorated with Roman artifacts, such as the **bas-relief** at Via Pier delle Vigne 26 (off Corso Appio); at number 34 on the same street is a picturesque Renaissance house with an arched courtyard designed by Guido da Maiano, and a few interesting churches. Particularly noteworthy are the six marble **busts** ★ gracing 16th-century **Palazzo del Municipio** on Piazza dei Giudici, off Corso Appio; they depict Jupiter, Neptune, Mercury, Juno, Ceres, and Mars and were taken from the Anfiteatro Campano of Santa Maria Capua Vetere.

Cattedrale di Santo Stefano e Sant'Agata ★ Also called the Duomo, this church was severely damaged by bombing in 1943, but an immense restoration campaign faithfully re-created it according to the original plan. The church dated from A.D. 856, with additions from 1120. The 11th-century atrium, built with columns and

Corinthian capitals from the 3rd century A.D., and the Duomo's 9th-century bell tower, supported at its base by four ancient Corinthian columns, are original. Among the medieval sculptures decorating the bell tower, you can admire three Roman bas-reliefs from the amphitheater in Santa Maria Capua Vetere (see "Anfiteatro Campano," earlier in this chapter).

Inside the church, a large range of artwork dates from the 12th century to the present. We love the splendid, lavishly decorated 13th-century **ceremonial candleholder** and the two columns supported by carved lions on the modern pulpit—all that remain of the original 13th-century **ambo.** Other parts of the original ambo, including some mosaics, were used to decorate the small chapel in the **crypt** under the presbytery. In the **Cappella del Sacramento,** at the end of the right-hand-side nave, is a beautiful **altar** made of marble and precious stones, while in the presbytery behind the altar, you'll find the *Assunta* painted by Francesco Solimena. We also recommend a visit to the **Museo Diocesano** (© 0823-961081; admission 3€; daily 9:30am–1pm and 3:30–7pm), housing the church's **treasure** inside the **Cappella del Corpo di Cristo,** adjacent to the cathedral. Among the objects on exhibit is a collection of Islamic carved crystal dating from the 11th and 12th centuries.

Piazza Landolfo (off Via Duomo). © **0823-961081.** Free admission. Daily 8–11am and 5:30–7:30pm.

Museo Campano ★ In the Palazzo Antignano (graced by an unusual 15th-century **portal** ★ in Catalán-Moorish style, at no. 76 of Via Roma), the museum, established in 1874, is dedicated to the art, religion, and history of Campania. Its wealth of holdings is divided into two sections: Archaeological finds are on the first floor, while medieval displays, including the parchment collection and the picture gallery are on the second.

The archaeology section includes Oscan (the Osci were the local Italic population), Etruscan, and Roman artifacts from a number of sites in the area. Among the Etruscan-Oscan pottery, we liked the beautiful black dishes decorated with fish and dating from the 4th century B.C. The most poignant artifacts, however, are *Le Madri* **(The Mothers)** ★★, in rooms five through nine. This is a whole group of statues and architectural structures with Oscan inscriptions that were found in a field near Santa Maria Capua Vetere. They pertain to an Oscan sanctuary that was active between the 6th and 1st centuries B.C. and was dedicated to the Italic goddess of fertility and maternity, Matuta. Several of these figures, carved in tufa stone, show mothers offering their children to view and (probably) thanking the goddess for the gift of maternity. The **Roman mosaic** on the second floor in room number 10 was found in the temple of Diana Tifatina, near Sant'Angelo in Formis (see "Sant'Angelo in Formis," below).

Among the holdings in the medieval section, the most famous is the collection of **Federician Sculptures** ★ in room number 26. Among this group of marble sculptures from the castle built by Federico II in 1239 in Capua are a few portraits of Federico himself. One of the greatest of medieval rulers, he was crowned king of Sicily at the age of 4 and became Holy Roman Emperor in 1220. He participated in the Sixth Crusade, and crowned himself king of Jerusalem in 1229. Called **Stupor Mundi** ("wonder of the world") by his contemporaries, he was also much distrusted by the papacy and was excommunicated twice.

Via Roma 68 (off Via Duomo). © **0823-961402.** Free admission. Tues–Sat 9am–1:30pm; Sun 9am–1pm.

Isolated on the slopes of Mount Tifata on the outskirts of Capua, this medieval church may be the most fascinating in Italy.

Essentials

GETTING THERE You can easily reach the village by **buses** that depart from in front of Capua's train station. It is also a stop on the **Metro Campania Nord-Est** line (© 800-053939 toll-free in Italy; www.metrocampanianordest.it) from Naples, Caserta, and Santa Maria Capua Vetere. **By car** from Capua, take Via Roma out of town following signs for S. ANGELO IN FORMIS.

FAST FACTS The nearest **hospitals** are in Caserta and Santa Maria Capua Vetere (see "Fast Facts," p. 286 and 293). For **first aid,** dial © **118.** You can call the **police** at © **113** or 112.

Exploring the Romanic Basilica

Enjoying an ideal position up the mountain overlooking Capua and affording, on clear days, a **view** ★ that stretches all the way to Ischia, this basilica was built over the ruins of the **Temple of Diana Tifatina,** the most important pre-Christian sanctuary in this region. Turned into a church sometime before the 10th century, it was then bequeathed to the nearby monastery of Montecassino. Its abbot, Desiderio of Montecassino, decided to establish the sanctuary as an important religious site, and had the basilica completely redone in 1073. Note how the lateral arches in the portico in front of the church are pointed arches typical of Islamic architecture. Under the portico you will see the first series of frescoes, with a wonderful **Saint Michael** ★ from the 11th century, and others from the 12th and 13th centuries. Inside, the basilica is divided into three naves by 14 columns topped with beautiful antique Corinthian capitals. The greatest attraction is really the **frescoes** ★★ that were painted by local art students. Along the sides of the central nave is the cycle depicting scenes from the Old and New testaments, and on the inner facade is the *Last Judgment.* Little remains of the 11th-century mosaic floor—you'll see some at the end of the right nave—and parts of the marble floor are original to the temple of Diana (dated by an inscription from 74 B.C.).

Piazza della Basilica di Sant'Angelo, Formis. © **0823-960492.** Free admission. Summer Mon–Sat 9:30am–noon and 3–7pm, Sun 10am–4pm; winter Mon–Sat 9:30am–12:30pm and 3–6pm, Sun 10am–4pm. Holidays 10am–4pm.

---

3 BEWITCHING BENEVENTO

51km (31 miles) E of Caserta; 86km (53 miles) NE of Naples

With its heritage of mysterious witchcraft and Roman art, this pretty hilltop town hides some wonderful artistic treasures, including the best-preserved ancient Roman arch in existence and an intriguing Longobard star-shaped church.

ESSENTIALS

GETTING THERE Benevento is well connected by **train,** with frequent service from Naples, Caserta, Avellino, and Rome. Contact **Trenitalia** (© 892021 in Italy; www.trenitalia.it) for fares and information. Trains arrive at Benevento's **stazione** (© 0824-50159) located in Piazza Colonna 2, to the north of town. Benevento is also served by the **Metro Campania Nord-Est** line (© **800-053939** toll-free in Italy; www.metro campanianordest.it) from Naples.

Marozzi (© 06-4742801; www.marozzivt.it) offers regular **bus** service to and from Rome; use **ETAC** (© **0824-28321;** www.etacsrl.it) to and from Salerno, or **AIR Auto-servizi Irpini** (© **0825-204250;** www.air-spa.it) to and from Avellino.

By **car,** take autostrada A16 to the exit signed BENEVENTO and continue on the short stretch of highway to the town.

GETTING AROUND   The center of Benevento is relatively small and accessible **on foot;** however, it extends uphill, so you might want to use public transportation as well. The town's **bus** system maintains a number of lines that crisscross the area; most leave from the hub across from the train station. Lines 1 and 7 both pass by Trajan's Arch, going up to the Rocca dei Priori in the heart of the historic district. You'll need to buy bus tickets at a tobacconist or a newsstand before boarding; tickets cost .65€ and are valid for 90 minutes. **Taxis** wait at the **stand** on Piazza Colonna, across from the railway station (or call © **0824-50341**).

You can rent a car in town with **Cardillo,** Via dei Mulini 91 (© **0824-359775**).

VISITOR INFORMATION   The excellent local **tourist office EPT,** Via Nicola Sala 31, 82100 Benevento (© **0824-319911;** www.eptbenevento.it) maintains an **information office** in Piazza Roma 11 (© **0824-319938**).

FAST FACTS   You'll find a **pharmacy** (© **0824-21590**) in Piazza Orsini 13. The hospital is **Ospedale Fatebenefratelli,** Viale Principe di Napoli 14–16 (© **0824-50374**). For an **ambulance,** dial © **118,** or call the **Croce Rossa Italiana** (© **0824-315000**). You can call the **police** at © **112** or 113**.** There is a **post office** (© **0824-24074;** Mon–Sat 8am–2pm) in Piazza Colonna Vittoria, by the railway station.

EXPLORING THE TOWN

On a hill at the heart of a hilly green valley, Benevento is a very pleasant town. Once completely enclosed by defensive walls, only fragments of them are still visible today, together with the fortress—**Rocca dei Rettori,** at Piazza IV Novembre—in the highest part of town. Built by the pope in 1321 over the preexisting Longobard and ancient Roman defensive structures, the fortress was recently restored and houses the provincial government; but some of it can be toured when special exhibits are hosted by **ARCOS** (Museum of Contemporary Art of Sannio). The **Villa Comunale** ★ is a delightful public garden, designed in the late 19th century and graced by elegant Liberty-style fixtures such as lamps and benches.

Arco di Traiano (Trajan's Arch) ★★★   This is quite simply the best conserved— it's practically pristine considering its 2,000 years of age—ancient Roman triumphal arch in the world. The lengthy restoration—mainly a careful cleaning that took 14 years—was completed recently (2001) and the arch is again visible in all its glory. Built between A.D. 114 and 117 by Rome to honor Emperor Trajan, it was at the beginning of the Via Traiana, what was then a new—and shorter—route that led from Benevento to Brindisi, the harbor that was Rome's gateway to the eastern Mediterranean. The arch's reliefs celebrate the deeds of this illuminated leader, who enlarged and strengthened the empire while implementing a generous social policy and numerous public works. During the Middle Ages, this superb work of art was enclosed in the city walls and used as the main gate into town (hence the local name for the arch: Port'Aurea), which contributed to its conservation. The nearby church, **Sant'Ilario a Port'Aurea** ★, Via San Pasquale, off the

Arco di Traiano (📞 **0824-21818;** free admission; daily 10am-1pm, in winter also 3-6pm, fall–spring 4-7pm, summer 5-8pm), a Longobard church from the 10th century, houses a permanent exhibit on the arch and on life in Rome under Emperor Trajan.

Via Traiano (off Corso Garibaldi).

Duomo ★ The first version of this church goes back to the 7th century A.D., when it had only a central nave. After consecration in A.D. 780, during Longobard domination, two naves were added in the 9th century and two others in the 12th century. The structure was then restored and redecorated in the 18th century, at which point it became known as one of the most beautiful Romanesque churches in Italy. However, the U.S.

Benevento History 101

A powerful Sannite town inhabited since the 7th century B.C., the original community was soundly defeated by the Romans in 275 B.C., after fierce opposition. The Roman Empire established a colony and changed the town's name from the original Malies, or Maloenton—which in Latin sounded like a bad omen—to Beneventum. Taken by the Goths at the decline of the Western Roman Empire, it was rescued by the Byzantines, who then relinquished it in turn to the Longobards. Finally, Benevento was absorbed into the state of the Church of Rome in the 16th century and remained relatively peaceful until it was almost completely destroyed by the earthquake of 1688. The city's archbishop—who, in later years, was to become Pope Benedetto XIII—rebuilt the city and supported its cultural and spiritual development. The reborn Benevento enjoyed a new period of prosperity until World War II, when the town was heavily bombarded by the United States in 1943—65% of it, including important monuments, was destroyed, and 2,000 people were killed. The town has since recovered and become a lively and pleasant provincial town with an interesting hinterland.

bombing in 1943 destroyed almost the entire ancient church, except for the bell tower and the elegant Romanesque facade, a 13th-century Pisan-style marvel of striped marble and rich carvings. The richly carved jambs of the central portal date from the 12th century; they once bracketed 13th-century sculpted bronze doors which were considered rivals of the famous ones of Florence's baptistery. They were blown to pieces by the bombing, and what was saved was painstakingly restored; you can now see the 72 frames that composed the doors displayed inside the church. The top 43 are decorated with scenes from the life of Christ, from the Annunciation to the Ascension, while the bottom 29 depict local religious personalities. The **Museo Diocesano**—housed partly in the crypt and partly in the adjacent Palazzo Arcivescovile, Piazza Orsini 27 (✆ **0824-54717**)—holds remains from the destroyed Duomo, including what was left of the extremely rich treasure. *Note:* At presstime, the Duomo had just closed for restorations and no date was given for the reopening.

Piazza Duomo. ✆ **0824-47591**. Free admission. Daily 9am–12:30pm and 5–7pm.

Museo del Sannio ★ In the former monastery of Santa Sofia (below), this museum holds a picture gallery and a good collection of archaeological and medieval artifacts. Among the most interesting items on display is the collection of Egyptian art coming from the local temple of Isis (built by the notoriously cruel Emperor Domitian in A.D. 88). It was decorated both with statues imported from Egypt and others produced locally in the Egyptian style—including a portrait of Domitian in Egyptian attire. The picture gallery has a collection spanning the 15th to the 20th centuries, including major names such as Francesco Solimena *(Madonna col Bambino e i Santi)* and Carlo Maratta *(Sacra Famiglia)*. Part of the collection is displayed in the elegant **cloister** ★, an interesting architectural merger of Moorish arches and Romanesque columns, carved with strange, fantastic, or everyday scenes, such as boar hunts and pilgrimages.

The museum's historical section (documents and signatures of famous historical figures) is in the scenic Rocca dei Rettori (access with the same ticket) on Piazza IV Novembre.

Piazza Santa Sofia. ✆ **0824-21818** or 0824-28831. Admission 4€. Tues–Sun 9am–7pm.

Santa Sofia ★   This medieval church is one of our favorites in Italy. Its unique design singles it out as an architectural marvel and shows the intermingling of Longobard and Christian cultures. Begun in 762 by the Longobard Arechi II when he became Duke of Benevento, the church's star-shaped structure is a central hexagon, covered by a dome, and supported by six powerful columns; around this are eight square pillars and two columns topped by Corinthian capitals. The pillars are aligned with the surrounding walls, which are part circle and part star, creating a strange perspective. In the apse are fragments of a great cycle of frescoes from the 8th century, representing, among other things, scenes of the life of Saint Zaccaria; the surrounding walls are decorated with representations of nature and symbols derived from the Longobard religion. The bell tower stands alone, isolated from the church; it was redone in 1703. Attached to the church is the monastery, now housing the **Museo del Sannio** (above). It was actually a Benedictine convent founded in conjunction with the church. It became one of the most powerful monasteries in Italy during the 12th century, famous for its type of writing, "scriptorium Beneventanum." *Note:* The church was undergoing restoration at press-time, with no date announced for the reopening.

Piazza Matteotti. ✆ **0824-21206.** Free admission. Daily 10am–noon and 4:30–7pm.

Teatro Romano ★   This is one of the largest well-conserved Roman theaters in Italy. Theater performances, including drama, comedy, and poetry as well as music, were very important to Roman culture and a matter of everyday life. Theaters (the classic hemi-cycle) were ubiquitous, to the extent that even little towns often had more than one. But while grandiose ruins remain of the great amphitheaters dedicated to contests and spec-tacles—such as Rome's Colosseum and the Anfiteatro Campano in Santa Maria Capua Vetere—most ancient Roman theaters have been integrated into later constructions. This makes Benevento's Roman theater an important exception. Built in the 2nd century A.D., it had a diameter of 90m (295 ft.) and could contain up to 20,000 spectators. Most of the original structure is still visible, and only the third floor was completely lost. The path that leads from the ticket booth to the theater takes you past assorted sculptures, capitals, and massive hunks of marble that once graced the structure. A portion of the second level also still stands, with corridors leading to the mostly intact seating area, still used during the summer for opera performances and classical dramas (contact the tourist office for a schedule of events).

Via Port'Arsa. ✆ **0824-47213.** Admission 2€. Daily 9am to 1 hr. before sunset.

WHERE TO STAY
Moderate
Grand Hotel Italiano ★   Offering lodging since 1920, this family-run hotel has been updated many times but retains its old-fashioned hospitality. It is not far from the train station, in a pleasant residential part of town with lots of shops; the town center is a 15-minute walk or a quick bus ride away. The large guest rooms are comfortable and modern, all with good-size bathrooms. In summer, the hotel offers discounted access to a nearby swimming pool and gym. The **restaurant** ★ on the premises is very good and quite popular among locals.

Viale Principe di Napoli 137, 82100 Benevento. ✆ **0824-24111.** Fax 0824-21758. www.hotel-italiano.it. 71 units. 88€ double. Rate includes buffet breakfast. Children 2 and under stay free in parent's room. AE, DC, MC, V. Limited free parking. **Amenities:** Restaurant; bar; concierge; Internet. *In room:* A/C, TV, minibar.

The Witches of Benevento

Legend has it that Benevento is a land of witches and has been for thousands of years. The origins of the legend lie with the Egyptian cult of Isis—goddess of magic and mystery among other things—which found fertile ground in Benevento during the Roman era. The cult remained an important force here even after the cult was replaced by Christianity in other parts of Italy. When the Longobards from Central Europe took the town in A.D. 571, they imported their own religion, a nature cult based on the adoration of the god Wothan and his sacred walnut tree. They elected an old walnut near the **Ponte Leproso** as the town's sacred tree. (The Ponte Leproso was a bridge built by the Romans over the Sabato River at the Via Appia's entrance to Benevento. The bridge is still in use today; you can see it by taking a short walk west of the Teatro Romano). Around this walnut tree—known as the Noce di Benevento—the Longobards held their nocturnal open-air rituals which, combined with knowledge of the cult of Isis and the vivid imagination of the locals, gave rise to the witchcraft legend.

The Longobards were converted to the Catholic religion by Saint Barbato, the town's bishop, in the 7th century A.D., and the bishop had the tree cut down. The dances stopped; yet, some say, the witches remained, and can still be seen dancing by the site on certain nights.

Hotel Villa Traiano   Aspiring to be the most elegant hotel in Benevento, this small hotel enjoys an excellent location near Trajan's Arch. In a neoclassical villa it affords charming public spaces. Guest rooms are good-size, elegant, and pleasant, with hardwood floors and reproduction furniture; most of the marble bathrooms are fairly spacious (some with shower only). The atmospheric **wine bar** in the cellar is a recent and welcome addition.

Viale dei Rettori 9, 82100 Benevento. ✆ **0824-326241.** Fax 0824-326196. www.hotelvillatraiano.it. 19 units. 150€–180€ double. Rates include buffet breakfast. AE, DC, MC, V. Parking 15€. **Amenities:** Restaurant; 2 bars; concierge; room service. *In room:* A/C, TV, hair dryer, minibar.

President Hotel   Right in the center of town, this hotel caters mostly to a business clientele, with a number of single rooms. Accommodations are comfortable and classically styled, with hardwood floors and simple but tasteful furniture.

Via Perasso 1, 82100 Benevento. ✆ **0824-316716.** Fax 0824-316764. www.hotelpresidentbenevento.it. 69 units. 115€ double; 130€ triple; from 150€ suite. Rates include buffet breakfast. Children 2 and under stay free in parent's room. AE, DC, MC, V. Free parking. **Amenities:** Bar; concierge; Wi-Fi. *In room:* A/C, TV (in some), minibar.

WHERE TO DINE

Benevento may be small, but dining is taken seriously at the many restaurants in town. Locals also are fond of dining excursions to the nearby villages (see "Farther Afield," p. 306).

Gino e Pina ★ PIZZA/SANNITE   A favorite with young and not-so-young locals, this excellent restaurant and enoteca (wine bar) serves well-prepared traditional dishes along with D.O.C. wines. Among the seafood, meat, and truly excellent pizza, standouts are *cavatelli con vongole e zucchini* (a short rolled pasta with clams and zucchini) and the delicious *agnello al forno* (roasted lamb). The restaurant doubles as a cultural center, with a **tourist agency,** a **shop** selling local products, and a **lounge bar.**

Viale dell'Università. ✆ **0824-24947.** www.ginoepina.it. Reservations recommended. Secondi 11€–22€; pizza 7€–10€. AE, DC, MC, V. Mon–Sat 12:30–3pm and 7:30–11pm. Closed 2 weeks in Aug.

Locanda delle Streghe ★ BENEVENTAN   Also popular with a mix of young and old, this atmospheric restaurant prides itself as a stronghold of local culinary tradition. Indeed, the menu includes time-honored dishes that are difficult to find elsewhere. We recommend, of course, the *zuppa delle streghe* (witch stew), a savory, thick soup made from a number of herbs and vegetables, with hot red pepper and cheese, but also the homemade *cavatelli alle erbe* (with wild herbs), and the splendid *pollo alla diavola* (spicy grilled chicken).

Via Manciotti 11. ✆ **0824-29873.** www.locandadellestreghe.it. Reservations recommended. Secondi 10€–20€. AE, DC, MC, V. Wed–Mon 12:30–3pm and 7:30–11pm.

Inexpensive

Nunzia ★ BENEVENTAN   This local institution is a family-run restaurant that is so welcoming it almost feels like the home of a Beneventan host. You'll also spend very little, so it's not surprising that this place is very popular among locals. The highlights are the *primi* and the soups, which might include tasty *spaghetti e piselli* (with peas), as well as meats, such as lamb and pork roast. If they have it, do not miss one of the specialties, *baccalá con capperi e olive* (salt cod in an olive-and-caper sauce).

Via Annunziata 152. ✆ **0824-29431.** Reservations recommended for dinner. Secondi 6€–12€. MC, V. Mon–Sat noon–3pm and 7–11pm. Closed 2 weeks in Aug.

Ristorante Pizzeria Traiano ★ BENEVENTAN/PIZZA   Excellent local cuisine and great pizza (available only in the evening) make this a popular place. Open the almost unnoticeable entrance door, and you'll find yourself in a crammed little restaurant with two small dining rooms, usually filled with people happily downing large dishes of food. This place is particularly famous for its variety of *antipasti* that comes either as

Strega—the Brew of Benevento

Appropriately named "witch," this local **liqueur** might well enchant you with its unique bittersweet taste. Concocted in the 17th century from a secret mixture of 17 herbs and spices, it is served as a digestive or to "correct" your espresso (adding a bit of alcohol to it); it is a good complement to fruit salads and ice cream, too. The liqueur also comes in a **cream** variety (similar to Baileys). It is also used for a proprietary candy—*caramella Strega*—an individually wrapped **hard candy** with a soft, creamy Strega-flavored center. All those goodies make excellent souvenirs and are for sale at local shops (see "Stocking up on Souvenirs," p. 306).

Stocking up on Souvenirs

Among the local specialties we absolutely love is *torrone*. Hard or chewy, this wonderful delicacy is a crumbly nougat made of egg whites, honey, and nuts—usually hazelnuts and almonds. A favorite in Roman times—historian Tito Livio mentions it in his writings—it reached European fame only in the 17th century, when the Beneventan candy makers created today's traditional varieties, which are covered with dark chocolate or with a special icing flavored with lemon, orange, or coffee. Among the best confectioners in town are **Alberico Ambrosino,** Corso Garibaldi 111; (✆ **0824-28546**); **Umberto Russo,** Via Gaetano Rumno 17 ((✆ **0824-24472**); and the **Fabbriche Riunite Torrone di Benevento,** Viale Principe di Napoli 113 ((✆ **0824-21624**), a consortium of local torrone producers. You will also find *torrone Strega,* and delicious *caramelle*—small hard candies with a soft center of "cream of Strega" (the Strega version of Baileys liqueur; see box, "Strega—The Brew of Benevento," earlier).

appetizers or as side dishes—try *involtini di melanzane* (eggplant rolls) if they have them. The restaurant is also famous for its homemade desserts. Both *antipasti* and desserts are on display near the entrance. Pasta dishes—such as *spaghetti alle cozze e vongole* (with mussels and clams)—are also excellent.

Via Manciotti 48. (✆ **0824-25013.** Reservations recommended for dinner. Secondi 6€–11€. MC, V. Wed–Mon noon–2:30pm and 7:30–11pm.

Taverna Paradiso ★ BENEVENTAN   This is one of our favorite places in the area, not least for its atmospheric setting in a historic tavern (for a long time it was a wine bar). The varied menu caters to most possible tastes and needs, from celiac to vegetarian to children. The dishes are simple, all based on the local tradition and using local ingredients. We recommend sampling the cured meats and cheese as appetizer, and then trying the *paccheri con pomodorini e caciocavallo* (fresh pasta with cherry tomatoes and local cheese), and a succulent *maiale farcito* (pork roasted stuffed with arucola and cheese).

Via La Vipera 33. (✆ **0824-42914.** www.taverna-paradiso.com. Reservations recommended for dinner. Secondi 8€–16€. AE, DC, MC, V. Wed–Mon noon–2:30pm and 7:30–11pm. Closed 3 weeks in Aug.

FARTHER AFIELD AROUND BENEVENTO: DISCOVERING SANNIO

The region around Benevento is a hilly area called **Sannio,** which is reputed for the production of some of Italy's best D.O.C. *(Denominazione di Origine Controllata)* wines. It is a perfect destination for wine lovers—as well as for those interested in its history, thermal waters, and genuine cuisine. In this authentic small town, it is not uncommon to be the only foreign tourist in a hotel. Local culture is very much alive, with each town claiming to be different from the rest of Italy, including other towns just a few miles away.

Although most of the villages are served by **SITA bus service** ((✆ **0892-26604;** www.sitabus.it), a **car** is the best way to explore the hills around Benevento (see "Fast Facts," p. 326, for car-rental companies, and "Getting Around," p. 300, for an agency in Benevento).

Dominated by the Monte Taburno, this valley extends southwest of Benevento. Take SS 7 (Via Appia) out of Benevento, going toward Capua, and you'll reach the village of **Montesarchio** ★. Ignore the modern area and proceed to the picturesque historic district with its imposing 15th-century **fortress.** For a good meal in the historic district, head to **Ristorante 'O Pignatiello** ★, Via Vecchia Annunziata 2 (✆ **0824-847470**). Another noteworthy restaurant is **Barry** ★ (which stands for "bar-ristorante") in the elegant **Cristina Park Hotel,** Via Benevento 102, 82016 Montesarchio (✆ **0824-835888;** fax 0824-835888; www.cristinaparkhotel.it; 105€ double).

The national park of **Monte Taburno** (1,394m/4,573-ft.; www.parcotaburno.it), just outside of town, is a good place for **hiking** ★. The easiest way to reach the trail head is by car, taking the scenic local road marked VITULANO at the eastern edge of Montesarchio; it skirts the fortress and climbs to Piano Caudio (14km/8¾ miles from Montesarchio). Here you bear left at the fork in the road, following the signs for **Rifugio-Albergo Taburno,** a bar/restaurant/hotel at an altitude of 1,050m (3,445 ft.) where the trail starts. From the *rifugio,* the climb is fairly easy and you will reach the top in about an hour; the **panorama** ★★ on a clear day is splendid. Incidentally, this mountain is the origin of the aqueduct that feeds the fountains of Caserta's Royal Palace (p. 286).

Continuing on road SS 7 and then turning on the local road, SP 125, you'll reach the pretty mountain town of **Airola,** dominated by its scenic castle. Its 16th-century church—**Chiesa dell'Annunciata**—is worth a visit, with a beautiful facade that is the handiwork of Luigi Vanvitelli, the same architect who designed the Royal Palace in Caserta and the artwork inside this church.

Farther along, you'll reach **Sant'Agata dei Goti** ★★, a scenic medieval town built on a high tufa-stone cliff. Despite having been severely damaged by the earthquake of 1980, the town is still very picturesque and unique, built along an unusual semicircular urban plan. It is famous for its many churches: The most attractive is the **Duomo** (originally from the 10th century), which retains some of its beautiful mosaic floor and, in the crypt, the original frescoes. Other noteworthy churches are the 13th-century **Chiesa dell'Annunziata** and 11th-century **Chiesa di San Menna.** Sant'Agata is also a reputed destination for wine lovers and foodies. The local vineyard **Mustilli** ★★, Via dei Fiori 20, 82019 Sant'Agata dei Goti (✆ **0823-717433;** www.mustilli.com), is renowned for its excellent Falanghina and several reds well worth tasting, as well as some outstanding grappa; we definitely recommend a visit to the cellar excavated from the tufa stone (call ahead for reservation). Mustilli also operates as *agriturismo* from the 18th-century **Palazzo Rainone,** the family's home in the historic center of Sant'Agata: The **restaurant** ★★ serves superb meals prepared with the products of the farm—homemade pasta *(ravioloni,*

CASERTA, BENEVENTO & AVELLINO

11

BEWITCHING BENEVENTO

The D.O.C. Wines of the Sannio

Benevento is the capital of the Sannio region, which is well-known for its wines, as it counts an uncommonly high number of D.O.C. vintages. Among the stars, are Aglianico del Taburno, Solopaca, Guardiolo, Sannio, Sant'Agata dei Goti, and Taburno. Another famous name is the refreshing Falanghina, a white wine with an aromatic bouquet and a dry flavor.

cavatelli, pacche) with seasonal sauces, such as wild mushroom in the fall and wild asparagus in the spring, and also *agnello* (lamb) and *arista di maiale* (pork roast). Guests sleep in six elegantly appointed rooms (90€ double; rates include buffet breakfast). Round off your gastronomic tour with the excellent ice cream at **Bar Gelateria Normanno,** Via Roma 65 (ℭ **0823-953042;** www.gelaterianormanno.it); among the many special flavors are *bacio normanno* (chocolate hazelnut) and *spumone all'Annurca* (a sherbet shake made with the renowned local apple variety).

Valle Telesina ★★

Spreading northwest from Benevento along route SS 372, this valley is well-known by wine lovers destined for **Solopaca,** the village that gave its name to the best of the region's D.O.C. wines. This is a charming valley of green hills dotted with hill-top villages. One of the most attractive is **Torrecuso ★,** with its medieval *borgo* crowned by a castle and great views from its cliff-top location. This is also the location of a reputed vineyard, **La Rivolta,** Contrada Rivolta (ℭ **0824-872921;** www.fattorialarivolta.it), the producer of an excellent Aglianico del Taburno: *Terre di Rivolta.* The charming 19th-century country residence **Le Vigne ★** (ℭ/fax **0824-872682;** www.levignetorrecuso.it) has elegantly appointed guest rooms a short distance from the vineyard.

Farther along is the popular **Telese Terme ★,** a green and pleasant little town, famous for its sulfuric springs—good for the skin and beneficial to ear ailments as well as respiratory illness—which sprung up after an earthquake in 1349. The largest spa is **Terme di Telese ★** (ℭ **0824-976888;** www.termeditelese.it), located in a beautiful park where pavilions and pools have been built over the natural springs, offering baths, mud applications, and a number of other therapies. We also recommend the smaller and more romantic **Aquapetra Resort & Spa ★★,** Strada Statale Telesina 1 (ℭ **0824-941878;** fax 0824-901557; www.aquapetra.com; 250€-350€ double). The best hotel in town is the elegant 19th-century **Grand Hotel Telese ★,** Via Cerreto 1, 82037 Telese (ℭ **0824-940500;** fax 0824-940504; www.grandhoteltelese.it; 180€ double, rates include buffet breakfast), near the Terme di Telese but offering its own small spa. Within walking distance of town are two other attractions: About 1km (a half-mile) to the southeast is the pretty **Telese Lake ★,** and a few miles to the west are the ruins of **Telesia ★,** a Sannite and then Roman town. For a typical Sannite meal and good local wine, head to the **Locanda della Pacchiana,** Viale Minieri 32 (ℭ **0824-976093**).

North of Telese, **Guardia Sanframondi** has a panoramic medieval castle that protected the surrounding *borgo.* The two churches **Chiesa dell'Annunziata** and **San Sebastiano** are worth a visit for the art that decorates them. Farther north is **Cerreto Sannita ★★,** a harmonious ensemble of late-baroque buildings. The village was rebuilt at the end of the 17th century, after an earthquake completely destroyed it in 1688. Many of its churches are worth a visit, including the **Cathedral, San Martino** and **San Gennaro.** The town is also renowned for its Capodimonte porcelain; local artists in Cerreto and in the nearby village of **San Lorenzello** continue the tradition today. You can admire the local craft at the **Mostra Permanente della Ceramica Antica e Moderna,** Piazza L. Sodo, off Corso Umberto I (ℭ **0824-861337** or 0824-861700), and the **Museo Civico e della Ceramica,** Corso Umberto I, inside the church of San Gennaro and the Convent of Sant'Antonio (ℭ **0824-815211**). To purchase some of the craftwork, head for **Keramos,** Via Nicotera 84 (ℭ **0824-861463**), one of the best showrooms in town. Last but not least, Cerreto is popular with locals for its restaurants: We recommend **Il Pozzo dei Desideri ★,** Via Michele

| Ciro the Dinosaur

East of the medieval village of Cusano Mutri is the **Geo-Paleontological Park of Pietraroja** ((*C* **0824-868000;** www.geologi.it/pietraroja). The area, rich in sedimentary rocks, has yielded many fossils, including a complete baby dinosaur of a unique species, *Scipionyx samniticus*. Locals are very proud of the discovery, and—with typical local enthusiasm—they nicknamed it Ciro, an endearing and very traditional local name.

Ungaro 122, across from San Martino church ((*C* **0824-816050;** closed Wed and 2 weeks in winter). It serves delicious homemade pasta, such as *pappardelle ai funghi porcini* (with porcini mushrooms) and a splendid *costata alla griglia* (grilled steak served with local olive oil). Juicy steaks and succulent pasta dishes attract locals from throughout the area to the **Agri Hotel's La Vecchia Quercia** ★, Via Cerquelle ((*C* **0824-861263;** fax 0824-816217; www.vecchiaquercia.com; closed Tues), on the hill overlooking the village, a short distance out of town.

We recommend pushing farther north to the picturesque village of **Cusano Mutri** ★★, with its stone houses and well-preserved Norman castle. Also worth a visit are the two churches: **Chiesa dei Santi Pietro e Paolo** and **San Giovanni.**

Val Fortore

Most of the visitors who pass through this valley, which spans north of Benevento along SS 212, make a pilgrimage to **Pietrelcina** (about 12km/7½ miles from Benevento), the home village of Padre Pio (a monk and a controversial figure, who died in 1968 and was canonized in 2002 by Pope John Paul II). The excursion is well worth it, if only for the ride alone, as the meandering road takes you through scenic green mountains. Should you need another reason to visit, we suggest sampling the cuisine at the impressive local **Boda de Ciondro** ★, Via Tratturo ((*C*/fax **0824-997601** or 0824-991327; Tues-Sat 6:30-11pm, Sun and holidays noon-4pm, closed 1 week in July).

Farther north is **San Marco dei Cavoti** ★, the destination of a different kind of pilgrim, one who comes to savor the delicious local specialty: *torroncini.* Made in small batches by local confectioners, these bite-size nougat candies are made with honey and nuts and often dipped in dark chocolate. While you can find *torroncini* in Benevento, only here can you sample a staggering variety. The best are the *baci* (kisses) from **Premiata Fabbrica Cavalier Innocenzo Borrillo,** Via Roma 66 ((*C* **0824-984060**), although his descendents are worthy competitors: **Anna Maria Borrillo,** Via Martiri di Bologna 18 ((*C* **0824-984939**), and **Dolciaria Borrillo,** Contrada Catapano 22 ((*C* **0824-995099**). The runner up is **Antonina Petrillo,** Vico San Vincenzo 2 ((*C* **0824-969266**), in Montefalcone di Val Fortore, a picturesque village nearby.

On the Way to Avellino ★

More than the scenic surroundings and local history, the real draw here are two **restaurants** that are among the best in the region. Both are very close to Benevento and make great dining excursions. In **Beltiglio,** a hilltop village near the small town of Ceppaloni, about 10km (6 miles) southwest of Benevento, is **La Rete** ★★, Via Masseriola ((*C* **0824-46574;** www.ristorantelarete.com; Thurs–Mon 12:30-2:30pm and

8-10:30pm). It features great cuisine, which is very authentic and made from the best local ingredients. The succulent appetizers include excellent local cheese, cured meats, and *bruschette* (grilled peasant bread with a variety of toppings), and the meal continues with the superb *fusilli porcini e salsiccia* (with porcini mushrooms and sausages), the unique *gnocchi al tartufo su salsa di parmigiano* (potato dumplings with truffle and parmesan sauce), or a delicious vegetarian lasagna (with ricotta, basil, and fresh tomatoes). For secondo, do not miss the grilled boar and lamb. **Children** will enjoy the outdoor **playground.**

The long-established **Antica Trattoria Pascalucci** ★★, Via Ianassi 17, Località Piano Cappelle, San Nicola Manfredi (© **0824-778400;** reservations recommended; secondi 12€–22€; daily noon–3pm and 7:30–11:30pm, closed Dec 24–25) is off SS 7 (Via Appia) about 4km (2½ miles) southeast of Benevento. The large menu includes tasty local peasant cuisine and seafood recipes from the Naples coast. Start with the *antipasti* for a taste of local cured meats and delicious *sottoli* (vegetables prepared and kept in olive oil). Continue with *tubetti alle cozze* (short pasta with mussels) or *fusilli ai funghi porcini* (with porcini mushrooms). You can then attack the secondo, choosing between perfectly grilled meats and daily catch *al forno in umido* (baked with tomatoes).

4 AVELLINO & THE HILL TOWNS OF IRPINIA

Surprisingly close to the northeastern outskirts of Naples, Irpinia is a mountainous region of medieval villages amid rolling hills. It is renowned among connoisseurs for its food and wine, considered the best in Campania and among the best in Italy. The capital of the region is **Avellino,** a town that was largely destroyed by earthquakes and was rebuilt with uninteresting modern buildings. The real attraction is the wilderness beyond, with its remote villages and authentic traditions.

AVELLINO

35km (22 miles) S of Benevento; 54km (34 miles) E of Naples

The capital of Irpinia, Avellino started as a Roman town—Abellinum—which was abandoned in early medieval times because it was too difficult to defend (p. 315). The population moved uphill to a Longobard fortified village (about 3km/2 miles to the west), with a strategic position controlling the road between Benevento and Salerno. The town is not much nowadays, victim of the numerous earthquakes that have hit the area—last and not least the one in 1980, whose terrible economic repercussions are still felt—and left little standing.

GETTING THERE   Avellino is easily reached by **train** from Benevento, Naples, and Salerno. Contact **Trenitalia** (© **892021** in Italy; www.trenitalia.it) for fares and information. Trains arrive at Avellino's train **station,** on Via Francesco Tedesco.

If you are arriving by **car,** take the AVELLINO exit off autostrada A16. You'll find a covered garage (© **0825-23574**) on Via Terminio 20.

GETTING AROUND   You can easily get around Avellino **on foot.** A number of **bus** lines (**SITA;** © **089-226604;** www.sitabus.it) leave from Avellino to serve most villages in the area. In addition to major **car-rental** companies (see "Fast Facts," p. 326), **Win Rent,** Corso Umberto I 89 (© **0825-756237**), is a good local agency.

VISITOR INFORMATION The local tourist office (© 0825-74732) is at Piazza della Libertà 50 and is open Monday through Friday 8am to 2pm and 2:30 to 4:40pm, Saturday 9am to 1pm. The **EPT** office (© 0825-74731 or 0825-74695; fax 0825-74757; www.eptavellino.it) for the province is at Via Due Principati 5.

FAST FACTS You'll find a **pharmacy** (© 0825-35097) in Corso Vittorio Emanuele II. You will find a number of banks and **ATMs** along Corso Vittorio Emanuele II, such as the **Banca di Roma,** Corso Vittorio Emanuele II 35 (© 0825-24737). The **hospital, San Giuseppe Moscati** (© 0825-23343 or 0825-36891), is at Via Cristoforo Colombo

20. For an **ambulance,** dial ✆ **118.** You can call the **police** at ✆ **113** or 112. The **post office** (✆ **0825-781209**) is at Via Francesco De Sanctis 3, off Corso Europa.

SPECIAL EVENTS   Avellino is famous for **Carnevale Irpino,** the festival organized for the celebration of Carnival. Included are traditional performances, the most famous of which is **Zeza.** Taking its name from the wife of Pulcinella, this musical farce narrates the adventures of the family when their daughter Porzia decides to get married to Don Zenobio. Contact the **EPT** (see "Visitor Information," above) for a schedule of events.

Exploring the Town

What remains of the historic district of Avellino is around **Corso Umberto I,** a street that crosses the medieval town and heads to the **Castello.** This was ruined not by earthquakes, but during the Spanish wars at the beginning of the 18th century.

Duomo, aka Cattedrale dell'Assunta ★   This 12th-century church was redone
and added to in following centuries. The elegant facade is neoclassical, as are the decorations inside. The cathedral holds many masterpieces, including a beautiful **tabernacle** by Giovanni da Nola that you can admire in the chapel to the right of the main one. Also take note of the 16th-century carved **choir** at the back of the church, in the apse. Under the Duomo, you'll find the Cripta dell'Addolorata, or Church of Santa Maria dei Sette Dolori. It was created in the 17th century by adding a nave to the original Romanesque crypt and is decorated with **frescoes** and with Roman and medieval capitals. From the presbytery, you can access the courtyard, where you can see remains of the original Longobard church and the partially restored Romanesque bell tower, decorated with Roman marble inscriptions from Abellinum.

Piazza Duomo. Free admission. Daily 9–11am and 5–7pm.

Museo Irpino ★★   Across from the public park of Villa Comunale, this modern
museum houses an important collection of fascinating artifacts dating as far back as 4000 B.C. The extensive archaeological collection is in the main building, together with the grandiose 18th-century artistic *presepio* and a rich collection of **porcelain** from the late 18th to the early 19th century. The **picture gallery,** with an ensemble of 17th-, 18th-, and 19th-century Neapolitan masters, has been moved to the **Carcere Borbonico** (Piazza d'Armi, off Via Mancini, same hours as the museum), an interesting hexagonal building that once housed the prisons of the Bourbon kings. In rooms two and three are the artifacts excavated from the Aeneolithic necropolis of Madonna delle Grazie (near Mirabella Eclano), including the reconstruction of a complete tomb of a tribal chief, buried with his dog. (By the way, "Aeneolithic" means the transitional period between the Neolithic and the Bronze ages; we looked it up.) A number of findings document life in the old Abellinum, including a great **mosaic ★** from the 1st century (in the entrance hall), ceramics, fragments of frescoes, and the funerary collection from the 2nd-century **tomb of a young woman ★,** all in rooms eight and nine. A new hall displays the recent findings from the Sanctuary of the Goddess Mefite, a cult going back to the 6th century B.C. that persisted through the Roman era. These were found in a site near the Passo di Mirabella.

Corso Europa. ✆ **0825-38582.** Free admission. Sun–Fri 8:30am–2pm.

Where to Stay

Hotel De La Ville ★   With its central location, luxury service, and elegant romantic
vibe, this glitzy modern hotel wins the prize for best in town. Comfortable guest rooms are large and well-appointed, and bathrooms are good size. Public spaces are spacious and

Pulcinella

Pulcinella, the famous white-dressed, black-masked, pizza-and-spaghetti-eating character, is the Campanian counterpart to the Venetian masks of the *Commedia dell'Arte*. His familiar figure has become a sort of local hero and plays an important role in celebrations, especially during **Carnival.** Many towns in Campania have claims for the paternity of this character—Capua for one—but the truth is more complicated. In Acerra (a little town just north of Naples), a tailor named Andrea Calcese "Ciuccio" is supposed to have invented Pulcinella sometime before his death around 1656 (you can still see his house in town at Via Suessola 6). Ciuccio did not actually invent Pulcinella; he popularized him after a farmer from Giffoni created him.

According to historians, though, the Pulcinella character already existed in the *Atellane* (traditional theatrical farces with typical characters, similar to the *Commedia dell'Arte,* which were common in Campania during the late Roman Empire), and that his name was derived from *pullicenus,* late Latin for "chick."

Whatever its origins, you will probably encounter Pulcinella at various turns, if you travel through this region.

furnished with elegance—down to a garden complete with swimming pool (heart shaped, no less). The hotel's restaurant, **Il Cavallino,** is excellent, serving traditional and historical Neapolitan and Irpinian dishes.

Via Palatucci 20, 83100 Avellino. *📞* **0825-780911.** Fax 0825-780921. www.hdv.av.it. 69 units. 230€ double; from 420€ suite. Rates include buffet breakfast. Children 2 and under stay free in parent's room. AE, DC, MC, V. Parking 10€. **Amenities:** Restaurant; bar; concierge; pool; room service. *In room:* A/C, TV, Internet, minibar.

Where to Dine

Antica Trattoria Martella ★★ IRPINIAN   This historic restaurant is prized by locals as the best in town for its difficult-to-find specialties, and the elegant yet unsophisticated setting. The vaulted ceilings, wooden chairs with straw seats, white tablecloths, and attentive service create an old-fashioned atmosphere, which is perfect for experiencing the seasonal local menu. If they have it, try the unusual *fusilli affumicati con ricotta e pancetta* (lightly smoked homemade pasta with ricotta and pork belly) or the *tagliatelle al tartufo nero,* seasoned with the famous local black truffles. We also recommend *coniglio ripieno con patate* (stuffed rabbit with potatoes).

Via Chiesa Conservatorio 10. *📞* **0825-32123.** www.ristorantemartella.it. Reservations recommended. Secondi 14€–18€. AE, DC, MC, V. Tues–Sat 1–3pm and 8–11pm; Sun 1–3pm. Closed Dec 24–26, Jan 1, and 1 week in Aug.

La Maschera ★★ **Kids** MODERN IRPINIAN   This is our favorite restaurant in town, both for its elegant setting and charming outdoor terrace, and for the variety of dining options. You can choose among several tasting menus, including a vegetarian and even a children's menu, and the daily menu is based on market offerings. The cuisine is a modern interpretation of the local traditions, offering lighter versions of many favorite dishes. We recommend *zuppa di cipolla di Montoro* (local onion soup), *ravioli di ricotta* *con punte d'asparagi di montagna* (with cheese and mountain asparagus), *pollo ruspante alle noci* (free-range chicken with walnuts), and *coniglio ripieno* (stuffed rabbit).

Rampa San Modestino 1. ✆ **0825-37603.** Reservations recommended. Secondi 11€–16€. AE, DC, MC, V. Mon–Sat 1–3pm and 8–11pm; Sun 1–3pm. Closed 10 days July–Aug.

SANTUARIO DI MONTEVERGINE ★★

Very close to Avellino, this sanctuary with an annexed monastery (✆ **0825-72924;** www. santuariodimontevergine.it) is famous for its art and for the splendid view, encompassing the entire valley down to Mount Vesuvius and the Gulf of Naples. On a sunny day, the panorama is beautiful enough—some say—to justify your whole trip to Campania; in really bad weather, we wouldn't even attempt the drive up.

Almost at the top of Mount Montevergine, at an altitude of 1,270m (4,167 ft.)—the summit rises 1,493m (4,898 ft.)—the sanctuary is a popular pilgrimage destination which attracts over a million people every year, especially between May and September.

Founded by Guglielmo da Vercelli in 1119, for his order of the Verginiani—June 25 is Saint Patron Day celebrating San Guglielmo—the sanctuary has a hostel, the monastery, a museum and gallery, and **two churches.** The smaller, original church was probably consecrated in 1124; the huge new basilica, finished in 1961, is nestled into the older one at a right angle, over the original church's left nave.

In the presbytery of the **New Church,** rich in marble decorations, you can admire the so-called *Throne of the Madonna,* the great 13th-century painting of the **Madonna di Montevergine** ★. On each side of the new presbytery, small doors lead to the **Old Church.** Built in the 12th century, the Old Church was completely redecorated in the 17th century but still shows its Gothic structure. In the presbytery, you will see the splendid 17th-century **main altar** ★, a masterpiece of intarsia in marble and precious stones. In the apse is a beautiful carved choir from the 16th century. At the end of the right nave is the Gothic **Cappella del Sacramento,** holding a magnificent 13th-century **baldaquin** ★ in mosaic, and the ornate 15th-century marble **cyborium** ★. The church is rich in funerary monuments with amazing stone inlay work, such as the grandiose **Monument to Caterina Filangeri** from the 15th century, located at the end of the right nave to the left, before the Cappella del Sacramento. The Gothic portal of the original church is also very beautiful, and warmer than the rather austere modern style of the new construction.

We also recommend a visit to the **museum,** which houses a small but interesting collection, including a beautiful *sedia abbaziale* **(abbey's throne)** dating from the 13th century. Male visitors also have access to the monastery itself, including the portions that date back to the 17th century. On nice days, we recommend the short 1.5km (.9-mile) **hike** to the mountain summit.

To reach the monastery from Avellino (21km/13 miles away), take SS 7 bis and then switch to SS 374 following signs for MERCOGLIANO; here you take the winding mountain road to MONTEVERGINE. Continuing up the road past the monastery, you'll reach, after 1.5km (.9 mile), the trail head to the mountaintop. The short walk takes only about 15 minutes, and from the summit, you can enjoy an even better panorama than from the sanctuary.

EN ROUTE TO MIRABELLA ECLANO ★★

Heading northeast from Avellino on SS 7 (Via Appia), or autostrada A16, you will eventually reach Benevento. The way is dotted with historic villages and towns. Down the hill from Avellino, about 3.5km (2 miles) to the east, is **Atripalda,** where, beyond the belt of modern construction, you can visit the **Collegiata di Sant'Ippolisto.** This church is particularly famous for its **crypt** ★★, which was part of the **Specus Martyrum,** the catacombs that hold the graves of Saint Ippolisto and the other martyrs of Abellinum, killed by the notoriously cruel emperor Domitian. It is decorated with a beautiful fresco of a Christ Pantocrator from the 14th century. Nearby are the ruins of **Abellinum** ★ itself, much damaged by the liberal use of the stones as building material throughout the centuries. Valleverde-Zi Pasqualina ★★, Via Pianodardine 112, off SS 7 (**©** **0825-626115;** www.ziapasqualina.it; reservations recommended; closed Sun and holidays), in the outskirts of Atripalda is a homey, welcoming trattoria-cum-enoteca that serves hearty portions of excellent local fare. The *antipasto della casa* is a medley of cheese, cured meats, and other local specialties; the homemade fusilli and ravioli are superb; and the *pollo alla cacciatora* (chicken stew) is a flavorful marvel. We also recommend a stop at **Mastro-berardino** ★★, Via Manfredi 80, 83042 Atripalda (**©** **0825-614111;** www.mastro berardino.com), a historic vineyard—it's 130 years old—that turns out some of the best traditional wines in the region. The Taurasi is superb, and the vineyard also manages and produces the Villa dei Misteri wine in Pompei (see p. 140). The frescoed aging cellars are also a gallery for fine Italian paintings. Call ahead for reservations for tours or tastings. (See their website for a list of news and scheduled events.)

A short distance east of Atripalda, following directions for Sorbo Serpico, you'll find another great vineyard, **Feudi di San Gregorio,** Localitá Cerza Grossa (**©** **0825-986683;** www.marenna.it), and its excellent restaurant **Marennà** ★★ (**©** **0825-986621;** Wed-Sat 12:30-3pm and 7:30–10:30pm, Sun 12:30–3pm, closed first week in Sept; reservations required), offering creative cuisine inspired by the local tradition and, of course, a great choice of wines.

Prata di Principato Ultra is a village about 10.5km (6½ miles) north of Avellino. The draw here is a visit to the **Basilica dell'Annunziata** ★★ (**©** **0825-961019**). The historic church was built by the Longobards over paleochristian catacombs and a 6th-century basilica. From the modern little church, you will access an elliptical **apse,** carved of tufa stone, probably dating from the 7th century, decorated with a fresco of *Madonna and Saints* dating to the 8th century. At the end of a courtyard to the left of the church is the entrance to the grotto, a Christian catacomb from the 3rd and 4th centuries that is decorated with frescoes, altars, and sarcophagi.

About 10km (6 miles) farther north, switch to the SS 90 toward Passo di Mirabella, a scenic road on the mountain slopes leading to an important archaeological area; the most important findings are conserved in the **Museo Irpino** (p. 312) in Avellino. A short distance before Passo di Mirabella, are the ruins of **Aeclanum** ★★ (**©** **0825-449175**), a Sannite/Roman town that was an important stop along the Via Appia. Destroyed in 662 during the wars against the Longobards, the town was rebuilt—and named Quinto-decimo—but was destroyed again in the 11th century during the war between the Byz-antines and Saracens. In the archaeological area, you can still see many remains of the Roman town, including segments of the walls, the theater, and the market square, as well as ruins of houses and shops. About 3.5km (2 miles) to the southwest, following signs for TAURASI, you'll come to the **Eneolithical Necropolis of Madonna delle Grazie** ★, with its tombs excavated in the tufa stone and dating back to 2000 B.C.

The lively little town of **Mirabella Eclano** is the heir of Aeclanum, and memories of the past decorate its streets, as marble carvings and inscriptions from Roman and medieval times were built into the walls of the houses. **Santa Maria Maggiore,** in the main square of the old town, features the 12th-century *Crucifix* ★★, a Romanesque masterpiece by a Campanian artist. A good spot for a meal or an overnight in Mirabella is **Radici Resort** ★★, Localitá Piano Pantano (🕿 **0825-431293;** fax 0825-431964; www. radiciresort.com), in the vineyard property of the Mastroberardino family (p. 315). This is where they make their excellent Taurasi and Fiano di Avellino Radici, D.O.C.G., or Vino a Denominazione di Origine Controllata e Garantita, similar to the D.O.C stamp of approval but the rules on D.O.C.G. eligibility are even more stringent (see box, "The D.O.C. Wines of Ischia," for more on D.O.C. requirements). The property includes six spacious guestrooms, a 9-hole golf course, a swimming pool, and the wonderful upscale **Morabianca restaurant.**

MONTEMARANO & SANT'ANGELO DEI LOMBARDI

South along the original route of the Roman Via Appia is the heart of Irpinia. Traveling here is a feast for the senses: You'll find art, history, and the region's best cuisine. The medieval town of **Montemarano** ★★ is dominated by its well-preserved **castle,** and the **Chiesa dell'Assunta** is graced by a nicely carved 16th-century portal. Inside the church is a delicately carved 15th-century **folding chair,** decorated with images of the *Sacra Famiglia* by Andrea Vaccaro; the seat was used by the bishop until recent times. This ancient little town is also famous for its **Carnival** celebrations: Festivities start on January 17—the feast of Sant'Antonio Abate—and continue until Mardi Gras. For days, groups of dancers and musicians guided by a Pulcinella (see box, "Pulcinella," p. 313) tour the little town asking for offerings, and as the Carnival ripens, more events take place, including ritual **tarantella** dances. A rare occurrence in modern times, this famous frenzied dance is still performed according to tradition and not as a tourist show. Among the lighter events are farcical performances and the traditional parade of the Pulcinella, where all the town's characters participate. Contact the UNPLI Provinciale, Via Derna 7 (🕿 **082-524013**) for a schedule of events. A number of great restaurants are in town. At Gastronomo ★★, Via Nazionale 39 (🕿 **0827-67009;** Mon–Tues and Thurs–Sat noon–3pm and 7:30–11pm; Sun noon–3pm), simplicity, a welcoming atmosphere, and excellent food and wine combine to make this place a local favorite. The pizza is very good, but we also like the *antipasto della casa,* a sampler of local cheese and cured meats. The homemade ravioli is delicious, and the lamb stew is superb.

Farther east is the delightful medieval town of **Sant'Angelo dei Lombardi** ★★, overlooking the surrounding valley from the top of its hill. Founded by the Longobards, the town is rich in historic monuments, most of which can still be enjoyed despite the severe damage caused by the 1980 earthquake. These include the scenic **Norman Castle** and the 11th-century **cathedral,** housing several funerary monuments such as the beautiful 17th-century **Sepolcro Cecere** found at the beginning of the right nave. About 6.5km (4 miles) out of town to the southwest, in Contrada San Guglielmo, is the **Abbazia di San Guglielmo al Goleto** ★★ (🕿 **0827-24432;** www.goleto.it; call for visits), justly considered one of the most scenic attractions of southern Italy. Founded around 1133 by the same San Guglielmo who founded Montevergine (p. 314), this is the monastery where the saint died in 1142. Originally a double monastery (for men and women), it was very influential until the end of the 14th century. The women's section was suppressed in 1505, while the men's half was annexed to the Monastery of Montevergine, and finally closed in 1807. The body of Saint Guglielmo was then moved to Montevergine, and the monastery was completely abandoned. The religious order, though, decided to save it from ruin, and—thanks to much restoration—it became the seat of a small religious community in 1989. The monastery is huge and surrounded by powerful walls that can be seen from a considerable distance. Originating as a double monastery, it is organized around two cloisters, while the two churches were built one over the other. The facade of both, the top one Gothic (from the 13th century), and the bottom one Romanesque (from the 12th century), can be viewed from the left-hand cloister. Also in this cloister are the ruins of the 18th-century church. Stone steps lead to the top church, a wonderful artistic masterpiece with harmonious proportions and elegant decoration. Around the second cloister is the abbey itself, with the massive defensive tower built in the 12th century with stones from a Roman mausoleum. The abbey is open daily (8am–1pm and 6–8pm). You can eat nearby in the memorable **Ristorante Il Porcellino** ★, Via Campoluongo (① **0827-23694**), where the local homemade cuisine is based on homemade pastas and a variety of grilled meats. In winter, there are wonderful soups.

Fast Facts & Websites

1 FAST FACTS: CAMPANIA & THE AMALFI COAST

AREA CODES **081** for the province of Naples (including Sorrento, Pozzuoli, Ischia, and Capri); **082** for the provinces of Caserta, Benevento, and Avellino; **089** for the province of Salerno (including the Amalfi Coast); and **097** for the Cilento. To call to and from this region, see "Staying Connected," p. 65, and "Telephone Tips" on the inside front cover of this book.

AUTOMOBILE ORGANIZATIONS Two organizations operate in Italy and offer memberships: **Automobile Club d'Italia (ACI;** *©* **803-116** toll-free within Italy; www.aci.it) provides road assistance throughout the country. Their offices also help with car insurance, registration, and other regulation-related issues. **Touring Club Italiano** (www.touringclub.com) publishes maps and guides and maintains useful databases of services for car travelers.

BUSINESS HOURS General business hours are Monday through Friday 8:30am to 1pm and 2:30 to 5:30pm. Banks are generally open Monday through Friday 8:30am to 1:30pm and 2:30 to 4pm. Some banks and businesses are also open on Saturday mornings. Shops are usually open Monday through Saturday from 8 or 9am to 1pm and 4:30 to 7:30 or 8pm, with one extra half-day closing per week at the shop's discretion. *Note:* A growing number of shops in tourist areas stay open during the lunch break and on Sunday.

DRINKING LAWS There's no legal drinking age in Italy. Alcohol is sold day and night throughout the year, and the only limitations are the operating hours of bars and shops (see "Business Hours," above). The law is extremely tough though on drunken behavior, and disturbance of the *quiete pubblica* (public quiet) will be punished with stiff fines and jail time. Littering (including potential littering such as drinking from your beer bottle while sitting on an ancient wall) is also severely penalized. Drinking and driving can result in jail time as well as loss of your driving permit.

DRIVING RULES See "Getting There and Getting Around," p. 44.

ELECTRICITY The electricity in Italy is an alternating current (AC), varying from 42 to 50 cycles. The voltage is 220. It's recommended that any visitor carrying electrical appliances obtain a transformer (laptop computers usually have one built in their cord; check on the back for allowed voltages). Italian plugs have prongs that are round, not flat; therefore, an adapter plug is also needed. You can purchase both transformer and adaptor in any local hardware store.

EMBASSIES & CONSULATES Embassies are located in Rome, but you'll find most consulates in Naples: The **U.S. Consulate** is at Piazza della Repubblica 2 (*©* **081-5838111;** fax 081-7611869; http://naples.usconsulate.gov); the **Canadian**

Consulate is at Via Carducci 29 (② **081-401338;** fax 081-406161; www.canada.it); the **U.K. Consulate** is at Via Crispi 122 (② **081-663511** or 081-663589; fax 081-7613720; www.britain.it).

EMERGENCIES ② **113** or 112 for the police; ② **118** for an ambulance; and ② **115** for a fire. For road emergencies dial ② **803-116.**

ETIQUETTE & SOCIAL CUSTOMS
Volumes have been written on Italian etiquette, as there are rules on everything. Yet, Italians are pretty forgiving of foreigners; and, if you are observant and mold your behavior to theirs, you'll stay away from most blunders.

Appropriate Attire: Italians tend to dress more formally, particularly in urban settings. Shorts and tank tops are reserved for the beach. Women tend to dress more conservatively, particularly if they are alone. The Catholic Church has strict dress codes for both women and men: No showing of shoulders or legs above the knee in a *chiesa* or on sacred ground.

Courtesy: Get up for anybody who's hampered by packages or children, for the elderly, and for women; and open doors for them especially if you are a man. Offer your seat to the elderly and to pregnant women, or anybody carrying a small child. Don't cut in line: Italians might not queue in an orderly manner like the English, but they respect the order of arrival at an establishment, from the ice-cream counter to the post office. Always acknowledge people when entering and exiting a place, such as a shop, with "Buongiorno" and "Grazie."

Gestures & Contact: Italians do gesticulate a lot, but pointing at someone with your index finger is considered rude. Shake hands with your right hand, and hugging and kissing on the cheek among friends is common.

Eating & Drinking: It is customary for two parties to "argue" over the dinner bill,

and you are expected to offer to pay, even if you won't be allowed. If you have been taken out for a meal, then it is good manners to return the invitation. If that is impossible, a small gift (flowers, for example) sent to their home (if it was a private party) or a thank-you note (if it was a business meal) will do the trick. If you are invited to someone's home, never go empty-handed: Flowers, pastries, chocolates, or a small gift for the children are the right way to go.

Photography: It is forbidden to take photographs of military, police, or transport (including subway and airport) facilities.

GASOLINE (PETROL) Gasoline sells on average for 1.35€ per liter and diesel for about 1.13€ per liter, with small variations depending on the location. Taxes are already included in the printed price. One U.S. gallon equals 3.8 liters or .85 imperial gallons.

HOLIDAYS Banks, government offices, post offices, and many stores, restaurants, and museums are closed on the following **national holidays:** January 1 (New Year's Day), Easter Monday, April 25 (Liberation Day), May 1 (Labor Day), August 15 (Ferragosto/Assumption of the Virgin), November 1 (All Saints' Day), December 8 (Feast of the Immaculate Conception), December 25 (Christmas Day), and December 26 (Santo Stefano). Closings are also sometimes observed on **feast days** honoring the patron saint of each town and village, when processions are organized through the historic district and around the town's main chiesa or cathedral. In Naples, September 19 is the Feast of St. Gennaro; in Salerno, September 21 is the Feast of St. Matteo; in Avellino, February 14 is the Feast of St. Modestino; Amalfi celebrates the Feast of St. Andrea on June 27 and November 30.

For more information on holidays see "Calendar of Events," in chapter 3.

INSURANCE Buying insurance is a personal decision. We find that trip-cancellation policies are a good idea, particularly if you are investing a lot of money in your trip and you have made plans way in advance.

One type of insurance you do need to have for your trip to Italy is **medical insurance** (see "Medical Requirements," p. 43). Few U.S. health plans provide coverage overseas, check with yours. Most of those that do provide coverage require you to pay up front and will reimburse you later, hence you might want to purchase additional health insurance. Check **MEDEX Assistance** (© 410/453-6300; www.medexassist.com) or **Travel Assistance International** (© 800/821-2828; www.travelassistance.com; for general information on services, call **Worldwide Assistance Services, Inc.,** at © 800/777-8710).

Canadians should check with their provincial health plan offices or call **Health Canada** (© 866/225-0709; www. hc-sc.gc.ca) to find out the extent of their coverage and what documentation and receipts they must take home if they are treated overseas.

European citizens are covered for necessary medical treatment in Italy but need to request a European Health Insurance Card (EHIC) from the health offices of their country of residence before their trip.

For information on traveler's insurance, trip-cancellation insurance, and medical insurance while traveling please visit www. frommers.com/planning.

INTERNET ACCESS Check the "Fast Facts" section for each destination throughout this book as well as "Staying Connected" on p. 65.

LANGUAGE Italian is the local language. English is generally understood at most hotels, in restaurants that cater to visitors, and by some personnel at attractions and transportation counters. All young doctors and pharmacists and many of the older ones understand English. Even if not all the staff at a restaurant or other business speak English, almost always one person does and can be summoned. The glossary in chapter 13 will prove helpful as you travel in remote towns and villages, and a Berlitz Italian phrase book is a handy accompaniment.

LAUNDROMATS Public laundromats are called *lavanderia a gettoni* and are extremely rare. The alternative is dropping your laundry at a dry cleaner, called *tintoria,* which provides wash-and-fold service. There is at least one of these in most locations.

LEGAL AID If you are pulled over for a driving offense, you'll have the choice to settle the fine right there on the roadside (you will be given a copy of the fine and an official receipt) or pay it at the post office (you will be given a form to fill out). If you are taken to the police office, you can ask for a translator to be sure you understand the situation. If you are actually arrested, the consulate of your country is the place to turn for legal aid, although offices can't interfere in the Italian legal process. They can, however, inform you of your rights and provide you with a list of professional attorneys. If you're arrested for a drug offense, the consulate will notify a lawyer about your case and perhaps inform your family.

MAIL Italian mail works well. Check with www.poste.it for any specific question. Postcards (not in regular letter envelopes) pay a reduced rate and are the slowest: Your family and friends back home might receive your postcards after your return. You are better off slipping your postcard in an envelope and sending it letter rate or higher. For international mail, we recommend the *Posta Prioritaria* rate. Your letter will take 3 to 8 days depending on the destination. Postcards and letters weighing up to 20 grams cost .65€ for Europe; .85€ for Africa, Asia, and the Americas; and 1€ for Oceania. You can buy stamps—regular rate and *Posta Prioritaria*—at all post offices and at *tabacchi* (tobacconist) stores.

MAPS   Tourist offices are the best places to find user-friendly local **maps,** usually available for free. If you are driving, the best maps are available from **Touring Club of Italy** (www.touring.it); buy directly from their website, at bookstores abroad, or from most bookstores and newsstands in Italy. **Michelin** maps are good but generally less detailed. Hiking and trail maps are available from local bookstores.

NEWSPAPERS & MAGAZINES   You'll find a large variety of magazines and newspapers in Italian at local newsstands and some bookstores. Those in cities and in tourist destinations also carry some international press. For instance you'll find the *International Herald Tribune* and sometimes *USA Today, Time,* and *Newsweek.*

PASSPORTS   See www.frommers.com/planning for information on how to obtain a passport. See "Embassies & Consulates," above, for whom to contact if you lose yours while traveling. For other information, please contact the following agencies:

For Residents of Australia: Contact the **Australian Passport Information Service** at ℰ **131-232,** or visit the government website at www.passports.gov.au.

For Residents of Canada: Contact the central **Passport Office,** Department of Foreign Affairs and International Trade, Ottawa, ON K1A 0G3 (ℰ **800/567-6868;** www.ppt.gc.ca).

For Residents of Ireland: Contact the **Passport Office,** Setanta Centre, Molesworth Street, Dublin 2 (ℰ **01/671-1633;** www.irlgov.ie/iveagh).

For Residents of New Zealand: Contact the **Passports Office** at ℰ **0800-225-050** in New Zealand, or 04/474-8100; or log on to www.passports.govt.nz.

For Residents of the United Kingdom: Visit your nearest passport office, major post office, or travel agency; or contact the **United Kingdom Passport Service** at ℰ **0870-521-0410;** or search its website at www.ukpa.gov.uk.

For Residents of the United States: To find your regional passport office, either check the U.S. State Department website or call the **National Passport Information Center** toll-free number (ℰ **877/487-2778**) for automated information.

POLICE   Dial ℰ**113** or 112 for emergencies.

SMOKING   Smoking still is very common in the region, but is forbidden in enclosed public spaces, except those with separate ventilated smoking areas.

TAXES   Taxes in Italy are usually included in the prices quoted, but some luxury hotels will show it separately on their bills. **VAT,** Value-Added Tax (called IVA in Italy) is imposed on most goods and services; the rate depends on the item and goes from 4% for basic food items to 20% for accessories and clothing. VAT is used in Italy for social purposes and, as a foreigner, you can ask for a refund: Non-E.U. (European Union) citizens are entitled to a refund of the IVA for purchases over 154.94€ before tax at any one store, on those goods you will take out of the country. To claim your refund, request an invoice from the cashier at the store and take it to the Customs office *(dogana)* at the airport to have it stamped before you leave. ***Note:*** If you're going to another E.U. country before flying home, you can have it stamped at the airport Customs office of the last E.U. country you'll be in (for example, if you're flying home via Britain, have your Italian invoices stamped in London). Once you're back home, mail the stamped invoice (keep a photocopy for your records) back to the original vendor within 90 days of the purchase. The vendor will send you a refund of the tax that you paid at the time of your original purchase. Reputable stores view this as a matter of ordinary paperwork and are businesslike about it. Less-honorable stores might lose your file. It pays to deal with established vendors on large purchases. You can also request that the refund be credited to the card with which you made the purchase; this is usually a faster procedure.

Many shops are now part of the "Tax Free for Tourists" network (look for the sticker in the window). Stores participating in this network issue a check along with your invoice at the time of purchase. After you have the invoice stamped at Customs, you can redeem the check for cash directly at the Tax Free booth in the airport (in Rome, it's past Customs; in Milan's airports, the booth is inside the duty-free shop) or mail it back in the envelope provided within 60 days. Check **Global Refunds** (www.globalrefund.com) for more information.

TELEPHONES See "Staying Connected," p. 65.

TIME Italy and Campania are 6 hours ahead of Eastern Standard Time in the United States and 1 hour ahead of Greenwich Mean Time in the U.K. (GMT+1). **Daylight saving time** in Italy is from the last Sunday in March to the last Sunday in October.

TIPPING Tipping is not required in Italy as service charges are usually included in your bills. It is customary, though to leave a small tip if you are satisfied with the service: give your hotel maid .50€ to 2€ per day, the doorman (for calling a cab) .50€, and the bellhop or porter 1€ to 5€ for carrying your bags to your room. A concierge might get up to 10% of his or her bill. In cafes you usually leave a small tip, such as .10€ if you had a coffee. In restaurants, your menu or your bill should say if the service charge is included; if

you're not sure whether it is, ask, "È incluso il servizio?" (ay een-*cloo*-soh eel sair-*vee*-tsoh). If it is not included, add 10% to 15% to your bill. An additional tip isn't required, but it's customary to leave the equivalent of an extra couple of euros, if you've been pleased with the service. Checkroom attendants expect .50€ to 1€, and washroom attendants should get at least .50€. Taxi drivers can be tipped 10% of the fare.

TOILETS Airports, train stations, museums, and major archaeological areas and attractions all have restrooms, often with attendants who expect to be tipped. Bars, nightclubs, restaurants, cafes, gas stations, and hotels should have facilities as well, but they are open only to customers. Public toilets are found near many of the major sights. Usually they're designated WC (water closet) and bear international symbols or the signs DONNE (women) and UOMINI (men). The most confusing designation is SIGNORI (gentlemen) and SIGNORE (ladies), so watch that final i and e! Many public toilets charge a small fee or employ an attendant who expects a tip. It's a good idea to carry some tissues in your pocket or purse—they often come in handy.

VISAS Information on tourist and other visas can be obtained at the nearest **Italian Embassy** or **Italian Consulate** in your country of residence (select the name of your country in the form at www.esteri.it/visti/rilascio.asp). **U.S.** citizens can obtain up-to-date visa information at the Italian Embassy, 3000 Whitehaven St., NW Washington, DC 20008 (© **202/612-4400;** www.ambwashingtondc.esteri.it) or at one of the following Italian Consulates: 535 Griswold, Buhl Building, Ste. 1840, Detroit, MI 48226 (© **313/963-8560;** www.consdetroit.esteri.it); 690 Park Ave., New York, NY 10065 (© **212/439-8607;** www.consnewyork.esteri.it); 600 Atlantic Ave., Boston, MA 02210

(📞 617/722-9201; www.consboston. esteri.it); 500 N. Michigan Ave., Ste. 1850, Chicago IL 60611 (📞 312/467-1550; www.conschicago.esteri.it); 1300 Post Oak Blvd., Ste. 660, Houston, TX 77056 (📞 713/850-7520; www. conshouston.esteri.it); 12400 Wilshire Blvd. No. 300, Los Angeles, CA 90025 (📞 310/979-5295; www.conslosangeles. esteri.it/consolato_losangeles); 4000 Ponce de Leon Blvd, Ste. 590, Coral Gables, FL 33146 (📞 305/374-6322; www.consmiami.esteri.it); Public Ledger Building, 150 S. Independence Mall W., Ste. 1026, Philadelphia, PA 19106 (📞 215/592-7329; www.consfiladelfia. esteri.it); 2590 Wester St., San Francisco, CA 94115 (📞 415/292-9214; www.cons sanfrancisco.esteri.it).

Australian citizens can obtain up-to-date visa information from the Italian Embassy, 12, Grey St., Deakin, ACT 2600, Camberra (📞 6-126-2733-333; www.ambcanberra.esteri.it); or at one of the Italian Consulates in the country: 509 St. Kilda Rd., Melbourne, VIC 3004 (📞 6-139-867-5744; www.consmelbourne. esteri.it); Level 45 Gateway 1 Macquarie Place, Sydney, NSW 2000 (📞 6-129-392-7900; www.conssydney.esteri.it); 398 Payneham Rd., Glynde, SA 5070 (📞 6-188-3370777; www.consadelaide.esteri.it); AMP Place, 10 Eagle St., 14 Level, Brisbane 4000 (📞 6-173-229-8944; www.consbrisbane. esteri.it); 1292 Hay St., Level 2, West Perth, WA 6005 (📞 6-189-322-4500; www. consperth.esteri.it).

British subjects can obtain up-to-date visa information at one of the following Italian Consulates: 32 Melville St., Edinburgh, EH3 7HA, Scotland, U.K. (📞 4-413-1220-3695; www.cons edimburgo.esteri.it); 136 Buckingham Palace Rd., London SW1W 9SA (📞 4-420-7823-6519; www.conslondra. esteri.it); Rodwell Tower, 111 Piccadilly, Manchester M1 2HY (📞 4-416-1236-9024; www.consmanchester.esteri.it).

Irish citizens can obtain up-to-date visa information through the **Italian Embassy** 63/65 Northumberland Rd., Dublin 4 (📞 3-531-664-2312; www.ambdublino. esteri.it).

Citizens of **New Zealand** can obtain up-to-date visa information from the Italian Embassy at 38 Grant Rd., Thorndon, Wellington (📞 644-474-0951; www. ambwellington.esteri.it).

VISITOR INFORMATION The **Italian National Tourist Board** (www.italian tourism.com) is a good source of information before you go.

In the United States: 630 Fifth Ave., Ste. 1565, New York, NY 10111 (📞 212/245-4822; fax 212/586-9249); 500 N. Michigan Ave., Ste. 2240, Chicago, IL 60611 (📞 312/644-0996; fax 312/644-3019); and 12400 Wilshire Blvd., Ste. 550, Los Angeles, CA 90025 (📞 310/820-1898; fax 310/820-6357).

In Canada: 175 Bloor St. E., South Tower, Ste. 907, Toronto, ON M4W 3R8 (📞 416/925-4882; fax 416/925-4799).

In Australia: Level 4, 46 Market St., NSW 2000 Sydney; PO Box Q802, QVB NSW 1230 (📞 02-92-621666; fax 02-92-621677).

In the United Kingdom: 1 Princes St., London W1B 2AY (📞 020-7408-1254; fax 020-7399-3567).

We also recommend writing directly (in English or Italian) to the local tourist boards for a variety of brochures as well as maps. The **Campania tourist board** covers the whole region; its address is Centro Direzionale Isola C/5, Napoli 80143 (📞 081-7968974; fax 081-7958576; www.regione.campania.it).

Campania is administratively divided into five provinces, each with its own **provincial tourist board** (Ente Provinciale per Il Turismo, or EPT):

EPT Napoli (covering Naples, Phlegrean Fields, Herculaneum, Pompei, Ischia, Capri, and the Sorrento peninsula): Piazza dei Martiri 58, 80121 Napoli

(© 081-405311; fax 081-401961; www. eptnapoli.info).

EPT Salerno (covering Salerno, the Amalfi Coast, and the Cilento): Via Velia 15, Cap 84125 Salerno (© **089-230411;** fax 089-251844).

EPT Caserta (covering Caserta, Caserta Vecchia, and Capua): Palazzo Reale, 81100 Caserta (© **0823-322233;** fax 0823-326300; www.casertaturismo.it).

EPT Avellino: Via Due Principati 5, 83100 Avellino (© **0825-74695;** fax 0825-74757; www.provincia.avellino.it and www.e-irpinia.it).

EPT Benevento: Via Sala 31, 82100 Benevento (© **0824-319911;** fax 0824-312309; www.eptbenevento.it).

In addition to the above, local tourist boards operate in all places of tourist interest; we have listed them in each individual chapter.

WATER In restaurants, most locals drink mineral water with their meals; however, tap water is safe everywhere, as are public drinking fountains. Some areas of Naples have had long-term problems with the water supply, and this is why all public establishments in the city—hotels, bars, cafes, restaurants, and so on—have their own filtering devices. If you are staying in a private home, though, make sure you ask about the water supply. Unsafe sources and fountains will be marked ACQUA NON POTABILE.

2 AIRLINE, HOTEL & CAR-RENTAL WEBSITES

MAJOR AIRLINES

Aeroméxico
www.aeromexico.com

Air Canada
www.aircanada.ca

Air China Ltd.
www.airchina.com.cn

Air France
www.airfrance.com

Air New Zealand
www.airnewzealand.com

Airoflot
www.airoflot.ru

Alitalia
www.alitalia.com

American Airlines
www.aa.com

Austrian Airlines
www.aua.com

British Airways
www.british-airways.com

China Airlines
www.china-airlines.com

Continental Airlines
www.continental.com

Cubana
www.cubana.cu

Delta Air Lines
www.delta.com

EgyptAir
www.egyptair.com

El Al Airlines
www.elal.co.il

Emirates Airlines
www.emirates.com

Finnair
www.finnair.com

Iberia Airlines
www.iberia.com

Icelandair
www.icelandair.com

Israir Airlines
www.israirairlines.com

Japan Airlines
www.jal.com

KLM (Royal Dutch Airline)
www.klm.com

Korean Air
www.koreanair.com

LAN Airlines
www.lan.com

Lufthansa
www.lufthansa.com

Malaysia Airlines
www.malaysiaairlines.com

Meridiana
www.meridiana.it

Mexicana
www.mexicana.com

Northwest Airlines
www.nwa.com

Qantas Airways
www.qantas.com

Qatar Airways
www.qatarairways.com

BUDGET AIRLINES

Aegean Airlines
www.aegeanair.com

Aer Lingus
www.aerlingus.com

Air Berlin
www.airberlin.com

Air Italy
www.airitaly.it

Air One
www.flyairone.it

AirVallee—Services Aeriens du Val D'Aoste
www.airvallee.com

Baboo
www.flybaboo.com

Blue Air
www.blueair-web.com

BMI
www.flybmi.com

Philippine Airlines
www.philippineairlines.com

Singapore Airlines
www.singaporeair.com

South African Airways
www.flysaa.com

Swiss Air
www.swiss.com

TAP Portugal
www.flytap.com

Thai Airways International
www.thaiair.com

Turkish Airlines
www.thy.com

United Airlines
www.united.com

US Airways
www.usairways.com

Virgin Atlantic Airways
www.virgin-atlantic.com

Brussels Airline
www.flysn.com

Cimber Sterling
www.cimber.com

easyJet
www.easyjet.com

FlyOnAir
www.flyonair.it

Jet2.com
www.jet2.com

Ryanair
www.ryanair.com

Southwest Airlines
www.southwest.com

Transavia
www.transavia.com

TUIfly
www.tuifly.com

Vueling
www.vueling.com

FAST FACTS & WEBSITES

12

AIRLINE, HOTEL & CAR-RENTAL WEBSITES

Wind Jet
www.volawindjet.it

Wizzair
www.wizzair.com

MAJOR HOTEL & MOTEL CHAINS

Accor
www.accorhotels.com

Best Western International
www.bestwestern.com

Clarion Hotels
www.clarionhotel.com

Comfort Inn
www.comfortinn.com

Crowne Plaza Hotels
www.ichotelsgroup.com/crowneplaza

Embassy Suites
www.embassysuites.com

Four Seasons
www.fourseasons.com

Hilton Hotels
www.hilton.com

Holiday Inn
www.holidayinn.com

Hyatt
www.hyatt.com

InterContinental Hotels & Resorts
www.ichotelsgroup.com

Jolly Hotels
www.jollyhotels.it

Marriott
www.marriott.com

Quality Inn Hotels
www.qualityinn.com

Radisson Hotels & Resorts
www.radisson.com

Sheraton Hotels & Resorts
www.starwoodhotels.com/sheraton

Starhotels
www.starhotels.it

Westin Hotels & Resorts
www.starwoodhotels.com/westin

CAR-RENTAL AGENCIES

Auto Europe
www.autoeurope.com

Avis
www.avis.com

Budget
www.budget.com

Europcar
www.europcar.it

Europe by Car
www.europebycar.com

Hertz
www.hertz.com

Kemwel (KHA)
www.kemwel.com

Maggiore
www.maggiore.it

National
www.nationalcar.com

Sixt
www.sixt.com

Travelcar
www.travelcar.it

Molto Italiano

Classified as a Romance language, Italian is closely related to Latin, French, Spanish, Portuguese, and Romanian. It arose from the Vulgar Latin of the late Roman Empire. The Italian alphabet has 21 letters. The letters **h, j, k, w, x,** and **y** are used only in words taken from other languages (such as jazz). Certain combinations of letters have special sounds in Italian, just as **ch, sh, th,** and **ng** have special sounds in English.

Italian has few pitfalls such as silent letters; a word's sound closely resembles its written form. Such straightforward pronunciation makes this melodious language accessible and appealing to even the most casual student. Often **c** and **g** are stumbling blocks for beginners. Both have a soft sound before **e** or **i**, a hard sound before **a, o,** and **u.** Think **cubo** *koo*-boh (cube) versus **arrivederci** ahr-ree-veh-*dehr*-chee (bye) and **gala** *gah*-lah versus **Luigi** loo-*ee*-jee. Double consonants should be pronounced twice—or lengthened and intensified. English speakers are already familiar with this from phrases such as gra**b b**ag, bla**ck c**at, goo**d d**ay, hal**f f**ull, goo**d j**ob, ho**t t**ea and ki**ds z**one.

1 BASIC VOCABULARY

English	Italian	Pronunciation
Thank you	**Grazie**	*graht*-tzee-yey
You're welcome	**Prego**	*prey*-go
Please	**Per favore**	*pehr* fah-*vohr*-eh
Yes	**Si**	see
No	**No**	noh
Good morning or Good day	**Buongiorno**	bwohn-*djor*-noh
Good evening	**Buona sera**	*bwohn*-ah *say*-rah
Good night	**Buona notte**	*bwohn*-ah *noht*-tay
How are you?	**Come sta?**	*koh*-may *stah*
Very well	**Molto bene**	*mohl*-toh *behn*-ney
Goodbye	**Arrivederci**	ahr-ree-vah-*dehr*-chee
Excuse me (to get attention)	**Scusi**	*skoo*-zee
Excuse me (to get past someone)	**Permesso**	pehr-*mehs*-soh
Where is . . . ?	**Dovè . . . ?**	doh-*vey*
the station	**la stazione**	lah stat-tzee-*oh*-neh
a hotel	**un albergo**	oon ahl-*behr*-goh
a restaurant	**un ristorante**	oon reest-ohr-*ahnt*-eh
the bathroom	**il bagno**	eel *bahn*-nyoh

English	Italian	Pronunciation
To the right	**A destra**	ah *dehy*-stra
To the left	**A sinistra**	ah see-*nees*-tra
Straight ahead	**Avanti** (*or* **sempre dritto**)	ahv-*vahn*-tee (*sehm*-pray d*reet*-toh)
How much is it?	**Quanto costa?**	*kwan*-toh *coh*-sta
The check, please.	**Il conto, per favore**	eel kon-toh *pehr* fah-*vohr*-eh
When?	**Quando?**	*kwan*-doh
Yesterday	**Ieri**	ee-*yehr*-ree
Today	**Oggi**	*oh*-jee
Tomorrow	**Domani**	doh-*mah*-nee
Breakfast	**Prima colazione**	*pree*-mah coh-laht-tzee-*ohn*-ay
Lunch	**Pranzo**	*prahn*-zoh
Dinner	**Cena**	*chay*-nah
What time is it?	**Che ore sono?**	kay *or*-ay *soh*-noh
Monday	**Lunedì**	loo-nay-*dee*
Tuesday	**Martedì**	mart-ay-*dee*
Wednesday	**Mercoledì**	mehr-cohl-ay-*dee*
Thursday	**Giovedì**	joh-vay-*dee*
Friday	**Venerdì**	ven-nehr-*dee*
Saturday	**Sabato**	*sah*-bah-toh
Sunday	**Domenica**	doh-*mehn*-nee-kah
January	**Gennaio**	jehn-*nah*-yoh
February	**Febbraio**	fehb-*brah*-yoh
March	**Marzo**	*MAHR-tso*
April	**Aprile**	ah-*pree*-leh
May	**Maggio**	*mahd*-joh
June	**Giugno**	*jewn*-nyo
July	**Luglio**	*lool*-lyo
August	**Agosto**	ah-*gohs*-toh
September	**Settembre**	seht-*tehm*-breh
October	**Ottobre**	oht-*toh*-breh
November	**Novembre**	noh-*vehm*-breh
December	**Dicembre**	dee-*chehm*-breh

NUMBERS

1 **uno** (*oo*-noh)
2 **due** (*doo*-ay)
3 **tre** (tray)
4 **quattro** (*kwah*-troh)
5 **cinque** (*cheen*-kway)
6 **sei** (say)
7 **sette** (*set*-tay)

8 **otto** (*oh*-toh)
9 **nove** (*noh*-vay)
10 **dieci** (dee-*ay*-chee)
11 **undici** (*oon*-dee-chee)
20 **venti** (*vehn*-tee)
21 **ventuno** (vehn-*toon*-oh)
22 **venti due** (*vehn*-tee *doo*-ay)

A Little Tip

By adding a diminutive suffix, **-ino -a, -etto -a,** or a combination of the two, you can make anything smaller or shorter. These endings replace the original *-o* and *-a*, respectively:

a really little bit   **pochino -a** *(poh-kee-noh -nah)*

a really teeny tiny bit   **pochettino -a** *(poh-keht-tee-noh -nah)*

30	**trenta** *(trayn-tah)*	90	**novanta** (noh-*vahnt*-tah)
40	**quaranta** (kwah-*rahn*-tah)	100	**cento** (*chen*-toh)
50	**cinquanta** (cheen-*kwan*-tah)	1,000	**mille** (*mee*-lay)
60	**sessanta** (sehs-*sahn*-tah)	5,000	**cinque milla** (*cheen*-kway *mee*-lah)
70	**settanta** (seht-*tahn*-tah)	10,000	**dieci milla** (dee-ay-chee mee-lah)
80	**ottanta** (oht-*tahn*-tah)		

2 A GLOSSARY OF ITALIAN ARCHITECTURAL TERMS

Abside (**Apse**)   Half-rounded extension behind the main altar of a church. Christian tradition dictates that it be placed at the eastern end of an Italian church, the side closest to Jerusalem.

Ambo or **Ambones**   Pulpit, either serpentine or simple in form, erected in an Italian church.

Atrio (**Atrium**)   Courtyard, open to the sky, in an ancient Roman house; the term also applies to the courtyard nearest the entrance of an early Christian church.

Baldacchino or *Ciborio* (**Baldachin, Baldaquin,** or **Ciborium**)   Columned stone canopy, usually placed above the altar of a church; spelled in English.

Basilica   Any rectangular public building, usually divided into three aisles by rows of columns. In ancient Rome, this architectural form was frequently used for places of public assembly and law courts; later, Roman Christians adapted the form for many of their early churches.

Battistero (**Baptistery**)   Separate building or a church area where the rite of baptism is held.

Calidarium   Steam room of a Roman bath.

Campanile   Church's bell tower, often detached.

Capitello (**Capital**)   Four-sided stone at the top of a column, often decoratively carved. The Greek classic architectural styles include three orders: Doric, Ionic, and Corinthian.

Cariatide (**Caryatid**)   Column carved into a standing female figure.

Cattedrale (**Cathedral**)   The church where a bishop has his chair.

Cavea   The curved row of seats in a classical theater; the most prevalent shape is that of a semicircle.

330 **Cella**   The sanctuary, or most sacred interior section, of a Roman pagan temple.

Chiesa   Church.

Chiostro **(Cloister)**   Courtyard ringed with a gallery of arches or lintels set atop columns.

Cornice   The horizontal flange defining the uppermost part of a building, especially in classical or neoclassical facades.

Cortile   Courtyard or backyard.

Cripta **(Crypt)**   A church's underground chapel, mostly used as a burial place, usually below the choir.

Cupola   Dome.

Duomo   A town's most important church, usually also a cathedral.

Foro **(Forum)**   The main square and principal gathering place of any Roman town, usually adorned with the city's most important temples and civic buildings.

Ipogeo **(Hypogeum)**   An underground chamber that is part of an ancient building. Often used as a tomb.

Loggia   Roofed balcony or gallery.

Navata **(Nave)**   Each of the longitudinal sections of a church or basilica, divided by walls, pillars, or columns.

Palazzo   Palace or other large building, usually of majestic architecture.

Pergamo   Pulpit.

Piano Nobile   The floor of a palazzo reserved for the owner's use (usually the second floor), as opposed to the floors used by the house staff and for other services.

Pietra Dura   Semiprecious stone, such as amethyst and lapis lazuli.

Portico   A porch with columns on at least one side, usually for decorative purposes.

Presbiterio   Area around the main altar of a church, elevated and separated by columns or, in the oldest churches, by a *transenna* (screen), which was traditionally reserved for the bishop and the officiating clergy.

Pulvino **(Pulvin)**   A typical structure of Byzantine architecture consisting of a four-sided stone, often in the shape of a truncated pyramid and often decorated with carvings of plants and animals, which connected the capital to the above structure.

Putto   Artistic representation of a naked small child, especially common in the Renaissance.

Stucco   A building compound composed of sand, powdered marble, lime, and water. Stucco is applied to a surface to make it smooth, or used to create decorative reliefs.

Telamone or **Atlante**   Statue of a male figure used as structural support.

Terme   Thermal baths or spa, such as those in ancient Rome.

Timpano **(Tympanum)**   The triangular wall—sometimes decorated with reliefs—between the cornice and the roof.

Transenna   Screen (usually in carved marble) separating the presbytery from the rest of an early Christian church.

Travertino **(Travertine)**   Type of porous limestone—white, pale yellow, or pale reddish in color—commonly found in central Italy.

MOLTO ITALIANO

13

A GLOSSARY OF ITALIAN ARCHITECTURAL TERMS

Acqua pazza   Light broth flavored with fresh herbs and tomato used to poach fish.

Agnello   Lamb, usually grilled or baked.

Antipasti   Succulent tidbits served at the beginning of a meal (before the pasta). The choices might be sliced cured meats, seafood (especially shellfish), and cooked and seasoned vegetables.

Aragosta   Lobster.

Babà   Puffy soft cake soaked in rum and served with pastry cream.

Baccalà   Dried and salted codfish usually prepared as a stew.

Braciola   In the rest of Italy this means chop, usually lamb or pork; here it refers to an *involtini* filled with raisins and pine nuts and cooked in *ragù* sauce, a meat-based tomato sauce.

Brasato   Beef braised in white wine with vegetables.

Bruschetta   Toasted peasant-style bread, heavily slathered with olive oil and garlic and often topped with tomatoes.

Bucatini   Thick hollow spaghetti.

Calzone   Filled pocket of pizza dough, usually stuffed with ham and cheese, and sometimes other ingredients. It can be baked or fried.

Cannelloni   Tubes of fresh pasta dough stuffed with meat, fish, or vegetables and then baked with cheese, tomato sauce, and sometimes béchamel (creamy white sauce).

Caprese   Salad of fresh tomatoes and fresh mozzarella, seasoned with fresh basil and olive oil.

Carciofi   Artichokes.

Carpaccio   Thin slices of raw beef, seasoned with olive oil, lemon, pepper, and slivers of Parmesan. Sometimes raw fish is served in the same style but without the cheese.

Cassuola   Small terra-cotta casserole; also the process of cooking something in terra cotta—usually squid or octopus.

Coniglio alla Cacciatora   Rabbit cooked in wine with olives and herbs.

Cozze   Mussels.

MOLTO ITALIANO

13

CAMPANIAN MENU TERMS

Do's and Don'ts

Italians measure foodstuffs by the kilogram or smaller 100g unit (**ettogrammo** abbreviated to *etto*: equivalent to 3.5oz). **Pizzerie al taglio** (pizza slice shops) generally run on this system, but hand gestures can suffice. A good server poises the knife, then asks for approval before cutting. **Più** (PYOO) is "more," **meno** (MEH-noh) "less." **Basta** (BAHS-tah) means "enough." To express "half" of something, say **"mezzo"** (MEHD-zoh).

Fagioli   Beans.

Fiordilatte   Type of mozzarella made with cow's milk.

Fragaglie   Very small fish, usually served deep-fried.

Fresella   Whole-wheat rustic bread served as a salad with fresh tomatoes, fresh basil, salt, and olive oil. The special bread is sold in the shape of flat rounds.

Friarelli   Local type of thin broccoli sautéed with olive oil, garlic, and red pepper and often served with sausages.

Frittata   Italian omelet.

Frittura   Deep-fried medley of seafood, usually calamari and shrimp.

Frutti di Mare   Translated "fruits of the sea," it refers to all shellfish.

Fusilli   Spiral-shaped pasta; the traditional one is fresh and homemade.

Gelato (Produzione Propria)   Ice cream (homemade).

Gnocchi   Dumplings usually made from potatoes (*gnocchi alla patate*) or from semolina (*gnocchi alla romana*) and often served with a tomato sauce.

Granita   Flavored ice, usually with lemon or coffee.

Insalata di Mare   Seafood salad (usually including octopus or squid) seasoned with olive oil, lemon, sometimes vinegar, and whatever the chef fancies—usually parsley and other herbs and spices.

Involtini   Thinly sliced beef, veal, pork, eggplant, or zucchini rolled, stuffed, and sautéed, often served in a tomato sauce.

Melanzane   Eggplant.

Minestra Maritata   Thick soup of pork meat and vegetables.

Minestrone   Rich and savory vegetable soup usually sprinkled with grated parmigiana.

Mozzarella di Bufala   Typical Campania cheese, this is an unfermented cheese, made exclusively from fresh buffalo milk, boiled, and then kneaded into a rounded ball, and served fresh. What is called mozzarella in the rest of Italy and abroad is mere *fiordilatte,* a similar kind of cheese made with cow's milk.

Panna   Heavy cream.

Panzerotti   Reminiscent of ravioli, *panzerotti* is half-round in shape and deep-fried. It can be savory—filled with ricotta, ham, and mozzarella—or sweet, in which case it is filled with jam.

Parmigiano   Parmesan is a hard and salty yellow cheese usually grated over pastas and soups but also eaten by itself; the best is *Parmigiano-reggiano*. A pale imitation is *grana padano*.

Pastiera   Sort of a thick pie filled with a creamy mixture of wheat grains, ricotta, and candied orange peels. Traditionally prepared for Easter but sold all the time now.

Peperoni   Green, yellow, or red sweet peppers (not to be confused with pepperoni, which doesn't exist in Italy).

Pesce al Cartoccio   Fish baked in a parchment envelope and seasoned with whatever the chef fancies.

Pesce Spada   Swordfish.

Pesto   Fresh basil, garlic, and olive oil, finely chopped into a paste.

Pizza   Among the varieties is *margherita* (with tomato sauce, cheese, fresh basil, and memories of the first queen of Italy, Marguerite di Savoia, in whose honor it was first made by a Neapolitan chef); marinara (with tomatoes and oregano); and *romana* (tomatoes, cheese, and anchovies). Quite hilariously, these are the same toppings that in Rome make the pizza *napoletana*.

Pizzaiola   Process in which something (usually a slice of beef or a filet of fish) is cooked in a tomato-garlic-oregano sauce.

Polipetti   Squid.

Polpo or **Polipo**   Octopus.

Ragù   Meat-based tomato sauce, where the chef's imagination rules.

Ricotta   Soft, bland cheese served very fresh and made from sheep's milk or, in lesser-quality versions, from cow's milk.

Risotto   Italian rice, cooked with wine and other ingredients to a creamy consistency.

Risotto alla Pescatora   Rice cooked with wine, a little tomato, and lots of fresh seafood.

Sartù   Delicious baked rice dish in which a crown of rice is filled with baby meatballs, mozzarella, sausages, and other ingredients.

Scapece   For this special preparation for zucchini and eggplants, the vegetables are fried, then seasoned with vinegar and fresh mint.

Semifreddo   Frozen dessert; usually ice cream with sponge cake.

Seppia   Cuttlefish (a kind of squid); its black ink is used for flavoring certain sauces for pasta and risotto dishes.

Sfogliatella   Flaky pastry filled with a sweet ricotta mixture.

Soffritto   Typical Neapolitan sauce made with pork tidbits cooked at length in a tomato sauce with olive oil and red pepper.

Sogliola   Sole.

Spaghetti   Long, round, thin pasta, served different ways: *al ragù* (meat sauce), *al soffritto* (see above), *al pomodoro* (with fresh tomatoes), *ai frutti di mare* (with a medley of sautéed seafood), and *alle vongole* (with clam sauce) are some of the most common.

Spiedini   Pieces of meat grilled on a skewer over an open flame.

Tagliatelle   Flat egg noodles.

Tonno   Tuna.

Torta Caprese   Rich cake made with chocolate and almonds.

Tortelli   Pasta dumplings stuffed with ricotta and greens.

Vermicelli   Very thin spaghetti.

Zabaglione or **Zabaione**   Egg yolks whipped into the consistency of a custard, flavored with Marsala, and served warm as a dessert.

Zuccotto   Liqueur-soaked sponge cake, molded into a dome and layered with chocolate, nuts, and whipped cream.

Zuppa Inglese   Sponge cake soaked in custard.

INDEX